DICTIONARY
OF
AMERICAN
HISTORY

SUPPLEMENT

Robert H. Ferrell and Joan Hoff, Senior Editors

PART 2
MacArthur Foundation—Zoology

Charles Scribner's Sons Reference Books
MACMILLAN LIBRARY REFERENCE USA
SIMON & SCHUSTER MACMILLAN
NEW YORK

SIMON & SCHUSTER AND PRENTICE HALL INTERNATIONAL
LONDON • MEXICO CITY • NEW DELHI • SINGAPORE • SYDNEY • TORONTO

Library of Congress Cataloging-in-Publication Data
Dictionary of American history. Supplement / Robert H. Ferrell and
  Joan Hoff, editors.
     p.   cm.
  Includes bibliographical references and index.
  Contents: pt. 1. AARP–Lyme Disease — pt. 2. MacArthur Foundation–Zoology.
  ISBN 0-684-19579-8 (set : alk. paper). — ISBN 0-684-80464-6 (pt.
1). — ISBN 0-684-80465-4 (pt. 2)
  1. United States—History—Dictionaries.   I. Ferrell, Robert H.
II. Hoff, Joan, 1939– .
E174.D52 1976 Suppl
973'.03—dc20   96-7844
                                           CIP

1 3 5 7 9 11 13 15 17 19 20 18 16 14 12 10 8 6 4 2

Printed in the United States of America

The paper used in this publication meets the minimum requirements of the American Standard for Information Sciences—Permanence of Paper for Printed Library Materials, ANSI Z39.48-1984.

DICTIONARY
OF
AMERICAN HISTORY

MacArthur Foundation–Zoology

M

MacARTHUR FOUNDATION "GENIUS" AWARDS.

Launched in 1981, the fellowship program of the John D. and Catherine T. MacArthur Foundation of Chicago annually awards "no-strings" grants of between $150,000 and $375,000 to creative individuals in all fields and supports them for five-year periods. Although the awards became popularly known as "genius grants," that is not a term encouraged by the foundation. The nomination process is secret but criteria include creativity, the person's contribution to society, and the potential effect on the recipient's career. The foundation was created by the billionaire founder of Bankers Life and Casualty, John D. MacArthur (1897–1978) and instituted upon his death. As of 1991 it was the fifth largest foundation in the United States. Of the 350 awards distributed between 1981 and 1991, 109 were in the sciences, 81 in the arts, 70 in the humanities, 53 in public affairs, and 37 in the social sciences.

[Anne Matthews, "The MacArthur Truffle Hunt," *New York Times Magazine* (June 7, 1992); Denise G. Shekerjian, *Uncommon Genius* (New York, 1990).]

JEFFREY M. MERRON

MAGAZINES.

Following World War II specialization became the route to success, or at least survival, for magazines. In the 1990s general interest weeklies such as the *Saturday Evening Post* were gone, but magazine racks groaned beneath the weight of new ventures, most of which quickly sank. Weeklies such as *Sports Illustrated* and *Money* attracted upscale readers that advertisers wanted to reach, as did such monthlies as *Bride's* and *Yachting*. *Time* and other giants changed ads and copy on selected pages in each weekly edition, and thus delivered issues customized geographically and according to readers' interests. For example, a college student's issue could differ from the one delivered that same week to his or her parents.

A few regional magazines prospered, notably *Sunset*, a home magazine for readers in the West, and *Southern Living*. Although most city magazines concentrated on listing restaurants and entertainment, a few, such as *Philadelphia Magazine*, won national reporting awards. Many specialized publications, such as *Engineering News-Record*, boasted large but controlled circulations, that is, they were mailed free to every individual in the defined field but others could not even buy a copy. Again, this served the advertisers who want to reach only their best prospects. Magazines for African Americans multiplied and also specialized. *Ebony* prospered as a general monthly, while other publications targeted black young women (*Essence*), businessmen (*Black Enterprise*), and scholars (*Black Scholar*).

As the number of newsstands began to diminish after World War II, retail stores, especially supermarkets, became major magazine outlets. Although supermarket tabloids look like newspapers, the Audit Bureau of Circulations classified them as magazines. In 1994 the six largest sold a total of 10 million copies a week, with the *National Enquirer* having the largest circulation. Comic books, many intended for adults, made a comeback in the 1980s. Illustration and text became more diverse in men's magazines. *Playboy*'s pages contained not only pictures of nude women and cartoons but also works by leading authors. Another showplace for writing was *Esquire*, whose contributors were at the center of the so-called "new journalism," in which writers immersed themselves in topics to convey the "true essence" to readers, even if it required invented dialogue and composite characters. Literary magazines, mostly quarterlies affiliated with universities, continued to publish fiction and poetry.

Reader's Digest continued to lead all general magazines in circulation, with a paid circulation in 1993 of more than 16 million copies. Although *Modern Maturity* had a larger circulation, it is tied to a membership organization, the American Association of Retired Persons. At the same time, *TV Guide* was the leading weekly. Women's magazines (*Better Homes and Gardens, Family Circle, Good Housekeeping*) were among the top ten magazines in 1993. *Time* continued to outsell other newsmagazines by more than 1 million copies, and its 1993 circulation of 4.1 million was followed on the list of leading magazines by *People,* with 3.4 million copies. Magazines in the 1990s were increasingly being published on CD-ROM for access by computers.

[Michael Emery and Edwin Emery, *The Press and America* (Englewood Cliffs, N.J., 1988).]

JOHN D. STEVENS

MAGNETIC RESONANCE IMAGING (MRI), first used for medical purposes in 1976, is based on the phenomenon of nuclear magnetic resonance reported in 1946 by Felix Bloch of Stanford University and Edward Purcell of Harvard University, physicists awarded the Nobel Prize in 1952. Using complicated equipment to measure resonating frequencies emitted by tissue components, images of those tissues are constructed in much the same way as in CAT (computerized axial tomography) scanning. Information can be obtained about the soft tissues of the body, such as the brain, spinal cord, heart, kidneys, and liver, but not bone. MRI does not involve ionizing radiations and is noninvasive.

[Joseph K. T. Lee, Stuart S. Sagel, and Robert J. Stanley, eds., *Computed Body Tomography with MRI Correlation* (New York, 1989).]

PETER H. WRIGHT

See also **SUPP:** Computerized Axial Tomography.

MAGNET SCHOOLS. *See* **Schools, Magnet.**

MAIL-ORDER INDUSTRY. The techniques for promoting, selling, and distributing products through the mail or private delivery services have become increasingly diverse and sophisticated since the 1970s. In addition to continued growth of established mail-order companies, many new ventures started as small businesses or as offshoots of larger businesses. L. L. Bean is perhaps the best-known example of a traditional company that grew into a successful national mail-order retailer. The Sharper Image is one of a new generation of mail-order retailers, specializing in unusual, upscale items. Mail-order hence became more important to many retailers whose businesses were primarily based on in-store sales. Social and economic trends such as the increased number of working couples with less time to shop stimulated mail-order sales. Business buyers began to rely on mail-order vendors when they purchased equipment and supplies. The proliferation of credit cards and other types of financing and introduction of toll-free long-distance 800 numbers made buying faster and easier.

Promotional mailings and advertising targeted demographic groups. Development of complex computer databases, comprehensive mailing lists, and other information technology allowed merchandisers to pinpoint the most likely buyers for their products based on income, past purchases, and personal interest. The comprehensive information-gathering methods and pervasive nature of the new forms of direct marketing raised some concern about individual privacy. One sign of the shift from mass merchandising to more specific approaches was the decision by two of the original mail-order giants—Sears (in 1993) and Montgomery Ward (in 1985)—to discontinue their large general catalogs. They formed partnerships with other firms to produce smaller, more specialized catalogs at lower costs.

Printed catalogs and order forms continued to be a mainstay of mail-order marketing, but other marketing techniques became important as postal rates and other mailing costs increased. Television became a powerful direct-sales tool. The Home Shopping Network pioneered this approach in 1985 with continual on-air sales pitches for products that viewers ordered directly by telephone. The distinction between commercials and other programming had not always been clear in the early days of television. Sponsors produced entertainment shows in which their products were prominently featured in the name of and during the show, such as Texaco's sponsorship of Milton Berle's variety hour. In the late 1950s and the 1960s regulations and industry standard brought more clear-cut separations between commercials and programming, but this changed in the mid-1980s, when program-length commercials, known as "infomercials," began to appear on cable networks and later on broadcast channels. Infomercials are often made to resemble newscasts, talk shows, or other programming but are actually half-hour commercials. Unlike earlier sponsor-identified shows that also provided entertainment, the sole purpose of infomercials is to sell specific products.

Computers emerged as a vehicle for direct marketing. On-line services (telephone-based commercial networks that link computer users) began to feature "electronic malls" with descriptions of products that people could order on their computers. Merchants began to experiment with electronic multimedia catalogs, with products presented on CD computer disks or videocassettes. Another form of direct sales was telemarketing, in which salespeople (or automated recordings) made unsolicited and often irritating sales pitches to potential customers by telephone. The growth of direct marketing slowed with the recession of the late 1980s and early 1990s, when some of the new companies using innovative marketing failed. Renewal of economic growth persuaded survivors to press on.

[Ed Burnett, *The Complete Direct Mail List Handbook* (Englewood Cliffs, N.J., 1988); Cecil C. Hoge, *The Electronic Marketing Manual* (New York, 1993); Erik Larson, *The Naked Consumer* (New York, 1992).]

JOHN TOWNES

See also **SUPP:** Advertising; Credit Cards; Direct Mail; Home Shopping Networks.

MAINE began to change in the 1970s in ways that by the end of the twentieth century necessitated a new image for a state with a heritage of community, friendliness, and independence. For a while, the economic scene was troublesome. The closing of many mills and other industries during the recession of the 1970s forced workers to accept lesser positions or unemployment checks. Many left the state. Cutbacks in defense spending forced layoffs at the Bath Iron Works and the Portsmouth Naval Shipyard in Kittery. Since 1985, however, people looking for a better way of life and a safe place to raise children moved into the state. Low bank-loan rates encouraged residential construction, providing many jobs for skilled workers. The cities of Maine saw many changes in the 1980s. Shopping malls expanded, forcing downtown retailers to close their doors. Community-supported arts flourished. Portland, Bangor, and Lewiston-Auburn drew visitors and local residents to art museums, a wide range of musical events, theater arts, and

dance company performances. Maine experienced a striking increase in tourism, especially to such ski resorts as Sugarloaf U.S.A.

Maine's population in 1990 was 1,233,223, and changing demographics had exacerbated social and economic divisions, giving rise to the terms "the two Maines" or "the other Maine." Many parts of the state remained economically undeveloped, with rural poverty in farming and seasonal employment in the tourist industry. Maine remained a nearly white state, with a minority population of 2.5 percent that included African Americans, Native Americans, and a slightly rising number of Asians and Hispanics clustering in the major cities. With the economic expansion in southern Maine, something of a north-south split evolved. Census information from 1989 indicated a substantial difference in median household incomes between York County in the southern part of the state ($32,432) and Washington County in the north ($19,993). For all their differences, most Maine residents remained committed to the preservation of the environment and the natural beauty and resources of the state. A significant portion of the economy continued to be based on the natural resources of land, rivers, and the sea. Access to wilderness areas for recreation and sport was a priority, even when economic development opportunities were in conflict. Education was also a high priority for the people of Maine, as state residents realized that quality public education and technical schools attracted businesses to the state, which created jobs for Maine in the competitive global economy. In the late twentieth century commercial fishing was still a vital part of the economic stability of the state. In 1989 commercial fishing produced a catch valued at more than $132 million, including $60 million from lobstering. Inland, the Maine forest industry provided a livelihood for more than 100,000 residents. Timber was harvested primarily for paper (1.3 million cords in 1989).

Politically, the once staunchly Republican state saw a rise in Democratic representation. In 1978 Maine voters elected Democrat Joseph Brennan as governor to succeed an independent, James Longley, who had promised to serve only one term. Without raising taxes, Governor Brennan restored many public services diminished during previous years. He was succeeded for two terms by John McKernan, the first Republican governor in twenty years. Appointed by Brennan to the U.S. Senate to fill the term of Edmund Muskie, George Mitchell went on to be elected Senate majority leader in 1988. His decision to leave the Senate in 1994 dramatically affected Maine politics, widening the pool of candidates seeking office, bringing new voices and ideas to lead Maine into the twenty-first century. Looking for new direction and the promise of broad-based nonpartisan leadership, the citizens of Maine rejected "politics as usual" in November 1994 and elected another independent, Angus King, as governor.

Property taxes rose dramatically in Maine from the 1970s to the 1990s, partly as a result of economic growth and reduced federal assistance. In 1988 the state legislature enacted a program that offered direct financial assistance for low- and moderate-income households and increased municipal revenue-sharing from sales tax and income tax collections. Middle-income property owners assumed most of the tax burden. In 1974 a state lottery began, and in 1994 proposals were presented for gambling casinos run by Native Americans.

[Richard Barringer, *Changing Maine* (Portland, Maine, 1990); Joseph McGonigle, *Maine's Changing Face* (Augusta, Maine, 1989); Neil Rolde, *Maine* (Gardiner, Maine, 1990).]

GAIL S. THOMPSON

MALLS, SHOPPING, have their predecessors in the covered bazaars of the Middle East, the arcades of Victorian England, and the skylighted galleries of Italy. The first shopping centers in the United States were located in the downtown sections of suburban areas, near major intersections, with free off-street parking. The Country Club Plaza, built in 1922 in Kansas City, is a Spanish-motif extravaganza extending over several city blocks that is still in operation. The first truly regional shopping center (which attracts consumers from a twenty-mile radius) was Northgate on the outskirts of Seattle (1950), with a long open-air pedestrian walkway and a large anchor department store surrounded by smaller shops. This was followed by the first completely enclosed shopping center, Southdale, in Edina, Minn., built in 1956. The 1970s and 1980s witnessed expanded construction of shopping centers, such as the Galleria in Houston and Woodfield near Chicago. Shopping malls proliferated from the mid-1970s until by the end of 1992, according to the National Research Bureau, there were 38,966 across the country, of which 1,835 were large regional malls.

Due to overbuilding and undue competition, shopping malls began to experience an economic downturn in the late 1980s. Pressed for time and short of money, exhausted consumers lost interest in leisure shopping and turned to factory-outlet centers such as Sawgrass Mills in Sunrise, Fla., which covers 120 acres and is the world's largest outlet mall. Catalog purchasing, home shopping networks on television, and specialty stores such as Home Depot and Price Club also diminished mall shopping. Mall builders soon realized that new marketing was necessary and started a bread-and-circuses approach, in some instances attempting to make malls into virtual tourist attractions. Malls such as that in Las Vegas, Nevada, have become popular vacation spots. They are esteemed for the variety of activities, number of stores, and quality of entertainment provided. These huge malls are true urban centers with post offices, hotels, and even amusement parks and schools in a weather-proof, safe, clean environment. They have became social centers where young people meet their friends and socialize rather than shop. Elderly people walk the malls for exercise, not merchandise. The mega-malls offer visitors such diversions as theme parks, miniature golf, bungee jumping, and water slides.

The Mall of America, which opened in the summer of 1992 on seventy-eight acres in Bloomington, Minn., is the largest enclosed shopping center in the United States. It is enormous—five times larger than Red Square in Moscow and twenty times larger than Saint Peter's Basilica in Rome—and covers 4.2 million square feet and cost $625 million to construct. It is a successful prototype of futuristic shopping, attracting 130,000 visitors a day, each of whom spends an average of four hours in the mall. Families and international tourists patronize restaurants, theaters, and fine stores and can go on amusement rides in the seven-acre Knott's Camp Snoopy, the nation's largest indoor theme park, with a carousel, log flume ride, and one-half-mile-long roller coaster.

[Joel Garreau, *Edge City: Life on the New Frontier* (New York, 1991).]

JOHN J. BYRNE

See also **SUPP:** Advertising; Home Shopping Networks; Mail-Order Industry; Retailing Industry.

MANNERS, as described in Edith Wharton's *The Age of Innocence* (1920) and Emily Post's *Etiquette* (1922), reflected a sense of propriety that was expected of everyone. Critics of the late twentieth century claimed that since then incivility has become more common than politeness. The alleged breakdown of family, church, and neighborhood led to a more individualized society, because of the protest spirit of the 1960s, which preached freedom for the individual from the constraints of societal conformity and which resulted in free love and the hippie movement. Responsibilities to the community, the critics said, were abandoned. In a time when presidents are called by their first names (Jimmy, Ron, Bill), or even by their nicknames ("Bubba"), and when sneakers have become the footwear of choice in workplaces, increasing casualness may be leading to widespread vulgarity. A 1993 poll by *Reader's Digest* revealed that both men and women swear an average of sixteen times a day. At home, preschoolers often adopt rude behavior and language, not realizing the consequences of their remarks. By emphasizing self-expression over manners, parents often do not train children early in politeness and courtesy. In business, managers claim they are too busy to be polite. Workers interested in career development are told they must adapt to the corporate culture with a take-charge attitude that often conflicts with good manners.

Nevertheless, people are social animals, and codes of conduct do exist in modern society. Business etiquette dictates a hierarchical seating at meetings, appropriate dress styles, and gifts to business associates and clients at holiday seasons. Restaurant etiquette requires that people cancel reservations that will not be kept, that they avoid inappropriate conversation and excessive noise, and that they dress appropriately. It is considered tacky to use a calculator to figure out a waiter's tip. Now that fitness centers have ceased to be dating facilities, gym manners have emerged, ranging from taboos on ridiculous dress to monopolizing mirrors. An unspoken hierarchy exists that dictates the closer one stands to the instructor, the fitter and more expert one must be. Advances in communications have required rules of etiquette regarding telephone call-waiting, cellular phones, television remote controls, answering machines, and electronic mail. Even to chat by computer, users need etiquette spelled out in an electronic rule book. Users of electronic bulletin boards must observe rules of behavior that include greeting the crowd upon "entering the room," reading before "speaking," avoiding defamatory statements and obscenities, and avoiding using all capital letters or "shouting." Camcorder users are expected not to block other people's views and always to ask permission before videotaping.

Technological advances also raised such questions of manners as where and when is it appropriate to wear beepers or Walkmans. Traditional rules of conduct may no longer apply, however, due to the changing mores. How does one congratulate an unmarried pregnant woman? What does one say to someone who has had plastic surgery? Must one ask if dinner guests are vegetarians? Such situations, which developed in the last quarter of the twentieth century, were addressed by etiquette author and columnist Miss Manners (Judith Martin), who wrote on subjects that did not exist in Emily Post's time, such as "significant others" and political correctness.

[David J. Knowles, *Etiquette of American Society* (Pittsburgh, 1993).]

JOHN J. BYRNE

See also **SUPP:** Fashion and Style; Political Correctness.

MANUFACTURING. During the late 1970s many economists and political leaders argued that U.S. manufacturing had lost its dominant position in the nation's and the world's economy. While others argued that U.S. manufacturers remained the world's leaders, the period from 1975 to 1995 showed two unmistakable trends: U.S. manufacturers needed fewer workers to maintain or improve output, while foreign manufacturers—especially companies based in Japan or Germany—either increased their ownership of U.S. manufacturers or built their own plants and factories in the United States. These trends, which many Americans felt personally with the closing of auto plants and steel mills in the Northeast and Great Lakes region, initiated a prolonged debate about whether the U.S. economy had declined, how to respond to foreign competition, and whether the government had a responsibility to help workers who lost jobs as manufacturers closed shop during the 1970s and 1980s.

According to the Bureau of Labor Statistics, in 1950 almost 34 percent of the nation's 45 million workers were engaged in some type of manufacturing; in 1970 manufacturing's share of that year's 71 million workers was 27.3 percent; by 1990, when the United States had almost 118 million workers, manufacturing claimed only 17.4 percent of the total. Moreover, between 1979 and 1992 U.S. manufacturing output annually grew 1.1 percent but employment fell 1.2 percent, with 3 million manufacturing jobs eliminated during that period. It is generally agreed that the jobs lost between 1970 and 1990—losses accelerated by economic recessions—provided good pay and benefits for unskilled and semiskilled workers and were jobs that had helped propel the booming U.S. economy during the first six decades of the twentieth century. Hardest hit during the decline were manufacturers that had produced most of that economic growth: steel and textile producers, automobile companies, and manufacturers of appliances, televisions, and radios. Makers of paper, chemicals, industrial and analytical instruments, production machinery, and metalworking equipment also suffered.

Many of the problems faced by these companies came from overseas competition. Japan used lower-cost labor and heavy investment in plant and equipment to produce higher-quality goods at more productive rates. By the 1980s overseas advances, coupled with changes in the tastes of U.S. consumers, allowed Japan, West Germany, Brazil, South Korea, and other countries to make significant headway in the sales of automobiles, steel, and televisions and other electronic equipment. Some economists, businessmen, and politicians, however, said manufacturing's problems in the 1970s and 1980s went deeper than foreign competition. They maintained that poor economic policies, such as an overvalued dollar, credit business cycles that disrupted capital formation needed for plant and equipment modernization, and tax and regulatory policies that rewarded consumption instead of production, had wounded U.S. manufacturing just as deeply. Other economists maintained that the nation was not deindustrializing but rather that production was moving to the southern and western United States, where nonunion labor (meaning lower wages and benefits) was available. Still other observers downplayed any decline in manufacturing. They argued that the country merely was going through a transition from an industrial society to an economy organized around information and services. Companies and workers ready to exploit the new economy would prosper as had the old-line manufacturers.

The burgeoning services sector did provide higher-paying jobs in such areas as law, accounting, and the medical professions. In addition, thanks to a postwar push toward higher education, some workers who in the past might have been consigned to factory jobs took advantage of new opportunities offered in the 1970s and 1980s by the professions. On the other hand, the growing services sector—12 percent of the 45 million jobs in the United States in 1950 and 19.1 percent of the 118 million jobs in 1990—was more often typified by low-paying, low-benefit jobs in restaurants, retail stores, and other service-oriented businesses. For workers with few skills and educational opportunities—workers who once found family-supporting wages at steel mills or auto plants—the change was ominous, even if the new work was safer.

By 1982 a withering recession brought on by high interest rates used to extinguish double-digit inflation, aggravated manufacturing's problems. Chemical plants reported operating at 67 percent of capacity, while machinery plants, which supplied manufacturers with equipment, slashed their workforces by about 30 percent. Steel mills were in the worst shape. They operated at 30 percent of capacity and 60 percent of the workforce was unemployed. Several mills appeared close to asking the courts for protection from creditors as the industry's financial losses ran close to $2.5 billion for 1982.

U.S. manufacturers did report success stories during the period. One study, comparing manufacturing in 1970–1972 and 1980–1982, showed that production of electronic products rose 19 percent; plastic products, 125 percent; office equipment, 87 percent; synthetic materials, 77 percent; chemical products, 63 percent; and communications equipment, 59 percent. These manufacturers were emblematic of the higher-tech companies—both in terms of the goods being produced and the way they were being produced—that were becoming successful as steel mills and textile plants closed. High-tech manufacturers, however, often had different work needs. They relied on higher-skilled workers with better reading and math skills and automated many processes that had previously been staffed by unskilled and semiskilled workers. One important sector of high-tech manufacturing—computer equipment manufacturers—suffered from foreign and domestic competition as well.

As the crisis in manufacturing became apparent in the early 1980s, manufacturers tried to alleviate their problems. They slashed costs, laid off workers, closed unproductive or outdated plants and renegotiated union contracts. They looked at how foreign competitors, especially the Japanese, organized production. New management techniques and theories flooded the workplace, such as just-in-time inventories, statistical process control, lean production, continuous improvement, and total quality management. Success stories cropped up. The Ford Motor Company, considered almost dead in the early 1980s, sprang back to life in 1985 with a popular line of new cars and trucks that competed effectively against imports. Specialty steelmakers built smaller, more efficient plants to compete against imports from Brazil, Spain, and South Korea.

By the early 1990s many U.S. manufacturers reported a much better economic climate. Overall, U.S. manufacturing production climbed 26 percent during a fifteen-year period. Output per employee improved 37 percent. Productivity in the early 1990s showed average increases of 3 percent per year. By 1994 the Big Three automakers—General Motors, Ford, and

Chrysler—showed improved market share and better profits. The automakers, which many had dismissed as incompetent and incapable of adjusting to rapidly shifting markets, rededicated themselves to producing better-quality cars and trucks and began reaping benefits from the new focus. In the final quarter of 1993, for example, Chrysler, which had tried to sell itself to the Italian automaker Fiat three years earlier, reported earnings of $777 million, its highest-ever quarterly profit. Automaking provided an interesting example of how manufacturing was changing in the United States. U.S. automakers increasingly shifted production to such foreign countries as Mexico while foreign automakers, especially the Japanese, began producing cars in the United States. Honda, for example, produced its Accord sedans at an Ohio plant.

The productivity and profitability increases for U.S. manufacturers, combined with never-ending competition from foreign and domestic manufacturers, meant that there would be no return to the employment levels that defined manufacturing from the beginning of the twentieth century to the 1970s. Bureau of Labor Statistics data showed what had happened—manufacturers could make more with less and production generally was cheaper. By the mid-1990s a new manufacturing industry had taken shape, with economists predicting that computer manufacturing would become increasingly important. Other durable-goods manufacturers were expected to prosper, such as electronics, transportation, and instruments. The fastest-growing areas of nondurables manufacturing included paper and allied products, printing and publishing, chemicals and related products, and rubber.

Although U.S. manufacturers rejoiced over their improved conditions in many areas, they still lagged behind their foreign competition, especially Japan. Despite financial and economic problems in Japan in the mid-1990s, its manufacturers still led their U.S. counterparts in such areas as output per employed person, output per hour, and unit labor costs. Moreover, the average Japanese worker in manufacturing was taking home much more real compensation than U.S. workers, while Japan's manufacturing employment continued to grow. Meanwhile, U.S. high-tech companies entered into joint ventures with the Japanese that called for the manufacturing of products in Japan. In 1992 Intel and three other U.S. producers of "flash" memory chip semiconductors announced joint ventures, and the following year IBM and Toshiba entered into a billion-dollar venture to build flat-panel computer displays.

[Robert W. Crandall, *Manufacturing on the Move* (Washington, D.C., 1993); *DRI Report on U.S. Manufacturing Industries* (New York, 1984); Paul Ingrassia and Joseph B. White, *The Fall and Rise of the American Automobile Industry* (New York, 1994).]

THOMAS G. GRESS

See also **SUPP:** Automobile Industry; Computer Industry; Foreign Investment in the United States; Labor Unions; Rustbelt; Unemployment.

MARATHONS. The long-distance foot race known as the marathon is named after the celebrated Athenian victory over Persian invaders near the Bay of Marathon in Greece in 490 B.C. It commemorates the fact that a Greek soldier ran the twenty-five miles from the battlefield to Athens with tidings of the victory, only to die of exhaustion. A marathon was incorporated into the Olympic Games when the modern series began in Athens in 1896 and has retained an important place in them. The first victor was a Greek, Spiridon Loues, who won in 2 hours, 58 minutes, and 50 seconds. A year later the Boston Marathon was established and is held annually on Patriots' Day; by the 1990s it was attracting 10,000 competitors. The New York Marathon, founded in 1970 by Fred Lebow, head of the New York Road Runners Club, draws about 25,000 entrants each year. The length of the marathon was fixed at 26 miles, 385 yards in 1908 when the British Olympic Committee determined that the race should commence at Windsor Castle and finish in front of the royal box at Shepherds Bush in London. Although no official records of marathons are kept because the courses are of varied difficulty, by 1995 the fastest recorded times were about two hours and seven minutes for a man and about two hours and twenty minutes for a woman. Violet Percy of Great Britain became the first woman to officially enter a marathon, the London Marathon, in 1926. In 1970 the Road Runners Club of America organized the first championship marathon for women, although it was not until 1984 that a women's race was included in the Olympic Games. In 1970 two women in the New York Marathon became the first to break three hours. Marathons grew in popularity in the United States after Frank Shorter won the marathon in the 1972 Olympic Games. The New York Marathon began to be televised in 1979, and the following year, after fraudulent finishes in both Boston and New York by Rosie Ruiz, videotaping became routine. Triathlons, such as the Ironman Triathlon World Championship held on the Kona coast of Hawaii, which began in 1978, incorporate a marathon, a 2.4-mile swim, and a 112-mile bicycle race. A related sporting challenge is the endurance marathon, in which the length of uninterrupted participation is the determining factor in any number of activities, from tiddlywinks to trampolining.

ROBERT GARLAND

See also **DAH** and **SUPP:** Olympics.

MARINE LIFE. *See* **Fish and Marine Life; Marine Sanctuaries.**

MARINE SANCTUARIES were created by Title III of the Marine Protection, Research, and Sanctuaries Act of 1972. Twenty years later the National Marine Sanctuary System, administered by the National Oceanic and Atmospheric Administration, included fourteen designated and proposed unique and threatened coastal locations. Designated sanctuaries included Monitor in Virginia, Gray's Reef in Georgia, the Florida Keys, Flower Garden Banks in Texas, the Cordell Bank, Gulf of the Farallones, and Channel Islands off California, and Fagetele Bay of American Samoa. Proposed sanctuaries include Thunder Bay (Great Lakes), Stellwagen Bank (Mass.), Norfolk Canyon (Va.), Northern Puget Sound and Olympic Coast (Wash.), Monterey Bay (Calif.), and Kahoolawe (Hawaii). The environmental movement prompted Congress to enact laws for environmental protection. Books such as *The Sea Around Us* (1951, rev. 1961) by Rachel Carson and television documentaries by the French undersea explorer Jacques Cousteau enchanted a wide popular audience with descriptions of marine organisms. Their works carried the message that human impacts on marine ecosystems affect human health. The 1972 legislation not only provided the mechanism for protecting the ecosystems of the U.S. coast through ocean sanctuaries but also mandated a federal marine research program and enabled the Environmental Protection Agency to regulate industrial and municipal disposal of wastes at sea.

[Samuel P. Hays, *Beauty, Health, and Permanence: Environmental Politics in the United States, 1955–1985* (Cambridge, Mass., 1987).]

DENNIS WILLIAMS

See also: **SUPP:** Environmental Protection; Fish and Marine Life; Wildlife Refuges and Sanctuaries.

MARRIAGE AND DIVORCE. Twentieth-century family trends in the United States, as in other industrialized countries, have been on a seesaw. In the nineteenth century and the first third of the twentieth century, average age at marriage increased, family size declined, and divorce became easier to obtain. After the Depression of the 1930s, however, all three of these trends turned around—the median marriage age for women dropped to near twenty, there was a "baby boom" in which the birth rate increased by 60 percent, and the divorce rate fell. By the late 1960s the seesaw reverted to its former position as the habits of previous decades reemerged. The baby boom now looked like an aberration, a reaction to the deprivations and disruptions of the Great Depression and World War II, when many could not plan on a stable future. The abrupt return to an older age at marriage, a decline in fertility, and rise in the divorce rate created a "crisis" atmosphere, leading many to fear the "end" of the family.

This decline in the centrality of marriage in adult lives reflected socioeconomic and demographic changes in American society beginning in the late 1960s, but the causal relationship between those changes and the decline was difficult to pinpoint. It may have been that many adults in the United States did in fact celebrate romance but at the same time placed a high value on personal freedom, particularly as the U.S. economy made that freedom possible. It was no longer necessary to find oneself trapped in an unhappy marriage. Another possibility was that the necessity for both partners to work to support themselves and their children in a way they deemed satisfactory, and the emphasis on commitment that characterized many occupations, led women and men to have little time for family life. The growth of organized leisure, sports, and other recreation provided many adults with absorbing alternatives to family life as well.

Perhaps two more phenomena account for the reduced importance of marriage in the lives of adults. First, changes in gender roles made marriages difficult to negotiate and maintain. In the nineteenth century industrialization took men away from the family to work, which deprived them of involvement with children and left the tasks and reward of child rearing to women. The result was that men were far less likely than women to see children either as a source of personal meaning, happiness, stability, or as a source of adult status in the community. As more and more women entered the workforce, people became confused about what the division of labor inside marriage should be. Some opted to form other relationships, cohabiting with others (of the same or opposite sex) or living alone.

The growth in the number of people living alone was another force influencing change in family life. The living arrangements of unmarried adults changed dramatically after World War II, with the result that in 1990 more than one-quarter of U.S. households contained only one person, compared with only 10 percent in 1940. Much of this increase reflected a decline in family extension among the unmarried, as those who once lived with available family members (parents, adult children, or other kin) were able to afford homes of their own. This change, however, meant that young adults no longer had to marry to leave their parents, and those contemplating ending a marriage had alternatives that preserved their privacy, autonomy, and adult status.

One result of the increase in the divorce rate has been the impoverishment of women. Professional women suffered inequalities of divorce settlements to be sure, but poor women suffered more, especially after the introduction of no-fault divorce in the late 1960s. The reason for impoverishment was in part visible in a statistic of the 1980s, namely, that less than 4 percent of divorced women received alimony, and only half of all women awarded child support received the full amount, with women receiving $2,500 annually on average.

The decline in marriage and remarriage has also meant that many children are raised by and often born into one-parent families. In 1991 the median family income of female-headed households with children was only 30 percent the level of income of households where both parents were living with children. In other industrialized countries, child poverty rates were a third or less than in the United States, because either the divorce rate was still low, as in Japan and southern Europe, or welfare programs supporting children were substantial. Children in the poorest U.S. communities have disproportionately suffered from these trends in poverty and family dislocation. Marriage declined dramatically in African-American communities. By 1990 more than half of all black children lived in one-parent families, compared with less than one-quarter of white or Hispanic children. About one-third of white children living with one parent were poor, while this was the case for nearly two-thirds of minority children.

By the 1990s many novelties accompanied the return of the marriage-trend seesaw. As divorces increased to nearly one of every two marriages so did remarriages. Although more than 70 percent of divorced men and women remarried, it was predicted 60 percent of those remarriages would fail, resulting in 1 million remarriages every year and leading to the practice known as "serial monogamy." Remarried couples suffer from more stress than those couples marrying for the first time, including greater financial problems, stepparenting, and dealing with former spouses. About 40 percent of remarriages in the 1990s involved stepchildren, and those couples experienced a higher divorce rate than childless remarried couples.

Another novel aspect of the post–baby boom era has been the increasing frequency of detailed contracts along with the general contract of marriage itself. Beginning in the colonial period, wealthy women tried to protect themselves with prenuptial agreements. These contracts fell into disuse, only to reappear and became quite common in the 1980s, as couples attempted to transform a relationship of love, or perhaps reinforce it, by resorting to economics. An economic agreement, it was believed, would protect both sides of a marriage. By 1995 all fifty states permitted such contracts, although only thirty recognized them as legal instruments.

Conservative commentators often urge that a return to the family patterns and gender roles of the 1950s, that is, yet another swing of the seesaw, is needed to preserve the family. Others argue that marriage and family life will need to continue to change to reflect the new realities of men's and women's lives. An altogether new equilibrium, centered on a family-friendly workplace in which men and women build long-term relationships around children, home, and community, is theoretically possible, although the complexities of the late twentieth century made the likelihood of its achievement uncertain.

[Andrew J. Cherlin, *Marriage, Divorce and Remarriage,* rev. ed. (Cambridge, Mass., 1992); Frances K. Goldscheider and Linda Waite, *New Families, No Families? The Transformation of the American Home* (Berkeley, Calif., 1991); David Popenoe, *Disturbing the Nest: Family Change and Decline in Modern Societies* (New York, 1988); Lenore J. Weitzman, *The Divorce Revolution: The Unexpected Social and Economic Consequences for Women and Children in America* (New York, 1985).]

FRANCES K. GOLDSCHEIDER

See also **SUPP:** Family.

MARYLAND, one of the smallest states in size, by the 1990s was one of the most divided. Since the 1970s urban Baltimore, once so dominant, rapidly declined in influence and increasingly became blue-collar. The five western counties were egalitarian and contentious. The twelve eastern and southern counties around Chesapeake Bay were hierarchical and conservative. The six counties of suburban Washington and Baltimore, surged in size and power with prosperous and mobile populations. The accommodation of such differences within one state gave Maryland a certain representativeness in the United States. Suburbanization characterized the state's post–World War II history. In the late 1940s the suburban population doubled, often with low-cost tract housing. In the 1950s and 1960s it doubled again as jobs and freeways extended and shopping centers developed. Split-level houses, cookouts, and station wagons became suburban symbols. Since 1970 the suburban population has doubled once more, bringing malls, office parks, and a demographic mix. By 1990 almost two-thirds of the state's population lived in the six suburban counties. Newcomers to the suburbs were usually young, upwardly mobile, liberal, eager for zoning and good schools, and often politically independent. Even with legislative reapportionment in the 1960s, their voices in state affairs were fewer than their numbers. It was not until the 1970s that they gained control of their counties from the old organizations of large landowners and developers.

The clash of the old politics of patronage and favors with the new politics of innocence and issues invited corruption, for which the state was briefly renowned. Spiro T. Agnew, elected in 1966 as a reform governor, was the first suburban representative to serve in that office, but he was unable to distinguish between campaign contributions and bribery. He was elected vice president of the United States in 1968, remaining a symbol of suburban probity until forced to resign for accepting a quarter of a million dollars from developers in return for favors. Agnew was succeeded as governor by Marven Mandel, an old-style machine politician from Baltimore, one of the ablest administrators the state ever had, progressive, and efficient. He took care of his friends as had his predecessors until he was convicted and imprisoned for violating the new conflict-of-interest laws he had championed. During the 1970s, a U.S. senator from Maryland, two congressmen, nine state legislators, and a score of lesser officials were convicted of crimes. For most of the United States, including Maryland, the 1970s was a discordant time, with Watergate, urban riots, and Vietnam protests. Maryland emerged from the 1970s with its innocence lost and its political machines broken but with some of the strongest laws governing political ethics in the country.

Along with the move to the suburbs came the transformation of an agricultural and manufacturing economy into a service economy. By the 1990s approximately 60 percent of the state's workers were employed by government or engaged in service work (including finance and transportation), 23 percent were engaged in trade, 10 percent in manufacturing or farming, and 6 percent in construction or other activities. Numerous federal agencies had offices throughout the state, including main offices of the Social Security Administration, the Bureau of the Census, the Bureau of Standards, the National Institutes of Health, and the National Archives.

One of the burgeoning new government services was environmental management. During the 1960s Maryland emphasized preservation of natural resources, soil conservation, halting strip mining, control of beach erosion, and rescue of the collapsing oyster fisheries. In the 1970s attention shifted toward appreciation of nature—expansion of state parks and forests, wildlife preserves, and care of waterfowl and endangered species. By the 1980s environmentalists were most concerned with pollution—control of industrial waste spewed into the air and waterways, toxic waste, sewage treatment, farm run-off, and recycling. The 1990s produced multistate agreements for control of Chesapeake Bay and state-sponsored research into marine life and biotechnology. Maryland was usually near the forefront of the environmental movement, and by most measures the environment was cleaner in the 1990s than in earlier decades.

During the 1980s incomes rose and political tensions lessened. Governor Harry Hughes was an appropriate symbol for the decade, clean cut and quiet spoken, neither liberal nor conservative, judiciously managing the legislature's expansion of health and welfare services, transportation, and schools and colleges. The real-estate boom of the early 1980s tempted the state's poorly regulated savings and loan associations to overexpand and by mid-decade some faced bankruptcy. The state froze assets, sent miscreants to jail, and established controls and depositor insurance, and the episode passed without lasting damage.

Prosperity encouraged the multiplication of cultural and recreational facilities. The Morris Mechanic Theater and the Meyerhoff Symphony Hall came to Baltimore and a major performing arts center to the University of Maryland; the Baltimore Museum of Art, the Walters Art Gallery, and many private galleries expanded; the Maryland Historical Society and the Hall of Records moved into splendid new facilities; the Maryland Arts Council and the Maryland Humanities Council took their activities into every county; and there were hundreds of historical restorations and reenactments of historical events. Ethnic pride increased and ethnic restaurants multiplied. In 1984 the state celebrated the 350th anniversary of its colonial founding. The Baltimore Colts football team left Maryland, but the state built a magnificent new stadium for the Baltimore Orioles baseball team and planned one for the Washington Redskins. Boating on the Chesapeake, hiking in the Appalachians, and sunning at Ocean City reached new peaks of popularity.

As Maryland suburbs soared, and suburban spillover allowed the western and eastern counties to hold their own, Baltimore declined despite valiant efforts at renewal. The city's population fell from 47 percent of the state population in 1940 to 23 percent in 1970 and 12 percent in 1994. As prosperous residents departed for the suburbs, urban tax revenues declined and the poor were left behind. William Donald Schaefer served as governor of Maryland from 1987 to 1995, mainly as a spokesman of economic development. He expanded the state's subsidy for Baltimore with a light-rail system to tie it to the suburbs, new stadiums for its harbor, and funds for schools, police, libraries, and parks. Convinced that universities were engines of economic growth, he combined the University of Maryland, with eleven state colleges, into a single system, hoping that unification would reduce costs and bring research into closer collaboration with business. The state also offered land and tax benefits to entice new businesses and, like the rest of the country, wrestled inconclusively with the problems of abortion, gun control, drunk driving, prostitution, the death penalty, and the right to die. In 1994 the Democratic candidate Parris Glendening, with a program similar to that of Schaefer, won a hairbreadth victory over a conservative Republican candidate.

[Robert J. Brugger, *Maryland* (Baltimore, 1988); George H. Callcott, *Maryland and America, 1940 to 1980* (Baltimore, 1985).]

GEORGE H. CALLCOTT

See also **SUPP:** Baltimore.

MASSACHUSETTS. One of the oldest settlements in British North America in the eighteenth century, the colony most associated with the American Revolution, and later the state most closely associated with the movement to abolish slavery, Massachusetts in the late twentieth century continued to be a national leader in business, politics, education, and the arts and sciences. The state's population grew moderately during the 1970s and 1980s, reaching 6,016,425 in 1990, when Massachusetts ranked sixth among the states in numbers of foreign-born residents and seventh in households with languages other than English. Immigration has continued from the Caribbean, Canada, Britain, Ireland, Italy, Portugal, the Cape Verde Islands, Poland, Russia, and Southeast Asia. African Americans constituted 5 percent of the state's population, Hispanics 4.8 percent, and Asians 2.4 percent. The state ranked third in population living in urban areas (84.3 percent) and sixth in median household income ($36,558). It was first in percentage of the population possessing college degrees.

With its highly concentrated population, Massachusetts nonetheless developed an awkward division between a predominantly white, financially comfortable, highly educated populace in urban and suburban areas, and a poor and much less educated population in the older manufacturing cities and former mill towns. This division may be the most important development in the state since the 1970s. Massachusetts has in effect two separate and unequal societies, one marked by people with excellent housing, schools, and libraries, surrounded by modern office buildings and laboratories, and the other in the older cities and towns plagued by poor housing, dismal schools, and all the economic and social problems that stem from them. Economic trends prior to World War II continued after 1970. There was continuing decline of the textile, shoe, machinery, and food-processing industries. High costs associated with lack of fossil fuels, cold winters, and a location distant from national markets and raw materials, together with unionized workers, made competition with Sunbelt states and newly industrial nations difficult. Most of the traditional manufacturing operations left the state and were replaced by high technology and service industries, which were crucial to the state's late twentieth-century prosperity.

During the recessions of the early 1970s and the late 1980s, state government was plagued by unbalanced budgets, high unemployment, and large increases in public assistance. The subsequent recovery has been called the "Massachusetts miracle." High technology began in the 1960s, supported by military research and breakthroughs in electronics and miniaturization, producing the economic turnaround. Expansion of architecture and engineering firms and centers for medical treatment and research also helped. Unemployment soared to 11.2 percent in 1975 but dropped to 3.2 percent in 1987. New office and hotel towers were built in Boston's business district, matched by office buildings, hotels, factories, and warehouses at almost every interchange of the state's metropolitan highway, Route 128, one of the highest concentrations of high-tech industries in the United States. The early 1990s were marked by cutbacks in military contracts and computer orders, and statewide unemployment reached 9 percent in 1991, but the downturn quickly came to an end. Highly important in the revival was the scientific and technological excellence of the state's universities, especially the Massachusetts Institute of Technology (MIT). Government-sponsored research conducted at MIT during World War II and the cold war decades produced many military breakthroughs with civilian applications. Another contribution was the region's skilled manpower, especially in machine tools, which provided an abundance of trained technicians.

State government may have been antiquated, burdened by patronage, and unable to plan continued economic development, but the Massachusetts Port Authority developed Logan Airport into one of the nation's most important. In the mid-1990s the Massachusetts Bay Transportation Authority operated four subway lines and had expanded rail and boat commuter lines and many bus routes in and around Boston. The state undertook the nation's most costly highway project, rebuilding Boston's Central Artery underground, together with construction of a third harbor tunnel, neither completed as of 1996. On the national political scene, Massachusetts' history of voting for Democrats gave it a reputation for liberalism. Although President Ronald Reagan carried the state with thin majorities in 1980 and 1984, Clinton's majority over George Bush in 1992 was larger than in any other state. In 1990 the state's entire delegation to Congress comprised liberal Democrats. The party held overwhelming majorities in both houses of the state legislature. Massachusetts Representative Thomas P. (Tip) O'Neill served as speaker of the U.S. House of Representatives from 1977 to 1987. All incumbent Massachusetts Democrats in the House were unseated, however, in the November 1994 election.

Republicans and conservative Democrats had remarkable successes in the last quarter of the twentieth century in winning state and local offices. In 1978 a conservative Democrat, Edward J. King, was elected governor. He was closely associated with Proposition 2½, which severely limited the powers of cities and towns to raise taxes on real estate and motor vehicles. A startling change in political sentiments was the downfall of Governor Michael S. Dukakis. His loss of the 1988 presidential election to Bush was attributed to his failure to respond to the Bush campaign's racist and jingoist tactics. For this Dukakis lost the respect of large sectors of a public that had elected him governor three times, and he served as a near powerless "lame duck" during his last two years in office. A Republican, William Weld, was elected governor in 1990, defeating the conservative John Silber, president of Boston University. Democratic leaders in both houses of the state legislature frequently were described as conservative. Conservatives have been notably successful in the state's nonpartisan local elections. Party loyalty weakened in Massachusetts because of an unusual ballot form that scatters party nominees almost at random across the ballot. Nonpartisan local elections deprived parties of support in odd-numbered years.

Culturally, Massachusetts continued to dominate New England in the late twentieth century. A 1971 addition to the Boston Public Library was followed by renovation of its magnificent 1887 building. New wings were added to Boston's Museum of Fine Arts, School of Art, Museum of Science, and the Clark Museum in Williamstown. The Boston Symphony Orchestra gained a new summer hall at Tanglewood in the Berkshires. The State Archives and Museum relocated from the State House in Boston to Columbia Point in Dorchester, joining the John F. Kennedy Library. Boston's Children's Museum relocated to an abandoned waterside warehouse, which it shared successively with the Museum of Transportation and the Computer Museum. In the 1980s community planning was barely mentioned, but a variety of planning proposals appeared in the 1990s. The most successful was the creation of the Cape Cod Commission, established to guide development of one of the state's most popular regions. To counter the continuing rise in automobile use and congestion, three rail transportation improvements were discussed during 1994. One, a rail connection between Boston's North and South Stations, would permit interstate trains to proceed across the city. A circumferential ring just outside downtown Boston would connect two medical centers, three universities, and Logan Airport with South Boston, Roxbury, and Chelsea. A third rail proposal looked to reconstruction of existing freight lines to accommodate passenger rail traffic and connect suburban towns in an arc eighteen to twenty miles west of Boston.

[Michael S. Dukakis and Rosabeth Moss Kanter, *Creating the Future* (New York, 1988); *Encyclopedia of Massachusetts* (New York, 1984); Lawrence W. Kennedy, *Planning the City upon a Hill* (Amherst, Mass., 1992);

David Lampe, ed., *The Massachusetts Miracle* (Cambridge, Mass., 1988); Richard Wilkie et al., *Historical Atlas of Massachusetts* (Amherst, Mass., 1991).]

ROGER FEINSTEIN

See also **SUPP:** Boston.

MEDICARE AND MEDICAID. In most industrialized countries, virtually everyone is covered by governmentally insured health care. The uniquely expensive U.S. medical system, however, consigns most citizens to private health insurance or to none at all. Medicare (government health insurance for the elderly and seriously disabled) and Medicaid (health coverage for the poor under welfare) stand as notable exceptions, accounting for almost one of every three dollars spent on health care in the early 1990s. Since the 1910s major government reform of the U.S. health care system has often seemed to be just around the corner, but, despite overwhelming public support, it has usually foundered on pressures from the medical establishment, crippling charges of socialized medicine, and predictions of greater expense and intrusive, impersonal bureaucracy. President Franklin D. Roosevelt thus omitted health insurance from his Social Security proposals in the 1930s, and President Harry S. Truman's plan in 1945 for national health insurance succumbed to conservative partisanship and an attack from the American Medical Association. With the vast expansion of private health insurance, particularly union-negotiated medical plans, in the 1940s, government plans seemed doomed, but in the 1950s key officials in the Social Security Administration, a group commonly at the core of U.S. welfare state expansion, shifted strategy. To make government health insurance more politically marketable, they proposed that it be confined to the elderly and tied to the increasingly popular old-age insurance program. After all, older Americans, who had to stretch incomes half the national average to cover medical expenses three times as great, could not easily be cast as unworthy welfare cheats. By the late 1950s Medicare was backed by organized labor and many Democrats, including candidate and future president John F. Kennedy. Kennedy never was able to push the program through either house of Congress, and even the legendary legislative skills of his successor, Lyndon B. Johnson, at first could only secure Senate passage. In 1965, however, Kennedy's martyred legacy combined with a strong economy and the overwhelming Democratic congressional majority elected on the coattails of Johnson's 1964 landslide to allow passage of the Social Security Act Amendments of 1965, which established both Medicaid and Medicare as part of Johnson's Great Society.

Medicaid's success came less controversially. Medical interests saw some virtue in the government picking up the tab for hospital or doctor bills of "charity cases," and confining government-funded health care to the poor was a common fall-back position for opponents of more wide-ranging plans. As early as 1950 states had been allowed to make payments under federally subsidized welfare programs directly to hospitals, nursing homes, and doctors. An amendment to the Social Security Act in 1960 (the Kerr-Mills program) beefed up these so-called "vendor payments" for the elderly poor while adding coverage of the "medically indigent" elderly, whose health care expenses would otherwise leave them impoverished. In 1965 a new medical assistance program (Medicaid) extended this coverage of the elderly poor's medical costs to low-income people of all ages who qualified under any federally subsidized, state-administered welfare program.

The Medicaid program had a marked impact. It allowed the poor to receive much more care from doctors and hospitals than previously, when they had often postponed treatment until they required emergency-room care. While two-thirds of its recipients by the mid-1990s were low-income women and children, half of its outlays went to nursing home and other long-term institutional services for the elderly, the disabled, and AIDS patients. It became, in short, a safety net for the American medical system, assisting in coverage ranging from the elderly poor's Medicare premiums and copayments to long-term institutional services for the developmentally disabled and AIDS patients. Medicaid, however, carried the stigma of welfare, and wide disparities among state programs assured that many who needed medical treatment would receive inadequate coverage or none at all. Medicare, by contrast, was a federally administered, contributory, social insurance program, provided to almost all Americans aged sixty-five and over as a right that they had purportedly earned through previous payments. Medicare opponents sought to limit government's role by proposing the alternative of government-subsidized voluntary private insurance that, they noted, would cover a wider range of medical services, including doctor bills, than the original Medicare plan. Wilbur Mills, chairman of the House Ways and Means Committee, cannily adapted this alternative into a new Part B of Medicare. Thus, Medicare Part A, financed by payroll taxes on employers and employees, reimbursed recipients for hospital and limited post-hospitalization home health care and nursing-home costs, while Part B offered older Americans cut-rate insurance policies (made possible by a 75 percent subsidy taken from government general-revenue funds) covering doctor bills, ambulance charges, and certain lab tests.

Despite, or perhaps because of, the gap between the perception of Medicare as an earned benefit and the reality that most of its costs had not been paid by the elderly themselves, the program became very popular, but it was also much more expensive than advocates had anticipated, even though the Social Security Administration's overhead to administer the program was gratifyingly low. To gain the acquiescence of medical interests, Medicare had no cost-control provisions to speak of. Guaranteed reimbursement of all customary or reasonable fees, hospitals and doctors cashed in, pushing up medical prices far faster than general inflation, and provided medical services, lab tests, and technologies that a more cost-conscious system might have precluded. Medicaid reimbursement rates soon became less generous, enough so that many doctors refused to participate. Even so, Medicaid expenditures also rocketed, fueled less by sensational cases of provider fraud than by a combination of greater use of medical services and a 700 percent increase in the number of recipients over the program's first fifteen years—a boon, to be sure, for the health of the poor, but an increasingly resented bust for state budgets. Facing mounting costs, Medicare kept increasing payroll taxes, deductibles, and copayments, and in 1983 and 1992 established systems to limit allowable charges by hospitals and doctors. By the mid-1990s Medicare, Medicaid, and medical costs in general approached financial crisis, assuring further reform.

[Edward D. Berkowitz, *America's Welfare State* (Baltimore, 1991); Sheri I. David, *With Dignity: The Search for Medicare and Medicaid* (Westport, Conn., 1985).]

MARK H. LEFF

See also **SUPP:** Health Care; Social Security; Welfare.

MEDICINE. In the United States as elsewhere, scientific medicine came of age in the twentieth century. Since its improvised colonial beginnings, medicine in America has evolved into an imposing system of skills and technology capable of delivering strikingly successful therapies, but its successes are increasingly powered by a large and complex scientific, commercial, and governmental establishment that many observers criticize as bureaucratic, depersonalizing, and unaffordable. Not coincidentally, the final decades of the twentieth century witnessed important transformations in the way in which medical care was delivered, who delivered it, and how it was financed.

Equally significant changes occurred in the nature of the diseases that affect us and the rate at which they occur. Some of these changes are also the paradoxical legacy of contemporary medicine's successes. As people live longer, the resulting increase in the number of aging Americans has led to a dramatic increase in the degenerative diseases of old age—cancer, heart and kidney disease, dementia, and stroke. Changing social realities have required that matters not previously considered medical, such as the use of tobacco products, become public health issues. A rapidly increasing alcohol- and drug-addicted population became a major public health concern, as did the shocking escalation in the number of injuries and deaths from firearms.

Acquired immune deficiency syndrome (AIDS), a disease first reported in 1981, quickly assumed epidemic proportions, particularly among gay men and intravenous drug users, but fifteen years later AIDS was spreading more rapidly among heterosexual women. By 1995 more than a quarter of a million people with AIDS had died in the United States, and about a million more were infected with the lethal virus, for which no immunization or cure has been discovered. Despite an impressive rate of improvement through use of new antipsychotic and antidepressant drugs, many people required care for mental illness.

Perhaps the most significant advance in medicine in the last quarter of the twentieth century was the burgeoning ability to study human genetic diseases, a breakthrough made possible by the development of recombinant DNA technology. The investigation of a number of devastating genetic diseases, including sickle-cell anemia, Down's syndrome, Huntington's disease, cystic fibrosis, and muscular dystrophy, was made possible by this technology. Historically, disease was dealt with by treating its overt symptoms. It appeared likely that the next advance would be the revolutionary ability to treat disease at its molecular level by introducing normal copies of defective genes into the existing, abnormal genetic structure. In the mid-1990s clinical trials were under way employing gene therapy in the treatment of rheumatoid arthritis, hemophilia, and some types of cancer, as well as sickle-cell anemia, cystic fibrosis, muscular dystrophy, and other conditions.

Important developments also took place in neurology and psychoneuroimmunology, with the discovery that the normal release of chemicals in the brain has an extremely far-reaching effect that influences most of the body's systems, nerve functioning, and emotional behavior. The development of medications that enhance or inhibit the production of serotonin, dopamine, and other neurotransmitters mitigated the debilitating neurological and psychological symptoms of disorders such as Parkinson's disease, Huntington's disease, and depression.

Other major advances occurred at the juncture of recombinant gene therapy, immunology, and virology. In 1994 vaccines were licensed for chicken pox and hepatitis A. A hepatitis B vaccine was licensed a decade earlier. The rapidly mutating influenza virus has defeated all efforts to bring it under effective control, but a global network of laboratories, led by the World Health Organization, began collaborating to identify new strains of influenza as they appear, saving many lives by minimizing the time between the beginning of epidemics and the production and distribution of appropriate vaccines. Although neither immunization nor a cure had been found for AIDS, the duration and quality of the lives of HIV and AIDS patients improved dramatically with the development of a number of drugs that inhibit reproduction of the virus at various stages of the disease.

A substantial number of the major breakthroughs in contemporary medicine were technological. Extremely sophisticated diagnostic techniques were developed, including nuclear medicine scanning tests and imaging devices such as magnetic resonance imaging (MRI) and computerized axial tomography (CAT scans), which provide images of the brain, heart, gastrointestinal tract, and other soft tissues. Advances in Doppler echo and other ultrasound technology provided a noninvasive technique for determining blood flow velocity in various locations in the body. This technology affords the opportunity for noninvasive anatomical evaluation in many fields, including obstetrics, gastroenterology, and urology. DNA science now permits replication of human genes and their transfer to products that can be used for therapeutic purposes. Furthermore, its diagnostic, predictive, and forensic uses have become increasingly refined. Equally sophisticated therapeutic and surgical procedures also rely on complex, advanced technology, such as organ transplantation.

One totally nontechnological field that came to the fore as an important part of medical intercession was prevention. Since the 1970s much emphasis is placed on educational programs designed to teach people proper nutrition and exercise in order to avoid illness. Nutrition and exercise were recognized as important in the prevention and control of heart disease, hypertension, diabetes, and other chronic diseases and in promoting health generally. Nonetheless, technology is central to contemporary medicine and is very costly. Reliance upon elaborate equipment and procedures resulted in a growing number of people receiving outpatient examination, testing, and treatment in hospitals rather than in doctors' offices or at home. The greatest increase in the cost of medical care since the 1960s was in hospital care. The enormous medical establishment that evolved in the last third of the twentieth century included pharmaceutical and medical equipment manufacturers, insurance carriers, and an abundantly supported research community, as well as federal, state, and local government.

The federal government is involved in important ways in the furnishing of health care. On the civilian side, through the Department of Veterans Affairs, it operates approximately 900 hospitals, nursing homes, ambulatory care clinics, and veterans counseling centers. It also directs the Indian Health Service, which provides comprehensive health care services to Native Americans. Through the Public Health Service, the federal government administers the Centers for Disease Control and Prevention (CDC) and the National Institutes of Health (NIH). The CDC is the federal agency charged with providing leadership and direction in the prevention and control of diseases and responding to public health emergencies. The NIH is the principal biomedical research agency of the federal government. Both were intimately involved in virtually all of the significant advances since the mid-1960s. The medical contributions of the military are not limited to the health services commands of the armed forces. Ultrasound technology, adapted from military sonar, is an example of an important military contribution to the health of the population as a whole.

Beginning in the 1970s, the trend among physicians toward specialization was reversed and more family practitioners, general pediatricians, and internists entered practice. Increasingly, too, physician assistants, nurse-practitioners, and nurse-midwives—often referred to as physician extenders—performed many procedures traditionally reserved to physicians.

Ethical issues have always been critical in medicine because they deal with matters of life and death, but the medical technology developed in the late twentieth century gave new urgency to ethical questions. The ability to prolong life for months and even years after a person's heart or lungs have failed recasts the question of what life is and when death occurs. Organ transplantation and human medical experiments generate great debate, and DNA science has raised a new world of ethical concerns.

[James H. Cassedy, *Medicine in America: A Short History* (Baltimore, 1991); Lester S. King, *Transformations in American Medicine* (Baltimore, 1991); Jeff Lyon and Peter Gorner, *Altered Fates: Gene Therapy and the Retooling of Human Life* (New York, 1995); Paul Starr, *The Social Transformation of American Medicine* (New York, 1982).]

JACK HANDLER

See also **SUPP:** Acquired Immune Deficiency Syndrome; Cardiovascular Disease; Centers for Disease Control and Prevention; Clinical Research; Computerized Axial Tomography; Euthanasia; Genetic Engineering; Health and Human Services, Department of; Health Care; Health Maintenance Organizations; Magnetic Resonance Imaging; Medicaid and Medicare; Medicine, Alternative; National Institutes of Health; Patients' Rights; Physician Assistants; Public Health Service; Surgery; Transplants and Organ Donation; Women's Health.

MEDICINE, ALTERNATIVE. In seeking to understand and treat their illnesses, Americans have always had recourse to a great variety of healing practices. Conventional physicians have had to compete with a wide range of alternatives, including folk healing, prayer, popular health manuals, midwifery, patent medicines, osteopathy, Christian Science, homeopathy, herbalism, water cure, and more recently Chinese medicine, Ayurveda, meditation, yoga, and an assortment of New Age practices. The list of available and emergent alternatives could be expanded indefinitely. Healing in America can take place in a clinic, home, community center, church, and temple. Despite the efforts of organized medicine to regulate access to health care providers, the medical marketplace in the late twentieth century remained as diverse and as crowded as ever.

When suffering from illness, people generally are pragmatic in seeking care. They might initially try self-treatment or ask advice from friends, family, and neighbors. Depending on the character, severity, and duration of the complaint, and in accordance with past experiences and trusted advice, they may then visit one or more health care providers, following an implicit hierarchy of resort. Most people do not use only one sort of health care for all the ailments they may suffer; for a chronic condition, a person will often seek out a variety of explanations and treatments. In practice, then, alternative medicine is more accurately described as complementary medicine. Since the 1980s surveys have shown that those with the most resources—the better educated and those with access to information networks—are more likely than the poor and less educated to use alternative medicine. The search for explanations and therapeutic experimentation are strongly associated with having the confidence and the knowledge to assert control over one's state of health.

There is no fixed definition of conventional scientific medicine. Indeed, some practices and theories, such as autointoxication, that once were impeccably conventional came to appear quite unconventional, while many previously alternative modalities, such as acupuncture, gradually gained biomedical validation. No medical intervention is inherently or self-evidently conventional or alternative. Accordingly, the best definitions of conventional medicine are those derived from its organizational or social features. A practice is conventional if it is taught in medical schools and is acceptable to the organized medical profession—in this context, the American Medical Association (AMA) and specialist groups.

Between the 1830s, when most states repealed medical licensing laws, and the 1870s, when licensure was gradually reintroduced, the medical profession was remarkably open. Orthodox physicians competed equally with nonorthodox or "sectarian" doctors; proprietary medical schools proliferated, often providing only perfunctory training; and many new healing practices were imported from Europe or were formulated locally. During this period orthodox physicians tried to develop a coherent and stable professional identity in order to distinguish themselves from sectarians. Orthodox medical training began to include more formal scientific education, often in universities rather than proprietary schools, and state medical associations made sure their members did not later stray onto the sectarian path. The AMA, established in 1847, campaigned vigorously against nonscientific competitors. By 1900 the organized medical profession could demand that anyone wanting to practice medicine show a diploma from a recognized medical school. Those who could not were deemed "quacks," a term that once had been applied to self-promoters and frauds of all persuasions (including those making fanciful claims for conventional therapies). When a healing practice could not be suppressed, many of its practitioners could be assimilated; thus, in 1903 the AMA welcomed into its ranks those homeopaths and herbalists willing to forsake their "speculations" for "science." Once the most liberal of medical marketplaces, the United States, after the orthodox backlash, began to restrict alternative medicine with a rigor rarely observed in comparable societies, such as Australia, Great Britain, and the rest of Europe.

Folk medicine has always been one of the more popular resources for understanding and treating disease in America. Unlike many modern alternatives, access to folk methods usually requires a long-standing and broad allegiance to a specific cultural group. Long before Europeans arrived with their folk medicines (and a more cosmopolitan elite medicine based on classical texts), Native Americans had developed their own healing traditions, which emphasized spiritual well-being and ecological integration, including the use of local botanical remedies. Over the past 300 and more years African Americans have constructed out of African and Christian traditions socially potent blends of herbal and spiritual healing, sometimes called hoodoo or rootwork. Like most folk medicine, this healing system gives its adherents an understanding and a sense of control of the community, the environment, and the spiritual world. Similarly, Hispanic folk medicine, which derives from indigenous herbal knowledge and Spanish humoral theories, has worked for many centuries as an adaptable and intellectually satisfying explanatory model of disease. Health, in this nonmedical model, is a state of balance between the four humors; if disturbed by a "cold" or a "hot" disease, the balance can be restored by using food or medicine with an opposing character. These are some examples of the more vigorous folk traditions. Every family and community in the United States retains elements of their folk medical heritage—even if only to "feed a cold and starve a fever."

Belief in miraculous, divine healing frequently has offered an alternative to the materialism of modern conventional medicine. Religious healing—oriented toward worship and devotion—finds expression in individual prayer, the Catholic tradition of pilgrimage, and the evangelical laying on of hands. In the late nineteenth century, Mary Baker Eddy drew on New England transcendentalism to fashion a belief system, Christian Science, that depended on religious faith to cure all disease. A form of radical idealism, Christian Science requires its followers to regard the body, disease, and death as illusions; any materialist preoccupation, such as an interest in conventional medical explanation, is assumed to impede spiritual healing. The great majority of alternative therapies, however, are not so exclusive.

One of the earlier semi-institutionalized alternatives to orthodox medical practices was botanical medicine, the systematic use of roots, herbs, and barks by lay healers. Formulated by Samuel Thomson in the early nineteenth century, this mild, herbal regime became a popular alternative to conventional "heroic" therapeutics, especially in rural areas of the West and South. By the 1840s botanical physicians had begun to form medical societies and issue diplomas, but the movement soon divided into factions and faded away at the end of the century. A more lasting challenge to conventional therapeutics came from homeopathy, the doctrine that disease could be cured only by very small doses of the drugs that produced in a healthy person the symptoms found in the sick. In other words, like cures like, using infinitesimal amounts. Derived from the experimental pharmacology of Samuel Hahnemann, homeopathy became popular among the urban elite in the northeastern United States soon after its introduction in the 1820s. By the 1880s most large cities had a homeopathic college, and in the 1890s examining boards were set up to license homeopathic physicians. Although most homeopathic institutions converted to conventional teaching in the early twentieth century, since the 1970s there has been a revival of interest in homeopathic principles.

In the twentieth century, osteopathy was the most significant institutionalized alternative to conventional medicine. When Andrew Taylor Still, a frontier physician, became dissatisfied with conventional "drugging" methods, he speculated that the underlying cause of illness was an obstruction to the flow of electricity through the body, leading to an imbalance of vital force that could be fixed only through spinal manipulation. By merging magnetic healing and the older technique of bonesetting and expressing his findings in religious language, Still attracted thousands of patients to his clinic in Kirksville, Mo., during the 1890s. In the twentieth century osteopathic medicine managed to maintain its schools, hospitals, specialty boards, and journals, although doctors of osteopathy increasingly provided the same services as medical doctors, with manipulation having only a small part in their repertoire. Chiropractics, which was developed by Daniel D. Palmer a few years after Still announced his new doctrine, has remained more focused on spinal manipulation but has not yet enjoyed the same institutional success as osteopathy.

In the late twentieth century, an interest in Asian healing systems emerged in the United States. Acupuncture has probably attracted more popular and scientific attention than any other recent introduction. Part of traditional Chinese medicine—along with acupressure, herbology, moxibustion, and dietetic regimes—the insertion of needles at certain acupuncture points is supposed to rebalance or unblock the flow of life energy (*chi*), which normally circulates through the body along the acupuncture meridians. According to this theory, illness develops from an obstruction of *chi* along one of the twelve double meridians. In the 1980s scientists began to try to provide more conventional explanations for the physiological changes observed in acupuncture.

Since the 1970s an eclectic holistic health movement promoted a broader health consciousness, drawing on a vast array of old and new alternative practices, including (but not limited to) naturopathy, meditation, yoga, acupuncture, "bodywork," biofeedback, flower essences, and exercise. The emphasis of this middle-class health reform movement was on the individual's responsibility for finding the right idiosyncratic mixture of holistic practices. Health was viewed as a positive physical and spiritual state, not just the absence of disease. This social movement had its information networks, metaphysical bookstores, health-food shops, informal groups, and journals, but unlike many nineteenth-century alternatives, it was not based itself on a conventional medical model.

[Norman Gevitz, ed., *Other Healers: Unorthodox Medicine in America* (Baltimore, 1988); Wayland D. Hand, ed., *American Folk Medicine: A Symposium* (Berkeley, Calif., 1976).]

WARWICK ANDERSON

See also **DAH:** Folk Medicine; Homeopathy; Indian Medicine; Medicine and Surgery; Osteopathy; **SUPP:** Medicine.

MEGALOPOLIS, a term coined from the name of a settlement in Peloponnese Greece meaning "great city," was first employed by the urbanist Lewis Mumford in *The Culture of Cities* (1938) as a metaphor for unnaturally large urban development. Such inorganic trends, he maintained, reflected "not a new kind of city on a supermetropolitan scale" but rather an "anti-city." Likened to one big "atomized container," megalopolitan areas, he warned, would produce "massive monotony" and result in "an increasingly homogenized urbanoid mass that lacks the complex social and cultural attributes of the city." With no nucleus, no organic nature, no essence of city, this process both "denatures the countryside and

mechanically scatters fragments of the city over the whole landscape."

In contrast, the American physicist J. Robert Oppenheimer and the French geographer Jean Gottmann contended in 1950 that the megalopolis should be seen more positively. In *Megalopolis* (1961), Gottmann challenged Mumford's gloomy forecast, saying that a continuous network of urban communities, such as that stretching from Boston to Washington, D.C., represented the blueprint for the future. He argued that this region constitutes one of the world's largest industrial belts and "the greatest financial and political hubs on earth." With a population exceeding 40 million in 1995, more the size of a nation than a metropolis, the Northeast corridor of the United States contains the world's most highly developed concentration of large urban centers, with an increasingly suburban, white-collar population.

In addition to this prototype there are eight other megalopolises around the globe with more than 25 million people each, the second largest being located in the "Tokaido" region of Japan stretching from the conurbation of Tokyo-Yokohama to Osaka-Kōbe. Others include the Great Lakes megalopolis, extending from Quebec City to Milwaukee; the urban constellation of Shanghai; the area of northwestern Europe from Amsterdam and the Ruhr to Lille; the English urban sprawl from Dover to Merseyside; the Italian plain of the Po River to the Mediterranean, from Genoa to Marseilles and Pisa; Rio de Janeiro to São Paulo; California from the Mexico border to the San Francisco Bay area, and, most recently, a megalopolitan region in India.

[Jean Gottmann, *Megalopolis: The Urbanized Seaboard of the United States* (New York, 1961); Jean Gottmann and Robert A. Harper, eds., *Since Megalopolis: The Urban Writings of Jean Gottmann* (Baltimore, 1990); Lewis Mumford, *The Urban Prospect* (New York, 1968).]

TIMOTHY C. COOGAN

See also **DAH:** Cities, Growth of; City Planning; Urban Structure; **SUPP:** Demographic Changes; Suburban Living; Urban Living.

MEMPHIS, the largest city in Tennessee and the eighteenth largest in the United States, experienced an economic and cultural resurgence from the late 1970s to the mid-1990s. A thriving port city because of its location on the east bank of the Mississippi River, Memphis languished during the 1970s but rebounded in the 1980s. It established itself as a major distribution center, especially as the central terminal of the delivery service Federal Express in the 1970s. During the 1980s the city's downtown area prospered. The historic Peabody Hotel was renovated, and the city spent $63 million constructing a museum on Mud Island, near the downtown area, that included a five-block-long model of the Mississippi River. Along the river itself, old cotton shippers' offices were restored, and the architecturally striking thirty-two-story Pyramid entertainment and sports arena was built. In 1991 the National Civil Rights Museum opened, occupying the shell of the Loran Motel, the site of the assassination in 1968 of Martin Luther King, Jr. Following the death of Elvis Presley at his Graceland estate on Aug. 16, 1977, Graceland became the most visited house in the United States, with 750,000 tourists in 1994. During Elvis International Tribute Week, held annually in mid-August, dozens of events attract 50,000 tourists. Memphis has retained its dominance in cotton marketing and hardwood lumber trading. By the early 1990s its largest industry was health care, with treatment, education, and research bringing $2.5 billion per year to the city's economy. The 1990 population of Memphis was 610,337, 54.8 percent of which were African Americans.

JEFFREY M. MERRON

See also **SUPP:** Tennessee.

MENTAL ILLNESS, a common reference for disorders of thought, mood, or conduct, including schizophrenia, which affects about 1 percent of the U.S. population at some time in their lives; bipolar disorder (or manic-depressive illness), which affects 1 to 2 percent; and major depression, which strikes about 5 percent. These disorders are considered major because when untreated they have devastating consequences. They can take a considerable economic and social toll and cause great personal suffering. The ability to work or to have stable relationships and families is often lost or severely impaired. Rates of suicide are very high (10 to 20 percent) in people with these diagnoses and early death is the norm. Treatment often requires hospitalization. Other important diagnoses associated with disability or suicide include borderline personality disorder, panic disorder, and obsessive-compulsive disorder. Alcoholism and drug abuse often are included among major psychiatric diagnoses. In the United States, 10 percent of the population meet the definition for alcohol abuse or dependence at some time in their lives and almost 6 percent for other drugs.

In the last third of the twentieth century, ways to define mental illness sharpened and led to widespread belief that some of the most important disorders are diseases. Although patterns of symptoms had long been recognized, such as "schizophrenia" or "manic-depressive illness," there was uncertainty as to whether a psychiatric condition was an "illness" or an understandable response to a disturbed familial and social environment. Three developments made these disorders appear as illnesses. First, as drug treatment developed, mental disorders responded to them. It became clear that tranquilizers are not just sedatives. They help schizophrenics organize their thoughts and behaviors and suppress or eliminate hallucinations. These drugs, commonly called neuroleptics, were introduced in the 1950s. Twenty years later lithium (a mineral) came into use as an aid to stabilizing mood swings of bipolar disorder. Research results on the response to these medications showed that people with schizophrenia and bipolar disorder are biologically different from each other, even though in the acute phase of illness they are not easy to tell apart. Second, the risk of developing one or the other of these diseases appears to be inherited. Epidemiological research conducted since the 1950s shows that there is a genetic component to these illnesses, although environmental influences, such as toxic exposures, may function as triggers. It is also apparent that psychological stressors initiate episodes of illness. Third, research in the neurosciences provided evidence that mental illnesses are associated with abnormalities in the brain. As imaging methods developed it became possible to demonstrate subtle structural damage in the brains of schizophrenics. Bipolar disorder, however, is associated with biochemical abnormalities.

The emerging belief that mental illnesses are specific disorders, often with a basis in biology, supported a shift in psychiatry. Whereas assignment to a diagnostic category often included inferences about the psychological processes of the patient, psychiatrists turned to a descriptive approach, using observable behavior and the course of the illness to establish a diagnosis. This change now appears in the *Diagnostic and Statistical Manual of Mental Disorders,* published by the American Psychiatric Association. The first two editions, 1952 and 1968, maintained a "process" orientation, whereas the third and fourth, in 1980 and 1994, emphasized a descriptive approach. These books, known as *DSM-III* or *DSM-IV,* have enormous influence on mental health practice. Insurance reimbursement usually requires a *DSM* diagnosis. Examinations to certify psychiatrists rely on familiarity with *DSM* criteria.

Years ago there were two avenues to treat major mental disorders. A "cure" could be attempted through restructuring the patient's experience, chiefly with psychotherapy or milieu treatment in an institution. If unavailing and the illness did not remit of its own accord the alternative was prolonged institutional care. The dichotomy between cure or custody was superseded by both medical and social approaches. Medication helped keep the mentally ill out of hospitals, often called "deinstitutionalization." The community mental health movement, originally focused on efforts to prevent mental illness, evolved in part into a philosophy of rehabilitation. The environment of a mental hospital itself produces dependency and disorganization. Allowing patients to live in the least restrictive environment compatible with their well-being proved more effective. There is evidence that people with chronic mental illness prefer being able to live outside a hospital, although deinstitutionalization has deprived many people of care and led to increased homelessness. Such was the case in the last quarter of the twentieth century in large cities, where political and economic exigencies (for example, overcrowding of institutions) rather than social or bureaucratic munificence prompted the emptying out of mental hospitals.

Although drugs for psychiatric disorders can have serious side effects, they can improve the quality of life for people with schizophrenia, major depression, or manic-depressive illness as well as anxiety disorders, obsessive-compulsive disorder, and other conditions, such as premenstrual dysphoric disorder (commonly referred to as PMS). The most important innovation in drug treatment since the late 1980s is the increasingly widespread use of clozapine (trade name Clozaril), a unique antipsychotic drug once thought to be too dangerous because of its ability to cause a dramatic and even lethal lowering of white blood cells. Research shows that clozapine benefits one-third of people with schizophrenia resistant to treatment with other medications. The drug requires a blood test every week.

Meanwhile there was a shift in ethical and legal attitudes. Individual autonomy increasingly received attention, even if the person's choice would not be seen by most people as in his or her own best interest. The right of a competent person to refuse medical treatment of any kind, even if it is life-saving, became established. Definitions of competence changed and many people with impairment due to mental ill-

ness are now considered competent to manage some of their affairs and particularly to refuse psychiatric treatment unless symptoms are so severe as to put life (their own or another's) at risk. Many more people with disturbing symptoms are now living independently, often in public view, rather than confined to hospitals.

[Michael J. Dear and Jennifer R. Wolch, *Landscapes of Despair: From Deinstitutionalization to Homelessness* (Princeton, N.J., 1987); James H. Kocsis et al., *Diagnosis and Treatment of Chronic Depression* (New York, 1995); Christian L. Shriqui and Henry A. Nasrallah, eds., *Contemporary Issues in the Treatment of Schizophrenia* (Washington, D.C., 1995); J. Mark G. Williams, *The Psychological Treatment of Depression,* 2nd ed. (New York, 1992).]

WILLIAM IRA BENNETT

See also **SUPP:** Psychiatry; Psychology; Substance Abuse.

MERCHANT MARINE, and to a lesser extent the seagoing shipping of other nations, underwent enormous change beginning in the second half of the twentieth century, including a veritable revolution in handling freight. Over the centuries, merchandise carried overseas went in break-bulk, that is, divided into parcels of varying size. Such handling continued during the age of steam and the diesel engine. Terminal activities in this scheme of moving goods were labor intensive. Cargoes should have been handled at a low cost with care and speed, but often this was not the case. Collective-bargaining agreements between shippers and unions increased longshoremen's hours for specific jobs. Work stoppages occurred on the docks. Moreover, break-bulk items were frequently damaged or lost due to poor handling or theft.

All this came to an end with the introduction of the container system, created by Malcolm McLean, a former truck driver and founder of McLean Trucking who knew little about shipping. (A container is a box up to forty feet long and eight feet wide and is transported on land by the use of a chassis that is pulled by a truck; containers are double stacked without a chassis when hauled by train.) McLean sought an inexpensive way to return containers from New York to Texas and fitted two tankers with platforms above the decks for carrying thirty-five-foot boxes. He purchased Pan-Atlantic Steamship Corporation and Waterman Steamship in 1955. In April of the next year, Pan Atlantic's *Ideal X,* the world's first container ship, sailed from Port Newark, N.J., to Houston. Pan-Atlantic announced that it would convert other ships into container ships. When these vessels went to sea, McLean told their captains not to bother him with nautical nonsense; they were ship drivers at sea. The first fully containerized vessel, *Gateway City*, began regular service between New York, Florida, and Texas in 1957. Pan-Atlantic Steamship Corporation changed its name to Sea-Land in 1960. In sending freight across the oceans, the container revolution proved as influential as the shift from sail to steam. In one brilliant leap McLean produced an entirely different type of ship. The *Gateway City* had a capacity for 226 thirty-five-foot containers. It could be turned around in one day by two shore-based gantry cranes. With break-bulk, this would have taken weeks. Once the system came into full operation, damage and pilferage decreased dramatically. Matson Navigation helped to make containerization a familiar word in the shipping industry; the company developed a gantry crane that could handle 520 containers every twenty-four hours.

Other developments quickly followed. During the early 1960s a division of American President Lines known as Pacific Far East Line (PFEL) transported military supplies to Vietnam. No one knew how long that war would last, and it seemed unwise to consider building docks and erecting gantry cranes at Cam Ranh Bay in South Vietnam. PFEL used a lighter aboard ship (LASH) system. Sea-Land, the original innovator, then introduced another novelty, this time in the pattern of trade employed by container ships voyaging to East Asia. Because Sea-Land ships were returning to Oakland, Calif., with empty containers, the company therefore sought business in Japan, and without waiting for cooperation from the Japanese government, it arranged gantry cranes and other container equipment in a Japanese port, thereby giving Sea-Land a profitable back haul. The result was worldwide competition. After Sea-Land's move in Japan, local shipping firms installed U.S. equipment. In a short time Japanese companies built container ships and were competing with U.S. companies. British shippers also moved to develop container capability.

McLean eventually overreached himself in attempting to create a worldwide line specializing in container ship commerce. After selling Sea-Land in May 1969 to the R. J. Reynolds Tobacco Company, which was seeking to diversify, McLean acquired the United States Lines and purchased another old American line, Moore McCormack. He signed contracts in 1983 for twelve new container ships, to be built in the huge Daewoo yards in South Korea. The $570 million order represented the largest single peacetime shipbuilding contract and the largest expansion of the U.S. Merchant Marine in its entire history. McLean conceived of a remarkable commerce, in which a Daewoo-built ship would depart an East Asian port for the Panama Canal, and after transit calls at East Coast ports, sail to Western Europe. After leaving the Mediterranean, passing through the Suez Canal, and calling at Middle Eastern ports, the ship would move on to the East Asian port of origin, thus completing a worldwide loop. He described the proposed route as his Sea Bridge. He would reach all areas of the world with the Sea Bridge except for West Africa, Australia, and New Zealand. The Sea Bridge operation began in December 1984, but after a few months of operation, McLean's venture turned into bankruptcy, with a loss of nearly $100 million in a single quarter. In 1987 the Econships, as they were known, were sold, then began operating under U.S. flag and Sea-Land ownership.

U.S. container ships continued to carry much world commerce. From 1985 to 1995 the volume of exports of containerized cargo from New York harbor alone jumped by 53 percent, from 2.68 million long tons to 4.1 million (a long ton, the traditional measure of shipping, is 2,240 pounds). The value of this shipping rose from $9.59 billion to $17.14 billion, a 32 percent increase after factoring in inflation. The Port Authority of New York and New Jersey estimated that it handled $56.31 billion in cargo in 1993, generating 180,800 jobs. Part of the Port Authority's increase in business was caused by modernization, including new railway links, crucial because containers go directly from freighters onto trucks and trains, all the while tracked by computers. Labor relations in the Port of New York area have improved, but the principal reason for the resurgence of the New York–New Jersey area has been the sheer efficiency of the container ships.

The leading U.S. ports on the East Coast are New York–New Jersey, with 38 percent of the North Atlantic trade, mostly containerized cargo, followed by Norfolk, Va., Philadelphia, and Baltimore. In the Gulf of Mexico, the principal port is Houston. New Orleans leads on the Mississippi. On the West Coast the leading ports are Seattle-Tacoma, San Francisco (including Oakland), Long Beach, and Los Angeles. The tonnage carried by the U.S. Merchant Marine has risen because of container ships. In the 1940s construction of mass-produced Liberty and Victory ships raised tonnage spectacularly, and as late as 1960 the Merchant Marine under U.S. registry stood at almost 25 billion gross tons. Twenty years later it had dropped to nearly 18.5 billion, but by 1993 it had reached the remarkable figure of almost 22.5 billion gross tons.

[René De La Pedraja, *The Rise and Decline of U.S. Merchant Shipping in the Twentieth Century* (New York, 1992); John Niven, *The American President Line* (Newark, Del., 1986).]

CHARLES V. REYNOLDS, JR.

MERCY KILLING. *See* **Euthanasia.**

MERGERS AND ACQUISITIONS. *See* **Leveraged Buyouts.**

MERITOR SAVINGS BANK V. MECHELLE VINSON, 477 U.S. 57 (1986), a Supreme Court decision that attempted for the first time to define what standard a court should use to determine sexual harassment under Title VII of the Civil Rights Act of 1964. The two main issues were whether a plaintiff's claim of sexual harassment could succeed if based on psychological aspects without tangible loss of an economic character, and whether employers are absolutely liable in cases of sexual harassment by supervisors. Mechelle Vinson was an employee at Meritor Savings Bank under the supervision of the vice president and branch manager, Sidney Taylor, and Vinson had earned various promotions on the basis of merit. Vinson testified that Taylor invited her to dinner, repeatedly proposed sexual relations, leading to forty or fifty occasions of intercourse, fondled her in front of employees, followed her into the women's restroom, exposed himself to her, and raped her on several occasions. At first Vinson resisted but ceased to do so out of fear of losing her job. She testified she never reported the incidents or used the bank's complaint procedure out of fear and because she would have to make the claim directly to her supervisor, Taylor. He stopped sexually harassing her when Vinson began dating someone steadily. She was fired for taking an excessive leave of absence.

Subsequently, she filed a sexual harassment claim for violations of Title VII. Both the bank and Taylor denied Vinson's accusations and insisted that the claim arose from a business-related dispute. The bank asserted that if Vinson's claims were true, the supervisor's activities were unknown to the bank's executive managers and engaged in without its consent. The federal district court held that for a sexual harassment claim to prevail the plaintiff had to demonstrate a tangible economic loss. The court also held that the bank was not liable for the misconduct of its supervisors. On both counts the circuit court reversed in favor of Vinson. The bank appealed to the Supreme Court, which in a unanimous decision decided for Vinson on the first point, but held that employers were not automatically liable for sexual harassment by supervisors. Similarly, however, absence of notice to an employer did not insulate the business from liability for the acts of supervisors. In such cases the issue was one of fact, which required meeting a burden of proof. The case placed sexual harassment resulting from a hostile work environment on an equal footing with sexual harassment resulting in the loss of job or promotion. The case put employers on notice that they must review supervisors' conduct because mere absence of notice of improper conduct is no longer a defense.

TONY FREYER

See also **SUPP:** Sexual Harassment.

MEXICAN AMERICANS represent both an old and a new ethnic group in the United States. Some can trace their backgrounds to the early Spanish-Indian encounters in both Mexico and the U.S. Southwest. Others migrated to the United States from Mexico in the twentieth century. It is this combination of old and new, past and present, that gives the history of Mexican Americans its character. Spain's conquest of Mexico and the Aztec empire in 1521 led to development of a mixed or mestizo people consisting of Indians and Spaniards. This encounter became the basis for the colonial missions and settlements that stretched from Texas to California. A Spanish-Mexican cultural presence was implanted that is visible today in the names of southwestern locations. These Spanish-Mexican settlements, however, were coveted by the United States following independence from Great Britain. The United States undertook an expansionist drive after the Louisiana Purchase (1803) from France placed the young nation in direct proximity to Spain's northern frontier. After Mexico's own independence from Spain in 1821, it came under increased U.S. pressure to cede its inherited northern borderlands. In 1836 Texas, under control of U.S. immigrants, established its independence, and in 1845 it was annexed by the United States. Coveting additional Mexican territory, the United States successfully waged war against Mexico in 1846–1848. The subsequent Treaty of Guadalupe Hidalgo provided for transfer of the balance of Mexico's northern lands, which included the present-day states of Colorado, Nevada, Utah, California, and most of Arizona and New Mexico. The resident Mexican population became U.S. citizens.

The period following the Mexican War marked a dark era in Mexican-American history. U.S. rule led to pressures on Mexican-American landowners resulting in loss of property to squatters, litigation, taxes, and market pressures. In addition, Mexican Americans were treated like second-class citizens. Mexican Americans might have become a footnote in U.S. history had it not been for a subsequent mass migration from Mexico. Pushed out of their own country by both poverty and the Mexican Revolution that began in 1910, immigrants were drawn into the United States because of the need for labor for U.S. railroads, mines, and farms. More than a million crossed the border between 1900 and 1930. They expanded older settlements in the Southwest, established new barrios, and renewed the Mexican-American cultural presence in the United States. The Great Depression stopped this migration and generated pressure to deport immigrants. In response, U.S.-born Mexicans launched a civil rights movement focusing on discrimination in education, jobs, wages, housing, political representation, and racial and cultural stereotyping. They sought integration in U.S. society. The move was vastly assisted by the involvement of thousands of Mexican Americans in World War II, in which many were awarded citations for bravery, including the Medal of Honor.

A new generation, that of Chicano Americans, appeared in the 1960s. Composed of children or grandchildren of immigrants, this generation of activists defiantly called themselves Chicanos (a working-class barrio term) and advocated cultural pride. Influenced by the struggle of farm workers led by Cesar Chavez, they brought pressure on schools to institute Chicano studies and bilingual education. They instituted a cultural and artistic resurgence centered on Chicano identity. There was a Chicano anti–Vietnam War movement and the beginning of a Chicano feminist movement. They established a Chicano political party (La Raza Unida). The most widespread Mexican-American protest movement in history, the Chicano movement brought the plight and aspirations of Mexican Americans to national and international attention. The Chicano movement of the 1960s and 1970s defeated some but by no means all forms of discrimination. The emergence of a more conservative U.S. political climate in the 1980s and 1990s made civil rights struggles more difficult. Still, Mexi-

can Americans continued to integrate into U.S. society while asserting their identity in a pluralistic nation, partly because of their and other Hispanics' growing numbers in the United States. By 1990 Mexican Americans constituted three-fifths of the twenty-two million Hispanics in the United States.

While Mexican Americans have constituted a permanent and settled part of the U.S. population for some time, immigration from Mexico has continued to reinforce this population and remains a key factor in Mexican-American life. During World War II, for example, thousands of braceros (contract workers) were imported into the United States from Mexico to work, especially in agriculture. The Bracero Program was maintained from 1942 to 1964. Many braceros did not return to Mexico at the prescribed time and remained in the United States without proper documentation. Moreover, the Bracero Program helped stimulate an increase in undocumented immigration; many who did not qualify for the program crossed the border illegally and undocumented immigration continued to escalate after the program ended. To deal with the impact of illegal immigration, Congress in 1986 passed the Immigration Reform and Control Act, which provided amnesty for those who could prove they had been working in the United States for a number of years.

[Mario T. Garcia, *Desert Immigrants: The Mexicans of El Paso, 1880–1920* (New Haven, Conn., 1981), and *Mexican Americans: Leadership, Ideology, and Identity, 1930–1960* (New Haven, Conn., 1989); Peter Skerry, *Mexican Americans: The Ambivalent Minority* (New York, 1993).]

MARIO T. GARCIA

See also **DAH:** Guadalupe Hidalgo, Treaty of; Mexican War; Texas; **DAH** and **SUPP:** Immigration; Mexico, Relations with.

MEXICO, RELATIONS WITH. U.S. relations with Mexico in the second half of the twentieth century were complicated, principally because the two nations, despite strikingly different cultures and often conflicting political agendas in the international arena, nonetheless created economic bonds of lasting importance. The modern relationship between Mexico and the United States took form during and after World War II, when Washington's need for strategic resources and cheap Mexican labor coincided with Mexican determination to achieve U.S. approval of its revolutionary agenda and to modernize its economy. The half century after World War II witnessed volatile political exchanges between Washington and Mexico City over cold war issues (such as the Cuban and Nicaraguan revolutions), immigration, trade, U.S. business in Mexico, debts, drugs, and political corruption—but the intertwining of the two economies continued. The approval of the North American Free Trade Agreement (NAFTA) in 1993 merely formalized this unequal economic union, particularly along the 2,000-mile border. By the year 2000, some observers believe, the 100-mile-wide swath on either side of the legal demarcation may be the most populated region in North America and will be filled with factories. Unlike its Canadian-U.S. counterpart, however, the Mexican-U.S. border embodies the anticipated social, cultural, and political dysfunctions that accompany the meshing of a postindustrial with a putative Third World economy.

Since the early 1970s the border industrialization program, which was designed to create jobs in Mexico and thus retard the flow of illegal entries into the United States, has instead exacerbated the problem. Confronting a financial crisis brought on by overspending and a $100 billion foreign debt, Mexican President José López Portillo nationalized his country's banks. The Mexican standard of living, particularly for the middle class, fell sharply. After more than a decade of debate, in 1986 the U.S. Congress passed the Immigration Reform and Control Act, establishing sanctions against U.S. employers who knowingly employ undocumented workers. Two years later, after a bitterly fought campaign laced with charges of fraud, Harvard-educated Carlos Salinas de Gortari, candidate of the ruling Institutional Revolutionary Party, became president of Mexico. Salinas committed his administration to a revival of the Mexican economy through strengthened economic ties with the United States. A decade earlier, a more bombastic Mexican leader had defied the United States, condemning its intervention in Central America and proclaiming Mexico as a leader in the Third World. Weathering the inevitable charges hurled at him by nationalists, Salinas endorsed an economic union with the United States and Canada.

President George Bush pushed hard for NAFTA and President Bill Clinton expended considerable political energy getting the measure through the U.S. Congress, despite opposition from environmentalists and organized labor. Unlike the European Economic Community, now the Economic Union of Nations, NAFTA does not erase national boundaries or create a common currency; rather, it represents the formalization of the symbiotic economic relationship that began during World War II. Continued charges of po-

litical corruption and socioeconomic injustice on the part of the Mexican government, which was unable to put down a revolt of Indians in the state of Chiapas in 1994, belie the positive image projected of Mexico during the NAFTA debates.

[Lester D. Langley, *Mexico and the United States* (Boston, 1991); Robert A. Pastor, *Integration with Mexico* (New York, 1993).]

LESTER D. LANGLEY

See also **SUPP:** El Paso; Mexican Americans; North American Free Trade Agreement.

MIAMI, city in southeastern Florida, was founded in 1896 by railroad and hotel baron Henry M. Flagler as a tourist destination at the terminus of Flagler's Florida East Coast Railway. Miami possesses sunshine, seashore, and a subtropical climate, and these amenities attracted vacationers by the hundreds of thousands as early as the 1920s. The Florida real estate boom of the 1920s helped push Miami's population to 110,000 by 1930, while stimulating the growth of such nearby communities as Miami Beach, Coral Gables, and Hialeah. Despite the Great Depression, the Miami area's permanent and visitor population continued on an upward spiral; between 1920 and 1940, Miami was one of the fastest-growing metropolitan areas in the nation. Implanted in the public consciousness by 1940, Miami's image was that of a glamorous resort catering to the rich and famous: business tycoons and movie stars, labor leaders and politicians, presidents and gangsters.

World War II had an important impact on the city. The establishment of military training facilities and numerous air and naval bases boosted the local economy during the war. More than one hundred hotels housed military trainees, providing year-round income to their owners. The big military payroll also stimulated the building and service trades, attracting civilian workers to south Florida. In addition, the war led Miamians to a greater appreciation of the importance of air travel, and from this period local boosters touted Miami as the aviation capital of the Americas and the "Gateway to Latin America." Miami experienced dynamic growth in the postwar era. The local economy became more diverse as construction, services, and light manufacturing complemented the tourist industry. The population of metropolitan Miami grew rapidly to 495,000 in 1950 and 935,000 in 1960. Developers subdivided the periphery to house residents and retirees from the Northeast and Midwest. Miami's population became more affluent and more liberal on political and social issues. Jewish migrants helped form the Miami chapter of the Congress of Racial Equality and joined with black activists in lunch-counter sit-ins, bringing civil rights issues to south Florida. In the late 1950s, urban reformers addressed the area's fragmented government, introducing the nation's first two-tiered, metropolitan or "metro" government in 1957.

The Cuban revolution of 1959 led by Fidel Castro initiated a massive exodus of Cuban exiles to the United States, totaling 900,000 by 1990. Most Cubans settled in metropolitan Miami, where they dramatically altered the city's character. Several hundred thousand exiles from other Caribbean nations and from Central and South America, added to the Cubans, constituted half of metropolitan Miami's 1990 population of 2 million people; according to the 1990 census, some 70 percent of Miami's population was foreign born. This demographic revolution made Miami a bilingual, multicultural city. Demographic patterns turned Miami into the economic and cultural capital of the entire Caribbean basin. International trade and banking surged beginning in the 1970s, as did foreign investment in Miami real estate. In the late twentieth century Latin American tourists mingled with northern vacationers. Although Miami came to be recognized for its new skyscraper skyline, there was a darker side to the city's history in the late twentieth century. Ethnic conflicts and economic disparities led to polarization, pitting Hispanics, blacks, and native-born whites against each other. Miami experienced four major race riots in 1980–1992, suggesting deep underlying tensions. Crime and murder damaged Miami's image, as did a persistent illegal drug trade. Rapid development of the urban periphery, especially along the fringes of the ecologically sensitive Everglades, has posed environmental dangers. Nevertheless, Miami still displayed the vitality that can accompany growth, change, and cultural diversity.

[Raymond A. Mohl, "Miami: The Ethnic Cauldron," in *Sunbelt Cities: Politics and Growth Since World War II,* edited by Richard M. Bernard and Bradley R. Rice (Austin, Tex., 1983); Nicholas N. Patricios, *Building Marvelous Miami* (Gainesville, Fla., 1994); Alejandro Portes and Alex Stepick, *City on the Edge: The Transformation of Miami* (Berkeley, Calif., 1993).]

RAYMOND A. MOHL

See also **SUPP:** Caribbean Policy; Cuban Americans; Florida; Hispanic Americans; Tourism.

MIAs. *See* **Prisoners of War and Missing in Action.**

MICHIGAN. During the 1970s the state endured a threefold increase in violent crime and the erosion of urban centers, the effects of which were most evident in industrial cities such as Detroit and Flint. Relocation of automotive plants and their suppliers from the cities to suburban areas and other states, combined with a decline in employment resulting from increased automation and advances in production techniques, created high unemployment, with nearly 50 percent of inner-city black youths jobless. Neighborhoods deteriorated and houses and shops became vacant. By the end of the decade, Detroit, which derisively had been dubbed "murder city" because of its 44.5 homicides for every 100,000 residents in 1975, had undergone a transformation. Under the leadership of its first black mayor, Coleman Young, elected in 1973, a business-hotel complex aptly named the Renaissance Center and the Joe Louis Sports Arena were erected and later showcased when Detroit hosted the 1980 Republican National Convention. Neighborhood revitalization was encouraged, and many young middle-class people returned to live in the city. Detroit's revitalization program served as an important model for a state with an urban population of 81.3 percent in 1980. Other communities followed Detroit's lead and by 1980 Michigan was making widespread efforts at urban renewal.

Another problem facing the state in the 1970s was the economic devastation caused by the October 1973 embargo on oil from the Middle East. Gasoline shortages, combined with threats of rationing, led to a reduction in new car sales. In addition, Michigan's billion-dollar-a-year tourist industry, especially critical to the economy of the upper peninsula, was crippled as concern over the availability of gasoline kept many travelers at home. By 1978 automobile production and sales had recovered, but the message of the 1970s was evident. If Michigan persisted in relying on the automobile industry, it would face stagnation or decline.

Two popular political leaders became prominent during the 1970s. William G. Milliken moved up from his post as lieutenant governor when Governor George Romney resigned in 1969 to become a member of President Richard Nixon's cabinet. A moderate Republican, Milliken held office for fourteen years. In 1976 liberal Democrat Philip Hart ended eighteen years of service in the U.S. Senate, where he had helped shape virtually every piece of legislation favoring civil rights, consumer protection, and regulation of big business. Michiganians also were proud of

Gerald R. Ford, who, after twenty-five years in Congress, became the first Michigan resident to serve as president of the United States.

The 1980s began on a sour note as spiraling inflation and soaring interest rates thrust the automobile industry into another nosedive. By mid-1980 more than 620,000 auto workers were jobless, the most since the Great Depression. As sales plunged and unemployment rose, state revenues plummeted, while demands for state assistance for the needy increased at a record pace. In 1982 Democrats took advantage of Michigan's having the highest unemployment rate in the nation (16 percent), Milliken's retirement, and a split in the Republican party to elect a Detroit congressman, James Blanchard, as their party's first governor in twenty years. The new governor inherited a $200 million deficit. Because the state constitution mandated a balanced budget, he proposed a temporary 38 percent increase in the state income tax, as well as additional cuts in state-supported programs. With this change in administration Michigan started on yet another slow road to recovery. Bond ratings were upgraded, funding for state services and education increased, and the Michigan Youth Corps was formed to offer temporary summer employment to more than 60,000 young people. Car sales, aided by a federal import quota on foreign automobiles, began to rise, unemployment declined to 14 percent, and Michigan was hailed as one of the nation's "comeback states." Refusing to ignore the lessons of the past, Blanchard outlined a program of economic strategies stressing diversification of industry, retraining of workers for high-technology jobs, and regional cooperation among the Great Lakes states to attract new industry. His ability to achieve these goals was hindered by an electorate angered by the tax increase. After an unsuccessful recall campaign against the governor, voters returned control of the state senate in 1983 to the more fiscally conservative Republicans. Blanchard was reelected in 1986, primarily because of another division within the Republican party, but his second term was marred before it even began. Two days after his reelection General Motors announced that it was closing seven plants in Michigan and laying off nearly 18,000 workers, an action that Blanchard had told voters would not occur.

The 1980s also saw a decline in the number of residents engaged in the state's third largest industry—agriculture. Farms declined during the decade from 66,000 to 55,000, and cultivated acreage fell from 11.4 million to 10.8 million. One of the state's major contributions during the decade was the creation of the Michigan Educational Trust Fund, which allowed parents to invest $3,000 per child and in return receive assurance that the child would receive a four-year education at any of Michigan's fifteen state-supported colleges beginning in the year 2005. This program was in the best tradition of Michigan's commitment to educational excellence. In 1980, 60 percent of Michigan's residents were high school graduates, and 14.3 percent had completed at least four years of college. Between 70 and 80 percent of Michigan's college students attend public, rather than private, institutions, a rate nearly 20 percent above the national average. The trust fund met the future needs of a population fearful of the spiraling costs of higher education.

In 1990, plagued by yet another decline in the automobile industry and facing charges that he had not done enough to remedy problems of inner-city minorities, Blanchard lost his bid for a third term to Republican State Senator John Engler by 17,000 votes. The new governor inherited a $1.8 billion deficit, which he sought to reduce through a program of cost-cutting and reorganization. In 1993 Michigan had the most robust economic growth of all industrial states. A record 4.35 million workers were employed, an increase of nearly 400,000 since 1991; unemployment was at its lowest level in fifteen years; and growth in personal income was nearly three times the national average. Michigan's turnaround was based on three factors. The first, welfare reform, was aimed at ending dependency on the state, and in 1991 general assistance welfare payments stopped for 83,000 single, able-bodied adults. Retraining programs and community service alternatives were instituted. The retraining worked so well that Michigan in 1993 led the nation in the number of welfare recipients employed and moving toward self-sufficiency. Second, a tax relief program, including a property tax freeze, a cut in the state small business tax, and elimination of inheritance taxes helped produce a $312 million surplus in 1993. Third, the state embarked on partnerships with private industries and privatized state services. Partnership with a pharmaceutical company made it possible to supply free vaccines to nearly all of the state's children, and Michigan contracted with the Salvation Army to provide shelter for 5,000 homeless persons. Education continued to be a popular program in the 1990s and was spared from budget cuts, receiving increases of more than $500 million over four years. In a bold move, Governor Engler in 1993 called for ending reliance on property taxes for school funding, and in 1994 he signed a bill establishing the most sweeping charter school act in the nation.

Despite its economic vicissitudes and political changes, Michigan continued to support cultural organizations and events. The Interlochen Center for the Arts maintained its status as one of the nation's premier music training centers, while art fairs and summer stock theater developed into summer showcases throughout the state. Two living history museums, Greenfield Village in Dearborn and Crossroads Village in Flint, enable visitors to experience life in pre-twentieth-century Michigan, and Detroit's Afro-American Museum and Holocaust Museum serve as reminders of the struggles of blacks and Jews everywhere. Ethnic cultural contributions are evident in events such as the Holland Tulip Festival, Frankenmuth's Oktoberfest, and Detroit's summer-long series of ethnic festivals.

[Richard J. Hathaway, ed., *Michigan: Visions of Our Past* (East Lansing, Mich., 1989); Bruce A. Rubenstein and Lawrence C. Ziewacz, *Michigan: A History of the Great Lakes State* (Arlington Heights, Ill., 1981).]
BRUCE A. RUBENSTEIN

See also **SUPP:** Detroit.

MICROBIOLOGY. During the last quarter of the twentieth century the biological sciences achieved a wealth of benefits from progress in microbiology, the study of living organisms invisible to the naked eye. Sophisticated electron microscopes, improved staining, cloning, sequencing, and the availability of computer graphics enabled scientists in the United States and elsewhere to learn more about the structure and composition of viruses, fungi, protozoa, bacteria, and other members of the microbial world. Such enlightenment contributed to efforts aimed at preventing, ameliorating, and curing certain diseases. Studies of microorganisms in the late twentieth century opened new areas of research in cell physiology, biochemistry, and genetics. Microbiological research enhanced molecular biology by leading to a more precise means of investigating the structure and functions of nucleic acids and proteins. The focus on the arrangement of genetic materials, including the nature of genes and mechanisms controlling their functions, also helped develop molecular genetics.

Microbiology research aided in clarifying the causes of diseases that drew national attention in the 1970s and 1980s, including Legionnaire's disease, a mysterious respiratory disease that struck 182 members of the American Legion at a convention in Phila-

delphia in 1976. By 1978 microbiologists at the Centers for Disease Control had isolated the *legionella* bacteria. Subsequent studies of the bacteria assisted health officials in identifying sources and victims. Research also helped scientists at the National Institutes of Health (NIH), the federal government's largest biomedical research center, identify certain microbes responsible for other human illnesses. In 1980 Robert Gallo and his team at the National Cancer Institute linked cancer to a virus. In 1982 Willy Burgdorfer of the NIH Rocky Mountain Laboratories in Hamilton, Mont., observed the spiral-shaped spirochete from a tick that caused Lyme disease. Burgdorfer's find led to more accurate diagnoses and treatment and to research for a vaccine.

One of the more notable advances was the use of the colon bacterium *Escherichia coli* (*E. coli*), especially for biotechnology. Because of the work of several Nobel Prize winners and their colleagues, including Marshall Nirenberg of the National Heart, Lung, and Blood Institute of NIH and Walter Gilbert of Harvard University, researchers recognized that strains of *E. coli* could house a variety of genes for testing. Scientists found that strains of *E. coli* could help develop processes for producing human insulin and possibly protective materials with the strength, resistance, and light weight of spider webs. Additional efforts resulted in the isolation of hepatitis viruses previously unrecognized, identification of an acquired immunodeficiency syndrome (AIDS) virus, and reconstruction of a major histocompatibility complex protein involved in immune responses to infection—studies that, among other improvements, contributed to the development of tests to make blood transfusions safer.

[Ronald M. Atlas, *Microbiology: Fundamentals and Applications* (New York, 1984); Wolfgang K. Joklik et al., eds., *Zinsser Microbiology* (Norwalk, Conn., 1992).]
RUTH ROY HARRIS

See also **SUPP:** Acquired Immune Deficiency Syndrome; Bacteriology and Virology; Legionnaire's Disease; Lyme Disease; Medicine; Toxic Shock Syndrome.

MIDDLE EAST, RELATIONS WITH. Prior to World War I the United States had few diplomatic relations with the Middle East. Only in major capitals such as Istanbul, Cairo, and Tehran was there a continuous U.S. diplomatic presence. Private citizens, archaeologists, a few businessmen, and, most important, Protestant missionaries and educators acted as unofficial representatives of the United States. Although few in number the latter exerted influence through their educational institutions, such as the American University of Beirut, Robert College in Istanbul, and Damavand College in Tehran, where they trained many future Mideast leaders. These U.S. citizens had political contacts in Washington and when occasion demanded could call upon the assistance of their government. In the early 1880s the missionary community of Iran prevailed upon President Chester A. Arthur to send a permanent diplomatic representative to Tehran. As in East Asia, missionaries often served as consuls in cities where there was no permanent U.S. representative in residence. In the years following World War I, U.S. oil companies became interested in regional resources. European companies had discovered oil in Iraq and neighboring Iran and arranged to keep control for themselves. Successive Republican administrations helped to open the door for U.S. capital, but the heyday of the nation's economic penetration would come after World War II, with the discovery that much of the region adjacent to the Persian Gulf was floating on a sea of oil.

World War II served as a catalyst for U.S. involvement in the Middle East. The administration of President Franklin D. Roosevelt helped to maintain a bridge to victory for the Allies from 1942, channeling military supplies through Iran to the Soviet Union. In 1943 important Allied meetings took place at Casablanca, Cairo, and Tehran, where leaders worked out strategies for defeating the Axis powers. As a sign of changing times Roosevelt met with King Abd al-Aziz Ibn Saud of oil-rich Saudi Arabia on his way back from the Yalta Conference in 1945. After the war the U.S. government would have been content to let Great Britain and France continue to represent Western diplomatic interests in the Middle East. Faced with the rising force of nationalism and demands for independence, however, the European colonial powers had neither the resources nor the energy to reimpose their domination. Great Britain withdrew from Palestine (now Israel, the West Bank, and Gaza) in 1948, Egypt in 1954, Aden (later the People's Republic of Yemen and now part of Yemen) in 1967, and the Persian Gulf in 1971. France withdrew from Lebanon in 1943, Syria in 1946, Morocco and Tunisia in 1956, and finally Algeria after a bloody struggle that raged from 1954 to 1962.

As the cold war with the Soviet Union intensified, only the United States had the power to oppose communist penetration of the region. Until the end of this struggle in the late 1980s, the two principles of U.S. Middle East policy were to contain the Soviets and guarantee regional oil supplies for the West. Many historians believe the cold war began in the Middle East, where the two superpowers openly disagreed over the issue of Soviet troop withdrawals from postwar Iran in 1945–1946. Then Great Britain, plagued by deficits, withdrew from Greece, where a civil war raged. President Harry S. Truman, believing that the Russians had instigated the turmoil there and that they also threatened neighboring Turkey, in 1947 announced the Truman Doctrine of economic and military assistance for the two states. In 1952 Greece and Turkey became members of the North Atlantic Treaty Organization (NATO), anchoring the eastern flank of the alliance.

Step by step the United States entered more deeply into regional affairs. No undertaking would be more decisive than Truman's support in 1948 of an independent Jewish state in the former British mandate of Palestine. A combination of factors inspired the president: sympathy for survivors of the Holocaust, lobbying by Zionists (supporters of a Jewish state) in the United States, a desire to thwart Soviet moves to befriend the Jewish settlers in Palestine, and a wish to nurture a stable, democratic, pro-Western state in the region. Although historians differ on the importance of these factors, they agree that the issue divided the Truman administration. Officials who opposed recognition feared it would antagonize the Arabs and push them into closer contact with the Soviets.

Since 1948, Arab hostility toward the United States, Israel's staunchest ally, has at times become intense and threatened to undermine U.S. goals in the region. Egyptian president Gamal Abdul Nasser tried to buy arms from Washington after an Israeli attack into the Egyptian-controlled Gaza Strip in February 1955. When President Dwight D. Eisenhower refused, Nasser purchased them instead from Soviet-controlled Czechoslovakia, inaugurating years of Soviet-Egyptian collaboration. Secretary of State John Foster Dulles decided to teach Nasser a lesson and withdrew U.S. support for the project to build a higher dam at Aswan on the Nile River. Nasser in turn nationalized the Suez Canal and contracted with the Soviet Union to complete the dam project. Great Britain, France, and Israel joined in a war against Nasser in October 1956. Eisenhower pressed them to withdraw. His action produced a surge of pro-U.S. sentiment throughout the Middle East but worsened relations with Washington's two European allies and Israel.

When the United States supported Israel in its June 1967 preemptive war against Egypt and Syria, many Arab states broke diplomatic relations. In the October 1973 Yom Kippur War, Nasser's successor, Anwar as-Sadat, sent Egyptian forces across the Suez Canal, taking Israeli defenders by surprise. Sadat wanted to regain the Sinai Peninsula, occupied by Israel since 1967. Arab states criticized President Richard M. Nixon's decisions in the middle of the war to release military supplies to Israel and to announce a large loan for Tel Aviv. This time the Arab states, led by Saudi Arabia, imposed an oil boycott on the United States, sending gasoline prices skyrocketing.

The United States tried repeatedly to work out a compromise that would reconcile the Arabs to the existence of Israel but the barriers were formidable and each initiative fell short of its goal. Democratic administrations, especially those of Truman, John F. Kennedy, and Lyndon B. Johnson, tended to look more favorably on the Jewish state than did Republican ones, in particular those of Eisenhower, Gerald R. Ford, and George Bush. Whenever the United States attempted negotiations the fate of the Palestinian Arabs proved the hardest issue to resolve. Displaced in the 1948 and 1967 wars, they had become part of a great diaspora; many lived in primitive refugee camps in states bordering Israel. In 1968 they selected the activist Yasir Arafat, founder of the guerrilla group Fatah, to lead the Palestine Liberation Organization (PLO). Rival Palestinian factions began to target Israeli and U.S. citizens in an effort to draw attention to their cause. Airliners and airports came under terrorist attack. For years the U.S. government refused all contact with the PLO, even after members of the League of Arab States recognized the organization as the sole legitimate representative of the Palestinian people. Washington was bound by a 1975 agreement with Israel not to negotiate with the PLO as long as the latter refused to recognize the existence of Israel. Secretary of State Henry Kissinger, renowned for his shuttle (airport-to-airport) diplomacy after the October War, had agreed to this demand to secure a partial Israeli withdrawal from the Sinai.

Only in 1988, as the Palestinian Intifada (uprising) raged in the Israeli-occupied West Bank and Gaza Strip, did the United States open talks with Arafat. Initiated by the Ronald Reagan administration and continued by President Bush and his secretary of state, James Baker, the talks resulted in a peace conference in Madrid and the September 1993 signing of an interim Palestinian-Israeli peace accord at a ceremony in Washington hosted by President Bill Clinton.

Despite early optimism in the United States, however, Israelis and Palestinians were far from a just and lasting peace. Much earlier the United States had achieved an important breakthrough with the Camp David Accords. In September 1978 President Jimmy Carter helped negotiate a treaty establishing peace and diplomatic relations between Egypt and Israel. Egypt thus became the first Arab state to recognize Israel. The agreement came at a high price for the United States, which consented to increase dramatically its economic and military assistance to the two signees. Thereafter they received more than half of all U.S. foreign aid. The Arab world ostracized Egypt for breaking ranks and Cairo consequently moved closer to Washington.

From the early post–World War II years the United States looked for friends in the region. As elsewhere in the world, it often found them in the ranks of conservative nations headed by hereditary rulers, such as Iran, Libya, and Saudi Arabia. This policy, which incidentally guaranteed access to vast oil reserves, often placed the United States in the position of supporting the status quo. Critics accused Washington of ignoring regional problems in pursuit of a global strategy of winning the cold war. The pro-Western king of Libya was overthrown in September 1969. Colonel Muʿammar al-Gadhafi, a young, militant Arab nationalist, replaced him as leader of the oil-rich state and immediately pressed the United States to evacuate its Wheelus Air Force Base. The crisis in U.S.-Libyan relations, however, came much later, during the Reagan administration. Gadhafi supported liberation movements around the world and reportedly had ties to the terrorist bombing of a West Berlin disco in April 1986 at which two U.S. soldiers were killed and many others were injured. Reagan, pursuing a tough policy on terrorism, ordered a massive retaliatory raid on Gadhafi's compound in Tripoli. The Libyan leader narrowly escaped, but U.S. bombs killed an adopted daughter and wounded two of his sons. After this attack, which received strong support in the United States but considerable criticism from U.S. allies in Europe and the Middle East, both nations pulled back from the brink of open hostilities.

In 1951 a crisis developed in Iran over the rights of the Anglo-Iranian Oil Company to monopolize production and sale of petroleum. An elderly nationalist leader, Mohammad Mosaddeq, ignited popular enthusiasm for nationalizing the company's holdings. Becoming prime minister in May of that year, he waged a two-year struggle to force the British, who had initiated a worldwide blockade of Iranian oil, to accept the takeover. At first the United States sympathized with Mosaddeq and urged Great Britain to compromise, but as the prime minister's internal support weakened and the local communist party, the Tudeh, seemed to gain ground, the new Eisenhower administration turned against him. The Central Intelligence Agency (CIA) plotted with groups of dissident Iranians to undermine the regime and restore Shah Mohammad Reza Pahlavi to power. After a coup d'état in August 1953, the United States consistently supported the increasingly dictatorial shah.

Many Iranians came to view the shah as Washington's puppet—which he decidedly was not—and their disillusionment with him and the United States increased. Opposition to the shah passed into the hands of the religious class, many of whom rejected the increasing secularization of the Pahlavi state. Ayatollah Ruholla Khomeini, an exile since 1964, organized his forces from afar to destroy the shah's regime. Suffering secretly from a terminal illness, the shah vacillated and the opposition took heart. After a series of blunders and with mixed signals from the Carter administration, which was divided on the issue, the shah fled the country in January 1979. Khomeini returned to establish an Islamic republic with himself as final arbiter. The U.S. government had few ties with the new Iranian leadership and officials in Washington were again divided over whether to adopt a hard-line or a conciliatory approach. When President Carter allowed the ailing shah to enter the United States in October 1979 for medical treatment, Iranians, remembering the events of 1953, feared a conspiracy to restore the ousted monarch. On Nov. 4, 1979, militant students seized the U.S. embassy in Tehran and took its occupants hostage. The ensuing crisis lasted until the end of Carter's term, helping to deny him reelection.

After 1981 the United States had several brushes with the prickly revolutionaries in Tehran. Diplomatic relations languished. U.S. officials feared the spread of militant Islam to neighboring states. Their concern brought closer ties with Iran's only Arab neighbor, Iraq. U.S.-Iraq relations have resembled the dips and rises of a roller coaster. Washington worked closely with the monarchy to establish the anti-Soviet Baghdad Pact in 1955 (Iraq, Iran, Turkey, Pakistan, and Great Britain), but three years later revolutionary forces overwhelmed the conservative, pro-Western regime of King Faisal II and Premier Nuri al-Said. At the same time Jordan's King Hussein faced increasing challenges. It seemed the royal dominoes were falling. Acting under the Eisenhower Doctrine an-

nounced in 1957 to block communist aggression in the region, the United States sent marines into Lebanon to strengthen its pro-Western president, who had come under attack. This also served as a gesture of support to other friendly regimes in the region. The crisis passed quickly and the marines soon went home but the U.S. action (and similar British steps in Jordan) left many Arabs bitter. Ostensibly the move was to thwart communists but the real threat, as Eisenhower knew, came from supporters of Egypt's Nasser, who preached a pan-Arab union, which they believed would restore past glories.

Ties with Iraq were never again as cordial as they had been prior to 1958. Baghdad broke relations in 1967 and they were only restored in 1984 during the Iran-Iraq War. Washington saw the Iraqi leader, Saddam Hussein, as a barrier to the spread of revolutionary ideas from Iran. The Reagan and Bush administrations overlooked the brutal, authoritarian character of the regime, seeing it as the cork in the Iranian bottle. Iraq also offered a lucrative market for U.S. business. The 1989 collapse of the Soviet Union, a longtime ally of Iraq, removed a restraining influence on Saddam Hussein. The United States seemed to offer no opposition to his hints of annexing tiny neighboring Kuwait, over which he had long claimed sovereignty. The U.S. message had been ambiguous, but once Iraq's army poured into Kuwait in August 1990, President Bush left no doubt about his policy. He condemned Iraq and rushed to organize an international coalition to force its withdrawal. In the ensuing Gulf War of 1991 the Iraqi army suffered near-total defeat. Kuwait was restored and Iraq was forced to accept a series of United Nations resolutions. President Bush stopped short of removing Saddam Hussein; he restricted U.S. ground forces to a zone in southern Iraq far from Baghdad. He did this because his Arab coalition partners disagreed and because of fears that removal might trigger a power struggle during which surrounding states, including Iran, would seek territorial gains at Iraq's expense. The success of the Gulf War gave impulse to plans to resolve the Palestinian-Israeli conflict. With the end of the cold war, Israel lost some of its leverage as a bastion of anticommunism in the region. One reason the United States moved with such speed against Iraq was the threat it posed to the oil-rich Gulf states adjacent to Kuwait. Despite attempts in the 1970s to lower imports of foreign oil and to develop energy alternatives, the 1980s saw increasing consumption of Middle Eastern petroleum. The United States had a vested interest in maintaining stability in the Persian Gulf.

After the cold war, President Bush and his successor, Bill Clinton, spoke of a new world order, but no one knew what was envisioned for the United States in this part of the world. As pressures for change built throughout the region, it was unclear how conservative regimes like Saudi Arabia would adjust. In states such as Egypt and Algeria the United States aligned itself with the status quo against Islamic activists. Some observers questioned whether these corrupt and inefficient regimes would be able to introduce much-needed reform. The United States risked being identified with governments that many believed served the interests of only a minority of their citizens.

[James A. Bill, *The Eagle and the Lion* (New Haven, Conn., 1988); John A. DeNovo, *American Interests and Policies in the Middle East, 1900–1939* (Minneapolis, 1963); George Lenczowski, *American Presidents and the Middle East* (Durham, N.C., 1990); William B. Quandt, *Decade of Decisions: American Policy Toward the Arab-Israeli Conflict, 1967–1976* (Berkeley, Calif., 1977); Barry M. Rubin, *Paved With Good Intentions: The American Experience and Iran* (New York, 1980); Steven L. Spiegel, *The Other Arab-Israeli Conflict* (Chicago, 1985); Robert W. Stookey, *America and the Arab States* (New York, 1975); Seth P. Tillman, *The United States in the Middle East* (Bloomington, Ind., 1982).]

JAMES F. GOODE

See also **DAH:** Arab-American Relations; **SUPP:** Arab Americans; Beirut Bombing; Foreign Aid; Gulf War of 1991; Hostage Crises; Iran-Contra Affair; Iranian Americans; Iran-Iraq War; Iraq-gate; Iraqi Americans; Israel-Palestine Peace Accords; Lebanon; Oil Crises; Palestinian Americans; West Berlin Disco Bombing.

MIDDLE EAST HOSTAGES. *See* **Hostage Crises.**

MIDWIFERY. *See* **Childbirth.**

MILITARY BASE CLOSINGS. By the late 1980s the United States had approximately 3,800 military installations within its borders, including army forts, navy and air force bases, supply depots, and building and repair facilities. Their locations had sometimes been a matter of national politics, because members of Congress regarded the establishment of a military base as a way of bringing federal money and jobs to their state or district as well as of creating additional employment for servicing the base's population. In

the late 1980s this protective attitude toward bases started to change. The conclusion of the cold war with the collapse of the Warsaw Pact and the Soviet Union ended a major threat to U.S. national security. A mounting federal budget deficit and a desire to redirect federal spending into domestic programs reinforced arguments to cut national defense spending. As a consequence, military base closings began, along with reductions in military personnel and weapons. Congress chose neither to allow the president or the Department of Defense to decide which bases to close nor to make such decisions itself. Instead, it voted in 1988 to create an independent, bipartisan advisory commission to the Pentagon to propose lists of bases for closure. The secretary of defense would announce the proposed list, and, provided Congress did not reject it within forty-five legislative days, the schedule for closings would become official. Three subsequent defense base closure and realignment commissions were established to act in 1991, 1993, and 1995. While some bases were shut down, others actually grew through realignment or the shifting of personnel and functions among installations.

Secretary of Defense Frank Carlucci announced, and Congress accepted, the first commission's list in 1989. Eighty-six bases were to be closed, five were to be partially closed, and fifty-four were to undergo realignment. The bases had at least four years advance notice, except for Pease Air Force Base in New Hampshire, which closed in 1991. In 1990 Secretary of Defense Richard Cheney announced a second list of proposed base closings without relying on a commission. This caused an outcry in Congress, where the Democratic majority thought the list contained too many bases in states or districts represented by Democrats. The chair of the House Armed Services Committee, Les Aspin of Wisconsin, recommended that a second commission propose another list. In October 1990 Congress approved the commission's creation. In 1991 the commission presented its list, which called for the closure of thirty-four bases and the realignment of another forty-eight. Congress accepted these recommendations.

Even though Congress had created the commission format, some senators and representatives were concerned about the impact of these closures on state and local economies. Legislators from the Philadelphia area, opposed to the closing of that city's naval shipyard, turned to the federal courts to determine whether base closure decisions should be subject to judicial review, but in May 1994 the Supreme Court unanimously ruled against this. Also, in approving closings Congress stated that the secretary of defense must consider closing overseas bases. The 1993 commission faced similar difficulties. Concerned about the loss of jobs and the economic impact on communities and states, Congress closely scrutinized the proposed list. Aspin, now secretary of defense, rebutted allegations that some of the closings were politically motivated. The third list affected 175 military installations, with some 30 major U.S. bases to be closed, 12 other major bases subject to realignment, and additional smaller bases being closed, realigned, or relocated. Congress accepted the list in 1993. In June 1995 the commission recommended closing 79 bases and realigning 26 others. Although President Bill Clinton expressed strong concern about the economic impact of base closings in Texas and California, he approved the recommendations in July. Later that month the House National Security Committee rejected proposed legislation that would have overturned the recommendations.

Base closings in themselves did not substantially reduce the annual defense budget. For example, closures announced in 1991 would save about $1.5 billion annually after 1997, and the 1993 list would save about $2.3 billion annually after 1999. It was more difficult to estimate the effect of base closings on local economies. States such as California, with more than 300,000 people employed at sixty-seven bases in 1991, felt the loss of jobs and income disproportionately. Including all base closures through the 1995 recommendations, Senator Diane Feinstein of California estimated that 108,900 Californians employed at these bases would lose their jobs. Evidence suggested, however, that base closings did not affect communities as seriously as layoffs in the defense industry. Military bases tended not to be as integrated into local economies as defense manufacturing. Many communities even hoped to benefit by acquiring the land once occupied by bases, although federal regulations often slowed up this process. A greater problem in this regard was perhaps the serious environmental hazards at military installations resulting from use of machinery and storage of solvents, fuels, and explosives. In the 1990s the cleanup of such hazards depended on the availability of federal funding.

[Andrew C. Mayer and George H. Siehl, *Military Base Closures: Issues for the 104th Congress* (Washington, D.C., 1995); U.S. Congress, Office of Technology Assessment, *After the Cold War: Living with Lower Defense Spending*, OTA-ITE-524 (Washington, D.C., 1992).]

KENNETH B. MOSS

See also **SUPP:** Defense, Department of.

MILITARY SERVICE, WOMEN IN. *See* **Women in Military Service.**

MILITIAS. Modern, private, citizen-organized militias have their roots in the post–World War II right-wing Patriot movement. Militia members and Patriots share a fear of a tyrannical federal government and domination of the United States by a global conspiracy controlled by the United Nations. While the majority of Patriots have historically sought to reverse these perceived trends through political organization and social movements, militia participants believe an armed citizenry is the only real defense against despotism. The bombing of the Oklahoma City federal building in April 1995 and the arrest of suspects and militia members Timothy McVeigh and Terry Nichols brought notoriety and public attention to the militia movement, but civilian paramilitary groups have been active in the United States at least as far back as the first Ku Klux Klan, formed just after the Civil War. Several armed groupings emerged in the late 1970s and 1980s, mostly identified with the racist, anti-Semitic far right. The FBI uncovered and disbanded the white supremacist Order, or Silent Brotherhood, after the group committed armed robbery, counterfeited currency, and murdered radio talk-show host Alan Berg, a Jewish liberal, in 1984.

In the mid-1990s white supremacy continued to have a profound impact on paramilitary groups, but the more recent militia movement has a broader base, resulting from two events. The first concerned the armed confrontation between federal agents and white supremacist Randy Weaver at Ruby Ridge, Idaho, in 1992 after he failed to appear for trial on weapons violations. In the resulting standoff a federal marshal, as well as Weaver's son and wife, were killed. Although Weaver was acquitted of the federal marshal's murder, his case became for many Patriots a symbol of governmental excess. In 1995 the Justice Department agreed to pay the Weaver family $3.1 million in damages without admitting wrongdoing. In the aftermath of Ruby Ridge, former Green Beret and right-wing Populist party presidential candidate James "Bo" Gritz mobilized supporters to form militias to defend their social status and constitutional rights. Those answering his call included farmers facing foreclosure, displaced industrial workers, gun-rights advocates, anti–income tax protesters, Christian millennialists, adherents of the confrontational wing of the pro-life movement, militant antienvironmentalists, states' rights advocates, and people who believe that the county is the highest acceptable level of government. While most members are white males, some local militias include African-American and female participants. The largest of the local paramilitary groups is John Trochman's Militia of Montana.

The second event spurring militia participation was the April 1993 siege of the Branch Davidian compound in Waco, Texas, by agents of the Bureau of Alcohol, Tobacco and Firearms, culminating in the deaths of cult leader David Koresh and seventy-seven of his followers. For many militia members and potential recruits, the Waco siege appeared to be a trial run by the federal government for imposition of national martial law. Gun control legislation was viewed as a part of the plot. In 1995 the estimated militia membership was between 10,000 and 40,000, with organizing activity probably occurring in every state.

[Michael Barkun, *Religion and the Racist Right* (Chapel Hill, N.C., 1994); Chip Berlet and Matthew N. Lyons, "Militia Nation," *The Progressive* (June 1995), and *Too Close for Comfort: Rightwing Populism, Scapegoating, and Fascist Potentials in U.S. Politics* (Boston, 1996); Daniel Junas, "Angry White Guys with Guns: Rise of Citizen Militias," *Covert Action Quarterly* (Spring 1995).]

ELLEN A. SLATKIN

See also **SUPP:** Fundamentalism; Gun Control; Oklahoma City Bombing; Vigilantes; Waco Siege; White Supremacists.

MILLENARIANISM, or millennialism, focuses on a thousand-year period of unprecedented peace and righteousness that some Christians believe will either precede or follow the return of Christ to earth, marking the end of history. In the twentieth century the most militant millenarians have been premillennialists—people who expect Christ to return and preside over the millennium. Some believers set dates for Christ's coming, as in Harold Camping's *1994?* (1992) or Edgar Whisenant's *Eighty-eight Reasons Why the Rapture Will Be in 1988* (1988). Inspired especially by events in the Middle East since the creation of the state of Israel in 1948, premillennialism has produced a vast literature speculating about current events and the end of history. The all-time best-seller was Hal Lindsey's *The Late Great Planet Earth* (1970). At the popular level, postmillennialism is perhaps most visible in advocates of reconstructionism, or ushering in the millennium through natural means by Christianizing the social and cultural institutions as well as humankind. Amillennialism assigns spiritual importance to one thousand years and empha-

sizes conforming the individual Christian's life to the rule of Christ within the heart.

[Timothy P. Weber, *Living in the Shadow of the Second Coming* (Chicago, 1987).]

EDITH BLUMHOFER

See also **SUPP:** Fundamentalism.

MILWAUKEE, the largest city in Wisconsin and the seventeenth largest in the United States, experienced a marked change of demographics since World War II. It began with a white exodus from the city's core areas in the years after the war. This exit accelerated following 1967 demonstrations over fair housing and race rioting; by 1985 Milwaukee was the nation's most segregated city, with 90 percent of its African-American population residing in the downtown core. The population declined from 717,000 in 1970 to 636,000 in 1980 and 628,000 in 1990, but the metropolitan area increased from 1,397,000 in 1980 to 1,432,000 in 1990. Milwaukee's traditional European image has altered in the last two decades, with the establishment of Hmong, Vietnamese, Hispanic, and Arab communities. These groups, along with the more established German, Italian, Polish, Irish, Native American, and African-American communities, celebrate their heritage annually in a series of ethnic galas, earning Milwaukee the title City of Festivals. For the city and metropolitan area, industry continued to be important and included production of machinery, fabricated metal products, and electrical and electronic equipment. Breweries, which once had made the city famous, were of lesser importance, although three remained. Milwaukee hosts the annual Great Circus Parade and is home to major league baseball and basketball teams. The city boasts two universities and is ranked high for housing affordability and quality of life. Municipal elections in Milwaukee are officially nonpartisan, but candidates usually represent moderate to liberal Democratic positions.

[Harry H. Anderson and Frederick I. Olson, *Milwaukee* (Tulsa, Okla., 1981).]

KATHLEEN FOSS-MOLLAN

See also **SUPP:** Wisconsin.

MINNEAPOLIS, a city located in southeastern Minnesota, derived its identity before World War II from milling and food processing (Pillsbury, General Mills) and its predominant German-Scandinavian-Lutheran-New England population mix. Since then, the population has become more mixed and less European. In 1980 the population was 87 percent white, 7.7 percent African American, 2.4 percent Native American, and 1.1 percent Asian; in 1990 the figures were 78 percent white, 13 percent African American, 3.3 percent Native American, and 4.3 percent Asian. Minneapolis's population decreased from 370,951 in 1980 to 368,383 in 1990; its county, however, has grown. Light manufacturing (Munsingwear, for example) declined, while the computer and financial services industries, medicine, and entertainment expanded. A downtown revival included renovation of the Orpheum and State Theaters and construction of the Jeune Lune Theatre, Orchestra Hall, new night spots, and the elimination of several unattractive buildings. The changes are highlighted on the landscape, dominated until 1973 by the Art Deco Foshay Tower, and in 1995 by a half-dozen pastel and glassed office buildings, the Humphrey Metrodome (home of baseball's Minnesota Twins and football's Minnesota Vikings), the Target Center (home of professional basketball's Timberwolves), and the Sculpture Garden. Ethnic and class differences have long marked Minneapolis's neighborhoods. "Nordeast" is predominantly eastern and southern European, while Kenwood is well-to-do; Native Americans increasingly moved to the area around the American Indian Center on Franklin Avenue; African Americans resided in south Minneapolis; gays and lesbians grouped around Loring Park; and middle-class whites lived in the suburbs. Magnet schools and the many lakes and parks reflect the city's aspirations. In 1993 Minneapolis elected Mayor Sharon Sayles Belton, the city's first female mayor and first African-American political leader, signaling a demographic change and growing liberalism.

[Larry Millett, *Lost Twin Cities* (Saint Paul, Minn., 1992).]

ANNETTE ATKINS

See also **DAH:** Twin Cities; **SUPP:** Minnesota.

MINNESOTA. Machinery Hill has been a farm-implement mecca at the Minnesota State Fair for nearly one hundred years, but at the 1993 fair, snowblowers and garden tractors replaced combines, harrows, and field tractors. Butter sculptures, Hardanger embroidery, and prize lambs still drew crowds, but bungee jumping, the midway, minidoughnuts, and the Beach Boys captured more fairgoers' attention. The fair draws more than 1.5 million visitors annually because, while catering to current tastes, it holds out images of an older Minnesota. Minnesotans make many claims

to the good life. On average they live two years longer than other Americans. They passed the trendsetting Clean Indoor Air Act in 1976. They point to the Mayo Clinic, the University of Minnesota Hospitals, the large number of doctors and dentists, pacemaker production (Medtronic), and pathbreaking work in open-heart surgery as examples of Minnesota's advantages. They cite the "Minnesota method" of addiction treatment pioneered at the Hazelden Institute. The state's crime rate has risen but remains low (forty-seventh nationally in 1970; thirty-sixth in 1990). Minnesotans even take a perverse pleasure in winter—ice fishing, cross-country skiing, and inventing and elaborating indoor shopping malls (Southdale in Edina was the first, built in 1956; Mall of America in Bloomington is the largest in the United States).

Governor Rudy Perpich (1977–1978, 1982–1990) called Minnesota the "brain-power state," and many take pride in the state's commitment to education. Minnesota ranks seventh in per capita funding of all education. In 1971 the state shifted from property-tax-based to income-tax-based school funding, thus equalizing school expenditures across school districts (at least through the 1970s). In the mid-1990s Minnesota supported forty-six state, community, and private colleges and universities and thirty-four technical colleges. Standardized test scores consistently ranked the state's students among the top five states in the nation. The computer-to-pupil ratio was third nationally. Of the state's over-twenty-five population, 85 percent were high school graduates.

Minnesota's economy in the nineteenth and early twentieth centuries depended on food, wood, and iron ore. The late-twentieth-century economy still did but had changed radically since World War II, when the state responded to the demand for weapons and defense systems. Minnesota businesses—Honeywell, Control Data, Cray Research, National Computer Systems—have pioneered in high tech and computer products and services. Minnesota also has strong service companies: Dayton Hudson, Ecolab, Lutheran Brotherhood, and the St. Paul Companies. More recently, the music industry has boomed in Minnesota, including such independent recording companies as Twin Tone Records and Red House Records, Minnesota Public Radio, and American Public Radio. This diversification made the economy partially recession-proof, but there were some casualties: high unemployment on the Iron Range; the decline of small towns; a bitter and protracted 1986 strike against the Hormel Company in Austin; and layoffs to make companies more competitive. These changes fractured lives, sometimes created less congenial workplaces, and bruised a state that has prided itself on corporate generosity and the family quality of its farms and businesses.

Minnesotans continued to struggle to define the proper relation between business and government. In the nineteenth century many viewed big business as a danger and government as a force for good. This suspicion and faith nourished a liberal tradition that in the twentieth century produced such nationally known politicians as Hubert Humphrey, Walter Mondale, Orville Freeman, Harold Stassen, Eugene McCarthy, and Paul Wellstone. In the 1990s many Minnesotans advocated an activist government, but others worried that the state's tax structure, workers' compensation, and generous state programs had created a chilly business climate. Minnesota politicians have worked since the 1970s to reduce taxes and tap the research and development talents of the University of Minnesota. They instituted the Minnesota Department of Trade and Economic Development and created regional initiative funds, enterprise zones, and business tax credits. The result of thirty years of focusing on the business climate (and arguing about it) was relatively high personal income taxes (but not the highest in the nation) and good state services.

Minnesota's political parties—Democratic Farmer-Labor (DFL) and Independent Republican (IR)—traditionally formed two coalitions: labor, Catholic, ethnic, farm people (DFL) and Protestant, business, small town (IR). In the mid-1970s the two parties underwent a major realignment when issues of abortion, feminism, and homosexual rights led to factional division and drove many religious conservatives from the DFL to the IR. In 1978 the IR candidates defeated their DFL opponents for the governor's seat (Albert Quie) and both senate seats (David Durenberger and Rudy Boschwitz). In the 1980s and 1990s women also became increasingly active in politics: Joan Growe was elected secretary of state continuously beginning in 1974; Dee Long took office as speaker of the house in 1992; Marlene Johnson was lieutenant governor from 1982 to 1990 and Joanell Drystad took over that office in 1992; and Sharon Sayles Belton became mayor of Minneapolis in 1994.

Minnesota was populated in the nineteenth century by Scandinavians, Germans, and Irish in farm and urban areas, and southern and eastern Europeans settled on the Iron Range and northern Minnesota. The largest groups of immigrants were Asians, Hmong people in particular, who, it was estimated, would outnumber the African-American population by the end of the twentieth century. Minnesota's 1990 population of 4,375,099 was 2.2 percent African American, 1.8 percent Asian, 1.2 percent Hispanic, and 1.1 percent Native American. Minnesota has held steady in the ranking of state populations since 1970 (nineteenth in 1970, twenty-first in 1980, and twentieth in 1990). Ojibwa and Dakota peoples originally populated the territory and near the end of the twentieth century were spread across eleven reservations-communities. Minneapolis has the largest urban population of Native Americans in the United States, perhaps accounting for the birth there of the American Indian Movement (AIM) in the 1970s. Poverty is the most immediate problem facing Native Americans, a problem in the midst of change as native groups opened casinos (eighteen in 1994) that attracted thousands of visitors and billions of dollars. Racism continued to be a problem in a state so predominantly white, although the first Urban Coalition chapter was founded in Minnesota following the 1966 and 1967 riots, and in 1993 Minneapolis elected as mayor an African-American women.

Minnesota's Twin Cities—Saint Paul and Minneapolis—are not identical. Minneapolis, the more Protestant, African American, and Native American, is the home of the University of Minnesota's main campus, the Lake Harriet Rose Garden, the Minnesota Orchestra (known until 1968 as the Minnesota Symphony), and many lakes. Its skyline, once dominated by the Foshay Tower, now shows off the IDS Tower, the First Bank Place, and the Norwest Center buildings, all housing financial services companies. Saint Paul, which is more Catholic, Jewish, and Hispanic, is home of the University of Minnesota agricultural campus, the State Fairgrounds, the Ordway Theater, and the Como Conservatory. The Minnesota capitol, Saint Paul Cathedral, Minnesota History Center, and Saint Paul Companies dominate the Saint Paul skyline. Bloomington, the state's third largest city and a Twin Cities suburb, sports mostly hotels, service companies, shopping centers, and the Mall of America. Duluth, which is more working class and is located on Lake Superior, supports itself with shipping and tourism, having weathered, if not recovered from, a near economic collapse that began in the 1970s. Its decline in relative size, from third to fourth in the state according to the 1990 census, signaled larger population shifts in the state toward the Twin Cities and their suburbs.

In the late twentieth century, audiences supported more than thirty theater companies, as different from each other as the Guthrie Theater Company, the Jeune Lune Theatre, the Heart of the Beast Puppet Theatre, Mixed Blood Theater, and the Children's Theater Company. Minnesota was also home to several small publishers (West, Graywolf, and Milkweed Editions, for example) and a variety of authors, including Jon Hassler, Louise Erdrich, Fred Manfred, Patricia Hampl, J. F. Powers, LaVyrle Spencer, Robert Bly, Peg Meier, and, perhaps best known, Garrison Keillor.

[Jo Blatti, *Women's History in Minnesota* (Saint Paul, 1993); Theodore C. Blegen, *Minnesota* (Minneapolis, 1975); Clifford E. Clark, Jr., ed., *Minnesota in a Century of Change* (Saint Paul, 1989); Elizabeth Ebbott, *Indians in Minnesota*, 4th ed. (Minneapolis, 1985); June Drenning Holmquist, ed., *They Chose Minnesota* (Saint Paul, 1980); Ramedo J. Saucedo, ed., *Mexican Americans in Minnesota* (Saint Paul, 1977); Barbara Stuhler and Gretchen Kreuter, eds., *Women of Minnesota* (Saint Paul, 1977); David Vassar Taylor, ed., *Blacks in Minnesota* (Saint Paul, 1976).]

ANNETTE ATKINS

See also **SUPP:** Minneapolis.

MINORITY BUSINESS. Enterprises owned or operated by members of racial and ethnic minority groups have historically been a distinctive element of U.S. business. The nature and role of minority businesses have evolved with changing social and political circumstances. Business activity among African Americans has been traditionally concentrated in small retail and personal-service firms serving a black clientele and usually located in inner-city ghettos. Most were less capitalized than white-owned firms operating in the same areas. As a result of the civil rights movement of the 1960s, the federal government began programs to actively encourage black business enterprise. In 1965 the Small Business Administration began to channel loans to minority businesses. In 1969 the Office of Minority Business Enterprise (OMBE) was created within the Department of Commerce to coordinate public and private initiatives in the development of minority business. Critics charged that the enthusiasm of politicians for black capitalism masked a lessening commitment to alleviating urban poverty through public employment and job training. They pointed out that the initial appropriation for the OMBE came from funds transferred out of the budget of the Office for Economic Opportunity. Nevertheless, independent surveys in 1981 by *Nuestro Business Review* and *Black Enterprise* showed that 45 of the top 100 Latino businesses had been formed between 1969 and 1976 and that 56 of the top 100 black firms had been established between 1969 and

1976, 30 of them between 1969 and 1971. In 1985, 1,000 African-American businesspersons gave a testimonial dinner praising the establishment of OMBE (now the Minority Business Development Agency).

While the traditional small retail business still accounts for more than half of black enterprises, in the 1970s and 1980s blacks established or expanded firms in construction, engineering, and business and professional services. Beginning with the administration of President Richard M. Nixon (1969–1974), their efforts were aided by minority set-aside programs of local, state, and federal governments that mandated a certain percentage of public contracts for minority firms. These set asides were justified as ways to overcome past racial discrimination, but in 1989, in *City of Richmond* v. *J. A. Croson Company,* the Supreme Court struck down such a program and ruled that public officials would have to offer evidence of past discrimination to justify such policies.

The law establishing the OMBE in 1969 also designated Hispanics, Native Americans, Asians, Aleuts, and Eskimos as minority groups eligible for assistance in business development. Small business entrepreneurship has often been associated with ethnic groups that are recent immigrants. Since the most recent period of large-scale immigration to the United States began in 1965, Koreans, Chinese, and Cubans have shown high levels of entrepreneurial activity. Using family members and relatives as employees and drawing on financial resources inside and outside the United States, they have been successful in retail and wholesale trade in urban areas where supermarkets and other stores belonging to regional and national corporations have departed. In some instances these businesses thrive by serving an ethnic clientele.

Since the 1960s small business in general has reversed an earlier decline and benefited from the shift away from manufacturing in industrial nations. Different racial and ethnic groups, however, have varying levels of success in business. Recent Asian immigrants, especially Koreans and Chinese, have percentages of population engaged in small business at levels higher than the national average, while the percentage is below the average for Mexican Americans and blacks. Participation and success in small business enterprise have depended on education, access to credit, and management experience. Blacks have historically lagged behind various Asian and European immigrant groups in each of these areas. One study conducted in 1989 found that banks loaned black-owned businesses located in minority neighborhoods an average of $40,000 less than black-owned businesses in predominantly white areas. The record shows that with more education and affluence, later generations of ethnic immigrant groups move out of small-business ownership and into higher-paying managerial and professional occupations.

[Timothy Bates, *Banking on Black Enterprise* (Washington, D.C., 1993); Roger Waldinger, *Ethnic Entrepreneurs: Immigrant Business in Industrial Societies* (Newbury Park, Calif., 1990).]

JOHN B. WEAVER

See also **SUPP:** African Americans; Chinese Americans; Cuban Americans; Korean Americans; Set-Asides.

MISSILES, MILITARY. *See* **Defense, Department of.**

MISSING IN ACTION. *See* **Prisoners of War and Missing in Action.**

MISSISSIPPI. The history of Mississippi during the last quarter of the twentieth century was dominated by two themes—racial change and economic progress. In the mid-1960s Mississippi was still a firm bastion—perhaps the firmest—of racial segregation, and many civil rights battles were fought out in the state, including the crisis in 1962 over James Meredith's admission to the University of Mississippi; the murder of civil rights leader Medgar Evers in 1963; and the violent resistance to voter registration drives in 1964. Segregation depended on an agrarian economy, and as Mississippi's civil rights battles were occurring, socioeconomic change was beginning, represented by the rise of an urban, industrial, and commercial culture that fundamentally altered Mississippi's institutions.

Mississippi was a one-party state from the end of Reconstruction until well after World War II. Loyalty to the Democratic party was almost universal among Mississippi's whites, while almost all blacks were denied the right to vote or to run for office. In the 1990s the state elected the first Republican governor (Kirk Fordice) and lieutenant governor (Eddie Briggs) since 1875. By the mid-1990s it also had two Republican senators (Thad Cochran and Trent Lott) and one Republican congressmen (Roger Wicker). Republican candidates have carried the state in every presidential election starting with 1980. Similarly, large-scale black voter registration in the 1960s changed Mississippi's politics. In 1971 Charles Evers became the first black to wage a vigorous, although unsuccessful, campaign for governor. Since that time

blacks have held positions as mayors, state legislators, and U.S. representatives. Mississippi Congressman Mike Espy served as secretary of agriculture in President Bill Clinton's administration.

After World War II, Mississippi's economy shifted from a one-crop cotton economy to a more diversified agricultural and industrial system. Tenancy and sharecropping disappeared, and agriculture became not only diversified but mechanized. Soybeans, rice, livestock, poultry, and fish farming replaced the old dependency on cotton. Individuals employed in agriculture dropped from 43 percent in 1950 to only 2.7 percent in 1990. Employment in manufacturing, trade, and government soared. In 1990, 24 percent of Mississippians were employed in manufacturing, 42 percent in trade, and 23 percent in government.

Mississippi has made important contributions to the nation's music and literature. Before World War II such blues musicians from the Mississippi Delta as "Big Bill" Broonzy and Charley Patton began a virtual revolution in American music that soon spread over the world. Similarly, Mississippi writers such as William Faulkner, Richard Wright, and Eudora Welty created a body of literature of unparalleled volume and power. Scholars still wonder how such an outpouring could come from so small and isolated a state. The influence of these writers continues in the work of such authors as Shelby Foote, Ellen Douglas, Ellen Gilchrist, and Beth Henley. Like Faulkner and Welty, the stories of this new generation of writers are rooted in the people and history of Mississippi.

In the years before World War II, Mississippi's schools suffered from segregation, poor funding, and rural isolation. During the 1950s and 1960s, the state's schools were wracked by confrontations over integration. By 1970 public schools and colleges alike were integrated, and remain so today. While Mississippi still ranks near the bottom among the states in total expenditures for education, it ranks near the top in per capita tax burden for education, and 45 percent of the state's budget goes for that purpose. Similarly, consolidation of rural schools, begun in the 1920s, has steadily eliminated the small schools and created larger ones with more diverse offerings. Colleges and universities admittedly have undergone less consolidation than the public schools. Three comprehensive universities—the University of Mississippi (Ole Miss), Mississippi State University, and the University of Southern Mississippi—are at the top of the educational hierarchy. Mississippi has five smaller regional universities with more limited offerings: Mississippi University for Women, Delta

State, Alcorn, Jackson State, and Mississippi Valley. The latter three are historically black colleges whose enrollments were still predominantly black in the 1990s. The state has thirteen public community college systems, which offer technical and vocational courses and the first two years of college courses. Enrollments in the public universities totaled 57,602 in the fall of 1994, and enrollment in community colleges totaled 76,900. In addition to the public colleges and universities, Mississippi has four-year and two-year denominational colleges, the largest of which are Mississippi College at Clinton (Baptist) and Millsaps College at Jackson (Methodist).

The state's population rose only modestly from 2,178,000 in 1960 to 2,573,000 in 1990. Mississippi always was and remains a rural state. In 1970 only 45 percent of Mississippians lived in towns and cities; by 1990 that figure had risen just slightly to 47 percent. Only three states—Vermont, West Virginia, and Maine—had smaller urban populations. These figures, however, must be qualified by two population trends. First, a great number of rural dwellers, perhaps as many as half, commuted daily to work in nearby towns and cities. Second, three metropolitan areas, Jackson, the Gulf Coast, and the Mississippi suburbs of Memphis contained 64 percent of Mississippi's urban population.

[Richard A. McLemore, ed., *A History of Mississippi*, 2 vols. (Hattiesburg, Miss., 1973); John R. Skates, *Mississippi: A Bicentennial History* (New York, 1979).]

JOHN R. SKATES

MISSOURI, the Show Me State, is centrally located and defined by its rivers, especially the mighty Mississippi along its eastern border and the Missouri, which flows west to east, cutting the 69,697-square-mile state in half. The topography varies from the rugged Ozarks in the south to rolling farm land in the north. In the last quarter of the twentieth century the state did fairly well economically, although not markedly so. In agriculture the cotton-producing Bootheel, jutting into Arkansas, had much in common with the lower South. In northern Missouri agricultural pursuits resembled those in neighboring Iowa and Nebraska, with soybeans the most important crop. The cost of machinery forced consolidation of some farms, and 10 percent of Missouri's farms accounted for 60 percent of sales in the 1990s, although the state's 107,000 farms were second in number only to Texas. Factories were located primarily in the state's two largest metropolitan areas, Saint Louis in the east and Kansas City in the west, and the principle manufactures were for transportation—motor

vehicles, railroad cars, and aircraft. Food processing, primarily dairy products, flour, and beer, and chemicals were next in importance in manufactures.

The state's two metropolitan areas were sizable; in 1992 Saint Louis had 2,518,528 residents and Kansas City had 1,616,930. Both metropolitan areas spill over into neighboring states, respectively, East Saint Louis, Ill., and Kansas City, Kans. Both Saint Louis and Kansas City have large international airports, and the huge Kansas City airport in the 1970s replaced a downtown airport with runways almost too short for jet aircraft. The state's smaller cities were hardly comparable to Saint Louis and Kansas City; Missouri's third- and fourth-largest cities, Springfield and Independence, had populations in 1990 of 140,593 and 112,301, respectively. Independence, an eastern suburb of Kansas City, grew notably, doubling and tripling from the earlier rural town.

Politically, in the 1970s, 1980s, and early 1990s, Missouri continued to display the same rural-urban antagonisms that had marked the state's history since statehood in 1821. With its two major metropolitan areas having more than 4 million residents in a state that contained a 1990 population of 5,117,073, the state government seemed incapable of bridging the rural-urban gap. It did not seem to matter much if governors were Republicans or Democrats. Starting in 1977 there was a Democratic governor, followed by two Republicans, then a Democrat; rural-urban antagonisms continued. The building of interstate highways, which promised to tie rural areas to metropolises, only accentuated the division in Missouri. While interstate highways ran through the middle of the state and along the eastern and western boundaries, large parts of the state remained without four-lane roads in the 1990s.

Environmental problems began to appear in the 1970s, caused by both city and rural practices, including the dumping of solid wastes (garbage) and the use of farm chemicals. The solid waste problem became massive, and the more than 100 landfills in the state were expected to be filled by the end of the twentieth century. Meanwhile, massive concentrations of the chemical dioxin were discovered at Times Beach and thirty other sites in the state in 1982. The problem was attacked at a cost of many millions of dollars, but in 1988 the state had twenty-one sites on the federal Superfund list of abandoned hazardous waste sites. Rural streams were badly polluted by acid runoff from abandoned coal mines. The Missouri and Mississippi rivers were also badly polluted.

Race relations in Saint Louis and Kansas City improved after desegregation in the 1950s and 1960s, but there were continuing problems. A significant school desegregation controversy arose in Kansas City in 1987. A federal judge ordered an increase in the city property tax and a surcharge on the state income tax, in order to provide money for Kansas City district schools. A federal appeals court upheld the property tax increase and authorized the district school board to set the tax rate but overturned the income tax surcharge. The Supreme Court upheld the appeals court in 1990, on the principle that constitutionally judges cannot set tax rates, although they can order local government bodies, in this instance the district school board, to do so.

In the mid-1990s Missouri continued to take an interest in its historical heritage, and the state attracts about 40 million tourists each year, which contributes approximately $6 billion per year to state revenues. The spectacular Gateway Arch at Saint Louis announces that city's historical role as the gateway to the West, and the city developed its Mississippi riverfront as part of the Jefferson National Expansion Memorial. On the western side of the state, the National Park Service developed a site near the Harry S. Truman Library and Museum in Independence that includes the president's house and the farmhouse where Truman once lived, now encircled by the Kansas City suburb of Grandview. In celebration of the state's most famous citizen, Northeast Missouri State University, located in the rural "outstate" town of Kirksville, became Truman State University in 1996.

[William E. Foley, *The Genesis of Missouri: From Wilderness Outpost to Statehood* (Columbia, Mo., 1989); William E. Parrish, ed., *A History of Missouri,* 5 vols. (Columbia, Mo., 1971–1986); William E. Parrish, Charles T. Jones, Jr., and Lawrence O. Christensen, *Missouri,* 2nd ed. (Arlington Heights, Ill., 1992).]

LAWRENCE H. LARSEN

See also **SUPP:** Branson; Kansas City; Saint Louis; Times Beach.

MONTANA, the fourth-largest state in area, remained lightly populated in 1970 with only 694,409 people. At that time its citizens began actively to explore how to balance economic growth with protection of their environment, a goal that was partly fulfilled in the decade that followed only to be dashed in the 1980s. The Montana of the 1990s was a state somber, cautious, and perhaps wiser for the experience. Economic, social, and political forces combined during the late 1960s and early 1970s to produce a popular revolution in Montana. Increasing numbers of the state's people recognized the consequences of a con-

tinued headlong depletion of the state's land. They supported the national movement to establish wilderness areas and preserve wild and scenic rivers and joined in a statewide effort to protect both the land and land-dependent employment. Politics embraced the popular sentiment. The state's 1972 constitution—containing significant changes from its 1889 predecessor—was noteworthy for protection of the environment. Two legislatures supported the environmental revolution, passing the Strip Mining and Reclamation Act (1973), the Water Use Act (1973), the Major Facility Siting Act (1975), and the Coal Severance Tax (1975). Suddenly Montana became a national leader on environmental and consumer protection issues.

Despite public support Montana's traditional, natural-resource extractive industries have stumbled or fallen since 1970. Hardrock mining, timber, petroleum, coal, and agriculture all experienced the downside of Montana's cyclical boom-and-bust economy. The 1980s proved particularly devastating. Reacting to national and international forces, Montana suffered from foreign economic fluctuations, reduced industrial demands, and rapidly changing technology. The state's major employer throughout the century—the Anaconda Copper Mining Company—departed during the 1970s. Its successor, the Atlantic Richfield Company (ARCO), closed its smelters and then terminated all operations in 1983, devastating such old mining towns as Butte. Champion International purchased the Anaconda Company's massive timber holdings, only to endure the national lumber market's disintegration through the 1970s and into the 1990s. These years marked the deindustrialization of Montana. Impressive petroleum discoveries in the 1970s and 1980s and a bituminous-coal boom in the early 1970s turned Billings, on the Yellowstone River, into Montana's largest and most affluent city. Despite drastic declines in the petroleum market and a reduction in coal production, Montana's energy reserves offer promise for development. Montana's future rests on the ability to handle such challenges as replacing traditional natural-resource-extractive industries and increasing per capita income. The latter in 1948 was 16 percent above the national average but by 1986 had dropped to 77 percent of the national average; by 1993 it had increased only to 84 percent, still far below what it once had been.

In the mid-1990s agriculture remained Montana's most lucrative basic industry. Farmers and ranchers adapted to technology, to special crops and breeds, to new farming and livestock techniques, and to international markets. Montana continued to rely on the wheat-beef-barley triumvirate but was quick to embrace such specialty crops as canola. In the 1970s a wet cycle and huge wheat sales to the Soviet Union produced an agricultural boom across the state, while the 1980s brought plummeting prices and the severe, lingering drought of 1985–1990. Agriculture continued to withstand the boom-and-bust cycle.

The constant in Montana through the 1970–1995 period was land, the state's ultimate natural resource. Montana offered the inhabitants of an increasingly pressurized nation its clean, quiet, open spaces, varied recreational opportunities, and scenic beauty. The realization by Montanans that open space represented a financial asset was a novelty in the 1990s. The new attitudes about Montana's land sustained the state's tourism. In 1970 nonresident visitors spent $75 million; in 1992 they contributed $930 million to the state's economy. Yellowstone National Park and Glacier National Park drew the most tourists, but other destination resorts, especially those for skiing, hunting, and fishing, extended tourism's bounties.

With a 1994 population of 856,000, Montana remained "a small city with very long streets connecting its neighborhoods." Increasingly both natives and newcomers have settled in the western Rocky Mountains, "yuppifying" Livingston and Bozeman on the borders of Paradise Valley and depopulating the eastern high plains. Despite vast space, few people, and no sales tax, Montana supported a diverse educational system. The state also became a haven for the arts, ranging from Western painting, photography, and regional literature to Hollywood film. With the withdrawal of the Anaconda Company from Montana politics, the few remaining large corporations had to share power with trade unions, consumer advocates, and single-issue coalitions. In the 1970–1995 period Montana tended to elect conservatives to state and local offices while sending liberal Democrats to Congress, including Mike Mansfield, Lee Metcalf, John Melcher, Max Baucus, and Pat Williams. The exception was Conrad Burns, a conservative who in 1994 became the only Montana Republican ever reelected to the Senate. Despite the state's slight increases in population, it lost one of its two seats in the House of Representatives in 1990.

[Harry W. Fritz, *Montana: Land of Contrast* (Woodland Hills, Calif., 1984); Michael P. Malone, Richard B. Roeder, and William L. Lang, *Montana: A History of Two Centuries* (Seattle, 1991); K. Ross Toole, *Montana: An Uncommon Land* (Norman, Okla., 1959).]

DAVID A. WALTER

See also **SUPP:** Butte.

MORMONS. *See* **Latter-day Saints, Church of Jesus Christ of; Reorganized Church of Jesus Christ of Latter-day Saints.**

MOTION PICTURES. *See* **Movies.**

MOUNT ST. HELENS, a stratovolcanic peak composed of alternating layers of lava and ash, in southwest Washington State, forty miles northeast of Portland, Oreg. Dormant since 1857, Mount St. Helens erupted on May 18, 1980. The eruption was triggered by a series of earthquakes below the volcano's peak and resulted in the release of a mushroom cloud of gases 63,000 feet high, carrying superheated ash and core particles. A lavalike mixture of glass, gas, and ash swept down the mountainside at speeds up to 100 miles per hour. The natural disaster killed 60 people, decimated several native animal populations, and destroyed $500 million worth of timber; economic losses to the region totaled $3 billion. Subsequent minor eruptions occurred on May 25, 1980, and April 11, 1981. In 1982 Mount St. Helens was declared a national volcano monument.

[Caroline D. Harnly and David A. Tyckoson, *Mount St. Helens, The 1980 Eruptions: An Annotated Bibliography* (Metuchen, N.J., 1984).]

CAROLYN BRONSTEIN

See also **SUPP:** Washington State.

MOVIES. Historians place the beginning of projected images in the mid-seventeenth century, when two Germans, Athanasius Kirschner and Johannes Zahn, first mounted figures on glass slides inside a rotating cylinder. Such "magic lanterns," lacking as they were in pliable celluloid film, electromotive force, and, not unimportantly, urban crowds large enough to support this machine-driven form of communication, could hardly be called motion pictures in any contemporary sense, but the optical principles that made Kirschner and Zahn's work possible pointed toward a future that included commercial movies made for mass audiences. Tinkerers and inventors of several European nations, along with several Americans, carried on their experiments. In 1877 Leland Stanford, the American railroad entrepreneur, commissioned an eccentric researcher, Eadweard Muybridge, to settle a bet on the question of whether or not the hooves of a galloping horse ever simultaneously left the ground; the issue was resolved in the affirmative when Muybridge caught the horse at full gallop by means of a row of cameras linked to trip wires over which the horse raced. By 1890 George Eastman had patented a reel of flexible celluloid that made possible exposing film in sequential frames, and beginning in 1896 movies were projected onto screens for audiences at Koster and Bial's Music Hall in New York City.

Inventor Thomas Edison managed to synthesize much research by engaging the scientist William Kennedy Laurie Dickson and by buying up patents for ancillary inventions filed by Thomas Armat, Woodville Latham, and others. At first Edison's firm focused only on his Kinetoscope, a hand-cranked device through which a single viewer peered at a few moments of motion—Annie Oakley firing a rifle, shots of the daily lives of Western Indians, and other fleeting vignettes. Patented in 1891, demonstrated at the Columbian Exposition of 1893 in Chicago, shown to a paying public in the spring of 1894 in New York City, the Kinetoscope peep shows quickly gave way to projected images, again invented by Edison, only two years later at Koster and Bial's. In 1902 Thomas L. Tally opened his Electric Theatre in Los Angeles, a debut soon followed by theater owners in McKeesport and New Castle, Pa., and eventually in every major city. These new theaters—Nickel Odeons, as they were called—helped establish movies as a medium distinct from performance theater, such as vaudeville. Movies soon began to appear in a complex national network of chain theaters supplied by distribution centers called "exchanges." Studios anticipated the Hollywood system of vertically integrated, script-to-screen enterprise.

To a great extent the early system of making and distributing movies was held in place by a patent pool, the Motion Picture Patents Company, led by Edison and other patent holders who used licensing fees as a means of restraining competition. Oddly, these inventive entrepreneurs were aesthetically conservative to the point that few of them thought audiences could tolerate feature-length movies. By 1913 the rivals of the pool had begun to make inroads into its market. Carl Laemmle moved his studio from the Midwest to southern California, where he could get 200 sunny shooting days per year, cheap real estate, and a haven remote from lawyers of the Patents Company. The pioneers included Samuel Goldwyn, Jesse L. Lasky, and Cecil B. DeMille, who together made one of the first features in Hollywood, *The Squaw Man* (1914). Parallel to this westward movement, other movie innovators, such as George Kleine and Adolph Zukor, imported lengthier and more presti-

gious films, with Zukor bringing in *Queen Elizabeth* (1912) with Sarah Bernhardt. The campaign against the patents trust was also assisted by the success of D. W. Griffith, J. Stuart Blackton, and others. They synthesized an emerging canon of cinematic techniques—narrative editing, expressive closeups, and mobile cameras—into an aesthetic that made possible the evolution of feature-length films. Moviemaking by 1915 had been transformed into the Hollywood system by circumstances seemingly unrelated. Griffith completed *The Birth of a Nation* (1915), his famous (and racist) jeremiad against Reconstruction, which demonstrated the political power of the medium and expanded its capacity for advertisement. Gradually the rebels against the mainly Anglo-Saxon patents trust evolved into a Jewish elite whose recent arrival in the United States inspired a broad synthesis of America that harmonized old and new, immigrant and settler, working class and middle class.

World War I stifled European moviemaking so much that American studios, by filling the void, assumed a dominant place in the international marketplace. By the time the United States entered the war in 1917, movies dominated popular culture and movie "stars" were engaged to sell millions of dollars worth of war bonds. By war's end the Hollywood system had become institutionalized, with power in the hands of such producers as Irving Thalberg of Metro-Goldwyn-Mayer. The movie business eventually generated 600 movies each year (some of which grossed millions of dollars), built 5,000 new theaters, raised capital totaling $2 billion, and dominated the world's markets. "The film is to America what the flag was once to Britain," warned the *London Post* in 1925. "By its means, Uncle Sam may hope some day . . . to Americanize the world." "Movies in the age of innocence" described the era when Hollywood's reach seemed limitless and its style universal. Westerns grew into vast epics, such as *The Iron Horse* (1924) and *Covered Wagon* (1923). *The Thief of Baghdad* (1924), *The Phantom of the Opera* (1925), and *The Hunchback of Notre Dame* (1923) filled screens with exotically romantic eras and places. The demimonde appeared in *Broken Blossoms* (1919) and *Beggars of Life* (1928). Racial tensions strained the fabric of *Showboat* (1929) and *Uncle Tom's Cabin* (1927). Social dramas played out in *Manslaughter* (1922) and *Male and Female* (1919). The Judeo-Christian Bible came vividly to life in *The King of Kings* (1927) and other spectacles. The system gradually stifled the artistic impulses of directors—Erich von Stroheim's movies were edited into miniatures and Griffith made his last film in 1931—all this in the name of profitability.

The coming into theaters of sound-on-films is more accurately explained by studio connections with brokers and bankers than by the old legend of a fiscally shaky Warner Brothers gambling everything on sound films as if on a last throw of the dice. Sound film had existed for years but proved usable only when accompanied by the wherewithal to wire thousands of theaters. Between 1926 and 1929, sound film came in the form of *Don Juan* (1926); Al Jolson in *The Jazz Singer* (1927); the first all-talkie, *Lights of New York* (1928), and the first attempts at depicting African-American life on film, all in 1929—*Hallelujah!*, *Hearts in Dixie*, and Bessie Smith's short film by Dudley Murphy, *The St. Louis Blues*. The quick success of sound film encouraged studios to try Herbert Kalmus's long-simmering Technicolor process. From the first Technicolor short, *La Cucaracha* (1934), to David O. Selznick's epochal *Gone with the Wind* (1939), color changed from a costly adventure in research and development into an increasingly common element in movie aesthetics. Here is another innovation best explained by a symbiosis between scientists and investors rather than by a romantic legend of bold moguls saving their studios.

With the coming of the Great Depression, Hollywood studios sought to move against the tide, and some actually made a profit. Only Paramount, overextended in theatrical realty, brushed against bankruptcy. Indeed, as sound film became conventional the studios extended their range into whole new genres. As the American theatrical stage became more naturalistic, its best works, such as Eugene O'Neill's *Anna Christie* and Sidney Kingsley's *Dead End*, came to the screen in 1930 and 1937, respectively, along with movie versions of such American novels as Sinclair Lewis's *Dodsworth* in 1936, Ernest Hemingway's *A Farewell to Arms* in 1932, and John Steinbeck's *The Grapes of Wrath* in 1940. At the same time, DeMille and other makers of movie epics adapted their silent movie styles to sound film in such works as *Cleopatra* (1934), *The Crusades* (1935), and *Union Pacific* (1939). Biographies from Abraham Lincoln to Lillian Russell emerged from every studio, especially Twentieth Century–Fox. The "star system" flourished, again particularly at Fox, in such Shirley Temple films as *The Little Colonel* (1934), *The Littlest Rebel* (1936), *Wee Willie Winkie* (1937), and a score of others. Will Rogers had his own genre of local color in such movies as *David Harum* (1934), *Judge Priest* (1934), and *The County Chairman* (1935).

Crime dramas that portrayed a dark underside of urban culture—*Scarface* (1932), *Bullets or Ballots* (1936), and *Public Enemy* (1931), to name but a few—became vehicles by which moviemakers addressed social dysfunctions brought about by the Great Depression. Even such musicals as *The Gold Diggers of 1933* (1933) served not only as escapist fare but as ideologically optimistic responses to the economic crisis. The Hollywood system reached an apogee of sorts in 1939, the year of *Gone with the Wind, The Wizard of Oz, Stagecoach, Wuthering Heights, Juarez,* and *Goodbye Mr. Chips*.

During this heady era, Hollywood studios reached a complex level of corporate structure. Each maintained a close affiliation with bankers and brokers on both the East and West coasts, a system of producer units on each lot, sales departments that presented their products to the world, stables of contractual stars and directors, adversarial links to many craft guilds, and influential links to movie fan magazines. Most compelling in defining the Hollywood product, however, was the Hays Office of the Motion Picture Producers and Distributors of America (MPPDA) (after 1945 known as the Motion Picture Association of America, or MPAA). Hollywood created the MPPDA in 1922 in response to scandals involving movie stars. Will H. Hays became its first president. When critics continued to charge that moviegoing caused moral and social decay, the movie industry adopted a production code in 1930. Heavily moral in emphasis but also politically conservative, the code was largely the work of a Jesuit priest, Daniel A. Lord. The ability of Hays and the MPPDA to enforce the code was strengthened in 1934 with the creation of the Production Code Administration (an arm of the Hays Office) and the Roman Catholic Legion of Decency (independent of Hays), which could organize some 8 million Catholics to boycott offensive movies. Thenceforth, evildoers met bad ends and virtue was rewarded on theater screens.

The movie industry entered World War II with considerable concern, generated by the prospect of federal interference. A newly minted Office of War Information (OWI) sought to prescribe Hollywood's contribution to the war effort. Even before the war, a Senate committee had investigated Hollywood's alleged "warmongering," and a House committee had probed a presumed infiltration of the movie industry by the Communist party. As it turned out, the OWI proved an accommodating monitor, and the congressional committees put aside their curiosity for the duration of the war. Furthermore, Hollywood's craft guilds, like most other trade unions, deferred strikes. Within their familiar formulas the studios produced simply phrased war movies, and satisfied audiences provided studios with their greatest profits ever. War movies typically ranged over a wide field to influence Anglophobes, draftees in search of war aims, African Americans in need of a reason to fight despite their oppression at home, and civilians who felt the loss of their men under arms. These movies also sometimes served the country simply by offering diversions from the stresses imposed by war. *Sergeant York* (1941) defined the notion of a "just war" in folkish terms; *Sundown* (1941) contained an implicit promise that a victorious Britain would find a way out of colonialism; *Sahara* (1943) and *Lifeboat* (1944) dramatized the virtues of allying against fascism; *Mrs. Miniver* (1942) and *In Which We Serve* (1942) revealed a Britain unified across class lines; *Bataan* (1943) and *Crashdive* (1943) placed black Americans in the military ranks; *Casablanca* (1943) traced the conversion of an American in Morocco from isolationism to action against the Germans; and *Since You Went Away* (1944) and *Gangway for Tomorrow* (1943) brought the war to civilians. At the same time, outside the circle of Hollywood studios the war stimulated a movement of documentary filmmakers toward a cinema of social advocacy. Responding to requirements of the Signal Corps, OWI, and other agencies, filmmakers turned out a sweeping range of propaganda movies, such as *The Negro Soldier* (1944), *The Battle of Midway* (1942), *With the Marines at Tarawa* (1943), and *The Memphis Belle* (1944). After the war these same filmmakers brought their training to bear on U.S. political and social issues in such films as *The Quiet One* (1947) and a generation of television documentaries such as *The Twentieth Century* (1957–1966).

Unfortunately for the Hollywood that America had come to know, the era of peace brought an irresistible assault of pent-up social forces. Simmering labor disputes produced strife at the studio gates, resulting in soaring labor costs; wartime savings led consumers on a binge of leisure-time spending, seemingly on everything but moviegoing, that brought a period of inflation, which meant another boost in moviemaking costs; Congress, freed from wartime pressures for unity, revived its inquiry into communism in Hollywood, this time with a vengeance that trampled on the civil rights of its victims; the Supreme Court, which had muted its opposition to trusts, handed down the 1948 *Paramount* decision that obliged studios to dismantle the vertical integration of the sys-

tem that had brought each movie from script to screen; and finally, the shaken system was first threatened, then dominated by the new medium of network television. Such innovations as stereophonic sound and widescreen processes, like CinemaScope, only momentarily gave movies an edge in the face of TV's popularity. In the twenty-five years after World War II, Hollywood lost hundreds of millions of dollars. Hollywood recovered, but at the price of transforming its very nature. Its will to survive drove it into the arms of television, first selling off its vast libraries of feature films and, second, becoming the principal producer of the thousands of hours of broadcast time that television required. The made-for-television movie and the miniseries became staples of the old studios, while hour-length serial dramas and "sitcoms" assumed the role of older, cheaply made B-movies.

The mainstream fare, with its undemanding embrace of middle American values, was challenged during the 1960s by theatrical movies that brought to the screen occasionally revolutionary ideas and images that could find no place on the TV schedule. *Bonnie and Clyde* (1967) celebrated the lives of two murderous bank robbers of the Depression era. *Easy Rider* (1969) sympathetically portrayed the romantic rebels known as "flower children." *Sweet Sweetback's Baadasssss Song* (1971) offered a violent depiction of a black assault on white oppressors personified in a sadistically brutal Los Angeles police force.

Accompanying this sectoring of the audience into interest groups of television viewers and newly selective and politically aware audiences, was an opening of the nation's screens to foreign films, often played in "art houses" set apart from the increasingly unused downtown "picture palaces." At their best they included psychologically and socially sophisticated fare from Europe, some of them—such as Jules Dassin's *Never on Sunday* (1960)—running for more than a year in a single art house. Some, like *La Chinoise* (1967), were highly charged leftist films, while others paid homage to older American forms, much as *Tirez sur le Pianiste* (1960) echoed American gangster movies and the bleak postwar detective movies that came to be known as film noir. Still other imports, such as *Rashomon* (1950) and *Pather Panchali* (1955), came from Japan and India, respectively. Each in its way undercut the market for American movies and all but drove Hollywood into other areas of entertainment, as in the case of MGM's hotels and casinos. In the 1970s a few studios recovered by reaching for a newly discovered audience, a disaffected, urban, black youth that embraced the violence of so-called "blaxploitation" movies, such as Gordon Parks's *Shaft* (1971), which simultaneously recast the private detective into black terms and saved MGM from closure.

In the Hollywood that survived, several trends marked off the new generation from the old. Directors and writers such as Martin Scorsese and Steven Spielberg came to Hollywood from university film schools rather than up through the studio hierarchies. Some came willing to take risks, as in the case of George Lucas, who used computer-generated techniques in *Star Wars* (1977). Both in television and movies, the makers embraced a strategy of betting resources on hoped-for "blockbusters"—impressively expensive theatrical films that earned hundreds of millions—or television miniseries during "sweeps weeks," when audience-sampling firms provided the networks with data on the nation's viewing habits upon which advertising rates were based. Because audiences were ever younger, the movie year took on a rhythm grounded in the hiatuses of the academic year. Prospective blockbusters opened in summer and at Christmas, while offbeat movies such as Spike Lee's *She's Gotta Have It* (1986) opened in the new off-seasons of fall and spring. By the 1990s Hollywood had taken on the traits of conglomeration, an international trend in corporate enterprise, so that studios often came to be owned by foreign firms such as Sony, energy firms such as Gulf and Western, and soft-drink companies such as Coca-Cola. Accompanying this trend toward conglomeration, however, there was also a small growth of independent cinema that offered hope for ethnic minorities and cinematic innovators.

[Robert C. Allen and Douglas Gomery, *Film History* (New York, 1985); David Bordwell, Janet Staiger, and Kristin Thompson, *The Classical Hollywood Cinema* (New York, 1985); Thomas Cripps, *Slow Fade to Black: The Negro in American Film* (New York, 1977); Douglas Gomery, *Movie History* (Belmont, Calif., 1991); Garth Jowett, *Film: The Democratic Art* (Boston, 1976); Robert Sklar, *Movie-Made America* (New York, 1975).]

THOMAS CRIPPS

See also **DAH:** Motion Pictures; **SUPP:** Television.

MRI. *See* **Magnetic Resonance Imaging.**

MTV. *See* **MUSIC TELEVISION.**

MULTICULTURALISM. In the 1990s multiculturalism dominated interpretive and curricular debates about history in schools and universities. The idea responds in part to the diversity of students, especially in urban areas, increasingly from African-, Hispanic-, and Asian-American backgrounds. Taken together, minority groups are nearing a majority in such major cities as New York and Los Angeles and in states including California, Texas, Florida, and New York. By the year 2000 non-European ethnic minorities are expected to make up one-fourth of the nation's population. State and federal education officials, test designers, and educational publishers are concerned by these changes. Since demonstrations at Stanford University in 1988, educators on campuses across the country have debated the extent to which a history curriculum should be Eurocentric, that is, be based on classical Western texts, take a triumphal view of national settlement or expansion by Europeans, or emphasize the history of U.S. political and economic elites. Some multiculturalists claim that white Americans of European heritage have unjustly tried to impose ethnocentric values on nonwhite Americans. They hold that the school-based imposition of Western history, literature, ideas, institutions, and values on children of non-European backgrounds is unjust and culturally biased. Other scholars assert that the nation's political institutions, language, cultural ideals, and economic system derive mainly from Europe, notably from England.

Multiculturalism emphasizes the recognition and study of national diversity, especially along lines of ethnicity and gender. Both pluralists and group separatists claim its philosophical foundations: Multiculturalism may acknowledge qualities of U.S. culture and politics that transcend group differences, or it may contend that racial, ethnic, sexual, religious, and other human characteristics create "separate realities" and "multiple cultural perspectives" of learning. Many multiculturalists reject the idea of a common culture, including older ethnic melting-pot ideals and the idea of pluralism. The multicultural concept is often linked to self-esteem training used to advance the self-image of minorities and women. Some educators envision multiculturalism as a tool to change the educational environment so that students from various groups and social classes will experience equal educational opportunity. According to a 1991 New York City Board of Education declaration, "Multicultural education is an interdisciplinary approach to education designed to foster intergroup knowledge and understanding, to engender greater self-esteem within the entire school community, and to equip students to function effectively in a global society." Some philosophers distinguish between multiculturalism and pluralism in that the former "repudiates the idea of national identity and the emotion of national pride." They worry that such a repudiation, if standard in history and government, invites social fragmentation and civil disorder, whereby students will identify with groups rather than through bonds of citizenship, language, and law.

GILBERT T. SEWALL

See also **SUPP:** Curriculum; Pluralism; Political Correctness; Women's Studies.

MUSEUMS. Although museums in the United States date back to the late eighteenth century, the great age of museum building occurred in the 1870s with the founding of such institutions as the Metropolitan Museum of Art and the American Museum of Natural History, both in New York City, the Art Institute of Chicago, and the Boston Museum of Fine Arts. These grand public buildings emphasized rare and exemplary objects of great beauty, technical importance, or historical relevance, chiefly from cultures abroad, past and present. By the early twentieth century, however, U.S. museums began to respond to broad reform currents with a greater emphasis on U.S. culture itself. John Cotton Dana's work at the Newark Museum, for example, attempted to reach out to recent immigrants. A new interest in ordinary objects, on period rooms and contextual display, on historic houses, and on U.S. arts and crafts manifested itself. The era saw the emergence of such specialized art museums as the Museum of Modern Art, the Whitney Museum of American Art, and the Boston Institute of Contemporary Art.

The focus on U.S. history and culture was taken a step further in the 1920s with the development of the outdoor museum. Colonial Williamsburg in Virginia and the Henry Ford Museum and Greenfield Village in Michigan were the most visible and the best financed. Such museums brought a history focused in part around the daily lives of ordinary people and sought to teach a common past to a population that had become heterogeneous. As collections of buildings brought together to form a single site, Williamsburg and Greenfield Village served as models for such later museums as Old Sturbridge in Massachusetts and Old World Wisconsin. During these years the New York State Historical Association, under Dixon Ryan Fox, also began to play a leadership role that extended into the second half of the century, fostering ties between museum and university historians, exploring further the history of ordinary Americans,

and eventually playing an important role in the development of history exhibitions and graduate education.

The 1930s brought several changes in museum management. The reorganization of the National Park Service in 1933 greatly expanded its responsibility for historic interpretation and preservation and marked the beginning of a larger role for the federal government in support of museum development. The Chicago Museum of Science and Industry opened in 1933, inaugurating a more interactive form of science education and leading to the development of science centers, many supported and programmed directly by business. The decade was marked by calls to make museums instruments of social change and by a deepening interest in the U.S. past, especially in its folk and populist roots.

After World War II collectors and philanthropists founded museums devoted to neglected areas of national culture. Among the most important were Electra Havemeyer Webb's collection of Americana at the Shelburne Museum in Shelburne, Vt., and the Henry Francis du Pont Winterthur Museum in Delaware. Museums of business and industry emerged in these years, including the Hagley Museum and Library in Wilmington, Del., the Slater Historic Site in Pawtucket, R.I., and the Saugus Iron Works National Historic Site in Saugus, Mass.

Since the 1960s there have been several new trends. The federal government assumed an even larger role, and the National Park Service began to operate visitor centers with museum-quality displays, the Department of Defense supported a large network of military museums, and the National Endowment for the Humanities, the National Endowment for the Arts, and the Institute for Museum Services have served not just as financial supporters but as standard setters for museums. With public funding came a stronger commitment to education and access as well as greater scrutiny. The increasingly public face of museums enhanced the roles of museum educators, exhibition designers, and visitor survey specialists. Museums also became more specialized. Museums of sports, of broadcasting, and of labor have taken their places alongside museums of art, history, and science. There has been a substantial growth in small, community-based museums, and the social movements of the 1960s have led traditional museums to be more inclusive of the U.S. populace in their showings. Among the most innovative new museums are the Exploratorium, the science teaching center in San Francisco; the imaginative and well-designed aquariums in Baltimore and Monterey, Calif.; the Holocaust Museum in Washington, D.C., the first major institution devoted to the understanding of human tragedy; and Manhattan's Lower East Side Tenement Museum, a new kind of historic-house museum. The growing movement of museums devoted to ethnic groups was given legitimacy by creation of the Museum of the American Indian, planned for the last open space on the Mall in Washington, D.C.

For art museums the 1970s and early 1980s marked an era of big and expensive loan exhibitions. Blockbuster shows on British country houses, impressionism, and Egyptian culture, among others, attracted huge crowds but strained museum resources. Smaller shows relying on in-house collections became the norm in the 1990s as museums struggled with lowered budgets. Venerable historical societies and urban history museums transformed themselves and their exhibitions in the 1980s in Pittsburgh, Richmond, and Minneapolis in an effort to reach a broader public. Not every such effort worked. The New-York Historical Society came close to failure as costs outran income. At the same time, however, natural history museums, among the most traditional and predictable of museums, put a renewed emphasis on education and imaginative exhibitions. Chicago's Field Museum was among the leaders. Far more than in the past, museums have become places of great controversy. Heated public debates in Madison, Wisc., accompanied the development of Old World Wisconsin. An exhibition of Robert Mapplethorpe's photographs in Cincinnati elicited a lawsuit for obscenity, and the funding practices of the National Endowment for the Arts came under harsh attack. The Smithsonian Institution's efforts to interpret the art of the American West and, through its Air and Space Museum, the bombing of Hiroshima and Nagasaki, produced intense public controversy.

[Warren Leon and Roy Rosenzweig, eds., *History Museums in the U.S.* (Urbana, Ill., 1989); Joel J. Orosz, *Curators and Culture* (Tuscaloosa, Ala., 1990); Michael Steven Shapiro, ed., *The Museum: A Reference Guide* (New York, 1990).]

GARY KULIK

See also **SUPP:** National Endowment for the Arts; National Endowment for the Humanities; Park Service, National; National Trust for Historic Preservation; Science Museums.

MUSEUMS, SCIENCE. *See* **Science Museums.**

MUSIC, BLUEGRASS, is a form of country music that emerged in the 1940s and 1950s from a group known as the Blue Grass Boys headed by Grand Ole Opry star Bill Monroe, who came to be known as "the father of bluegrass." The music in its definitive form was first heard in Nashville, Tenn. Early bluegrass was distinctively flavored by Appalachia, where such groups as the Stanley Brothers and their Clinch Mountain Boys and Lester Flatt, Earl Scruggs, and the Foggy Mountain Boys performed on radio station WCYB in Bristol on the Tennessee-Virginia border. Several characteristics define bluegrass style. A typical band consists of four to seven players and singers who use acoustic rather than electrical instruments. Bluegrass is pitched high and requires more than one voice to sing something other than harmony parts. The guitar, mandolin, banjo, string bass, and fiddle play both melody and provide rhythm and background for vocal soloists. Through recordings, television, tours, and festivals, bluegrass performers have gained a national and even international constituency. An establishment consisting of several recording companies (Country, Rebel, Rounder, Sugar Hill, and others), clubs, and magazines, such as *Bluegrass Unlimited*, developed as the bluegrass festival movement spread in the 1960s. In the 1970s performances departed from the traditional form with "new grass," using rock repertoire and techniques.

[Neil V. Rosenberg, *Bluegrass: A History* (Chicago, 1985).]

CHARLES A. WEEKS

MUSIC, CLASSICAL, encompasses instrumental and vocal music written by trained composers. It expresses more fully the artistic values of composers than music of an essentially commercial nature (popular) or music that develops anonymously and is transmitted aurally (folk). In the United States classical music has appealed to fewer people than popular or folk music. In the eighteenth century, classical music could be heard in Boston, Philadelphia, New York, Williamsburg, Charleston, and New Orleans and elsewhere in the houses of the well-to-do. Composers such as William Billings, Francis Hopkinson, and Alexander Reinagle produced hymns, songs, instrumental music, and opera similar in style to that of European contemporaries but noteworthy for a degree of originality. None of these composers could make a living from compositions; Billings died penniless. Much of their best music went unpublished in their lifetimes, as was the case with a Reinagle piano sonata that was not published until 1978. The music of such Europeans as George Handel, Antonio Vivaldi, Arcangelo Corelli, Luigi Boccherini, Jean-Philippe

Rameau, and Joseph Haydn was probably better known and more often played in these coastal cities and in the houses of talented amateur musicians, such as Robert Carter and Thomas Jefferson, both of Virginia.

Composition of American classical music in the nineteenth century was dominated by a group of people eager to emulate the European masters, particularly those in the Germanic tradition. Many studied with teachers in Germany and did not deviate from what they learned. John Knowles Paine, the first musician to hold a professorship in a university (Harvard), became the prototype of the academic composer and, along with Dudley Buck, Edward MacDowell, Horatio Parker, Amy Cheney Beach, and George Whitefield Chadwick, wrote symphonies, concertos, songs, and choral music in the style of European contemporaries. Some African-American composers, beginning with Harry Thacker Burleigh, practiced more compositional diversity in an effort to express their African-American heritage. A significant result of this endeavor was William Grant Still's "Afro-American Symphony" of 1930.

Audiences, performing venues, and important musical organizations emerged in the nineteenth century. The predecessor of the New York Philharmonic, the Philharmonic Society, gave its first concert in 1842. Orchestras were established in Boston (1881), Chicago (1891), St. Louis (1893), and Cincinnati (1895). As early as the 1790s operas were performed in New Orleans and Philadelphia. In New York City opera was performed in theaters and the Academy of Music. The Metropolitan Opera House opened in 1883 and in 1910 transmitted a radio broadcast. Performers went on tour, the most famous being the Swedish singer Jenny Lind, promoted by the greatest of all entertainment entrepreneurs of the century, Phineas T. Barnum. Very little music, however, by native composers was performed.

In the twentieth century, opera flourished in the United States. An early work, *Treemonisha,* by composer and popularizer of ragtime Scott Joplin, received a limited production in 1915, and George Gershwin's *Porgy and Bess* was first heard in 1935. A new Metropolitan Opera House opened in 1966 with a production of *Antony and Cleopatra,* written by Samuel Barber in the tradition of European grand opera. In 1957 Barber had composed *Vanessa,* which was performed at the Metropolitan and elsewhere. Other composers of opera were Marc Blitzstein (*Regina,* 1949), Leonard Bernstein (*Trouble in Tahiti,* 1952), Douglas Moore (*The Ballad of Baby Doe,*

1956), Gian Carlo Menotti (*The Medium,* 1945; *The Consul,* 1949; *Amahl and the Night Visitors,* composed for television in 1951), Virgil Thomson (*Four Saints in Three Acts,* 1934), Philip Glass (*Einstein on the Beach,* 1975; *Satyagraha,* 1981; *The Voyage,* 1992), John Adams (*Nixon in China,* 1987; *Death of Klinghofer,* 1991), John Corigliano (*The Ghosts of Versailles,* 1991), and Hugo Weisgall (*Six Characters in Search of an Author,* 1956; *Esther,* 1987).

American composers produced a wealth of instrumental music over the course of the twentieth century. Some sought to innovate; others enriched European tradition. Most taught at universities or such conservatories as Juilliard (established 1905), the Eastman School of Music (1919), and the New England Conservatory (1867). The giant of American innovative composers was Charles Ives, whose music had to wait until after his death in 1951 for full recognition, as did that of Charles Tomlinson Griffes, who died in 1920, and Carl Ruggles, who died in 1971. French-born Edgar Varèse took up residence in the United States in 1915 and influenced native composers, notably Henry Cowell and Harry Partch, to write music to unsettle, shock, disturb. Two other innovators were John Cage and Milton Babbitt, whose 1989 work "Transfigured Notes" was unplayable because of limited rehearsal time by the Philadelphia Orchestra. Leonard Bernstein and Aaron Copland, who many have characterized as the dean of American composers, stand out because of the quantity and variety of their compositions and because of their roles as performers and advocates of music.

Among the best representatives of postromantic and expressionist music are Roger Sessions, called the greatest of American symphonists; Roy Harris; Howard Hanson; Peter Mennin; Walter Piston; and David Diamond. Leslie Bassett and Elliott Carter might also be placed in the expressionist tradition. Harris, composer of fourteen symphonies, and Robert Palmer wrote music showing the influence of central European nationalism. Barber and Hanson, who for forty years headed the Eastman School of Music, sustained an Italian, Scandinavian, and Russian romanticism. The career of George Rochberg encompassed experiments with atonality, but most of his output is expressionistic and romantic.

Much American classical music found audiences because of the large numbers of American symphony orchestras—1,400 by the late twentieth century. Radio and television disseminated music, as illustrated by the Metropolitan Opera's Saturday afternoon radio broadcasts beginning in 1940 and such public television series as *Great Performances* and *Live from Lincoln Center*. New halls and cultural centers opened in New York, Washington, Atlanta, San Francisco, Los Angeles, Dallas, and other cities; older halls, including former movie theaters, were renovated and restored in Detroit, Pittsburgh, Oakland, and St. Louis.

Despite observations suggesting trouble in the world of classical music (the recital and symphony orchestra dead or dying, for example), enrollment in conservatories and music schools and attendance at a growing number of summer music festivals increased. Many orchestras expanded seasons, encouraged new music through composer-in-residence programs, and showed a remarkable ability to innovate in programming and format. Classical music at the end of the twentieth century remained a vital part of the musical culture of the United States.

[Gilbert Chase, *America's Music: From the Pilgrims to the Present*, 3rd rev. ed. (Chicago, 1992); Richard Crawford, *The American Musical Landscape* (Berkeley, Calif., 1993); John Dizikes, *Opera in America: A Cultural History* (New Haven, Conn., 1993); Monroe Levin, *Clues to American Music* (Washington, D.C., 1992); Stanley Sadie and H. Wiley Hitchcock, eds., *The New Grove Dictionary of American Music*, 4 vols. (New York, 1986).]

CHARLES A. WEEKS

MUSIC, COUNTRY AND WESTERN, often referred to just as country music, eludes precise definition because of its many sources and varieties. It can best be understood as a style of popular music that originated in the folk culture of the rural South, a culture of European and African origin. Fiddlers, banjo players, string bands, balladeers, and gospel singers drew upon existing music to develop materials suitable for performance at family and community events. As southerners migrated to northern cities in the early twentieth century, their music went with them; and, beginning in the 1920s, radio and recordings did much to popularize and diversify this music. Musicians from Texas, Louisiana, and Oklahoma were especially innovative with regard to developing and promoting this essentially rural form of entertainment. In 1934, when a radio hillbilly singer from Texas named Orvon Gene Autry went to Hollywood, the era of the great cowboy singer in the movies began. The Grand Ole Opry in Nashville, beginning in the 1940s, made that city a mecca for country music fans, many of whom listened religiously to its performances on the radio. The popularity of rock and roll through the revolution in popular music begun by Elvis Presley in the mid-1950s posed a challenge to country music, but it was countered in part by development of a new style known as country pop or the Nashville Sound. By the 1990s country and western music had an international following.

[Bill C. Malone, *Country Music, U.S.A.: A Fifty-year History*, rev. ed. (New York, 1985).]

CHARLES A. WEEKS

See also **SUPP:** Music, Bluegrass; Music, Rock and Roll.

MUSIC, JAZZ, is characterized by improvisation, bent pitches or blues notes, syncopation, and polyrhythms. It first appeared in the southern part of the United States during the late nineteenth century, blossomed in New Orleans at the turn of the century, and spread to other cities between 1890 and 1920, as dance halls, cabarets, restaurants, and theaters proliferated to satisfy a growing demand by Americans for pleasure and self-expression. The first jazz recording was made in New Orleans by the Original Dixieland Jazz Band in 1917, and during the 1920s jazz and jazz-influenced dance music became the popular music of the United States. F. Scott Fitzgerald entitled a collection of his short stories *Tales of the Jazz Age* (1922), and the phrase became part of the lexicon of the decade. In the next two decades the success of jazz was assured by the big swing bands. By the end of World War II, bebop, which originated in the practice of vocalizing or singing instrumental lines and was played by small groups of three to six members, was becoming popular among musicians who disliked the size and formality of the swing bands. Another style, cool jazz, emerged at the same time. By the 1960s rock and rock-based styles had displaced jazz as the popular music of the United States. Since the 1970s many styles have flourished, including modal jazz, an avant-garde free jazz, and jazz rock or fusion. Beginning in the 1980s a movement emerged to preserve a purer or classical jazz against attempts to fuse it with rock or rhythm and blues.

[Frank Tirro, *Jazz: A History*, 2nd ed. (New York, 1993).]

JOSHUA L. COX
CHARLES A. WEEKS

MUSIC, NEW, in the most comprehensive sense, is music produced each time a composer puts notes to paper. Music can, however, stand out because of its departure from norms. Creators of such music may be responding to new social and economic conditions or they may simply set out to invent something not heard before. Prior to the twentieth century, religious and ethnic groups constituted important sources of new music. African Americans adapted the music they brought with them to serve new needs and produced a distinctive dance and vocal music. Some of this music evolved into the spirituals of the nineteenth century and the blues, ragtime, jazz, and soul music of the twentieth century. Beginning with the Second Awakening, the great religious revival of the early nineteenth century, evangelical religion, with its camp and revival meetings, produced revival hymns and spiritual songs. Southern and midwestern rural singers, tunebook compilers, and singing-school teachers developed a system of notation, the shape note, that designated a body of semifolk music and a style of singing known as fasola-folk or sacred-harp singing, after the most widely used shape-note tunebook, *The Sacred Harp* (1844).

Technology and social changes in the twentieth century created a time of ferment and encouragement in the production of new music. Recordings, radio, television, movies, and electronics all influenced the composition and performance of music. In the first two decades of the twentieth century such composers as Charles Ives, Carl Ruggles, Wallingford Riegger, Ruth Crawford Seeger, and Henry Cowell began employing atonality, the absence of a tonal center, with little or no knowledge of similar experiments in Europe. Ives experimented freely with tonality and rhythm, taking a cue from his father, who believed there were no rules in music. Cowell emerged as a major advocate of the unorthodox in music; his *New Music Quarterly* championed the music of Ruggles, Seeger, and other innovators.

Jazz emerged in the first three decades of the twentieth century from the dance and vocal music of nineteenth-century African Americans and entered into the composition of operas. Scott Joplin, the ragtime composer, published the opera *Treemonisha* in 1911, but it was almost forgotten until its revival in the 1970s. George Gershwin's opera *Porgy and Bess* (1935) similarly departed from European models by incorporating native materials. Beginning in the 1920s Gershwin, and later Richard Rodgers, Harold Rome, Jerome Kern, Cole Porter, Frank Loesser, Leonard Bernstein, Stephen Sondheim, and others, made music theater a part of cultural life in the United States.

Experimentation and innovation continued in the late 1940s and 1950s, to include electronic music, that is, music composed or altered by electronic apparatus. The tape recorder was the first device employed for this novel purpose. By the 1960s the synthesizer and similar instruments expanded possi-bilities, as illustrated by the Columbia-Princeton Electronic Music Center headed by composer Milton Babbitt, a rigorous exponent of serial music and its disregard for tonality. After World War II Harry Partch and John Cage experimented similarly with chance or aleatoric music. In popular music, another innovation of the 1950s was rock and roll, popularized by singer Elvis Presley.

While many of these experimental traditions continued into the last quarter of the century, new music became a conservative reaction against atonality, serialism, and chance music. In 1964 "In C" by Terry Riley heralded the advent of minimalism, music characterized by repetitions of a motif or group of motifs coupled with strict adherence to tonality. The best-known composers of this genre, in addition to Riley, were La Monte Young, Steve Reich, and Philip Glass. In popular music perhaps the most significant innovation of the 1980s was rap music, an urban African-American form said to be as important to its period as jazz was to an earlier time. Innovation continued in the music of Pulitzer Prize–winning classical composers Elliott Carter, Dominick Argento, Ned Rorem, Joseph Schwantner, David Del Tredici, Ellen Taaffe Zwilich, and William Bolcom. In their work one can note a preference for tonality and form, perhaps complementing a conservatism found in politics, religion, architecture, and the visual arts. Musical styles of the late twentieth century thus showed a distinct preference for earlier aesthetics.

[Gilbert Chase, *America's Music: From the Pilgrims to the Present,* 3rd ed. (Urbana, Ill., 1992); David H. Cope, *New Directions in Music,* 6th ed. (Madison, Wis., 1993); Paul Griffiths, *Modern Music: A Concise History from Debussy to Boulez* (New York, 1978); Joan Peyser, *The New Music: The Sense Behind the Sound* (New York, 1971); John Rockwell, *All American Music: Composition in the Late Twentieth Century* (New York, 1983).]

CHARLES A. WEEKS

See also **DAH:** Awakening, Second; Camp Meetings; Hymns; Music; Music, Afro-American; Singing Schools; **SUPP:** Music, Classical; Music, Jazz; Music, Rock and Roll; Music Festivals.

MUSIC, RHYTHM AND BLUES. The term "rhythm and blues" was first used by the popular music magazine *Billboard* in 1949 to replace its category of "race records." By then and continuing into the 1950s, blues artists, who drew on a musical heritage that originated in the rural South, were incorporating the rhythms of jazz to produce a commercial urbanized music. It drew styles and performers from the big bands, such as Count Basie and His Orchestra; pop groups, such as the Inkspots; and blues men, such as Joe Turner, Jimmy Rushing, B. B. King, and Bobby Bland. It also produced such major stars as Ray Charles, who used jazz instrumentation and urbanized blues and gospel idioms, and such balladeers as Percy Mayfield and Ruth and Charles Brown. Promoters and recording entrepreneurs Phil Spector and Jerry Wexler promoted markets for these styles, and through the 1960s such groups as the Clovers, Orioles, and Jackson Five penetrated mass markets. As with other popular music idioms, rhythm and blues blurred in the 1960s as its elements merged with other commercial art forms and as new urban social systems and values developed. Even by the mid-1950s such rhythm and blues performers as Fats Domino and Little Richard had crossed over to rock and roll, which was initially a country music–based genre. Memphis Minnie, a rhythm and blues artist, had a profound influence on Elvis Presley. By the 1970s the term "rhythm and blues" had lost its original meaning and was retained only to indicate commercial music by African-American performers.

[Peter Grammond, *The Oxford Companion to Popular Music* (New York, 1991); L. E. McCutcheon, *Rhythm and Blues: An Experience and Adventure in Its Origins and Developments* (Arlington, Va., 1971).]

JOHN DAVIS

See also SUPP: Music, Jazz; Music, Rock and Roll.

MUSIC, ROCK AND ROLL, reflected youth and social change in post–World War II America. It integrated musically blacks and whites in the mid-1950s, was pivotal in the youth counterculture and protest movements of the mid-1960s through the early 1970s, and reflected societal divisions from the 1970s through the 1990s. Elvis Presley helped create rock and roll with "That's Alright Mama" (1954), "Mystery Train" (1955), and other recordings for Memphis-based Sun Records, which also produced the Jerry Lee Lewis classics "Whole Lot of Shakin' Going On (1957) and "Great Balls of Fire" (1957). Presley's blend of blues and country smashed the color barrier between black and white musical styles, triggering a musical revolution that was amplified by Chuck Berry, a black guitarist who drew heavily from white country music when writing such enduring standards as "Johnny B. Goode" (1958). White youths increasingly embraced black music, from the smooth harmonies of the Drifters to the hyperkinetic screams of Little Richard (Richard Penniman), whose "Tutti Frutti" (1965) stunned unprepared listeners. By 1956,

when Presley began to enjoy massive national popularity, black and white music were achieving an integration rare in the larger society.

The early 1960s heard the Beach Boys harmonizing about a mythic California; Phil Spector's "wall of sound," which exploded with the Crystals epic "Then He Kissed Me" (1963); the Ventures' influential instrumental rock, and the emergence of such Motown Records stars as Smokey Robinson and Marvin Gaye. It was the Beatles, however, who defined rock and roll in a way no act has before or since. They not only dominated the American popular music charts (beginning with their 1964 hit "I Want to Hold Your Hand") but also helped lead the music's expansion from simple adolescent love songs to complex aggressions that could reflect the social and political changes sweeping the United States. Bob Dylan's stunning *Highway 61 Revisited* (1965) and *Blonde on Blonde* (1966) were pivotal albums in this transformation, which was accelerated by other albums, such as the Beatles' *Rubber Soul* (1965) and *Sgt. Pepper's Lonely Hearts Club Band* (1967) and the Rolling Stones' *Aftermath* (1966) and *Let It Bleed* (1969). Despite growing diversity, rock and roll did not seem fragmented at the end of the 1960s. The Woodstock music festival (1969) was able to encompass Jimi Hendrix's guitar explosions, the Grateful Dead's folk-rock, Sly Stone's eclectic funk, Credence Clearwater Revival's straightforward rock, Janis Joplin's anguished blues, the Who's furious intellectualism, and much more.

By the 1970s, however, rock's fault lines grew. The disco music of Donna Summer and others was reviled by the heavy metal fans of Led Zeppelin, while devotees of such introspective singer-songwriters as Paul Simon or Joni Mitchell were at best puzzled by the Sex Pistols, Patti Smith, Television, and other pioneering punk rockers. New-wave bands, such as the Talking Heads, expanded rock's musical vocabulary, but they too spoke to one part of what had once seemed a unified audience.

In the 1980s Madonna (Madonna Louise Ciccone) combined sexual provocation and steely business acumen to win huge commercial success, while rap music restored distinctly black music to a central place in rock. Although such rappers as Run-DMC developed an interracial appeal, other hip hop artists seemed to encourage an animosity toward whites that was unknown to such earlier black music exemplars as Aretha Franklin and James Brown, and many whites remained hostile to rap. Rock artistry thrived in the 1990s, from Prince's (Prince Rogers Nelson) infectious fusion of musical styles to Nirvana's incendiary mix of punk and heavy metal, but no one could rejoin the splintered rock audience. Such top acts as Michael Jackson and REM spoke to different musical worlds, while Bruce Springsteen, one of the most popular and important artists of the 1980s, sang only to that fraction of listeners eager to hear him. The music that had grown out of the integration power of Elvis and had reached its mythic unifying peak at Woodstock was deeply divided as the United States faced a new millennium.

[Greil Marcus, *Mystery Train: Images of America in Rock 'n' Roll Music,* rev. ed. (New York, 1982); Ed Ward et al., eds., *Rock of Ages: The "Rolling Stone" History of Rock & Roll* (New York, 1986).]

ANDREW L. AOKI

See also **SUPP:** Music, Rhythm and Blues.

MUSIC EVENTS. *See* **Benefit Concerts; Music Festivals.**

MUSIC FESTIVALS commemorate anniversaries, celebrate religious or ethnic traditions, or offer music of a composer, period, or type; they can range from a single event to many events encompassing days or even a season. The earliest festivals in the United States date from the eighteenth century and had religious, social, or pedagogical functions. The first were associated with singing schools, to promote the singing of psalms according to established rules and order. Folk music began in the eighteenth century in the form of fiddlers' contests, many expanding to several days and involved instrumental music and community audiences. Several large events took place beginning in the middle of the nineteenth century. In 1856 the Boston Handel and Haydn Society presented three major choral works—Haydn's *The Seasons*, Handel's *Messiah*, and Mendelssohn's *Elijah*. In 1869 the bandmaster Patrick S. Gilmore arranged a National Peace Jubilee in Boston comprising 20,000 instrumentalists. During the 1876 centennial of independence, Philadelphia sponsored a major music festival. Worcester, Mass., in 1858 and Cincinnati, Ohio, in 1873 inaugurated festivals that have continued to the present day. Four festivals that came out of the tradition of singing schools continued into the twentieth century: the Messiah Festival in Lindsborg, Kans. (1882), the Big Singing Day in Benton, Ky. (1884), the Ann Arbor May Festival (1894), and the Bethlehem, Pa., Bach Festival (1900).

Festivals proliferated in the twentieth century. Many occur in rural settings during summer months and feature classical music, jazz, folk, bluegrass, country, cajun, and light or pops. Commercial motives and entrepreneurial talent have been a significant force in their promotion. Major symphony orchestras that employ musicians year-round include summer seasons that have become virtual festivals. Beginning in 1936 the Chicago Symphony Orchestra has played in Ravinia Park north of Chicago. Tanglewood, in the Berkshire Hills of western Massachusetts, has been the summer home of the Boston Symphony Orchestra since 1936; in 1940 its former music director, Serge Koussevitzky, opened the Tanglewood Music Center. Meadowbrook became the summer home of Detroit's orchestra in 1964; the Blossom Music Center between Cleveland and Akron became the summer residence of the Cleveland Orchestra in 1968. The Philadelphia Orchestra has given free concerts at the Mann Music Center in Philadelphia and since 1966 has performed at Saratoga Springs, N.Y. In that year the annual Mostly Mozart Festival became a major offering of the Lincoln Center for the Performing Arts in New York City. Many of these summer centers have expanded to offer jazz, folk, and rock music. Smaller festivals have grown out of centers that specialize in the study of particular styles of music. The Marlboro School in Vermont has stressed chamber music since 1950. The National Music Camp at Interlochen, Mich., has offered a variety of musical programs since 1928. The Brevard Music Center in western North Carolina has sponsored festivals since 1936. A number of festivals center on opera. Since 1920 the Cincinnati Summer Opera Festival has offered a series of productions, while Santa Fe (1957) has featured little-known operas. Beginning in 1975 the Seattle Opera offered Richard Wagner's *Ring Cycle*, first in German, then in English, in an event that has become the Pacific Northwest Festival. Contemporary or new music is offered in programs in California—Ojai since 1947 and Cabrillo since 1963. New Music Across America began as a festival in New York in 1979 and has emphasized works by composers using new techniques and new instruments; in 1992 the festival took place simultaneously in many sites across the country.

Festivals of indigenous or folk music have similarly increased in the twentieth century. Building on the tradition of fiddlers' contests, the Old Time Fiddler's Convention began in North Carolina in 1924. The National Folk Festival first took place in St. Louis in 1934 and in 1971 moved to Wolf Trap Farm Park southwest of Washington, D.C. The Kool Jazz Festival, founded in 1954 as the Newport Jazz Festival in Rhode Island, moved to New York City in

1972, and, on the Pacific coast, the Monterey Jazz Festival began in 1958. Rock music promoters staged big events in the 1960s, notably the 1967 Monterey International Pop Festival in California and the Woodstock, N.Y., Music and Arts Fair in 1969, which was the biggest rock concert ever organized, attracting about 400,000 representatives of the counterculture of the decade. The Woodstock event took on iconic status for many and was commemorated in 1994 by a second concert.

[Robin Carol Price, *Music Festivals in America,* 4th ed. (New York, 1990).]

CHARLES A. WEEKS

See also **DAH:** Fiddlers and Fiddle Tunes; Singing Schools; **SUPP:** Woodstock.

MUSIC INDUSTRY, the business of selling music, in the nineteenth century was often the domain of composers, who assumed the role of entrepreneur to ensure dissemination of their music. In the twentieth century the business became more specialized and organized. What eventually emerged was a complex musical culture of composer, performer, marketer, consumer and writer. In 1896 the American Federation of Musicians brought performers together in the first union. In 1914 artists helped found the American Society of Composers, Authors, and Performers (ASCAP), a performing rights organization. Broadcast Music Inc. (BMI) was established in 1940 for the same purpose. A recording industry defined in the 1920s and 1930s by such major companies as Victor and Columbia and a large number of smaller firms by the 1980s provided a significant outlet for music. Talent representatives and organizations, such as Community Concerts and Columbia Artists, established by Arthur Judson in 1928 and 1931, respectively, promoted the performance of music in communities throughout the country. Beginning in the 1920s radio, movies, and television provided other outlets for music, often influencing its character. From the 1960s onward, cultural centers in large cities, notably Lincoln Center in New York, provided new venues for performance, achieving national scope when assisted by radio and television. While universities, conservatories, private persons, and government have supported in the twentieth century a significant amount of financial and artistic autonomy for composers and performers, music in the United States continues to be influenced significantly by the opportunities and pressures of the market.

[Richard Crawford, *The American Musical Landscape* (Berkeley, Calif., 1993); Harvey Rachlin, *The Encyclopedia of the Music Business* (New York, 1981).]

JOSHUA L. COX
CHARLES A. WEEKS

MUSIC TELEVISION (MTV), the first all-music television network, began broadcasting on Aug. 1, 1981, and targeted an audience aged twelve to thirty-four. The network's programming comprised back-to-back videos created by record companies to promote their artists. MTV was troubled in its early years by accusations of racism, concerning failure to broadcast videos by black artists. The founders, among them Robert Pittman, prescribed a policy of "narrowcasting" drawn from radio, which aired only a restricted range of music. British "new pop" acts such as Duran Duran and the Thompson Twins were so heavily programmed that observers credited MTV with launching a second "British invasion" (the first being the Beatles in the 1960s) of the U.S. music marketplace. Because music videos are primarily advertisements for recording artists, MTV has been frequently criticized for commercialism. It was also criticized by women's groups for sexism. Following the sale of MTV from Warner-Amex to Viacom International in 1986, the network diversified its output, expanding into nonmusic programming and encompassing a broader range of music. Heavy metal was for some years the staple, and following the success of *Yo! MTV Raps* in 1989 (for some time the most popular show on the network), many rap artists concluded that MTV was responsible for introducing this form to Middle America. In 1987 MTV launched MTV Europe and began a period of world expansion. By 1994 it was available in fifty-eight countries to a potential audience of 240 million households. It continued to expand nonmusic programming (notably with its highest-rated show, the controversial cartoon *Beavis and Butt-head*) and was credited with mainstreaming the "grunge" rock of Nirvana, Pearl Jam, and Soundgarden. News coverage on MTV stressed social and political issues relevant to young people. In 1992 MTV's "Rock the Vote" campaign was credited by President Bill Clinton with helping increase the youth vote.

[Andrew Goodwin, *Dancing in the Distraction Factory* (Minneapolis, 1992).]

ANDREW GOODWIN

See also **SUPP:** Music, New; Music, Rock and Roll; Music Industry; Television.

N

NAACP. *See* **National Association for the Advancement of Colored People.**

NADER'S RAIDERS. *See* **Consumer Protection.**

NAFTA. *See* **North American Free Trade Agreement.**

NAMING. American personal names typically include a given name, middle name, surname, and occasionally suffixes. Anglo-American surnames can be traced back to the English adoption of surnames after the Crusades in the thirteenth century. Traditionally, American surnames are transmitted along the male line, and at marriage women usually assume husbands' surnames, although many women retain their natal surnames after marriage or hyphenate their surname with that of their husband. Middle names appeared in the United States and Great Britain at the end of the eighteenth century. By the end of the nineteenth century most Americans received middle names, and by the end of the twentieth century, fewer than 5 percent of Anglo-American children lacked such names. Middle names and suffixes were first popular among the elite and later were adopted generally.

Most twentieth-century American given names trace to three sources: a small stock of traditional Anglo-Saxon names popular in England before the Norman Conquest in 1066, a stock of Norman names introduced following the Conquest, and a stock of biblical names from both the Old and New Testaments. Throughout the nineteenth century the stock of American given names continued to grow as names were introduced by immigrant groups (especially German and Scotch-Irish), surnames occasionally were used as given names, masculine names were transformed to feminine forms (Roberta, Michelle), and many new names were coined. In the twentieth century the pool of American given names greatly expanded, especially since the 1970s. While many traditional names continued in popularity, especially among religious groups who preferred biblical names or those of saints, names gained and lost popularity with increasing speed. In the 1990s the ten most popular names for men and women were given to 20 to 30 percent of children, down from 50 percent or more two centuries ago. There were two notable trends in naming in the late twentieth century. First, while parents continued to name children after relatives (especially sons after fathers), family names were more often used as middle names and less often as first names. Second, Americans increasingly selected names that express identification with or pride in ethnic, racial, or religious groups. African Americans, for example, after a century of preference for traditional given names, began to draw names from a wider variety of sources and to coin new names.

[Richard D. Alford, *Naming and Identity: A Cross-Cultural Study of Personal Naming Practices* (New Haven, Conn., 1988); George R. Stewart, *American Given Names* (New York, 1979).]

RICHARD D. ALFORD

NASHVILLE. Speculators settled Nashville in 1779 on the Cumberland River in central Tennessee. Principally a place of commerce, it grew slowly, despite becoming the state capital in 1843. Indeed, throughout the nineteenth century it was a traditional southern town. Matters changed during the Great Depression of the 1930s with an infusion of federal money for the Tennessee Valley Authority. The end of segregation in the 1960s also gave the city a lift, what with removal of uneconomic hiring practices and thereby new livelihoods for many of its citizens. Nashville technically became Nashville-Davidson after the creation of a metropolitan government in 1963, with a mayor, vice mayor, and a forty-member metropolitan council. Thereafter the city boomed. In some ways development had an ironic twist, because as the boom spread throughout the entire South, Nashville lost some of its former stature to other cities, but the local boom was undeniable, and in 1990 the city's population reached 488,374, the Nashville-Davidson area 985,026. Nashville's reputation steadily increased, for the city was the site of the Grand Ole Opry, a household name known worldwide for country music. In this respect Nashville rivaled Los Angeles and New York in music recording, publishing, distribution, and production. In the years before the Civil War, Nashville had become known for its political figures—Andrew Jackson, James Polk, and Sam Houston. In the 1990s, because of country music, the well-known names were Dolly Parton, Chet Atkins, Loretta Lynn, Hank Williams, and Johnny Cash.

The city's economy in 1990 was primarily service oriented, with 28 percent of the workforce so employed. Retail-wholesale trade was not far behind, at 25 percent of the workforce. Manufacturing industries employed 17 percent of the population and the government 12 percent. In a 1992 survey of top U.S. cities for business, Nashville ranked second for pro-business attitude and race relations, third for labor-management relations, and ninth for vocational training of workers. Its central location helped, having brought into the vicinity two large automobile plants. The diverse economy of the metropolitan area included banking, health care, and a large religious publishing and printing industry.

[Anita Shafer Goodstein, *Nashville, 1780–1860: From Frontier to City* (Gainesville, Fla., 1989).]

LAWRENCE H. LARSEN

See also **SUPP:** Tennessee.

NATIONAL AERONAUTICS AND SPACE ADMINISTRATION (NASA). *See* **Space Program.**

NATIONAL ASSOCIATION FOR THE ADVANCEMENT OF COLORED PEOPLE (NAACP). Since 1975 the NAACP has continued to fight for equal rights for African Americans but internal divisions and lack of funding have stifled its progress. Although the NAACP's victories historically came through litigation in the courts, the organization found it increasingly difficult to sustain such activity in the 1970s and 1980s. Much of this resulted from a rift between the NAACP and the independent NAACP Legal Defense and Educational Fund (LDF). Disagreement became so intense that in May 1982 the NAACP sued the LDF in an effort to control the LDF's activities. The split shifted the NAACP's focus from legal action to lobbying against federal policies that threatened existing civil rights legislation and affirmative action programs.

In 1993 the NAACP's longtime executive director, Benjamin Hooks, retired and was succeeded by Benjamin F. Chavis. An aggressive civil rights activist and head of the United Church of Christ's Commission for Racial Justice, Chavis in 1982 coined the term "environmental racism," to describe the tendency of manufacturing and other companies to dump toxic waste in or near areas where racial minorities resided. Chavis promised to revamp the NAACP by developing a marketing plan targeted at the younger generation through music videos, by promoting health care reform, and by embracing issues of global human rights. When Chavis took office the NAACP had shown little growth since the 1970s and had only 500,000 members with about 2,000 chapters nationwide. He was determined to recruit not only more African Americans, but Latinos, Asian Americans, and people of color around the world.

Chavis immediately ran into criticism for embracing Louis Farrakhan, minister of the Nation of Islam; for producing a deficit of $3 million; and for his lobbying efforts on behalf of corporations attempting to avoid paying for toxic waste cleanup. He was fired in 1994 for not informing the NAACP board of directors that he had agreed to pay more than $300,000 in NAACP funds to a former female employee who had charged him with sexual harassment. William F. Gibson, chair of the NAACP board of directors since 1985, supported Chavis until his ouster, only to find himself under investigation for excessive spending. With the future of the NAACP in doubt, Myrlie Evers-Williams, civil rights activist and widow of Medgar Evers, unseated Gibson as chair by one vote in February 1995. She faced the challenge of a $4.5 million deficit, falling contributions because of the perceived state of disarray within the organization, and the task of finding a new executive director. In February 1996 Democratic Congressman Kweisi Mfume of Maryland resigned his seat in the House to take over the executive directorship of the NAACP.

Mfume, former leader of the congressional black caucus, promised to rehabilitate the NAACP and unite it for aggressive action and embarked immediately on a voter registration drive.

[Lynne Duke, "What Is Happening to the NAACP?," *Washington Post National Weekly Edition* (Jan. 16–22, 1995); Kenneth Goings, *The NAACP Comes of Age* (Bloomington, Ind., 1990); Matthew S. Scott, "Chavis to Lead NAACP into New Era," *Black Enterprise* (July 1993); Hanes Walton, Jr., *When the Marching Stopped: The Politics of Civil Rights Regulatory Agencies* (Albany, N.Y., 1988).]

JILL WATTS

See also **SUPP:** Affirmative Action; African Americans; Civil Rights Movement.

NATIONAL ENDOWMENT FOR THE ARTS (NEA), an independent agency of the federal government created in 1965 along with the National Endowment for the Humanities. The NEA began with a budget of $2.5 million, and support rose to $175 million in 1991, before cutbacks to $167.6 in 1994. Although the NEA has had critics throughout its existence, it became a center of controversy in the late 1980s as questions arose over grants for controversial works and the propriety, in general, of federal financial support for the arts. The NEA funds an array of works and activities, including music, theater, and visual and performance arts. It also distributes funds to smaller organizations, which grant them to individual artists and organizations. Proponents argue that the NEA is essential because grants provide "seed money" necessary for raising private donations. NEA officials estimate that recipients are able to generate $11 to $26 in private money for every dollar given by the NEA. Critics claim that the NEA is an unfair tax on the many to support the tastes of a few, and that although grants for controversial works admittedly make up only a tiny portion of total NEA funding, they remain an inappropriate use of taxpayer money.

Controversy came to a boil in 1989 as opponents focused on works of art they termed obscene and immoral. These included a photograph by Andres Serrano, entitled *Piss Christ,* that showed a plastic crucifix immersed in a jar of the artist's urine; a display by art student Scott Tyler, entitled *What Is the Proper Way to Display a U.S. Flag?,* which allowed people to comment on the question while stepping on an American flag placed on the gallery floor; and a series of photographs by Robert Mapplethorpe that contained sadomasochistic and homoerotic images, as well as pictures of nude children. Some members of Congress, most notably Republican Senator Jesse Helms of North Carolina and Republican Representative Dana Rohrabacher of California, used the controversy to attack NEA funding. Some conservative legislators and activist right-wing Christian groups endorsed moves to cut funding or attach content restrictions to grants, measures that were opposed by artists, arts organizations, and gay and lesbian alliances.

The NEA changed its procedures in response to congressional pressure. One of the most disputed reforms involved an "obscenity pledge," requiring grant recipients to sign a statement promising their work would not be obscene. John Frohnmayer, named NEA chairman by President George Bush in 1989, drew fire from artists and arts organizations for denying certain grants recommended by NEA panels. Critics accused Frohnmayer of using political criteria in denying the funding. In 1990 Dennis Barrie, director of Cincinnati's Contemporary Art Center, was arrested and tried on obscenity charges for exhibiting Mapplethorpe's work. Organization of the touring exhibition had been partially supported by an NEA grant. The acquittal of Barrie and his center later that year brought to a close the arguments about the obscenity of Mapplethorpe's work, but congressional interest in NEA grants did not wane.

Senator Helms continued to introduce bills and amendments to limit grants for works that were sexually oriented or that denigrated religion. In 1990 the House and Senate passed a three-year reauthorization of the NEA that eliminated restrictions on the sort of art the endowment might fund, but Congress required "general standards of decency and respect for the diverse beliefs and values of the American public." The NEA then eliminated its obscenity pledge. A few organizations, artists, and panel members continued to protest by declining to accept endowment funding.

In 1994 Congress renewed its attack on the NEA. The endowment already received a 2 percent targeted budget cut, from $171 million to $167.6 million, because of an NEA grant to a performance artist, Ron Athey, who at the Walker Art Center in Minneapolis carved a pattern on another artist's back, wiped the blood with paper towels, and hung the latter on a clothesline over the audience. Although only $150 of NEA money went to support the performance, many lawmakers were outraged. The budget cut was in visual arts, theater, performance art, and photography. In 1995 the head of the NEA, Jane Alexander, testifying before a Senate committee, stressed how the NEA benefited the nation. She estimated that the per capita contribution was sixty-four cents and that without such support arts organizations would be less able to raise private money. Opponents argued that the endowment needed to monitor funds and refuse grants for works that depict controversial issues or endorse controversial views. Other proposals included supporting the NEA for a limited time until it could become a private corporation or support itself from copyright fees.

[Livingston Biddle, *Our Government and the Arts* (New York, 1988); Richard Bolton, ed., *Culture Wars: Documents from the Recent Controversies in the Arts* (New York, 1992).]

KATHLEEN B. CULVER

See also **SUPP:** National Endowment for the Humanities; Philanthropy.

NATIONAL ENDOWMENT FOR THE HUMANITIES (NEH), established by Congress in 1965, provides funds for research, education, and public programs to such individuals, groups, and institutions as schools, museums, and libraries. It is headed by a chairperson appointed by the president. Chairs since 1965 have been Barnaby C. Keeney (administrations of Lyndon B. Jackson and Richard M. Nixon), Ronald Berman (Nixon administration), Joseph D. Duffey (Jimmy Carter administration), William J. Bennett (Ronald Reagan administration), Lynne V. Cheney (Reagan and George Bush administrations), and former University of Pennsylvania President Sheldon Hackney (Bill Clinton administration). The NEH is directed by a twenty-six person council whose members are appointed to rotating six-year terms by the president. It is often confused with the National Endowment for the Arts, a separate institution. During the 1993 fiscal year the NEH distributed $132 million in grants, fellowships, honoraria, and awards. Of this amount $28 million went to state programs, $25 million to public programs, $18 million to fellowships and seminars, $21 million to education programs, and $17.8 million to research programs.

The two most prestigious annual awards by the NEH are the Jefferson Lecture, established in 1972, and the Charles Frankel Award, established in 1988. The lecture, which carries a $10,000 honorarium and is the highest award that the U.S. government confers in the humanities, recognizes an intellectual leader who combines the virtues of thinker, scholar, and citizen in the tradition of Thomas Jefferson. The Charles Frankel Award honors individuals who have made outstanding contributions to public understanding of history, literature, and philosophy. Recipients of the Jefferson Lecture award include poets, historians,

novelists, philosophers, and social critics. Women received five of the twenty-three awards made between 1972 and 1994. Recipients were Lionel Trilling (1972), Erik Erikson (1973), Robert Penn Warren (1974), Paul A. Freund (1975), John Hope Franklin (1976), Saul Bellow (1977), C. Vann Woodward (1978), Edward Shils (1979), Barbara Tuchman (1980), Gerald Holton (1981), Emily Townsend Vermeule (1982), Jaroslav Pelikan (1983), Sidney Hook (1984), Cleanth Brooks (1985), Leszek Kolakowski (1986), Forrest McDonald (1987), Robert Nisbet (1988), Walker Percy (1989), Bernard Lewis (1990), Gertrude Himmelfarb (1991), Bernard M. W. Knox (1992), Robert Conquest (1993), and Gwendolyn Brooks (1994). Thirty individuals, including nine women, received the Charles Frankel Award between 1989 and 1994: Patricia L. Bates, Daniel J. Boorstin, Willard L. Boyd, Clay S. Jenkinson, and Américo Paredes (1989); Mortimer J. Adler, Henry Hampton, Bernard M. W. Knox, David Van Tassel, and Ethyle R. Wolfe (1990); Winton Blount, Ken Burns, Louise Cowan, Karl Haas, and John Tchen (1991); Allan Bloom, Shelby Foote, Richard Rodriguez, Harold K. Skramstad, Jr., and Eudora Welty (1992); Ricardo Alegría, John Hope Franklin, Hanna Holborn Gray, Andrew Heiskell, Laurel Thatcher Ulrich (1993); Ernest L. Boyer, William Kittredge, Peggy Whitman Prenshaw, Sharon Percy Rockefeller, and Dorothy Porter Wesley (1994).

ELIZABETH V. BURT

NATIONAL INSTITUTES OF HEALTH (NIH) has changed since the mid-1970s, although its objective has remained constant—to recruit high-quality biomedical researchers in the service of health for Americans—and two new funding programs were created to achieve this objective. The intramural program supports research in NIH laboratories on the Bethesda, Md., campus, and the extramural program distributes grants to university investigators across the United States and makes collaborative arrangements with researchers in other countries. The NIH annual budget in the early 1990s was more than $8 billion, and personnel on the Bethesda campus numbered more than 16,000. In 1993 Congress directed the NIH to include more women in research designs and analysis instead of continuing to concentrate on studies involving only men. Other changes since the mid-1970s include organizational shifts of the different institutes, centers, divisions, and offices that comprise the NIH. In 1994 the NIH consisted of seventeen institutes (Aging; Alcohol Abuse and Alcoholism; Allergy and Infectious Diseases; Arthritis and Musculoskeletal and Skin Diseases; Cancer; Child Health and Human Development; Deafness and Other Communication Disorders; Dental Research; Diabetes and Digestive and Kidney Diseases; Drug Abuse; Environmental Health Sciences; Eye; General Medical Sciences; Heart, Lung, and Blood; Mental Health; Neurological Disorders and Stroke; and Nursing Research); two divisions (Computer Research and Technology and Research Grants); four centers (Center for Research Resources; John E. Fogarty International Center; National Center for Human Genome Research; and Warren Grant Magnuson Clinical Center); three offices (Women's Health; Alternative Medicine; and Minority Health); the National Library of Medicine; and the Children's Inn at NIH. The NIH also funds three field units (the Gerontology Research Center in Baltimore, Md.; the Rocky Mountain Laboratories in Hamilton, Mont.; and the NIH Animal Center in Poolesville, Md.). NIH has joined with other agencies to advance biomedical research. In one of the larger projects, NIH and the Howard Hughes Medical Institute launched a multimillion-dollar cooperative program to encourage physicians to enter research.

As of 1995 there had been four Nobel Prize laureates among NIH researchers who were intramural scientists as well as seventy-one laureates whose projects were supported by NIH grants. Much intramural research includes bench research, which takes place in laboratories on campus. Such research has resulted in prominent scientific advances. In 1984 National Cancer Institute scientists headed by Dr. Robert Gallo, Jr., uncovered evidence that variants of a human cancer virus (called HTLV-III) are the primary cause of acquired immunodeficiency syndrome (AIDS). Beyond bench research NIH supports clinical research, including patient studies and experimental treatments. A landmark treatment took place in 1991, when cancer patients were treated with the first human-gene therapy. Much clinical research takes place in the Warren Grant Magnuson Clinical Center involving surgery, outpatient clinics, diagnostic radiology, clinical pathology, and nuclear medicine.

[Edward H. Ahrens, Jr., *The Crisis in Clinical Research* (New York, 1992); William N. Kelley et al., *Emerging Policies for Biomedical Research* (Washington, D.C., 1993); U.S. Department of Health, Education, and Welfare, Public Health Service, National Institutes of Health, *NIH Almanac* (Washington, D.C., 1992).]

CHERI L. WIGGS

See also **SUPP:** Acquired Immune Deficiency Syndrome; Health and Human Services, Department of; Public Health Service.

NATIONAL ORGANIZATION FOR WOMEN. *See* **Women's Movement.**

NATIONAL PARKS. *See* **Parks, National; Park Service, National.**

NATIONAL PUBLIC RADIO (NPR) is a private, nonprofit corporation serving more than 470 member radio stations throughout the United States. Founded in 1970, NPR initially served primarily as a producer and distributor of programs for public radio stations. It won critical acclaim for its thoughtful, in-depth news programming, such as the evening news magazine *All Things Considered,* which debuted in 1971. In the late 1970s NPR began serving the broader needs of its member stations, providing them with program promotion, training, and management assistance. It has been in the forefront of technological innovation, for example, setting up a satellite system for program distribution in 1979 and producing or distributing radio dramas, live concert performances, and even a humorous program focusing on automobile repair. By the early 1990s NPR's member stations reached more than 14 million listeners each week. Headquartered in Washington, D.C., NPR was formed in response to the Public Broadcasting Act of 1967, which authorized federal financing of public television and radio. Republican administrations, beginning with that of Richard M. Nixon in 1969, often questioned such funding, but no administration has succeeded in its elimination.

From their beginnings, many of the nation's public radio stations were affiliated with colleges and universities. They filled a small but important niche by providing educational programming (such as on-air classes for rural populations), news, and classical music. Federal funds allowed NPR to expand the role of public radio—an alternative to commercial radio fare, most of which by the early 1970s consisted of disc-jockey programs and brief newscasts. NPR established a reputation with news and information programming. *All Things Considered* combined news headlines with reports from NPR staff members and part-time correspondents. The program included incisive and often decidedly offbeat features. Reporters did lengthy profiles of prominent newsmakers and ventured afield to cover such topics as Appalachian folkways, the ravages of drug addiction, and life on an Iowa farm, bringing about a new style of radio reporting—one that relied on sound, not just narrative, to tell stories. Many of the NPR reporters credited the influence of Edward R. Murrow, the noted CBS correspondent of earlier years. As a radio reporter during World War II, Murrow had placed his microphone in the street to let his audience hear the sounds of the bombing of London. Murrow's style of reporting had disappeared from commercial radio, where tight formats discouraged long stories. It was revived and refined at NPR, first on *All Things Considered,* then on *Morning Edition,* a program launched in 1979. By the 1990s NPR had news bureaus in Chicago, New York, Los Angeles, London, and Moscow, and a corps of part-time correspondents in nearly every corner of the world. In the 1980s and 1990s NPR focused on innovative cultural and information programming, in part mirroring the nation's ethnic and racial diversity, as well as reaching younger listeners. Public radio's traditional focus on classical music was augmented by NPR programming featuring jazz, blues, and contemporary African music. *Car Talk,* hosted by the Magliozzi brothers of Cambridge, Mass., invited listeners to phone in their questions about auto repair. NPR documentaries and talk shows in the 1990s placed attention on contemporary social concerns, particularly environmental protection.

Besides producing its own programming, NPR distributes programs produced by its member stations and independent producers. In 1992 NPR launched its Hothouse Project, which provides money and technical assistance for development of new radio programming. The project's first undertaking was a program about the sacred music traditions of African Americans. From 1983 to 1986 NPR withstood a severe financial crisis—a deficit of several million dollars—that was widely blamed on poor management and nearly bankrupted the organization. In order to survive NPR dismissed more than 100 employees and instituted tough financial controls. The crisis also prompted a fundamental change in the financing of public radio in the United States. The Corporation for Public Broadcasting (CPB), an agency of the federal government, granted a loan to NPR and later began funneling public money to individual public radio stations, rather than to NPR. The stations used the money to acquire national programming. The move was intended to give public stations a greater voice in the governance of NPR and other program suppliers. Since the early 1980s public radio as a whole has relied less on government support and more on contributions.

[Mary Collins, Murray Bognovitz, and Jerome Liebling, *National Public Radio: The Cast of Characters* (Washington, D.C., 1993); Mel G. Grinspan, ed., *News and Views from National Public Radio* (Memphis, 1987); Susan Stamberg, *Talk: NPR's Susan Stamberg Considers All Things* (New York, 1993).]

JAMES KATES

See also **SUPP:** Radio.

NATIONAL RIFLE ASSOCIATION (NRA) was founded in 1871 to encourage marksmanship and is the largest organization in the United States opposed to gun control. The NRA lobbies to protect the rights of gun owners and to oppose more stringent gun controls through its Institute for Legislative Action and its literal interpretation of the Second Amendment to the U.S. Constitution ("the right of the people to keep and bear Arms, shall not be infringed"), contrary to the Supreme Court interpretation of the amendment. The organization has its largest following in small town and rural areas. For many years the NRA was considered one of the most powerful lobbying groups in Washington, but its failure to prevent passage of the Brady Handgun Violence Prevention Act (Brady Bill) in 1993 and the federal Crime Bill in 1994 was seen by many observers as evidence that the NRA's influence had diminished, while public concerns about crime had increased.

[Osha Gray Davidson, *Under Fire: The NRA and the Battle for Gun Control* (New York, 1993); Gary Kleck, *Point Blank: Guns and Violence in America* (Hawthorne, N.Y., 1991); James D. Wright, Peter H. Rossi, and Kathleen Daly, *Under the Gun* (Hawthorne, N.Y., 1983).]

JAMES D. WRIGHT

See also **SUPP:** Brady Bill; Gun Control.

NATIONAL SCIENCE FOUNDATION. Establishment of the National Science Foundation (NSF) in 1950 resulted from concern during and after World II about the role of the U.S. government in supporting scientific research and a science policy that would answer the needs of national security, industry, and the general concerns of U.S. scientists. Led by a presidentially appointed director, who works with a twenty-four-member National Science Board, the NSF concentrates on supporting basic research rather than applied research, which seeks a particular application of the findings. Because universities are the setting for most basic research in the United States, the NSF is especially important to those institutions. Although the NSF provided only 3 percent of the governments research and development funding in the mid-1990s, that figure represented nearly one-fourth of the government's support of university research. More than 2,000 colleges, universities, and research institutions in the United States have received grants or contracts from the NSF. None of the laboratories administered by the federal government is operated by the NSF, but it does support national research centers, often located at major universities, and some Antarctic research stations and oceanographic vessels. NSF's focus remains basic research, but in 1968 Congress changed its charter to enable support of applied research and in 1986 added engineering to NSF's mission.

Such changes reflected the growing concern in the United States about its ability to compete against Japanese and European industry in particular and the growing conviction in Congress during the 1980s and early 1990s that the government should act through more funding and changes in laws to strengthen research and development that could benefit U.S. industry. Thus, even during the administration of President George Bush (1989–1993), who was not a strong advocate of a government industrial policy, the NSF was supporting research in high performance computing and communications, which, after Bill Clinton became president in 1993, was part of the attempt to create a national information infrastructure—the so-called information highway. NSF was also supporting research in new manufacturing technologies, robotics, and advanced materials and actively studying the state of U.S. education in science and math in order to make recommendations on how to improve the curricula. Clinton placed far more emphasis on government support for industry. Nevertheless, NSF money still backed significant basic scientific research at universities and other centers. For example, ongoing efforts to determine the origins, age, and size of the universe depended in part on NSF funds, as did research attempting to assess the extent and implications of global environmental change. By the late 1990s, however, pressure to reduce significantly the size of government, as well as the level of funding for it, and a simultaneous debate over the role and means by which government should aid science and industry, created questions about the future course of NSF. Although not targeted for elimination, NSF could not forecast how much money it would have in the future and the degree to which it could support basic research at universities and applied research and engineering.

[George T. Mazuzan, *The National Science Foundation* (Washington, D.C., 1988); National Science Board, *Science and Engineering Indicators, 1993* (Washington, D.C., 1993); Bruce L. R. Smith, *American Science Policy Since World War II* (Washington, D.C., 1990).]

KENNETH B. MOSS

See also **SUPP:** Research Laboratories.

NATIONAL TRUST FOR HISTORIC PRESERVATION. Since its founding by Congress in 1949 as a private, nonprofit organization, the trust has acquired eighteen historic properties that it maintains as house museums, including Decatur House, its Washington, D.C., headquarters. To continue to carry out its goal of preserving the historical and cultural foundations of the nation, the trust established its Main Street program in 1980. The program has involved more than 800 communities in forty-five states, which have invested nearly $3 billion in historic business districts. As a result, there have been 21,000 building rehabilitations and the creation of 51,700 jobs and 14,800 new businesses. The trust's budget ($33 million in 1994) comes principally from private sources, including dues from 250,000 members, corporate and foundation grants, endowment income, and merchandise sales. Congress contributes about one-fifth of the trust's income in the form of matching grants through the Department of the Interior.

[David E. Finley, *History of the National Trust for Historic Preservation, 1947–1963* (Washington, D.C., 1965); Elizabeth D. Mulloy, *The History of the National Trust for Historic Preservation, 1963–1973* (Washington, D.C., 1976).]

EDWIN C. BEARSS

NATIONAL WEATHER SERVICE. *See* **Weather Service, National.**

NATION OF ISLAM. *See* **African-American Religions and Sects; Islam.**

NATIVE AMERICAN CHURCH has continued to provide religious experience and community to hundreds of thousands of American Indians through the ritual ingestion of peyote since its incorporation in 1918. Peyotism's legal standing, however, met a serious challenge in 1990. In 1984 Al Smith was fired in Oregon when his employer learned of his participation in Native American Church rituals and enforced its policy that employees be drug free. Although twenty-three states and national law protected peyote use in the Native American Church, Oregon law barred the use of peyote without exceptions. When

Smith sought unemployment benefits, the state refused them. Upon appeal the U.S. Supreme Court decreed in *Employment Division* v. *Smith* (1990) that the free exercise clause of the First Amendment did not exempt Smith from a neutral, generally applicable criminal law. The decision placed minority religions in jeopardy. In response, Oregon passed a 1991 law permitting the sacramental use of peyote by American Indians in the state, and Congress passed the Religious Freedom Restoration Act in 1993, which required the government to demonstrate a compelling state interest to justify any measure restricting religious practices.

[Christopher Vecsey, *Handbook of American Indian Religious Freedom* (New York, 1991); Christopher Vecsey and Omer C. Stewart, *Peyote Religion* (Norman, Okla., 1987).]

CHRISTOPHER VECSEY

See also **SUPP:** Freedom of Religion; Native Americans.

NATIVE AMERICANS. The U.S. census of 1990 enumerated some 2 million Native Americans, a more than 40 percent increase over 1980, making them one of the fastest-growing ethnic groups in the country, although they constitute less than 1 percent of the total U.S. population. The Cherokee (308,000) and Navajo (219,000) are the largest tribal groups. More than 60 percent of Native Americans live in such cities as Los Angeles, Chicago, and New York. The urban environment fosters contacts and cultural exchange through such institutions as the American Indian Community House in New York City. Native Americans generally return home to reservations each year, and some attempt to relocate to home reservations at some time in their lives.

Reservation environments, always fragile, have felt the impact of industrialization. Oil wells, coal mines, and the extraction of natural gas and uranium have disrupted environments from the Navajo and Hopi reservations in the Southwest to Inuit communities at the edge of the Arctic Sea. Hydroelectric projects have decimated fish populations in the Northwest, and pollution has had a deleterious effect on reservation ecologies. The expanding U.S. population in the Southwest has placed severe constrictions on water use, and Indians have had to sue for their water rights, sometimes successfully. The Clean Air Act of 1977 made it possible for the Northern Cheyenne to shut down or alter the operations of factories polluting their territories. The Exxon Corporation agreed to pay $20 million when the Exxon *Valdez* oil spill in 1989 ruined Alaskan hunting and fishing grounds at least in the short run. In some communities people were contaminated by nuclear radiation as a result of mining operations, particularly the Navajo. Others, such as the Chickasaw, offered to store nuclear waste to make money from government contracts, much to the dismay of local environmentalists and some tribal members.

Since the 1970s the past generation of Native Americans has attempted to revive such religious rituals as pipe ceremonies, spirit dances, sweats, and vision quests. Programs have sprung up to record and pass down tribal languages. Nonetheless, various forms of Christianity have become "traditional" in virtually every community, and perhaps only 100 of the 300 or so aboriginal languages are still spoken, many only by a handful of elders. At most, one of three Native Americans speaks a native language. Traditions are always in danger, especially when half of marriages are to non-Indians.

In 1977 the American Indian Policy Review Commission recommended that the United States recognize greater Native American sovereignty. The next two decades witnessed a marked growth in Indian sovereignty, despite congressional reluctance to accept the commission's report. Tribes possess the right to determine membership; 147 tribal courts have power not only over members but nonmembers in their territories. Tribal governments possess a right to tax their members. Reservation businesses have an exemption from state sales taxes. By 1995 federally recognized tribes had increased to 547, an increase of 22 since the federal acknowledgment process began in 1978. In the mid-1990s more than 100 other groups were seeking recognition. In 1994 President Bill Clinton issued a directive to federal agencies to treat the tribes with the same deference given to state governments.

Based on the Indian Claims Commission (ICC) Act (1946), tribes have pressed suits against the United States and individual states for recompense or return of lands taken illegally. In 1978 the ICC expired, after hearing 670 cases, with another 80 cases appealed. It had awarded $774 million to claimants. In the next decade the courts awarded another $487 million. From the Penobscot in Maine to the Puyallup in Washington, tribes have received substantial payments. Some tribes, such as the Sioux in South Dakota, have refused cash settlements, holding out for return of lands. Award money has helped tribes establish investment schemes and social service systems.

Titles to lands have increased, so that 4 percent of U.S. land in 1995 was held by tribes on 267 reservations. Some 140 of the total 287 reservations in the United States are entirely tribally owned.

The Indian Gaming Regulatory Act of 1988 encouraged Indian nations to establish gambling casinos, with the approval of and regulation by individual states. By 1995 seventy-four tribes had opened casinos, none more successful than the 300-member Mashantucket Pequot, who earned $600 million in profits in 1993 alone and who provide $80 million from these earnings each year as a "gift" (technically not a tax) to the state of Connecticut. Their $10 million bequest to the Smithsonian Institution (to help create the National Museum of the American Indian) was the largest donation ever received by the Smithsonian. By the mid-1990s Native American gaming was a $6 billion industry. Gambling is not the only form of economic enterprise on reservations. The Mescalero Apache maintain resorts; the Ak-Chin Pima and Maricopa grow cotton; the Choctaw assemble wire devices for automobiles; the Skagit make decorative boxes and sell salmon; and the Turtle Mountain Chippewa build house trailers. The Passamaquoddy hired investment bankers who helped boost the tribe's portfolio to $100 million. The Cherokee produce parts for military contractors. Native American art earns $500 million a year, protected from forgeries by the 1990 Indian Arts and Crafts Act.

Since the mid-1970s public and governmental sympathy for Native American culture has been growing, and the American Indian Religious Freedom Act (1978) attempted to direct governmental agencies to protect Indian spiritual interests, such as sacred sites. In 1992 the Columbus Quincentenary was marked by a debunking of Columbus's accomplishments, as tribes asserted the value of their ways of life. When the film *Dances with Wolves* played to packed movie houses in 1990, audiences applauded the deaths of white soldiers at the hands of the noble Lakota Sioux. Not everyone applauds Indian commerce. The Interstate Congress for Equal Rights and Responsibilities has attempted many times since its founding in 1976 to abrogate Native American treaties and hence destroy the underpinnings of recognition and sovereignty. The landmark decision in *United States* v. *Washington* (1979) gave half of the salmon catch in the state of Washington to Native Americans based upon treaty rights, which not only helped Northwest Indian economies but aroused the fury of non–Native American fishermen from Washington to Wisconsin.

Since the 1970s there has sometimes been violence within Indian communities, such as among the Mohawk at Akwesasne, N.Y. Several times in the 1970s and 1990s fighting broke out, and violence occurred in 1990 over the issue of gambling. Alcoholism continued to plague Native American communities throughout North America, with rates three times those in U.S. society as a whole. Suicides, accidental deaths, and arrest rates are connected to alcohol, and fetal-alcohol-syndrome births were distressingly high, as many as one-fourth of all births on some reservations.

Indians are the poorest population group in the United States, with 31 percent living in poverty in 1990. On reservations the median household income per annum was $13,000, per capita income was under $5,000, and unemployment was as high as 80 percent. The poorest county in the United States (Shannon, S.Dak.) was that of the Pine Ridge Lakota Sioux Reservation, where two-thirds of the population lived below the poverty line and per capita income was $3,000. In 1978 Congress passed the Tribally Controlled Community College Assistance Act; in 1995 there were twenty-six Native American–run colleges or junior colleges from the state of Washington to Michigan, most of them on the northern Great Plains. Only three are four-year institutions, including Sinte Gleska University in Rosebud, S.Dak. About 13,000 students attend these colleges. Tribal colleges emphasize Native American values and traditions, as well as training Indians for jobs in the modern world.

[Mary B. Davis, ed., *Native America in the Twentieth Century: An Encyclopedia* (New York, 1994); Marlita A. Reddy, ed., *Statistical Record of Native North Americans* (Detroit, 1993).]

CHRISTOPHER VECSEY

See also **DAH:** Indians, American, of the 1970s; **SUPP:** *Exxon Valdez;* Gambling; Native American Church; Poverty.

NATO. *See* **North Atlantic Treaty Organization.**

NEA. *See* **National Endowment for the Arts.**

NEBRASKA, bordered on the east by the Missouri River, on the south by Kansas and Colorado, on the west by Colorado and Wyoming, and on the north by South Dakota, has led some commentators to assert that the state, with only the Missouri River as a natural boundary, has had trouble gaining an identity.

Several factors, however, have created a sense of community. Almost all of the state's 77,227 square miles are on the Great Plains, sloping upward and westward from the Missouri. The state's severe winters and hot summers, with an average mean rainfall of roughly 32 inches in the east to 15 inches in the west, have led to an economy dominated by grain and livestock production. Population stabilized during the twentieth century, standing at 1,192,214 in 1910 and moving slowly ahead to 1,325,510 in 1950 and 1,578,385 in 1990. Lincoln, the state capital, and Omaha grew moderately, remaining the state's principal cities and having the only metropolitan areas in Nebraska. Omaha's population in 1990 was 335,795, with the metropolitan area at 618,262; Lincoln's city and metropolitan populations were 191,972 and 213,641, respectively. The next largest city is Grand Island, with a population in 1990 of 39,386. Because of the huge rural area to the west of the two principal cities, Nebraska as a whole had a population of 20 persons per square mile.

Agriculture has dominated the state, as evidenced by the fact that 95 percent of the state's total acreage is devoted to agricultural use, including the extensive production of cattle. The state ranked second in cattle ranching in 1990, and nearly half the state's acreage was grassland. Farmland throughout the state occupied 45 million acres, of which one-third is cropland. The principal farm crop is corn, followed by sorghum, soybeans, and wheat. Farm supports have ensured acceptable prices for producers. In keeping with national trends, single-family farms declined, replaced by huge corporate farms that are regulated by computers, connected with market information by radio and television, and farmed by employees. A small number of farms—fewer than 1,300 of the state's total of 56,000—account for 40 percent of farm income. The concentration of farms led to passage by the state legislature and approval by referendum of the Family Farm Preservation Act in 1982, which permits the acquisition of additional farmland only by Nebraska family-farm corporations. Local opinion has differed over the act's success, with some Nebraskans celebrating the limiting of farm corporations and others believing that the state's land values have been harmed.

While most of the state's industry is in services of one sort or another, agriculture accounts for 11 percent of the state's gross product, and much of that product has been related to the processing of food, especially the processing of corn for livestock feed. Manufacturing also made some advances, notably in printing and publishing and the manufacture of machinery. By the early 1990s Omaha had become a center for the manufacture of telecommunications equipment, surpassing meat-packing in employment. Nebraska is the only state in which all electric utilities are publicly owned and operated. Nuclear power supplies 35 percent of the state's electrical power. Transportation has long relied on the Missouri River, with bulk products passing down to Saint Louis. As in all states, Nebraska has seen a decline in railroad trackage, which stood at 4,150 miles in 1989. Roads have accounted for some of the decline, with the state having 92,405 miles of road in the 1990s, including 482 miles of interstate highways.

The politics of Nebraska have been predominantly Republican, with that party filling most state offices and congressional seats, although from the late 1970s to the early 1990s Democrats have primarily filled the governor's seat and those of the U.S. Senate. Nebraska is the only unicameral state legislature in the United States and elections to that body are officially nonpartisan. As might be expected in an agricultural state, the Nebraska environment has had its ups and downs, mostly the latter. More than 80 percent of Nebraskans drink groundwater, and almost half of it is contaminated by pesticides. More than 2,100 miles of streams are contaminated by agricultural pollutants. Only 9 percent of solid waste is recycled, and several hundred small municipal landfills have been exempted from state regulation since 1972. In the mid-1990s six hazardous waste sites were on the federal Superfund list. The state's important libraries are at the University of Nebraska campuses at Lincoln and at Omaha, where that city also maintains a large public library. The two cities maintain noted museums and symphony orchestras, and Omaha has an opera company. The state's largest festival is the annual state fair at the capital in Lincoln, and an important attraction is the greatly upgraded Omaha Zoo. The most important unifying factor among state residents is the University of Nebraska's football team (the Cornhuskers), which won the national championship in 1995.

[Robert W. Cherny, *Populism, Progressivism, and the Transformation of American Politics, 1885–1915* (Lincoln, Nebr., 1991); Lawrence H. Larsen and Barbara J. Cottrell, *The Gate City: A History of Omaha* (Boulder, Colo., 1982).]

LAWRENCE H. LARSEN

See also **SUPP:** Omaha.

NEH. *See* **National Endowment for the Humanities.**

NEO-ISOLATIONISM, a belief that grew out of disillusionment with the Vietnam War, is marked by a reluctance toward large-scale U.S. involvement in security matters involving foreign countries that could be costly in lives, equipment, and dollars. The term is often used in derision by those who favor a particular intervention opposed by others. Advocates of a more cautious policy prefer such labels as "interest-based policies," "strategic disengagement," "strategic independence," or "national strategy." Neoisolationism can include repudiation of "universal containment" and "indiscriminate globalism"; withdrawal from alliance systems, security agreements, and international organizations; and limiting defense to the Western Hemisphere. Advocates frequently differ but seldom repudiate U.S. trade relations, military aid, economic sanctions, or even combat forces. Because of neoisolationism's specific opposition to the intervention in Vietnam in the 1960s and 1970s and the opposition of conservatives in the 1980s to U.S. intervention in Haiti, Somalia, and Bosnia, it has little if any connection with U.S. isolationism of the nineteenth century or between World Wars I and II.

[Wayne S. Cole, "United States Isolation in the 1990s?," *International Journal* 48 (Winter 1992–1993); Earl C. Ravenal, *Never Again: Learning from America's Foreign Policy Failures* (Philadelphia, 1978); Robert W. Tucker, *A New Isolationism* (New York, 1972).]

JUSTUS DOENECKE

NEVADA. Since the 1960s Nevada's two principal urban centers, Las Vegas and Reno, have grown at an astounding pace. Despite this, the state's politics revolve around the use and ownership of Nevada's vast nonurban areas. With 82.9 percent (fiscal 1991) of the state's land owned by the federal government, primarily military installations and three areas administered by the National Park Service, numerous conflicts have erupted between state officials and federal agencies concerning the use and ownership of that land. Although economic diversification has long been the state's professed goal, in the mid-1990s Nevada remained heavily dependent on tourism and gambling as well as on the federal government's large military presence. Because Nevada's population increased so dramatically beginning in the 1950s, a relatively small percentage of residents are native to the state. Between 1980 and 1990 the state's population increased by 50.1 percent to 1,201,833, the highest increase recorded by any state in that period. By the late 1980s Nevada's urban population outnumbered its rural population by nine to one. According

to the 1980 census, a majority of Nevada's residents lived in southern Clark County, where the Las Vegas Metropolitan Statistical Area is located; the state legislature was reapportioned in 1981 to reflect this fact, giving Clark County a majority in both houses. The concentration of the state's population in and around Las Vegas and on the eastern slopes of the northern Sierra, where both Reno and the state capital, Carson City, are situated, left much of the remainder of the state open to ranching and mining. A significant portion of Nevada's rural lands was used by the Department of Energy and by the air force and the navy for testing weapons and training pilots. Despite the absence of settlement, little of Nevada's sagebrush desert remained unaffected by human projects.

Nevada has struggled to make the best of its close relation to the federal government. In 1977 Nevada took the lead among western states, in what was known as the Sagebrush Rebellion, to weaken the Bureau of Land Management's control over land within their borders. The movement faltered in 1981 when attempts failed to prove the bureau's control over western lands was unconstitutional. The Sagebrush Rebellion lost political steam, but many Nevadans continued to resent the bureau's presence. Nevada in the early 1990s found itself pitted against the federal government over whether the Department of Energy would continue with its plans to open a high-level nuclear waste repository at Yucca Mountain, seventy miles northwest of Las Vegas. Although Nevada has the right to veto construction of a repository within its boundaries, its veto can be overridden by a simple majority in the U.S. Senate. Extensive excavations began at the site in April 1993, but it was expected that safety tests would not be completed until 1998. An overwhelming majority of Nevadans opposed the project, although a vocal minority of residents who lived close to the site supported it because of the potential economic boost. Nevada's conflicts with the federal government are best understood as expressions of a state political culture that emphasizes local control and limited government. Brothels, for example, are permitted in Nevada by county option. The state's legislature is still confined to biennial sessions, despite the considerable difficulty of fashioning a biennial budget for a state that has been growing so rapidly.

In 1988 voters, by an overwhelming margin of four to one, approved a constitutional amendment prohibiting a state income tax. Nevada's economy, therefore, continued to be dominated by tourism and the casino industry, with the great majority of Nevada's workforce employed in casino or casino-related service jobs. The increased gambling revenue collected by the state, although considerable (more than half the state's annual general-fund revenue), threatened to be outstripped by the growing population's need for services. The military is a significant employer in some areas of Nevada, notably at Nellis Air Force Base, northeast of Las Vegas, and at the Fallon Naval Air Station, east of Reno. The Department of Energy's Nevada Test Site, northwest of Las Vegas, is a major employer for southern Nevadans. In addition, Nevada's mining industry, which appeared to be dying in the first half of the twentieth century, experienced a boom in the 1980s, especially in gold and silver mining, but the industry accounted for a meager 3 percent of Nevada's jobs in 1990. Nevertheless, the industry's growth had a dramatic influence on northeastern towns such as Elko, whose population almost doubled between 1980 and 1990 to 33,530. Despite its rapid population growth, Nevada remained overwhelmingly white. According to the 1990 census, 84.3 percent of Nevadans were white, 6.5 percent were African American, and 10.1 percent were Hispanic. Despite the presence of four reservations in the state, Native Americans made up only 1.7 percent of the population. At the same time Nevada had a small but visible Basque population.

[James W. Hulse, *The Silver State: Nevada's Heritage Reinterpreted* (Reno, 1991); Wilbur S. Shepperson, ed., *East of Eden, West of Zion: Essays on Nevada* (Reno, 1989).]

EMILY HAUPTMANN

See also **SUPP:** Las Vegas.

NEW AGE MOVEMENT, an international social movement that began in the late 1960s when Eastern religions became popular in the United States. It combined earlier metaphysical beliefs such as Swedenborgianism, mesmerism, transcendentalism, and theosophy. As expressed by Baba Ram Dass (born Richard Alpert), its first recognized national exponent, the New Age movement believes in the totality of the human body, mind, and spirit. The movement may be defined by its experience of transformation through rebirthing, meditation, possessing a crystal, or receiving a healing. Projecting from the concept of personal transformation, New Agers envision a new era that will witness a universal religion placing emphasis on mystical self-knowledge and belief in a pantheistic god as the ultimate unifying principle. The New Age movement is perhaps best known for its emphasis on holistic health, which emphasizes the need to treat patients as persons and offers alternative methods of curing, including chronobiological diet, naturopathy, vegetarianism, and a belief in the healing process of crystals and their vibrations, which restore the balance of bodily energy. New Age techniques include reflexology, which involves foot massage; acupuncture; herbalism; shiatsu, a form of massage; and Rolfing, a technique named after Ida P. Rolf, the originator of structural integration, in which deep massage aims to create a structurally well-balanced human being. Music is also used as therapy and as a form of meditation. While the term "New Age music" in the mid-1990s was a marketing slogan that included almost any type of music, true New Age music carries no message and has no specific form because its major use is as background for meditation.

[J. Gordon Melton et al., *New Age Encyclopedia* (Detroit, 1990).]

JOHN J. BYRNE

See also **SUPP:** Medicine, Alternative.

NEWARK, New Jersey's largest city, in the last quarter of the twentieth century tried to erase the stigma of being the nation's worst and unhealthiest city. Commenting on Newark's spreading black ghetto, one city official declared in 1970 that "wherever American cities are going, Newark will get there first." That haunting image confronted Kenneth Allen Gibson, Newark's first black mayor (1970–1986), as he fervently tried to resuscitate the racially torn, financially strapped, and socially bankrupt city, while bitterly fighting the economic retrenchment policies of the state capital at Trenton and the federal government. Defeated in the 1986 mayoral election by black Councilman Sharpe James, Gibson helped Mayor James launch and oversee the "new Newark." The city's massive restructuring of its downtown involved the investment of hundreds of millions of dollars to develop the Gateway–Penn Station area, Newark International Airport, the College of Medicine and Dentistry, Rutgers University's Newark campus, New Community Corporation properties, and an industrial parks program. The city's metamorphosis and urban "renaissance" earned Newark an All-American Cities Award, especially because it was selected as the site for a $300 million cultural complex, to be funded by the state, and for such strategic corporations as Prudential. Newark's administrators carefully crafted their policies to fit an urban population that had declined nearly 30 percent between 1967 and 1990, from 390,000 to 275,221. In 1990 Newark reported 78,771 whites, 160,885 blacks, 71,761 Hispanics, and a foreign-born population of 18.7 percent.

[Gordon Bishop, *Greater Newark* (Chatsworth, Calif., 1989); John T. Cunningham, *Newark,* rev. ed. (Newark, 1988); Stuart Galishoff, *Newark* (New Brunswick, N.J., 1988); Clement Alexander Price, "Newark and the Rhetoric of Optimism," in Gary Jardim, ed., *Blue Newark Culture* (Orange, N.J., 1993).]

TIMOTHY C. COOGAN

See also **SUPP:** New Jersey.

NEW HAMPSHIRE. Dramatic population and economic growth in the 1970s and 1980s, followed by reversals in the early 1990s, are the most striking features of New Hampshire's history since 1976. In 1990 the population rose for the first time to more than one million. Between 1980 and 1990 the state experienced the sixth highest rate of population growth, 20.5 percent, of any state, which was also the highest in the Northeast, but there was a slight decline in the early 1990s. One feature of New Hampshire's growth in the 1980s was a marked increase in the Asian, Hispanic, and African-American populations. Although none of these groups exceeded 1 percent of the total population in the 1990s, and although New Hampshire had the third highest concentration of non-Hispanic whites of any state, the rate of growth among ethnic minorities far exceeded that of whites and was among the fastest in the United States. Because the population boom resulted mainly from migration across the southern border with Massachusetts, the greatest social and demographic changes were concentrated in the south-central and southeastern parts of New Hampshire, the so-called "golden triangle." Clustered within this area were most of the newer electronics firms, other high-technology industries, suppliers of components for products ranging from computers to automobiles, and other manufacturing and service industries that for a time supported an almost fully employed and well-paid population. The abrupt transition in this part of New Hampshire, which is connected handily by highway with metropolitan Boston, led some Massachusetts émigrés to use their new homes in southern New Hampshire as part of the commuting suburbs, which gave rise to the "two New Hampshires" theory. According to that theory, the "golden triangle" differed not only socioeconomically but also in its orientation toward greater Boston and potentially in political attitudes from the more rural, less prosperous, and traditionally Yankee northern and western parts of the state.

These underlying economic and demographic tendencies, combined with nationwide concerns over energy and the environment, account for two especially dramatic controversies over further industrial development during the last quarter of the twentieth century. In 1974 the residents of Durham protested angrily against a plan by Greek tycoon Aristotle Onassis to build the world's largest oil refinery in their coastal town. Against the backing of Republican Governor Meldrim Thomson, Jr., and the powerful *Manchester Union Leader,* the state legislature voted down by more than two to one a bill that would have allowed the state to override local preference on such matters, and the refinery plan collapsed. This assertion of traditional home rule, however, was not enough to defeat the protracted construction of a nuclear power plant in the coastal town of Seabrook, from 1976 to 1986; the plant began generating electricity in 1990. The long construction process was marked by frequent interruptions, mass protests and mass arrests, conflict over the question whether consumers should pay construction costs while the work was still in progress, an interstate battle over the project between New Hampshire Governor John Sununu and Massachusetts Governor Michael S. Dukakis, court actions over the decisions of federal agencies, and the bankruptcy in 1988 of the Public Service Company of New Hampshire, the sponsoring power company. The economic downturn of the late 1980s was exacerbated by the closing in 1990 of Pease Air Force Base in Portsmouth and Newington, one of the first major military base closings of the post–cold war era. Much study and debate have gone into the problem of how to convert this large military facility to civilian uses, in order to revive the economy in southeastern New Hampshire.

Between 1976 and 1994 New Hampshire voters seldom strayed from their traditional Republican preferences. Democrat Hugh J. Gallen was elected governor in 1978, partly by opposing the proposed consumer charges for construction works in progress at Seabrook. He was reelected in 1980 but lost the 1982 election to Republican Sununu, a strong supporter of the Seabrook project and opponent of new state taxes. Gallen died at the end of December, leaving State Senate President Vesta Roy to fill in as governor until Sununu took office in January 1983. After serving three terms and playing a prominent role in the presidential campaign of George Bush in 1988,

NEW JERSEY

Sununu became chief of staff in the Bush White House. In 1990 President Bush appointed David H. Souter, a respected New Hampshire jurist little known outside his own state, to the U.S. Supreme Court. In 1992 the New Hampshire spring presidential primary, which the legislature had repeatedly moved to earlier dates in order to retain its claim of being the first in the nation, lost some of its cachet as an election forecaster. Since the state's first presidential primary in 1952, no candidate had been elected president without first having won his party's primary election in New Hampshire, but the Democratic winner in New Hampshire in 1992 was not Bill Clinton, who won his party's nomination and the presidency, but Senator Paul E. Tsongas of Massachusetts. Tsongas remained a familiar figure in the state through his association with former New Hampshire Republican Senator Warren Rudman in the "Concord Coalition," a movement against federal budget deficits.

Questions of public finance were also high on New Hampshire's internal agenda in the mid-1990s. With the soaring costs of public education, the state's heavy reliance on local real estate taxes for school funding prompted taxpayer revolts in some communities and a lawsuit demanding greater state contributions to school costs. In late 1993 the New Hampshire Supreme Court ruled that the state bore a constitutional duty to assure adequate and equal schools for every community. The overwhelming reelection of Governor Stephen Merrill and heavy Republican legislative gains in the 1994 election nevertheless appeared to endorse New Hampshire's historic opposition to any form of broad-based state tax.

[Henry F. Bedford, *Seabrook Station: Citizen Politics and Nuclear Power* (Amherst, Mass., 1990); Nancy Caffey Heffernan and Ann Page Stecker, *New Hampshire: Crosscurrents in Its Development* (Grantham, N.H., 1986).]

CHARLES E. CLARK

NEW JERSEY. Ranked eighth nationally in 1978 with 7.5 million people, New Jersey had already become America's most urbanized state (even though 42 percent of its land remained forested and it still had 8,000 farms). By decade's end New Jersey had also developed into four distinct topographical areas: the Hudson-to-Trenton manufacturing hub, with its heavy concentration of chemical and pharmaceutical companies (New Jersey ranked first in the nation in both industries), petroleum, apparel, and glass industries; the Atlantic coastal region (from New York harbor to Atlantic City and Cape May), the state's vaca-

tionland; the Pinelands; and southern, western, and northern regions, composed primarily of farms, forests, and expanding wealthy suburbs.

The removal, relocation, and decentralization of the state's old manufacturing plants, away from older areas in or near the major cities, caused dramatic shifts in New Jersey's industrial economy, forcing the legislature in Trenton to adopt new policies toward wholesale, retail, service, transportation, utilities, and finance sectors. Although urban populations have declined since World War II (Camden, 13.4 percent; Jersey City, 6.7 percent; and Newark, 7.4 percent), commercial activities in the state's tertiary sector provided jobs for an even larger share of the labor force than industry. Hudson County (Jersey City) suffered the heaviest job loss (it grew by just 2.1 percent in the 1980s and projections suggested a mere doubling of that figure in the 1990s). Only two major cities experienced growth during these years—Paterson by 2.8 percent and Elizabeth by 6.3 percent. An equally severe drop in population was predicted for the 1990s in the largest cities: Camden, Newark, Hoboken, Jersey City, Bayonne, Trenton, Passaic, and Paterson. These changes, along with decreasing fertility rates, a reduced movement of jobs into New Jersey from New York City and Philadelphia, a marked decline of jobs in the Middle Atlantic states, and the state's transient status, should assure only modest population growth in the near future. During the 1980s New Jersey's population increased only 5 percent, from 7,365,011 to 7,730,188.

While cities lost population from the 1970s to the 1990s, New Jersey also developed into the nation's most suburbanized state. In 1990 it ranked ninth nationally, with nearly 90 percent of the population classified as living in urban areas. New Jersey had the seventh highest population density, an unemployment rate of just 5 percent, and a per capita personal income second only to Connecticut. The state's largest ethnic group remained Italian Americans, while African Americans constituted 13.4 percent and Hispanics 9.7 percent of the population. Manufacturing employed one-third of the state's workforce, headed by electronic equipment and followed by chemicals. Nearly 10 percent of the nation's research dollars were spent in New Jersey research facilities and laboratories, while the resort industry emerged as a major factor in the state's economy. Accompanying these developments was the opening of the Garden State Arts Center and the completion of the Meadowlands Sports Complex, both of which helped to dispel the state's battered image. New Jerseyans continued to pack themselves into the center of a massive megalopolis that stretches from Boston to Washington, D.C. The state has come to epitomize urban sprawl, with its population density, housing shortages, water and air pollution, transportation gridlock, and urban crime and decay. Clearly, no matter how one characterizes it—as dormitory, garden, playground, workshop, or, in the words of Senator Dick LaRossa, "one big city"—New Jersey is a multifaceted place.

In order to reverse the negative trends, Republican Thomas H. Kean (acting governor, 1973; governor, 1981–1989) signed the controversial income tax of 1976 to help alleviate dependency on property taxes. Previously, the state had collected its revenue from corporate and nuisance taxes, and since 1966 from the equally unpopular sales tax. Kean's commitment to higher education, open government, and environmental protection also signaled greater government intervention and larger budgets. Kean's administration promoted an economic climate conducive to creating more skilled jobs, but it also slashed industrial jobs, closed manufacturing plants, and squandered much-needed tax revenues. To combat the recession, in 1981 the legislature established the Department of Commerce and Economic Development to bring in new jobs and rebuild the state's crumbling infrastructure. Governor Kean urged the creation of an infrastructure bank for New Jersey but the legislature voted it down.

Economic recession in the early 1980s precipitated increases in sales and income taxes during Governor Kean's stewardship, as New Jerseyans also experienced rising costs in health insurance and federal, state, and local taxes. These developments resulted in a doubling of unemployment, a precipitous fall in construction, plummeting real estate values, and a terrible decline in retail sales. State banks suffered from unpaid land and construction loans and had to be seized by federal marshals. Similar problems plagued the state's major insurance companies as well. The boom years of 1983–1988, however, saw the state budget double (from $5.5 billion to $11 billion), property taxes soar 160 percent (reaching $9.7 billion), extensive construction of commercial and residential buildings, and a reduction in unemployment from 7 percent to 3.5 percent.

The fastest growing areas of the state budget included aid for primary and secondary education, penal incarceration, and health costs. Medicaid alone rose from $500 million to $1.2 billion, while school expenses climbed $1 billion from 1985 to 1990. Another recession, with state revenues having been reduced to a deficit of roughly $1 billion, coupled with a new constitutional mandate to balance the budget, forced the legislature to slash expenditures by $600 million and dip into the 1989 "undesignated" (surplus) funds of $400 million. Democratic Governor Jim Florio (1990–1994) was embarrassingly forced to admit a budget shortfall of $700–$800 million for the fiscal year 1991 and had to cope with a projected $1 billion deficit in the 1992 budget. In a doomed effort to help the poor and eliminate the budget deficit once and for all, Florio raised taxes by a record $2.8 billion. His approval rating plunged below 20 percent.

Meanwhile, voter anger mounted against higher public spending and taxation, an outcry that Republican gubernatorial candidate Christine Whitman best expressed and capitalized on. A former member of the New Jersey Assembly (1967–1977), she had come out of nowhere in a losing 1990 senatorial race against incumbent Democrat Bill Bradley but charged back to defeat the unpopular Governor Florio in 1994. Following her election Whitman claimed that she wanted to be a record-breaking budget cutter. She became the first woman governor of New Jersey and was the Republicans' only woman governor in the United States. Governor Whitman made good on her campaign promise to cut taxes by signing an across-the-board 5 percent income tax cut, the state's first income-tax reduction. She told the state assembly that "this tax cut is a down payment on my promise to cut income taxes by 30 percent for most New Jerseyans." With Republicans a majority in both chambers of the legislature, Whitman received a line-item veto to do as she pleased. Her pledges implied annual cuts of $600 million for three years from the $15 billion budget. She also had to reduce New Jersey's annual $1 billion structural deficit. The Republican experiment appeared to rest more on faith in a resurgent economy, which would raise tax revenues, than on any blueprint, but Whitman's efforts made her one of the most powerful governors in the country.

[Helen M. Kushner, ed., *New Jersey Spotlight on Government,* 4th ed. (New Brunswick, N.J., 1983); Gerald M. Pomper, ed., *The Political State of New Jersey* (New Brunswick, N.J., 1986); Barbara Williams Prabhu, ed., *Spotlight on New Jersey Government,* 6th ed. (New Brunswick, N.J., 1992); Barbara G. Salmore and Stephen A. Salmore, *New Jersey Politics and Government* (Lincoln, Nebr., 1993); Joel Schwartz and Daniel Prosser, eds., *Cities of the Garden State* (Dubuque, Iowa, 1977); Karen A. West, ed., *New Jersey Spotlight on Government,* 5th ed. (New Brunswick, N.J., 1985).]

TIMOTHY C. COOGAN

See also **SUPP:** Atlantic City; Newark.

NEW MEXICO is called the "land of enchantment" for its scenic beauty and rich history of three cultures—Native American, Mexican, and Anglo. It is the fifth-largest state in terms of size, but with a 1993 population of 1,616,483 (up 19 percent from 1980) it ranks only thirty-sixth in number of residents. The population, reflecting the history of settlement in the state, is 76 percent white, 38 percent Hispanic, 9 percent Native American, and 2 percent African American. In the 1990s about three-quarters of the population lived in urban areas, especially Albuquerque, Santa Fe, Las Cruces, Roswell, Farmington, and Rio Rancho. Rapid housing and office construction began in the 1970s in Santa Fe, Las Cruces, and especially Albuquerque. The latter, New Mexico's largest city, grew by more than 50 percent between 1970 and 1990.

Since 1970 the primary economic change in New Mexico has been the rise of the service industry and the decline of ranching, farming, and mining. By the 1990s services, concentrated in the state's urban areas, provided about 70 percent of New Mexico's gross product. The oil-boom days following the 1973 and 1979 oil embargoes led to short-term economic gains, but by the mid-1980s competition from new oil fields and the surplus of oil and natural gas in world markets had depressed this sector. Production of potash and uranium also declined. In 1995 the state government employed more people than any other single economic activity. Sharply increased defense budgets created or expanded military bases, nuclear energy research at Sandia National Laboratories and White Sands Missile Range, and space research. President Ronald Reagan's 1983 proposal to develop the Strategic Defense Initiative led to substantial expansion of defense-related research. State government and private business made a concerted effort to make the corridor between Albuquerque and Santa Fe a high-tech center of the Southwest. The area became noted for manufacture of military communication systems, silicon chips for computers, appliances, and telephone equipment. New Mexico's scenery, mild climate, rich history, and cultural attractions made the tourist industry an important part of the economy. In the 1970s and 1980s developers built resorts and improved services to areas such as Ruidoso, with its quarter-horse races and skiing; Red River, with its spectacular mountain scenery and skiing; and Santa Fe, with its outdoor opera and museums. A major issue for the 1990s was balancing the desire for more tourists and winter resorts with the need to protect natural resources.

[Calvin A. Roberts, *New Mexico* (Albuquerque, 1988); Marc Simmons, *New Mexico* (Albuquerque, 1988).]
ALFRED L. CASTLE

See also **SUPP:** Albuquerque.

NEW ORLEANS between 1970 and 1990 suffered a 26 percent loss of its white population to adjoining Louisiana parishes, despite the continuing attraction of its central area to U.S. and foreign tourists. During the same period the city's total population decreased from 593,471 to 496,938. In 1990 the city's population was 61.9 percent black, 34.9 percent white, and 6.7 percent other ethnic groups. The median income was $16,465, with 33 percent of households living on an annual income below $10,000. The city's political and business leaders sought to create jobs and raise tax revenue through increased tourism. The Louisiana World Exposition opened in 1984; after its close, the fair's New Orleans Convention Center continued to function, accommodating 7 million visitors each year, who spend $1.8 billion. The nearby Superdome, completed in 1975, is used for the New Orleans Saints professional football games and numerous other sporting and entertainment events. A shopping mall, the Riverwalk, and the Aquarium of the Americas were built along the Mississippi River to attract visitors, as well as a recreation park along the French Quarter riverfront. New Orleans's largest tourist attraction, the carnival activities leading up to Mardi Gras, underwent a significant change in December 1991, after a controversial city ordinance was passed that prohibited race and sex discrimination by carnival organizations that parade on the city streets. As a result, three of the oldest and most prestigious groups—Comus, Momus, and Proteous—withdrew from parading. Most carnival organizations abided by the ordinance. In addition to the Mardi Gras festivities, New Orleans also attracts crowds to its Jazz and Heritage Festival every spring. First held in 1970, the Jazz Fest makes its home at the Fair Grounds racetrack, and its audiences number about 250,000 people over the weeklong festival.

The local maritime industry has changed considerably since the 1970s, particularly the containerization by 1990 of most cargo and the subsequent loss of wages previously paid to longshoremen. The port of New Orleans also transferred some of its wharves from the Mississippi to the Industrial Canal and the Mississippi River–Gulf Outlet, but it remained second only to the New York–New Jersey port in total tonnage and was the acknowledged national leader in the movement of such bulk cargoes as grain, oil, and coal. Politics in New Orleans kept pace with the population changes. In 1977 Ernest N. ("Dutch") Morial was elected the first black mayor of the city. He was followed eight years later by another black mayor, Sidney Barthelemy, whose successor in 1994 was Marc Morial, son of Dutch Morial. The major problems that faced New Orleans in the 1990s were public housing, crime, and maintaining public services. In addition to the upturn in the depressed oil industry in the early 1990s and the increasing importance of tourism, the city pinned its hopes for future revenue beginning in 1992 on casino gambling boats and on construction of the world's largest land-based casino on the site of the Rivergate convention and exhibition center.

[Bethany Ewald Bultman, *New Orleans* (Oakland, Calif., 1994); Arnold R. Hirsch and Joseph Logsdon, eds., *Creole New Orleans: Race and Americanization* (Baton Rouge, 1992).]

JOY J. JACKSON

See also **SUPP:** Louisiana

NEWSPAPERS. By the early 1990s there were 9,000 newspapers published in the United States, about 1,600 of them dailies. Both their number and combined circulation of 60 million have changed little since the 1950s. Newspapers still receive the lion's share of dollars invested in advertising. In the mid-1990s most newspapers earned handsome profits, but the industry was gloomy because circulation had grown more slowly than the population, and papers were not attracting young readers. With increased competition for advertising money from television and magazines (usually three-quarters of a paper's income), some publishers tried to reach nonsubscribers with "shoppers," inserts filled with retail ads, while others changed content to match reader survey responses.

Other changes since the 1970s included the adoption in 1973 by journalists of a new voluntary code of ethics, and in several cities they published journals, including the *Columbia Journalism Review* and *American Journalism Review,* in which they criticized their own publications. The National News Council, which investigated complaints of unethical behavior against the largest newspapers and the wire services, was abandoned after eleven years in 1984, but a few publishers supported local versions. In 1995 newspapers employed fewer than 500,000 staff and other workers nationwide. The newspaper as a local institution changed in 1982 when Gannett Company, the largest newspaper chain, launched *USA Today,* which quickly became the number two newspaper in the country. Like the *Wall Street Journal,* which has the highest circulation, *USA Today* utilizes satellites to print in several locales. These two national dailies are followed by the *Los Angeles Times* and the *New York Times,* both with circulations of more than a million, The *Washington Post,* the *New York Daily News,* and *New York Newsday* reported circulations in excess of 750,000. More than 100 others exceed 100,000. Smaller dailies received the Pulitzer Prize for Meritorious Public Service during the 1970s and 1980s, including the *Anchorage Daily News* (1976, 1989), the *Lufkin (Texas) News* (1977), the *Jackson (Miss.) Clarion-Ledger* (1983), and the weekly *Point Reyes (Calif.) Light* (1979).

The decades-long rush toward chain ownership abated in the early 1990s, in part because there were few privately owned dailies left to acquire. Only a handful of cities still supported competing dailies, leading many papers to avoid endorsing political candidates. Instead, many added op-ed pages, in which they publish columnists with diverse views. By the late 1980s computer terminals had replaced typewriters in newsrooms and offset printing was almost universal, which led to the increased use of color in photographs, illustrations, and maps. Technological improvements weakened the printing craft unions, causing the number of labor strikes to decline. The foreign-language press changed to serve the immigrants from Asia and Central America, and the *Miami Herald,* among others, prints editions in Spanish. The African-American press became more economically viable, thanks to increased advertising, and there was a trend toward consolidation. The *Afro-American* published editions in Washington, Baltimore, and other cities, while the *Chicago Daily Defender* acquired the *Michigan Chronicle* in Detroit.

[Newspaper Association of America, *Facts About Newspapers* (Reston, Va., 1994); Richard A. Schwarzlose, *Newspapers: A Reference Guide* (New York, 1987).]

JOHN D. STEVENS

NEW YORK CITY has changed very little geographically since 1975, although the borough of Staten Island initiated a plan of secession in the early 1990s. Demographically, however, there have been major changes; the city's population fell from 7,894,862 in 1970 to 7,071,639 in 1980, then rebounded to 7,322,564 in 1990. There were significant changes in the city's ethnic composition. The white population dropped from 4,972,509 (63 percent of total) in 1970 to 3,163,125 (43.2 percent) in 1990. The black population grew by 9 percent, reaching 1,847,049 in 1990. The Hispanic population grew by more 26 percent, to 1,783,511, making up 24 percent of the total population. In a change from post–World War II patterns, the biggest increase came from non–Puerto Rican Hispanics, whose numbers virtually duplicated Puerto Ricans by 1990, increasing 64 percent, to 886,748. Asians swelled from 115,830 in 1970 to 489,851 in 1990, a 63 percent increase. The 1980 census revealed the impact of the 1965 federal Immigration Act on New York City. Since 1970, 754,000 immigrants entered the New York–New Jersey metropolitan area. Of these, 116,500 (15 percent) came from Europe, traditionally the largest source of new city residents. In the 1970s, however, 168,000 (22 percent) came from Asia, with Hong Kong and India supplying the most. Of the 267,600 arrivals from North and Central America, Dominicans and Jamaicans accounted for 128,000. Newcomers from South America were led by Colombians, Ecuadorans, and Guyanans.

Despite the one-day stock-market crash in October 1987, New York remained the nation's economic and communications center. By 1990 the Manhattan central business district employed 2 million people in 600 million square feet of office space; more than 8 million more people worked in the greater metropolitan area, producing a gross regional product of $425 billion in 1985. A large force in the global economy, New York is the focus of major foreign investment in real estate and banking. Important accounting, advertising, and legal firms are based in New York. Beginning in the 1960s New York City changed from a manufacturing to a service economy. Although nearly a million persons worked in goods production and distribution in 1990, that figure was less than half the 1970 total. Corporate workers, management consultants, accountants, engineers, architects, and building and personnel service operatives became by 1989 the largest employment sector in the city. Gains were also made in entertainment, tourism, education, and research. The number of federal employees dropped from 106,000 to 76,000 by 1989, with further cuts in the early 1990s. In office work gender and race were major variables. Women were the overwhelming majority of secretaries, information clerks, and records processors. White women made up more than 60 percent of women clerical workers, down from 78.2 percent in 1970. Among computer operators, white workers declined from 84.2 percent in 1970 to 47.9 percent in 1990.

Following a fiscal crisis in the mid-1970s, during which the city faced bankruptcy, a period of prosperity emerged in the 1980s. More New Yorkers held jobs, household incomes rose, and housing improved. At the same time, inequality widened for blacks and Latinos and the population was afflicted with AIDS, drugs, and homelessness. The last of these social ailments provides a good example of the paradox of wealth: Single-room occupancy hotels housing the dependent elderly, deinstitutionalized mentally ill persons, and drug addicts were converted to luxury apartments and condominiums, pushing the former tenants into the streets. Similarly, the co-op conversion boom produced soaring property values and skyrocketing rents.

Local politics since the 1970s were characterized by mounting racial polarization. After Abraham Beame's single term as mayor, a coalition centered in the white neighborhoods of Queens and Staten Island brought three terms for Ed Koch, a neoconservative. Koch built a political coalition based on white, ethnic, middle-class voters and pursued policies promoting private investment and jailing of large numbers of criminals. By 1988 Democratic party liberals, disaffected by Koch's administration, nominated and elected the city's first black mayor, David Dinkins. Combining a resurgent black and Latino vote and a significant white vote, Dinkins barely defeated Republican Rudolph Giuliani. Four years later, after the bloom faded from the prosperous 1980s and following the ugly confrontation between blacks and Jews in 1991 in the Crown Heights section of Brooklyn, Giuliani narrowly defeated Dinkins by campaigning for reduced taxes and government spending, reversing affirmative action, and tougher law enforcement.

Widening economic and social gaps created an image of New York as a dual city, composed of prosperous and poor residents. Social disparity emerged in the 1989 "wilding" attack by a group of black teenagers on a female Wall Street investment banker in Central Park; social tensions later led to murders of black men by white mobs in Howard Beach in Queens and Bensonhurst in Brooklyn. Other indicators of poverty included a sharp increase in the number of female-headed households, low labor-force participation rates from virtually all subgroups of the population, mounting numbers of illegal immigrants unable to obtain the benefits of citizenship, and exclusion of blacks and Latinos from the rapidly growing and remunerative occupations of the postindustrial city. These groups were disproportionately represented in the informal economy that existed in sweatshops and petty criminal activities.

Such demographic and economic tensions were reflected in New York's cultural contributions. There was little change in performances at Lincoln Center, although jazz was newly represented. Broadway continued to produce elaborate musicals. The East and West Villages produced vanguard culture. Downtown, Joseph Papp's Shakespeare Festival remained the home of innovative theater. The Conversations with Writers series at the New School and "poetry slams" at the Nuyorican Theater reinvigorated public readings. Keith Haring and Jean-Michel Basquiat translated the visual language of city streets into paintings. Performance and conceptual art arose from the East Village. Punk music developed among self-consciously alienated art students in the Lower East Side and the new gallery district south of Houston Street, called Soho. West Indian immigrants popularized reggae music. New York was a major center of rap music, which combines storytelling over simple bass lines with distorted samplings of other musical artists.

[John Hull Mollenkopf, *A Phoenix in the Ashes: The Rise and Fall of the Koch Coalition in New York City Politics* (Princeton, N.J., 1992), and *New York City in the 1980s* (New York, 1993); John H. Mollenkopf and Manuel Castells, eds., *Dual City: Restructuring New York* (New York, 1991).]

GRAHAM RUSSELL HODGES

See also **SUPP:** New York State; World Trade Center Bombing.

NEW YORK STATE slipped from first in national population rankings to third by 1994, behind California and Texas, dropping from 18,241,391 in 1970 to 17,990,072 by 1990. The vast majority of New Yorkers lived in metropolitan areas, with only 1,605,000 persons living in rural areas. About 40 percent of New Yorkers live in New York City. The census of 1990 listed five cities with populations over 100,000, one less than in 1980. During the 1980s cities of 50,000 people showed declining populations. Hardest hit were Buffalo (–.083 percent), Rochester (–4 percent), and Syracuse (–4 percent). Much of New York was still rural; more than one-quarter of the state's total area was farmland and more than 180 villages had fewer than 1,000 people. Projections forecast continued slow population growth, reaching only 18,456,000 by 2010. In 1990 the population was 74 percent white, 16 percent black, 12 percent Hispanic, 4 percent Asian, and 3 percent Native American. Despite its stagnant population growth, New York remained among the most important states in the union. Although it placed thirty-eighth among "most livable

states" in 1994 (*State Rankings, 1994: A Statistical View of the 50 United States*), it ranked second in Internal Revenue Service collections, at $109 million (10.1 percent of the national total). New York was first in federal corporate tax collections in 1991, second in social security contributions, and third in IRS individual liabilities, at $5,900 per person. In 1992 New Yorkers' annual pay averaged over $30,000, third in the nation.

New York State continued to emphasize public spending for education. Overall it ranked second in the nation in 1992 in annual appropriations for public schools and second and third, respectively, in public elementary and secondary school enrollment. Salaries for classroom teachers trailed only that of California. New York had the highest number of institutions of higher education and was first in annual appropriations for libraries. The state and New York City shared responsibilities for higher education; the State University of New York and City University of New York systems were the largest in the nation.

New York has been plagued by social problems. It ranked first in 1992 in total crimes and second in violent crimes, third in murders, and second in robberies. It suffered the highest rate of robberies per capita of any state in the nation. In 1993 New York had the third-largest prison population in the country. It employed nearly 67,000 state and local police and expended more than $3.5 billion on law enforcement. With almost 8,400 prisoners serving life sentences, New York reinstated the death penalty in 1995. Since the 1970s upstate New York has experienced rapid construction of prisons, employing erstwhile farmhands to guard inmates from inner cities. More than 70 percent of inmates come from New York City.

Economically, the state, led by New York City, moved from manufacturing to service industries, followed by finance, insurance, and real estate. New York State underwent deindustrialization, manifested by declines in iron, steel, textiles, and apparel manufacturing. Trade declined by 18 percent from 1975 to 1988. The proportion of New Yorkers employed in the total population was 46 percent in 1990, below the national average. Annual employment growth of under 2 percent has trailed national rates, as have start-ups of new firms. Agriculture remained the state's largest industry. New York led the nation in production of cottage cheese and cream cheese and was second in apples, tart cherries, fresh market sweet corn, maple syrup, and cabbages. New York ranked third in production of milk, ice cream, cheeses, grapes, cauliflower, and snap beans. The state's 48,000 farms employed 200,000 people.

New York's senators in 1995, Democrat Daniel Patrick Moynihan and Republican Alfonse D'Amato, were long-term officeholders. From 1975 until 1995 the Democratic party controlled the governorship. Hugh Carey served two terms from 1975 to 1983, and Mario Cuomo held office for three terms until Republican conservative George Pataki defeated him in 1994. Cuomo suffered from anti-incumbency sentiment, while Pataki campaigned for restoration of the death penalty and lower taxes. Much of state politics revolved around the relationship between New York City and the rest of the state. In many ways the city seems independent of the state. The city's giant bureaucracy was 42 percent larger than the state government. Moreover, the city's ethnic profiles and religious and political preferences differ sharply from upstate. These cleavages impede agreement on social issues, such as homosexual rights, abortion, welfare, and the death penalty. During the 1980s and 1990s, when state assistance replaced federal grants, New York, a problem-ridden city, was often forced to turn to the state for relief. Consequently, a cordial relationship between the city's mayor and the state's governor was required. In 1994 Republican Mayor Rudolph Giuliani endorsed Democrat Cuomo over Republican Pataki on the grounds that Cuomo would be better for the city.

In Albany, the state capital, the legislature shapes life in the cities. Reapportionment battles have restrained the power exercised by New York and other cities. Nonetheless, New York State led the nation in welfare and education assistance to cities. The state constitution enables state officials to intervene in matters of local government. Home rule has little basis in the constitution. The governor and state assembly control agencies affecting city dwellers, such as the Port Authority of New York and New Jersey, which constructs and manages tunnels and bridges in the city, and the Metropolitan Transportation Agency, which controls buses and subways.

State financing affects city expenditures. The state takes major responsibility for highways and bridges, environmental conservation, and prisons. New York City does have the power to tax personal income, business, and sales. The city and state share responsibility for social services. The city has a very large health care system, with an average hospital size of more than 400 beds. The city used to maintain this system alone, but after passage of the federal Medicare program in the 1960s, expenditures soared. In the early 1980s the state obtained a federal waiver of policy and took control of hospital revenues. Simi-

larly, the state provides care for the mentally disabled. Following a court order in 1972, the state released tens of thousands of mentally disabled people from institutions. Using only drug therapy, the state in effect dumped patients onto the streets, creating a large component of its homelessness. Other state-city partnerships included housing, criminal justice, and child welfare. State and local expenditures for public welfare programs amounted to $18 billion in 1991.

The federal government is a critical part of state expenditures. Although federal activity on behalf of cities decreased, it still expended massive amounts in New York State. The federal government expended $77 billion in New York in 1991, the second highest in the nation. Direct payments to individuals for social security, Medicare, and other entitlement programs totaled $41 billion. Federal grants accounted for nearly a quarter of the state budget, and the federal government contributed almost 20 percent of the city budget. Still, the federal decline in expenditures dramatically altered the relationship between New York State and New York City. The process began in 1975 when the city's fiscal crisis alienated lenders, forcing it to the brink of bankruptcy. Preferring new state-authorized lending agencies to a federal bankruptcy judge, the city ceded power over major municipal policy to the Emergency Financial Control Board, dominated by the governor and his appointees. It was not until 1986 that the city government was able to regain autonomy. In the early 1990s the state economy showed signs of revival, although the 1992 election of Bill Clinton to the presidency did not bring a return of massive federal assistance. Upstate cities such as Buffalo, Syracuse, and Binghamton remained in the economic doldrums, whereas New York City exhibited a resurgent economy.

[Gary Alampi, ed., *Gale State Rankings Reporter* (Detroit, 1994); Gerald Benjamin and Charles Brecher, eds., *The Two New Yorks* (New York, 1988); Peter W. Colby and John K. White, eds., *New York State Today*, 2nd ed. (Albany, 1989); Edith R. Hornor, ed., *Almanac of the 50 States* (Palo Alto, Calif., 1994); Jerry Mumpower and Warren F. Ilchman, eds., *New York State in the Year 2000* (Albany, 1988).]

GRAHAM RUSSELL HODGES

See also **SUPP:** Buffalo; New York City.

NICARAGUA, RELATIONS WITH. As in Cuba in 1959 and Haiti in 1986, excesses of a despotic regime in Nicaragua compelled the United States to withdraw support from a longtime ally. During the 1970s the strongman of Nicaragua, Anastasio Somoza Debayle, a graduate of the U.S. Military Academy at West Point, N.Y., with many friends in Washington, D.C., could no longer control the country. Like Fulgencio Batista in Cuba and the Duvalier family in Haiti, the Somoza family not only had controlled political power but also used it to amass great wealth for itself and its close friends. What little economic progress occurred was concentrated in the capital city of Managua. The rest of the country was left to languish in poverty—ill-nourished, uneducated, and underemployed. Even Managua, devastated by an earthquake in 1972, came to be neglected by Somoza. Relief money sent from the United States and elsewhere to rebuild the city and aid its citizens disappeared or was diverted to other projects. Opposition to the dictatorial Somoza escalated from the mid-1970s until 1978, when the murder of popular journalist Pedro Joaquim Chamorro triggered a civil war. Sympathy within and outside Nicaragua turned toward the Sandinista National Liberation Front, which took its name from Augusto Sandino, the rebellious leader of the 1920s and early 1930s who had opposed the Nicaraguan government and its military supporter, the U.S. marines. Somoza and his henchmen left Nicaragua in 1979. The Sandinistas marched into Managua promising health care, literacy, agrarian reform, and elections within five years. Initially, relations between Washington and the Sandinista government were cordial. Simultaneously seeking aid from communist countries, Nicaragua's new rulers courted the administration of President Jimmy Carter,which responded with $8 million in emergency aid and $75 million in loans. The Sandinista leadership appeared to have learned from the Cuban example and avoided nationalizing all private enterprises or relying on one trading or ideological bloc.

The election of President Ronald Reagan in 1980 signaled a change in U.S. policy, which had emphasized human rights and tolerated some political pluralism in Central America. The new president was far less tolerant of a regime that openly adhered to Marxist principles. Exaggerated and often unsubstantiated accounts of Sandinista aid to leftist guerrillas in neighboring El Salvador provided justification as Reagan and his advisers became mired in a futile covert effort to dislodge the Sandinistas. The economy of Nicaragua and the prospect of a better life for the majority of the population declined sharply from 1981 to 1986, due in part to Sandinista mismanagement and a drop in prices for Nicaragua's agricultural products but also to the prolonged civil war promoted

by the United States and the trade embargo enacted in early 1985. Gradually, opposition to continued involvement in Nicaragua's affairs began to mount in the United States. Funds to the Contras, those fighting the Sandinistas, began to be withdrawn by Congress. Exposure in 1986 of a connection between continued aid to the Contras and sale of munitions to the government of Iran—both of which by then were illegal—created a political uproar in the United States.

In 1987 Central American governments moved to take the initiative in resolving the Nicaraguan civil war. Concerned with the threat of U.S. intervention, President Oscar Arias of Costa Rica proposed a peace plan for the entire region with specific proposals for Nicaragua. All Central American governments endorsed the plan, and seven South American countries and Mexico formed the Rio Group to support the initiative as well. Nicaraguan elections in 1990 resulted in defeat of the Sandinistas and the victory of Violeta Barrios de Chamorro, widow of the slain journalist, who immediately sought to deal with the troubled economy. Nicaraguans were weary of war but yearned for the unfulfilled promises of the revolution. By 1994 Chamorro was still trying to revive the economy and fulfill the promises. Meanwhile, many of the advances made by the Sandinistas in education and health had evaporated. Unemployment was high and the country remained tied to an external debt of $10 billion, a huge sum for a small country. An agreement with the International Monetary Fund cleared the way for $140 million in loans over the next three years as well as other foreign loans and aid. Nicaragua's economic future was by no means assured, because its export earnings were insufficient to meet its obligations. Continued economic uncertainty was accompanied by political squabbling that further hampered Chamorro's efforts. Such squabbling, however, provoked little concern in Washington. Democracy had been restored in Nicaragua, and the United States, for the first time in more than half a century, appeared ready to adhere to a strict policy of nonintervention in Nicaragua's internal affairs.

[E. Bradford Burns, *At War in Nicaragua* (New York, 1987); Anthony Lake, *Somoza Falling* (Boston, 1989); Neill Macaulay, *The Sandino Affair* (Durham, N.C., 1985).]

MARY COMMAGER

See also **SUPP:** Cuba, Relations with; Iran-Contra Affair.

NIH. *See* **National Institutes of Health.**

NOBEL PRIZES. In 1975–1995, 109 U.S. citizens won or shared a total of sixty-nine Nobel Prizes. During this period, only one American—Holocaust survivor, author, and human rights advocate Elie Wiesel—received the Nobel Peace Prize (1986). The other American winners of the Nobel Prize were:

Literature: Saul Bellow (1976); Isaac Bashevis Singer (1978); Czeslaw Milosz (1980); Joseph Brodsky (1987); Toni Morrison (1993).

Economic Science: Milton Friedman (1976); Herbert A. Simon (1978); Lawrence R. Klein (1980); James Tobin (1981); George Stigler (1982); Gerard Debreu (1983); Franco Modigliani (1985); James M. Buchanan (1986); Robert M. Solow (1987); Harry M. Markowitz, William F. Sharpe, and Merton H. Miller (1990); Ronald Coase (1991); Gary S. Becker (1992); Robert W. Fogel and Douglass C. North (1993); John F. Nash and John C. Harsanyi (1994); Robert Lucas (1995).

Chemistry: William N. Lipscomb (1976); Herbert C. Brown (1979); Paul Berg and Walter Gilbert (1980); Roald Hoffmann (1981); Henry Taube (1983); R. Bruce Merrifield (1984); Herbert A. Hauptman and Jerome Karle (1985); Dudley R. Herschback and Yuan T. Lee (1986); Donald Cram and Charles J. Pedersen (1987); Thomas R. Cech and Sidney Altman (1989); Elias James Corey (1990); Rudolph A. Marcus (1992); Kary B. Mullis (1993); George A. Olah (1994); F. Sherwood Roland and Mario Molina (1995).

Physics: James Rainwater (1975); Burton Richter and Samuel C. C. Ting (1976); Philip W. Anderson and John H. Van Vleck (1977); Arno Penzias and Robert W. Wilson (1978); Steven Weinberg and Sheldon L. Glashow (1979); James W. Cronin and Val L. Fitch (1980); Nicolaas Bloembergen and Arthur L. Schawlow (1981); Kenneth G. Wilson (1982); Subrahmanyan Chandrasekhar and William A. Fowler (1983); Leon M. Lederman, Melvin Schwartz, and Jack Steinberger (1988); Norman Ramsey and Hans G. Dehmelt (1989); Jerome I. Friedman and Henry W. Kendall (1990); Joseph H. Taylor and Russell A. Hulse (1993); Clifford G. Shull (1994); Martin Pearl and Frederick Reines (1995).

Physiology or Medicine: David Baltimore, Howard M. Temin, and Renato Dulbecco (1975); Baruch S. Blumberg and D. Carleton Gajdusek (1976); Rosalyn S. Yalow, Roger Guillemin, and Andrew V. Schally (1977); Daniel Nathans and Hamilton Smith (1978); Allan M. Cormack (1979); Baruj Benacerraf and George D. Snell (1980); Robert W. Sperry and David H. Hubel (1981); Barbara McClintock (1983); Michael S. Brown and Joseph Goldstein (1985); Rita Levi-Montalcini and Stanley Cohen (1986); Gertrude B. Elion and George Hitchings (1988); J. Michael Bishop and Harold E. Varmus (1989); Joseph E. Murray and E. Donnall Thomas (1990); Philip A. Sharp and Richard J. Roberts (1993); Alfred G. Gilman and Martin Rodbell (1994); Edward Lewis and Eric Wieschaus (1995).

[Sharon McGrayne Bertsch, *Nobel Prize Women in Science* (Secaucus, N.J., 1993); Bernard S. Schlessinger and June H. Schlessinger, eds., *The Who's Who of Nobel Prize Winners: 1901–1990,* 2nd ed. (Phoenix, 1991).]

ELIZABETH V. BURT

NOISE POLLUTION is generally defined as unwanted sound produced by people and their activities, unwanted in that it interferes with communication, work, rest, recreation, or sleep. Unlike other forms of pollution, such as air, water, and hazardous materials, noise does not remain long in the environment. Its effects are both immediate in terms of annoyance and cumulative in terms of temporary and permanent hearing loss. Society has attempted to regulate noise since the early days of the Romans, who by decree prohibited the movement of chariots in the streets at night. In the United States, communities have for many years enacted ordinances against excessive noise primarily in response to complaints by residents. It was not until the late 1960s, however, that the U.S. government officially recognized noise as a pollutant and began to support noise research and regulation. Public laws leading to federal action against noise pollution include the National Environmental Policy Act of 1969, especially sections concerning environmental impact statements; the Noise Pollution and Abatement Act of 1970; and the Noise Control Act of 1972, which appointed the Environmental Protection Agency (EPA) to coordinate federal research and activities in noise control. The EPA received the assignment to establish federal noise-emission standards, identifying both major sources of noise and appropriate noise levels that would not infringe on public health and welfare.

The EPA's so-called Levels Document, which provided information concerning noise descriptors and safe noise levels, is the standard reference in the field of environmental noise assessment. In it the EPA established an equivalent sound level (Leq) and a day-night equivalent level (Ldn) as measures and descriptors for noise exposure. Soon thereafter most federal agencies adopted either the Leq, Ldn, or both, including levels compatible with different land uses. The Federal Aviation Administration (FAA) uses Ldn as the noise descriptor in assessing land-use compatibility with various levels of aircraft noise. Support for Ldn as the descriptor for environmental noise was provided in 1978 by Theodore J. Schultz, whose synthesis of many social surveys on noise annoyance showed a relation between Ldn and people highly annoyed by noise in their neighborhoods. The Schultz curve became a basis for noise standards.

As part of the effort to identify major noise sources in the United States, the EPA set about determining the degree to which noise standard could contribute to noise reduction. During the 1970s EPA-sponsored research on major noise sources led to regulation of the products that most affected the public, including medium and heavy trucks, portable air compressors, garbage trucks, buses, and motorcycles. Missing from the list was aircraft, which was considered the responsibility of the FAA. During the administration of President Ronald Reagan in the 1980s, the power of the EPA and its Office of Noise Abatement and Control was curtailed and most of its noise regulations rescinded, but efforts continued to curb noise pollution. The Department of Transportation maintains standards for highways, mass transit, and railroads, as well as aircraft. The environmental review process in accordance with the National Environmental Policy Act of 1969 remains the single most effective deterrent against noise pollution.

[Environmental Protection Agency, *Information on Levels of Environmental Noise Requisite to Protect Public Health and Welfare with an Adequate Margin of Safety* (Washington, D.C., 1974); Theodore J. Schultz, "Synthesis of Social Surveys on Noise Annoyance," *Journal of the Acoustical Society of America* 63 (August 1978).]

CARL E. HANSON

See also **SUPP:** Environmental Protection Agency.

NORTH AMERICAN FREE TRADE AGREEMENT (NAFTA). The General Agreement on Tariffs and Trade (GATT), which went into effect in 1948 in the wake of World War II, sought to expand free trade by reducing tariffs between the twenty-three signatory nations. With the gradual privatization of state-run industries and economies, its membership expanded to ninety-six nations in 1988, and tariff barriers were reduced. A strong supporter of GATT throughout its history, the United States in 1986 began to urge that GATT move beyond the reduction of trade barriers and that its agenda include foreign investment, services, agriculture, and intellectual property rights. Many viewed this as an attempt to loosen environ-

mental and social regulations that might hamper access to resources throughout the world. While perhaps seeking to increase investment opportunities for corporate interests, the United States by the mid-1980s was clearly on the defensive economically. Once the leading creditor nation in the world, it had become the largest debtor nation and suffered from what some feared was a perpetual trade deficit.

Increasing competition from Pacific and European countries caused the United States to begin trying to assemble a dollar-dominated block in the American hemisphere. This desire led first to the Free Trade Agreement (FTA) with Canada, which went into effect on Jan. 1, 1989, and then to an expanded trilateral agreement with Canada and Mexico, the North American Free Trade Agreement, which went into effect on January 1, 1994. A multivolume, fifteen-pound document, NAFTA at its simplest level set up a schedule for the elimination of tariffs over a fifteen-year period. Given the earlier agreement between the United States and Canada, NAFTA dealt primarily with restructuring trade between the United States and Mexico and between Mexico and Canada. All tariffs between the United States and Canada would end by the year 1998; those between the United States and Mexico would be eliminated by 2008. The agreements, however, much like the expanded agenda for GATT, covered more than the elimination of trade barriers and led to divisive debate in all three countries. While few objected to freer trade, the opponents of the FTA with Canada and, later, NAFTA were many and vociferous. Concerns among Canadians in 1988 and Mexicans in 1992 reflected a lingering view of the United States as a powerful nation that might yet seek to swallow up or strangle its neighbors. While some critics employed a powerful emotional rhetoric reminiscent of the days when the United States was roundly condemned as the Colossus of the North, others focused on the perceived need to protect Canadian and Mexican sovereignty, which they saw as threatened by expanded U.S. investment in such crucial national resources as oil and in institutions such as banking. Given the unequal status between themselves and their powerful neighbor, these opponents argued, both Canada and Mexico risked becoming in effect economic colonies of the United States.

In 1988 Canadians voiced many of the same concerns expressed by labor leaders and environmentalists in the United States in the early 1990s. Because Canada was already part of GATT, Canadians questioned the necessity of the FTA and the benefit to

Canada of tying itself more closely to the largest debtor nation in the world. They argued that the movement of jobs from Canada to the United States, already a problem because of lower U.S. labor costs, would accelerate and that Canada's higher standards of environmental regulation and social programs would be threatened by U.S. investment and business practices. The debates over NAFTA that raged in all three North American countries in the early 1990s thus reflected not only old suspicions and prejudices but the confusion and uncertainty engendered by the end of the cold war, the increasingly global problems of overpopulation and pollution, and the growing interdependency of economies, as well as suspicion that the only ones who would benefit from the new agreements would be the transnational corporations, which many observers considered already too powerful and unregulated. By far the most emotional issue in all three countries was the effect of NAFTA on employment. While proponents of NAFTA stressed that implementation would ultimately create jobs, the fear of job loss inspired many opponents. The negotiations commenced and continued during a period of global recession and high unemployment. While the movement of jobs from Canada to the United States and from the United States to Mexico had preceded the FTA and NAFTA negotiations, labor groups in both the United States and Canada were unshakable in their opposition.

As the leaders of both Mexico and the United States sought to assuage the fears of those at home who opposed NAFTA, the fate of the pact had implications beyond the borders of North America in the early 1990s. When President George Bush and Mexican President Carlos Salinas de Gortari announced in June 1990 the possibility of a free trade agreement between Mexico and the United States, Bush also announced the Enterprise for the Americas Initiative, which envisioned a free trade block stretching from Alaska to Tierra del Fuego. This announcement preceded a dizzying number of new trading alignments within Latin America, including the agreement among Argentina, Brazil, Paraguay, and Uruguay in March 1991 to establish MERCOSUR, which pledged to integrate their economies by 1995, and numerous framework trade agreements between the United States and its southern neighbors. Most of these proposals received little attention, and public debate remained focused on the free trade agreement with Mexico.

Throughout the course of the NAFTA negotiations, which began in February 1991, more than economics was at stake. The creation of a multinational trading bloc represented a political as well as an economic objective. Correctly or not, Latin American leaders by the early 1990s had come to see the opportunity to move closer to the United States economically as a way to move their countries politically along a modern path of reform. At stake, then, was more than an economic reordering of the relationship among the three North American countries; achievement of a foreign policy objective—strengthening political ties throughout the hemisphere—was also on the line. NAFTA was approved by the U.S. Congress in November 1993. A complicated and cumbersome document largely unread by proponents and opponents alike, it included concessions made on all sides, because leaders in the United States, Mexico, and Canada sought to effect its passage, promote their own economies, and protect the frailest components of those economies.

[Marjorie Montgomery Bowker, *On Guard for Thee: An Independent Review of the Free Trade Agreement* (Quebec, 1988); Victor Bulmer-Thomas, Nikki Craske, and Monica Serrano, eds., *Mexico and the North American Free Trade Agreement: Who Will Benefit?* (New York, 1994); John Cavanagh et al., eds., *Trading Freedom: How Free Trade Affects Our Lives, Work, and Environment* (San Francisco, 1992).]

MARY COMMAGER

See also **SUPP:** Canada, Relations with; General Agreement on Tariffs and Trade; Mexico, Relations with; Trade, International.

NORTH ATLANTIC TREATY ORGANIZATION (NATO). The signing of the North Atlantic Treaty on Apr. 4, 1949, marked the end of a tradition of nonentanglement with European powers that had begun in 1800 with the termination of the Franco-American alliance of 1778. The treaty linked the United States with eleven other nations—Canada, Iceland, the United Kingdom, France, Belgium, the Netherlands, Luxembourg, Norway, Denmark, Portugal, and Italy. The proximate cause of this transformation in U.S. foreign relations was the Soviet communist menace to Western Europe. Initiative for the alliance came from Europe. In 1947 the administration of President Harry S. Truman had announced the Truman Doctrine, which established the principle of providing assistance to countries threatened by communist takeover, and the Marshall Plan, a program for the economic reconstruction of Europe that also included containment of communism as one of its goals. Worried that these measures did not provide sufficient security against communist subversion or Soviet pressures, however, the European nations sought a binding pledge from the United States. They received it in the form of Article 5 of the treaty, which stated that an attack on one member would be considered an attack on all. The allies in turn pledged to build their defenses, integrate their military forces, and prove through self-help and mutual assistance to be worthy of the U.S. commitment.

The alliance itself had little military significance in 1949. Its members assumed that the fact of U.S. adherence to the treaty would be sufficient to deter external attack and that a modest U.S. military assistance program would be sufficient to inhibit internal subversion. In 1950 the Korean War shattered these assumptions. If the Soviets were testing American resolve in a divided Korea, they might conceivably make their next move in a divided Germany. Fear of attack impelled the allies to expand the alliance into a military organization, under a Supreme Allied Commander in Europe (SACEUR) and in the Atlantic (SACLANT). A political headquarters was established in Paris in 1952. A vast military assistance program begun in the summer of 1950 was to raise the size of the ground forces to fifty divisions to cope with a potential Soviet invasion of the West. Greece and Turkey were brought into the alliance in 1952 to shore up the southeastern flank of NATO. West Germany entered the alliance in 1955 only after resistance from its neighbors, France in particular, had been overcome. From 1950 onward the purpose of the alliance was military rather than political. Throughout the 1950s and 1960s the SACEURs, beginning with General Dwight D. Eisenhower, were dominant figures, overshadowing the civilian secretaries-general. Although the drive to build up a large standing army waned in the 1950s, to be replaced by emphasis on nuclear weapons—tactical, intermediate, and by the end of the decade, intercontinental—the concern of the NATO allies remained centered on military security and U.S. authority remained self-evident.

By the late 1950s, however, there were clear signs of discontent among the allies, which gathered strength in the 1960s. Part of the problem was the increasing resentment of the U.S. nuclear monopoly as expanding economies in the European Economic Community generated a self-confidence that had been lacking earlier. At the same time Soviet technological achievements, epitomized by the Sputnik earth satellite in 1957, both stimulated interest of the allies in building their own nuclear weapons and cast doubt on the support of the United States if its own cities were vulnerable to Soviet intercontinental ballistic missiles (ICBMs). Efforts on both sides of the Atlantic to shore up the alliance faltered in the face of a rising Soviet threat. An ambitious attempt to create a multilateral force in Europe, armed with nuclear weapons, collapsed in 1964 because of U.S. unwillingness to turn over control of the weapons to the allies. President Charles de Gaulle's France withdrew its military participation in 1966 but remained a member of the NATO alliance, and NATO's headquarters moved in the following year from Paris to Brussels.

In 1967 the Harmel Initiative, named for Belgium's foreign minister, reinvigorated the alliance by having NATO use détente as well as defense as a major objective. On the assumption that coexistence with the Soviet bloc was a reality, the NATO allies in the 1970s negotiated with the Soviet-controlled Warsaw Pact nations on such issues as reducing nuclear and conventional weaponry and accepting the postwar boundaries of East Germany and Poland. The periodic crises in the 1950s and 1960s over the status of West Berlin, which had led to the Berlin Wall and confrontation between Soviet and American tanks in 1961, seemed to have ended. There was still an uneasiness among the allies when détente did not prevent the Soviet Union from building up offensive nuclear weapons at a time when the United States was reducing its own defense effort. Chairman Leonid Brezhnev's Soviet Union was less volatile than that of Premier Nikita Khrushchev but was no less threatening. Europeans were particularly worried about intermediate-range ballistic missiles targeted on their cities. Soviet behavior induced the allies to follow a dual-track system of both increasing defenses and reviving détente. Although ICBMs based in the United States and Polaris missiles on U.S. submarines effectively neutralized Soviet missiles, European insecurity required deployment of U.S. cruise and Pershing II missiles in five European countries to ease their fears. The United States asked for major increases in NATO defense expenditures, and, in the administrations of Presidents Jimmy Carter and Ronald Reagan, committed itself to massive increases. The Soviet Union at first refused to accept mutual reductions, on the mistaken assumption that Western antinuclear public opinion would prevent the deployment of U.S. missiles. When President Mikhail Gorbachev came to power in the mid-1980s, however, he sought to deescalate the conflict; the Soviet economy could not withstand new burdens that would result from further military competition with the United States. Negotiations that had been interrupted in 1983 while the Soviets attempted to intimidate the West resumed in 1985.

The rush of events at the end of the 1980s—reunification of Germany and dissolution of the Warsaw Pact and of the Soviet Union itself—ended in NATO's achievement of its initial goal, removal of the communist menace. In the mid-1990s NATO's sixteen nations, including Spain since 1982, were seeking new functions for the organization. Until such could be found, the disarray in the former Soviet empire postponed any measures to terminate the Atlantic alliance.

[David P. Calleo, *Beyond American Hegemony: The Future of the Western Alliance* (New York, 1987); Lawrence S. Kaplan, *NATO and the United States* (New York, 1994); Stanley R. Sloan, *NATO's Future* (Washington, D.C., 1985).]

LAWRENCE S. KAPLAN

See also **SUPP:** Arms Race and Disarmament; Cold War; Eastern Europe, Relations with; Soviet Union.

NORTH CAROLINA. Since 1976 remarkable changes have occurred in North Carolina politics, especially in the movement toward a two-party system. Although Republicans have elected many key officials, they have yet to control the General Assembly. Since 1968 the state has voted Republican in every presidential race except 1976. First elected in 1972, U.S. Senator Jesse Helms has been repeatedly reelected. His strongest opponent was Governor James B. Hunt in 1984, whom he defeated in a mean-spirited and expensive campaign. Supporting other conservative Republican candidates with his National Congressional Club, Helms secured the election of two Senate colleagues—John East in 1980 and Lauch Faircloth in 1992. In 1972 James Holshouser became the first Republican elected governor since 1896; James G. Martin, elected in 1984 and 1988, became the second. The Republicans have usually controlled only three U.S. House seats, in the mountains and urban areas, but in 1994 eight of twelve congressmen elected were Republicans. Although the state legislature included only 10 Republicans in 1977, their numbers increased to 67 of 120 representatives and 24 of 50 senators in 1995.

Another important political development was the rise in importance of the black electorate. African Americans were elected mayors of Chapel Hill, Raleigh, and Charlotte and won more legislative seats (from three in 1977 to fourteen in 1991). The numbers of state and local offices held by African Americans increased from 247 in 1980 to 1,086 in 1992. Daniel T. Blue, Jr., was elected the first black speaker of the house in 1990, and Harvey B. Gantt ran a strong race against Senator Helms in 1992, receiving 48 percent of the vote. The black electorate benefited from a U.S. Supreme Court decision in 1986 that declared four North Carolina legislative districts in violation of the Voting Rights Acts of 1965 and 1982. In 1992 the legislature created two oddly shaped congressional districts with black majorities to assure the election of the first black candidates since 1901, Eva M. Clayton and Mel Watt. In addition, the political consciousness of women in North Carolina greatly increased. From 1973 to 1983 many women in North Carolina campaigned unsuccessfully for the legislature to ratify the Equal Rights Amendment. Regarded in the 1940s as a progressive plutocracy, in the 1970s North Carolina was called a "progressive paradox" or a "progressive myth," despite the political changes. Critics cited much evidence to show increasing conservatism, including the election of Senator Helms, the conviction of the Wilmington 10 for arson in 1972, and the acquittal of Ku Klux Klan defendants charged with killing Communist Workers Party members in Greensboro in 1979.

Developments in education were mixed. The state created a new university system, expanded community colleges, and tried to upgrade public schools. Higher education expanded in the 1960s, and rising enrollments created demands in the twelve state colleges for university status, but only campuses in Asheville, Charlotte, and Wilmington were placed in the University of North Carolina (UNC) system. The other nine campuses achieved status as regional universities. Because the fight for funds was fierce and the quality of education was threatened, Governor Robert E. Scott demanded and secured in 1971 a university system ruled by a board of governors. Thereafter the University of North Carolina, a system of sixteen institutions under Presidents William C. Friday and C. D. Spangles, achieved a very good national reputation. The five predominantly black state universities were not happy with this system. The National Association for the Advancement of Colored People brought suit to deny federal funds to the UNC system because it was racially segregated. At issue was more than money for the black students. After fighting the suit for years in the federal courts, the university system in 1981 agreed to a consent decree. It required the state to upgrade the black institutions and take steps to integrate all campuses. The state also created a system of community colleges. Starting in the 1960s as industrial education centers, these institutions grew into fifty-eight two-year technical and community colleges. Operating at first under local boards of trustees, they were brought under a state board of community colleges in 1981. Between 1975 and 1991 community colleges tripled their enrollments, serving more than 230,000 students in 1991–1992.

Public schools were not as successful as higher education, but the needs of gifted students were met partly by summer governor's schools in the 1960s and the creation in 1981 in Durham of the School of Science and Mathematics, which provides a free education for selected students at a residential campus and receives the most National Merit Awards in the state. Public schools have emphasized recruiting and retaining good teachers. Besides upgrading teacher certification standards, the state created the Center for the Advancement of Teaching, where the best teachers receive a week's intellectual stimulation and encouragement. In 1985 the legislature started funding a basic education program, providing smaller classes, teachers' aides, foreign language instruction in lower grades, and achievement testing. Complaining of the poor education of high school graduates, the university system offered many remedial courses. The system required all enrollees to complete a college preparatory curriculum. Despite these efforts, the public was shocked when the state's students received the lowest SAT scores in the nation in 1989 and low scores on standard essay tests in 1993.

North Carolina's economy has performed well since the end of the 1970s. Personal income (in constant dollars) rose from $66 billion in 1980 to $98 billion in 1992, a 3.3 percent increase per year; only four states exceeded this rate. There was little change, however, in the types of employment. Manufacturing, trade, and government were the largest employers in 1976; in 1990 services moved up to third place, increasing from 285,400 to 568,800 jobs. In manufacturing, textiles, apparel, and furniture remained the top three employers, but the machinery industry was growing rapidly. Two geographical areas led the economic growth—Charlotte-Mecklenburg and the Research Triangle—and both areas became regional airline hubs. Economic growth produced population growth, and between 1980 and 1990 Charlotte increased from 315,000 to 396,000 and Raleigh from 150,000 to 208,000. The major population trend was a 35 percent increase in Hispanics and a 250 per-

cent increase in Asians. The state population grew from 5.9 million to 6.6 million, an 11 percent increase.

The crime rate also increased, from 4,121 crimes per 100,000 people in 1985 to 5,889 in 1991. The increase prompted debate about the death penalty. Although the U.S. Supreme Court declared the state's death penalty unconstitutional in 1976 and the legislature enacted a new law in 1977, executions did not resume until 1984. The executions seemed to have little impact on the crime rate. A celebrated legal case in the 1980s involved the Charlotte television evangelists Jim and Tammy Bakker. The federal government prosecuted Jim Bakker for mail and wire fraud, resulting in his conviction and imprisonment. In 1994, for the first time in state history, the governor called a special session of the legislature to address the problem of crime.

An enthusiasm for sports swept the state. North Carolina collegiate teams won the men's NCAA basketball championship five times from 1982 to 1993—the University of North Carolina twice, Duke University twice, and North Carolina State once. The latter's coach, Jim Valvano, was released from his position because his program ran counter to the university system's emphasis on the academic success of athletes. The state's best-known sports figure was Michael Jordan. Charlotte investors established two professional teams—the Charlotte Hornets basketball team in 1988 and the Carolina Panthers football team in 1993.

[John L. Bell and Jeffrey L. Crow, *North Carolina* (Montgomery, Ala., 1992); Eric B. Herzik and Sallye B. Teater, comps., *North Carolina Focus* (Raleigh, 1981); Paul Luebke, *Tar Heel Politics* (Chapel Hill, 1990); North Carolina General Assembly, *North Carolina Manual* (Raleigh, 1977–1991).]

JOHN L. BELL

See also **SUPP:** Charlotte; Raleigh.

NORTH DAKOTA. Contrasts have always typified the state of North Dakota, such as the weather, which varies dramatically. The fourth driest year on record (1976, with 12.04 inches of precipitation) was followed by the wettest (21.67 inches). When weather fluctuates, so do harvests of wheat, the state's primary crop, ranging from 156 million bushels in 1970 to 328 million in 1981. Since the 1970s the economy fluctuated similarly. Wheat brought $1.45 per bushel in 1970 but rocketed to $4.82 in 1974, when, with good harvests and prices, federal government payments were 1.2 percent of total cash income for farmers. After the 1988 drought, however, federal payments were 23 percent of total income. Social and economic contrasts abounded. Although nicknamed the "Peace Garden State," during the 1960s and 1970s North Dakotans joked that if the state seceded from the union, it would be the world's third-largest nuclear power. In 1991 it ranked first in the percentage of eighteen-year-olds in college, but thirtieth in residents with bachelor's degrees and forty-eighth in teachers' salaries. In 1977 it was the first state to complete the total interstate highway mileage assigned in the Federal Controlled Access Highway System, and in 1985 it was the last to report an AIDS case. Although outraged when decreasing population led *Newsweek* to label North Dakota and other states "America's outback," residents proudly sported buttons proclaiming "40 Below Keeps Out the Riffraff!"

Although 1980 saw the first population gain since 1930 (from 617,761 in 1970 to 652,717), 1990 recorded a decline to 638,800. By 1990 the state's urban population (53 percent) exceeded the rural (47 percent). From 1970 to 1990 the largest city, Fargo, grew from 53,365 to 74,111, and the capital, Bismarck, grew from 34,703 to 49,256. Demographically, North Dakota remained homogeneous. In 1990 the three largest ancestral groups were Germans (51 percent), Norwegians (30 percent), and the Irish (8 percent). In contrast, only 4 percent were Native Americans, and Hispanics, African Americans, and Asian Americans accounted for less than 1 percent each. Native Americans have struggled economically, despite five tribal community colleges, military manufacturing contracts, and casino gambling on reservations. In 1990 half lived below the poverty line, one-fourth were unemployed, and per capita income was only 31 percent of the state average.

Since the 1970s the state has depended heavily on the federal government. Agricultural price supports stabilized the farm economy but also increased its vulnerability to federal policies. Farmers benefited enormously from Soviet purchases, which drove wheat prices to $4.82 per bushel in 1974. When President Jimmy Carter embargoed grain sales to the Soviets in response to their invasion of Afghanistan, farmers suddenly found themselves with bulging grain bins. Despite the dependence and vulnerability accompanying them, federal funds generally benefited North Dakota. In 1992 the state ranked eighth in the nation in per capita federal funds received. Although agriculture remained the core of the state's economy, it had changed dramatically. The propor-

tion of agricultural workers fell from 21 percent in 1970 to 10 percent in 1990, the number of farmers decreased from 43,000 to 29,000, and farms dropped from 45,500 to 33,000. The average farm size increased from 920 acres in 1970 to 1,224 acres in 1993. U.S. Air Force bases and Minuteman missile silo complexes were another example of federal dependence. In the 1980s the proportion of the labor force in the military was almost twice the national average.

North Dakotans continued to favor Republicans for president, but in the late 1980s most officials were Democrats. Voters regularly reelected U.S. senators of either party whose seniority brought federal dollars home. Senator Milton R. Young, a conservative Republican in office from 1945 to 1980, gained the nickname "Mr. Wheat" for his devotion to North Dakota's agricultural interests. The liberal Democratic Senator Quentin N. Burdick (1960–1992), Young's political opposite on almost every issue, earned similar distinction. National legislators continued to hold town hall meetings to gauge public opinion and keep voters informed. State politics retained a populist streak, with minimum voter registration procedures and high voter turnout. Permissive initiative and referendum requirements allowed direct participation in lawmaking, and citizens had sometimes restructured the tax system to the dismay of legislators.

Energy development was a veritable economic roller coaster after 1970. Production expanded of lignite, a soft, low-sulfur coal found close to the surface and ideal for strip mining. The construction of enormous lignite-powered electrical-generation plants, exporting electricity to neighboring states, caused a steady increase in tons of coal mined, from 5 million in 1970 to 32 million in 1992. Crude oil production was 22 million barrels in 1970 and remained stable until the late 1970s, when it increased dramatically. It peaked at 52.7 million barrels in 1984, then fell to 32.9 million by 1992, as the world price of crude oil collapsed. The reduction devastated western North Dakota, leaving many towns with rows of empty houses and abandoned businesses. On the other hand, North Dakotans prided themselves on their high quality of life. In 1991 the state had the lowest violent crime rate and the third-highest rate of church membership in the nation. The proverbial "good place to raise children," it had reasonable taxes, wide-open spaces, clean air, and friendly people.

[*North Dakota Centennial Blue Book, 1889–1989* (Bismarck, 1989); University of North Dakota, Bureau of Business and Economic Research, *Statistical Abstract of*

North Dakota, 1988, 3rd ed. (Grand Forks, 1988); Robert P. Wilkins and Wynona Huchette Wilkins, *North Dakota: A Bicentennial History* (New York, 1977).]

LARRY R. PETERSON

NPR. *See* **National Public Radio.**

NRA. *See* **National Rifle Association.**

NRC. *See* **Nuclear Regulatory Commission.**

NSF. *See* **National Science Foundation.**

NUCLEAR POWER, in physics, refers to energy produced by fission, when atoms are split, or by fusion, when two nuclei of a light atom are fused to form a single nucleus. The energy produced can be used for weapons or for peaceful purposes. The phrase is also used to designate those nations that have nuclear weapons. The nations that have declared they have nuclear weapons are China, France, the former Soviet Union, Great Britain, and the United States. The breakup of the Soviet Union in the early 1990s resulted in the addition of Byelarus, Kazakhstan, and Ukraine as nuclear-weapon states because the nuclear missiles and storage sites placed on their territory by the Soviet Union became the property of these newly independent states. All three have declared their intention to transfer their weapons to Russia. In addition, a number of nations, such as India, Pakistan, and North Korea, are believed to have the capacity to develop nuclear weapons within a few months. Others, such as Israel, are suspected of having developed one or more such weapons secretly.

Nuclear power also refers to plants and industry that generate electric power from nuclear sources. Nuclear power plants differ from hydroelectric plants, which generate electricity from the force of flowing water, and coal-, oil-, or gas-fired electric plants, which generate electricity from the heat drawn from burning fossil fuels. Nuclear power plants generate steam to drive electric turbines by circulating liquid through a nuclear reactor. The reactor produces heat through the controlled fission of atomic fuel. Normally the fuel for power reactors is slightly enriched uranium. In 1951 the U.S. Atomic Energy Commission built the first nuclear reactor to generate electric power. The increasing availability of uranium ore at that time and the resulting reduction in price of this essential fuel increased interest in commercial exploitation of the new technology. Nuclear reactors have several advantages over power generation using other fuels. Unlike fossil fuels, nuclear fuel does not foul the air and is not dependent on oil imports from unstable parts of the world. The rising costs of the world's diminishing coal, oil, and natural gas resources and the limitation on the number of hydroelectric power plants that can be built could be overcome by nuclear plants. The attraction of electricity generated by nuclear power was not limited to the United States. Industrial and some developing nations embarked on ambitious programs of their own. By 1966 nuclear power generators were being built or operating in five countries. By the beginning of the 1980s there were 100 nuclear power plants in the United States.

One of the by-products of nuclear power generation is plutonium, a material that can be chemically processed for use in nuclear weapons. The danger of such use by nonnuclear nations led to international safeguards under the 1968 Nuclear Nonproliferation Treaty. In Article III signatory nations agreed to inspections by the International Atomic Energy Agency (IAEA), "with a view to preventing diversion of nuclear energy from peaceful uses to nuclear weapons or other nuclear explosive devices." Most of the world's nuclear and nonnuclear nations signed this treaty. Iraq in 1992 and North Korea in 1994 were subjected to IAEA inspections that proved treaty violations in the former and raised serious suspicions about the latter. Both nations were signatories of the treaty, although North Korea announced its withdrawal some months prior to inspection. Iraq's nuclear-weapon production facilities were discovered as a result of a series of highly intrusive IAEA inspections and were subsequently destroyed by the United Nations.

When Congress passed the Atomic Energy Act of 1954, it approved President Dwight D. Eisenhower's Atoms for Peace program, which included commercial development of nuclear reactors for the purpose of generating electric power. During the 1960s electricity generated by nuclear power contributed 1 to 2 percent of the nation's energy total. Since then that percentage has grown steadily, surpassing the proportion from hydroelectric sources in 1984. By 1990 nuclear power amounted to one-fifth of the nation's total generation of electricity. By 1992 nuclear generation reached 619 billion net kilowatt hours, more than double the amount generated in 1979, when the Three Mile Island accident produced an adverse effect on U.S. development of nuclear power plants.

NUCLEAR REGULATORY COMMISSION

In reaction to the 1973 oil embargo, U.S. consumers temporarily used less energy, which diminished the rate of growth in electricity generation. As a result of this and other factors, such as higher construction costs, delays brought on by antinuclear protests, increased operating costs resulting from new federal regulations, and uncertainties about disposal of high-level radioactive waste, no requests for construction of new nuclear power plants had been received by the Nuclear Regulatory Commission since 1978. The level of generation was still rising, however, because plants started in the 1970s had gone on-line, and modernization after 1979 made power plants more efficient. The rising production trend was expected to continue until the beginning of the twenty-first century, then level off and begin to fall, unless more nuclear plants were built.

[Department of Energy, Energy Information Administration, *Annual Energy Outlook 1994* (Washington, D.C., 1994), and *1992 Energy Facts* (Washington, D.C., 1993); Daniel Deudney and Christopher Flavin, *Renewable Energy: The Power to Choose* (New York, 1983); Peter Mannfield, *World Nuclear Power* (New York, 1991).]

ROBERT M. GUTH

See also **SUPP:** Arms Race and Disarmament; Energy Industry; Energy Policy; Hazardous Waste; Nuclear Regulatory Commission; Strategic Arms Limitations Talks; Three Mile Island.

NUCLEAR REGULATORY COMMISSION (NRC). The attraction of nuclear power has been dimmed since its beginnings by the danger of accidents. Governments faced a dilemma between promoting what was for many years seen as the promise of clean and cheap power and the need to regulate commercial development to protect public safety and the environment. The Nuclear Regulatory Commission was created as the U.S. government's regulator. Established under the Energy Reorganization Act of 1974, it inherited licensing and regulatory authority from its predecessor, the Atomic Energy Commission. The NRC licenses and regulates the construction and operation of civilian nuclear reactors and the possession, use, processing, handling, and disposal of nuclear materials. It issues rules and standards to protect public health and safety and the environment from the dangers of commercial nuclear programs and inspects them for adherence to NRC rules. The five commissioners are appointed by the president (who also selects the chair) for five-year terms. A maximum of three commissioners may be of the same political party. The NRC's major program responsibilities are administered by the Offices of Nuclear Reactor Regulation and Nuclear Material Safety and Safeguards. Field operations are conducted from regional offices in Atlanta, Philadelphia, Chicago, Dallas, and San Francisco. NRC headquarters is in Bethesda, Md. The Office of Nuclear Reactor Regulation licenses construction and operation of nuclear reactors and seeks to ensure their safe and environmentally sound operation. Since the late 1970s, however, applications for new construction of nuclear power plants have dwindled to the point where safety of operations and environmental inspections and reviews have become the office's principal business. The Office of Nuclear Material Safety and Safeguards oversees uranium mines, mills, and recovery facilities for the proper processing, handling, transportation, storage, and prevention of theft and sabotage of nuclear materials. The Office of Nuclear Regulatory Research develops safety and environmental standards for the operation of nuclear facilities and management of nuclear waste. It sponsors research on which to base standards and to support the NRC's responsibilities for evaluating accidents and predicting risk.

Established to relieve tension between the development and regulation of nuclear power, the NRC found itself divided between responsibilities for safety and environmental protection and the profitability of the nuclear power industry. Public confidence in nuclear power was undermined by the Mar. 28, 1979, accident at the Three Mile Island nuclear plant near Harrisburg, Pa., in which a cooling-system failure of one reactor led to a partial exposure of its uranium core, threatening an explosion and wide release of radioactivity until the crisis was contained twelve days later. The NRC received scathing criticism for lax enforcement and poor preparation for emergencies from the commission investigating the accident. Inevitably more stringent regulation followed, leading to increased costs for new plants. Industry budgets had to deal with lengthening start-up times that were already seen as excessive and account for expensive cleanup in the event of another accident. As of 1995 no applications to build new commercial nuclear power plants had been received since the 1979 accident and projects for the construction of new plants were abandoned in the 1980s. The cost of electricity produced by earlier plants and those completed since the accident rose steadily into the 1990s and were projected to continue rising. Environmental concerns linked to fossil fuels may well drive costs of nonnuclear power generation up to the point where nuclear generation again may look commercially attractive.

[Philip L. Catelon and Robert C. Williams, *Crisis Contained: The Department of Energy at Three Mile Island* (Carbondale, Ill., 1982); Fred Clement, *The Nuclear Regulatory Commission* (New York, 1989); Union of Concerned Scientists, *Safety Second* (Bloomington, Ind., 1987).]
ROBERT M. GUTH

See also **DAH:** Atomic Energy Commission; **SUPP:** Energy, Department of; Energy Industry; Energy Research and Development Administration; Hazardous Waste; Nuclear Power; Three Mile Island.

NUCLEAR WASTE. *See* **Hazardous Waste.**

NURSING. Since the 1960s nurses have expanded their knowledge, practice, and independence. With congressional legislation authorizing Medicare and Medicaid, enormous numbers of people sought primary-care services. Aware that there were not enough physicians, Congress authorized federal funding to hospitals, clinics, and schools of nursing that offered training in ambulatory, primary care to nurses. In the ensuing years, certified nurse practitioners (CRNPs) developed specialties in pediatrics, geriatrics, and women's health, joining nurse-midwives, visiting nurses, and nurse-anesthetists who had practiced more independently than other nurses from the early years of the twentieth century. Nurses' roles in the acute care of hospitalized patients also enlarged. Advances in medical science and technology from World War II greatly increased the invasiveness of procedures and risk to patients of hospital care. Nurses and physicians worried about patients residing unobserved in semiprivate rooms, as patients utilized the coverage offered by health-insurance plans to avoid hospitalization in wards. Nurses responded by grouping their sickest patients in areas that could be more intensely monitored. The first such arrangements took the form of recovery rooms following surgery. Coronary-care units followed, and by the 1990s critical-care units existed for patients with almost every kind of organ dysfunction. Intensive nursing care gave these units their character, and critical care evolved as a specialty of expert nurses. The American Association of Critical Care Nurses, founded in 1969, began the journal *Heart and Lung* and rapidly became nursing's largest specialty organization.

The two major nursing fields started to merge in the 1990s. Hospitals began to hire nurse practitioners in specialties as substitutes for medical house staff

residents. Clinical nurse specialists began to develop physical examination and diagnostic skills. Hospitals thus hired nurses to deliver medical services and often chose minimally trained substitutes to give nursing care. In the 1960s the American Nurses' Association and the National League for Nursing recommended the baccalaureate degree for beginning professional nurses. Community college and hospital program graduates were to be designated "technical nurses." Licensed practical nurses would continue to graduate from hospital and high school programs. State legislatures balked at passing such proposals, and by 1994 only North Dakota had passed the legislation. Although enrollments in programs that prepared registered nurses reached an all-time high of 257,983 in 1992 (from 230,803 in 1973), only 102,128 were baccalaureate enrollees, 132,603 were associate degree candidates, and 23,252 were hospital diploma program participants. Men comprised 12 percent of these enrollees, up from 7 percent a decade earlier. Meanwhile, graduate nursing programs were increasing. In 1973 eight doctoral programs in nursing enrolled 375 students. By 1992 fifty-four doctoral programs had 2,727 students enrolled. By the mid-1990s employers generally required nursing researchers, educators, and administrators to hold doctorates.

[Barbara Melosh, *"The Physician's Hand": Work Culture and Conflict in American Nursing* (Philadelphia, 1982); Susan M. Reverby, *Ordered to Care: The Dilemma of American Nursing* (New York, 1987).]
ELLEN D. BAER

See also **DAH:** Medical Education; Nursing; **SUPP:** Health Care; Physician Assistants.

NUTRITION. While the federal government continued its food-stamp and Women, Infants, and Children food-aid programs in the last quarter of the twentieth century, nutritional emphasis in the United States had changed since the 1970s. The government and scientific groups, such as the National Academy of Sciences, raised alarms about the effects of poor diets on health, while pharmaceutical companies promoted megavitamins and weight-reduction diets. Beginning in 1973 the Food and Drug Administration required exact nutrient labeling of all foods with added nutrients or nutritional claims. In 1977 the Senate Select Committee on Nutrition and Human Needs established quantitative goals for consumption of protein, carbohydrates, fat, fatty acids, cholesterol, sugars, and sodium. Nutritionists disagreed with some of the findings, and the U.S. Department of Agriculture

(USDA) found it impossible at the time to use the 1977 goals to revise its food guide, which had been in existence since 1916. The goals induced the department to pay more attention to health and to make more specific dietary recommendations to the public. Consequently, the department issued a series of dietary guidelines for maintenance of a healthy weight and a diet with a variety of foods, low in fat and cholesterol, and moderate in sugar, sodium, and alcoholic beverages.

Interest in promoting quantitative nutritional information prevailed. In 1990 Congress passed the Nutrition Labeling and Education Act, which required processed-food labels to state the amounts of daily intake of nutrients. The USDA had been working on the revision of its food guide for several years and issued its new food guide "pyramid" in 1992. This new daily guide and an accompanying brochure increased the categories of foods and drinks from four to six. The department recommended fats, oils, and sweets (sparingly); milk, yogurt, and cheese (two to three servings); meat, poultry, fish, dry beans, eggs, and nuts (two to three servings); vegetables (three to five servings); fruits (two to four servings); and bread, cereal, rice, and pasta (six to eleven servings). Of all the nutritional issues raised during this period, cholesterol received most attention from biomedical researchers. The Nobel Prize–winning (1985) cholesterol research of Doctors Michael S. Brown and Joseph Goldstein of the University of Texas Health Science Center in Dallas led to an understanding of the genetic involvement of cholesterol and ultimately to treatment for high blood cholesterol. Studies of cholesterol culminated in a 1985 conclusion by a conference sponsored by the National Institutes of Health that lowering blood cholesterol could prevent heart disease.

Consumption of excess fat also aroused concern. A 1991 survey of U.S. high school students by the Centers for Disease Control showed that a median of 69 percent reported eating two or fewer servings of high fat foods each day. The federal government established national health objectives for persons over two years of age to reduce fat in their diets and increase complex carbohydrate and fiber-containing foods. Meanwhile, the American Cancer Society listed among its goals a desire to bring up to 80 percent the proportion of teenagers eating no more than two servings a day of high fat foods. Thus, while Americans received more information about nutrition by the 1990s, the results seemed uncertain. One-third of all Americans were overweight, according to statistics released in 1994; reduction of fat consumption did not solve weight problems because sugars and carbohydrates also add weight to the consumer.

[J. Campana, "Participation in School Physical Education and Selected Dietary Patterns Among High School Students—United States, 1991," *Journal of the American Medical Association* 268 (Sept. 16, 1992); Susan O. Welsh et al., *USDA's Food Guide* (Hyattsville, Md., 1993); Jack Zeev Yetiv, *Popular Nutritional Practices* (Toledo, Ohio, 1986).]

RUTH ROY HARRIS

See also **SUPP:** Food, Fast; Health Food Industry.

O

OAKLAND, a major California urban area located on San Francisco Bay's east shore and the thirty-ninth largest city in the United States, had a population of 372,242 in 1990. African Americans made up 44 percent of the population and white residents one-third. The Asian (15 percent) and Hispanic (14 percent) communities have grown rapidly since the 1970s. Originally home to the Ohlone people, the area now comprising Oakland was included in an 1820 Spanish land grant given to Don Luis Maria Peralta. A supply and departure point for the 1849 gold rush, Oakland was chartered in 1852 and incorporated as a city in 1854. Selected as the western terminus of the first transcontinental railroad in 1869, the city grew as an industrial center in the early twentieth century. Attracting residents and businesses from across the bay following the 1906 earthquake, Oakland's growth accelerated during World War I and after the completion of the San Francisco–Oakland Bay Bridge in 1936. As a port for container ships and a railroad terminus, it serves as a link for Pacific trade. Although propelled by the World War II boom, Oakland has struggled since the 1960s. While manufacturing still accounts for one of every five jobs, plant closings and cutbacks cost the city 20 percent of its manufacturing jobs in the 1980s. Job growth was in the public sector and low-paying service and retail sectors. The local school system, suffering from inadequate resources, racial tensions, and mismanagement, was taken over by the state in 1989. Responding to neighborhood deterioration and declining public services, officials and residents initiated a variety of neighborhood organizations and development projects, such as Preservation Park. Oakland's troubles were compounded by the earthquake of 1989, during which the Nimitz Freeway collapsed, and wildfires in 1991. A center for African-American culture and politics, Oakland was the birthplace of the Black Panther Party in 1966. Since the 1970s African-American politicians have led the city government (Mayors Lionel Wilson and Elihu Harris) and represented Oakland in Congress (Democrat Ron Dellums). The city hosts a number of African-American museums and performing arts groups, as well as a variety of ethnic festivals. Oakland benefits from a temperate climate, striking natural features such as Lake Merritt, and ties to nearby cities through a complex of freeways, bridges, and the Bay Area Rapid Transit system.

[Beth Bagwell, *Oakland: The Story of a City* (Novato, Calif., 1982); Marilyn S. Johnson, *The Second Gold Rush: Oakland and the East Bay in World War II* (Berkeley, Calif., 1993).]

ERIC FURE-SLOCUM

See also **DAH** and **SUPP:** California; San Francisco; **SUPP:** Earthquakes.

OBSERVATORIES. In the first half of the twentieth century, U.S. astronomers were the world champions among builders of large telescopes. The 100-inch reflector at Mount Wilson Observatory, near Los Angeles, was a technological marvel when it opened in 1917. In 1948 a 200-inch reflector was completed at the Palomar Observatory outside San Diego. Astronomers continued to want larger telescopes to examine fainter and more distant celestial objects. Unfortunately, the technology of the 1950s through 1970s was not up to the task. Russian astronomers built a

236-inch telescope in the mid-1970s, but it proved too massive and unwieldy, and offered less-than-ideal performance. Later technology ushered in a new era of large-telescope building. In 1979 scientists at the University of Arizona and the Smithsonian Astrophysical Observatory completed the multiple-mirror telescope on Mount Hopkins near Tucson, Ariz. It combines six 72-inch mirrors into one instrument with the light-gathering power of a 176-inch telescope but the weight of the smaller one at Mount Wilson. Other new designs incorporate largely hollow, honeycomb (hexagonal) mirrors; very thin mirrors; or giant mirrors made from many smaller pieces. · Simple, lightweight mountings controlled by computers can maintain the mirrors' precise optical shapes and keep the entire telescope pointed at a celestial target for hours at a time. By the year 2000 there should be at least ten telescopes around the world with apertures ranging from 250 to 630 inches. All but two will be built mainly by U.S. astronomers, although some will be located in other countries to study parts of the sky not visible from the United States. In 1991 the W. M. Keck Telescope atop Mauna Kea, Hawaii, became the world's largest at about 400 inches. A twin telescope (Keck II) was scheduled to open on the same site in 1996. Plans were drawn up in the early 1990s for the National Optical Astronomy Observatories to build two 300-inch reflectors, one each in the Northern and Southern Hemispheres, in the hope that astronomers could use these and other glass giants to solve cosmic mysteries.

[Kevin Krisciunas, *Astronomical Centers of the World* (New York, 1988).]

RICHARD TRESCH FIENBERG

See also **DAH:** Observatories, Astronomical; **DAH** and **SUPP:** Astronomy.

OCEANOGRAPHIC SURVEYS. Since the mid-nineteenth century oceanographic surveys for military, scientific, and commercial purposes by major countries of the world have proliferated, with the United States leading these efforts. Investigations have included the water masses, ocean floor, and ocean surface. Surveys by the U.S. Naval Oceanographic Office have covered a large portion of the major oceans. Since the 1970s massive data-gathering efforts have been made with great navigational precision. The U.S. military has employed satellites to measure ocean surface characteristics. Results are largely classified, although some of that data has been included in the maps and charts of the U.S.

Navy and the National Oceanic and Atmospheric Administration (NOAA). Information acquired by non-military agencies and research groups has rivaled the amount collected by the military. In the mid-1990s academic researchers in the United States had available twenty-six research vessels and several research submarines as well as data from satellites of NOAA and the National Aeronautics and Space Administration. The U.S. Geological Survey published detailed bathymetric surveys (measurement of water depth) of much of the United States Exclusive Economic Zone, an area that extends 300 miles off the Atlantic, Gulf, Pacific, Alaskan, and Bering Sea coasts. Spatial locations are accurate to a few tens of meters. Data taken by the military services is deposited with the Defense Mapping Agency with offices in and near Washington, D.C. Federally funded civilian agencies or groups deposit their data at appropriate national archives, which include the National Geophysical Data Center (Boulder, Colo.), the National Oceanographic Data Center (Washington, D.C.), and the National Space Science Data Center (Greenbelt, Md.).

J. R. HEIRTZLER

See also **DAH:** Oceanographic Survey; **DAH** and **SUPP:** Oceanography.

OCEANOGRAPHY. Oceanographic science is divided into the subfields of physical, chemical, and biological oceanography and marine geology and geophysics. As an exact science oceanography began in the latter part of the nineteenth century when activities were directed at learning the depth of the oceans, their systems of currents and water masses, and major chemical and biological components. During World War II it became essential to understand the acoustic transmission properties of ocean waters for submarine warfare and to predict sea surface conditions for ocean ship traffic. In contrast, coastal oceanographic studies have always differed from deep-water oceanography because they are concerned with erosion and coastal damage. By the late 1950s a large amount of marine geophysical data had been collected, including measurements of the ocean floor's sediment thickness, magnetic field anomalies, and heat flow from the floor. With new knowledge about internal currents of the oceans, calculations of mass and energy balance could be made. The Global Positioning System, a method of determining one's latitude and longitude precisely by observing signals from U.S. Navy satellites whose orbits are accurately known, allowed a new precision (to a few dozen meters) in open-water navigation, and computers organized these data. It was possible to confirm theoretical ideas of sea floor spreading and continental drift.

In 1964 oceanographers initiated the Deep Sea Drilling Project, originally a cooperative endeavor between four U.S. oceanographic institutions. It was enlarged and sponsored by many U.S. institutions and several foreign governments. A large, specially equipped ship was used to drill holes of up to several kilometers in the ocean floors of the world. Drill cores were analyzed to determine ocean sediments and to reconstruct their history. This project, continued under the title of Ocean Drilling Project, has bored several thousand holes. Because ocean sediments have been laid down in a systematic manner and are less disturbed than sediments on land, core analysis has yielded much information on paleoceanography and paleoclimatology. Global change has been an important area of investigation since the 1960s, when man-made changes in the earth's atmosphere became evident. The oceans are believed to be an important sink (carbon is taken from the air by ocean surface water, which then sinks, thereby reducing carbon in the air) in the global carbon cycle, regulating the greenhouse effect. Oceanographers have also been observing a coupling of oceanic and atmospheric effects in the South Pacific called El Niño, which has far-reaching effects on fishing and climate.

In the 1970s oceanographers discovered geothermal vents at the axis of the midocean ridges. Ocean chemists and biologists found organisms there that receive nourishment directly from hydrogen sulfide rather than from photosynthetic processes. In another development, satellites that scan ocean color and temperature have enabled biologists to determine much about the biological productivity of the ocean surface layer. In the 1980s and 1990s an effort developed to coordinate oceanic cruises with special oceanic satellites. The cruises ensured temporal and global coverage (measuring all of the oceans at all times), while satellites recorded the variability of oceanic surface and atmospheric conditions. It was thereby possible to determine the elevation of the surface (accurate to a few centimeters), analyze ocean currents and their eddies, and learn details of the ocean floor as reflected in the shape of the ocean surface.

[National Research Council, *Oceanography in the Next Decade: Building New Partnerships* (Washington, D.C., 1992).]

J. R. HEIRTZLER

See also **SUPP:** Oceanographic Surveys.

OFFICE TECHNOLOGY evolved rapidly, beginning in the 1970s, and incorporated ever greater automation, principally through computers. The result was greater productivity as well as changes in work patterns. Offices have long relied upon telephones, copiers, and calculators, and when commercial computers appeared in the 1950s businesses were early customers for so-called mainframes, which are large devices that serve multiple users simultaneously and can store large quantities of data. Advancing technology has replaced mainframe computers in many offices. The first replacement was the minicomputer, smaller and less expensive than mainframes but still serving multiple users. In the 1980s microcomputers, also known as personal computers, supplanted mainframes and minicomputers. A personal computer generally has only one user, although advances in networks now allow users to communicate easily and share data. In 1977 Apple Computer introduced the first in a series of highly popular personal computers. International Business Machines (IBM), long the dominant maker of mainframes, launched its first personal computer in 1981. Although IBM computers have not captured a dominant share of the market, other companies copied IBM's technical standards. IBM-compatible computers and software prevail in U.S. offices today. Because of the large investment that companies have made in hardware, software, and employee training, IBM compatibles are likely to retain their market domination.

Early personal computers had only rudimentary capabilities, but engineers have radically improved the chip inside the device that serves as its processing unit. A typical computer on an office desk in the mid-1990s had more power than a 1960s-era mainframe. The wider availability of hardware also encouraged new software. A key example is the spreadsheet, developed for personal computers, which manipulates numerical data, such as in preparation of a budget. Spreadsheets can now accommodate text and graphics. The first spreadsheet was Lotus 1-2-3, which captured the lion's share of the market after 1982. Personal computers equipped with word-processing software and printers have virtually replaced typewriters. A computer can store an electronic copy of a document, making it easy to revise without retyping. Word-processing software frequently includes spell-checkers, which search for misspelled words and typographical errors. Another category of software attributable to the rise of personal computers is desktop publishing, in which an operator can produce a professional-quality document, such as a newsletter or book, that incorporates text, pictures, and graphics, without conventional printing equipment. Yet another type of office software is the database program, which stores information in retrievable fashion. Databases were available in some mainframes, but it was not until the advent of personal computers that software allowed searches for information that met wide specifications. The first database developed for personal computers was dBase, which became one of the most popular computer programs.

Another milestone in office technology was xerography, a copying process used in most photocopying machines. Xerox Corporation's 914 copier, the first xerographic office copier, appeared in 1959 and made seven copies per minute. Advances in computers and electronics breathed new life into the facsimile (fax) machine, developed early in the century. In the 1980s technology expanded the capability of fax machines, and industry-wide design standards ensured that virtually all fax machines could communicate with one another, transmitting pictures and text digitally over telephone wires. Developments in computers and telecommunications led to voice mail, answering machines shared by all telephones in offices that offer individualized messages for each phone, and electronic mail (E-mail), messages sent between computer users via a computer data network. Advances in miniaturization of electronic components made possible mobile devices, such as the laptop computer, the beeper, and the hand-held cellular phone. New techniques for mass-producing inexpensive communication satellites have encouraged companies to plan global satellite networks that allow executives to communicate with home offices at any time from any point on the planet.

[U.S. Congress, Office of Technology Assessment, *Automation of America's Offices* (Washington, D.C., 1985).]

VINCENT KIERNAN

See also **SUPP:** Communications Industry; Computers; Electronic Mail; Internet; Telecommunications.

OFFSHORE OIL and gas development in the United States since the mid-1970s has been shaped largely by tensions generated by the efforts of the federal government to reduce dependence on foreign oil on one hand and pressures from environmentalists and conservationists to reduce energy consumption, especially of fossil fuels, on the other. Except during the Arab oil embargo of 1973–1974 and the U.S. embargo on Iranian oil, in effect from 1979 to 1981, the trend in the industry has been toward low prices and

oversupply of foreign crude oil. It was not until the oil shocks of the 1970s that there was an incentive to expand offshore exploration and production. With the low prices that have prevailed since 1986, expensive and labor-intensive recovery techniques have lost their economic feasibility. Since the 1970s U.S. energy policy has emphasized environmental protection and the conservation of U.S. reserves. The federal government has developed stringent environmental regulations governing the exploration and development of offshore crude oil fields in the lower forty-eight states and in Alaska. Opposition to offshore drilling is strong, especially in California, where there are large untapped offshore reserves. As early as 1975 California's State Lands Commission halted drilling of fifty-three offshore wells in the Santa Barbara Channel, and the National Energy Policy Act of 1992 came close to banning offshore drilling. Federal regulations imposed a leasing moratorium on sections of the Outer Continental Shelf and in the Arctic National Wildlife Refuge east of Alaska's Prudhoe Bay.

[Michael L. Godec and Khosrow Biglarbig, "Economic Effects of Environmental Regulations on Finding and Developing Crude Oil in the U.S.," *Journal of Petroleum Technology* 43 (1991).]

STEPHEN J. RANDALL

See also **DAH** and **SUPP:** Petroleum Industry; **SUPP:** Energy, Renewable; Energy Policy; Oil Crises.

OHIO entered the 1970s after three decades of economic and population growth, propelled by World War II and the postwar expansion of its large industrial sector. Employment peaked in 1967, however, and by the early 1990s had declined by more than 25 percent. Although Ohio's 1990 population of more than 10.8 million was slightly higher than it had been twenty years earlier, the state dropped in rank to seventh place, falling behind Texas and Florida. With the decline of the steel, automobile, and rubber industries, large industrial cities such as Cleveland, Akron, and Youngstown lost population. Only the state capital, Columbus, countered the downward urban trend, thanks in part to aggressive annexation of suburbs. Despite some gentrification—the return of middle- and upper-income persons to restored neighborhoods—Ohio's largest cities followed the national pattern of housing a disproportionate number of the poor and unskilled. Increasingly, jobs as well as people migrated to the suburbs, which now include retail and commercial centers that equal or even eclipse the older downtown core areas. Ohio's central cities responded by trying to revitalize downtown areas with office, retail, and residential construction. Success was mixed but certain entertainment and business activities remained uniquely situated in urban centers, ensuring continued vitality.

The quest for economic development has been a theme in state politics since 1970. Political leaders used incentives, such as tax concessions, employee training, and infrastructure improvements, to hold on to old industries while luring in new ones. These efforts did not completely reverse underlying trends, but there were notable successes, such as the decision of the Japanese carmaker Honda to locate most of its U.S. manufacturing in Ohio in the early 1980s. Much of this job growth occurred in rural and small-town areas where pressures for unionization and higher wage levels were weaker.

Historically, Ohio politics have followed moderately conservative lines, and pragmatic considerations have been important. Known as a bellwether Republican state in the early twentieth century, Ohio began to shift toward the Democrats in the 1940s, and by the 1970s and 1980s the Democratic Party was leading the state in the direction of liberal reform. During the administration of Governor John J. Gilligan (1971–1975), Ohio joined other industrial states in levying a personal income tax. With the support of organized labor, Gilligan used the increased revenue to improve state services. In 1972 the Democrats gained control of the state legislature, and Vernal G. Riffe, Jr., speaker of the Ohio House of Representatives (1975–1994), became a powerful figure in allocating state resources. The popular Republican governor of the 1960s, James A. Rhodes, returned to office with a narrow victory over Gilligan in 1974. Rhodes's decision to send National Guard troops to quell student unrest at Kent State University in 1970, which culminated in the deaths of four students, tarnished his record as the longest-serving governor in Ohio history (1963–1971, 1975–1983). Ironically, a tremendous expansion in public higher education was one of his greatest achievements as governor. In the 1970s and 1980s he also emphasized economic development, such as negotiations with Honda and other Japanese firms. Democratic Governor Richard F. Celeste, elected in the midst of the severe economic recession of the early 1980s, emphasized further liberal reform, supporting a move to allow state employees to strike and increasing state programs. A former Rhodes scholar and Peace Corps director, he injected a new style into Ohio politics.

Scandals involving his political backers, such as the Home State Savings collapse in 1985 and some political appointments, tarnished his overall record.

At the national level Ohio's political leaders were not as prominent in leadership as in earlier times. In 1973, during the Watergate crisis, Senator William B. Saxbe resigned to become the last attorney general in President Richard M. Nixon's beleaguered administration, a position he retained during part of Gerald R. Ford's presidency. John H. Glenn, the first U.S. astronaut to orbit the Earth, became the first Ohio senator elected to a fourth consecutive term in 1992. He had made little headway, however, in his unsuccessful bid for the 1984 presidential nomination. The more liberal Howard M. Metzenbaum retired from the U.S. Senate in 1994 after three terms. Supported by organized labor and liberal interest groups, he often challenged business corporations. Lagging population growth between 1970 and 1992 reduced Ohio's delegation in the House of Representatives from twenty-four to nineteen.

Compared to other states, Ohio's moderate politics usually did not place it in the forefront of progressive innovation, but changes since the 1970s have led Ohioans to expect more help from government in enhancing the quality of life. One such area of concern has been environmental protection. By the late 1960s lack of attention had given Ohio a national reputation for dirty air and water, best symbolized by the "death" of Lake Erie and the 1969 fire on the Cuyahoga River in Cleveland. The state legislature created the Ohio Environmental Protection Agency, and in 1972 a strip mining reclamation program. By the 1990s billions of dollars had been spent on cleanups. Air quality showed improvement, especially in the heavily industrial Upper Ohio Valley. Concern remained about hazardous waste dumps (subject to regulation through the federal Superfund program) and the quality of drinking water. Still, Lake Erie and the state's rivers had improved so substantially that they were once again viable resources. In 1974 Congress established Ohio's first national park, the Cuyahoga Valley National Recreation Area, 32,512 acres of scenic gorge and forest land located near the 4 million residents of the Cleveland and Akron metropolitan areas.

Education was another area of concern to Ohioans. In the post–World War II era, Ohio led the national average in rates of high-school graduation but lagged in college attendance, a predictable pattern in a state with a large blue-collar workforce. State support for elementary and secondary education increased after 1970, but much of the money continued to come from local property taxes, with a resulting disparity between wealthier and poorer districts. Proceeds from the state lottery, begun in 1974, were earmarked for education but represented a small part of the state's contribution. Teachers demanded higher salaries and in some communities defied the ban on strikes. Problems involving finances, declining student achievement, drugs, and violence were acute in urban districts, but few if any schools were immune from such woes. In the 1990s judicial remedies were introduced to address the problem of inequitable funding. Beginning in 1994 high-school graduation was denied any Ohio student who failed mandated examinations in mathematics, reading, writing, and citizenship. Meanwhile, like most other states, Ohio attacked its crime problem with a massive increase in prison construction. In 1990 a Republican former mayor of Cleveland who had worked actively to revitalize that city in the 1980s, George V. Voinovich, succeeded Governor Celeste. Voinovich promised to "do more with less" by maintaining and managing state programs efficiently, without major tax increases. Republicans looked forward to the prospect of other electoral gains, as leading Democrats retired and others faced questions regarding conduct in office. The Ohio legislature passed a more stringent ethics enactment in 1994.

[George W. Knepper, *Ohio and Its People* (Kent, Ohio, 1989); Carl Lieberman, ed., *Government and Politics in Ohio* (Lanham, Md., 1984); Leonard Peacefull, ed., *The Changing Heartland: A Geography of Ohio* (Needham Heights, Mass., 1990).]

JOHN B. WEAVER

See also **SUPP:** Cincinnati; Cleveland; Columbus; Rustbelt; Superfund; Toledo.

OIL CRISES. In 1973–1974 and 1979 the United States experienced shortages of gasoline and other petroleum products because of reduced domestic oil production, greater dependence on imported oil, and political developments in the oil-rich Middle East. Historically, the United States had supplied most of its own oil, but in 1970 U.S. oil production reached full capacity. Imported oil, especially from the Middle East, rose from 19 percent of national consumption in 1967 to 36 percent in 1973. The Arab-Israeli War of 1973 contributed to the first oil crisis. At that time, Saudi Arabia controlled 21 percent of the world's oil exports. After Egypt and Syria attacked Israel in October and the United States came

to Israel's aid, oil ministers from the five Persian Gulf states and Iran cut their monthly production by 5 percent to discourage international support for Israel. They banned oil exports to Israel's allies, including the United States, the Netherlands, Portugal, South Africa, and Rhodesia (Zimbabwe). World oil prices jumped from $5.40 per barrel to more than $17. Retail gasoline prices in the United States increased 40 percent, and consumers often faced long lines at service stations. To conserve gasoline and oil, President Richard M. Nixon reduced the speed limit on national highways to 55 miles per hour and encouraged people to carpool and to lower their house thermostats. It was Israeli victories and U.S. arrangement of Arab-Israeli negotiations and not domestic programs, however, that helped end the embargo in March 1974.

The Organization of Petroleum Exporting Countries (OPEC) continued to keep world oil prices high, which slowed the world economy. In 1973–1975 the U.S. gross national product declined by 6 percent and unemployment doubled to 9 percent. The economies of Europe and Japan also suffered, but the developing countries that lacked money to pay for expensive oil suffered most. In 1975 Congress established fuel-efficiency standards for U.S. automobiles to reduce energy costs and dependency on foreign oil. President Jimmy Carter urged additional steps. By the late 1970s the United States was exploring both old (coal) and new (solar, thermal, and wind) sources of energy.

A second oil crisis followed the collapse of the government of the shah of Iran and suspension of Iran's oil exports in December 1978. Iran was the world's second-largest exporter of oil. If buyers, including oil companies, manufacturers, and national governments had not panicked, however, this second oil shortage would not have been so severe. Gasoline prices rose, and people again waited in lines at service stations. These factors, combined with the hostage crisis in Iran, contributed to President Carter's defeat in the 1980 election. The worst of the second crisis was over by 1980. In late 1985 a drop in world oil prices (from $32 to $10 per barrel) gave American consumers a sense that the crisis had ended, but concerns about the increasing U.S. dependence on foreign oil remained in the 1990s.

[Daniel Yergin, *The Prize: The Epic Quest for Oil, Money, and Power* (New York, 1991).]

KENNETH B. MOSS

See also **SUPP:** Energy Industry; Energy Policy; Hostage Crises; Middle East, Relations with; Petroleum Industry.

OIL INDUSTRY. *See* **Offshore Oil; Oil Crises; Petroleum Industry.**

OKLAHOMA, the Sooner state, lies between the Midwest and South, the Great Plains and the arid Southwest. The rolling, tree-covered hills of its eastern and southern counties resemble the Ozark regions of bordering Missouri and Arkansas. As it follows an upward slope to the north and west the land becomes more level, the rainfall much lighter, and the trees and streams scarce. The western and panhandle counties are extensions of the Texas plains and Kansas prairies. The entire western half is one of the nation's leading producers of winter wheat and beef cattle, both increasingly capital-intensive industries. Agriculture in the eastern section tends to be more diverse but less demanding of heavy investment. One consequence is that per capita incomes are almost always higher in western than in eastern counties. Ironically, although both areas lost population, the western counties were most affected by a steady depopulation trend that began with the Great Depression and accelerated thereafter. In both cases the migrants generally preferred to stay close to home, which is why Oklahoma City, Tulsa, and other cities experienced slow but consistent growth between 1970 and the mid-1990s. During that period the state population increased from just over 2.5 million to 3.1 million. Its Native American population (252,089 in 1990) was the largest in the nation.

Those years also witnessed a continuation of the state's familiar pattern of boom and bust economic cycles. Massive grain sales to the Soviet Union and others pushed wheat and other grain prices to near-record levels during the 1970s. At the same time, the 1973 Arab oil embargo and insatiable energy demands propelled crude oil prices to unheard-of levels. At the decade's end unemployment was all but nonexistent in the state, per capita income for the first time reached the national average, public services expanded, and teachers and other public employees moved toward competitive salaries.

All of that changed abruptly in the mid-1980s. International oil prices dropped from a 1978 high of $42 per barrel to $30.90 in November 1985. Within seven months, they slid to $10.25. Grain prices took similar hits as the price of wheat plummeted in a matter of months from $5.60 per bushel to $2.70 by the summer of 1986. The effects were felt in every sector of the state's economy. Oil industry jobs evaporated by the tens of thousands. Family farms, many of them dating to the famous nineteenth-century land runs, disappeared. Merchants and others dependent upon the regular flow of oil and wheat money went bankrupt. Before it was over, auto dealerships, implement sellers, entire shopping malls, and several dozen state banks all had gone under. The collapse of one of those banks—Oklahoma City's Penn Square Bank—was the first domino to fall in a chain of bank failures that went on to claim as its final and greatest casualty what had been the nation's fourth-largest bank, Continental Bank of Illinois.

The economic disorder magnified and accelerated changes already transforming state politics. With rare exceptions, Oklahoma had been part of the Democratic Solid South since it entered the Union in 1907. This pattern remained unchanged until Oklahoma's electoral votes went to Republican Dwight D. Eisenhower in the 1950s and then Richard M. Nixon in 1960. Subsequent elections proved these were no temporary aberrations. Lyndon B. Johnson returned Oklahoma to the Democratic column in 1964 as part of his national landslide, but Johnson proved to be the only Democrat to win Oklahoma's electoral votes between 1952 and 1992, a record of Republican support exceeded only by that of Arizona. "Presidential Republicanism" quickly became gubernatorial and senatorial Republicanism. Sooners elected their first Republican governor in 1962 and voted Republican in the next three gubernatorial elections. The GOP also claimed seven of the ten races for U.S. Senate seats between 1968 and 1995. In the latter year Republicans held the governorship, both Senate seats, and five of six House seats.

The shift in party dominance owed much to the increasingly conservative national mood and to Oklahoma's economic dislocations. During the boom years, the state coffers were full. When the collapse came, the government suddenly was confronted with a staggering $350 million annual shortfall. Disaster was averted only by two bitterly fought tax increases recommended by a Republican governor (Henry Bellmon) and approved by Democratic legislatures. Taxpayers thereupon exercised their traditionally populist aversion to taxes and politicians and amended the constitution to limit legislative terms and require voter approval of nearly all subsequent tax increases.

In the 1970s and 1980s voters were further angered by a series of political scandals. The largest of these involved the state's county commissioners, who fell victim to a Justice Department probe that uncovered years of systematic corruption, primarily involving contracting kickbacks. In all, between 1977 and

1987, 246 sitting officials were convicted of federal crimes, and a number of others were convicted of state offenses, including two governors, a speaker of the state house, and several state legislators, whose misdeeds ranged from election rigging to narcotics trafficking.

[W. David Baird and Danney Goble, *The Story of Oklahoma* (Norman, Okla., 1994); David R. Morgan, Robert E. England, and George G. Humphreys, *Oklahoma Politics and Policies* (Lincoln, Nebr., 1991); Howard F. Stein and Robert F. Hills, eds., *The Culture of Oklahoma* (Norman, Okla., 1993).]

DANNEY GOBLE

See also **SUPP:** Oklahoma City; Oklahoma City Bombing; Tulsa.

OKLAHOMA CITY, capital of the state of Oklahoma, sprang into existence with the land run of April 22, 1889, when more than 10,000 settlers established a tent city on the site in one day. From the beginning its government was dominated by businessmen, who scored a coup in 1910 when they wrested the state capital from Guthrie. With the discovery of oil in 1928, Oklahoma City's economy came to rest primarily on oil-related activities and its politics controlled by oilmen, bankers, and merchants. Since the 1970s fluctuating international oil prices created a boom-and-bust economic cycle. In politics Republicans asserted their domination of the city, using the rising prosperity to attract voters and then blaming the decline on Washington and Oklahoma's long tradition of Democratic rule. The population in 1990 was 450,000: 74 percent white, 16 percent African American, 5 percent Hispanic, and 4 percent Native American. Oklahoma City was rather typical of the nation's medium-sized cities, except that the median household income did not place it in the top 500 of U.S. cities.

[Odie B. Faulk et al., *Oklahoma City* (Northridge, Calif., 1988).]

DANNEY GOBLE

See also **DAH** and **SUPP:** Oklahoma; **SUPP:** Oklahoma City Bombing.

OKLAHOMA CITY BOMBING (April 19, 1995), in which a bomb composed of a fertilizer called ammonium nitrate mixed with fuel oil destroyed the Alfred P. Murrah federal building in Oklahoma City, Okla., killing 168 people, including fifteen children in a day-care center. The building housed branches of federal departments including the Bureau of Alcohol, Tobacco, and Firearms, thought initially to be the target of the bomb. The worst act of terrorism in U.S. history, the blast sent Americans into mourning and deep apprehension over civil disorder. President Bill Clinton led a national day of sorrow on Sunday, April 23. For seventeen days after the explosion rescue teams from around the nation combed the rubble seeking survivors and excavating bodies, often under hazardous conditions. Shortly after the blast Federal Bureau of Investigation agents arrested Timothy McVeigh, a former U.S. Army sergeant with extreme right-wing views, as the principal suspect in the bombing. McVeigh, authorities believed, rented a truck in Kansas, filled it with the combustible mixture, and drove it to Oklahoma City. He allegedly parked the truck in front of the Murrah building, lit the fuse, and walked away; witnesses identified him at the scene. Federal authorities believed he acted to avenge destruction of the Branch Davidian cult in Waco, Tex., which took place on the same date two years earlier, and because he feared federal revocation of the constitutional right to carry guns. On Aug. 16 McVeigh and a friend from his time in the army, Terry Nichols, were arraigned in federal court under extraordinary security; both pleaded not guilty to charges that they had carried out the terrorist attack in Oklahoma City. Another army friend, Michael Fortier, under threat of indictment, testified to government officials against McVeigh and Nichols. Fortier reportedly was promised lesser charges in exchange for testimony. After eliminating leads concerning other unknown participants (John Does) in the bombing, federal investigators declared that McVeigh and Nichols acted alone and not in conspiracy with any organization. Attorney General Janet Reno announced that the government would seek the death penalty if the pair were convicted. McVeigh's extreme views directed media attention to conservative radio talk-show hosts and "citizen militias" vowing to execute federal agents infringing Second Amendment Rights, although all disavowed any connection with the bombing. Incredibly, one talk-show host blamed the government for the explosion while another, G. Gordon Liddy, advised on the best methods to assassinate federal agents. The FBI sought links between McVeigh and far-right militia groups. President Clinton called for stronger antiterrorist laws, although support for additional statutes was lukewarm among Republicans and civil rights proponents.

GRAHAM RUSSELL HODGES

See also **SUPP:** Militias; Oklahoma City; Terrorism; Waco Siege.

OLYMPIC GAMES. By the 1970s the Olympics had become the largest multisport event in the world and through satellite technology attracted a worldwide television audience. The 1972 Olympic Winter Games were held in Sapporo, Japan, the first Winter Games awarded to an Asian city. Unprecedented achievement and controversy occurred at the 1972 Summer Games in Munich, Germany. U.S. swimmer Mark Spitz won a record seven gold medals, while his teammates lost the first-ever Olympic basketball game in a controversial gold medal contest with the Soviet Union. A tragic event cast a pall over the Munich games when on Sept. 5, 1972, Palestinian terrorists kidnapped and murdered eleven members of the Israeli team. Competition was suspended for an entire day, although a call to discontinue the games was ignored by International Olympic Committee (IOC) President Avery Brundage of the United States. Amid tight security, in 1976 a thousand athletes from thirty-seven countries gathered for the Winter Games at Innsbruck, Austria. The Summer Games later that year in Montreal were mired in debt and reduced international interest in hosting the Olympics. In the summer of 1978 the United States Olympic Committee (USOC) moved its headquarters from New York City to Colorado Springs. The Amateur Sports Act, enacted by Congress in 1978, named the USOC the coordinating body of sports in the Pan American Games and the Winter and Summer Olympics and recognized national governing bodies for sports in these competitions.

At the 1980 Winter Games in Lake Placid, N.Y., U.S. speed skater Eric Heiden won an unprecedented five gold medals, and the U.S. hockey team won its first gold medal in twenty years with a dramatic final-round victory over the Soviet Union. Because of the Soviet invasion of Afghanistan, President Jimmy Carter called for a boycott of the 1980 Moscow Summer Olympics. For the first time in modern Olympic history, the United States, joined by sixty-one other boycotting nations, did not participate.

A turning point in the Olympics occurred in 1984 when the Los Angeles Summer Olympics, although boycotted by the Soviet Union and most other eastern bloc countries, produced a $225 million profit, largely because of the contributions of commercial sponsors. Joan Benoit won the first women's Olympic marathon, and the U.S. women's basketball team claimed the first gold medal by the United States in that competition. The U.S. women's basketball team took the gold again in 1988, as did the men's basketball team in 1984 and 1992. Sprinter and long jumper Carl Lewis began his collection of Olympic gold medals by winning four in Los Angeles. He added two more gold medals and a silver medal in 1988 and claimed two more gold medals in 1992. Also at Los Angeles, Mary Lou Retton won the first gold medal in women's gymnastics. A highlight for the U.S. team during the 1984 winter competition, held in Sarajevo, Yugoslavia, was the gold medal victory in the men's figure skating competition by Scott Hamilton, who had begun ice skating as therapy for an intestinal disorder.

Four years later the games were held in Calgary, Alberta, Canada. For a decade Brian Boitano of the United States and Brian Orser of Canada had been figure skating rivals, and in 1988 both skaters presented exemplary performances, but Boitano edged out Orser for the gold medal. By the time of the 1988 Summer Olympics in Seoul, South Korea, professional athletes had become more visible in the Olympic movement. The IOC had decided to let professionals participate in the Olympic Games in an effort to attract the best athletes. Diver Greg Louganis became the second U.S. Olympian to achieve a "double-double," when he repeated his 1984 victories in springboard and platform diving at the Seoul Olympics. Louganis's springboard victory came a day after he accidentally hit and cut his head on the board during a dive, an event that gained significance in 1995, when Louganis revealed publicly that he was aware at the time that he was HIV-positive but did not inform the physicians who treated him. Also in 1988 Jackie Joyner-Kersee began her dominance of the heptathlon and made two additional Olympic appearances, winning two gold medals and a silver in the event.

The CBS television network paid $243 million for the rights to televise the 1992 Albertville Winter Games in France, while NBC paid a record $401 million to televise the 1992 Summer Olympics in Barcelona, Spain, the last time that summer and winter competitions were held in the same year. The IOC voted to separate the competitions by two years in order to generate more television revenue. In 1992 Kristi Yamaguchi became the first American woman since Dorothy Hamill to win an Olympic figure skating title. At the 1992 Summer Olympics in Barcelona the U.S. basketball team, composed of professional players (the "Dream Team"), won the gold medal.

Three-time gold medal winner Bonnie Blair became the leading gold medalist among American women when she won two more gold medals in speed skating at the 1994 Winter Games in Lillehammer, Norway. Tommy Moe became the first American downhill skiing gold medalist since Bill Johnson a decade earlier; he also won a silver medal in the super giant slalom. After two disappointing Olympic appearances, Dan Jansen, in his last Olympic race, finally reached the top of the medal podium, winning the 1,000-meter speed skating championship in Lillehammer. In an incident that attracted widespread attention in the weeks leading up to Lillehammer, U.S. figure skater Nancy Kerrigan was attacked during the Olympic trials and sustained a leg injury. The husband of rival U.S. figure skater Tanya Harding was later convicted of conspiring to injure Kerrigan. Because the USOC did not have evidence to implicate Tanya Harding, she was allowed to compete in Lillehammer. Kerrigan claimed her second singles silver medal, while Harding finished in sixth place. Harding was later implicated in the plot to injure Kerrigan and was expelled from the U.S. Figure Skating Association, thus ending her amateur career.

The 1996 centennial Olympics were awarded to Atlanta, Ga., and the 1998 Winter Games to Nagano, Japan.

U.S. gold medalists from 1984 to 1994 were:

Archery: Darrell Pace (1984); Jay Barrs (1988).

Boxing: Tyrell Biggs (1984); Mark Breland (1984); Paul Gonzales (1984); Steven McCrory (1984); Meldrick Taylor (1984); Jerry Page (1984); Frank Tate (1984); Henry Tillman (1984); Pernell Whitaker (1984); Andrew Maynard (1988); Kennedy McKinney (1988); Ray Mercer (1988); Oscar De La Hoya (1992).

Canoeing: Greg Barton (1988); Joe Jacobi and Scott Strausbaugh (1992).

Cycling: Connie Carpenter-Phinney (1984); Alexi Grewal (1984); Mark Gorski (1984); Steve Hegg (1984).

Diving: Greg Louganis (1984, 1988); Mark Lenzi (1992).

Equestrian: Karen Stives (1984); U.S. team jumping and three-day event team classification (1984).

Figure Skating: Scott Hamilton (1984); Brian Boitano (1988); Kristi Yamaguchi (1992).

Gymnastics: Mary Lou Retton (1984); Bart Conner (1984); Trent Diamas (1992).

Rowing: U.S. women's eight-oar team (1984).

Shooting: Pat Spurgin (1984); Matthew Dryke (1984); Edward Etzel (1984); Launi Meili (1992).

Skiing: Bill Johnson (1984); Phil Mahre (1984); Donna Weinbrecht (1992); Diann Roffe-Steinrotter (1994); Tommy Moe (1994).

Speed Skating: Eric Heiden (1980); Bonnie Blair (1988, 1992, 1994); Cathy Turner (1992, 1994); Dan Jansen (1994).

Swimming: Theresa Andrews (1984); Tracy Caulkins (1984); Tiffany Cohen (1984); Mary T. Meagher (1984); Carrie Steinseiffer (1984); Mary Wayte (1984); U.S. women's relay teams (1984, 1992); Janet Evans (1988, 1992); Nicole Haislett (1992); Summer Sanders (1992); Mike Barrowman (1992); Matthew Biondi (1984, 1988, 1992); Richard Carey (1984); George DiCarlo (1984); Steve Lindquist (1984); Pablo Morales (1984, 1992); Michael O'Brien (1984); U.S. men's relay teams (1984, 1988, 1992); Nelson Diebel (1992); Mel Stewart (1992).

Synchronized Swimming: Candy Costie (1984); Tracie Ruiz (1984); Kristen Bob-Sprague (1992); Karen and Sarah Josephson (1992).

Tennis: Zina Garrison (1988); Pam Shriver (1988); Ken Flach (1988); Robert Seguso (1988); Jennifer Capriati (1992); Gigi Fernandez (1992); Mary Jo Ferguson (1992).

Track and Field: Evelyn Ashford (1984, 1988, 1992); Joan Benoit (1984); Valerie Brisco-Hooks (1984); Benita Fitzgerald-Brown; Florence Griffith Joyner (1988); Jackie Joyner-Kersee (1988, 1992); Louise Ritter (1988); Gail Devers (1992); Gwen Torrence (1992); U.S. women's relay teams (1984, 1988, 1992); Alonzo Babers (1984); Al Joyner (1984); Roger Kingdom (1984, 1988); Carl Lewis (1984, 1988, 1992); Edwin Moses (1984); Joe DeLoach (1988), Steven Lewis (1988); Andre Phillips (1988); Mike Conley (1992); Mike Marsh (1992); Mike Stulce (1992); U.S. men's relay teams (1984, 1988, 1992); Quincy Watts (1992); Kevin Young (1992).

Wrestling: Ed Banach (1984); Lou Banach (1984); Bruce Baumgartner (1984, 1992); Jeffrey Blatnick (1984); Steven Fraser (1984); Randy Lewis (1984); David Schultz (1984); Mark Schultz (1984); Robert Weaver (1984); Kenneth Monday (1988); John Smith (1988, 1992); Kevin Jackson (1992).

Yachting: U.S. teams (1984, 1988, 1992).

[International Olympic Committee, *Olympic Charter* (Lausanne, Switzerland, 1992); U.S. Olympic Committee, *Legacy of Gold* (Clearwater, Fla., 1992).]

PAULA D. WELCH

See also **SUPP:** Sports, New; and individual sports.

OMAHA, founded on July 2, 1854, in the newly established Nebraska Territory at a ferry crossing on the Missouri River, was a frontier village when eastern capitalists selected it as the eastern terminus of the first transcontinental railroad, the Union Pacific, constructed between 1862 and 1869. Omaha, located across the Missouri River from Council Bluffs, Iowa, had no special natural advantages, but Omaha was at the start of the Mormon Trail and was the winter quarters for Mormon migrants heading for Utah in 1846–1848. Omaha served as the capital of the territory until 1867, when Nebraska became a state, and was incorporated as a city that same year. During the last quarter of the nineteenth century, the city became an important transportation and meat-packing center and overcame severe depression conditions in the 1890s. A symbol of Omaha's recovery was the highly successful Trans-Mississippi and International Exposition of 1898. Between 1900 and 1940 Omaha's population increased from 102,555 to 223,844, and the city endured social and racial tensions. In 1909 rioters drove several hundred Greek immigrants out of town, and in 1919 a mob estimated at 20,000 watched the brutal lynching of a suspected African-American rapist. A powerful political machine, headed by Thomas Dennison, dominated Omaha politics during the first thirty years of the twentieth century. The conservative business community fought hard but unsuccessfully to keep out unions. The economy surged following the outbreak of World War II, led by construction of a bomber plant that employed 20,000 workers. In the immediate postwar period the Strategic Air Command moved its headquarters to the Omaha area at Offutt Air Force Base. In the 1950s and 1960s new agribusiness endeavors contributed to the steady expansion of the private sector. Federal projects, especially highway construction, funneled great sums into Omaha. Although most of the packing plants closed in the 1960s, a large insurance industry flourished, and corporations established regional headquarters in Omaha. In 1990, with a population of 335,719, Omaha was the center of a metropolitan area of 639,580.

[Lawrence H. Larsen and Barbara J. Cottrell, *The Gate City: A History of Omaha* (Boulder, Colo., 1982).]

LAWRENCE H. LARSEN

See also **SUPP:** Nebraska.

OPEC. *See* **Middle East, Relations with; Oil Crises; Petroleum Industry.**

OPINION POLLS in the United States primarily involve measuring public views through surveys. Polling gained legitimacy after the 1936 presidential election, when three pollsters, including George H. Gallup, correctly predicted Franklin D. Roosevelt's victory. The *Literary Digest* incorrectly picked Roosevelt's opponent, basing its forecast on responses mailed in by 2 million Americans. The pollsters instead used scientific sampling, which established that predictions made from polling a small random sample, usually 1,200 people, can be equally or more valid than asking a million respondents. When pollsters incorrectly predicted the 1948 presidential election results, picking George Dewey over Harry S. Truman, it was not because samples were too small but because they were improperly drawn and thus not representative. The 1948 embarrassment led to procedures that resulted in increasing acceptance. Polling organizations now emphasize reliability, whether similar results would occur if the same survey was conducted repeatedly, and validity, whether the survey measured what it was designed to measure.

From its onset, polling raised concerns about the effect on voting and other public behavior. Some early critics argued that polls did not merely measure opinion but affected it. Later research found that while voters may be influenced by poll results early in a campaign, the effects decrease as election day nears. Many observers voiced concerns following the 1980 presidential election about exit polling, interviews conducted as people left voting sites, fearing that early reports of the results could affect voter turnout in later time zones. Although exit polls are still conducted, many feel that their impact has been exaggerated. Of greater concern during and since the presidency of Ronald Reagan (1981–1989) has been the inclusion of communication, polling, and media specialists in the White House who have become barriers between the president and the public. The combined expertise of these specialists, who favor nostalgic posturing, sound bites, and negative advertising, may be responsible for even lower voter turnout. After reaching new heights in the 1988 and 1992 presidential campaigns, negative ads and polls influenced by them became even more prevalent in the 1994 midterm elections when 70 percent of campaign budgets for national office went to media and polling consultants. "There's not a competitive race in the country that doesn't use a poll," Democratic pollster Mark Mellman said in 1994, adding, "You've got to point out the faults of your opponent or you'll get creamed." The marketing of modern politicians as though they were commercial products, using computerized mass mailings and phone banks, minimizes discussion of serious issues, dehumanizes politics, and devalues leadership. As of the mid-1990s neither the American people nor their elected representatives seemed prepared to question the impact of polling and negative advertising on the U.S. political system.

KATHLEEN B. CULVER

See also **DAH:** Public Opinion; **SUPP:** Campaigns, Presidential.

OPTICS, FIBER. *See* **Fiber Optics.**

OPTIONS EXCHANGES. In the increasingly complex U.S. financial markets, options are a major innovation. Option trading began in the United States in 1973 with the opening of the Chicago Board Option Exchange. The logic of the option market is simple but the dynamics are difficult for the average investor to understand. An option gives a purchaser the right to buy or sell a specified security (or commodity) during a particular time for a specific amount. An option is attractive to institutional investors who want to reduce risks by protecting against major price changes and market fluctuation. Options exchanges are in most major financial markets including those in New York, Chicago, Philadelphia, Minneapolis, Kansas City, and San Francisco. Options are sold on major stock indexes, bonds, foreign currencies, and commodities. The option buyer makes a calculated decision on what direction—up or down—the actual price change for the security or commodity will go. Buyers purchases "call" options if they want to buy during the specified period, or "put" options if they want to sell. Buyers pay close attention to the exercise price, that is, the price at which the stock can be bought (call) or sold (put). An exercise price determines when the option can be executed. Failure to reach the price on a put can result in a quick and severe loss. Options are different from futures contracts that obligate both buyers and sellers to purchases and prices at a later date. Although they are listed in the major financial newspapers along with stocks and mutual funds, options clearly are for sophisticated investors. The volume of options contracts grew dramatically with the development of more options offered along with investor education and confidence. Option volumes in 1995 were expected to exceed the previous record of 164 million contracts set in 1987.

[Merton H. Miller, *Financial Innovations and Market Volatility* (Cambridge, Mass., 1991).]

BRENT SCHONDELMEYER

See also **SUPP:** Banking and Finance; Financial Exchanges; Financial Services Industry; Wall Street.

OREGON. Although more than 90 percent of Oregon's 1994 population of 3,080,000 was white, minority groups have grown in numbers since the 1960s and have obtained greater political and economic opportunities. Hispanic Americans, once largely migratory workers, have settled as permanent residents and in the 1990s made up the state's largest minority. African Americans worked to obtain their civil rights through such organizations as the National Association for the Advancement of Colored People, the Urban League, and the Black United Front. Several Native-American tribes, including the Siletz, Grande Ronde, and Klamath, reorganized in order to obtain recognition from the federal government, which carries economic benefits. Support of public libraries and bookstores is far above the national average, and Oregonians have attained national and international distinction in literature and the arts. Don Berry published a trilogy of historical novels about the pioneer era including *Trask, Moontrap,* and *To Build a Ship,* while Ken Kesey received acclaim for *One Flew Over the Cuckoo's Nest* and *Sometimes a Great Notion,* both made into motion pictures. Ursula Le Guin was one of the world's most popular authors of science fantasy as evidenced by her winning all of the major awards in this genre. Sallie Tisdale is a recognized writer of nonfiction, and Barry Lopez is an internationally acclaimed essayist on science and the environment. In architecture, Pietro Belluschi founded the Northwest style, which uses regional materials to construct churches and residences that fit their natural surroundings.

Oregon became nationally known for its political progressivism in the 1960s and 1970s, when the legislature established the first system of statewide land-use planning in the United States, sought to preserve wild rivers, and created the Willamette River Greenway. The state was largely Republican in the first half of the twentieth century, then established a two-party system in which elections were closely contested. During the 1980s and early 1990s, Oregon politics became more conservative as voters became less willing to spend tax dollars. In 1990 a property tax limitation was adopted as a constitutional amendment, which had the effect of crippling government services. On the national scene Senator Bob Packwood was a proponent of tax simplification, while Senator Mark O. Hatfield was best known for championing a noninterventionist foreign policy. Liberal Democratic Governors Neil Goldschmidt (1987–1991) and Barbara Roberts (1991–1995) were able to accomplish little because of conservative strength in the state legislature. Oregon's economy depends on natural resources and the condition of the national economy. Agriculture, forest products, and tourism are the principle industries. Increasingly, manufacturing jobs have been replaced by lower-paying service and retail jobs. The state's economy grew during the years after World War II but plummeted between 1979 and 1982, primarily because of a near-collapse in the forest-products and construction industries. Recovery began in 1983, however, and since 1986 the state's employment growth has outpaced that of the nation as a whole.

[Gordon B. Dodds, *The American Northwest: A History of Oregon and Washington* (Arlington Heights, Ill., 1986).]

GORDON B. DODDS

See also **SUPP:** Portland.

ORGAN DONATION. *See* **Transplants and Organ Donation.**

ORGANIC FARMING coalesced as a movement in the United States in the 1940s with the work of J. I. Rodale of Emmaus, Pa., who followed the British agriculture botanist Sir Albert Howard in the belief that healthy soil produces healthy people. Rodale published a magazine dedicated to organic gardening and farming that drew subscribers ranging from home gardeners to truck farmers. Spurning synthetic fertilizers, he advocated natural soil-builders, such as composted organic materials and ground rock. He and his disciples reacted against synthetic pesticides, such as DDT, and livestock antibiotics, such as penicillin, which were just finding their way onto farms and into farm produce. After the publication of Rachel Carson's *Silent Spring* (1962), many Americans became concerned with human health and permanence. Thus, organic farming found many adherents in the late 1960s and the 1970s among both antitechnology members of the counterculture and environmentally concerned consumers. Synthetic agricultural chemicals, which had become a staple in U.S. agriculture in the post–World War II period, increasingly came under attack as scientists recognized many of them as carcinogenic. The back-to-basics philosophy of the environmental movement boosted the popularity of organic agriculture as a healthy alternative to the seemingly apocalyptic results of high technology.

For decades the U.S. Department of Agriculture (USDA) had advocated use of synthetic agricultural chemicals while bemoaning the loss of humus and topsoil. Responding to environmental concerns, petroleum shortages, and rampant inflation in the 1970s, the USDA began to advocate research into conversion of urban and industrial organic wastes into composted soil-builders that farmers could use to increase fertility and restore structure. The Organic Foods Production Act of 1990 called for federally funded pilot projects to help introduce organic techniques as supplements to chemical-intensive agriculture. Supporters maintained that organic farming would support family farms by lowering costs, increasing yields, and raising quality, as well as assisting farmers to conserve soil and other natural farm resources. By the mid-1980s organic techniques such as low-till and no-till farming, in which farmers leave crop residues in fields to increase humus and to decrease water and wind erosion, were common practice among cereal farmers in the Midwest.

Public awareness of these issues continued to grow. In the late 1980s there was a widely publicized controversy over Alar, a chemical sprayed on apples and other produce to enhance color and prolong shelf life, which had been linked to cancer in laboratory studies. The Environmental Protection Agency attempted to reconcile 1950s legislation prohibiting carcinogenic pesticide residues on food with the highly sensitive measuring devices of the 1990s. Projects such as Biosphere 1 and 2 experimented with a sustainable lifestyle in a closed ecosystem. Organic farmers hoped to tap into the antichemical sentiment that drove these activities by selling produce labeled "organically grown" in supermarkets. Initially organic farming was an attempt to preserve "good farming" practices in the face of a rapidly changing agriculture. In the 1990s organic farming techniques gained acceptance as a result of environmental regulation, rising energy prices, and consumer demand.

[Samuel P. Hays, *Beauty, Health, and Permanence: Environmental Politics in the United States, 1955–1985* (New York, 1987).]

DENNIS WILLIAMS

See also **SUPP:** Agriculture; Biosphere 2; Fertilizers; Health Food Industry; Hydroponics.

ORGANIZATION OF PETROLEUM EXPORTING COUNTRIES (OPEC). *See* **Middle East, Relations with; Oil Crises; Petroleum Industry.**

OZONE DEPLETION. Ozone, a denser form of oxygen that is designated by the chemical notation O_3

and that shields the Earth from excessive ultraviolet radiation from the sun, became a concern of environmentalists in the 1980s. As early as the 1950s scientists had detected substantial fluctuations in the amount of ozone in the atmosphere over Antarctica between summer and winter. In the 1970s some chemists, notably Sherwood Rowland and Mario Molina of the University of California, blamed the lower level of ozone over Antarctica in the winter on the rapidly increasing use of chlorofluorocarbons (CFCs), as refrigerants and propellants in aerosol cans and in the manufacture of plastic foam products. This charge was confirmed by the National Academy of Sciences in 1976. The process of depletion, as described by Rowland, involves the migration of the highly stable CFC molecules to the stratosphere, where, moved by global air circulation patterns, they collect over the Antarctic ice cap during the cold winter months and become fixed on polar stratospheric clouds that, because of their cold temperature, are isolated from the normal atmospheric circulation. When sunlight returns to Antarctica in early spring, the ultraviolet rays bring about a chemical reaction that in turn releases a chlorine-oxide free radical that precipitates a chemical chain reaction breaking up the oxygen molecules that form the ozone layer. A world that has been producing and releasing into the atmosphere 1 million tons of CFCs per year has seen a rise in the reservoir of these chemicals in the atmosphere from 0.8 parts per billion by volume in 1950 to 4 parts per billion in 1990. This accumulation is expected to continue to rise in the twenty-first century.

A greater sense of urgency about ozone depletion arose after scientists stationed in Antarctica reported in 1985 a virtual disappearance of ozone from the Antarctic stratosphere in winter. This announcement was confirmed by measurements taken in 1986 and 1987. The United Nations Environmental Program had registered concern about ozone depletion as early as 1977, and its administrators began negotiations that led in 1985 to the Vienna Convention, signed by twenty nations agreeing to take action to phase out the use of CFCs. In 1987 all major industrial nations signed the Montreal Protocol, agreeing to deadlines for ending the use of CFCs. These deadlines were advanced in an agreement, signed in Copenhagen by eighty nations, calling for the almost total elimination of CFCs, as well as methyl chloroform and carbon tetrachloride, by 1996. Major chemical companies around the world proposed as substitutes for CFCs another group of chemicals known as HCFCs. Although these chemicals also contain chlorine, the chemical responsible for ozone destruction, they also contain hydrogen, which speeds up their dissolution before they reach the stratosphere. Production of HCFCs is to be capped at the level of output achieved in 1996, and they are subject to a gradual phaseout beginning in 2004 and terminating in 2030.

Scientists have determined that the ozone layer in the stratosphere is diminishing worldwide at a rate of between 2 and 3 percent per year. In the late 1980s it was feared that an ozone "hole" comparable to that over the Antarctic might develop over the Arctic, but subsequent measurements have indicated that the risk is not as great; the Arctic does not become as cold as the Antarctic and warms sooner in spring, so there is less time for the ozone-destroying chain reaction created by chlorine free radicals to do its work. Scientists remain concerned, however, about the general reduction in the ozone layer, since it creates a risk of greater penetration of the lower atmosphere by ultraviolet radiation from the sun. They predict an increase in skin cancer because measurements in temperate latitudes in fact show increasing penetration by ultraviolet radiation.

[Seth Cagin and Philip Bray, *Between Earth and Sky: How CFC's Changed Our World and Endangered the Ozone Layer* (New York, 1993); F. Sherwood Rowland, "Stratospheric Ozone in the 21st Century: The Chlorofluorocarbon Problem," *Environmental Science and Technology* 25 (1991).]

NANCY M. GORDON

See also **SUPP:** Air Pollution.

P–Q

PACIFIC, TRUST TERRITORY OF THE. *See* **Trust Territory of the Pacific Islands.**

PACIFIC RIM, a region described as that bordering the vast Pacific Ocean—Asia, along with North and South America. Geologically the region contains four-fifths of the world's seismic activity. It is the region's economic activity, however, that has given the geological term currency in international business and in world politics, especially with regard to Asia. In sheer rate of economic growth the Asian countries in the Pacific Rim have begun to outperform those of all the rest of the world. Asian economies went from producing just 4 percent of the world's overall economic output in the 1960s to 25 percent in the 1990s. By the early 1990s U.S. exports to Asia exceeded those to Europe; transpacific trade had become more important than transatlantic. The region's economic growth was not confined to the economic miracle of Japan. This ferocious growth was led by the four "little dragons," Singapore, Hong Kong, South Korea, and Taiwan, which rapidly industrialized. Closely following in their wake were Indonesia, Malaysia, and Thailand, which initially provided inexpensive labor and undertook only industrial assembly operations but soon developed industries using the latest technology. Adding to the importance of the region was the increasing involvement of China in international trade as it reluctantly began to open its market of 1.1 billion consumers to outside trade. The Pacific Rim nations in 1989 formed the Asia-Pacific Economic Cooperation (APEC), and in 1994 this eighteen-nation group signed an accord to achieve "free and open trade and investment" in the region among its industrialized countries while giving its developing nations until the year 2020 to comply. The hope was that the agreement would transform the region into the world's largest free-trade area.

[Alexander Besher, *The Pacific Rim Almanac* (New York, 1991).]

BRENT SCHONDELMEYER

See also **SUPP:** China, Relations with; Japan, Relations with; North American Free Trade Agreement; Trade, International; Trade Agreements.

PACs. *See* **Political Action Committees.**

PAINTING. In the last third of the twentieth century U.S. painters occupied a prestigious place within the Western art world. Aided by growing public appreciation, art in general and painting in particular enjoyed a remarkable popularity. A uniquely American art is impossible, because the physical size of the country, the diversity of its population, and desire for freedom of expression works against conformity. A stunning array of styles has emerged, ranging from superrealism to the farthest reaches of the abstract. Viewers confront paintings that are variously material- or process-oriented, deliberately casual or overtly formal, political or apolitical, or contrived through craft-based mixed media. Whereas art lovers once had to visit institutions or studios to see original works, near the end of the twentieth century they needed only have access to the art walks that appeared in every major city during the 1970s and 1980s. An outgrowth of politics of the 1960s, street art brought the visual expressions of the poor and dispossessed to public attention.

Painters made a radical departure in expressing their understanding of urban subjects. Instead of the exalted roles accorded to people in the work of Robert Henri or the reverential stance toward the metropolis assumed by John Marin, street artists turned to such commonplace subjects as structural and street deterioration, garbage heaps, and haphazard human presence, all underneath the intrusive glare of commercial signs. With brilliant colors and bold forms they splashed their messages across framed canvases and murals, occasionally mixing the results with participatory theater in a fashion reminiscent of the composer John Cage's "happenings" in the 1950s. In similar fashion more mainstream artists scrutinized the forces within their own lives. The clarion call came from New York, where artists painted and sculpted soup cans, cigarette butts, comic book characters, and giant hamburgers. Aware of the role played by the media in shaping moods and attitudes, the first "pop art" practitioners challenged the notion that complexity (of theme, technique, content, execution) necessarily connotes seriousness of purpose.

The marriage of street art and pop art philosophies produced superrealism, a style characterized by excruciatingly detailed images achieved by colors applied with equal brightness across a canvas. As in the photorealism movement earlier in the century, superrealists paint from models and photographs. Superrealists strive to deliver pointed messages. One of the most compelling examples of this style is Jack Beal's *History of American Labor,* a four-panel commission for the General Services Administration building in Washington, D.C., which captures the optimism-turned-pessimism-turned-confusion experienced by workers in the face of labor trends (the fight for unions, the dominance and decline of same, and the subsequent allegiance to the old views of individual initiative and self-reliance) over the course of the twentieth century. Scattered amid the avant-garde paintings is a respectable showing of works in traditional styles. In any urban center at virtually any time viewers can see settings, thoughts, and issues in every style from baroque to cubism. A typical encounter could bring a side-by-side view of a realist, an expressionist, and a minimalist, all interpreting the same scene or idea.

If there is a thread running through the art annals of the United States it is the decided preference of Americans for figurative painting. Artists have expanded the conventions of figurative painting by using collages, photomontages, and found objects in their compositions. One of the most favored painters in the latter genre was Romare Bearden, an African American respected for provocative depictions of religious events, conjuring women, and not-so-placid garden scenes. An emerging element of importance was the push for egalitarianism in the arts. Although the idea is old, contemporary artists have challenged the exclusionary policies and economic controls practiced by galleries, although many artists benefited during the 1980s from the highly inflated climate created and sustained largely by such gallerists as Mary Boone. The feminist movement brought about intriguing developments in art. Such artists as Judy Chicago and Miriam Schapiro developed pattern painting, a style that features human forms, floral patterns, and an endless litany of nonobjective shapes arranged in configurations similar to wallpaper. Contrived through mixed-media designs of needlework, cloth, and other crafts associated with women, feminist paintings often appear under the guise of performance pieces written and choreographed by other feminist artists.

The interaction between artists and the ease with which artists moved among media continue to alter modern painting. Surfaces sculpted for texture and alternative views toward line, balance, and form hint of aesthetic vistas yet unexplored. The increasing popularity of art in public places could lead to greater intimacy between painters and viewers. All told, the painter of the future may be forced to abandon the garret and seek succor from the streets.

[Daniel M. Mendelowitz, *A History of American Art,* 2nd ed. (New York, 1970); Barbara Rose, *American Art Since 1900,* rev. ed. (New York, 1975); John Wilmerding, *The Genius of American Painting* (New York, 1973).]

EVELYN S. COOPER

See also **SUPP:** Folk Art; Graffiti; National Endowment for the Arts; Sculpture.

PALEONTOLOGY. Although the last dinosaur died 65 million years ago, the decades of the 1970s, 1980s, and 1990s can be called the dinosaur age. Some, although not all, of the interest in dinosaurs stemmed from the theory that the creatures may have been destroyed by a meteorite or comet that hit the earth. A large fossil crater underlying the Yucatán peninsula has been identified with a catastrophe at the end of the Cretaceous period, but some paleontologists defend the role of vulcanism as an alternative scenario for the extinction of the dinosaurs, and still other paleontologists suggest that such factors as climate change or disease killed off this group. Arguments as to whether birds are allied to or directly descended from dinosaurs have whetted the public's appetite for surprisingly sophisticated general discussions of the intricacies of evolution. The collection of dinosaur bones in the West has spurred at least one court case over ownership of the skeleton of a Tyrannosaurus rex, valued at several million dollars.

Invertebrates have not generated quite as much fervor as dinosaurs, but an account published in 1989 of bizarre fossil animals found in the Burgess Shale in Canada from the Middle Cambrian period (520 million years ago) reached the New York Times bestseller list. The book's commercial success was aided by reports of similar although slightly older Early Cambrian fossils found in China, Australia, Canada, and Greenland. These fossils have pointed up the problem posed by the abrupt appearance of skeleton-bearing animals at the base of the Cambrian. No adequate theory accounts for why or how some groups developed hard parts, while others, such as worms and jellyfish flourish without a skeleton. Progress has been made on the study of Precambrian fossils, forms older than 540 million years. The Ediacaran fauna first described in Australia in the 1950s has been recognized worldwide in rocks from 650 to 550 million years old. Some of the fossils may be allied to jellyfish, but others have no living counterparts. With one dubious exception, none of these early animals has a mineralized skeleton. They show no close relation to the atypical Early and Middle Cambrian fauna mentioned earlier, and it has even been suggested that some kinds formed a separate kingdom of organisms.

The low price of crude oil and its abundant supply since the mid-1980s resulted in reduced employment opportunities for paleontologists in the oil industry, especially micropaleontologists. Partly offsetting this loss was the Deep Sea Drilling Project (DSDP), the latest phase in drilling in the ocean for scientific results that began in the 1960s. The DSDP has achieved remarkable biostratigraphic precision in dating some microfossils, with some dated to intervals of 100,000 years and even less. At the same time, there has been a dramatic shift in the profession away from stratigraphic investigations. The emphasis in the 1990s was on evolutionary studies, spurred by the debate over "punctuated equilibrium," which suggests an abrupt appearance of new forms, versus gradual change; the problem of interpreting mass extinctions; and questions about predator-prey relationships. Pa-

leoecological studies and functional morphology systematic studies increased, while classic monographic systematic studies declined. New sections of the Treatise on Invertebrate Paleontology, which began in 1953, continued to be published, with paleozoologists producing new summary volumes of groups and revising previously published sections.

Studies of former plant life continued into the 1990s, including the search for ancestors of angiosperms; the coal-forming forests of the past were being interpreted with the ideas of modern ecology; and remarkably well-preserved fungi more than 300 million years old were added to the geologic record. Artifacts from the Precambrian, nine-tenths of the time of earth, were slowly yielding information on the origin and the early evolution of life. Team studies of the Archean (1983) and the Proterozoic (1992) periods clarified earlier hypotheses about early life and documented much of its course from the appearance of life 3,500 million years ago. Studies of other planets have emphasized the uniqueness of life on earth and its effect on the planet.

[Stephen Jay Gould, Wonderful Life: The Burgess Shale and the Nature of History (New York, 1989); J. W. Schof, ed., Earth's Earliest Biosphere: Its Origin and Evolution (Princeton, N.J., 1983); J. W. Schof and C. Klein, eds., The Proterozoic Biosphere: A Multidisciplinary Study (Cambridge, 1992).]

ELLIS L. YOCHELSON

See also DAH and SUPP: Archaeology and Prehistory.

PALESTINE LIBERATION ORGANIZATION (PLO). See **Israel-Palestine Peace Accords; Middle East, Relations with.**

PALESTINIAN AMERICANS. There have been four waves of Palestinian immigration to the United States. The first occurred following creation of the state of Israel in 1948, which made many Palestinians refugees. The second occurred in the early 1970s following the 1967 Arab-Israeli Six-Day War, when immigrants were fleeing the Israeli occupation of the West Bank and Gaza. The third wave was a result of the 1987 popular uprising (intifada) against the Israeli occupation. A fourth immigrant group arrived after the Gulf War of 1991, expelled from Kuwait and the Gulf region. Although Palestinian Americans have deep roots in Arabic culture and often maintain their language and customs, they have excelled in U.S. schools and universities. Notable Palestinian American academicians are the literary scholar Edward Said, the historian Walid Khalidi, and the writer Ibrahim Abu-Lughod. Palestinian Americans also have prospered as entrepreneurs, especially in the food, clothing, and electronics industries.

[Samia El-Badry, *Fitting In: An Analysis of Socio-Economic Attainment Patterns of Foreign Born Arab Americans and Other Nationalities in the United States* (Austin, Tex., 1987).]

SAMIA EL-BADRY
SAMAR SAKAKINI

See also **SUPP:** Arab Americans; Middle East, Relations with.

PALIMONY, a term derived from "alimony," is the legal action upholding oral agreements between unmarried couples to share property and earnings acquired while the couple shared the same abode. In 1976 Michelle Triola Marvin sued actor Lee Marvin, claiming that she abandoned her own singing career to serve as his companion, cook, and confidante and that in return he agreed to share his earnings. She eventually sued Marvin for close to $2 million for "services" as his "wife" and loss of her career. The California courts let her sue under the theory that the couple had an oral contract. In the end she won $104,000. Palimony is misnamed in that it implies the equivalent of alimony when unmarried couples break up. The legal basis of palimony suits where states allow them is an oral contract for services, other than sexual, provided during cohabitation.

PAUL FINKELMAN

See also **SUPP:** Marriage and Divorce.

PANAMA CANAL TREATY (1977). The genesis of the 1970s agreements between Panama and the United States lay in increasing Panamanian discontent over existing treaty relationships with the U.S. government. The 1903 Hay-Bunau-Varilla Treaty had granted "in perpetuity" to the United States a canal zone within which the United States could exercise "all the rights, power, and authority" of a sovereign state. Severe rioting in January 1964 led to twenty-one Panamanian deaths and considerable destruction of U.S.-owned property. In December of that year President Lyndon B. Johnson promised negotiations to abrogate the 1903 treaty. The following year Johnson and Panamanian President Marco Aurelio Robles announced agreement on a set of principles to guide subsequent negotiations. Draft treaties were

completed and initialed by late June 1967, but leakage of the terms to the press stirred opposition in both countries and led to the shelving of the covenants.

An October 1968 coup in Panama brought to power Guardia Nacional Colonel Omar Torrijos Herrera. A chance conversation two years later between President Richard M. Nixon and Panamanian President Demetrio Lakas led to resumption of negotiations between the two countries. In May 1973 Panamanian Foreign Minister Juan Antonio Tack formulated a set of principles (similar to the Johnson-Robles principles of 1967) to undergird any U.S.-Panama agreement. Secretary of State Henry Kissinger signed a modified version of the Tack principles in 1974. The administration of President Gerald R. Ford could not obtain Pentagon support for the proposed treaties until the autumn of 1975. President-elect Jimmy Carter in January 1977 requested a review of negotiations and subsequently authorized a resumption on the basis of the Tack-Kissinger principles. Treaties following the terms of the 1967 principles were signed by Carter and Torrijos on Sept. 7, 1977.

The Panama Canal Treaty stated that the United States would maintain control of the waterway until Dec. 31, 1999, and Panama would assume a greater role in the canal's operation, maintenance, and defense. An increasing percentage of canal revenues would accrue to Panama during the transition period. A second agreement, the Neutrality Treaty, required Panama to keep the canal neutral and open to all nations, with the United States and Panama pledged to guarantee neutrality. A Carter-Torrijos "statement of understanding" was issued as a clarification of two articles of the Neutrality Treaty. Each country could act to defend the canal "against any aggression or threat," although this did not mean that the United States could intervene in Panama's internal affairs. Both treaties were approved by plebiscite in Panama on Oct. 23, 1977, but final congressional approval took two years. Republican Senator Dennis DeConcini of Arizona proposed an amendment to the Neutrality Treaty stating that in the event of the closure of the canal the United States and Panama independently had the right to take any necessary steps to reopen it, including use of force. With this amendment the U.S. Senate approved the Neutrality Treaty on Mar. 16, 1978, by a vote of 68 to 32. The Canal Treaty was ratified by the same margin on April 18. It contained an amendment introduced by the Senate leadership stating that nothing in either treaty would have as its purpose or would be interpreted as a right of intervention in the internal affairs of Panama. President George

Bush may have violated this amendment when he ordered the invasion of Panama in 1989 to capture General Manuel Antonio Noriega. Enabling legislation for the two treaties passed the House and Senate late in September 1979; both treaties went into effect on Oct. 1, 1979.

[William J. Jorden, *Panama Odyssey* (Austin, Tex., 1984).]
RICHARD W. TURK

See also **DAH:** Panama Canal; Panama Revolution; **SUPP:** Panama Invasion.

PANAMA INVASION (1989). The invasion of Panama by U.S. forces in December 1989 was designed in part to end the rule of General Manuel Antonio Noriega. A graduate of the Peruvian Military Academy in 1962, he had supported Colonel Omar Torrijos Herrera, the ruler of Panama, during an attempted coup against the latter in 1969. Noriega soon became head of the Panamanian military intelligence service and served Torrijos for a decade as chief of security. Two years after Torrijos's death in an airplane crash in 1981, Noriega became commander of the Guardia Nacional, renamed the Panama Defense Forces (PDF). Torrijos and subsequently Noriega aided the U.S.-sponsored Contras with arms and supplies in their struggle against the Sandinista regime in Nicaragua. Noriega's involvement with the Medellín drug cartel in the 1980s and the emergence of Panama as a money-laundering site proved far more lucrative than receiving U.S. support because of assistance to the contras.

In 1987 a feud between Noriega and his chief of staff, Roberto Diaz Herrera, led to Diaz's publicly charging Noriega with crimes and encouraged Panamanian opponents to demand Noriega's resignation. Noriega responded with arrests and brutality. Secret negotiations between Panamanian and U.S. representatives designed to facilitate Noriega's departure broke down. The U.S. Justice Department filed indictments against Noriega in federal court; soon afterward the U.S. government imposed a series of economic sanctions. The United States sent additional military forces to the Canal Zone in Panama, recalled its ambassador, and encouraged PDF officers to overthrow Noriega. An attempted coup in 1989 failed and led to executions. The media criticized President George Bush and Secretary of Defense Richard Cheney for failing to provide more support to the coup leaders. The U.S. military drew up plans for an invasion, which began when a U.S. serviceman died from gunfire outside PDF headquarters on Dec. 16, 1989.

Operation Just Cause began December 20 and lasted through December 24. The PDF numbered 5,000, augmented by 8,000 paramilitary troops organized in "dignity battalions." The 13,000 U.S. troops stationed in Panama were reinforced by an additional 9,000. Fighting centered around Noriega's headquarters in Panama City. Noriega took refuge with the papal nuncio (the Vatican's representative in Panama), but surrendered on Jan. 3, 1990. Twenty-three U.S. soldiers were killed during the invasion. Panamanian deaths—military and civilian—exceeded 500. U.S. public opinion supported the operation but many foreign governments did not. A new civilian regime took control in Panama and the country experienced severe economic problems and a troubled security situation for months afterward. Noriega became a federal prisoner in Miami on Jan. 4, 1990; he was tried and convicted in April 1992 of cocaine smuggling and imprisoned. Political and economic stability remained an elusive commodity in Panama; nationalist resentment against the United States surged, and by 1995 Noriega's adherents may have regained a degree of authority in Panama.

[Edward M. Flanagan, Jr., *Battle for Panama: Inside Operation Just Cause* (Washington, D.C., 1993).]
RICHARD W. TURK

See also **DAH:** Panama Canal.

PAN AM FLIGHT 103, a U.S. passenger jet, was destroyed by a terrorist bomb on Dec. 21, 1988, over Lockerbie, Scotland, killing 259 passengers and crew and 11 residents. The incident ignited a protracted international effort to bring the suspected Libyan perpetrators to trial and marked a shift from hijacking to sabotage in terrorist attacks against Western targets. Passengers included thirty-five foreign-study students from Syracuse University who were en route to New York from London's Heathrow Airport when their aircraft was "decapitated" by a plastic explosive concealed in a forward cargo bay. Relatives of the dead blamed U.S. authorities for failing to make public information warning of a terrorist attack on a flight originating in Frankfurt, Germany. Bomb experts later confirmed that the explosive, hidden in a radio cassette player inside a suitcase, had been smuggled aboard in Frankfurt. Because West German authorities had arrested members of the Popular Front for the Liberation of Palestine–General Command earlier in 1988 and found plastic explosives in their possession, it first was thought that Palestinians were behind the bombing. Speculation also centered on Tehran, presumably in retaliation for the accidental downing of an Iranian passenger jet by the USS *Vincennes* in the Persian Gulf in July 1988. In 1991, however, the United States and Scotland indicted two Libyan intelligence agents for the bombing of Pan Am Flight 103. For the first time in its history the United Nations Security Council ordered one nation, in this case Libya, to surrender citizens to another nation. When Libya refused, the Security Council imposed an air and arms embargo on the country. Intelligence sources in the United States believe Libyan leader Mu'ammar al-Gadhafi ordered the bombing in retaliation for a U.S. air raid on Tripoli in April 1986. That attack was in turn a response to Libya's alleged bombing of a West Berlin discotheque that targeted off-duty U.S. servicemen and women.

[Steven Emerson and Brian Duffy, *The Fall of Pan Am 103: Inside the Lockerbie Investigation* (New York, 1990).]
BRUCE J. EVENSEN

See also **SUPP:** Middle East, Relations with; Terrorism.

PARENTAL CHOICE IN EDUCATION. *See* **Education, Parental Choice in.**

PARENTHOOD, SURROGATE. *See* **Surrogate Parenthood.**

PARKS, NATIONAL. Of the 83.3 million acres in the National Park System in 1994, 50.4 million were in the fifty-four national parks and 2.06 million in the seventy-three national monuments. The remaining acres can be accounted for in other areas in the system—such as national seashores, national scenic trails, and national historic sites—that are not designated as national parks or national monuments. During the administrations of Richard M. Nixon, Gerald R. Ford, Ronald Reagan, and George Bush, national monuments were created by congressional action. President Jimmy Carter, acting under the powers assigned presidents by the Antiquities Act of 1906, created national monuments in Alaska by proclamation.

Between 1974 and 1994 fifteen areas that were formerly national monuments became national parks: Badlands, Biscayne, Channel Islands, Death Valley, Dry Tortugas, Gates of the Arctic, Glacier Bay, Great Basin, Katmai, Kenai Fjords, Kobuk Valley, Joshua Tree, Lake Clark, Saguaro, and Wrangell–St. Elias. The Theodore Roosevelt National Memorial park,

created in 1947, was redesignated a national park in 1978, and in 1988 the National Park of American Samoa was established. The two largest National Park Service areas in 1995 were Wrangell–St. Elias and Gates of the Arctic, both in Alaska. In 1977 the National Park Service classification system that divided units into natural, historical, and recreational areas was abolished because these categories became difficult to apply, as some areas contained multiple attributes. National parks and national monuments are often, however, classified informally according to their primary attributes.

The twenty-nine national monuments categorized as primarily natural areas are Aniakchak, Alaska; Chiricahua, Organ Pipe Cactus, Sunset Crater Volcano, Arizona; Devils Postpile, Lava Beds, Muir Woods, Pinnacles, California; Black Canyon of the Colorado, Gunnison, Dinosaur, Florissant Fossil Beds, Great Sand Dunes, Colorado; Craters of the Moon, Hagerman Fossil Beds, Idaho; Agate Fossil Beds, Nebraska; Capulin Volcano, El Malpais, White Sands, New Mexico; John Day Fossil Beds, Oregon Caves, Oregon; Congaree Swamp, South Carolina; Jewel Cave, South Dakota; Cedar Breaks, Natural Bridges, Rainbow Bridge, Timpanogos Cave, Utah; Buck Island Reef, Virgin Islands; Devils Tower, Fossil Butte, Wyoming.

The forty-three national monuments categorized as primarily historical areas are Russell Cave, Alabama; Cape Krusenstern, Alaska; Canyon de Chelly, Casa Grande Ruins, Hohokam Pima, Montezuma Castle, Navajo, Pipe Spring, Tonto, Tuzigoot, Walnut Canyon, Wupatki, Arizona; Cabrillo, California; Hovenweep, Yucca House, Colorado; Castillo de San Marcos, Fort Matanzas, Florida; Fort Frederica, Fort Pulaski, Ocmulgee, Georgia; Effigy Mounds, Iowa; Poverty Point, Louisiana; Fort McHenry, Maryland; Grand Portage, Pipestone, Minnesota; George Washington Carver, Missouri; Little Bighorn Battlefield, Montana; Homestead, Scotts Bluff, Nebraska; Aztec Ruins, Bandelier, El Morro, Fort Union, Gila Cliff Dwellings, Petroglyph, Salinas Pueblo Missions, New Mexico; Castle Clinton, Fort Stanwix, Statue of Liberty, New York; Fort Sumter, South Carolina; Alibates Flint Quarries, Texas; Booker T. Washington, George Washington Birthplace, Virginia.

The most significant service acquisitions between 1974 and 1994 were in Alaska. Under the Alaska Native Claims Settlement Act of 1971 the secretary of the interior was given the discretion to withdraw up to 80 million acres of Alaskan lands that would qualify as units operated by one of the following agencies: National Park Service, Forest Service, or Fish and Wildlife Service. In 1973 Secretary Rogers C. B. Morton recommended that 32.3 million acres be withdrawn for parks. Congress had five years to act on the secretary's recommendation, which would double the size of the lands administered by the Park Service. There was strong opposition from commercial interests and from hunters who urged Congress to create preserves that permitted sport hunting and trapping, rather than parks that prohibited those activities. Representative Morris K. Udall of Arizona drafted a bill that created national preserves but it was defeated in May 1978.

It appeared that the five-year limit for Congress to act would expire and the withdrawn areas would revert to public lands. On Dec. 1, 1978, President Jimmy Carter proclaimed fifteen new national monuments and made additions to two others. He proclaimed the withdrawn lands as monuments to allow Congress time to draft legislation concerning their status. In 1980 Congress agreed to an Alaskan lands bill, and on December 2 President Carter signed the Alaska National Interest Lands Conservation Act into law, redesignating seven monuments as national parks and increasing the acreage of the National Park Service by more than 47 million, much more than the 32.3 million Secretary Morton had recommended for withdrawal. Five of the seven parks were accompanied by national preserves, allowing sport hunting and trapping.

[Barry Mackintosh, *The National Parks: Shaping the System* (Washington, D.C., 1991); National Park Service, *The National Parks: Index 1993* (Washington, D.C., 1993).]

JON E. TAYLOR

See also **DAH:** Parks, National, and National Monuments; Park Service, National, and National Park System; **SUPP:** Park Service, National.

PARK SERVICE, NATIONAL. Crowding in the national parks has placed pressure on their resources and exacerbated the tension inherent in the National Park Service's dual mission of preservation and public enjoyment. A major construction program—Mission 66—to accommodate visitors in the 1950s and 1960s was followed by an era of environmental concern that greater use and related facility development jeopardized park values. In the mid-1970s, during the bicentennial of the American Revolution, the two dozen historical parks commemorating the Revolution benefited from an extensive development pro-

gram. At Independence National Historical Park in Philadelphia, the Park Service reconstructed the house where Thomas Jefferson drafted the Declaration of Independence, installed elaborate exhibits at the site of Benjamin Franklin's house, and moved the Liberty Bell to a new pavilion outside Independence Hall. On July 4, 1976, President Gerald R. Ford spoke at Independence Hall and signed legislation making Valley Forge a national historical park.

Beyond routine protection, management, and upkeep, Park Service personnel engage in a range of more specialized activities, from erection of fire lines to control damage to surface artifacts (for example, during the 1977 fire at La Mesa in Bandelier National Monument, near Los Alamos, N.Mex.) to an ongoing program of cyclical prospecting—identifying vertebrate fossils at risk from damage by natural causes—in the John Day Fossil Beds, Badlands National Park, S.Dak. Wilderness preservation received an enormous boost with the Alaska National Interest Lands Conservation Act of 1980, which, with the addition of Denali and Wrangell–St. Elias and five other preserves, more than doubled the size of the National Park System.

Because the Park Service's funding and staffing had not kept pace with its growing responsibilities, the administration of President Ronald Reagan and Congress in the 1980s sought to slow the system's expansion. Rather than creating more parks, they backed the Park Restoration and Improvement Program, which allocated more than $1 billion over five years to resources and facilities in existing parks. Beginning in Reagan's second term the National Park Service sought a greater role in educating the public about American history and environmental values. The service also returned to a more expansionist posture, supporting such additions as Great Basin National Park, Nevada, and Steamtown National Historical Site, a railroad connection in Scranton, Pa. The latter was a costly venture and was much criticized as an example of "pork barrel" politics, casting into doubt the national significance of other proposed parks that seemed primarily driven by local economic-development interests. During the presidency of George Bush (1989–1993) the National Park Service leadership spoke out against such a "thinning of the blood" of the National Park System and sought to regain the initiative from Congress in charting its expansion.

In 1990 the Richard King Mellon Foundation made the largest single park donation yet: $10.5 million for additional lands at Civil War battlefields and at

Shenandoah National Park. In all, ninety-seven units were added to the National Park System between 1975 and November 1994, including the National Mall in Washington, D.C.; Canaveral National Seashore, Florida; recreation areas in rural pockets of New Jersey, Georgia, New York–Pennsylvania, Nebraska, West Virginia, and Minnesota and in Guam; and Wrangell–St. Elias National Preserve and Denali National Preserve, both in Alaska. Denali, the fourth largest unit in the system and site of North America's highest mountain, Mount McKinley, brings in more than fifty buses, each carrying approximately forty people, every day. In 1996 the system comprised 369 areas—80 million acres—featuring resources as diverse as the Grand Canyon and the Statue of Liberty.

[Barry Mackintosh, *The National Parks* (Washington, D.C., 1991).]

EDWIN C. BEARSS

See also **DAH:** Park Service, National, and National Park System; Parks, National, and National Monuments; **SUPP:** Conservation; Parks, National.

PATIENTS' RIGHTS, a movement that was an outgrowth of the movement for individual rights of the 1960s and 1970s that gave rise to the idea of a set of rights for protection of medical patients and succeeded in having those rights enacted into law in many states. Although medical and hospital patients in most states were beneficiaries of common-law rights well before the 1960s, these protections were limited to the right not be treated without consent, the confidentiality of statements made to a physician during treatment, the right to damages in event of malpractice, and, to some extent, the confidentiality of a patient's hospital records. An advance in patients' rights occurred in 1973 when the American Hospital Association (AHA) approved a bill of rights for adoption by member hospitals. It promised patients considerate and respectful care, the right to know hospital rules and regulations relating to patient conduct, the right to know the identity of the physician in charge of care, sufficient information to enable patients to make informed decisions with respect to their treatment, the right to obtain information concerning diagnosis and treatment as well as prognosis if medically advisable, the right not to be a subject of experiment, the confidentiality of clinical records, and the right to receive an explanation of the hospital bill.

Although the AHA represented almost all of the 5,300 nonprofit, general, and investor-owned hospitals in the United States in the 1990s, the bill of rights adopted by most of the association's members was of little or no legal value because it was voluntary. Nonetheless, it established public awareness of patients' rights and set the stage for a second advance that took place between 1975 and 1985, when one-third of the states enacted patients' rights statutes. Although these statutes varied, they all incorporated the AHA pledges and generally went beyond them to guarantee the right to prompt emergency attention, the right to examine one's clinical chart during the course of treatment and to obtain a copy of it, the right (within limits) to privacy during the hospital stay, the right to receive an itemized bill, and the right to receive information about financial assistance and free care. The most important aspect of these statutes was that they were enforceable. California, Colorado, Illinois, Maryland, Massachusetts, Michigan, Minnesota, New York, Pennsylvania, and Rhode Island were some of the states that enacted statutes. In most instances the statutes were also applied to nursing homes. The right to refuse treatment extended to psychiatric patients if they were competent. By the 1990s federal law required hospitals and nursing homes to advise patients of their right to refuse care and their right to execute living wills or to name proxies if they become unable to make life-and-death treatment decisions.

[George J. Annas, *The Rights of Patients,* 2nd rev. ed. (Totowa, N.J., 1992).]

JACK HANDLER

PDA. *See* **Pregnancy Discrimination Act.**

PEACE CORPS. As an idea, the Peace Corps originated with Democratic Representative Henry S. Reuss of Wisconsin and Senator Hubert H. Humphrey of Minnesota in the late 1950s. Both advocated sending U.S. volunteers into developing nations to help alleviate poverty, illiteracy, and disease. Democratic presidential candidate John F. Kennedy adopted the idea in 1960. The Peace Corps appealed to Kennedy's notion of service to country and humanity; it also had the potential for encouraging goodwill for the United States among developing nations. The Soviets and Chinese, in Kennedy's opinion, were far ahead of the United States in cultivating friendships among nations emerging from colonialism after World War II. He wanted the Peace Corps to counter communist aims in developing nations by demonstrating U.S. democratic values. President Kennedy moved quickly, appointing his brother-in-law, Sargent Shriver, to create the Peace Corps. Shriver built the agency in a matter of weeks. The president signed an executive order on Mar. 1, 1961, temporarily establishing the Peace Corps, and in September, Congress voted to create a permanent corps. Appointed its first director, Shriver worked to develop a system for recruiting, training, transporting, supplying, and caring for overseas volunteers. His drive helped the Peace Corps gain independent status from other U.S. foreign policy agencies. Although directors of the Peace Corps are political appointees and have changed the focus of the organization somewhat as presidential administrations changed, the Peace Corps has remained relatively free from use as a direct foreign policy instrument.

After the end of the cold war the Peace Corps' goals remained unaltered. It seeks to promote world peace and friendship through interaction of the volunteers with their hosts. Volunteers spend two years in a host country that requests Peace Corps help, aiding in whatever ways the host desires. Tasks range from teaching and community organizing to assistance in agriculture. The corps concentrates on small, personal projects and has three broad aims—providing trained workers for developing nations, promoting understanding of the United States and its values, and increasing volunteers' understanding of the perspectives and values of people in developing nations. Despite attacks, low funding, and internal problems the Peace Corps survives as a popular agency. Since 1961 it has sent more than 140,000 volunteers to ninety-nine nations. The agency cannot keep pace with demands for volunteers. Charges of cultural imperialism have been leveled, but the agency responds that it does not seek to replace traditional societies' values with those of the United States but rather to act as a bridge between cultures. The Peace Corps continues to receive bipartisan congressional support.

[Gerard T. Rice, *The Bold Experiment: JFK's Peace Corps* (Notre Dame, Ind., 1985).]

JOEL D. SHROCK

PEACE MOVEMENTS. U.S. citizens take part in peace movements for a variety of reasons. Some limit their commitment to specific antiwar activities, particularly during military conflicts. Others champion internationalism, supporting worldwide peace organizations. Many are pacifists, religious or secular. Some believe that large standing armies pose a threat to liberty and democracy. Many link peace to such other interests as feminism, socialism, civil rights, or environmentalism. With the end of the Vietnam War

in 1975 the broad coalition of peace activists who had come together to protest the longest conflict in U.S. history broke down once again into smaller groups addressing a range of concerns.

Protests against the nuclear arms race, which had been a focus of peace groups since the 1950s, intensified in the 1980s in response to the Ronald Reagan administration's buildup of the U.S. nuclear arsenal. In the early 1980s the nonviolent Livermore Action Group sought to close the Lawrence Livermore National Laboratory in California, which produced nuclear weapons. Such actions reinforced the wider nuclear freeze campaign, a movement that in November 1982 led to the largest voter referendum on any issue in U.S. history. More than 11.5 million Americans, 60 percent of those voting on the freeze issue, supported the measure. The freeze issue appeared on the ballot in states and localities across the country. Twelve state legislatures, 321 city councils, 10 national labor unions and international bodies endorsed the effort by the United States and Soviet Union to ban mutually the testing, production, and deployment of nuclear weapons. One result of the movement was the Intermediate-Range Nuclear Forces (INF) Treaty of 1988 with the Soviet Union.

Activists also linked the huge U.S. military budget with neglect of such human needs as education, health care, and housing for the poor, which led to ambitious campaigns against such costly projects as the B-1 bomber, the MX missile system, and the Strategic Defense Initiative ("Star Wars"). Peace groups were critical of U.S. military interventions in Grenada (1983) and Panama (1989), and to a lesser extent, in Somalia (1992), challenging the morality as well as the effectiveness of using military means to achieve political, economic, or even humanitarian ends. Although the brief Gulf War of 1991 elicited overwhelming public support in favor of halting Iraq's aggression against Kuwait, many peace activists criticized the George Bush administration for engaging in a war they believed was more about U.S. dependency on Middle East oil than about freedom for the citizens of Kuwait. Elsewhere, protests were aimed at the Reagan administration for its support of the Contras seeking to overthrow the Sandinista government in Nicaragua, where in 1990 U.S. peace organizations monitored free elections.

A unique aspect of the peace movement since the 1970s has been the surge of feminist involvement. Awareness generated by the 1975–1985 United Nations Decade for Women resulted in international networks concerned with global issues of war, economic crises, and the rights of women. In 1980 and 1981 women encircled the Pentagon to oppose war. New York State in 1983 witnessed the massive Women's Encampment for the Future of Peace and Justice sited next to the Seneca Army Depot, a nuclear weapons storage facility. The 1987 Mother's Day action at the Department of Energy's nuclear test site near Las Vegas enlisted thousands of women from throughout the country. As in the past, peace movements appealed most to middle-income women, clergymen, educators, college students and people in their twenties, and some business leaders. Geographically, their centers of strength were in college towns, the large metropolitan areas of the Northeast and Midwest, and along the West Coast.

[Charles Chatfield, *The American Peace Movement: Ideals and Activism* (New York, 1992); Barbara Epstein, *Political Protest and Cultural Revolution* (Berkeley, Calif., 1991); Charles F. Howlett, *The American Peace Movement: References and Resources* (Boston, 1991); Lawrence S. Wittner, *Rebels Against War: The American Peace Movement, 1933–1983* (Philadelphia, 1984).]

CHARLES F. HOWLETT

See also **SUPP:** Arms Race and Disarmament; Grenada Invasion; Gulf War of 1991; Haiti, Relations with; Human Rights; Nicaragua, Relations with; Panama Invasion; Somalia, Relations with; Strategic Defense Initiative; Women's Movement.

PEARL HARBOR FIFTIETH ANNIVERSARY (Dec. 7, 1991) commemorated the bombing of the Pearl Harbor naval base in Hawaii on Dec. 7, 1941, and U.S. entry into World War II with an address by President George Bush. Along with 2,000 veterans who survived the Japanese attack he hailed the 1,177 Americans who died aboard the USS *Arizona* on the "date which will live in infamy." A navy pilot who had enlisted after Pearl Harbor, Bush avowed that fifty years later he held "no rancor in my heart toward Germany or Japan." He praised Japan's recent acknowledgment of "responsibility" for starting the Pacific War. Scholarly conferences, including one at Hofstra University, also remembered Pearl Harbor in the United States. There were no commemorative events in Japan.

J. GARRY CLIFFORD

See also **DAH:** Pearl Harbor; **SUPP:** War Memorials.

PENNSYLVANIA. William Penn, the founder of Pennsylvania, sought to balance goals of justice, political equality, and tolerance of religious diversity and hoped to establish a divinely inspired commonwealth where people would respect differences and reject ideological extremes stridently proclaimed as undeniable truths elsewhere. Three centuries later the Pennsylvania novelist John Updike described the state as one of "mild, misty, doughy middleness" where moderates rule. The events of the late twentieth century support this dual image of diversity and moderation. Pennsylvania voters tended to hold moderate positions and cared most about bread-and-butter issues. Pennsylvania politicians therefore stood in the center with the voters, avoiding ideology and focusing on jobs and services to communities and individuals. Consistent with this concrete service orientation was the political tradition of helping one's friends and providing favors, which in turn has led to tolerance of a degree of corruption neither Penn nor Benjamin Franklin would have found acceptable.

Indicative of political moderation is the outlook of the state's governors and senators. Governor Milton J. Shapp, a Democrat, promoted a moderate liberal agenda from 1971 to 1979. During his two terms the state passed a sunshine law for open government, established the Department of Aging, expanded women's legal rights, removed children from adult jails, and greatly increased government support for the arts and for handicapped children. During the 1970s, however, nearly 300 public officials at all levels of government admitted to, were convicted of, or pleaded no contest to corruption. Democratic Congressmen Joshua Eilberg and Daniel J. Flood accepted bribes, Republican Congressman J. Irving Whalley demanded kickbacks from staff members, and Republican Senator Hugh D. Scott accepted illegal gifts of $10,000 annually from the Gulf Oil Corporation. There were fewer corruption scandals in the 1980s but the bizarre suicide of Republican State Treasurer R. Budd Dwyer was particularly shocking. Convicted of accepting a $300,000 bribe, Dwyer shot himself before television cameras during a 1987 press conference. By dying before his sentencing Dwyer ensured that his family would receive pension benefits of more than $1 million.

Republican Richard Thornburgh was governor from 1979 to 1987. Thornburgh, who would later serve as Attorney General in the George Bush administration, campaigned as a moderate who pledged to end corruption and administer progressive social programs. His progressive appeal was so successful that he won the votes of traditionally Democratic African-American voters. His gubernatorial campaigns stressed moderate themes. Democrat Robert P. Casey continued the tradition of two-term governors. In both his campaigns Casey emphasized that his administration would work with business leaders to preserve jobs and create new ones. The voting records of Pennsylvania's senators since 1980 are consistent with the theme of moderation. Republicans H. John Heinz and Arlen Specter were among the Republican senators most likely to oppose the conservative positions of the Ronald Reagan and Bush administrations. After Senator Heinz died in a 1991 plane crash, Democrat Harris Wofford defeated former Governor Thornburgh to fill the final three years of Heinz's term. Wofford proposed health care reform and an activist government to promote jobs.

Part of Pennsylvania's moderation is its willingness to embrace standards that are more symbolic than tangible. Pennsylvania joined most other states in re-establishing the death penalty, for example, but the state government nonetheless has hesitated to execute anyone. Another area of symbolic standards with little tangible policy impact is abortion policy. In the 1970s the Pennsylvania Catholic Conference lobbied legislators to enact pro-life policies. Overriding Governor Shapp's veto, the legislature passed an antiabortion bill so extreme that the Supreme Court ruled it unconstitutional. In the 1980s the Court began to expand the scope of abortion legislation that could be enacted by the states. The Pennsylvania chapter of the National Abortion Rights Action League (NARAL) and other pro-choice groups, however, organized to challenge the influence of the Catholic Conference. After *Webster* v. *Health Reproductive Services* (1989) allowed states to place restrictions on women obtaining abortions, the legislature approved some of the measures favored by the Catholic Conference. A federal judge struck down portions of the law but the state appealed. The Supreme Court ruled in *Planned Parenthood of Southeastern Pennsylvania* v. *Casey* (1992) that spousal notification was unconstitutional but upheld other provisions, including a twenty-four-hour waiting period, informed consent of one parent of pregnant teenagers, and various reporting requirements. Finally implemented in 1994, the law has had little impact on abortion practices.

Pennsylvania's economy in the last quarter of the twentieth century shifted from manufacturing to services. The city of Pittsburgh reflected the change by surviving the demise of its steel industry through the development of diversified services. The loss of higher-paying union manufacturing and mining jobs (only 27,000 of the latter remained in 1990) was enormous, but creation of nonunion, low-paying service jobs was so great that Pennsylvania's unemployment figures were not significantly higher than national averages. At the beginning of the 1990s there were 1.5 million service and 1.2 million wholesale and retail trade jobs, compared with 1 million manufacturing jobs. Agriculture continued to be the largest single occupation in the state, with 800,000 people employed and 57,000 farms. The state's mushroom industry was the largest in the country. Still, the loss of manufacturing jobs brought considerable pain. There were also great regional disparities as many industrial counties of western Pennsylvania suffered high unemployment and declining populations at the same time southern counties outside Philadelphia thrived.

In 1992 the state's population stood at 12,009,361, with a higher proportion of elderly citizens than in most states. Nine percent of Pennsylvanians were African Americans. The Amish still drove their buggies. Ethnic neighborhoods existed both in the cities and towns. Mahanoy City, a typical anthracite (coal-mining) town of 5,200 residents, boasted a dozen churches and a half-dozen fire companies representing different ethnic groups. These traditional cultures continued to enrich Pennsylvanians as they encountered the challenges of modern society with its diversified economy.

[Paul B. Beers, *Pennsylvania Politics Today and Yesterday* (University Park, Pa., 1980); Philip Klein and Ari Hoogenboom, *A History of Pennsylvania,* 2nd ed. (University Park, Pa., 1980).]

ROBERT E. O'CONNOR

See also **SUPP:** Philadelphia; Pittsburgh; *Planned Parenthood of Southeastern Pennsylvania* v. *Casey*; Three Mile Island; *Webster* v. *Reproductive Health Services.*

PENSION PLANS. Usually involving employers or government or both, pension plans provide periodic payments to employees or their families after retirement or in the event of death or disability. In some cases, usually among the self-employed, these arrangements are individual. Plans may be funded through employer set-asides, deferred profit sharing, or employee savings. Social security, a federal pension program for most working Americans established by the Social Security Act of 1935, may augment employer or private pension plans. Separate government pension plans exist for federal, state, and local government employees and the military. Individuals may augment their pensions through individual retirement accounts (IRAs) as well as 40l(k) or other thrift plans. Such savings strategies are a growing segment of the U.S. retirement system, offering tax deferrals and the promise of increased pension income as individuals reach qualifying age.

In 1991, 68 percent of U.S. workers were covered by employer-provided pension plans (although only 53 percent of these elected to participate in such plans), compared to just 19 percent who were covered at the end of World War II. One consequence of increased participation in pension plans is that the age at which many Americans choose to retire is now less than sixty-five, an age that previously was considered early retirement. Inflation, which greatly increased during the 1970s, led to automatic increases in many pension plans, which, together with the increased longevity of senior citizens, threatened the stability of some pension funds.

ROBERT M. GUTH

See also **SUPP:** Cost of Living Adjustment; Set-Asides; Social Security.

PENTECOSTAL CHURCHES. The Pentecostal movement emerged out of small beginnings in 1901 in Topeka, Kans. It had nineteenth-century antecedents, especially among clusters of holiness advocates in Tennessee and North Carolina but its defining doctrinal tenet first was advanced by Charles F. Parham (1873–1929) in Topeka. At the turn of the century scattered groups of populist radical Protestants sought a religious experience they called "the baptism with the Holy Spirit." Parham concluded that such baptism would always be manifested by speaking in tongues. Pentecostals were radical evangelicals who accepted as biblical Parham's view that tongues speech evidenced Spirit baptism. Their general beliefs and practices closely paralleled those of many others in their religious subculture. Only gradually did a Pentecostal movement disentangle itself from related and similar movements in the contemporary popular religious culture.

In the 1990s Pentecostalism was found all over the world. Seventy-five percent of all Protestants in South America (regardless of denomination) subscribed to Pentecostal beliefs. In parts of Africa huge indigenous churches were essentially Pentecostal in belief and worship style, as was a large portion of the Christian community in China. In the United States the charismatic renewal in mainstream denominations since the 1960s brought emphasis on beliefs and practices usually associated with Pentecostalism. The term generally is used to describe a movement that acknowledges Parham and the revival meetings his views influenced at the Azusa Street Mission in Los Angeles in 1906. Adherents believe all Christians should have an experience of baptism with the Holy Spirit and that tongues speech is the "uniform initial evidence" of this baptism. They hold this view in a larger theological context shaped by premillennialism, advocacy of divine healing, and expectation of the presence among them of the "gifts of the Spirit" listed in the New Testament. Pentecostals emphasize evangelism and some denominations sponsor a strong missionary presence abroad. Their focus on spiritual gifts usually resulted in distinctive styles of worship. They tend to be verbal and expressive of faith and may vent feelings in hand clapping, tears, shouts, falling, dance, song, tongues, and other responses to what they believe to be the Holy Spirit's presence among and within them.

Despite such commonalities Pentecostalism historically has been divided. The first division stemmed from the first decade of the movement when it attracted people from various backgrounds whose unity was rooted in the quest for a particular experience. It soon became evident that disagreement over the timing and understanding of baptism with the Holy Spirit was deep and abiding. Some believed that the experience of Spirit baptism was authentic only if it followed two definite, instantaneous experiences—conversion and sanctification. Others held that Spirit baptism followed conversion and that sanctification was progressive. In the mid-1990s the largest groups holding to three experiences are the Church of God in Christ, headquartered in Memphis, Tenn., and the Church of God in Cleveland, Tenn. The best-known denomination advocating two crisis experiences is the Assemblies of God.

Another division emerged in 1913 when a sizable group opted to follow teaching that denied the Trinity in favor of emphasizing Jesus' name. Known as Oneness or Jesus Only Pentecostals, this segment of Pentecostalism remained apart from the movement as a whole because of its anti-Trinitarian stance. It historically has divided along racial lines. Among larger Oneness groups are the Pentecostal Assemblies of the World headquartered in Indianapolis, Ind., and the United Pentecostal Church centered in St. Louis, Mo. The third division was along racial lines. During the brief heyday of the Azusa Street revival (1906–1908), blacks and Anglo-Americans sometimes shared leadership. The acknowledged head of the Azusa Street Mission was an African American, William Seymour, who expelled Hispanics from the mission. In general,

Pentecostalism comprises denominations that are primarily black, primarily white, or primarily Hispanic. The Church of God in Christ has been primarily black, for example, whereas the Assemblies of God is primarily white, with a sizable Hispanic membership organized in separate districts and generally served by separate schools and publications.

Over the years black Pentecostals, Oneness and Trinitarian, have had limited contact with one another. Trinitarian white Pentecostals met annually beginning in 1948 through the Pentecostal Fellowship of North America until that organization disbanded in 1994. In its place, in a display of interracial goodwill, black and white Trinitarian Pentecostals created the Pentecostal-Charismatic Churches of North America. Trinitarian Pentecostals worldwide have an opportunity every three years to gather in the World Pentecostal Conference.

Most U.S. Pentecostal denominations oppose the ecumenical movement and distance themselves from the National Council of Churches and the World Council of Churches. At the local level and in local causes Pentecostals often participate in ministerial associations and church councils. Although the charismatic renewal provides limited opportunities for relationships with some mainline Protestants, most Pentecostals nurture stereotypes of mainstream denominations as "dead" and "cold" with little to offer people who have discovered the "full" gospel. Pentecostalism of the late twentieth century demanded far less separation from the culture at large, such as amusements, sports, entertainment, and fashion, from adherents than the movement once did. This, together with an openness to popular culture and readiness to answer all questions, made Pentecostalism attractive. Growth in membership in the United States has been flat since the early 1980s, but in the non-Western world Pentecostalism continued to thrive.

[Robert Mapes Anderson, *Vision of the Disinherited* (New York, 1979); Edith L. Blumhofer, *Restoring the Faith* (Urbana, Ill., 1993); Harvey Cox, *Fire From Heaven* (New York, 1994).]

EDITH BLUMHOFER

See also **SUPP:** Fundamentalism; Millenarianism; Religion.

PERSIAN GULF WAR. *See* **Gulf War of 1991.**

PERSONAL ADS. Advertisements placed by young women who had been left "destitute of Fortune and Friends" appeared in the United States as early as 1790. The *Philadelphia Public Ledger* was the first publication to devote a separate department to classified advertising, and by the end of the nineteenth century newspaper ads placed by "young masseuses" were common, as were ads placed by lonely men in the frontier West who were seeking companionship and marriage. Personal ads have been the basis for such motion pictures as *Sea of Love* (1989) and *Loves Music, Loves to Dance* (1991) about serial killers who find their victims through the papers. In addition to growing numbers of newspaper and magazine "personals," cyberspace users can search for love among millions of people around the world on the Internet and on independent computer bulletin boards.

[Frank Luther Mott, *American Journalism,* 3rd ed. (New York, 1962).]

JOHN J. BYRNE

PERSONAL COMPUTERS. *See* **Computers.**

PERSONNEL ADMINISTRATOR OF MASSACHU-SETTS V. FEENEY, 442 U.S. 256 (1979), a Supreme Court case that considered whether a Massachusetts law giving veterans a lifetime preference in filling open civil service positions violated the equal protection clause of the Fourteenth Amendment. Helen B. Feeney was a civil servant who received higher grades on civil service examinations than male veterans. Because of the preference law, however, males repeatedly were promoted over her. Twice the federal district court declared the law unconstitutional. The state of Massachusetts, supported by the solicitor general of the United States, appealed to the Supreme Court. The Court in a seven-to-two decision sustained the law. A basic question was whether the effect of the preference classification was "purposeful discrimination." The law violated the Fourteenth Amendment only if the claimant could prove that the discriminatory purpose was because of, not merely in spite of, its adverse effect on the employment opportunities of women. The history of the Massachusetts law indicated that the statute created "a preference for veterans of either sex over women." The law affected adversely more women than men because until 1967 there had been a 2 percent quota on women in the military. Male nonveterans, however, suffered from this preferred treatment as much as female nonveterans. Although the lower court initially applied this principle to decide in favor of Feeney, after appeals by the state she lost. The case clearly stated that in gender-discrimination suits mere foreseeability of a law's consequences does not establish the needed discriminatory purpose. The case supported state assistance to veterans even if discrimination toward women was a result. It also established a greater burden of proof on plaintiffs.

[Bruce E. Rosenblum, "Discriminatory Purpose and Disproportionate Impact: An Assessment After *Feeney*," *Columbia Law Review* 79 (November 1979): 1376–1413.]

TONY FREYER

See also **SUPP:** Affirmative Action; *Equal Employment Opportunity Commission* v. *Sears, Roebuck and Company*; Women's Movement; Women's Rights.

PESTICIDES are chemicals that destroy organisms that compete with human activity. Seventy percent of all pesticides used in the United States are employed in agriculture to control insects, weeds, and fungi. Other uses include lawn maintenance and disease control. Since the development of synthetic chemicals in the 1940s, the use of chemical pesticides has increased dramatically. Between the early 1950s and the 1990s, agricultural use of pesticides, by weight, increased 900 times. The use of pesticides produces many short-term economic benefits. Pesticides clear areas of pests and are easy to transport, store, and apply. Pesticides contribute to increased crop yields; the annual U.S. investment of $3 billion in pesticides leads to $12 billion in increased agricultural revenues. The U.S. Department of Agriculture estimates that without pesticide use and sophisticated storage and transportation technologies, food prices would be 30 to 50 percent higher.

Concern over the long-term costs of pesticide use has increased since the early 1960s, when the warnings contained in Rachel Carson's *Silent Spring* (1962) led to critical examination of pesticide use. Research in ecology, economics, and public health during the 1970s and 1980s demonstrated the detrimental effects of pesticides. Pesticide practices prevalent in the 1990s compromised the ecosystem in several ways. Many pesticides kill a variety of species in addition to the target organism. Application of pesticides can be inefficient, contaminating soil and water supplies. Populations of pests often develop genetic immunity to pesticides. By 1990 almost 500 insect pest species had developed genetic resistance to pesticides. Moreover, the concentration, and thus the potential for harm, of pesticides increases as they move through organisms up the food chain. The integrity of ecosystems suffers as pesticides interfere with ecological relationships between organisms.

Humans, equally dependent on healthy ecosystems, are also harmed by exposure to pesticides.

In response to environmental and health concerns and decreased efficacy of chemical pesticides, the Environmental Protection Agency banned the use of several pesticides, including DDT in 1973 and ethylene dibromide in the early 1980s, although export to foreign countries is still legal. The Department of Agriculture supports research on alternative pest control strategies. Traditional methods of cultivation used prior to the advent of pesticides, such as crop rotation and crop diversity, were reemerging, and cross-breeding and genetic engineering were producing plants that are more resistant to specific pests. Biological controls include the use of bacteria, viruses, natural predators, pheromones that attract insects to traps, and development-arresting hormones. These techniques are combined through integrated pest management (IPM) programs that examine the ecological relationships of pests, crops, and other organisms and produce control strategies utilizing a variety of nonpesticide techniques to raise crop yields. Government policy in the 1990s, through subsidies and price supports, still favored chemical pesticide use and production. There was, however, also a clear movement to develop techniques that ultimately may make pesticides obsolete.

[Walter H. Corson, ed., *The Global Ecology Handbook* (Boston, 1990); G. Tyler Miller, Jr., *Environmental Science* (Belmont, Calif., 1991); Sandra Postel, "Controlling Toxic Chemicals," in *State of the World, 1988*, edited by Lester R. Brown, Linda Stark, and Edward C. Wolf (New York, 1988).]

DAVID W. CASH

See also **DAH** and **SUPP:** Agriculture; Ecology; Insecticides and Herbicides; **SUPP:** Environmental Movement.

PETROLEUM INDUSTRY. The embargo of oil exports to the United States by Middle East Arab nations in the aftermath of the 1973 Arab-Israeli War was the most dramatic catalyst in shaping the global and U.S. petroleum industry in the 1970s and 1980s. Nominal prices of crude petroleum and petroleum products rose dramatically from less than $5 per barrel in the late 1960s to almost $40 per barrel in 1980 before tapering off in the late 1980s and early 1990s to approximately $15 a barrel. The rapid rise of crude oil prices drove gasoline prices to unprecedented levels in the 1970s and 1980s, contributing in 1973 and again in 1979–1980 to long lines for consumers at the gas pumps. Between 1970 and 1980 U.S. gasoline prices increased from less than $.40 a gallon to almost $1.40 a gallon before declining in the mid-1980s to under $1. Such significant increases in prices did not derive primarily from a decline in world production levels, although U.S. production did vary over the 1970–1990 period, adding additional uncertainty to the market. U.S. crude oil production declined in the 1970s from approximately 9.6 million barrels a day in 1970 to 8.6 barrels in 1980, following an even sharper decline to 8.2 in 1976. In 1976 the United States also fell to third place among world producers, behind the Soviet Union and Saudi Arabia. After a brief recovery to 8.9 barrels in 1985, production declined again to 7.3 by 1990. The initial fear of international oil shortages contributed to a quadrupling of prices between 1972 and 1982 before rapidly declining in the mid-1980s. World production levels (including the United States) continued impressive levels of growth to 1980, rising from 45.8 million barrels a day in 1970 to 59.35 a decade later. They then declined slightly before surpassing 1970 levels by 1990.

In 1971 the administration of President Richard M. Nixon imposed price controls on oil as part of the president's larger anti-inflation program. This measure, however, contributed to higher levels of consumption at the same time that it discouraged domestic producers. With the 1973 international crisis over supplies, demand increased sharply with the result that independent refiners experienced difficulty obtaining adequate supplies. In 1973, responding to political pressure to remove price controls, the Nixon administration introduced a voluntary allocation system and abolished the import quotas established a decade earlier by the administration of Dwight D. Eisenhower. Both measures were designed to improve access to supplies of crude oil, although the long-standing tension remained between a policy that encouraged domestic production by restricting imports and thus reducing dependency on foreign oil and a policy that encouraged imports both to protect domestic reserves and also to encourage lower prices for domestic use.

In late 1973 President Nixon addressed this issue in his first major address on energy, in which he called for Project Independence to make the nation self-sufficient in oil by 1985. That goal was to be achieved by increasing domestic supplies, developing alternative sources of energy, and through domestic conservation. In 1975 the administration of President Gerald R. Ford and Congress instituted price and allocation controls in the Energy Policy and Conservation Act. The legislation provided that the controls would be

phased out by mid-1979. The Ford administration also sought to reduce imports by reducing demand and stimulating domestic production, transporting oil from Alaska, leasing the outer continental shelf, and reconsidering the effects of environmental controls. In the same year the administration established the Strategic Petroleum Reserve to reduce dependence on foreign supplies of crude oil.

President Jimmy Carter's administration was even more strongly committed to energy self-sufficiency. The President's National Energy Plan in 1977 identified as goals the reduction of vulnerability to interruption of supply, promoting conservation, and shifting to renewable or inexhaustible resources. The administration proposed taxes to reduce demand and force consumers to pay the full cost of energy. Price controls were recommended to prevent windfall profits to producers from radical increase in prices. Even more than the initiatives under Nixon and Ford, the Carter policies were intended to shift consumption from imports to domestic sources and toward coal and nuclear energy and away from oil and natural gas. The Carter proposals resulted in the 1978 National Energy Act, which incorporated in broad outline the Carter proposals, although it tended to weaken them. The legislation provided for reduction of electrical generation by oil and natural gas and tax incentives to encourage conservation, but oil and gas price controls were not continued. There were no provisions to develop alternative energy sources and only limited resources were allocated to research and development on alternative energies. The 1980 Energy Security Act established the Synthetic Fuels Corporation to provide financial support to the private energy sector.

Such initiatives had little impact on imports from the Organization of Petroleum Exporting Countries (OPEC), which continued to increase. In 1973 the United States imported 1.2 billion barrels of crude oil, more than one half coming from the Americas, and almost 300 million barrels from the Middle East. In 1979 imports rose to 2.4 billion barrels. By that date, however, Africa was the leading source of supply with 900 million barrels, followed by the Middle East with 750 million barrels. The Americas had fallen back to slightly more than 400 million barrels.

Government regulation of the industry in the 1970s had a variety of objectives, including reducing import dependency, encouraging domestic production, and attempting to stabilize prices. Higher prices for domestic refined oil in the United States encouraged producers and refiners to process oil that at lower prices would have been uneconomical. One effect of feared oil shortages during the decade along with high demand and rising prices was to increase corporate profits, although there is debate among specialists whether the refining or producing sectors benefited more. One evaluation of twenty-four major firms indicated an increase of net income for those firms from $6.4 billion in 1971 to $9 billion in 1973, $11.4 billion in 1974, and $16.3 billion in 1980.

Oil shortages occasioned by the curtailment of Iranian supply because of the 1979 revolution in that country produced the second major oil shock within ten years and for three years drove prices to unprecedented levels. Although a reduction in prices after 1982 encouraged greater U.S. economic growth in the 1980s, there was a disincentive to continue the conservationist and alternative energy initiatives of the Nixon through Carter administrations. President Ronald Reagan's administration also was committed to free-market conditions to resolve national energy problems, with more exploitation of oil, natural gas, coal, and uranium on public lands. The Reagan administration deregulated oil prices, although it increased contributions to the Strategic Petroleum Reserve. The Reagan and George Bush administrations, with their emphasis on market forces and deregulation, abandoned the effort to establish a clear, long-term national oil and energy policy, assuming that supply and price were under control. One result was that oil imports by the 1990s were on the rise again. In 1985 total imports of crude oil had fallen to the 1973 level of 1.2 billion barrels, with a reduced dependency on the Middle East as a source of supply (fewer than 100 million barrels compared with more than 600 million from the Americas). In 1990 Middle East supplies constituted 600 million of the 2.2 billion barrels imported. The United States was again dependent on foreign supplies for half its oil requirements.

One of the most dramatic and significant developments of the mid-1980s in the oil sector was the collapse of world and domestic prices—the third oil shock following those of 1973 and 1979–1980. The crisis was stimulated in large part by the rift within OPEC, between Saudi Arabia and other OPEC producers over market share, with OPEC objectives shifting from price control to markets. OPEC also began to increase production in 1985–1986. One result was that in 1985 the price of West Texas Intermediate oil fell sharply to $10 a barrel from a high in excess of $31. The consequences of this price decline of course varied within the U.S. economy; for consumers the decline was a boon, while for producing regions of the United States where there was a heavy reliance on the industry for employment and revenues the collapse meant severe recession.

The Gulf War of 1991 rekindled concern over security of supply and led the Bush administration to inaugurate a national energy strategy. The main objective of the strategy was to reduce the importance of oil in the U.S. economy and, accordingly, mitigate the vulnerability of the United States to foreign oil supply disruptions. Legislation under that initiative passed Congress in October 1992, although the legislation dealt less with oil and gas than with electric utility reform and nuclear power and authorized more research and development funds for alternative fuels and conservation. With the victory of the Republicans at the polls in the 1994 midterm elections and the movement of Republicans into key committee chairmanships in Congress, it was anticipated that the highly conservationist orientation of the previous decade would come under challenge from the 104th Congress. Congress moved quickly to end restrictions on exports of oil from the Alaska North Slope and to implement some royalty relief for deepwater projects in the Gulf of Mexico. It was also anticipated that there would be a strong effort to take a conservative stance on environmental regulation and enforcement. In 1995 oil industry specialists predicted a shift of the industry focus away from the oil and gas sectors in the Gulf of Mexico to Alaska and California, where the main interest is crude oil production.

The dilemma that confronted the industry and government was tension between those goals and economic and security interests. The Arctic National Wildlife Refuge was considered to be the most promising area for oil development in the twenty-first century. Given the high demand for oil and oil products and declining levels of U.S. domestic production (from 9 million barrels a day in 1985 to a projected 5 million in 2000), the tension between environmentalism and economic interest promised to be the main issue of the next decades.

[Joseph P. Kalt, *The Economics and Politics of Oil Price Regulation* (Cambridge, Mass., 1981); Peter Odell, ed., *Oil and World Power: Background of the Oil Crisis,* 8th ed. (New York, 1986); Daniel Yergin, *The Prize: The Epic Quest for Oil, Money and Power* (New York, 1991); Daniel Yergin and Barbara Kates-Garnick, eds., *The Reshaping of the Oil Industry: Just Another Commodity?* (Cambridge, Mass., 1985).]

STEPHEN J. RANDALL

See also **SUPP:** Energy, Department of; Energy, Renewable; Energy Industry; Energy Policy; Energy

Research and Development Administration; *Exxon Valdez*; Gulf War of 1991; Middle East, Relations with; Offshore Oil; Oil Crises.

PHARMACEUTICAL INDUSTRY. A wide variety of effective, high-quality products for both human and veterinary use are produced by the U.S. pharmaceutical, or drug, industry, including nonprescription, over-the-counter drugs marketed directly to the public, as well as ethical drugs, which require a prescription and are therefore marketed to the medical profession. After the introduction of sulfa drugs in the 1930s and such antibiotics as penicillin in the 1940s, the drug industry grew rapidly and began to produce a host of new products that were effective in the prevention, treatment, and in some cases eradication of many deadly diseases. Drug therapy became important, widespread, and generally cost effective. The drug industry in the late twentieth century was a large, highly profitable, socially important, and politically powerful entity. As a result of these successes and some widely publicized failures, drug company activities are highly politicized.

The largest and most sophisticated multinational drug companies combine research and development with an elaborate network for distribution of information and products. Although most of these companies are in Western Europe, the United States, and Japan, the industry has become increasingly international. Sixty countries have an annual production of at least $100 million. Worldwide production doubled between 1975 and 1990, reaching $150 billion. Market growth proved nearly as robust during the same period; worldwide per capita consumption jumped from $17 to $29. Debate continued as the twentieth century drew to a close about the extent and appropriateness of the high profits of the industry, which were well above the average for all manufacturing industries as well as for Fortune 500 companies. In 1992 the U.S. drug industry's return on sales was 11.5 percent, four times the average of Fortune 500 companies. During the 1980s drug prices did not rise as fast as overall health care costs but exceeded significantly the rate of inflation.

By the end of the 1980s public concern over the cost of health care and growing interest in health care reform had increased markedly. This concern politicized federal agency and industry decisions. For example, the Food and Drug Administration responded to the AIDS epidemic by developing guidelines for an accelerated approval process. In 1987 Burroughs Wellcome marketed AZT, the first anti-AIDS drug approved in the United States. The company's decision to price a year's supply at $8,000 to $10,000 was widely criticized as a rapacious pricing strategy. Drugmakers typically have offered price breaks to large buyers, such as hospitals and health maintenance organizations (HMOs), but pharmacists often face huge markups—sometimes 1,000 percent—over prices paid by hospitals and HMOs. In the early 1990s retail pharmacists and others brought price-discrimination suits against drug manufacturers. Analysts doubted the pharmacists would prevail in court, arguing that the real intent behind such suits may have been to keep pressure on Washington to include some limits on differential pricing practices as part of health care reform.

Conservatives and industry spokespeople argued against government interference in the market, particularly through price controls, the most common form of intervention in other countries. They claimed that without high profits there would be little innovation. Liberals and consumer advocates pointed to the monopoly benefits of patent protection, evidence of oligopolistic behavior, and extensive government subsidization of research costs to back their claims that there should be price controls or profit limits set by the government.

Pricing decisions have always taken place within the context of patent laws, and in industrial countries patent protection usually lasts sixteen to twenty years from the date of application (seventeen years from the date of grant in the United States). During this period—part of which is taken up by testing and approval—the company has exclusive marketing rights. Once the patent expires a drug is much less profitable. Even when prices are high, companies may claim products are cost-effective by pointing to the cost of alternative methods such as surgery and other treatments. This tactic was used in defending the price of AZT. The industry estimated the annual cost of standard AIDS treatment at $43,000 and defended the $8,000 to $10,000 annual price tag for AZT as a comparative bargain. Since the 1950s debate over pharmaceutical profits has been tied to the question of whether there is competition in the drug industry or if high profitability is the result of monopoly or oligopoly. It is doubtful that any firm enjoys monopolistic status, but evidence suggests that some enjoy considerable market power. New products sometimes generate high profits for particular firms, industry profitability is high, and the market position of major firms has remained stable.

The largely cordial relationship between government and the drug industry began to change in 1959 with the congressional investigations known as the Kefauver hearings. Questions emerged about research practices, drug safety and effectiveness, and price disparities between brand-name drugs and generic equivalents. The Thalidomide disaster, widely publicized in 1961, heightened public concern. Although not approved for use in the United States, the sedative Thalidomide led to birth defects in 12,000 children worldwide. Such events led to a more complex approval process and stricter manufacturing guidelines in the attempt to ensure both the safety and efficacy of drugs.

Drug manufacturers have complained about such regulations as lengthy approval processes, claiming they prevent marketing of potentially beneficial drugs. Many new drugs, however, are "me too" drugs that are often essentially equivalent to existing drugs and are not necessarily more effective. The FDA replaced 308 of 348 new drugs brought to market between 1981 and 1988 in this category. The industry has often benefited from government policies. Pharmaceutical manufacturers have rightly noted that research and development is risky and expensive, but much of the risk associated with the research and development of new drugs is borne by university laboratories, small companies, and the National Institutes of Health (NIH). These organizations do much of the initial screening of compounds for possible therapeutic efficacy. Once a promising compound is discovered it can be sold or licensed to the large drug companies. While the research costs for many new drugs are not subsidized by government funds, the government does provide roughly half of all U.S. health-related research money, largely through the NIH. The NIH conducts drug-related research, and when promising compounds appear, companies bid for a license to market them. Consumer advocates claim that the licensing fees do not reflect the value of the research and that drug companies fail to pass on such savings to the public. The industry benefits from a variety of tax breaks. Large companies have long taken advantage of Section 936 of the U.S. Internal Revenue Code. Intended to promote economic development in Puerto Rico, Section 936 allows U.S. industries partial tax exemption on profits from operations in Puerto Rico and other U.S. possessions. In late 1995, citing concerns about "corporate welfare" and the budget deficit, Congress considered elimination of Section 936. These and other issues continued to be debated as consumer advocates and policy-makers addressed the rising costs of health care in the late twentieth century.

[Robert Ballance, Janos Pogany, and Helmut Forstner, *The World's Pharmaceutical Industries* (Brookfield, Vt., 1992); Milton Silverman, Philip R. Lee, and Mia Lydecker, *Pills and the Public Purse* (Berkeley, Calif., 1981).]

M. SEAN DONNELLY

See also **SUPP:** Acquired Immune Deficiency Syndrome; Bacteriology and Virology; Food and Drug Administration; Hospitals; Insurance; Medicine; National Institutes of Health.

PHILADELPHIA. Between the 1970s and 1990s the City of Brotherly Love moved from a period of racial divisiveness and financial crisis to a less turbulent era of accommodating social relations and financial stability. In the 1970s the flamboyant Mayor Frank L. Rizzo linked crime and race as tensions heightened in a city where the minority population would soon reach 40 percent. In the 1980s African-American Mayor W. Wilson Goode won acclaim for handling race relations well but received criticism for alleged administrative incompetence. In the early 1990s, Mayor Edward G. Rendell took office with broad support from every racial and ethnic group. Financial problems reached their peak in 1991 when the city borrowed $150 million at an effective interest rate of 24 percent in order to avoid bankruptcy. The state provided funding to the city, required Philadelphia to plan balanced budgets for five years, and created a financial oversight board with the power to stop state funding if the plans were not implemented. Philadelphia temporarily lost some of its freedom but began to reestablish a sound financial position.

Migration of many middle- and upper-income Philadelphians to the suburbs was one cause of Philadelphia's financial woes. The city lost 6 percent of its population from 1980 to 1990. An even bigger decline of 13 percent took place from 1970 to 1980. The 1990 population of 1,585,577 was down from more than 2 million in the 1960s. The metropolitan area had between 5 and 6 million residents in 1990.

The dominant Philadelphian in the 1970s was Mayor Rizzo. A former police commissioner, he inspired both affection and enmity. His supporters applauded his intention to take forceful measures to reduce crime. Opponents believed his statements exploited racial tension by defending police brutality directed at African Americans. Rizzo left office in 1979 after voters rejected a charter amendment that would have allowed mayors to serve more than two consecutive four-year terms. The dominant Philadelphian in the 1980s was Mayor Goode, the city's first African-American mayor, who served two terms. Despite campaign themes that emphasized good management, deepening fiscal problems and administrative difficulties marked the Goode years. Symbolic of these years and the most memorable event of the 1980s was the MOVE (Community Action Movement) tragedy of May 1985. In trying to evict MOVE, a radical commune living in a Philadelphia row house, the police dropped a bomb on the building. The ensuing fire killed eleven MOVE members, including children. Sixty-one adjacent buildings also burned down, leaving 250 people homeless. After winning the 1991 Republican primary, Rizzo (a former Democrat) suffered a fatal heart attack. Rendell, a white Democrat, defeated two black candidates to win the Democratic nomination. He defeated the Republican candidate, Joseph M. Egan, with two-thirds of the vote and focused on economic concerns, including efforts to keep Philadelphia's sports teams in the city.

[Russell F. Weigley et al., eds., *Philadelphia: A Three-Hundred-Year History* (New York, 1982).]

ROBERT E. O'CONNOR

See also **SUPP:** Pennsylvania.

PHILANTHROPY. Charitable giving has been the subject of more study since 1970 than at any time in U.S. history. This popular and scholarly attention, reflected in a spate of books, articles, and university courses on the subject, have enriched our understanding of a national characteristic often overlooked. One hotly debated issue for scholars studying the role of charity in national institutions is whether philanthropy preserves economic inequalities in a capitalist society. Critics of Western democratic capitalism see private philanthropy as one of the many ideological means by which the capitalist class maintains its privileged status. In Western societies of the past, religion supplied the dominant ideology by which the lower classes were reconciled to their fate on earth with the promise of heavenly rewards. In contemporary U.S. society such principles as equality of opportunity, economic growth, individual initiative, and the absolute value of private property integrate citizens into a belief system that makes the financial success of some and the failure of others appear natural, inevitable, even just. From this viewpoint, a commitment to philanthropy—as opposed, for example, to efforts to achieve a more equal distribution of wealth—serves the interests of the capitalist class.

Defenders of philanthropy, however, argue that the right to associate freely and to support formally such associations is a key to safeguarding American liberties. Conservatives may also find philanthropy, with its frequent progressive agenda, suspect, but they argue that volunteer associations provide a critically needed layer between citizens and government. The right of people to "vote their values" through charitable giving is viewed as essential in a pluralistic democracy. Another major issue is the public's lack of understanding of the important role philanthropy has played historically in shaping U.S. history. More universities, however, began studying charitable giving in order to understand its effect on the nation's past and present. Excellent programs in nonprofit management and philanthropy exist at Yale University, Indiana University, and the University of San Francisco, among others.

The range, extent, and growth of giving in the United States is astonishing. Donors gave an estimated $124.3 billion to charity in 1992, 6.4 percent more than in 1991. According to *Giving USA,* an annual report on U.S. philanthropy, donations outpaced inflation despite a weak economy from 1970 to the mid-1990s. Foundation giving represented nearly 6 percent of this total, corporate giving 4 percent, and individual giving and bequests 90 percent. These percentages have been remarkably stable since 1970. Giving by the nation's 22,000 active grant-making foundations ($8.7 billion in 1992) has increased more than other sources of contributions since 1990. The continuing importance of foundation giving lies in the ability to concentrate funds on selected projects, call attention to trends in social needs, and venture capital on unproven solutions to social problems. Formation of new foundations in the 1980s and early 1990s, as well as more openness and accountability among smaller nonprofit organizations, is a trend that should continue. Corporate giving continues to raise controversy. In an era of downsizing, corporate officers have reduced charitable budgets, putting emphasis on gifts that enhance the marketability of their products and advance their business agenda. Short of cash, many corporations emphasize cause-related marketing partnerships with prestigious nonprofits from major universities or human service groups such as the Red Cross. The connection between giving and corporate interest has increased criticism of this sector. Should corporations engage in philanthropy with the funds of stockholders? Is corporate philanthropy just a marketing tool?

Much scholarly attention has focused on characteristics of individual donors. Considering that 90 percent of total funds donated come from this source, scholars and nonprofit professionals have begun asking questions and offering data about who gives, why, and in what areas. Although such research is still relatively new, patterns are emerging. A comprehensive survey of giving for the period 1987–1989 by the Gallup Organization–Independent Sector showed that U.S. households gave an average of $734, up 31 percent from $562 two years earlier. Seventy-five percent of households—94.6 million—made charitable deductions in 1989, up from 71 percent in 1987. Among demographic groups showing substantial gains in giving were baby boomers born between 1946 and 1964 (86 percent gave), those with household incomes between $75,000 and $100,000 (92 percent gave), and African Americans (61 percent gave). The largest increases went to environmental, health, educational, and human services needs, while international causes and arts groups saw declines in giving. These trends continued without substantial change into the 1990s.

Surveys show that activities and attitudes strongly correlate with charitable giving. In 1990, 100 million adults volunteered time to charities, a substantial increase from the 80 million who volunteered in 1987. Volunteers gave an average of $1,022 in 1989, nearly three times the $357 average contribution for nonvolunteers. Employers and charities benefited by encouraging volunteerism among underrepresented groups, including African Americans, youths ages eighteen to twenty-four, and people with household incomes below $20,000. When asked to volunteer, people from these groups did so at rates similar to other demographic groups. Surveys by the Council on Foundations and the Independent Sector indicate that another key variable in charitable giving is religious worship and church membership. Perhaps 70 percent of the population attends churches, synagogues, or mosques. People who worship regularly make 70 percent of all contributions to charity and give more to nonreligious charities than do nonworshipers. In 1989 members of congregations gave an average 2.4 percent of household income to charity, compared to 0.8 percent from households with no formal religious connection. Motives for giving are complex. Surveys agree that giving correlates with identifiable attitudes and feelings. Citizens who believe that those possessing wealth are responsible for the less fortunate tend to give more; those with well-defined personal philanthropic goals or who are concerned about reinforcing traditional moral values tend to give more; those giving for religious reasons give more.

Americans continued to support charities in record numbers and record amounts despite the 1986 Tax Reform Act, under which Congress disallowed tax deductions to donors qualifying for itemization of deductions on their returns. Tax considerations can affect the timing and amount of gifts but are not more important than a host of other donor motives, including a sense of personal satisfaction; furthering activities of institutions from which the donor benefited; responding to the request of a friend, influential business associate, or employer; and creating a memorial to a family member.

The changing culture of philanthropy helps define the ethos of the country as a whole as well as its regions. Historians, philosophers, economists, and sociologists are interested in what attitudes, beliefs, values, and expectations shape giving and receiving of gifts. Scholars such as James Joseph and Michael O'Neill provided perspectives on how, why, and where ethnic and racial groups define and support communities. Solid information about trends among groups other than traditional Catholic, Protestant, and Jewish donors was still sketchy in the mid-1990s, but scholarly attention began focusing on African-American, Hispanic, Asian-American, Native American and other groups heretofore underexamined. Clearly traditional philanthropy, which tends to dictate solutions "from the top of society down," is less important. Complex social problems require sensitivity to multiculturalism, grass-roots community planning, and multisector (private, government, and nonprofit) funding.

With the return of Republican control of Congress in the 1994 elections and fewer public resources for a host of familiar programs in support of the arts, education, health, and welfare, the 1990s witnessed a renewed debate about philanthropy's role. Many conservatives argued that reduced government spending would be adequately replaced by private giving. With a slow-growth economy and lingering recession in key states, such as California, there was no likelihood that giving rates could keep pace with human needs. Indeed, the traditional debate about the proper mix of public sector and private sector responsibility for the welfare of the country was revived. Many, particularly in the charitable foundations sector, continued to feel that organized philanthropy is best limited to social research, development, and innovation with government remaining responsible for social maintenance. The outcome of the debate promised to help shape policy in important ways as the twentieth century drew to a close. Philanthropy in the United States continued to help characterize its society. It is not likely that voters will allow government to restrict free association of the right of donors to help shape their communities by expressing values through giving. For all the imperfections and its occasional waste, philanthropy will continue to help define the United States as a culturally distinct part of the world.

[Robert H. Bremner, *American Philanthropy* (Chicago, 1988); Robert A. Nisbet, *The Making of Modern Society* (New York, 1986); Michael O'Neill, *The Third America* (San Francisco, 1989); Burton A. Weisbrod, *The Nonprofit Economy* (Cambridge, Mass., 1988).]

ALFRED L. CASTLE

See also **DAH:** Philanthropy and Benevolence; **SUPP:** Volunteerism.

PHILIPPINE ISLANDS remained an important outpost for U.S. naval and air forces until the end of the 1980s. To preserve its bases the United States supported the dictatorship of Ferdinand Marcos until 1986 and then managed the transition to an unstable democracy headed by Corazon Aquino. By the early 1970s U.S. investments in the islands had been surpassed by Japanese and Taiwanese capital, and, as the cold war came to a close, U.S. strategic interest in the islands diminished. As Catholic clergymen and members of the elite became increasingly vocal in their criticism of the government in the mid-1970s, Marcos intensified state repression. The Philippine military killed at least 2,255 persons in extrajudicial executions known as "salvagings," and as many as 70,000 persons may have been imprisoned. Eager to avoid conflict during talks on the military bases, including Clark Air Force Base and the Subic Bay Naval Station, the administration of President Jimmy Carter refrained from criticizing the Philippine record on human rights. A new accord on the bases was signed in January 1979, and U.S. loans, foreign aid, and trade rights continued to support the Philippine economy.

President Ronald Reagan openly embraced Marcos, inviting him for a state visit and declaring him a major ally, but administration officials worried about growing opposition to Marcos within the Philippines. In 1983 opposition leader Benigno Aquino was assassinated at the Manila airport by military conspirators close to the Philippine president. In the following months the armed insurgency of the New People's Army (NPA), a Maoist organization, gathered strength throughout the country. The NPA initiated hundreds of raids against military garrisons and controlled large portions of the countryside and even some cities. In July 1985 analysts for the U.S. Central Intelligence Agency predicted that the NPA might seize power in five years, and in October Reagan sent Senator Paul Laxalt to Manila to express concern over the deteriorating situation. Two weeks later Marcos announced a presidential "snap election" to be held in February 1986. Aquino's widow, Corazon, led a united opposition ticket. On election day, news of widespread fraud incited massive street demonstrations. Catholic bishops denounced the election and called for civil disobedience. On February 22 two leading military officials, Fidel V. Ramos and Juan Ponce Enrile, defected, sealing themselves in a military camp in central Manila. Thousands rushed to the camp to protect Ramos and Enrile from army units loyal to Marcos, while other demonstrators seized broadcast stations and marched on the presidential palace. At Reagan's urging, Marcos fled to Hawaii on February 25.

The new government, headed by Corazon Aquino, maintained strong ties to the United States, allowing the United States to keep its military installations despite increasing opposition to the bases from Filipinos. The Aquino administration endured a string of unsuccessful military coups, the boldest of which, in December 1989, was suppressed with the help of planes dispatched by President George Bush. The end of the cold war coincided with negotiations to renew the bases treaty, and by 1991 it was evident that President Bush was unwilling to offer sufficient aid to gain approval of the treaty from the Philippine senate. In June the eruption of Mount Pinatubo destroyed Clark Air Force Base and damaged the naval station at Subic Bay, further diminishing their value. Unsatisfied with the proposed terms for renewal, the Philippine senate rejected the new treaty in September; the last U.S. forces left the Philippines in November 1992. Relations between the two countries remained cordial, although the United States closed many of its aid programs and consulates, reflecting the Philippines' diminished importance for U.S. foreign policy. In 1992 Filipinos elected Ramos, who had been endorsed by Aquino, to the presidency.

[David Wurfel, *Filipino Politics: Development and Decay* (Ithaca, N.Y., 1988).]

NICK CULLATHER

See also **SUPP:** Filipino Americans.

PHILOSOPHY in the United States since the 1960s has been characterized by diversity and pluralism in the subjects studied and the methods employed, by a significant increase in the number of its practitioners, by a growing influence within colleges and universities, and by a waning influence in the larger society. Analytic philosophy, which dominated philosophic thought in the United States in the middle of the twentieth century, remained important, but wider diversity was brought about by other approaches, such as continental European thought; renewed interest in pragmatists and other historical figures; applied philosophy, including ethics; and new voices espousing feminism, environmentalism, and animal rights. In the 1990s philosophy seemed secure within institutions of higher education; the membership of the American Philosophical Association, most of whom teach in a college setting, climbed from 2,888 in 1975 to 8,792 in 1990. Philosophers also found an audience outside their own departments, as nonphilosophers took up such subjects as semiotics, feminism, and rights and the study of European philosophers, such as Ludwig Wittgenstein, Friedrich Nietzsche, Jacques Derrida, Michel Foucault, and Martin Heidegger. Outside the academic world, however, the specialized and often highly technical studies published by philosophers found only a small audience. The broader audience that earlier read Ralph Waldo Emerson, William James, or John Dewey had largely vanished.

Analytic philosophy, with its analysis of language, concepts, and logic, appeared in the writings of such practitioners as W. V. O. Quine, Hilary Putnam, Donald Davidson, and Robert Nozick. Work in logic and the mathematical analysis of language contributed to the study of artificial intelligence. Philosophers were in the forefront of the effort to explore the meaning of the mind and intelligence in an era of increasingly more powerful computers. Other philosophers, however, such as Richard Rorty, who returned philosophy to its broadly humanistic roots and concerns, rejected the analytic goal of transforming philosophy into a science. Rorty, in his influential *Philosophy and the Mirror of Nature* (1979), urged his colleagues to put aside their epistemological and analytic interests in favor of participation in the "conversation" that constitutes culture. According to Rorty, the best one can hope for is not some absolute, scientifically determined truth that accurately mirrors nature and the "real world," but edification—the effort to find newer, better, and more productive ways of talking about human interests and problems. Phenomenology and existential philosophy were two European imports that contributed to this reorientation of philosophical thought. Not all philosophers were willing

to put aside analysis for edification, but Rorty's work helped spur on a diversification of philosophical approaches.

Pragmatism experienced something of a revival beginning in the 1970s. Often regarded as the most important contribution of the United States to philosophic thought, pragmatism was developed at the turn of the twentieth century by Charles S. Peirce, James, and Dewey. Such neopragmatists as Rorty and Richard J. Bernstein hark back to Dewey's broad philosophical outlook. Other scholars found in Peirce valuable logical insights and a well-developed theory of signs, or semiotics. Peirce, ignored for decades, was finally recognized as perhaps the greatest American philosopher. His seminal work in semiotics influenced such diverse fields as literature and anthropology. The revival of pragmatism was aided by the publication of modern scholarly editions of the works of James, Dewey, and Peirce.

The interrelated approaches of ethics, moral theory, and applied philosophy received renewed attention. Fields such as biomedical and business ethics brought philosophy out of the classroom into operating rooms and corporate board rooms. John Rawls's *A Theory of Justice* (1971) reconfigured debates in moral and legal theory. The study of rights moved beyond abstraction to the consideration of the rights of particular groups, such as the disadvantaged, the disabled, women, animals, and the environment. These discussions had more than scholarly impact; many philosophers sought to ground existing law or policy or to advocate expanding the concept of rights and legal protection to previously unprotected categories.

Philosophy became increasingly decentered as philosophers asked new questions and adopted new perspectives and standpoints. The philosophy of science, building on the work of Thomas S. Kuhn, raised serious questions about the objectivity of science. Feminist philosophy, as practiced by Alison Jagger and Sandra G. Harding, for example, challenged the patriarchical assumptions undergirding most philosophical work and asserted the importance of women's ways of knowing. African-American philosophers, such as Cornel West, sought to counter Eurocentrism with insights from an Afrocentric perspective. Animal rights advocates, such as Peter Singer and Tom Regan, asserted the rights of nonhuman sentient beings. Environmental philosophers adopted a biocentric perspective, putting nature rather than humanity at the center of philosophic vision. By asking new questions and challenging old assumptions, these new perspectives enlivened philosophic debate and made philosophy more relevant for previously marginal groups. Pluralism and fragmentation were characteristic of philosophy in the United States near the end of the twentieth century. While the analysis of concepts, language, and logic remained important, the weakening of the analytic tradition and the rise of new voices and perspectives encouraged philosophers to participate in a broader humanistic conversation that was often international in scope.

[John Rajchman and Cornel West, eds., *Post-Analytic Philosophy* (New York, 1985); John Rawls, *A Theory of Justice* (Cambridge, Mass., 1971); Richard Rorty, *Philosophy and the Mirror of Nature* (Princeton, N.J., 1979).]

DANIEL J. WILSON

PHOENIX. During and after World War II the Arizona capital became a major military and high technology center due to massive federal funding. Phoenix moved to the top of the urban hierarchy in the desert Southwest in the 1950s and secured its hold on that position during the next thirty years as a center of manufacturing, tourism, and agriculture. The mass production of air conditioners in the 1950s made Phoenix livable in summer as well as winter. The population was 789,704 in 1980, up from 439,170 in 1960 and 65,414 in 1940. By 1980 the city ranked as the ninth-largest in the nation. The boom continued during the 1980s, and Phoenix expanded in size and prominence. A combination of economic opportunities and amenities attracted newcomers, and political changes and cultural developments appeared to the satisfaction of many residents. As Phoenix became a sprawling, multicentered metropolis, however, it served as an example of the problems as well as the progress of the new urban United States. City services often lagged behind growth. Critics complained but few were heeded. In the late 1980s recession brought hardship to Phoenix but by 1992 another economic boom and population explosion was under way. In that year Phoenix was declared the eighth-largest city in the country with a population of more than 1 million; the metropolitan area contained more than 2 million. In the mid-1990s the major problem facing Phoenix was the conflict between the area's two most cherished values—growth and the good life. The challenge was to handle growth in ways that would improve the quality of life rather than harm it.

[Bradford Luckingham, *Phoenix: The History of a Southwestern Metropolis* (Tucson, Ariz., 1989).]

BRADFORD LUCKINGHAM

See also **SUPP:** Arizona; Sunbelt; Tucson.

PHOTOGRAPHY. During the final decades of the twentieth century photography became easy for unskilled practitioners. The cumbersome method introduced by Louis J. M. Daguerre in 1839 had given way to affordable 35-mm compact automatics. Photographic images in silver, color dyes, and printers' ink had spread around the world. Innovations in moving film made faraway events accessible through simultaneous broadcast. Professional photographers were typically in the forefront of technology and trends. To compensate for the disappearance of skilled portraiture and documentation in the wake of the 35-mm revolution, photographers turned to publishing and advertising. Their camera of choice was a $2\frac{1}{4}$-inch format equipped with motor drives and used with multiple lenses and sophisticated artificial lighting. Fine-art photographers devoted considerable energy to experimenting with equipment, format, film, and paper, and their subjects tended toward the eclectic. Since the late 1940s they have attempted to capture "private realities," a quest that drew inspiration from such sources as Eastern religious philosophies, psychoanalytic theory, and abstract expressionist painting. The popularity of this form in the United States stemmed from the postwar economic boom, the ability of former military personnel to attend art schools and colleges at federal expense, and the founding of the Institute of Design, the Western Hemisphere version of the Bauhaus, which advocated a "new vision" of interpreting common places in personal ways. New vision photographers experimented with equipment and format, frequently contriving a final image from collages, montages, and multiple exposures.

The straight tradition popularized by Edward Weston remained the dominant but far from the only style in professional photography in the late twentieth century. A gifted photographer, educator, and author, Minor White, encouraged his followers to reveal "things for what they are" as well as "for what else they are." His advocacy of the "equivalent image" produced a cultlike following in the 1960s that continued into the 1990s. White's influence led photographers with a mystic bent to seek spiritual oneness with nature. With large-format cameras they photographed such natural phenomena as gnarled trees, tumultuous ocean waves, and dew-tinged leaves and petals. Photographers like Walter Chappell and Paul Caponigro struggled to evoke the mystic divinity of nature itself. Aerialists like Bradford Washington went aloft to invest nature with stunning abstractions of shifting land masses and geometrical farmlands.

Photographers took to the streets in the 1950s and 1960s using handheld units to frame reality with sardonic or ironic twists. Like the painter Andy Warhol, these photographers opted for the vernacular and emblems of popular culture. Modern masters like William Klein, Garry Winogrand, and William Wegman chose human (and in Wegman's case, canine) interaction among artifacts, whereas Elliott Erwitt, who beginning in the late 1940s has taken pictures of everyday scenes from around the world, preferred symbols largely free of human encroachment, although one well-known sequence shows the world of humans from a dog's point of view. Bruce Davidson and Diane Arbus sought odd faces in out-of-the-way places and captured them with a dignity previously reserved for the wealthy and classically beautiful.

Underlying the achievements of all photographers since the 1970s were technological improvements in cameras. The single-lens reflex camera became smaller and more reliable, with large-format cameras revamped to fit the computer age. In 1972 the Polaroid camera was improved with the SX-70 system, which was in turn supplanted by the 600 system, featuring automatic focus, electronic flash, and battery together with high-speed color film. In the last quarter of the twentieth century both black-and-white and color-positive-and-negative film vastly improved in speed and resolution. Infrared film sensitive to light invisible to the human eye had wide use in science. In the 1990s both Agfa and Ilford marketed wide-latitude film that joined dye couplers with silver halides to form images.

Electronic cameras, introduced in the early to mid-1990s, became increasingly sophisticated and easy to use, producing high-resolution photos and spelling the end of film photographic processes in certain quarters, notably news coverage. In 1987 United Press International and Associated Press, the largest news wire services in the United States, began transmitting pictures electronically. Still-picture versions of camcorders or videocameras (which themselves gained wide use as observation and surveillance tools in prisons, hospitals, courts, schools, and banks and were employed to help diagnose injuries and perform such surgery as laparoscopy) came into being, and digital cameras enabled photographers to store pictures on computer chips, which can be downloaded and tinkered with on a personal computer, obviating the need for the darkroom. Despite industry predictions that digital cameras were poised to do to the traditional silver halide photography market what camcorders did to Super-8 home movies, their high

cost made acquisition prohibitive to the average consumer, although a camcorder could be converted into a digital camera for under $200. Digital imaging and computer manipulation of photos led to the use of faked and "enhanced" pictures in magazines, on television, and in newspapers. A 1994 *Time* magazine cover featured a digitally altered image of O. J. Simpson's mug shot, taken when he was arrested for the murder of his former wife and one of her friends. Among applications by the scientific community was the use in 1994 of digital image processing of conventional photographs to reveal detailed views of the sun's corona during an eclipse.

[Ian Jeffrey, *Photography: A Concise History* (New York, 1981); Beaumont Newhall, *The History of Photography: From 1839 to the Present,* 5th ed. (Boston, 1982); Johann Willsberger, *The History of Photography* (Garden City, N.Y., 1977).]

EVELYN S. COOPER

PHYSICIAN ASSISTANTS (PAs), persons trained, certified, and licensed to take medical histories, conduct physical examinations, and diagnose and treat medical problems under the supervision of physicians, thereby extending the capacity of physicians to provide care. In the mid-1990s there were more than 20,000 PAs practicing in the United States in all areas served by physicians, including primary care, internal medicine, surgery, geriatrics, psychiatry, and pediatrics. The creator of this profession was Eugene A. Stead, chairman of the Department of Medicine at Duke University in the mid-1960s. A 1959 Surgeon General's report indicated that the nation faced a shortage of medical personnel, particularly among such traditionally underserved populations as the rural and inner-city poor and elderly. Stead's idea was that returning medical corpsmen from Vietnam, with their experience treating illness and injury, could be trained to work in health care facilities in less time than that required to complete an entire medical and residency program. In 1965 four medical corpsman entered the first PA program under Stead's direction at Duke; thirty years later there were fifty-eight such programs throughout the United States.

The American Medical Association officially recognized the profession in 1971 and began working on the process of PA certification. PA training has not changed a great deal since. Most programs require two years and include intensive clinical rotations under physician supervision. Physician supervision continues throughout the careers of PAs, making them "dependent practitioners" along with nurses. PAs see patients with routine and minor complaints, freeing physicians to see more serious cases, and provide continuity for regular patients in settings with medical residents and interns whose positions turn over rapidly. Malpractice claims against PAs have been few; insurance analysts consider PAs low-risk providers because they are dependent practitioners. PAs work in virtually all health care settings, including rural communities in which they may be the only practitioners. All states except Mississippi license and regulate PA practice and most allow PAs to write prescriptions. Work opportunities are extensive. The American Academy of Physician Assistants claims six jobs for every graduating PA and the Department of Labor projects a 44 percent increase between 1990 and 2005. PAs are no longer an experiment but an important part of mainstream medical care.

[Gretchen E. Schafft and James F. Cawley, *The Physician Assistant in a Changing Health Care Environment* (Rockville, Md., 1987).]

SUSAN ANDREW

See also **SUPP:** Health Care; Hospitals; Medicine.

PHYSICS. In the last quarter of the twentieth century, physicists expanded the range and power of the laser, learned how to obtain controlled nuclear fusion for short intervals, manufactured several new transuranium elements, discovered that certain exotic mixtures could be superconducting at relatively high temperatures, formulated the theory of quarks, and found a series of massive nuclear particles to confirm the augmented theory of atomic nuclei. U.S. theorists took the lead in establishing and developing the nuclear theory that is now called "the standard model," and U.S. scientists won the majority of Nobel Prizes in Physics during this period.

Lasers, invented in the early 1960s, were commonplace by the 1980s, used in bar-code readers and compact disk players. In the 1970s physicists discovered how to make tunable lasers, which greatly increased the possible color range, and by 1980 lasers could be used to make individual atoms stand still. The first successful X-ray laser was built in 1984. These can be so powerful that they were studied both as weapons for destroying enemy missiles (as part of the now-defunct Strategic Defense Initiative) and as tools for the production of controlled nuclear fusion.

Meanwhile, physicists, notably at Princeton University, developed the tokamak, a donut-shaped magnetic enclosure in which ionized matter could be contained and heated to the very high temperatures necessary for nuclear fusion to take place. By 1977 they obtained temperatures of 27 million kelvins. (For fusion to take place, 100 million kelvins are required.) Within a few years the Princeton experiments reached 80 million kelvins, and by 1991 Princeton physicists sustained fusion for two seconds. In May 1994 the Princeton tokamak momentarily generated nine megawatts of power by transforming hydrogen isotopes into helium.

In 1972 a group of Americans won the Nobel Prize in Physics for their work on the theory of superconductivity, the phenomenon where, at very low temperatures, electrical resistance ceases. The next year physicists discovered that a combination of the elements niobium and germanium became superconducting at 22.3 K, about 2 degrees higher than the previous record. In the late 1980s, however, scientists unexpectedly found other combinations with much higher (but still very cold) temperatures—above 120 K—that still lacked electrical resistance.

The greatest success in theoretical physics was in the understanding of the particles that compose the atomic nucleus and their interactions. By the 1960s physicists knew that in addition to the protons, neutrons, and electrons that had been used to explain atomic nuclei for several decades, there was a confusing number of additional particles that had been found using electron and proton accelerators (popularly known as "atom smashers"). A pattern, called the eightfold way, was discerned by the California Institute of Technology physicist Murray Gell-Mann and the Israeli Yuval Ne'eman. Gaps were noticed, predictions of a new particle were made, and the particle (the so-called Omega-minus) was promptly discovered. To explain the pattern, Gell-Mann postulated the existence of some underlying but unobserved elementary particles that he called "quarks."

Quarks carry electrical charges similar to protons or electrons, but the amounts of the charges are one-third or two-thirds of the charge of the electron or proton. Gell-Mann postulated several different kinds of quarks, giving them idiosyncratic names such as up, down, and strange. Protons and neutrons are clusters of three quarks. Protons are made of two up quarks, each with a charge of plus two-thirds, and a single down quark with a charge of minus one-third, so the total is plus one. Neutrons are made of one up quark and two down quarks, so the total charge is zero. Another group of particles, the mesons, are made up of quarks and antiquarks. More massive particles, such as the ones found independently by Burton Richter at the Stanford Linear Accelerator and

Samuel C. C. Ting at Brookhaven National Laboratory in 1974, fit into the picture as being made from charm quarks. Two years later Ting and Richter shared the Nobel Prize in Physics. The masses of these particles, like the spectrum of the hydrogen atom used by Niels Bohr many decades earlier to elucidate the quantum structure of the outer parts of electrons, now provided a similar numerical key for understanding the inner structure of the atom. Six different "flavors" of quarks are required to account for these heavy particles, and they come in pairs: up-down, charm-strange, and top-bottom. The first member of each pair has an electrical charge of two-thirds and the second of minus one-third.

Meanwhile, Sheldon Lee Glashow at Harvard University, Steven Weinberg at the Massachusetts Institute of Technology, and Abdus Salam at Imperial College in London in 1968 independently proposed a theory that linked two of the fundamental forces in nature, electromagnetism and the so-called weak nuclear force. Their proposal, known as quantum field theory, involved the notion of quarks and required the existence of three massive particles to "carry" the weak force, two charged particles (W+ and W–) and one neutral particle (Z). These particles are short-lived, massive versions of the massless photons that carry ordinary light. All of these particles are called bosons, or more precisely, gauge bosons, because the theory explaining them is called a gauge theory. The name, which comes about for purely historical reasons, refers to a type of symmetry in which labels of the particles can be interchanged according to rules suggested by quantum mechanics, and the resulting forces (and gauge bosons) are found as a consequence of the symmetry requirements.

By 1972 indirect evidence for the existence of the Z particle was found in Geneva at the European Centre for Nuclear Research (CERN), and the 1979 Nobel Prize in Physics went to Glashow, Weinberg, and Salam. It was not until 1983 that the Z particle itself was found, also at CERN, and close on the heels of this discovery came the detection of the W particle. Carlo Rubbia, a Harvard colleague of Glashow and Weinberg and leader of the successful discovery team, remarked to them, "Now you won't have to give back the prize!" A year later Rubbia himself shared the Nobel Prize in Physics.

In January 1987 the Tevatron proton-antiproton accelerator at the Fermi National Accelerator Laboratory (Fermilab) in Illinois came into operation. Having narrowly missed out on some of the earlier discoveries, the Fermilab scientists were particularly keen to find evidence for the postulated top quark, the only one of the quarks not yet measured and a particle so massive that only the most powerful accelerators could produce enough energy to find it. Their search at last succeeded in 1995.

Along with the quarks and bosons, a third type of particle completes the present roster: the lepton, of which the electron, positron, and a group of neutrinos are the best known examples. The leptons and quarks provide the building blocks for atoms. The gauge bosons interact with the leptons and quarks, and in the act of being emitted or absorbed, some of the gauge bosons transform one kind of quark or lepton into another. In the standard model, a common mechanism underlies the electromagnetic, weak, and strong interactions. Each is mediated by the exchange of a gauge boson. The gauge bosons of the strong and weak interactions carry electrical charges, whereas the photon, which carries the electromagnetic interactions, is electrically neutral.

In its simplest formulation, the standard model of the strong, weak, and electromagnetic interactions, although aesthetically beautiful, does not agree with all the known characteristics of the weak interactions nor can it account for the experimentally derived masses of the quarks. Nuclear theorists hoped that the Superconducting Super Collider under construction in Texas in the late 1980s would provide data to extend and correct the standard model. They were highly disappointed when Congress cut off funding for this expensive atom smasher.

The standard model is one of the great achievements of the human intellect. It will be remembered—together with general relativity, quantum mechanics, and the unraveling of the genetic code—as one of the outstanding intellectual advances of the twentieth century. It is not, however, the "final theory," because too many constants still must be empirically determined. A particularly interesting development since the 1970s is the joining of particle physics with the astrophysics of the earliest stages of the universe. The early universe may provide the laboratory for exploration of the grand unified theories (GUTs) at temperatures and energies that are and will remain inaccessible in terrestrial laboratories.

[Frank Close, Michael Marten, and Christine Sutton, *The Particle Explosion* (New York, 1987); P. C. W. Davies, *The New Physics* (New York, 1989); Gary Taubes, *Nobel Dreams* (New York, 1986); Peter Watkins, *The Story of the W and Z* (New York, 1986); Steven Weinberg, *Dreams of a Final Theory* (New York, 1992).]

OWEN GINGERICH
S. S. SCHWEBER

See also **SUPP:** Astronomy; Cold Nuclear Fusion; Fermi National Accelerator Laboratory; Laser Technology; Superconducting Super Collider; Superconductivity.

PHYSIOLOGY. Advances in technology and microbiology contributed to the great strides taken by U.S. scientists in animal and plant physiology during the latter part of the twentieth century. Recognition of such accomplishments resulted in dominance of the United States in Nobel Prizes for medicine and physiology from 1975 to 1993; twenty-eight U.S. citizens won those awards during that period. U.S. progress in basic research helped combat serious diseases. In 1976 the Nobel Prize in physiology and medicine went to went to Baruch S. Blumberg and Daniel Carleton Gajdusek of the National Institutes of Health (NIH) for identification of the origin and dissemination of infectious diseases. That same year, by identifying interleukin-2, a protein factor promoting growth of human T cells in culture, Robert C. Gallo and his group at the National Institute of Allergy and Infectious Diseases opened the way for identifying human retroviruses. Also in 1976 J. Michael Bishop and Harold E. Varmus discovered the cellular origin of cancer-causing genes known as oncogenes, found in retroviruses, work that won them the Nobel Prize in 1989. There were also achievements in physiology affecting the heart. In 1980 Baruj Benacerraf and George D. Snell shared the Nobel Prize with Jean Dausset of France for their explanation of how cell structures relate to organ transplants and diseases. For clarification of the cholesterol metabolism, Michael S. Brown and Joseph L. Goldstein received the Nobel Prize in 1985. The U.S. Department of Agriculture also won recognition. In the 1940s and 1950s Nobelist (1983) Barbara McClintock experimented with corn and found that genes in corn chromosomes moved and could cause mutations in future generations of plants descending from the parent with mobile genes.

[I. Edward Alcamo, *Fundamentals of Biology,* 3rd ed. (Redwood City, Calif., 1991); Maya Pines, *Inside the Cell: The New Frontier of Medical Science* (Washington, D.C., 1978).]

RUTH ROY HARRIS

See also **SUPP:** Acquired Immune Deficiency Syndrome; Bacteriology and Virology; Cancer; Cardiovascular Disease; Clinical Research; Epidemiology; Genetic Engineering; Human Genome Project; Medicine; Microbiology; National Institutes of Health; Research Laboratories.

PITTSBURGH, the second-largest city in Pennsylvania, in 1970 represented the potential of post–World War II urban renewal for American cities. A twenty-five-year program, engineered by the partnership of Richard K. Mellon, a powerful Republican financier, and David L. Lawrence, mayor of Pittsburgh from 1945 to 1958 and the local Democratic party leader, cleaned the city's air and rivers, revitalized the downtown area, and rebuilt the infrastructure. Despite this renaissance, as the redevelopment was called, industry expanded slowly, the city lost population, and the metropolitan area's population barely increased. After 1970 Pittsburgh's steel industry collapsed, and electrical equipment, glass, and coal-mining corporations shuttered old plants. The steel industry was hampered by excess capacity, obsolete technology, and high labor costs. More than half the metropolitan area's manufacturing jobs disappeared, 90,000 in primary and fabricated metals alone. By 1990 manufacturing employed 12 percent of the labor force. Plant closings mirrored the decline in the number of corporate headquarters located in Pittsburgh, which dropped from third to eighth rank among U.S. cities in the number of Fortune 500 corporate headquarters.

As both young people entering the labor market and middle-aged workers left Pittsburgh in search of employment opportunities, the five-county metropolitan area by 1990 lost more than 300,000 residents from its 1950 population, a 12 percent decline; the population of the city of Pittsburgh plunged to 370,000, half the figure in 1950. Although the African-American community did not grow in absolute numbers, its proportion of the city's total population rose to more than 25 percent. Few Hispanic or Asian migrants came to the city.

Pittsburgh's leaders drew upon the earlier renaissance to address the economic challenge. Democratic Mayor Richard Caligiuri rebuilt the partnership with corporate leaders, encouraged office construction in the downtown business section known as the Golden Triangle, supported a light rail and subway system as well as a new airport, and cooperated with foundations to develop cultural facilities. Called Renaissance II, this redevelopment initiative supported a burgeoning banking, legal, and business services sector. Moreover, higher education and medical institutions generated growth from medical research, advanced technology, and health care businesses. In

1990 services employed one-third of the metropolitan area's labor force. With a low crime rate, affordable housing, and cultural amenities, Pittsburgh received the mantle of America's most livable city in the mid-1980s.

The service sector softened the city's precipitous industrial decline, but development across the region was uneven. In the 1990s older towns of the industrial river valleys remained depressed, while suburbs with interstate highway access, Pittsburgh's downtown and university districts, and the airport corridor flourished. Pennsylvania state programs, economic and community development organizations, and foundations struggled to help depressed mill towns and create a regional perspective that would allow Pittsburgh and communities in the metropolitan area to work together.

[John P. Hoerr, *And the Wolf Finally Came: The Decline of the American Steel Industry* (Pittsburgh, 1988); Stefan Lorant, *Pittsburgh* (Lenox, Mass., 1988).]

EDWARD K. MULLER

See also **SUPP:** Pennsylvania.

PLANNED PARENTHOOD OF SOUTHEASTERN PENNSYLVANIA V. CASEY, 112 Supreme Court 2791 (1992) is best known for what it did not do—overrule *Roe* v. *Wade* (1973). By 1992 five associate justices had been appointed to the Supreme Court by Presidents Ronald Reagan and George Bush, both of whom pledged to select judges committed to overturning *Roe,* which had legalized abortion. Reagan had named William Rehnquist, one of the original dissenters in *Roe,* as chief justice in 1986. *Webster* v. *Reproductive Health Services* (1989) and *Rust* v. *Sullivan* (1991) had upheld laws limiting access to abortion and seemed indicators of doctrinal shifts. The Pennsylvania Abortion Control Act at issue in *Casey* did not ban abortion, but the Court upheld all of the restrictions on abortion imposed by Pennsylvania except for mandatory husband notification. These included a twenty-four-hour waiting period, informed consent of one parent for pregnant teenagers, reporting requirements, and a state-scripted warning against the medical procedure. As a result of *Casey,* restrictions on abortion would no longer be judged by a strict scrutiny standard requiring a "compelling state interest," as did restrictions on other constitutional rights. Instead, an "undue burden" standard was substituted, allowing states to place restrictions on abortion unless they posed "substantial obstacles" to a woman's right of privacy recognized in *Roe.* For

Justices Sandra Day O'Connor, Anthony Kennedy, and David Souter, all appointed by Presidents Reagan and Bush, "the reservations any of us may have in reaffirming the central holding of *Roe* are outweighed by the expectation of individual liberty." Hence, *Casey* was a defeat for both sides on the abortion issue. It represented a victory for centrist judicial politics.

[Barbara Hinkson Craig and David M. O'Brien, *Abortion and American Politics* (Chatham, N.J., 1993).]

JUDITH A. BAER

See also **SUPP:** Abortion.

PLURALISM, a concept that recognizes and affirms racial, ethnic, and religious diversity within U.S. society, has been a prominent mode of thought in political science and philosophy since the 1950s, when scholars first argued that individual and group differences have a self-correcting and synergetic effect on a common national culture. Multiculturalism, which gained currency on college campuses in the 1980s, sought to replace a "patriarchal" and "ethnocentric" national history with a "curriculum of inclusion" that emphasizes the struggles and achievements of neglected social groups and societies. Pluralism, however, usually emphasizes commonalities among U.S. citizens that multiculturalism does not. While pluralism legitimizes diversity and difference, it also assumes the necessity for intergroup toleration and cooperation in the larger framework of society. In a pluralistic society self-identified groups maintain autonomy while assimilated within a common national identity. Pluralism is the attempt to make the United States what the philosopher Richard Rorty calls "a community of communities, a nation with far more room for difference than most." Pluralism maintains that the United States inherits a complex, commonly held political philosophy resting on the rules of law, contract, and property, encased in a federal structure of limited government, on citizen-based consent. Pluralism operates on the system of representative democracy and citizen-based rights, liberty, equality, reform, and progress. These ideas overarch and unite citizens of different ethnicities, social backgrounds, and religions, strengthening the position of the individual and collective society. They draw strength from tolerance and inclusion. Some political theorists seek pluralism's political authority and legitimacy in the different communities that bind individuals and groups on the basis of religion, race, ethnicity, and other differences. Other theorists emphasize the pluralist values of ethnicity, localism, religion, and kinship, relying on informal customs, folkways, and habits of mind to sustain liberty and to moderate invasive national laws or administrative regulations.

GILBERT T. SEWALL

See also **SUPP:** Curriculum; Multiculturalism.

POLICE. In the early 1990s, the United States had more independent police agencies than any other country. Estimates have been as high as 40,000, but contemporary estimates range from 20,000 to 25,000. These figures contrast with such countries as Ireland and Israel, which have single national police forces, and with those countries whose multiple forces are centrally coordinated, such as France and Great Britain. It is at least partly by design that the United States has neither a single national police force or a centrally coordinated system of multiple agencies. Local control of police appeared to be a guarantee against the acquisition of too much political power by police. The Federal Bureau of Investigation has some characteristics of a national police force, but its jurisdiction is limited by other federal police agencies, as well as by state and local police forces. Many critics use what they regard as the serious abuses of power by J. Edgar Hoover, who headed the FBI for forty-eight years (1924–1972), to argue against greater centralization.

In 1995 there were more than sixty federal agencies with law enforcement powers. The FBI, U.S. Marshals Service, Immigration and Naturalization Service, and Drug Enforcement Administration are in the Department of Justice. Within the Department of the Treasury are the Secret Service, Customs Service, and Bureau of Alcohol, Tobacco and Firearms. The police power of this last agency was brought to the attention of the American public by its 1993 raid on the Branch Davidian complex in Waco, Texas. Federal police agencies have specialized law enforcement functions, but their geographical jurisdiction extends throughout the United States. Although the jurisdictions of state and local agencies are limited to territory governed by state or local political authorities, they have general law enforcement powers within their territories. There are some legal extensions to the geographically limited authority of local police. Buffer zones can extend beyond city or county lines within which police have full authority, and officers often have the authority to engage in "hot pursuit" of a suspect across boundaries that would

normally define their jurisdiction. The Texas Rangers, founded in 1835, before Texas became a state, became the first state police force. Pennsylvania established a state police force in 1905, and the other states, except for Hawaii, have followed suit. The law enforcement powers of state police vary from one state to another. State National Guard units, normally federally controlled army or air force units, can also be used by the governors of states as domestic police agencies in times of emergency. Sheriffs are county officials, generally elected to office. Although the list of tasks typically performed by sheriff departments is long, responsibilities vary from one department to another. In addition to law enforcement, sheriffs usually have charge of county jails and can be officers of the county court, enforcing courtroom security and serving legal notices, such as warrants, subpoenas, and foreclosures. Sheriff departments sometimes receive criticism because of their connection to politics and frequent failure to uphold professional standards for recruitment and training.

Police departments have become more professional by raising recruitment standards, increasing recruit training, and using advanced technology and the results of specialized research. Scientific police work began in Europe, with development of fingerprinting and other modern methods of crime detection, and U.S. police departments began to adapt the European model to the United States in the early twentieth century. There has been an increase in use of technology, from the introduction of radio-dispatched patrol cars in the 1930s to the use of computerized databases in the 1990s. Many police agencies now require recruits to have college degrees, and a growing number of programs in criminal justice have attracted students hoping to pursue careers in police work. The professionalization of the police was in response not only to the technical demands of law enforcement but also to repeated discoveries of corruption in police departments. In New York City the 1972 report of the Knapp Commission, appointed to investigate the corruption allegations of Detective Frank Serpico, stated that 15,000 New York City police officers, half the members of the department, were taking illegal payoffs. In 1986 police officers in Boston were found to have been stealing and fixing police promotion exams, and officers in New York and Philadelphia were accused of participation in gambling and drug operations. The beating of Rodney King in 1991 by Los Angeles police officers led to widespread investigations throughout the country of police racism and excessive use of violence.

Since the early 1970s police departments have recruited more women and minorities through the efforts of progressive police leaders and because of the legal requirements for equal employment and affirmative action. Recruitment of minorities was part of attempts to improve relationships between police and communities. Such incidents as the videotaped beating of King dramatized the need for police who are both highly professional and committed to the welfare of people within their jurisdictions. After the riots following acquittal of the officers who beat King, former Philadelphia Police Commissioner Willie Williams was appointed the first African-American police chief in the history of Los Angeles.

[David H. Bayley, *Patterns of Policing: A Comparative International Perspective* (New Brunswick, N.J., 1995); Randy LaGrange, *Policing American Society* (Chicago, 1993).]

RICHARD W. MOODEY

See also **SUPP:** Crime; Federal Bureau of Investigation; Justice, Department of; Los Angeles Riots; Waco Siege.

POLISH AMERICANS. The arrival of Poles at the Jamestown colony in Virginia on Oct. 1, 1608, initiated the Polish presence in America. The London Company recruited Poles, most probably to manufacture pitch, tar, and soap. When the hard-working Poles were denied the vote in the Virginia House of Burgesses in 1619, they objected and won the franchise. Few Poles, however, reached the colonies before the American Revolution. Kazimierz Pulaski and Tadeusz Kościuszko were the earliest Polish political émigrés. Pulaski served as a volunteer in the Continental army from 1777 to 1778 and then was made a general and ordered to organize a cavalry corps; he was mortally wounded at the Battle of Savannah in October 1779. Kościuszko was appointed colonel of engineers in the Continental army in 1776, and his fortifications at Freeman's Farm (Bemis Heights), N.Y., ensured the American victory at Saratoga in 1777. A scattering of exiles and émigrés followed in the first half of the nineteenth century.

The character of Polish migration changed in 1854, when 150 Silesian peasants settled Panna Maria, Texas, near San Antonio. Driven by what was unavailable at home, especially after the Polish Insurrection of 1863, Poles came to the United States, according to Henryk Sienkiewicz, a Nobelist in literature (1905), "in search of bread and freedom." They planted urban villages in the midwestern industrial states of Illinois, Michigan, Wisconsin, Ohio, Minnesota, and Indiana and in the Atlantic coast states of New York, Pennsylvania, New Jersey, Massachusetts, Connecticut, Maryland, Delaware, Rhode Island. Polish settlements were particularly dense in metropolitan New York, Chicago, Detroit, Philadelphia, Milwaukee, Buffalo, Pittsburgh, Cleveland, Minneapolis–St. Paul, Boston, and Baltimore. They labored in steel and linen mills, factories, and mines, while only 10 percent made their way into agriculture. Polish immigrants organized a complex community infrastructure between 1854 and World War II. More than 950 Roman Catholic and Polish National Catholic parishes, 585 parochial schools, national insurance fraternal organizations (Polish National Alliance, Polish Roman Catholic Union, Polish Women's Alliance, and Polish Falcons), a Polish language press, and athletic, cultural, social, and political clubs and organizations. The 1930 U.S. Census counted 3,342,198 Polish immigrants and their descendants.

During World War I (1914–1918), Polish Americans lobbied the administration of President Woodrow Wilson on behalf of Poland's independence. In the interwar period, the Polish-American community pursued domestic priorities. Citizens clubs helped members acquire citizenship and political recognition. During and after the Great Depression, Polish Americans voted for Franklin D. Roosevelt and his New Deal and joined labor unions. By 1945 they constituted nearly 10 percent of the Congress of Industrial Organizations. The outbreak of World War II in September 1939 altered the Polish-American community's development. Following the Soviet occupation of Poland in 1944, 190,771 political émigrés, soldier-exiles, and displaced persons entered the United States between 1949 and 1956. The Polish American Congress, founded in 1944, articulated postwar Polish-American concerns, including the socioeconomic advancement of Americans of Polish origin. Polish settlements in the United States declined after World War II, as educational levels rose and Polish Americans joined the exodus from inner cities. A limited ethnic revival occurred in the 1970s, a response to the blight of ethnic humor in the media. The election of Pope John Paul II in 1978 stimulated Polish-American pride, as did the creation of the Solidarity movement in Poland in 1980.

Most descendants of pre–World War I Polish immigrants became Americanized, but the appearance of a more liberal communist government in Warsaw in 1956 reopened direct migration from Poland, reinforcing declining Polish communities in the United

States. The Immigration and Naturalization Act of 1965 also shaped Polish migration to the United States. Between 1965 and 1990 there were 178,384 immigrants, along with 957,360 nonimmigrants, temporary visitors who claimed to be tourists but actually sought work. In addition, 35,131 Solidarity-era political refugees arrived in the 1980s. The arrival of more than one million immigrants, nonimmigrants, and refugees helped Polish-American communities survive. The 1990 U.S. Census recorded 9.4 million Americans of Polish descent.

A century ago peasants and unskilled laborers were the majority in the immigrant community. Since World War II, however, Polish Americans' income, education levels, and occupational mobility increased, as did their percentages in the professions, management, research and education, and in technical jobs. Americans of Polish origin who have achieved professional acclaim include Senator Edmund S. Muskie and Representative Dan Rostenkowski; Stanislaw Ulam (physics); Zbigniew Brzezinski (political science); Arthur Rubenstein, Liberace, and Bobby Vinton (music); Pola Negri, Gloria Swanson, and Charles Bronson (motion pictures); Nobel laureate Czeslaw Milosz and novelist Jerzy Kosinski; General John Shalikashvili; and baseball's Stan Musial and Carl Yastrzemski, while Polish Americans have played on every National Football League team.

Polish Americans in the 1990s were still concentrated in the states where their ancestors settled, but they joined the migration to the Sunbelt states. They are part of the American tapestry, but retain ties to their ancestral homeland. Polish Americans hailed the fall of communism in 1989 but remained anxious about Poland's security and lobbied for Poland's admission to the North Atlantic Treaty Organization and European economic and political associations.

[Andrzej Brozek, *Polish Americans, 1854–1939* (Warsaw, 1985); John J. Bukowcyzk, *And My Children Did Not Know Me: A History of Polish-Americans* (Bloomington, Ind., 1987); Waclaw Kruszka, *A History of Poles in America to 1908* (Washington, D.C., 1905–1908), trans. and repr., James S. Pula, ed. (1993–1995); W. S. Kuniczak, *My Name Is Million: An Illustrated History of the Poles in America* (New York, 1978); Helena Znaniecka Lopata, *Polish Americans,* rev. ed. (New Brunswick, N.J., 1994); James S. Pula, *Polish Americans: An Ethnic Community* (New York, 1995).]

STANISLAUS A. BLEJWAS

POLITICAL ACTION COMMITTEES (PACs), groups that collect monies from their members or politically like-minded citizens, represent a single interest group, such as a labor union, corporation, or industry, or such socioeconomic issues as abortion or the environment. PACs use their monies to influence the legislative and executive branches of government. Even foreign powers have PACs working in the halls of state legislatures and Congress. Participation in PACs is not always voluntary. Groups put pressure on the men and women who work for them by inviting them to participate either monetarily or as volunteers. The hidden message often is that those who give money to PACs will be looked upon favorably by the organization in the form of promotions and pay raises. PACs attempt to gain support for their interests by contributing to political campaigns, hoping that their favors will be returned once candidates reach office. Even when candidates eschew PAC money, the very existence and need for that money assures that, for the most part, only independently wealthy candidates can compete with those who take PAC money. The most insidious thing about PACs is that they continue to be part and parcel of a political process that assures that those with the most money will have the most access and influence in the system.

The origin of PACs can be traced to the American labor movement and the Congress of Industrial Organizations (CIO). The first political action committee was formed during World War II, after Congress prohibited the assets of organized labor from being used for political purposes. The CIO created a separate political fund in 1943 to receive and spend voluntary contributions and called it the Political Action Committee. After the CIO merged with the American Federation of Labor, a political action committee called the Committee on Political Education (COPE) was formed in 1955. Other PACs, such as the American Medical Political Action Committee (AMPAC) and the Business-Industry Political Action Committee (BIPAC), were formed in the 1950s and 1960s, but it was not until the reform legislation of the 1970s that the number of PACs began to increase significantly.

While labor unions formed PACs during the 1940s, corporations were not allowed to support candidates until the Federal Campaign Act (FECA) of 1971, which allowed corporations to use their money to set up PACs. In 1974 and 1976 FECA was amended, giving trade associations and corporations a new role in politics. As a result, FECA changed its guidelines for raising political money, sparking a tremendous growth in the number of PACs and the amount of money spent to influence the political system. Even though revisions in FECA set limits on the amount of money PACs could contribute to individual candidates and political campaigns ($5,000) and set a $1,000 limit on individual contributions per candidate per election, PACs were able to get around these limitations and still influence the political system. In fact, PACs often receive guidance from the lobbyists who work directly in the halls of state legislatures and Congress. While it is conflictive and often forbidden to have labor unions, for example, use their members' dues for political influence, there is no question that such arrangements are made.

Observers have argued for reform of the election process, insisting that PAC money should be eliminated or at least severely limited. Even where there are legal limits, individuals and groups have gotten around them by giving so-called "soft money" to political parties instead of directly to candidates. Officially, soft money is supposed to be used for party housekeeping, but in fact parties manage to pass on their cash to candidates. Gifts of soft money tend to obligate party managers to PACs and their political goals. In fact, the very existence of PACs since the 1970s has run up the tab on elections to the point that a single congressional contest may involve the expenditure of $1 million or more. For example, in 1974 approximately 600 PACs gave $12.5 million to congressional candidates. In 1988 the number of PACs had increased seven times (approximately 4,200 with $132 million in contributions to primarily incumbents). This increase raised public criticism of PACs and led to congressional proposals to eliminate them in 1991–1992, but no significant action was taken. According to the Center for Responsive Politics, there were 3,954 registered PACs in existence at the end of 1994, but only 3,001 were active.

[W. Lance Bennett, *The Governing Crisis: Media, Money, and Marketing in American Elections* (New York, 1992); William J. Keefe and Morris S. Ogul, *The American Legislative Process: Congress and the States,* 5th ed. (Englewood Cliffs, N.J., 1981); Frank J. Sorauf, *Money in American Elections* (Boston, 1988); F. Wertheimer and Susan Weiss Manes, "Campaign Finance Reform," *Columbia Law Review* 94 (May 1994).]

ALAN CHARTOCK

POLITICAL CARTOONS. The history of American political cartoons can be divided into three eras, defined by the medium in which the cartoons were presented to the public—as prints, in magazines, and in newspapers. In the first era, which spanned from the 1750s to the 1870s, most cartoons were sold as steel engravings or, after 1820, lithographs. During the second era, from the 1840s to the beginning of the twentieth century, most cartoons appeared in magazines, either as woodcuts or lithographs. This was the first golden age of the political cartoon, when Thomas Nast of *Harper's Weekly* and Joseph Keppler of *Puck* made the political cartoon a tool for reform. The third era dawned in 1884, when publisher Joseph Pulitzer began printing political cartoons on the front page of the *New York World.* Since then the political cartoon has become a staple of the editorial pages of daily newspapers. Important newspaper cartoonists of the late nineteenth century and the first half of the twentieth century include Homer Davenport *(New York Journal),* John T. McCutcheon *(Chicago Tribune),* Jay Norwood ("Ding") Darling *(Des Moines Register),* and Daniel Robert Fitzpatrick *(St. Louis Post-Dispatch),* the last three of whom received Pulitzer Prizes. The cartoons of Herbert L. Block ("Herblock"), who received the first of three Pulitzers in 1942, have appeared in the *Washington Post* since 1946.

Many critics regard the period from the mid-1960s to the mid-1990s as the second golden age of cartooning. The period began when Patrick Oliphant emigrated from Australia to the United States in 1964 to work for the *Denver Post.* Unlike his predecessors, who tended to support one political party or the other, Oliphant made fun of all politicians. His satiric cartoons, full of demeaning caricatures of well-known politicians, prompted a generation of Americans once again to regard the political cartoon as a tool of reform. Those who have followed in Oliphant's footsteps include Jeff MacNelly *(Richmond News Leader* and later *Chicago Tribune),* Mike Peters *(Dayton Daily News),* Tony Auth *(Philadelphia Inquirer),* Doug Marlette *(Charlotte Observer, Atlanta Constitution,* and later *New York Newsday),* and Jim Borgman *(Cincinnati Enquirer),* all of whom have won the Pulitzer Prize for Editorial Cartooning. None of these cartoonists' work, however popular, had the impact of Garry Trudeau's comic strip "Doonesbury," which began in 1970 and was the first comic strip to be awarded the Pulitzer for editorial cartooning (1975). Because of its treatment of such controversial content as abortion, "Doonesbury" has been "censored" with some frequency (that is, certain strips have not been included by some newspapers that routinely run the strip). By the mid-1990s "Doonesbury" was appearing daily in more than 1,000 newspapers.

[*The Best Editorial Cartoons of the Year* (Gretna, La., annually since 1972); Stephen Hess and Milton Kaplan, *The Ungentlemanly Art: A History of American Political Cartoons* (New York, 1975); Richard Samuel West, *Satire on Stone: The Political Cartoons of Joseph Keppler* (Urbana, Ill., 1988).]

RICHARD SAMUEL WEST

POLITICAL CORRECTNESS (PC). Originally a term of approval used by old-guard communists to mean toeing the party line, "political correctness" was resurrected in the 1970s and early 1980s by leftist writers and activists who used it in an ironic sense among themselves to mock the Left's tendency toward dogmatic adherence to "progressive" behavior and speech, particularly with regard to the politics of race, gender, sexual orientation, labor, the Third World, and the environment. The term entered general use, however, in the late 1980s, when neoconservatives adopted it as a disparaging description of what they believed was rigid adherence to multicultural ideals on college campuses. Allan Bloom's *The Closing of the American Mind* (1987) and Dinesh D'Souza's *Illiberal Education* (1991) became best-sellers indicting academic political correctness. Both writers argued that PC stifled intellectual creativity on campuses. Among their complaints was the substitution in the undergraduate curriculum of recent literature by women and minorities for the classics of Western civilization. Bloom and D'Souza regretted the fall from grace of the "DWEMs" (Dead White European Males), claiming that multicultural "diversity" and "pluralism" had achieved iconic status. The most freely satirized element of political correctness was the use of such euphemisms as "vertically challenged" for short, "differently abled" for handicapped, and "companion animals" for pets.

[William Bennett, *The Book of Virtues* (New York, 1994); Paul Berman, ed., *Debating P.C.* (New York, 1992); Allan Bloom, *The Closing of the American Mind* (New York, 1987); Dinesh D'Souza, *Illiberal Education: The Politics of Race and Sex on Campus* (New York, 1991).]

PATRICK ALLITT

See also **SUPP:** Conservatism; Curriculum; Multiculturalism.

POLITICAL PARTIES. *See* **Democratic Party; Republican Party; Third Parties and Independents.**

POLLUTION. *See* **Air Pollution; Noise Pollution; Water Pollution.**

POPULATION. *See* **Demographic Changes.**

PORNOGRAPHY, written or visual images intended to excite sexually. In the 1990s hard-core pornography was widely accessible and often depicted nonconsensual sexual intercourse in violent graphic images, whereas at the beginning of the twentieth century that which was merely "immoral" or "sensational," such as a hazy drawing of a seminude woman, was viewed as pornographic. Thus, historically a far broader range of literature and visual images was subject to legal governmental regulation, from erotic photographs to literary classics. A provision of the 1842 Tariff Act restricted "obscene" pictures and prints from entering the United States. The government became more interested in pornography during the Civil War, when soldiers began trading and collecting French postcards of pictures of nude and seminude women. The U.S. postmaster general in 1865 received a limited right to confiscate "obscene" materials in the mail. The Comstock laws of 1873 went further by making it illegal to sell or distribute through the mail a multitude of images in literature and art, as well as information on birth control or abortion.

From the 1870s through the mid-1930s, legal regulation of printed material and motion pictures was at its most restrictive. During this era the Supreme Court did not use arguments based on free speech and the First Amendment to challenge or modify obscenity laws and postal restrictions on literature or visual images. Until 1957 the Court accepted with only slight modification the British 1867 definition of "obscenity," which based censorship rulings on whether the written or spoken word (or visual representation) was intended to "deprave and corrupt those whose minds are open to such immoral influences, and into whose hands such a publication might fall." In effect, the Supreme Court upheld a definition of obscenity that created a standard for culture based on the lowest common denominator of acceptability—one that would not impair the moral development of children.

Before 1933 some novels that are now regarded as classics could not be distributed in the United States. The situation changed dramatically for literature in that year when federal judge John M. Woolsey, ruled that Irish author James Joyce's *Ulysses* was not obscene, arguing that the work should be taken as a whole, and prosecutors could not quote passages out of context as proof a book was obscene. On its first case against motion pictures in 1915, the Supreme Court ruled that the movie industry was a profit-inspired business, not an art form, and therefore subject to regulation. This allowed censorship by review boards before distribution of movies to the public by any state or local government that deemed it necessary or desirable. Beginning in 1934 the movie industry practiced rigorous self-regulation, through the Motion Picture Association of America and its Production Code, trying to avoid federal censorship.

At the turn of the century, censorship was popularly viewed as a device for social change. Groups such as the Woman's Christian Temperance Union joined vice societies to advocate censorship of literature and art. The American public has continued to support laws restricting the access of youth to pornographic films, as well as harsh action against anyone who creates or distributes child pornography. Like earlier reformers, Americans in the 1990s argued that censorship was necessary to protect children and family values. With *Miller* v. *California,* however, which was decided by the Supreme Court in 1973, the only adult pornography subject to governmental regulation became that which an "average person" deemed was without literary, artistic, political, or scientific value. The so-called LAPS test was weakened in 1987 when the court in *Pope* v. *Illinois* ruled that because community views varied, "reasonable person" should be substituted for "average person." Combinations of sex and violence soon began permeating not only low-budget pornographic films but mass-distributed movies, videos, and magazines, making violent portraits of adult sex readily available. By the 1990s pornographic materials were a $10 billion operation in the United States alone.

Late-twentieth-century adherents of the women's movement had divided opinions about pornography. Because of increasing violence against women, many feminists believed that pornography, especially images depicting violence against women or nonconsensual sex, are often harmful to female actors and, more broadly, to all women. This belief in the danger of pornography is based on the assumption that male viewers watch and read pornography as if it were a manual or an instruction guide to behavior, including relations between the sexes. Although the most extreme antipornography activists asserted that men learn to rape by watching and reading pornography, no study has proven a direct link, although many researchers have indicated that pornography diminishes male sensitivity to women's legal rights including the right to withhold consent to sex. Feminists Catharine MacKinnon and Andrea Dworkin oppose pornography both as "injurious speech," because it condones and encourages violence against women, and as a violation of women's civil rights. In the 1980s they successfully lobbied for ordinances in Minneapolis, Bellingham (Washington State), and Indianapolis. All were subsequently ruled unconstitutional on First Amendment grounds.

Anticensorship feminists who focus on the First Amendment argue that pornography should remain nonetheless a protected form of speech. Rejecting the idea that people respond to pornographic movies or books by trying to emulate the characters, they argue that pornography may serve as a safety valve, preventing violence against women by serving as a form of fantasy and as "safe sex." Some anticensorship feminists also doubt the efficacy of censorship and dislike its tendency to be used against such political minorities as homosexuals. They suggest that pornography's most objectionable images could be counteracted if feminist women and men produced their own pornography that challenged patriarchal and heterosexual notions about women's place in society. Anticensorship feminists point out that violence against women was a problem before pornography became as available and graphic as it has since the 1960s and conclude that banning pornography would probably not solve the physical abuse of women.

[Edward De Grazia, *Censorship Landmarks* (New York, 1969); Susan Gubar and Joan Hoff, eds., *For Adult Users Only: The Dilemma of Violent Pornography* (Bloomington, Ind., 1989); Susan Kappeler, *The Pornography of Representation* (Minneapolis, 1986); Laura M. Lederer, ed., *Take Back the Night* (New York, 1980); Lynne Segal and Mary McIntosh, eds., *Sex Exposed: Sexuality and the Pornography Debate* (London, 1992).]

ALISON M. PARKER

See also **DAH:** Censorship; **DAH** and **SUPP:** Freedom of the Press; **SUPP:** Prostitution; Women's Movement; Women's Rights.

PORTLAND, largest city in Oregon, located at the confluence of the Willamette and Columbia rivers, is named for Portland, Maine. Incorporated in 1851, the city has depended on trade throughout its history. The city tapped the wheat belt of the surrounding country to supply the California gold miners, then provided supplies to the miners of Idaho and Montana in the 1860s, as it did for Alaskan miners at the end of the nineteenth century. After the Civil War, the city drew the Columbia River and railroad wheat traffic of eastern Oregon and southeastern Washington. In 1905 the city sponsored the Lewis and Clark Centennial Exposition, and it profited from shipbuilding during World War I. The next boom came from the rebirth of shipbuilding under the leadership of Henry J. Kaiser's corporations during World War II. Substantial numbers of defense workers from many parts of the United States moved to Portland. To house the war workers, the new community of Vanport (between Portland and Vancouver, Wash.) was created, a town swept away by Columbia River floodwaters on Memorial Day 1948. During the 1970s and 1980s the city was substantially revitalized. Neighborhoods were preserved, a downtown transit mall was developed, and the city participated with regional governments to provide recreational, waste disposal, and mass transit facilities. Portland's principal industrial employers in the 1990s were wholesale and retail trades, services, and manufacturing, and the city has a vibrant artistic, literary, and musical life. Principal social problems that arose in the 1980s and 1990s included the decline in quality of the public schools because of voter insistence on cutting property taxes, the rise in the number of racial and ethnic gangs, and the loss of low-cost housing stock as neighborhoods began "gentrification." The city's population in 1990 was 437,319.

[Carl Abbott, *Portland: Gateway to the Northwest* (Northridge, Calif., 1985), and *Portland: Planning, Politics, and Growth in a Twentieth-Century City* (Lincoln, Nebr., 1983).]

GORDON B. DODDS

See also **DAH** and **SUPP:** Oregon.

POSTAL SERVICE, UNITED STATES. Since its establishment in 1970, the United States Postal Service (USPS), an independent agency of the executive branch of the government, has become a self-supporting corporation. Although the Postal Service is legislatively enjoined to achieve and maintain financial independence, unlike private corporations, it must provide cost-effective service and carry out federal policies. When the USPS sought to reduce costs during the 1970s and 1980s by consolidating services and closing local branches, public disapproval caused Congress to override such plans. As a self-sustaining corporation operating within the competitive private sector, the USPS strives for efficiency and innovation. It has computerized its operations; added Express Mail, an overnight service and the first new official class of mail since 1918; introduced Mailgrams, electronic messages delivered but not originating in writing; and in 1983 expanded the ZIP (Zone Improvement Program) code sorting system, first introduced in 1963 from five to nine digits. Despite competition from private-sector carriers, the USPS in the 1990s was the largest carrier of the world's mail (161 billion pieces annually), at rates lower than those of nearly all other letter carriers worldwide. The USPS achieves this standard even as its status as a federal agency imposes additional demands. The USPS must publicize and enforce legislation concerning interstate commerce, narcotics trafficking, business fraud, selective service registration, and the distribution of materials deemed pornographic. In 1992 there were 39,595 post offices, stations, and branches in the United States and possessions; in 1993 the USPS employed almost 780,000 employees, second only to the Department of Defense.

[United States Postal Service, *History of the U.S. Postal Service 1775–1981* (Washington, D.C., 1982).]

KERRY A. BATCHELDER

POST-STRUCTURALISM, an eclectic school of thought that significantly influenced literary and cultural theory in the 1970s and 1980s. It emerged as a reaction against the claims of 1960s French structuralism to scientific rigor, objectivity, and universal validity. Structuralism convinced many theorists that the key to understanding culture lay in the linguistic systemization of interrelationships in language. Building on the theories of the Swiss linguist Ferdinand de Saussure, the French anthropologist Claude Lévi-Strauss, and Russian Formalism, the structuralists found the clue to literary and cultural analysis in the phoneme, a unit of sound meaningful only because of its differences from other phonemes. Phonemes exemplify the elements in a cultural system that derive meaning from relations and contrasts with other elements. Structuralists determine meaning not by correlation to external reality but by analyzing its functions within a self-contained, culturally constructed code. Linguistic meaning is often established through binary opposition—the contrast of opposites, such as cold-hot and nature-culture. A critic who understands the underlying rules or "language" determining individual utterances will understand meaningful combinations and distinctions.

Post-structuralism was in part a reaction to structuralism's claim to comprehensive and objective exploration of every cultural phenomenon. This countermovement denied the objectivity of linguistic and cultural codes, language, and categories of conceptualization. It emphasized the instability of meanings, categories, and the inability of any universal system of rules to explain reality. The result was a radically nonhierarchical plurality of indeterminate meanings. Central to post-structuralist thought is Jacques Derrida's deconstructionism. Influential among literary critics at Yale University in the 1970s and 1980s, deconstructionism indicts the Western tradition of thought for ignoring the limitless instability and incoherence of language. The dominant Western logocentric tradition sought a transcendent center or primal guarantee for all meanings. Logocentric thinking, common since Plato, attempts to repress the con-

135

tingency and instability of meaning. Thus, any privileging of some terms as central to truth is denied as being merely arbitrary (for example, male over female, white over black). In the United States, literary critics used post-structuralist analysis to challenge the boundary between criticism of literature's subjectivity and objectivity, while elevating figurative language and interpretation. For post-structuralists there is no God, Truth, or Beauty—only gods, truths, and beauties. In the early 1990s post-structuralism underwent an intense critique from a range of social critics. Aside from the obscurantism of the movement, it seemed ahistorical, dogmatic, willfully nihilistic, and unable to provide a critique of moral and social injustice. Perhaps a part of the hedonistic flight from social responsibility of previous years, the movement seemed to slow down.

[Jonathan D. Culler, *Structuralist Poetics: Structuralism, Linguistics, and the Study of Literature* (Ithaca, N.Y., 1975); Edith Kurzweil, *The Age of Structuralism: Lévi-Strauss to Foucault* (New York, 1980); Selden Raman and Peter Widdowson, *A Reader's Guide to Contemporary Literary Theory* (Lexington, Ky., 1993).]

ALFRED L. CASTLE

See also **SUPP:** Literature.

POST-TRAUMATIC STRESS DISORDER (PTSD)

is a psychological condition in people who have suffered threats to life or bodily integrity and feel helplessness or terror; the syndrome may also appear in people who have witnessed horrifying events and feel unable to escape or alter them. Features of PTSD include intrusive memories or thoughts about the event, efforts to avoid thinking about it, a general numbing of emotional responsiveness, and a constantly heightened level of arousal. Dissociation, a sense of detachment from the reality of surroundings, is a way people often cope with repeated trauma. The full syndrome may only develop over months or years. PTSD as the explanation for "hysteria" emerged in the research of French psychologist Pierre Janet and, early in his career, Austrian psychoanalyst Sigmund Freud. During World War I, PTSD was common in soldiers; it came to be called combat neurosis or, colloquially, "shell shock" or "battle fatigue." The concept was developed by American psychiatrist Abram Kardiner in his book *The Traumatic Neuroses of War* (1941). The American Psychiatric Association accepted PTSD in 1980 as an official diagnosis, largely in response to descriptions of returning Vietnam War veterans. The revival of the feminist movement in the late 1960s led

to heightened awareness of domestic violence and abuse, whose victims are now recognized as often suffering a severe and persistent form of PTSD. The limits of the diagnosis, although not its fundamental validity, were still being debated as the twentieth century came to a close.

[Joel O. Brende, *Vietnam Veterans* (New York, 1985); Judith Lewis Herman, *Trauma and Recovery* (New York, 1992).]

WILLIAM IRA BENNETT

See also **SUPP:** Domestic Violence; Prisoners of War and Missing in Action; Psychiatry.

POVERTY,

especially in its most tangible forms of hunger and homelessness, continued to plague the United States as the twentieth century drew to a close. Poverty challenges the belief that hard work will be rewarded, and that all U.S. citizens have equality of opportunity. Poverty is defined as either a relative measure of money or material goods of one person in relation to others or as an absolute measure of how a person can meet the minimum requirements for survival. The most commonly used, although widely disputed, measure of poverty in the United States is an absolute measure, known as the poverty line. This is an amount of money calculated by multiplying the Department of Agriculture's Economy Food Plan by three (assuming therefore that food constitutes one-third of a family's expenditures). Developed for purposes of research, the measure was never meant to mark eligibility for social programs. The poverty threshold in 1994 was $15,141 a year for a family of four. In that same year, and by that measure, 14.5 percent of Americans lived in poverty. The poverty rate was not evenly distributed throughout the U.S. population. In 1994 it was 11.7 percent among whites, 30.6 percent among African Americans, and 30.7 percent among Hispanics. Also of concern was that 21.8 percent of all children in 1994 were poor.

The first large-scale effort to confront poverty on a national basis in the United States was during the Great Depression of the 1930s, when as much as 25 percent of the workforce was unemployed. No longer were religious and voluntary associations, which had given charity to the "deserving" poor, able to provide for those out of work. The Great Depression also underlined the structural problems (epitomized by the stock market crash of 1929) creating poverty, as opposed to the wage earner's lack of morality or personal failings. The Social Security Act of 1935 introduced the nation to social insurance, unemployment insurance, and public assistance. During the early 1960s President John F. Kennedy helped focus the nation's attention on the 22.2 percent of the population (in 1960) living in poverty. During President Lyndon B. Johnson's administration (1963–1969), legislation collectively known as the War on Poverty increased federal spending for the poor and helped bring the poverty rate down to 12.1 percent by 1969. One of the philosophical innovations of this era was the concept of "maximum community participation" of the poor. The poor became community action workers and sat on boards of antipoverty agencies.

Throughout the 1970s and 1980s there was widespread disillusionment with antipoverty efforts and a disdain for welfare programs that many observers saw as sapping people's work ethic. Under the administration of Richard M. Nixon (1969–1974), spending for the poor increased, contrary to the public impression of that Republican president's policies. Ronald Reagan's administration (1981–1989), however, promoted a "new federalism" to reduce the federal role in providing for the poor. Programs for the poor remained, but with restricted eligibility. During the administration of Bill Clinton, the Republican Congress, in alliance with Republican governors, continued the effort to transfer the responsibility for the poor from the federal government to the states, over the objections of the Democratic minority and President Clinton.

In the 1990s Americans were still debating ways to battle poverty. Especially disturbing was the homelessness and lack of opportunity facing the inner-city poor. Measures such as eliminating the welfare program available in some states for single, chronically unemployed persons, limiting the duration of receipt of welfare, or tying eligibility to work training or educational programs were hotly disputed. The most radical of the new proposals was the elimination of the federal commitment to provide subsistence payments to poor children through the Aid to Families with Dependent Children program. Instead, states would be given smaller sums of money and be allowed to decide who would get benefits and how much they would get, and benefits would not go to children born to teenage mothers or to children born to women already receiving assistance. Self-help and empowerment again become key phrases in discussions of antipoverty efforts and were implemented by agencies such as Habitat for Humanity, which involved the poor in rehabilitating housing.

[Irene Glasser, *Homelessness in Global Perspective* (New York, 1994); Michael B. Katz, *The Undeserving Poor: From the War on Poverty to the War on Welfare* (New York, 1989); Sar A. Levitan, *Programs in Aid of the Poor*, 6th ed. (Baltimore, 1990); William Julius Wilson, *The Truly Disadvantaged: The Inner City, the Underclass, and Public Policy* (Chicago, 1987).]

IRENE GLASSER

See also **SUPP:** Reaganomics; Unemployment; Welfare.

POWs. *See* **Prisoners of War and Missing in Action.**

PREGNANCY DISCRIMINATION ACT (PDA), a 1978 amendment to Title VII of the Civil Rights Act of 1964, prohibits workplace discrimination on the basis of pregnancy. The issue arose in 1976 when the Supreme Court in *General Electric* v. *Gilbert* decreed that denial of benefits for pregnancy-related disability was not discrimination based on sex. This reasoning recalled past management decisions by which married women faced job discrimination and pregnant women were routinely fired. By 1977 women made up more than 45 percent of the labor force, but only one-quarter had insurance plans that allowed sick leave for pregnancy-related illness. Women's organizations, feminists, labor and civil rights advocates, and some right-to-life groups formed a coalition known as the Campaign to End Discrimination Against Pregnant Workers to seek legislative relief from the Court's decision. In 1977 the original PDA that Congress considered sought to prohibit discrimination against pregnant women in all areas of employment, including hiring, firing, seniority rights, job security, and receipt of fringe benefits. More controversial aspects of the bill required employers offering health insurance and temporary disability plans to give coverage to women for pregnancy, childbirth, and related conditions. Although major corporations already provided such benefits, business associations argued that pregnancy was a "voluntary condition," not an illness, and that the bill would raise insurance costs. A more critical problem arose when congressmen attached an antiabortion rider disallowing benefits for elective abortions. After considerable debate the House and Senate passed versions that permitted employers to choose to provide abortion benefits but ambiguously told employers that they could rate a first pregnancy "more or less favorably" than other disabilities. The law took effect on Oct. 31, 1978, affecting only those companies with disability plans, thus failing to cover some 60 percent of female workers. Since passage, states and feminist groups have disagreed over how it should be applied, whether to protect pregnant women or to treat them equally.

[Joyce Gelb and Marian Lief Palley, *Women and Public Policies,* rev. ed. (Princeton, N.J., 1987); Joan Hoff, *Law, Gender, and Injustice* (New York, 1991).]

GRAHAM RUSSELL HODGES

See also **SUPP:** Family and Medical Leave Act; *General Electric Company* v. *Gilbert;* Women's Movement; Women's Rights.

PRESIDENCY. The American presidency has undergone a major transition since the 1970s. The president has vastly greater power than any official to lead the citizenry by setting the national agenda and determining foreign policy. Far more than his predecessors, however, the contemporary president must negotiate with Congress, the judiciary, cabinet departments, and executive and independent agencies, all of which have become more assertive. The president also faces ever-greater pressure from an electorate increasingly less loyal to political parties, from special interest groups that are well-financed and from media that are investigative. The president's international influence has been eroded by the rise of other industrial nations and Third World countries. Further, although the United States has unrivaled military strength and the world's largest economy, in the post–cold war era the president's command of nuclear weapons and foreign aid is not as effective as before to resolve conflicts and align nations, and the public is reluctant to approve U.S. participation in international peacekeeping or nation-building operations.

President Franklin D. Roosevelt (1933–1945) established the modern presidency. He acted as chief legislative whip and established the executive office of the president by moving the Bureau of the Budget into the White House offices in 1939, thereby expanding federal authority. His administrators managed New Deal programs and a wartime economy, and he exercised extraordinary diplomatic-military authority through executive agreements and summit conferences. Presidents expanded their power in the next decades by using the Bureau of the Budget and Council of Economic Advisers to assess the costs of legislative programs and national economic policy, marshaling federal authority to enforce Supreme Court desegregation rulings and civil rights laws and commanding television time for addresses and press conferences to advocate policies. Notably, President Lyndon B. Johnson (1963–1969) focused his politi-cal-legislative skills on his Great Society's commitment to voting and social welfare rights.

Presidential power over foreign affairs grew even more markedly. Harry S. Truman (1945–1953) became the first president to send troops to fight a major war—in Korea—and to station them abroad—in Western Europe—without formal approval from Congress. President Dwight D. Eisenhower (1953–1961) unilaterally approved military and covert actions against foreign governments. President John F. Kennedy (1961–1963) denied Congress a role in crises over Cuba and Vietnam. President Johnson used an incident in the Gulf of Tonkin in 1964 to persuade Congress to authorize almost unlimited retaliation, which led to a decade of war in Vietnam. Mounting protest against the Vietnam War, which television brought graphically into American homes, forced Johnson to forgo a reelection bid in 1968.

Richard M. Nixon, a Republican with a "southern strategy," was elected president in 1968 by promising not only to end the Vietnam War but to maintain a "law and order" administration, to reduce executive branch intervention in economic and social welfare matters, and to appoint conservative Supreme Court judges who would not "legislate" from the bench. Despite these pledges, the Nixon presidency (1969–1974) proved to be as "imperial" as any other. It enlarged and delegated authority to White House staff, expanded the Bureau of the Budget in 1970 into an even more powerful Office of Management and Budget (OMB), and impounded congressionally allocated funds, a virtual line-item veto. In 1971 Nixon instituted wage and price controls, suspended international convertibility of the dollar, and imposed a surcharge on imports. At the same time he outspent Johnson's Great Society, becoming the only cold war president to spend more on human resources programs than defense. Under Nixon the White House dominated foreign policy. It expanded the Vietnam War by secretly bombing Cambodia, intensified the warfare in Laos, and vastly increased bombing of North Vietnam. He restructured the National Security Council (NSC) to rival the Department of State and authorized his NSC adviser to use secret diplomacy to destabilize other governments, opened relations with the People's Republic of China, and negotiated to conclude the Vietnam War. Nixon also established a tenuous détente with the Soviet Union.

Congress gradually reasserted its authority at home and abroad during the Nixon era. It refused to confirm two Supreme Court nominees (although Nixon did appoint four justices who greatly influenced

Court opinions) and passed the Budget and Impoundment Control Act of 1974, creating the Congressional Budget Office to counter OMB functions. In 1969 the Senate resolved that a national commitment to use U.S. forces or finances to aid another country required formal approval from Congress. In 1970 congress repealed the Gulf of Tonkin Resolution and prohibited use of past or present appropriations to finance U.S. combat in Laos, Cambodia, and North and South Vietnam after August 1973. The Case-Zablocki Act of 1972 mandated that the president report all executive agreements to Congress within sixty days. The War Powers Act of 1973, passed over Nixon's veto, limited the president's use of troops abroad without formal congressional approval to sixty to ninety days, although the law conceded the president's authority to commit troops initially. In 1983 the Supreme Court, in an unrelated case, ruled that legislative vetoes (that is, Congress's right to overturn executive branch action either by withholding approval or voting to disapprove) such as provided in the War Powers Act were unconstitutional. In addition, since 1973 every president has sent troops abroad with scant reference to the War Powers Act.

The Watergate scandal during Nixon's second term brought the presidency into disrepute. White House aides and other officials were convicted for sanctioning or covering up a break-in at Democratic National Committee headquarters during the 1972 presidential campaign, a grand jury named the president an unindicted co-conspirator, and the House Judiciary Committee voted impeachment articles. In August 1974 Nixon became the first president to resign the office. Watergate was the worst White House scandal in U.S. history because it violated civil liberties and the political process and produced enduring public cynicism about the presidency and politics, but it also created a framework for scrutinizing alleged presidential transgressions. This included investigation by congressional committees and special prosecutors and a unanimous Supreme Court ruling that the president's executive privilege does not reach to withholding evidence in a criminal proceeding.

The presidency in the decade following Watergate and the end of the Vietnam War appeared at least temporarily weakened. President Gerald R. Ford (1974–1977) lacked a national constituency when he assumed the office following Nixon's resignation, and he undercut his support by pardoning Nixon. Ford's successor, President Jimmy Carter (1977–1981), lacked congressional allies, and his call for zero-based budgeting won no favor with federal officials, but he was able to broker Middle East peace accords and gain passage of the Panama Canal Treaty in 1978. His presidency foundered on matters beyond White House control: an energy crisis; inflation; the Soviet invasion of Afghanistan; and a revolution and hostage-taking in Iran.

Ronald Reagan won the presidency in 1980 by promising to minimize the size and scope of the federal government and to restore marketplace freedom and offering a foreign-military policy to regain U.S. global primacy. He identified closely with his party and capitalized on resurgent Republicanism in the older South as well as in newer Sunbelt regions and on rising religious fundamentalism. His victory catalyzed growing opposition to higher taxes and social welfare payments, administrative agency rulemaking, judicial decisions giving legal status to socially based rights, and animus toward the Soviet Union and terrorism. Reagan used both old and new political devices to strengthen his presidential power. He galvanized popular support with media messages, and used OMB's fiscal analyses and oversight of agency budgets and legislative proposals to slash social welfare, reduce taxes, and increase military spending. His economic policies, dubbed "Reaganomics," led to record budget deficits that necessitated cuts in social programs, prevented new entitlements, and created policy formation by budget priority. Reagan speeded deregulation. During his eight-year presidency, he appointed more than half of all federal judges—although Congress in 1987 rejected his controversial Supreme Court nominee, Robert Bork, who favored recent Supreme Court decisions that narrowed individual rights.

In foreign affairs Reagan undertook a vast nuclear weapons buildup, deployed forces to Lebanon, invaded Grenada, bombed Libya, and approved extensive covert activity in Central America. After difficult summit meetings with Soviet leaders, he reversed course in 1987–1988 to effect the most significant nuclear arms reduction since the start of the cold war. His presidency was jolted by the revelation that NSC officials had broken the law and lied under oath to Congress while exchanging arms for hostages with Iran and supporting covert actions in Central America. Congressional and blue-ribbon panel investigations of the Iran-Contra scandal proved only that the president gave his aides license, not instruction, to violate the law.

The popular Reagan propelled Vice President George Bush into the White House in 1988. Bush's forceful foreign policies against dictators in Panama and Iraq raised his standing to extraordinary heights in 1991, but he lost reelection a year later to a relatively unknown Democrat, Governor Bill Clinton of Arkansas, whose campaign emphasized domestic issues and benefited from sharp criticism of Bush's economic policies by an independent presidential candidate, billionaire businessman Ross Perot. Despite initial difficulties, Clinton won passage of the North American Free Trade Agreement in 1993 and a sharply modified economic program that raised taxes on high incomes, reduced burdens on lower income groups, and slowed the growth of annual budget deficits, but also included only modest appropriations for education and job programs. Clinton also appointed two moderate Supreme Court justices, Ruth Bader Ginsburg and Stephen G. Breyer. Most significantly, however, after appointing his wife, Hillary Rodham Clinton, to head a task force on national health care reform, the president failed to gain necessary support for its complex proposal intended to guarantee health coverage for all Americans and to contain health care costs, which had risen to 14 percent of the gross national product.

The Clinton presidency achieved moderate success in foreign policy despite a setback in 1993 when eighteen U.S. soldiers, part of a United Nations mission in Somalia, were killed by rebel forces, leading to the withdrawal of U.S. troops. Nonetheless, the Clinton administration helped to broker historic accords, signed at the White House, that initiated mutual recognition between Israel, the Palestinian Liberation Organization, and Arab autonomy on the West Bank and Gaza Strip. In 1994 Clinton effected a successful military—and peaceful—intervention to restore a democratically elected government in Haiti. The Clinton administration also fostered negotiations in 1995 intended to end four years of raging civil-religious war among Croatians, Bosnian Muslims, and Bosnian Serbs in the former Yugoslavia.

The Clinton presidency suffered a sharp political decline when the Republicans, who promoted term limits for federal officials and vastly reduced federal commitment—and greater state control—over social welfare programs, swept the congressional elections in 1994 and gained control of both houses of Congress for the first time in forty years. The Republican victories shifted the initiative for legislation from the White House to Congress, which rejected term limits but by the end of 1995 had prepared an economic program that proposed a balanced budget within seven years, lower taxes for high-income earners, and greatly reduced federal expenditures but more lati-tude for state controls for entitlement programs, including welfare (Aid for Families with Dependent Children) and Medicare and Medicaid. As 1996 opened it was unknown whether the president would try to compromise with Congress or veto the legislation and seek a new political mandate in the presidential election in the fall.

Post-Watergate presidents seem subject to unrelenting investigation of their personal as well as political behavior by Congress, special prosecutors, newspapers, and TV and radio talk shows. By 1995 the branches of government were more separate than ever before. Congress was voting programs and agency administrators and federal judges were making decisions that showed little deference for White House policy. A better-informed public was ready to change parties because of issues. The president still had unrivaled power to command public and congressional attention with policy statements, whether from the Oval Office or on talk shows. He had assistants to draft legislation and form political strategy. The OMB could bargain with congressional budget committees. The president retained almost unlimited power in foreign policy crises and great latitude in general to advance the national interest, even by reversing course with former adversaries, as Nixon did with China and Reagan did with the Soviet Union. Although constraints on presidential authority induced more accountability, they did not weaken the presidency, but even with great power, future presidents may find it more difficult to effect solutions to such problems as crime, poverty, drug addiction, and racial antipathy, as well as civil-religious wars, human rights violations, and nuclear proliferation.

[Ryan J. Barrileaux, *The Post-Modern Presidency: The Office After Ronald Reagan* (New York, 1988); Fred I. Greenstein, ed., *Leadership in the Modern Presidency* (Cambridge, Mass., 1988); Richard E. Neustadt, *Presidential Power and the Modern Presidents: The Politics of Leadership from Roosevelt to Reagan,* rev. ed. (New York, 1990); Malcolm Shaw, ed., *The Modern Presidency: From Roosevelt to Reagan* (New York, 1987).]

ARNOLD A. OFFNER

See also **SUPP:** Budget, Federal; Campaigns, Presidential; Democratic Party; Deregulation; Iran-Contra Affair; Reaganomics; Republican Party; Special Prosecutors; Third Parties and Independents; War Powers Act; Watergate, Aftermath of.

PRESIDENTIAL SUMMITS. *See* **Summits, Presidential.**

PRESS, FREEDOM OF THE. *See* **Freedom of the Press.**

PRINTING INDUSTRY was the fastest-growing manufacturing industry in the United States in the 1980s, but that growth was slowed by the recession late in the decade and in the early 1990s. By the early 1990s there were 64,000 commercial printing shops in the nation, and many other businesses that provided related services. Computers and other technologies changed the printing industry, automating older mechanical printing crafts, such as typesetting and page layout. Known as "desktop publishing," computerized print-related software and equipment became accessible to businesses and individuals outside the printing industry. The roles of printers and customers began to overlap because writers, designers, and other clients could now handle much prepress production themselves. Word processing and graphics programs made it possible to create and manipulate text and graphics completely within offices or on home computers and bypass steps (such as typesetting copy) traditionally handled by skilled workers in the printing crafts. Laser printers and other new copying equipment offered high-quality duplication of desktop-created computer files and other documents. This trend accelerated in the 1990s, with the advent of "paperless" multimedia publishing. Such documents and publications exist only "on line" in electronic and digital form, are distributed via computer disks or telephone lines, and are viewed on computers rather than on paper.

Technology reduced the need for professional printing services and crafts. It created business opportunities within the printing industry. Demand for printing services was bolstered by desktop publishing, because its ease and low cost prompted people to create publications, business documents, and other printed material that formerly required offset printing and other professional services. Many commercial printers adapted by offering desktop publishing and complementary services and by investing in advanced technology that remained too expensive and complex for clients. Specialized shops formed to handle pre- and postpress operations, such as color processing. Printing firms managed mailings and databases. Printers developed the capability to produce the new forms of electronic multimedia publications. Other trends stimulated the need for high-volume, high-quality printing, and special production methods. Magazine advertising began to include imbed-

ded fragrances and other features that relied on sophisticated printing techniques. Targeted marketing and advertising prompted more flexible methods of high-volume printing that could create versions of a publication or document, including printing methods that could make changes to individual copies within a single press run. With increased environmental concern and regulation, the printing industry faced the need to develop less toxic inks and other chemicals, more effective methods of waste disposal, and cater to the desire of many users for recycled paper.

[Nancy Aldrich-Ruenzel, ed., *Designer's Guide to Print Production* (New York, 1990); Liane Sebastian, *Electronic Design and Publishing: Business Practices* (New York, 1992).]

JOHN TOWNES

See also **SUPP:** Computers; Office Technology; Publishing Industry.

PRISONERS OF WAR AND MISSING IN ACTION (POWs and MIAs), an important legacy of the Vietnam War, with ramifications for both American domestic politics and U.S. relations with Vietnam. By the terms of the Paris Peace Accords of 1973, which ended U.S. involvement in Vietnam, the Democratic Republic of Vietnam (North Vietnam) agreed to release all American POWs that it was holding. North Vietnam, although having acceded to the Geneva Convention of 1949, which classified prisoners of war as "victims of events" who were entitled to "decent and humane treatment," had insisted that the crews of U.S. bombers were guilty of "crimes against humanity," and returning POWs told stories of mistreatment by their captors. The emotions stirred by evidence of mistreatment were magnified by reports that not all POWs had been returned and that Americans were still being held captive. These impressions of an inhumane Vietnamese government (officially called the Socialist Republic of Vietnam following the North's victory of 1975, which reunified the country) were reinforced by the plight of "boat people" fleeing Vietnam and Vietnam's invasion of Cambodia in 1978. These events helped to solidify public and congressional support for nonrecognition of Vietnam and a trade embargo.

The United States made "full accountability" of MIAs a condition of diplomatic recognition of Vietnam. At the end of the war, 1,750 Americans were listed as missing in Vietnam (another 600 MIAs were listed in neighboring Laos and Cambodia). The United

States also insisted that Vietnam assist in the recovery of remains of MIAs who were killed in Vietnam and in the return of any individuals who might have survived the war. Of particular concern were the "discrepancy cases," where individuals were believed to have survived an incident (for example, bailing out of an aircraft and having been reportedly seen later) but were not among the returning POWs.

The POW and MIA controversy triggered a rigorous debate and became a popular culture phenomenon in the late 1970s and 1980s, despite Pentagon and congressional investigations that indicated there were no more than 200 unresolved MIA cases out of the 2,266 the Department of Defense still listed as missing and about a dozen POWs unaccounted for. (Approximately 300,000 North and South Vietnamese are still considered MIAs.) President Ronald Reagan, speaking before the National League of POW/MIA Families in 1987, stated that "until all our questions are fully answered, we will assume that some of our countrymen are alive." The Vietnam Veterans of America, which sent several investigating groups to Vietnam in the 1980s, helped renew contacts between the U.S. and Vietnamese governments. Accordingly, agreements were reached between Vietnamese authorities and representatives of the Reagan administration that resulted in cooperation in recovering the remains of American casualties. Several hundred sets of remains were returned to the United States beginning in the late 1980s. In addition, progress was made in clarifying "discrepancy cases." The question resurfaced in the 1990s about whether President Richard Nixon and Secretary of State Henry Kissinger had done all they could during peace negotiations to free servicemen "knowingly" left behind or whether they both were so desperate to get out of Vietnam that they sacrificed POWs. Both Nixon and Kissinger maintained that it was the "doves" in Congress at the time who prevented any effective military action to find out the truth about POWs when it was still possible to do so in the summer and spring of 1973. On Feb. 3, 1994, with the approval of the Senate and business community, President Bill Clinton removed the nineteen-year trade embargo against Vietnam, and the Vietnamese government cooperated with veterans groups in locating the remains of U.S. soldiers and returning remains to the United States for burial, including those of nine soldiers in October 1995.

[Frederick Z. Brown, *Second Chance: The United States and Indochina in the 1990s* (New York, 1989).]

GARY R. HESS

PRISONS AND PRISON REFORM. Since the 1970s the goal of U.S. prisons has changed from rehabilitation to punishment. Most efforts at prison reform before that decade had been to introduce presumably better methods of turning criminals into good citizens. Beginning in the first quarter of the nineteenth century, reformers have debated the merits of the Pennsylvania (solitary confinement) and Auburn (separate and silent) systems, both designed for rehabilitation, but by the 1970s a number of academic studies concluded that none of the programs for rehabilitation had been successful. The studies came at a time when the national political climate was becoming conservative, with an emphasis on punishing rather than reforming criminals. A radical prisoners movement combined with academic studies and political conservatism to discredit rehabilitation.

Inspired by the civil rights movement and aided by the greater willingness of courts to intervene in supporting rights of prisoners, prisoners had become politically active beginning in the late 1960s. They protested against what they saw as the unfairness of indeterminate sentences, which were a part of the emphasis on rehabilitation. Convicts served unequal amounts of time for similar crimes, depending on the judgment of "experts" as to whether they had reformed. Activists believed that the length of time served should be proportionate to the seriousness of the crime. Court decisions supporting religious freedom in prison for Black Muslims and the rights of prisoners to sue prison officials led to increased activism in the 1970s, as well as frequent resentment on the part of many prison officials and guards who felt they were losing authority and respect. Prison demonstrations and rebellions of this period were not just about better physical conditions but also about greater rights for prisoners. Events at California's Soledad prison in 1969–1970 led to the organization of supporters outside the prison, the Soledad Brothers Defense Fund. Lists of demands at Soledad were echoed by inmates at California's Folsom Prison later in 1970, and at New York's Attica in 1971. Soledad, Folsom, and Attica became symbols of a movement that activists, outside prisons as well as inside, believed would radically change the nature of prisons in the United States.

Prisons did change but not in the direction desired by activists. An ironic effect of prisoner opposition to indeterminate sentences provided support for a conservative movement to "get tough" on criminals. By the end of the 1970s both the activist movement and the goal of rehabilitation had greatly weakened. The

1980 riot in the New Mexico State Penitentiary at Santa Fe contrasted with the Attica riot of 1971. Both were bloody, but at Attica most of the killing was done by officers of the law, whereas at Santa Fe prisoners tortured and killed other prisoners. The Santa Fe riot symbolized the end of hopes for prisoner activism. Mandatory sentencing became the norm in many states, and in 1987 guidelines for mandatory sentences for federal crimes were approved by the House of Representatives. Sentencing guidelines were not implemented in support of prisoners' rights but were part of the movement toward making prisons simply places of punishment.

The more punitive approach to imprisonment did not reduce the national crime rate, but it had noticeable effects upon rates of imprisonment. Rates remained steady during the 1960s but rose sharply in the early 1970s. The United States had about three times as many inmates in the 1990s (almost 800,000) as in the 1970s and more prisoners per capita than any other industrial democracy. For every 100,000 people, the United States has 300 in prison. Canada has the next highest rate, at 100 per 100,000, while that of the Netherlands is the lowest, fewer than 50 per 100,000.

Rates of imprisonment are not inevitable consequences of natural forces but the results of policy. They explain historical changes in imprisonment rates in Great Britain and the United States in terms of changes in policies in both countries. Punitive policies in Great Britain resulted in a rapid rise in the rate of imprisonment in the nineteenth century until about 1878. After that time different policies resulted in decreasing rates until about 1930, when they began to rise again. U.S. policies since the 1980s have resulted both in an extraordinarily high rate of imprisonment and serious levels of overcrowding. While there is general agreement that overcrowded prisons are inhumane and dangerous, there is little agreement about what ought to be done. Public opinion in the 1990s continued to support stiff sentences for individuals convicted of serious crimes but opposed tax increases to construct more prisons. Legislators responded by passing punitive laws but refused to appropriate funds and legislate taxes necessary to support these laws humanely.

[William Selke, *Prisons in Crisis* (Bloomington, Ind., 1993); Michael Sherman and Gordon J. Hawkins, *Imprisonment in America: Choosing the Future* (Chicago, 1981); Larry Sullivan, *The Prison Reform Movement* (Boston, 1990).]

RICHARD W. MOODEY

See also **DAH:** Auburn Prison System; Crime; Pennsylvania Prison System; **SUPP:** Crime.

PRIVATE SCHOOLS. *See* **Schools, Private.**

PRIVATIZATION, a term coined in 1969 by Peter F. Drucker in *The Age of Discontinuity* (actually "reprivatization") at the time U.S. government officials first considered privatizing goods and services. Privatization of government services involves selling, leasing, or contracting to a private company a service or product that had previously been performed or produced by the public sector. Until the twentieth century, government provided few services that could even be considered for privatization. Policy for 150 years was dictated by the principles of Adam Smith's *Wealth of Nations,* published in 1776. Smith argued that the "invisible hand" of a free marketplace was the most efficient way to maintain a country's economy. Intervention by government in the marketplace, in the form of regulations, public services, or public projects, he wrote, serves as a drag on the economy. This view prevailed, resulting in a tiny federal government that until the early twentieth century financed its operations almost exclusively with tariffs (with the exception of the Civil War). While state and local governments offered more services than the federal government, their activities were also narrow by modern standards.

Around the turn of the century, however, opinion began to change with the growth of the Progressive movement. While most people agreed that a free marketplace was the most efficient way to run an economy, the Progressives pointed out that it was not the kindest or best way to run a country. Public intervention became acceptable for the sake of safety and health, the maintenance of living standards, land conservation, and other areas of public good that would go unheeded by the private sector. At the same time the need for public facilities became more obvious as the nation's economy and its cities grew. Public lighting, well-maintained streets, police departments, water and sewer systems, and other services became pressing needs that the public demanded.

President Franklin D. Roosevelt took the Progressive movement one step further with the New Deal beginning in 1933. Through massive federal intervention in the form of public projects, Roosevelt aimed to take the nation's economy out of the Great Depression. For the next fifty years, government at the federal, state, and local levels took on responsibilities to provide goods and services for the marketplace. This trend eventually reversed itself, but it did so slowly. In 1955 the Bureau of the Budget issued a statement discouraging federal agencies from producing any "product or service [that] can be procured from private enterprise through ordinary business channels." In 1964 Republican presidential candidate Senator Barry Goldwater of Arizona called for sale of the Tennessee Valley Authority to private companies. The idea was rejected, even by his Republican colleagues. By 1980, however, privatization was a plank in Ronald Reagan's domestic platform in his bid for the presidency.

As government spending soared in the 1980s, more and more people went back to Smith's view that the private sector was a more efficient way of providing services than the government. In an often cited case, the city of Phoenix allowed private companies in the late 1970s to bid against its Public Service Department for local trash collection. The department lost the right to serve two of the city's five districts. Stung by the loss, the department took steps to improve service and cut costs. It later regained the lost districts. In 1984 the President's Private Sector Survey, known as the Grace Commission, called for adoption of private management practices in federal government and the sale of selected government services. In 1987 the government sold its 85 percent stake in Conrail for $1.65 billion, considered the largest privatization in U.S. history. One year later the President's Commission on Privatization made seventy-eight recommendations to privatize the federal government including sale of Amtrak, the repeal of statutes giving the U.S. Postal Service a monopoly on delivering letter mail, and the sale of a $250 billion loan portfolio of housing, business, agricultural, and education loans. President George Bush continued Reagan's efforts by making it easier for local and state government to privatize through regulatory changes. Reagan and Bush pushed for a school voucher system in which schools would compete with each other for students, introducing market forces into public education. President Bill Clinton also adopted many privatization initiatives after his election in 1992 through his efforts to "reinvent government."

Privatization took hold in the early 1990s, especially on state and local levels. Indianapolis Mayor Stephen Goldsmith undertook to privatize services ranging from sewer billings to operation of city parks. His efforts were followed by other large-city mayors, including New York City Mayor Rudolph W. Giuliani and Chicago Mayor Richard M. Daley.

Many cities and towns adopted versions of school choice or hired private companies to manage public schools. States joined the wave of privatization, shedding public management of road construction and maintenance and operation of prisons, state parks, and recreational facilities. Critics of privatization say the efficiencies gained from private sector involvement versus public sector are minimal. They cite the massive spending and fraud by defense industries as examples of private sector inefficiency. Unions note that private companies often underpay employees and are less inclined to hire women and minorities or provide basic workers' rights. Critics also argue that in many cases, such as operation of prisons, greater public goals, such as reforming criminals, are sacrificed for the sake of saving money.

[John D. Donahue, *The Privatization Decision* (New York, 1989); "Privatization," *Congressional Quarterly Researcher* 2 (Nov. 13, 1992).]

ERIK BRUUN

See also **DAH:** New Deal; Progressive Movement; Public Ownership; Public Utilities; **SUPP:** Education, Parental Choice in; Schools, For-Profit.

PRIZEFIGHTING generally means professional boxing, but other less savory matches featuring individual sparring include professional wrestling, strong-man competitions, televised gladiator contests, and illicit no-holds-barred fights produced for credulous audiences. Immensely popular and a recognized Olympic sport, boxing is an attack event in which a fighter punches to hurt and disable his opponent. Gloves are worn to protect the knuckles, not the adversary's chin or brain, as one commentator noted. The most visible survival of eighteenth-century English "blood sports," professional boxing is a fast-moving, exciting, aggressive challenge between two highly skilled, physically fit men. Amateur boxing is a fast-growing and popular sport among men and women.

Boxing suffers from a poor public image. Loosely organized in the 1990s by three associations, the World Boxing Council, the World Boxing Association, and the International Boxing Association, prizefighting is actually barely regulated. There is no national commission; each state has its own codes, permitting badly damaged fighters to compete frequently under false names, merely by crossing state lines. Unsavory promoters control the careers of boxers through options on future fights and powerful influence over television appearances. Whereas in other professional sports, athletes merely appearing with gamblers or criminals risk banishment, boxing matches are held in gambling casinos with heavy wagering. Since the mid-1970s, in an effort to increase the number of champions, boxing officials have subdivided older weight classifications into thirteen classifications bounded by flyweight (112 pounds) to heavyweight (no weight limit) with subdivided categories such as super middleweight. Boxing has suffered from fixing scandals, sham championship tournaments, and several deaths from fight injuries. In 1983 the *Journal of the American Medical Association* urged banning boxing because of evidence of chronic brain damage from fights.

Despite its many woes, boxing has produced important champions. The most prestigious title, the heavyweight championship, has lately been dominated by black pugilists including the great Muhammad Ali, Joe Frazier, Larry Holmes, Evander Holyfield, and Mike Tyson. White challengers such as Gerry Cooney have often garnered considerable attention. Perhaps the most famous white boxer since the 1970s was not really a boxer at all, but actor Sylvester Stallone, who immortalized an underdog champion in his Rocky movies. Major heavyweight matches have included Ali's recapturing the title by knocking out George Foreman in 1974; Ali's 1975 conquest of Frazier in the "Thrilla in Manila"; Ali's recapture of the crown from Leon Spinks in 1978; and Holmes's victory over Ali in 1980. Tyson seemed invincible from 1986 until Buster Douglas upset him in 1990. Tyson was convicted of rape in 1992 and sentenced to prison; following his release in 1995, the twenty-eight-year-old Tyson planned to resume his boxing career. In 1994 the forty-five-year-old Foreman regained the championship he lost twenty years earlier. Other legendary boxers since the 1970s have included Sugar Ray Leonard, Marvelous Marvin Hagler, Roberto Duran, and Thomas "Hit Man" Hearns. In 1980 Duran beat Leonard for the welterweight championship; six months later Leonard conquered Duran when the latter conceded, stating *"no mas"* (no more), allegedly suffering from stomach cramps. Leonard won a third fight in 1989 and fought other important matches against Hearns. Physical disabilities have hampered champions and opponents. Ali contracted premature Parkinson's disease from head punches; Leonard suffered a detached retina.

[Thomas Hauser, *The Black Lights: Inside the World of Professional Boxing* (New York, 1986); Joyce Carol Oates, *On Boxing* (Hopewell, N.J., 1994).]

GRAHAM RUSSELL HODGES

See also **SUPP:** Olympic Games.

PRO-CHOICE MOVEMENT, initiated primarily by such feminist groups as the National Organization for Women in response to the antiabortion pro-life movement that developed after the Supreme Court gave abortion constitutional protection in 1973. Pro-choice was the language activists used to highlight the central place of women in the abortion debate. They believe that women should have control over their reproductive lives, as a legal fact and fundamental right, and that abortion should be available to all women. The pro-choice movement is one part of the larger movement for reproductive rights that also opposes policies such as welfare measures penalizing women for childbearing.

[Ruth Colker, *Abortion and Dialogue: Pro-choice, Pro-life, and American Law* (Bloomington, Ind., 1992); Barbara Hinkson Craig and David M. O'Brien, *Abortion and American Politics* (Chatham, N.J., 1993); Faye D. Ginsburg, *Contested Lives: The Abortion Debate in an American Community* (Berkeley, Calif., 1989).]

NANCY B. PALMER

See also **SUPP:** Abortion; *Griswold v. Connecticut; Roe v. Wade; Rust v. Sullivan; Webster v. Reproductive Health Services;* Women's Health; Women's Movement.

PRODUCT TAMPERING, the deliberate and intentionally harmful alteration of consumer products, first took place in the 1890s, the most famous incident being the poisoning of two bottles of Bromo Seltzer with cyanide of mercury, which resulted in one death. The modern age of "consumer terrorism" began in Chicago, Ill., in 1982, with the injection of poison into packages of the painkiller Tylenol. Immediately following these incidents, more than 270 tampering episodes were reported, involving over-the-counter pharmaceuticals and packaged drinks and foods. Congress responded by passing the Federal Anti-Tampering Act of 1983, which made it a crime to tamper with products or to make false claims of tampering. The legislation made convictions punishable by three years in prison and a $10,000 fine for an attempted tampering; twenty years in prison and a $100,000 fine if serious injury occurs; and life imprisonment if there is a death. The threat of tampering alone can result in five years in prison and a $25,000 fine. Nevertheless, product tampering became a major cultural phenomenon in the United States. Motives have included murder, extortion, stock market manipulation, insurance fraud, and serial mayhem. Incidents of product tampering have been followed by public hysteria, copycat cases, and hundred of false reports. In 1993 false reports were made in twenty-three states that syringes were found in cans of Pepsi-Cola.

[Henry Glowa, "Criminal Product Tampering," *Southwestern University Law Review* 17 (Summer 1988); Barry Logan, "Product Tampering Crime," *Journal of Forensic Sciences* 38 (July 1993).]

ROBERT KRAIG

See also **SUPP:** Consumer Rights and Protection.

PRO-LIFE MOVEMENT, a grass-roots movement that developed in reaction to the 1973 Supreme Court ruling in *Roe* v. *Wade* that gave constitutional protection to legalized abortion. While the goal of the movement is to overturn *Roe,* participants have used direct action and the language of the civil rights movement to obstruct abortion clinics by harassing personnel and clients. Since the launching of Operation Rescue in 1987 by Randall Terry and Joseph Scheidler, violence against clinics has escalated to the extent that the 1990s witnessed murders of doctors performing abortions as well as of clinic personnel.

[Faye D. Ginsburg, *Contested Lives: The Abortion Debate in an American Community* (Berkeley, Calif., 1989); Kristin Luker, "Abortion, Motherhood, and Morality," in *Women's America: Refocusing the Past,* 4th ed., Linda K. Kerber and Jane Sherron De Hart, eds. (New York, 1995).]

NANCY B. PALMER

See also **SUPP:** Abortion; Adoption; Pro-Choice Movement; *Roe* v. *Wade; Rust* v. *Sullivan; Webster* v. *Reproductive Health Services.*

PROSECUTORS, SPECIAL. *See* **Special Prosecutors.**

PROSTITUTION, the exchange of money for sex, is illegal in every state with the exception of thirteen of sixteen counties in Nevada. In those states, closely associated crimes include pandering, or procuring prostitutes, and pimping, or living off the earnings of prostitutes. Between 1975 and 1991 there were an average of 89,000 annual arrests in the United States for male and female prostitution. Prostitution is overwhelmingly an urban phenomenon, with arrests far greater in cities of more than 250,000 people. Unlike Nevada, where prostitutes are carefully regulated, or San Francisco, where neither police enforcement or prosecution is actively pursued, most cities use an unofficial policy of enforcement to confine sexual commerce to "red light" districts. Most Americans do not worry greatly about prostitution unless activity is

nearby. Prosecution can be politically advantageous for local politicians, but it is usually inconsistently pursued. Raids often become symbolic gestures, an unintended, negative effect of which is to consolidate a prostitute's self-identity. Critics of current law enforcement policies also argue that prosecution and incarceration expenses should be applied to drug treatment and job training. In the politics of the United States, legalization of prostitution in the 1990s was as remote as it was in the 1890s.

An average of 62,000 women, but few "Johns," are arrested each year. Female prostitution is hierarchical and male dominated. At the top are call girls, available by appointment through a madam or high-class male pimps. Fees may run into thousands of dollars. A similar system involves escort services, through which customers may hire a woman (or a man) for companionship or sex. Escort services operate superficially within the law and may even advertise in newspapers and in telephone directories. Far below escort services are strip joints and massage parlors, functioning in tawdry, unsanitary conditions. A related activity is telephone sex, emerging from the threat of disease, particularly AIDS, by which a customer receives verbal stimulation of fantasies from a distant voice. At the bottom of the hierarchy are streetwalkers. Protected only by a pimp, streetwalkers charge little, accept nearly all customers, and perform their work in cars, alleys, or cheap hotels. New York City authorities estimate that one-third of street prostitutes carry the HIV virus, which causes AIDS. Streetwalkers are 10 to 20 percent of all prostitutes, but account for 90 percent of arrests; a disproportionate number of the detained are women of color.

Prostitution is a transaction superficially involving mutual choice. Young men still regard visits as rites of passage; older men ostensibly work out marital and sexual difficulties. Customers include disabled, single men unable to find legitimate sex partners. Women enter prostitution for myriad reasons, the fundamental nature of which is controversial. Divisions exist as to whether female prostitutes seek financial gain otherwise unavailable or are pushed into this life because of high unemployment, particularly among minority women. The belief that prostitutes are oversensual females is now invalidated, but a link with childhood sexual abuse at home is accepted. Prostitution is recurrently connected to other criminal activities, including credit card forgery and extortion. Little joy seems attached to the work, and interviews emphasize ancillary entertainment over sexual pleasure.

Despite disagreements within the feminist movement over whether prostitution should be legalized (women controlled by state) or decriminalized (permitting women to control this oldest of professions), the institution has entered politics. In 1973 Margo St. James, a San Francisco prostitute, organized COYOTE (Call Off Your Old Tired Ethics), urging decriminalization through the magazine *COYOTE Howls.* Priding itself as a union local, PONY (Prostitutes of New York) also favors decriminalization and works with United Nations groups to fight international trafficking in women and children. WHISPER (Women Hurt in Systems of Prostitution Engaged in Revolt) opposes prostitution, while other groups offer counseling to help young women quit the life. The political and legal impact of these organizations has been minimal. Still, the most significant organization at the street level is the exploitative control of the pimp.

The world of male prostitutes is more shadowy. The male prostitute is generally a lone individual, although connections with escort services are possible. Arrests of male prostitutes and their male partners are on the rise because law enforcement has become more gender-neutral while public acceptance of homosexuality is greater, permitting homosexual prostitutes more visibility, and because male prostitution, like female, may be linked to patterns of drug trafficking. Male prostitutes, like female, work in pornographic productions, strip houses, and phone sex.

The most notorious type is the child prostitute, who has left or been exiled from home, fleeing sexual abuse or other mistreatment or homes broken by a parent's drug or alcohol abuse. The AIDS epidemic has made child prostitutes more desirable for customers who believe incorrectly that children are less likely to pass on the disease. Increasing numbers of streetwalkers are runaway children. In New York City in the early 1980s, Eighth Avenue and Forty-second Street, adjacent to the Port Authority Bus Terminal, the arrival point for many runaway children, was known as the "Minnesota Strip," because of the many runaways enlisted and working there as prostitutes. In contrast to its ambiguous treatment of adult pornography, the Supreme Court grants no Constitution protection to child pornography, and police are especially vigilant toward child prostitution, because many of these children also work in child pornography media.

[Kathleen Barry, *Female Sexual Slavery,* rev. ed. (1994); Nanette J. Davis, ed., *Prostitution: An International Handbook on Trends, Problems, and Policies* (Westport, Conn., 1993); Judith Ennew, *The Sexual Exploitation of Children* (New York, 1986); Eleanor M. Miller, *Street Women* (Philadelphia, 1986); "Special Issue on Prostitution," *CQ Researcher* 3 (June 11, 1993); Samuel M. Steward, *Understanding the Male Hustler* (New York, 1991).]

GRAHAM RUSSELL HODGES

See also **DAH:** Mann Act; Prostitution; Sexual Attitudes; Venereal Disease; **SUPP:** Acquired Immune Deficiency Syndrome; Women's Movement.

PROTESTANTISM. All Christians believe that there is one God, that God is revealed in Jesus of Nazareth, the Christ, and that the purpose of the church is to worship God and live in the way of Christ. Historically, three different Christian faith communities—Roman Catholic, Eastern Orthodox, and Protestant—developed, each with a distinctive way of understanding and living out those beliefs. The word "protestant" was applied to Martin Luther and others who in the Reformation of sixteenth century Europe protested certain beliefs and practices of the Roman Catholic church. Protestants came to North America from Europe to gain religious and economic freedom. They helped shape the New World forms of capitalism and democracy as well as religion. Protestants were in turn changed and shaped by pioneer life, democracy, the federal form of government, capitalism, and slavery. The historic Protestant theological foundation rests on three "alones" and one "all." A person is saved (reconciled with God, others, and self) through God's grace (unearned love) rather than through human works, rituals, sacrifices, or beliefs (grace alone). Such grace is available to anyone through trust in God (faith alone). God is revealed in the Bible (Scripture alone). Every believer has equal access to God, especially by reading the Bible, without going through the priests and rituals of the church (the priesthood of all believers). Thus, Protestantism is a faith of freedom and a faith in freedom. There exists in its very nature, however, a paradox that hovers over the line between inclusion and exclusion. The doctrines of grace alone, faith alone, and the priesthood of all believers are inclusive. The doctrine of Scripture alone, however, is exclusive. If God is revealed in the Bible, then everyone has access to the one revealed truth. Those who do not choose to accept it are excluded by their own choice.

Protestants have never resolved the tension between the inclusive and exclusive dimensions of their faith. Sidney Mead described the United States as "a nation with the soul of a church." This soul was expressed politically in democracy and personal responsibility. It took form culturally in the ethic of hard work and personal morality. The United States was formed largely by this basic Protestant principle of individual freedom and responsibility, producing a new "social contract." Nonetheless, exclusion was built into this religious social contract because it existed primarily for white males and not even for all of them. Indentured servitude was a part of early U.S. life. Immigrant groups such as the Irish had to struggle against severe prejudice before being accepted into the contract. Native, African, Asian, and Hispanic Americans were both overtly and covertly omitted from the American dream. Although women of all races often worked as equal partners with men under harsh conditions, they had very few legal rights and their social position was severely circumscribed. The U.S. story, however, despite the marginalization of many people, was one of expansion and growth. Protestant churches, especially those that adapted to frontier conditions, participated in that growth. By 1960 approximately 60 percent of all U.S. citizens identified themselves as Protestant.

In 1993, according to the *Yearbook of American and Canadian Churches,* the largest Protestant religious groups in the United States were Baptist (33.5 million), Methodist (14.6 million), Pentecostal (10.1 million), Lutheran (8.3 million), Latter-day Saints (4.5 million), and Presbyterian (4.2 million). These and other groups were further divided into approximately 150 groups of associated churches, ranging in size from the 15 million members of the Southern Baptist Convention to the 420 members of the United Christian Church.

Since the 1960s, however, Protestantism has divided not along traditional denominational lines of theology but along the battle lines of social issues. Fewer Protestants think of themselves as Baptist or Methodist or Presbyterian. They identify themselves, consciously or unconsciously, as conservative or liberal, moderate or fundamentalist, charismatic or feminist, Native American or African American. Divisions have focused on issues of abortion, the cold war, consumerism, politics, race, television, family values, gambling, gender, and homosexuality. Religious differences have centered on such issues as inclusive (that is, not exclusively male) language, especially about God; prayer in public schools; biblical inerrancy; ecumenism; denominational control; church growth or lack of it; the role of women, especially in the ministry; and theology, especially specifically focused theologies such as liberation, feminist, and black.

These are all issues of inclusion and exclusion. Can women, homosexuals, fetuses/unborn children, eth-

nic minority persons, or communists be included in the church and the social contract? Should those be excluded who do not believe the Bible is without error, or those who participate in politics, get divorces, have children out of wedlock, or believe in evolution? Who is excluded by the nature of those prayers, or by prayer itself? Denominations, as associations of churches with common beliefs and practices, once provided fairly clear lines of inclusion and exclusion. In the 1990s, however, they were more administrative than theological.

Protestantism also has been shaped by religious consumerism. People choose a congregation because it meets their current needs and beliefs, not because of its denomination. They "church shop" and pick the congregation with the best youth program, the newest music, or the most congenial preaching. Even after making their choice they may not know what, if any, denomination they have selected. They tend to choose large congregations rather than small ones, causing decline in older denominations that have many small churches.

Since the 1970s population has shifted from the Northeast and Midwest to the Sunbelt. The shift from rural areas to large metropolitan areas has continued. Such older mainline denominations as Methodists and Presbyterians were heavily invested in church buildings and institutions in the industrial Rustbelt and in declining agricultural areas. As in earlier periods of U.S. history, newer, more conservative groups, such as pentecostals, were able to respond more readily. They established congregations where the people went. They grew as the more established denominations declined. Many of the most noticed churches do not even belong to denominations but are "megachurches" founded by entrepreneurial ministers who use television and modern fund-raising to build independent ministries. A large pool of new members for Protestant churches is composed of former Roman Catholics who no longer feel comfortable with the Catholic hierarchical structure, theology, or certain Catholic social stances, especially abortion, celibate clergy, and the place of women in church leadership.

In the 1960s and 1970s, several formal denominational mergers took place. Many Protestants talked about an "ecumenical imperative" to overcome denominational differences and witness to the unity of Christ through the unity of the church. Interdenominational ecumenism has now become almost irrelevant, however, because denominations no longer provide religious and social identity. This new ecumenism operative in Protestantism is based on individual Christians or, in some cases, congregations, joining together around issues. This creates tensions within denominations as their members are no longer united by theology but divided by issues of biblical inerrancy, speaking in tongues, abortion, homosexuality, women in ministry, and so forth. Almost every denomination has two or more groups in constant conflict with one another over who controls the denominational administration, theological schools, and missions.

Protestants are still individualistic, but it is an individualism based more on experience, practice, and social stance than upon theology. Protestants are as informed in spiritual practice by popular psychology and television talk shows as they are by traditional Christianity or denominational programs and literature. Although Protestants cannot agree on who should be excluded, there is considerable agreement on who should be included. Few denominations and congregations have succeeded in becoming interracial, but many have admitted women to full positions of leadership, both lay and clergy. They are increasingly sensitive to other marginalized persons, such as the physically challenged. They have transformed orphanages into homes for abused children and created retirement facilities for the burgeoning elderly population. Conservatives, liberals, moderates, charismatics, and feminists join together across lines of exclusion to feed the hungry, strengthen families, encourage the addicted, and comfort those afflicted by natural disasters.

[Harold Bloom, *The American Religion: The Emergence of the Post-Christian Nation* (New York, 1992); Roger Finke and Rodney Stark, *The Churching of America 1776–1990* (New Brunswick, N.J., 1992); George W. Forell, *The Protestant Faith* (Englewood Cliffs, N.J., 1960); C. Eric Lincoln and Lawrence H. Mamiya, *The Black Church in the African American Experience* (Durham, N.C., 1990); Sidney E. Mead, *The Nation with the Soul of a Church* (New York, 1975).]

JOHN ROBERT McFARLAND

See also **DAH:** Adventist Churches; African Methodist Episcopal Church; Afro-American Church; Baptist Churches; Church of Christ, Scientist; Congregational Churches; Cumberland Presbyterian Church; Disciples of Christ; Episcopal Church; Jehovah's Witnesses; Lutheranism; Mennonites; Methodists; Presbyterianism; Puritans and Puritanism; Quakers; Reformed Churches; Religion; **DAH** and **SUPP:** Latter-day Saints, Church of Jesus Christ of; Pentecostal Churches; Reorganized Church of Jesus Christ of Latter-day Saints; **SUPP:** African-American Religions and Sects; Fundamentalism; Millenarianism; Religion; Televangelism; Women in Churches.

PSYCHIATRY. Between 1900 and 1920 medicine rapidly redefined itself as scientific. Psychiatry lagged behind other specialties in this regard, partly because it was broadening its scope to include social issues rather than confining its attention to the mainly biological. Although they began their careers by focusing primarily on biological aspects of mental illness, some leaders of the field, including Adolf Meyer and Elmer E. Southard, went on to write and speak expansively about mental health. Even as psychiatry widened its focus, psychiatrists were losing status as specialists of medicine. They responded with an effort to strengthen their organization and tighten their standards. In 1921 the American Medico-Psychological Association was renamed the American Psychiatric Association, which became more active, and its journal became the *American Journal of Psychiatry*. In 1934 the American Board of Psychiatry and Neurology was founded to provide certification for practitioners specializing in their respective fields.

These developments were not much influenced by the emergence of psychoanalysis in Europe at the beginning of the twentieth century, although Sigmund Freud's visit to the United States in 1909 drew some attention, and a few American psychiatrists or neurologists began to experiment with psychoanalytic treatment. In the 1930s, however, an influx of European psychoanalysts fleeing the Nazis brought Freudian thought to the United States, and this group achieved considerable prominence. For a generation psychoanalysis was the dominant intellectual current in American psychiatry, and the two terms, psychiatry and psychoanalysis, became all but synonymous in training programs and in popular culture, although there continued to be a group of psychiatrists who managed mental hospitals, administered biological treatments, and espoused non-Freudian approaches.

The scope and authority of psychiatry (and psychology) were greatly enhanced during World War II. The discovery of high rates of psychiatric disorder in men between the ages of eighteen and forty-five being screened for the military heightened awareness of the problems treated by psychiatrists. Psychological management of the troops came to be seen as crucial to the war effort. Psychiatrists influenced criteria for induction and managed psychological responses to military experience, thus acquiring governmental recognition of their professional competence. Also in this period, both psychological and pharmacological developments were increasing the effectiveness of psychiatric treatments.

An antipsychiatry movement emerged in the 1960s and 1970s, led in part by disaffected psychiatrists and psychologists. Psychiatric practice was criticized as an insidious form of social control based on a pseudoscientific medical model. A few critics claimed that mental illness is an intellectual construct and that it represents a valid alternative to ordinary thinking and behavior. In this period the hold of psychoanalysis also began to wane. Research showed that its claims had been overly broad; biological treatments proved effective; and economic forces made long-term, labor-intensive treatment impractical for all but a few.

Since World War II the intellectual content of psychiatry appears to have been reinvigorated, with enormous advances in both biological and psychological knowledge. Nevertheless, in the mid-1990s it was one of the three lowest-paid medical specialties (along with primary care and pediatrics), and with the loss of the psychoanalytic mystique, it declined in public esteem. Psychiatry appeared to be entering yet another crisis. The effort to contain health care costs targeted psychiatric treatment, in part reflecting the success of psychiatry with the public; demand for mental health services was seen as being high and thus costly to insure. Benefits for such treatment were being curtailed, and there was pressure to shift much psychiatric care into primary practice (for example, by training primary practitioners to diagnose and treat depression). Some predicted that the number of practicing psychiatrists would diminish markedly by the early decades of the twenty-first century, although the demand for psychiatric services did not appear to be waning.

[Daniel Blain and Michael Barton, *The History of American Psychiatry* (Washington, D.C., 1979); Ralph Colp, Jr., "History of Psychiatry," in *Comprehensive Textbook of Psychiatry,* edited by Harold I. Kaplan and Benjamin J. Sadock, 5th ed., 2 vols. (Baltimore, 1989); Gerald N. Grob, *Mental Illness and American Society, 1875–1940* (Princeton, N.J., 1983).]

WILLIAM IRA BENNETT

See also **SUPP:** Mental Illness; Psychology.

PSYCHOLOGY. From 1975 to 1995 there was tremendous growth of interest in psychology and its applications in advertising, mental health, and the courts. The relationship between genetics and psychology addressed the enduring question of nature versus nurture (heredity versus environment). While the hereditarian chose the former explanation, the behaviorist chose the latter, but evidence from both areas shows there is a strong interplay between genes and environment in molding human personality and intelligence. Tensions developed between experimentalists and clinician practitioners, and by 1988 the differing viewpoints became so marked that academic and research-oriented psychologists broke away from the venerable American Psychological Association (now dominated by clinician practitioners) to found the American Psychological Society.

Many experimentalists have used materials and settings applicable to those in the real world. Experimental findings from the laboratories (the principles of learning and conditioning discovered by Ivan Pavlov and B. F. Skinner) have not only been used for what is considered the public good but also to influence consumer decisions. A considerable part of the billions spent each year in the United States on advertising pays for messages conveyed by persuasive techniques derived from psychological principles. Health psychology, developed to alleviate mental or physical illnesses, has brought parts of its terminology into everyday vocabulary. Perhaps the most notable discovery in this regard was the correlation between personality type and health. Interestingly, it was published not by psychologists, but by two cardiologists, Meyer Friedman and R. H. Rosenman, who in 1974 identified characteristic behavior patterns known as Type A and Type B personalities; Type A patterns are risk factors for coronary heart disease.

Since the 1970s practitioners of what is called forensic psychology have offered court testimony regarding competency of defendants, which has been used for and against the insanity defense. Expert testimony has been also been offered regarding the plausibility of witness or client testimony. Examples that have captured the public's attention include sexual abuse charges, brought up by adults after recovering memories of childhood incidents during therapy. Clinical psychologists have offered testimony documenting such repressed memories, but experimentalists have offered data suggesting that what is sometimes revealed are false memories implanted during therapy. This debate over memories recalled after decades of amnesia continues. In a 1994 landmark case, Gary Ramona won damages after his daughter accused him of sexual abuse based on recovery of repressed memories during therapy; the court's verdict, against his daughter's therapists and the medical center where they worked, considered that these memories were implanted.

Another controversial area has been the enduring question of nature versus nurture. Identical twins separated soon after birth have provided a laboratory for separating the effects of genetics versus upbringing and environment. Such evidence has been beneficial in terms of explaining and treating schizophrenia as well as severe alcoholism. Intelligence differences between groups have also been examined by correlating IQ test scores of identical versus fraternal twins (research resumed in 1994 by Richard Herrenstein and Charles Murray in *The Bell Curve*). The validity of this evidence, however, has been hotly debated. The debate has also raged over the origins of psychological traits, with some researchers pointing to environmental factors and others to genetics. In particular, a team led by Thomas J. Bouchard, Jr., at the University of Minnesota, concluded in a 1990 article in the journal *Science:* "The effect of being reared in the same home is negligible for many psychological traits." Most scientists suggest, however, that evidence supports that there is a strong interplay between genes and environment.

Because of the unusual range of phenomena studied by experimental psychologists, divisions exist among them, and psychology has evolved into fields that are too disparate to fit into a single theory. According to the American Psychological Association, psychology has branched into fifty-eight fields, grouped into the study of personality, development, social psychology, perception, neuroscience, motivation and emotion, cognition, psychometrics, psychopathology, and psychotherapy.

One of the most dramatic and productive changes has been the wedding of cognitive psychology to neuroscience. Cognitive psychology developed in the 1970s to study questions about mental life, and cognitive psychologists expounded theories to explain how people plan, think, remember, and make decisions. Neuroscience, which studies the physiology of the brain, is a much older study, dating to the seventeenth-century French mathematician and philosopher René Descartes. Late-twentieth-century technological advances changed much of what neuroscientists could examine. Techniques developed in the 1980s and early 1990s, such as positron emission tomography (PET) and magnetic resonance imaging (MRI), allow neurologists and psychologists to look into a brain and observe its functioning. Related developments came from other

quarters outside psychology. The partnership between cognitive psychology and computer science resulted in remarkable insights. A generation ago it seemed that the computer was the model for the mind, but that order has been reversed, with the mind as the model for the computer. Computer engineers began building computers to simulate aspects of human thinking (artificial intelligence).

[Howard Gardner, *The Mind's New Science: A History of the Cognitive Revolution* (New York, 1985); Henry Gleitman, *Psychology,* 4th ed. (New York, 1995); L. S. Hearnshaw, *The Shaping of Modern Psychology* (London, 1987); Morton Hunt, *The Story of Psychology* (New York, 1993).]

CHERI L. WIGGS

See also **SUPP:** Mental Illness; Psychiatry.

PUBLIC HEALTH SERVICE began in 1798 as the Marine Hospital Service, a program established within the Treasury Department for the care and relief of sick and disabled seamen. It was not until the 1870s that the service was formally organized as a national hospital system with a central headquarters in Washington, D.C., under the direction of a supervising surgeon (later known as the surgeon general). As the duties of the service grew in the late nineteenth century to include authority for quarantine, medical inspection of arriving immigrants, and operation of a hygienic laboratory, its name was changed to Public Health and Marine Hospital Service in 1902 and to Public Health Service (PHS) in 1912. The PHS assumed increasing responsibilities for public health. In 1930 its Hygienic Laboratory became the National Institute (later Institutes) of Health, which evolved into the nation's largest center for carrying out and funding biomedical research. A malaria control program during World War II grew into another PHS agency, the Centers for Disease Control and Prevention. In 1955 the service assumed responsibility for American Indians and Alaskan natives under the program now known as the Indian Health Service. In 1968 the Food and Drug Administration became part of the PHS. Four other PHS agencies are the Agency for Health Care Policy and Research, the Agency for Toxic Substances and Disease Registry, the Health Services and Resources Administration, and the Substance Abuse and Mental Health Administration. The PHS became part of the newly created Federal Security Agency in 1939. It was incorporated into the Department of Health, Education, and Welfare (now the Department of Health and Human Services) when the department was established in 1953. The service was directed by the surgeon general until 1968, when a reorganization placed it under the leadership of the assistant secretary for health. The surgeon general continues to play an important role as an adviser to the public on health matters. In the 1990s the PHS agencies reported to the secretary of health and human services.

[Bess Furman, *A Profile of the United States Public Health Service, 1798–1948* (Washington, D.C., 1973); Fitzhugh Mullan, *Plagues and Politics: The Story of the United States Public Health Service* (New York, 1989); Ralph Williams, *The United States Public Health Service, 1798–1950* (Washington, D.C., 1951).]

JOHN PARASCANDOLA

See also **DAH:** Public Health; **SUPP:** Centers for Disease Control and Prevention; Food and Drug Administration; Health and Human Services, Department of; National Institutes of Health.

PUBLISHING INDUSTRY. Book publishing in the United States is among the most stable industries, but since the 1970s it has undergone enormous changes from top to bottom. Mergers and acquisitions among the largest houses have, according to some critics, increased profits for "blockbuster" best-sellers but decreased the volume of worthy and important, if less popular, works of fiction and nonfiction. In the 1990s about 50,000 new titles were published in the United States each year, but only half the public bought books. Most sales were in nonfiction (83 percent, with biography and autobiography dominating). Only 17 percent of books purchased were fiction, poetry, and drama, with mysteries topping the fiction category. While large publishing houses dominate sales, approximately 3,000 publishers bring out more than three books a year. Most are specialty firms that place emphasis on editor-author relations. They rely on a large profit margin per title and print runs are in the thousands.

Despite corporate takeovers in the 1980s, including the acquisition of William Morrow by Hearst; the takeover of Crown, Knopf, Pantheon, and Ballantine by Random House; the purchase of Charles Scribner's Sons by Macmillan and subsequent purchase of Macmillan by Paramount, many traditions of the historically family-owned houses persisted. The proliferation of mergers may have been offset by startup firms. These new houses have continued to publish books of merit despite financial risk. Because large publishers concentrate on promoting potential best-sellers, many midlist titles—those that sell reasonably well in the long term—are available to smaller publishers.

The typical bookstore today looks radically different from what it did in the 1970s. It is likely part of a large chain, such as Walden Books, B. Dalton Booksellers, Crown, or Barnes and Noble. At the beginning of the 1990s, the Walden Books chain boasted 1,000 outlets and B. Dalton claimed 800. Superstores carrying tens of thousands of titles were rapidly proliferating. Inside the stores, paperback titles dominated. From 1980 to 1985, paperbacks jumped from 30 percent of all books in print to 40 percent, and sales jumped ahead of hardbacks. Consolidation in retail has not meant savings for the consumer—the average title in 1995 cost twice as much as it did in the late 1970s. Bookstores prominently display items like coffee mugs and t-shirts with "literary" figures on them, board games like Trivial Pursuit, designer bookmarks, clip-on reading lights, audiocassettes, and videocassettes.

The hardcover book has far from disappeared. In most bookstores hardcover titles from such perennial best-selling authors as James Michener, Robert Ludlum, and Stephen King are prominently displayed and usually deeply discounted. They sell millions of copies and can make huge profits for the publisher through the sale of rights to republish the book in serial form in magazines and in editions for trade paperbacks, mass-market paperbacks, large type, and book clubs. Income for big sellers also includes movie rights and adaptations to formats such as CD-ROM and audiocassette.

The book publishing industry has been influenced by radical changes in other media, including television, radio, and films. It faced competition in the 1990s for attention and money from media that did not exist or were in their infancy in the 1970s: video games, computer bulletin boards and information services, cable television, and videocassettes. One justification, and possible benefit, of the merger mania of the 1980s is that publishers were able to use the resources of parent companies that owned other media outlets. Once Time merged with Warner to become Time Warner in 1989, the magazine publishing, film, and broadcast divisions could provide marketing and management for Time-Life Books; Little, Brown and Company; and the Book-of-the-Month Club. As a result of mergers and the proliferation of media, authors and publishers began creating or adapting their work in different formats. Art Spiegelman's critically acclaimed *Maus* (1986), an account of the Holocaust told in comic book format, was released in CD-ROM with supplementary sketches, interviews, and other materials. Reference works like the *American Heritage Dictionary, Grolier's Encyclopedia,* and the *Hammond World Atlas* adapted their offerings to CD-ROM, sometimes combining print and CD-ROM versions in one package. An entirely new medium, CD-ROM books, emerged, enabling authors to combine photos, text, sound, and graphics in a multimedia format for readers interested in interactive experience. Although the staying power of such technologies is questionable, the Book-of-the-Month Club's decision to start carrying CD-ROMs shows the format's strength. (The club's first offering in May 1994 was "Poetry in Motion," which features eighteen poets reading and discussing their works.)

The combination of new formats and increasing influence of corporations dependent on earnings forecasts led the industry to promote books as never before. Publishing houses in the past resisted market research and other preliminaries to publicity, but with books increasingly seen as properties and commodities, houses put greater effort into publicizing their output. They sought displays in bookstores and eagerly arranged for authors to appear on television and radio talk shows before, during, and after a book's release. More attention went to cover art, which can determine the browser's decision to purchase.

Best-sellers, fueled by the increasing influence of superstores carrying tens of thousands of titles, retail chains, and discount chains, and the continuing influence of book clubs, helped the industry survive difficult times in the 1980s and early 1990s. In 1994 a record seventeen books sold more than one million copies, compared to nine in 1993. During the same year a record 183 books sold more than 100,000, compared to 157 in 1993. (In 1983 the top ten best-sellers sold only 4.3 million copies combined.) Most of the blockbusters were by longtime favorite authors, such as John Grisham, Tom Clancy, Danielle Steel, and Ken Follett, indicating the increasing importance of authors as "brand names."

Book clubs, notably the Time Warner-owned Book-of-the-Month Club (which includes both the above-named club and eight others, such as the History Book Club and the Quality Paperback Book Club), changed their operations during the 1980s. The Book-of-the-Month Club used to stress low prices, and the club and its eight "siblings" boasted 3.5 million members in 1993. In the 1990s, however, it could no longer compete with deep discounts by the chains. The club responded by stressing gift wrapping, book

searching, and an "800" number for easier ordering. Special-interest inserts in catalogs used market research to appeal to each customer's particular preferences, such as books about music.

Publishers continued to face problems, both economic and cultural, in the mid 1990s. The economic problems centered around competition for readers' attention from traditional and new media. Censorship remained a cultural issue, especially in schools, where more than 200 incidents of book banning in some form or another were reported in 1991. Among titles removed from school bookshelves were classics like *The Adventures of Huckleberry Finn.*

[Kenneth C. Davis, *Two-Bit Culture: The Paperbacking of America* (Boston, 1984); N. R. Kleinfield, "The Supermarketer of Books," *New York Times Magazine* (Nov. 9, 1986); Walter W. Powell, "The Good Books Business: The Perils of Publishing, Part 2," *New Republic* (Sept. 15, 1986); John Tebbel, *Between Covers: The Rise and Transformation of Book Publishing in America* (New York, 1987).]

JEFFREY M. MERRON

See also **DAH:** Book Publishing; **SUPP:** CD-ROM Technology; Communications Industry; Freedom of the Press; Magazines; Newspapers.

PUERTO RICAN AMERICANS. Although Puerto Ricans began migrating to the United States soon after the turn of the twentieth century (2,000 from 1900 to 1909), it was not until the 1940s that they did so in large numbers (151,000 from 1940 to 1949). Puerto Ricans settled in major cities, including New York, Chicago, Boston, and Philadelphia, as well as such smaller cities as Albany and Buffalo, N.Y.; Cleveland; Hartford, Conn.; and Worcester, Mass. There was a decrease in the number of migrants in the 1960s (145,000), but that trend reversed in the 1970s, although some 160,000 mainland residents returned to Puerto Rico during that decade. In 1994 Puerto Ricans and those of Puerto-Rican descent in the United States numbered close to 3 million.

Studies of the Puerto Rican population in the United States have commonly treated it either as a divided nation or as an ethnic minority. The first conceptualization considers the migratory experience within the context of international capitalism. Expanding urban industry absorbed surplus labor from the "colony" during and after World War II. Shrinking economic opportunities on the mainland beginning in the 1960s halted the flow and eventually resulted in return migration, a phenomenon peculiar to Puerto Ricans because of their status as U.S. citizens since 1917. In the 1970s and 1980s, however, a "brain drain" occurred in Puerto Rico because of limited employment opportunities in certain fields for overqualified individuals, causing many in search of more competitive salaries and higher standards of living to move to U.S. cities. The second scholarly construction treats migrants as an ethnic minority being integrated into mainstream American culture. It emphasizes the conditions Puerto Ricans encountered when they arrived and explains their adaptation in terms of the available resources and social-service programs. This interpretation attributes return migration either to the failure of Puerto Ricans to adapt to the host country and their desire to seek refuge among family and friends on the island or to the inability of U.S. agencies to provide the necessary wherewithal for integration.

Government officials on both the mainland and the island have considered migrants and return migrants as a problem. In U.S. cities the first wave of Puerto Ricans became the target of much discrimination because of skin color, level of education, and cultural differences. The second and third generation reacted by developing "cultural" traits that would ensure survival. Gang violence, later connected to drug use, was one of the coping strategies stereotyped by sensational and insensitive media. Equally recognizable has been ghettoization, social marginalization, unstable household income, and high levels of unemployment and high school dropout rates. On the island a large number of Puerto Ricans rejected the first wave of return migrants. Most natives' understanding of and sympathy for the mainland experience was limited. To them, *nuyoricans* seemed aggressive, lacking in culture, and, probably most important, unable or unwilling to speak Spanish. The sources of conflict did not disappear and the situation became more manageable in the late 1980s only because it was more familiar.

On their part, migrants and their descendants have created a distinctive culture by appropriating elements from the societies of origin and destination. In every large U.S. city Latin markets provide ingredients for a diet in which indigenous and African food conforms to more American tastes. Church and community organizations promote traditional religious and social rituals, such as christenings or young women's fifteenth-birthday celebrations, and coordinate the commemoration of important U.S. events, such as the birthday of Martin Luther King, Jr., or Independence Day. Salsa, the Afro-Latin rhythm born in Spanish Harlem, became a popular staple of the U.S. commercial music world. Moving comfortably among constituencies and the larger American public, Puerto-Rican educators, politicians, and civil servants reinforced and even institutionalized these rich cross-cultural contributions.

[José Hernández Alvarez, *Return Migration to Puerto Rico* (Berkeley, Calif., 1967); Center for Puerto Rican Studies, *Labor Migration Under Capitalism: The Puerto Rican Experience* (New York, 1979); Luis Nieves Falcón, *El Emigrante Puertorriqueño* (Rio Piedras, P.R., 1975).]

TERESITA MARTÍNEZ-VERGNE

See also **SUPP:** Education, Bilingual; Hispanic Americans; Puerto Rico.

PUERTO RICO. The world rise in oil prices in 1973–1974 shattered Puerto Rico's industrial model, known since the 1940s as Operation Bootstrap. Based on external capital investment, it had raised per capita income but had not significantly lowered unemployment. The oil crisis brought a sharp decline in Puerto Rico's industrial production, increased unemployment, and brought a marked increase in migration to the mainland United States. To reduce unemployment, the Commonwealth of Puerto Rico generated public-sector jobs at enormous expense, resulting in a disproportionately high growth of government compared to other sectors of society. To stimulate the stagnant economy of the island, Puerto Rico, with support from U.S. corporations, petitioned Congress for revisions in the tax code to encourage corporations to reinvest their earnings. The subsequent changes in 1976 resulted in a noticeable influx of capital to banks already established in Puerto Rico and an expansion of pharmaceutical and electronics companies. Apparel and other labor-intensive industries benefited much less, and the much-needed increase in employment thus fell short of what was predicted.

Meanwhile, Puerto Rican politics changed markedly. After the pro-statehood New Progressive Party (PNP) defeated the pro-Commonwealth Popular Democratic Party (PPD) for the first time in 1968, a two-party system became firmly entrenched. Between 1972 and 1992 each party won three elections. The Puerto Rican Independence Party (PIP) maintained its 5 percent share of the voters throughout this period. Political discussions revolved around whether islanders should reform the Commonwealth, become a state of the Union, or aspire to independent status. A December 1991 referendum asked Puerto Ricans whether future votes on the status of the island must offer the choices of statehood, commonwealth, and independence. (A choice would have to carry more than 50 percent of the vote to win.) Had the voters approved, any direct "yes" or "no" vote on statehood would have been prohibited. To most people's surprise, the proposal was defeated. In November 1993 the voters chose to retain the island's commonwealth status by a slim 2 percent margin over statehood. The option of independence received 4.4 percent of the vote. Some analysts concluded that these two referenda indicated that the average voter was much less interested in changing the island's relationship with the United States than were the leaders of the PNP and PIP.

In November 1994 Puerto Ricans turned down two propositions. One proposed increasing the number of judges on the Commonwealth Supreme Court; the other limited the right to bail. The statehood party supported both amendments. Against all predictions both proposals were defeated. One of the most publicized political events in Puerto Rico during the last quarter of the twentieth century concerned the death in 1978 of two young pro-independence Puerto Ricans at what is known as the Cerro Maravilla. Accused of sabotaging communication towers, they were killed by policemen in what seemed an execution. Legal action was taken against those involved.

Puerto Rico's population increased from 2,722,000 in 1970 to an estimated 3,621,000 in 1993. Because of the mainland's sagging economy in the 1970s, more Puerto Ricans returned home than left the island. In the 1980s the normal pattern of a net outmigration to the mainland resumed. The migrants of that decade were wealthier and better educated than those of previous years. Estimates in 1990 stated that 2.7 million Puerto Ricans lived on the mainland. In 1980, 43 percent of the mainlanders resided in New York. By 1990 that figure was down to 39.8 percent, as migrants moved to such states as Florida, Massachusetts, Connecticut, and Pennsylvania. If the trend of overall population growth among mainland Puerto Ricans continues, by the year 2010 there will be more Puerto Ricans living on the mainland than in Puerto Rico. One possible reason for migration is the several natural disasters that struck Puerto Rico beginning in the late 1970s. In 1979 Hurricane David and Tropical Storm Federico left 4 people dead and millions of dollars in damages. In 1985 torrential rains from Tropical Storm Isabel caused floods and left 500 dead. In 1989 Hurricane Hugo left at least 50,000 people homeless and caused 7 deaths; damages were in the hundreds of millions of dollars. In

1994 a prolonged drought forced authorities to ration water for almost three months in the northeast. Rationing in areas of low rainfall continued into 1995.

[Arturo Morales Carrión, *Puerto Rico: A Political and Cultural History* (New York, 1983); James L. Dietz, *Economic History of Puerto Rico* (Princeton, N.J., 1986); Edwin Meléndez and Edgardo Meléndez, eds., *Colonial Dilemma: Critical Perspectives on Contemporary Puerto Rico* (Boston, 1993).]

MAYRA ROSARIO

See also **SUPP:** Hurricanes; Puerto Rican Americans.

PULITZER PRIZES, endowed by newspaper publisher Joseph Pulitzer following his death in 1911, are awarded each May by the president of Columbia University on the recommendation of the Pulitzer Prize Board for meritorious work done during the preceding year in journalism, letters, and music. The prizes, each $3,000 (except for the meritorious public service award, which is a gold medal) have varied over the years but in 1995 numbered fourteen in journalism, six in letters, one in music, and four fellowships of $5,000. Three fellowships are awarded to Columbia University graduates for travel and study abroad, and one is for specialization in drama, music, literary, film, or television criticism. The journalism prizes began in 1917 with awards for reporting and editorial writing. Since then the prizes have included awards for meritorious public service by a newspaper (1918), editorial cartooning (1922), correspondence for Washington or foreign news coverage (1929), spot news photography (1942), national reporting (1942), international reporting (1942), feature photography (1968), criticism and commentary (1970), feature writing (1979), explanatory journalism (1985), and specialized reporting (1985). Sometimes a citation award (1938) is given for work in more than one year and includes journalists as well as novelists, composers, photographers, and even press cartographers (1945).

Since 1917 Pulitzer Prizes have been given for works of letters in history of the United States. Twice the award for history has included diaries—C. Vann Woodward's *Mary Chestnut's Civil War* (1982) and Laurel Thatcher Ulrich's *A Midwife's Tale: The Life of Martha Ballard, Based on Her Diary, 1785–1812* (1991). Other letters awards since 1917 have gone to an American author for a distinguished biography or autobiography. One recipient was John F. Kennedy for *Profiles in Courage* (1957). Since 1918 a prize has been given annually for the best work of fiction by an American author and dealing with American life. Recipients have ranged from Edith Wharton (*The Age of Innocence,* 1921) to Toni Morrison (*Beloved,* 1988) and Alice Walker (*The Color Purple,* 1983). An exception occurred in 1977, when the overseeing board could not agree with the fiction jury about awarding the prize to Norman Maclean for *A River Runs Through It,* and no award was given that year. The poetry prize, established in 1922, has been awarded to Robert Frost (1924, 1931, 1937, 1943), Carl Sandburg (1951), Robert Penn Warren (1958, 1979), Sylvia Plath (1982), and Rita Dove (1987). In 1962 the category of general nonfiction was added and that award has gone to authors such as Studs Terkel (*The Good War,* 1985) and Neil Sheehan (*A Bright and Shining Lie: John Paul Vann and America in Vietnam,* 1989). Prizes have been given since 1918 for drama, preferably an original play and one dealing with American life. Receiving the award twice or more were Eugene O'Neill (1920, 1928, 1957), Robert Sherwood (1936, 1941), Tennessee Williams (1948, 1955), Edward Albee (1967, 1975), and August Wilson (1987, 1990). An award in music has been given since 1943 to an American composer, including a special posthumous award to ragtime composer Scott Joplin in 1976.

[J. Douglas Bates, *The Pulitzer Prize: The Inside Story of America's Most Prestigious Award* (New York, 1991).]
BETTY HOUCHIN WINFIELD

PURE FOOD AND DRUG MOVEMENT. The 1980s was a decade of retrenchment for the pure food and drug movement, the effort of individuals and organizations to ensure the healthfulness of food and drugs. It was a decade of frustration for activists, partly because of conservative leadership in national politics. Nonetheless, significant public action took place. Democratic Representative John Dingell of Michigan, chairman of the Committee on Energy and Commerce, led an effort in Congress to bolster regulation of food and drugs. He exposed inadequate safeguards against the spread of the AIDS virus through the nation's blood supply and the virtual corruption by drug manufacturers of the Food and Drug Administration's generic drug approval process. Despite Dingell's public committee hearings, tainted blood infected between 12,000 and 20,000 people with the AIDS virus during the decade.

The election to the presidency of Governor Bill Clinton of Arkansas in 1992 released the pent-up energies of pure food and drug activists. There followed such an outpouring of reform proposals that the Clinton administration publicly urged activists to let up. One area of concern in the 1990s was the nation's program of meat inspection, which is under the jurisdiction of the U.S. Department of Agriculture. In 1993–1994 an outbreak of illness, affecting 1,672 people, with 19 deaths, occurred because of inadequately inspected meat. This seemed merely the tip of an iceberg, and in 1993 some statisticians predicted that 8 million people would be stricken with food-borne illnesses each year and 9,000 would die annually.

Among the movements in the area of food and drugs is the Pure Food Campaign (PFC). Founded in 1992 under the leadership of Jeremy Rifkin, it fights against the use of bovine somatotropin, or bST, a genetically engineered hormone to increase milk production in dairy cows. The Food and Drug Administration approved the hormone late in 1993, and within months many dairy herds were given it, with marked increases in milk yields. The PFC also opposes genetically engineered vegetables, which Rifkin dubbed "Frankenfoods." The PFC also opposed food irradiation, a proposed method for killing bacteria in meat and poultry.

[Herbert Burkholz, *The FDA Follies* (New York, 1994); Elizabeth Amy Poyck, Marshall Alexander Smith, and Alison Toledo, "Federal Food and Drug Act Violations," *American Criminal Law Review* 26 (Spring 1993).]
ROBERT KRAIG

See also **SUPP:** Acquired Immune Deficiency Syndrome; Agriculture, Department of; Consumer Protection and Rights; Food and Drug Administration; Genetic Engineering; Product Tampering.

PYRAMID SCHEMES are frauds that pay a hierarchy at the top of the triangle out of investments made by those at the bottom. Often confused with legitimate multilevel marketing, pyramids are felonies in most states. In most scenarios, a pyramid is set up by a few people offering a seemingly attractive product or service. They recruit people to sell that product but require an investment for participation. Those investors are then encouraged to recruit still more participants. In legitimate multilevel marketing, profit comes from sales to actual customers. With pyramids, most of the money comes from cash investments of recruited participants and product sales to those recruits, often required. Eventually, the pool of recruits dries up, leaving latecomers unable to recoup their investments. Since the mid-1970s, regulators have unearthed large pyramid schemes, although investigators admit that most go undetected. Many that slip through the cracks involve small numbers of investors bilked by con artists who move from state to state. One popular small operation involves a plane scenario. A "pilot" sits atop the pyramid, the next level has two "copilots," the third level four "flight attendants," and the fourth and bottom level eight "passengers." Each passenger pays an entry fee, usually a few thousand dollars. The money is given to the pilot, who "jettisons" with huge profits. The plane then breaks into two new pyramids, with each copilot now sitting as the pilot. The new flight attendants then recruit fresh passengers, usually friends and relatives, and the scheme continues until it collapses under its own weight.

[Joseph Bulgatz, *Ponzi Schemes, Invaders from Mars, and Other Extraordinary Popular Delusions and the Madness of Crowds* (New York, 1992).]

KATHLEEN B. CULVER

QUALITY CIRCLES, a term used in the field of human resources management that refers to the technique of motivating workers by allowing them input into decisions concerning the production process, thereby increasing productivity and profits. Originat-ing in Japan in 1962, quality circles were introduced in the United States in the early 1970s. By the mid-1990s thousands of manufacturing plants, banks, hospitals, and government agencies had implemented quality circles. A circle typically consists of three to twelve employees from a given department and a representative of management. The circle meets on a regular basis on company time to examine a limited range of issues related to the department, identify and analyze problems, and propose solutions. The focus of the circles is on improving both the quality of the product and the production process. The underlying premise is that productivity will increase because the person best able to decide the most efficient way to do a job is the person who does it for a living. Another premise is that if employees have greater control over the product, they will be more committed and effective workers.

[David Hutchins, *Quality Circles Handbook* (New York, 1985).]

JACK HANDLER

QUOTAS. *See* **Affirmative Action; Civil Rights Movement.**

R

RADIO. When radio first appeared in the United States in the early 1920s, it created an entirely new medium of entertainment—a "theater of the mind." By the 1930s listening to the radio became the most common home activity of families. All network programming was planned around the family. Women were offered daily dramatic serials during mornings and afternoons, nearly all sponsored by manufacturers of soap or detergent products ("soap operas"). Children were served adventure shows in the late afternoons. News and commentary programs followed. From 7:00 P.M. on, dramas and variety shows were broadcast for the entire family. Programming by and large was controlled by four national networks: the Radio Corporation of America's (RCA) National Broadcasting Company, with two networks (NBC-Red and NBC-Blue); the Columbia Broadcasting System (CBS); and the Mutual Broadcasting System (MBS). Because RCA owned two networks, the Federal Communications Commission ordered it to divest one, which it did in 1943, with NBC-Blue becoming the American Broadcasting Company.

Radio produced its own celebrities, few of whom could duplicate their successes in motion pictures. Jack Benny, Fred Allen, George Burns and Gracie Allen, Major Bowes, and Fanny Brice became extensions of virtually every U.S. family during radio's "golden age." For a time the most popular program featured a ventriloquist, Edgar Bergen, whose inability to keep his lips from moving doomed his attempts in later years to translate his show to television. It was the overwhelming popularity of Bergen and his dummy, Charlie McCarthy, a show that attracted one-third of all radio listeners, that may have prevented a national panic on Halloween of 1938. That night actor Orson Welles, whose "Mercury Theater on the Air" attracted a mere 3.6 percent of the national radio audience, broadcast a dramatization of the science-fiction book *War of the Worlds* by British author H. G. Wells that caused a near panic among the audience. A newspaper headline next day related that "Radio War Terrorizes U.S."; another read, "Panic Grips Nation as Radio Announces 'Mars Attacks World.'" The program demonstrated the power of radio's possible manipulation of the public's imagination.

Radio has had a marked effect on politics and reporting. President Franklin D. Roosevelt, whose voice rivaled those of the actors of the day, mobilized support for his New Deal in the 1930s by taking his message directly to the electorate via radio in "fireside chats." In the 1940s he used them to arouse the nation's patriotic ardor. When war came, first to Europe, then to the United States, radio was brought into the living rooms of Americans with on-the-scene reports from such correspondents as Edward R. Murrow, Walter Cronkite, William L. Shirer, Howard K. Smith, and Eric Sevareid.

With the advent of television—and concurrent development of the transistor—following World War II, radio was transformed into a portable jukebox, with networks becoming little more than headline news services. Independent stations appealing to niche audiences developed—stations with music appealing to older listeners, stations aimed at teenagers, and stations directed at ethnic minorities. With the emergence of new stations on the FM band by the 1970s, the niches were themselves partitioned. Stations were classified as "contemporary," "adult," "album-oriented," "urban," or described by a dozen other tags. FM broadcasting, with its superior fidelity, overtook established AM stations, in numbers and popularity. Between 1975 and 1995 FM stations in the United States nearly doubled to 5,000, and AM stations declined from 4,700 to 4,200.

With broadcasting companies downgrading their radio networks to insignificance, independent syndicators in the 1970s began providing special programming. A program hosted by Los Angeles disc jockey Casey Kasem, featuring a "countdown" of the top forty songs of the week, became the first program to attract a sizable national audience since radio's heyday in the 1930s and 1940s. In the mid-1970s a program syndicator, Westwood One, achieved a dominant position, eventually purchasing Mutual and NBC radio and signing Kasem to a long-term, multi-million-dollar contract. Its success was attributed to cost efficiencies achieved by distributing programs via satellite rather than by land lines. In 1980 Sony introduced the Walkman, a transistorized radio-cassette player that provided concert-hall sound in a package weighing only a few ounces. Demand became so great that a year after its introduction, there was still a month-long wait at many retailers. Ironically, competition with Walkman-type devices in the 1980s came from hefty portable players, or "boom boxes," that could blast the sound of popular radio stations through entire neighborhoods.

Because of the inferior tone quality of AM, many radio stations on that band turned to all-news and all-talk formats, where high fidelity was of little importance. News stations rehashed summaries of the day's events every twenty minutes—presumed to be the average length of an automobile commute. Indeed, all radio programmers recognized that most of their audiences listened in cars, so frequent traffic reports also became obligatory.

Initially, talk shows appealed to middle-aged audiences that appeared to delight in airing their personal problems through call-ins to station hosts, but in the early 1990s two utterly dissimilar national talk-show personalities, Howard Stern and Rush Limbaugh, rose to national prominence, overhauling the medium in the process. Stern's scatological satires made him the most listened-to personality on the air—even as federal regulators fined stations he appeared on for broadcasting obscene material. Limbaugh's humorous conservative broadcasts similarly caught on and produced a host of imitators. He and his cohorts were widely credited with helping the Republican party win a majority in both houses of Congress in 1994.

[Erik Barnouw, *A History of Broadcasting in the United States,* 3 vols. (New York, 1966–1970).]

LEW IRWIN

See also **SUPP:** Music Industry; National Public Radio; Talk Shows; Television; Voice of America.

RADON. *See* **Air Pollution.**

RAINBOW COALITION, a group developed within the Democratic Party during the 1984 presidential election. Led by African-American civil rights activist Jesse Jackson, it attracted blacks, Latinos, Asian Americans, American Indians, and poor whites. As the coalition's spokesperson (and candidate for president in the Democratic primaries), Jackson criticized the administration of President Ronald Reagan and called for cuts in defense spending, strengthening of affirmative action, and federal assistance for urban workers and farmers. Although he received 3.3 million votes in 1984 and 6.8 million in a second presidential bid in 1988, the coalition's alliance fragmented, its influence greatly diminishing by 1992. That year Jackson did not enter the presidential race. Perhaps in recognition that electoral campaigns could not fulfill its larger purpose, the coalition in 1993 turned to an outreach program for inner-city youth.

[Sheila Collins, *The Rainbow Challenge: The Jackson Campaign and the Future of U.S. Politics* (New York, 1986).]

JILL WATTS

RALEIGH. Founded in 1792 as North Carolina's first permanent capital, Raleigh evolved in the nineteenth century as a center of government, higher education, printing, and railroad transportation. In addition to the capitol, the state established a prison; an institution for the deaf, dumb, and blind; and a hospital for the insane. Raleigh's phenomenal growth, making it the state's second largest city after Charlotte, began in the 1960s, after the creation of the nearby Research Triangle Park. This 6,800-acre park attracted about eighty research institutions 35,000 employees and promoted the growth of scores of businesses outside the park. Expanding state government services, retailing, air transportation, and manufacture of electronics and textiles sustained the growth. The airport became a regional hub in 1987 and a gateway to Europe in 1988. A twenty-block state office complex employed more than 10,000 workers. North Carolina State University's student enrollment grew from

17,000 in 1975 to 27,500 in 1995. The city's population mushroomed from 47,000 in 1940 to 208,000 in 1990.

Since the early 1970s Raleigh has experienced rapid change. A political revolution in 1975 gave control of city government to a pro-growth faction that annexed large areas and expanded the city's infrastructure. Notable were completion of a beltline and a new reservoir. A major project was the revitalization of the downtown, which had been adversely affected by the opening of outlying malls and shopping centers. By 1994 successful revitalization encompassed a pedestrian mall, a civic center, a city market, high-rise offices and hotels, improved housing, and a state museum of history. The 1993 city elections resulted in the election of a Republican mayor—the first in a century. African Americans, about one-fourth of the population, have become better integrated. City and county schools merged in 1976 to provide more effective desegregation, and the city pledged itself to the hiring of more black police and firemen. Raleigh elected a black mayor in 1973 and a black sheriff in 1978. Plans for the future include an outer beltline to ease traffic congestion, better crime control, and sustained economic growth, partly through development of an additional 755-acre campus at North Carolina State University that will permit research support of private industry.

[Moses N. Amis, *Historical Raleigh from Its Foundation in 1792* (Raleigh, 1902); David Perkins, ed., *The News & Observer's Raleigh: A Living History of North Carolina's Capital* (Winston-Salem, N.C., 1994); Steve Stolpen, *Raleigh: A Pictorial History* (Norfolk, Va., 1977).]

JOHN L. BELL

See also **SUPP:** North Carolina.

RAPE as a political and social issue was transformed by the women's movement of the 1960s and 1970s. Rape is now increasingly interpreted as a crime of violence and control against women rather than a pathological sexual act that they invite. Activists have created rape crisis centers to help victim-survivors and their close friends and family. Following a comprehensive overhaul of rape law in Michigan in 1974, states revised their statutes and legal practices. Although reform has been uneven, state legislatures and court rulings have modified the definition and proof needed to establish rape. Shield laws now prevent all or much of a victim's previous sexual history from being introduced in court. Requirements for witnesses, use of physical force by the rapist, evidence

of resistance, and prompt complaint have been dropped in most states. Rape under the law now includes nonconsensual sex with spouses. It also includes such sex with acquaintances, since the vast majority of victims are raped by men they know, not by strangers. Some jurisdictions provide advocates to help women when reporting rape, gathering medical evidence, and meeting prosecutors. Although some research suggests that convictions are now easier to obtain, others find that juror and judicial attitudes block convictions. Rape remains statistically contentious. Estimates for lifetime chance of rape for women range from 5 to 25 percent. In the 1990s date rape on campuses and elsewhere appeared to be endemic, but some argued that its extent has been overblown. Celebrated cases involving William Kennedy Smith, Mike Tyson, John Wayne Bobbitt, and the gang rape of a jogger in New York City's Central Park raised public awareness and controversy.

[Julie A. Alison and Lawrence S. Wrightsman, *Rape: The Misunderstood Crime* (Newbury Park, Calif., 1993); Carole Goldberg-Ambrose, "Unfinished Business in Rape Law Reform," *Journal of Social Issues* 48 (1992): 173–185.]

AMY FRIED

See also **SUPP:** Domestic Violence; Rape Crisis Centers; Women's Movement.

RAPE CRISIS CENTERS started in 1972, when the first such service opened in Washington, D.C.; twenty years later there were more than 550 centers. Their origin lay in the commitment of the women's movement's to "personal politics," which redefined problems experienced by individual women as public issues. Rape crisis centers, like women's health clinics and battered women's shelters, were designed for empowering and serving women. Centers counsel victim-survivors, provide information about medical and legal procedures, and act as advocates in hospitals and police stations and with prosecutors. At the outset centers were staffed by community volunteers with erratic funding. In the 1990s many were run by universities or local governments and employed professional counselors.

AMY FRIED

See also **SUPP:** Rape; Women's Rights.

RAPID TRANSIT. In the prosperous decade of the 1950s, the United States traveled a different road than most other nations in developing a transportation system, building an interstate highway system satisfying the needs of individual automobile owners across the country. Although other countries also invested in highways, they put considerable resources into public transportation systems such as subways and aboveground trains. For Japan and several European countries, these investments ultimately paid off in what are known as "bullet trains," trains capable of reaching speeds greater than 150 miles per hour, whisking people quickly between cities. Environmental and energy concerns, combined with the problem of traffic congestion in many cities, piqued interest among transportation and public planning officials in deploying the high-speed trains in the United States, but the U.S. transportation system generally relied upon automobiles.

Most public planning experts consider mass transit—everything from buses and subways to aboveground trains, trolley cars, and light rail systems—as the best way to transport people at the least expense, including such nonfinancial "expenses" as pollution and depletion of energy sources. Mass transit prevailed in many U.S. cities before World War II. After 1945 Americans began moving in droves to suburbs. This, combined with the postwar prosperity that raised incomes for working Americans, led to the boom in individual automobile ownership and a decline in urban mass transit systems and passenger train service. Environmental and energy concerns did not stop the postwar automobile boom because gasoline was inexpensive. Passenger train travel dwindled until no private companies were involved in the business; instead, the federal government subsidized Amtrak, which provided passenger trains. Federal, state, and local governments also subsidized bus services, subways, and elevated trains for transporting people in city and suburban areas. Such services, however, generally were associated with poor people, and most working Americans outside of major cities preferred their cars for travel. More cars meant more miles; the number of automobile miles driven increased from 901 billion in 1970 to 1,525 billion miles in 1990, and further increase at the same rate appeared likely.

Public planners looked to high-speed bullet trains as a good alternative to the highway system and to airplanes for long-distance travel, and environmentalists supported them because they lowered energy and pollution costs. Amtrak and several states—including Texas and Florida—announced bullet-train initiatives. Proponents of high-speed trains gained an interesting and powerful ally in defense industry contrac-

tors, who hoped to switch their production facilities to building high-speed trains as a way of replacing defense spending cutbacks following the end of the cold war. Even with the defense industry's support, however, development of high-speed trains in the United States seemed doubtful in the 1990s. Texas dropped its plans after the airline industry expressed opposition to the idea. The cost makes many of the projects prohibitive. Supertrains and light rail systems such as those in Portland, Oregon, and Los Angeles require new tracks, which could cost up to $100 million per mile in cities. Also, the federal government's budget deficit and conservative attacks on spending threatened subsidies for public transportation.

[Brian J. Cudahy, *Cash, Tokens, and Transfers: A History of Urban Mass Transit in North America* (New York, 1990); George W. Jernstedt, *Give the City Back to People: New Mobility Can Make Our Cities a Joy Again* (Bolivar, Pa., 1994).]

THOMAS G. GRESS

See also **SUPP:** Transportation, Department of; Transportation Industry; Urban Living.

REAGANOMICS is the broad term used to describe President Ronald Reagan's economic policy during the 1980s. It was outlined in a document presented to Congress shortly after the 1980 election, entitled *America's New Beginning: A Program for Economic Recovery.* The program called for budget reforms to cut the rate of growth in federal spending; a series of steps to cut personal income taxes and business taxes; a far-reaching program of regulatory relief; and a commitment to a monetary policy for restoring a stable currency and healthy financial markets. Based largely on the principles of supply-side economics, the program was designed to lift the nation's economy out of its deepest recession since the Great Depression by reducing the federal government's economic role. By shifting federal revenues to a less restricted private sector through tax reduction, President Reagan expected to reinvigorate the economy. At the same time he hoped to reduce, or even eliminate, the federal deficit, a task made more difficult by another political goal—increasing defense spending.

With assistance from the Republican minority and a cadre of conservative Democrats, many of Reagan's congressional initiatives were passed. Although the nation remained mired in recession for the first two years of his administration, a robust recovery soon turned into the longest peacetime economic expansion in U.S. history, ending only in 1990. More than

18 million jobs were created during the economic expansion from 1983 to 1990, unemployment fell, and inflation dropped from 12.5 percent in 1980 to 4.4 percent in 1988, but the growth came at a price. Unable to cut federal spending, Reagan oversaw a tripling of the federal debt to $2.7 trillion and a quadrupling of the annual trade deficit to $137 billion. The legacy of Reaganomics is a matter of intense debate. In 1980 George Bush, an unsuccessful presidential candidate in the Republican primaries, dubbed Reagan's policies "voodoo economics." Bush and others were skeptical about whether Reagan could cut taxes, increase defense spending, and balance the budget. Critics charge that government spending cuts came at the expense of the poor and that tax cuts almost exclusively benefited the wealthy, increasing the gap between rich and poor. Reagan's economic policies, they add, unleashed a "decade of greed" and rampant speculation that led to the 1987 stock market crash and the 1990 recession. Further, they say, the federal deficit will serve as a drag on the nation's economy for generations. Reagan's supporters say that virtually all sectors of the economy benefited from his economic policies, that he reduced the rate of federal spending growth, and that the federal debt as a percentage of the nation's gross national product decreased. They add that the Democratic majority in Congress thwarted Reagan's efforts to make deeper cuts in federal spending and eventually undermined his tax policies with tax reforms in 1986 and 1990.

[Lou Cannon, *President Reagan: The Role of a Lifetime* (1991); "The Real Reagan Record," *National Review* (Aug. 31, 1992).]

ERIK BRUUN

See also **SUPP:** Balance of Trade; Black Monday Stock Market Crash; Financial Exchanges; Stagflation; Supply-Side Economics; Unemployment; Wall Street.

REAL ESTATE INDUSTRY. Real estate includes land, buildings, water, and other property physically or legally connected to them. While property values and the pace of construction have always fluctuated, they became especially volatile between the 1960s and 1990s, a fact that affected many aspects of national life. The estimated nationwide median price of a new house increased from $23,400 in 1970 to $122,900 in 1990. The value of land and other properties also rose. Development and construction increased markedly. Despite slowdowns and regional differences, values and activity continued upward until a dramatic decline in the late 1980s. A combination of social and economic conditions created this situation, among them a surge in the demand for housing among the large generation born after World War II. Real estate markets also reflected population movements from depressed rural and industrial communities to fast-growing metropolitan areas and rural resorts. Increasing retail, recreational, and other commercial activity prompted development of shopping centers, resorts, and office complexes. In addition, financing became more available to home buyers and commercial real estate ventures through government and the private sector. New federal income tax deductions in 1981 stimulated investment in real estate.

As a result, real estate became increasingly speculative. Instead of purchasing homes as residences and long-term investments, more individuals bought and sold housing essentially because it was a general trend, not a universal motivation for people buying housing, and to capitalize on rapidly rising prices. Real estate developers invested in ambitious development projects, often using elaborate financing. They developed large tracts for new housing and other purposes while renovating older sites and structures and giving them new identities, as with the conversion of old factories and railroad stations into theme shopping complexes. Individuals and businesses profited from these trends. Jobs were created, communities and neighborhoods revitalized, but the loss of open land and local character, plus other environmental, social, and economic issues, sparked controversy. Rising property values made it difficult for longtime, but less affluent, residents to remain in some rapidly changing neighborhoods. An increasing number of young people could no longer afford housing. As the economy entered a recession in the late 1980s real estate activity declined significantly, with wide-ranging consequences. The shift first became noticeable in the South and Southwest around 1985 and in other regions over the next several years. Many individuals and investors had overextended themselves. A surplus of new homes appeared, and costly ventures such as suburban malls became unprofitable. All this occurred when many savings and loan institutions were collapsing. Lenders became more stringent about financing and repayments. The Tax Reform Act of 1986 removed real estate investment incentives. In this environment foreclosures, bankruptcies, high vacancy rates, and other real estate failures became more common. Although the situation began to improve in 1992, the mood had shifted from aggressive optimism to caution and conservatism.

[Steve Lohr, "Banking's Real Estate Miseries," *New York Times* (Jan. 13, 1991); Martin Mayer, *The Builders: Houses, People, Neighborhoods, Governments, Money* (New York, 1978); Lawrence J. White, *The S&L Debacle* (New York, 1991); Suzanne Woolley, "A Firm Footing At Last," *Business Week* (Dec. 27, 1993).]

JOHN TOWNES

See also **SUPP:** Banking and Finance; Housing; Savings and Loan Crisis.

RECREATION. The first emigrants from Europe to settle on the northeastern seaboard of what would become the United States brought with them a distinctive view of the place of work and recreation in life. Traditional recreation, such as dancing (between men and women), gambling, some sports, and smoking tobacco (except at dinner), were banned in New England at one time or another, and a work ethic was embraced in its stead. Puritans, Quakers, and other radical Protestant groups regarded idleness as a source of vice while honest toil characterized members of God's elect. While the Puritans never comprised a majority in the colonies, their values with respect to work and recreation proved widely influential. Even in Puritan New England, however, adults often enjoyed dining, riding, moderate exercise, and even alcoholic beverages.

The nineteenth century saw a mixed attitude toward work and recreation. The work ethic characterized the urban industrial order that emerged in England during the mid-1700s and arrived in the United States in the early 1800s. By that time the industrial revolution was well under way and with it "clock time" to regulate the work schedule. Many religious leaders believed factory work provided discipline, and they often advocated long hours of work while criticizing recreation and play. Nevertheless, many entertainments, including music, minstrel shows, the circus, and theater became popular in the early nineteenth century, while participatory and professional sports flourished during the century's second half. Universities and colleges included athletics in their extracurricular activities and the Young Men's Christian Association (YMCA), founded in London in 1844 and introduced to the United States in 1851, soon developed a program based on athletics and physical recreation. The Young Women's Christian Association (YWCA) was established in Great Britain in 1855, and its first program in the United States opened in Boston in 1866. While one of the goals of the YWCA in the 1990s was to empower women, partly through programs in sport, physical education, and recreation, athletics in the late nineteenth century was still strongly male oriented. Although vigorous physical activity was commonly thought to be unsuited to the female constitution, athletics gradually became part of women's recreation. Women played croquet and lawn tennis after the 1860s, and sex-segregated sports appeared in progressive women's colleges, such as Vassar, by the end of the century.

Concern for the continuing education of adults brought about the lyceum movement, founded in 1826 to bring public lecturers to communities to speak on a range of topics including history, philosophy, science, women's rights, temperance, prison reform, and the abolition of slavery. This movement was concomitant with efforts by labor to reduce the workday from twelve to fourteen hours down to ten. Increased free time was not to be spent in recreation, however, but in intellectual cultivation that would make one a more responsible citizen. The growing exploitation of natural resources led to concern for the nation's natural heritage. In 1864 Congress set aside in California the Yosemite Valley and the Mariposa Grove of Big Trees (later Sequoia National Park) as wilderness areas. Yellowstone (in Wyoming, Idaho, and Montana) became the first national park in 1872. Interestingly, the initial purpose of parks and other wildlife areas was not recreation, but the preservation of wildlife and natural areas as part of the nation's heritage. Central Park in New York City, the first municipal park in the United States, was established in 1856. The need for safe play space for children in cities, especially in poor districts, culminated in the playground movement. The Boston Sand Garden, opened in 1885, was the earliest response to this need. The New York Society for Parks and Playgrounds set up small playgrounds in the city in 1889 and 1891, while the Outdoor Recreation League founded the Seward Park playground in 1893.

The recreation movement visible by the end of the nineteenth century is usually described as a humanitarian reaction to urban circumstances. Reformers first attempted to improve working conditions and unhealthy living conditions and to prevent social disorders by providing modest outlets for recreation. Their efforts constituted a form of social control, as wholesome recreation was presumed to redirect impulses that led to delinquency and crime. Access to public and commercial recreation programs and facilities has increased greatly since World War II. Concern for physical fitness and assistance for individuals with physical, mental, or emotional disabilities expanded markedly during the 1950s and 1960s. Subsequently, the recreation movement suffered setbacks because of economic recessions that led to reduced budgets to support recreation programs. Nevertheless, losses in public recreation were more than compensated for by gains in commercial and consumer-oriented recreation. Consumer spending on recreation rose from about 3 percent of income early in the twentieth century to just under 5 percent by 1929. Although it has shown minor fluctuations over time because of economic conditions, recreation spending in the United States has remained about 7 percent since World War II. Much of this spending is directed at the media, including books, magazines, films, and television, but also toward tourism, such fashionable forms of exercise as jogging, tennis, aerobics, and membership in exclusive sports clubs. These latter forms of recreation commonly represent personal expressions of taste and status.

Drinking and gambling were frequent components of male recreation in colonial America. Although both have been opposed at times by social movements that achieved success, such as Prohibition and efforts to outlaw gambling, alcohol use in the 1990s was a common part of the recreation of both men and women, while legalized gambling was one of the fastest growing industries in the United States. In addition, since the 1960s the recreational use of drugs, including marijuana, cocaine, amphetamines, barbiturates, and various hallucinogens, experienced a phenomenal increase, peaking at 24.3 million users in 1979. Largely a middle-class phenomenon, recreational drug use dropped to a low of 11.4 million users in 1992, although it was suspected to be on the rise again.

Several conflicting trends characterized recreation in the early 1990s. After decades of declining influence, the work ethic reappeared; the leisure age predicted in the late 1960s never arrived. At the same time recreation seemed increasingly a commodity: people work hard not necessarily because it is satisfying, but to purchase recreation, spending some $500 billion per year in the process. Most of recreation continued to take place in the home, although the videocassette recorder (VCR), home computer, and access to multichannel cable television meant that the content of recreation was changing. After the neglect of the 1980s, concern over the environment was intensifying, although the carrying capacity of many national parks and other wilderness areas was being reached or exceeded. While expenditures on public facilities rose only modestly, commercial recreation enterprises were among the fastest growing in the economy.

[Gary Cross, *A Social History of Leisure Since 1600* (State College, Pa., 1990); Foster Rhea Dulles, *A History of Recreation,* 2nd ed. (New York, 1965).]

GARRY E. CHICK

See also **SUPP:** Fitness, Physical; Parks, National; Sports, New.

RECYCLING. The term "recycling" was virtually unknown before the 1970s, although within industry it has been practiced for many years, in some cases centuries. The first American paper mill, built near Philadelphia in 1690, used rags as its raw material. Rags continued to be the basis of paper manufacture until the development of the sulfite process for making wood pulp in the mid-nineteenth century. By the twentieth century, the use of scrap material in industry was common. Scrap dealers in metal have been part of the industrial scene for many years; the metal in "junk" cars has been reprocessed ever since World War II, and many of the parts are remanufactured for sale to repair shops.

National consciousness about recycling is a product of the environmental movement, which can be dated from 1970, the first year Earth Day was celebrated and the year the federal Environmental Protection Agency (EPA) was established. The environmental movement focused attention on the problem of both industrial wastes, notably chemicals seeping into the ground and affecting drinking water, and solid waste, the trash generated by households ending up in the municipal dump or landfill. By 1990 the amount of what the EPA called municipal solid waste amounted to 180 million tons per year and was rising. Under the Resource Conservation and Recovery Act, first passed by Congress in 1976 and reauthorized several times after, the federal government sponsored recycling to restrict the growth of landfills. In 1989 the EPA set a national goal of 25 percent recycling by 1995, that is, the diversion of at least 25 percent of material that would otherwise become municipal solid waste and the reprocessing of it to make other consumer items.

The definition of recyclable material remains in dispute. The EPA includes only material in the municipal solid waste stream, otherwise known as postconsumer waste. The U.S. Bureau of Mines, however, includes industrial scrap in its definition of recyclables, as well as junk cars and other metal products that never end up in landfills. Because of this diversity of meanings, figures on recycling are unreliable. The principle recycled commodities are various metals, paper products, old automobile tires, used automobile batteries, and textiles and chemicals, including plastics. The most recycled material is steel, largely because its magnetic property makes it easy to recover from mixed trash. Three-fifths of the steel used in the United States is recycled, and half of steel products made in the United States is produced from scrap steel and iron. One-third of scrap steel and iron is postconsumer, largely "tin" cans, much of which has been recycled since the late 1980s. Aluminum, primarily in the form of aluminum beverage containers, is substantially recycled. The economic incentive is strong because recycled aluminum costs much less than "virgin" aluminum. The bottle deposit laws in many states have promoted the recycling of aluminum cans; Oregon passed the first such law in 1971. Scrap copper sells for a high price, so significant quantities are recycled. About one-third of copper manufactures is composed of recycled scrap copper.

Paper products are the largest single item (by volume) in municipal solid waste; about 40 percent is recycled. The major difficulty in paper recycling is the many forms in which paper appears—newspaper, corrugated boxes, advertising material, packaging, and writing paper. Corrugated boxes can be and often are reprocessed into new corrugated material. Nearly 50 percent of newsprint is recycled. The major problem in recycling paper is the need to de-ink it first; the paper industry is slowly increasing the number and capacity of its de-inking plants. Automobile tires and automobile batteries have been banned from landfills since the late 1980s. Batteries are reprocessed through the original manufacturers. The United States generates about one old tire per inhabitant per year, and they have proved a problem because, while barred from landfills, when stored above ground they are breeding grounds for rodents and insects. Many truck tires and some auto tires are retreaded; more recently many tires have been shredded and incorporated into road asphalt. Tires contain petrochemical material, and some old tires are burned as fuel.

Some textiles are recycled in the form of clothing shipped to Third World countries. Others are reconstituted as wipe cloths for industry. Most toxic chemicals are reprocessed by the chemical industry, particularly since congressional legislation in the 1970s held manufacturers liable for any residual chemicals found in the ground. Polymer chemicals, the basis of the plastic containers widely used in the twentieth century, are increasingly recycled. The first two-liter plastic bottle was produced in 1978, and as more and more states have passed bottle deposit laws, these have been remanufactured rather than discarded. Two types of plastic are suitable for recycling: PET, used in soda bottles, and HDPE, used in milk jugs. PET can be remanufactured as soda bottles and has many fiber applications; HDPE can be made into many products, such as fences and park benches.

Postconsumer recyclables are collected through municipal recycling programs mandated in many states. Minnesota had the highest recycling rate in 1994 at 38 percent, followed by New Jersey, Washington state, Massachusetts, and Maine. The principal barriers to increased recycling have been the uncertain quality of the material collected and the difficulty of marketing it. In many cases industry is not equipped to use recycled material. Still, the demand is growing, particularly as governments require that the products they purchase contain recycled material. Consumer attitudes toward recycling are gradually becoming more favorable.

[David R. Powelson and Melinda A. Powelson, *The Recycler's Manual for Business, Government, and the Environmental Community* (New York, 1992).]

NANCY M. GORDON

See also **SUPP:** Environmental Business; Environmental Movement; Environmental Protection Agency; Waste Disposal.

REED V. REED, 404 U.S. 71 (1971), a Supreme Court case that represented a departure from sixty years of sex discrimination doctrine. Previously, the Supreme Court had consistently affirmed the ruling in *Muller* v. *Oregon* (1908), in which the Court ruled that "protective" labor laws for women were justified by physical differences between the sexes. The Court subsequently went further, invoking this precedent to uphold laws whose primary effect was to restrict women's work opportunities, such as a prohibition on women bartenders (*Goesaert* v. *Cleary*, 1948) and even laws that had nothing to do with work, such as restrictions on women's jury service (*Hoyt* v. *Florida*, 1961). Lower courts followed this lead. Opinion after opinion stated that sex was a reasonable basis for classification, whatever the specific issue. Sex-based discrimination received only the minimal scrutiny, in contrast to those cases involving constitutional rights or racial discrimination, which receive strict scrutiny. The receptivity to individual rights under Chief Justice Earl Warren did not extend to women's rights, but this was not entirely the Court's fault. Years of undeviating leniency to sex discrimination had dried up the flow of appeals, so that the Court had to wait until the reemergence of the feminist movement for new litigation and an opportunity to reconsider the issue.

Reed v. *Reed* marked the first time the Court used the equal protection clause of the Fourteenth Amendment to invalidate a state statute on the grounds of sex discrimination. *Reed* is a decision whose importance stems far more from its historical interest than from its effect on public policy or doctrine. The case presented a factual situation unlikely to arise often. An Idaho law gave automatic preference to men over equally qualified women in appointing the administrator of a dead person's estate ("qualification" being defined as relationship to the deceased by blood or marriage). Cecil and Sally Reed, who were divorced, both applied to become administrator of their deceased son's estate. Cecil was appointed and Sally sued. The state argued that administrative convenience (removing the need to choose among applicants) and family harmony (removing the potential for conflict) provided rational bases for the law. The Supreme Court disagreed. The short, unanimous opinion implicitly accepted the rational basis test as the appropriate standard for sex discrimination cases but found the necessary reasonableness lacking. "To give a mandatory preference to members of either sex," the Court declared, "is to make the very kind of arbitrary legislative choice forbidden by the equal protection clause." *Reed* did not change constitutional doctrine on sex discrimination; that development had to wait for later cases. In effect, the Court distinguished this case from the precedents and opened the door for what would become a new tier or level of scrutiny in sex discrimination cases with *Craig* v. *Boren* (1976). The decision's impact on future rulings was unclear, both because few laws were as arbitrary as Idaho's and because *Reed* was decided by only seven justices.

[Judith A. Baer, *The Chains of Protection: The Judicial Response to Women's Labor Legislation* (Westport, Conn., 1978), and *Women in American Law: The Struggle Toward Equality from the New Deal to the Present* (New York, 1991); Joan Hoff, *Law, Gender, and Injustice* (New York, 1991).]

JUDITH A. BAER

See also **SUPP:** *Craig* v. *Boren;* Women's Movement; Women's Rights.

REFUGEES. Between 1946 and 1993 the United States admitted 2,855,087 refugees for permanent resettlement. During this period both the annual numbers and national origins of refugees have varied dramatically. During the decade following World War II, more than 90 percent of refugees came from European countries; after 1960 the geographic composition changed. Migration from Cuba rose and continued into the 1990s. Large-scale resettlement of Indochinese refugees began in 1975 and continued into the mid-1990s but at lower annual levels. Admission of refugees from countries in Eastern Europe and the Soviet Union increased during the 1970s and again during the 1990s with the dismantling of communist governments. Other groups that resettled in the United States from the 1970s to the mid-1990s included Iranians, Afghans, and Ethiopians.

The mechanisms for admitting refugees to the United States have also undergone significant changes since World War II. A common theme throughout U.S. refugee policy, however, was a focus on the selective admission of refugees for permanent resettlement in the United States. Only in recent years has the role of the United States as a country of asylum emerged as an important policy consideration. Moreover, until 1980 and the passage of the Refugee Act, U.S. refugee policy was intertwined with and often constrained by immigration procedures.

In 1875 Congress passed the first immigration legislation, specifying reasons for denying the entry of aliens. Prior criminal convictions were grounds for exclusion, but political refugees were the exception to this law. Alien criminals were defined as "persons who are undergoing a sentence for conviction in their own country of felonious crimes, other than political or growing out of or the result of political offenses." Political refugees were also excepted from the requirements of the Literacy Act of 1917. In 1921 legislation was passed regulating not only the moral and political character of aliens seeking admission to the United States but the number and national origins of immigrants. A system of quotas for each country was instituted that favored countries in northwestern Europe, restricted immigration from southern, eastern, and central Europe, and effectively banned Asians. Between 1921 and 1946 aliens seeking entry to the United States as political refugees were admitted primarily within the limits of annual quotas for the country of origin. Policy during this period reflected isolationist currents in U.S. foreign policy and public sentiment. During the years just prior to U.S. entry into World War II, for example, special legislation for the admission of European refugees, including children, was routinely defeated in Congress.

The aftermath of World War II revealed to U.S. government officials the problematic connection between political stability and displaced populations.

REFUGEES

Between 1946 and 1965 the relationship between U.S. foreign policy and refugee policy and programs was strengthened. The ineffectiveness of immigration policy for dealing with refugee resettlement was also made clear. The McCarran-Walter Act, passed over President Harry S. Truman's veto in 1952, served to reinforce the quota system and made no provisions for the demand for refugee migration to the United States. The postwar period was thus characterized by special presidential initiatives and legislation for the resettlement of Europeans. For example, more than 40,000 refugees were admitted under the Presidential Directive of 1945, nearly 410,000 aliens under the Displaced Persons Act of 1948, and 189,000 refugees under the Refugee Relief Act of 1953.

In 1956 President Dwight D. Eisenhower used the Immigration and Nationality Act for the temporary admission of individual aliens in order to admit approximately 31,000 Hungarians involved in the uprising of November 1956. Special legislation was then required to "adjust" their temporary parolee status to permanent resident or immigrant status. The mechanism was also used for admission of Cubans beginning in 1959 with the fall of Fulgencio Batista's government in Cuba. Cubans arriving initially were admitted as temporary visitors, whereas from 1960 until 1980 Cubans were paroled into the United States. As with the Hungarians, it was necessary for Congress to pass special legislation in order for Cubans to be granted U.S. immigrant status. Between 1967 and 1993, 512,000 Cubans became permanent residents under the Cuban Adjustment Act of 1966.

Support from Congress and the executive branch for the revision of immigration and refugee policy culminated in amendments to the Immigration and Nationality Act in 1965, which had eliminated the national quota system and established numerical limits for annual immigration from the Eastern and Western hemispheres, respectively. Immigrant visas were distributed according to a system that emphasized family reunification. Within that system, 10,200 annual visas were allocated for refugees, a recognition of the responsibility of the United States for refugee resettlement. The connection of refugee policy to foreign policy interests, however, remained consistent with the cold war. Refugees were defined as aliens who "because of persecution or fear of persecution on account of race, religion, or political opinion may have fled (1) from any Communist or Communist-dominated country or area and (2) from any country within the general areas of the Middle East . . . or . . . are uprooted by catastrophic natural calamity." Because political persecution was tied to communism, the U.S. definition was not consistent with the 1967 United Nations Protocol Relating to the Status of Refugees, ratified by the United States in 1968.

The limitations of the 1965 legislation for meeting the need for refugee resettlement became clear. Demand for refugee migration from the Soviet Union during the 1970s exceeded available visas; between 1972 and 1980, 53,500 Soviet émigrés were paroled in the United States. The parole authority was also used for the admission of refugees fleeing Indochina after 1975. Again, special legislation was passed to permit these and other groups to achieve immigrant status, and approximately 175,000 refugees became immigrants under the Indochinese Act of 1977 and another 139,000 under the Refugee-Parolees Adjustment Act of 1978, which included refugees from Indochina as well as such areas as Chile, Uganda, and Romania.

The Refugee Act of 1980 sought to disentangle U.S. refugee policy from the constraints of annual immigration admissions. The category for refugees within the family reunification–based system was replaced with a consultation process between Congress and the executive branch to set annual levels of refugee admissions. In 1993 the annual ceiling for refugees admissions was 132,000 allocated by geographic region as follows: Asia, 7,000; East Asia, 51,000; Eastern Europe, 2,725; Soviet Union, 49,775; Latin America and the Caribbean, 4,500; Near East and south Asia, 7,000; unallocated, 10,000. The 1980 act removed the requirement for flight from a communist country, making the U.S. definition of a refugee consistent with the UN protocol. Under the act aliens within the United States can apply for asylum. Aliens granted refugee status may apply for adjustment to permanent resident (immigrant) status after one year in the United States. Between 1980 and 1990, 778,000 aliens received permanent resident status. Of these, 44,000 or 5.6 percent were aliens granted political asylum. From 1991 to 1993 more than 365,000 refugees received permanent resident status; 45,000 or 12.3 percent were granted political asylum.

The extent to which refugee policy continues to serve foreign policy interests is an important consideration. Between 1981 and 1990, 90 percent of refugees and those seeking political asylum who were granted permanent resident status came from communist countries; 150,000 refugees were admitted from Eastern Europe, nearly 643,000 from Indochina and China, and 113,000 from Cuba. In 1993, 94 percent of the 56,000 applications for refugee status of persons from Eastern European countries and areas comprising the former Soviet Union were approved by the Immigration and Naturalization Service; 89 percent of applications from persons from Vietnam, Cambodia, and Laos were approved. Requests for refugee status from aliens from noncommunist countries such as El Salvador and Haiti have not been approved in such proportions. For example, between 1981 and 1990, just under 1,400 refugees from El Salvador were granted permanent resident status; from 1990 to 1993 the number was 2,800. Between 1991 and 1993, 32,000 applications for asylum were filed by El Salvadorans. The approval rate was 13 percent. A low proportion of applications from Haitians was approved during the early 1990s. In 1993 the figure was 10 percent.

Questions about refugee policy for different national groups have arisen concerning the government's response to Central American refugees and U.S. support for the government of El Salvador during the 1980s. During the 1990s similar concern arose about the strikingly different policy for Cuban and Haitian refugees. The unsympathetic response to requests for asylum led to an increase in undocumented immigrants from Central America and Haiti. Since the mid-1980s credible estimates of the number of undocumented El Salvadorans residing in the United States range between 300,000 and 500,000, many of whom applied for asylum; in 1992 between 50,000 and 100,000 undocumented Haitians were estimated to be residing in the United States.

[Peter H. Koehn, *Refugees from Revolution* (Boulder, Colo., 1991); Gil Loescher and John A. Scanlan, *Calculated Kindness* (New York, 1986); Robert W. Tucker, Charles B. Keely, and Linda Wrigley, eds., *Immigration and U.S. Foreign Policy* (Boulder, Colo., 1990); Aristede R. Zolberg, Astri Suhrke, and Sergio Aguayo, *Escape from Violence* (New York, 1984).]

ELLEN PERCY KRALY

See also **DAH** and **SUPP:** Immigration; **SUPP:** Asian Americans; Cuba, Relations with; Cuban Americans; Eastern Europe, Relations with; El Salvador, Relations with; Haiti; Latin America, Relations with; Soviet Americans.

REFUGES. *See* **Wildlife Refuges and Sanctuaries.**

RELIGION. For most of American history a Judeo-Christian heritage shaped public discourse. The dominant culture paid little attention to Native American or world religions. A change in immigration laws in 1965 opened the way for an influx that has changed the religious landscape. By the mid-1990s temples and mosques were scattered across the United States rather than confined to coastal cities, as Middle Eastern and Asian religions gained adherents. The resulting pluralism challenged both traditional religious communities and public institutions, raising issues of intolerance and harassment. Cultural tensions related to religious pluralism were influenced by several factors. First, people whose understanding is molded by Judeo-Christian thinking expressed alarm about cultural loss. While most of them did not advocate intolerance, they did advocate prayer in schools. Second, increasingly violent religious tensions abroad often raised fears in the United States. Americans cherish religious freedom. Tensions over pluralism found their source in ritual and social dimensions rather than in the experiential and ethical.

U.S. politics have often been marked by religious debates. Most conservative Protestants identify with the Republican party, while many Catholics and liberal denominations choose the Democratic party. By the 1990s, however, traditional party alignments were breaking down. Since the 1970s religious activists have fought over abortion, homosexuality, prayer in public schools, and creationism in the school curriculum. Polls taken from 1975 to 1995 indicate that the percentage of Americans who identified with a church or synagogue was fairly stable, ranging from 71 percent in 1975 to about 69 percent in 1995. While the percentage of Protestants and Catholics declined slightly, Jews remained at a constant 2 percent of the twenty-year period. Gallup polls pointed to a modest increase (3 percent over twenty years) in the number of Americans who identified with non-Western religions and to a similar increase in those surveyed who claimed no religious attachment at all. Attendance at religious services was a different matter, as were the churchgoing habits of regular attendees. While many churches abandoned all but Sunday morning worship, for example, some offered Saturday evening options. In any one week, however, more Americans found their ways to houses of worship than the citizens of other Western nations.

[Catherine L. Albanese, *America, Religions and Religion*, 2nd ed. (Belmont, Calif., 1992); Stephen L. Carter, *The Culture of Disbelief: How American Law and Politics Trivialize Religious Devotion* (New York, 1993).]

EDITH BLUMHOFER

See also **SUPP:** African-American Religions and Sects; Asian Religions and Sects; Catholic Church;

Cults; Freedom of Religion; Fundamentalism; Islam; Jews, American; Judaism; Latter-day Saints, Church of Jesus Christ of; Native American Church; Pentecostal Churches; Protestantism; Reorganized Church of Jesus Christ of Latter-day Saints; Televangelism.

RELIGION, FREEDOM OF. *See* **Freedom of Religion.**

REORGANIZED CHURCH OF JESUS CHRIST OF LATTER-DAY SAINTS (RLDS), the second-largest group tracing its heritage to the Mormon prophet Joseph Smith, Jr. (1805–1844), whose three sons succeeded him as RLDS president and sought to define the institution as somewhere in the middle between Mormonism and Protestantism. In 1978 Wallace B. Smith, the great-grandson of Joseph Smith, Jr., became president. He increasingly moved the church into mainstream Protestantism and in 1984 pressed for the ordination of women. In the same year the church opened its communion service to nonmembers. By the late 1980s the RLDS, based in Independence, Mo., had a worldwide membership of about 240,000 (90 percent in North America) and had abandoned many of their Mormon doctrines and practices in favor of greater ecumenism.

[Richard P. Howard, *The Church Through the Years*, vols. 1 and 2 (Independence, Mo., 1992–1993); Roger D. Launius, *Joseph Smith III: Pragmatic Prophet* (Urbana, Ill., 1988).]

ROGER D. LAUNIUS

See also **SUPP:** Church of Jesus Christ of Latter-day Saints.

REPRODUCTIVE TECHNOLOGY, broadly defined, includes any medical intervention in the processes of conception, pregnancy, and birth. More commonly, the term refers to techniques used by a third party (physician, donor, or both) to assist in the human processes of conception and gestation, usually in cases of infertility, where reproductive organs do not function normally. Artificial insemination (AI), in which sperm from a donor is injected, usually by a doctor, into a woman's uterus just before ovulation, was first performed in the United States in 1884. The first sperm bank opened in 1950 at the University of Iowa, and the first major commercial sperm banks opened in 1971 in New York City and Minnesota. In 1980 one California sperm bank gained national attention by seeking donations of sperm from Nobel Prize win-

ners. The age of so-called "test-tube babies" began in 1978 in England with the birth of Mary Louise Brown, who was conceived by the process of in vitro fertilization (IVF), in which a physician combines a woman's egg with sperm in a petri dish and then introduces the resulting early embryo into the mother's uterus. The first IVF clinic in the United States was opened in Virginia in 1981. The year 1978 also marked the first birth by a surrogate mother whose services were contracted for by an infertile couple through an intermediary. A surrogate agrees to bear a child (conceived by AI or IVF) and then to relinquish it at birth. In the mid-1980s two new processes were developed: gamete intrafallopian transfer (GIFT) and zygote intrafallopian transfer (ZIFT), in which the insertion of the gametes (egg and sperm) or the zygote (fertilized egg) into the fallopian tubes approximates the natural process of conception more closely than IVF.

None of these procedures has been introduced without controversy, and several individual cases have received tremendous media coverage. The birth of Louise Brown caused an international sensation. When a surrogate mother refused to surrender her child to its father and his wife in 1986, the ensuing legal battle over "Baby M" made headlines. Although the federal government does not fund research involving human embryos, it has left legislative decisions about reproductive technology to individual states. By 1994 ten states had laws mandating medical coverage for infertility treatments, and fifteen states had passed legislation regulating contracts and compensation in surrogacy arrangements. The legal, ethical, medical, social, and psychological implications of reproductive technologies have been hotly debated. Advocates argue that medical science has expanded the range of options for infertile couples, offering them the possibility of having children genetically related to at least one of the parents. Opponents point to the high cost of IVF and question the use of limited medical resources for such purposes. Feminists are concerned that reproductive technology reinforces the pronatalist bias in U.S. society, thereby stigmatizing those who choose to remain childless. They point out that reproductive technology is generally available only to heterosexual married couples and not to people in nontraditional relationships. Another concern is that this technology may lead to the commercialization of reproductive processes and products (that is, surrogacy, sperm, eggs, and embryos) and the removal of reproductive control (and possibly of reproduction itself) from women. Opponents fear that reproductive technology is one more step toward genetic engineering and warn that, with embryos in petri dishes, Aldous Huxley's brave new world of mechanically produced life may be dangerously close to reality.

[Dianne M. Bartels, Reinhard Priester, Dorothy E. Vawter, and Arthur L. Caplan, eds., *Beyond Baby M: Ethical Issues in New Reproductive Technologies* (Clifton, N.J., 1990); Elaine Hoffman Baruch, Amadeo F. D'Adamo, Jr., and Joni Seager, eds., *Embryos, Ethics, and Women's Rights: Exploring the New Reproductive Technologies* (New York, 1988).]

ELIZABETH WATKINS

See also **SUPP:** Fertility; Surrogate Parenthood; Women's Health.

REPUBLICAN PARTY. With the exception of Jimmy Carter's one term as president (1977–1981), Republicans dominated the presidency from 1968 until 1992. This record stood in striking contrast to the previous thirty-six years, when only one president, Dwight D. Eisenhower, carried the Republican banner. On all other levels of competition since the 1970s—party registration, seats in Congress, governorships, and state legislatures—Republicans as a rule ran behind the Democrats, although the discrepancy varied with each category and from year to year. In the 1980s the party undertook a shift to the ideological right, leading to virtual disappearance of a familiar force in American politics—the liberal Republican. Republican gains at the start of the 1970s stemmed as much from problems of the Democrats as from broad approval of Republican policies. The Republicans did profit from an end to the once "solid" Democratic South, at least in presidential politics. While southern Democrats continued to dominate on a reduced scale in state and local contests, a solid Republican South emerged in presidential races. Republican planners in the early 1970s hoped for a "southern strategy." More important to Republican fortunes was the Democratic association with the Vietnam War and its consequences in the late 1960s and early 1970s—demonstrations and riots, youth rebellion, emergence of a radical left—all of which divided the Democrats and seemed to challenge revered American principles.

In turning in 1968 to a centrist presidential candidate, Richard M. Nixon, Republicans sought to end their internal divisions of the 1960s. Brought into office in a close contest, the ticket of Nixon and Governor Spiro T. Agnew of Maryland overpowered the Democrats four years later with 61 percent of the popular vote. Democratic candidates Senator George McGovern and Sargent Shriver won only Massachusetts and the District of Columbia. Although Nixon had initially been elected on a law-and-order southern strategy campaign, desegregation continued in the southern states, albeit at times with little assistance from the president. His record on social and economic programs was mixed, but it contained more than expected by either conservatives or liberals. While he abolished the Office of Economic Opportunity, he proposed a family assistance plan, which failed to pass Congress, and supported proposals for environment control and consumer protection. Nixon was the only post–World War II president whose budgets, from 1970 through 1975, contained more spending on human resource programs than for defense.

Nixon's most visible achievements were in foreign affairs, where moves to reverse twenty years of hostility with the People's Republic of China and to pursue détente with the Soviet Union surprised liberals and caught rightist critics off guard. While the war in Vietnam continued through his first term, Nixon's plan of Vietnamization steadily reduced the U.S. commitment. By 1972 he could claim that peace was within sight. Although no viable peace was achieved, the margin of victory occurred because of the division of the opposition and a perception of the Democrats as the party of disorder and of McGovern as the candidate of the radical left. Nixon's victories brought factions within the Republican party together after Barry Goldwater's defeat by Lyndon Johnson in 1964. Republicans elected 192 members of the House of Representatives in 1968 and again in 1972, the largest number since 1956 and the largest until the 1990s. Between 1970 and 1992 in the House, only in 1972 did the margin by which Democrats outnumbered Republicans drop beneath fifty, and the number frequently stood at 100 or more. During the Nixon years the party had a deficit of at least ten seats in the Senate.

Rather than build on their gains, Republicans squandered them in the scandals of the early 1970s. First came the problems of Vice President Agnew, who, faced with charges of receiving bribes, pleaded no contest and resigned in October 1973. Nixon was by this time deeply involved in the Watergate affair, illegal activities against the Democrats and efforts to hide the truth. The Watergate tapes—secret recordings in the Oval Office—revealed that Nixon had obstructed justice by participating in efforts to conceal the origins of the scandal and repeatedly lied about the Watergate cover-up from June 1972 to August 1974. Rather than face impeachment and likely removal from office, he resigned on Aug. 9, 1974. The Watergate scandal went beyond the president. Republicans faced charges ranging from arrogant and mean-spirited behavior to shadowy fund-raising and various forms of illegal activity. Several government officials went to prison. The political fallout was immediate. The Republicans lost five Senate seats in 1974, leaving Democrats in control, 60–37. The Democratic margin in the House grew from 49 to 147. Republicans controlled legislatures in only five states, and whereas in 1970 they outnumbered Democrats in governorships by thirty-two to eighteen, in 1975 there were thirty-six Democratic governors to thirteen Republicans. Lopsided Democratic majorities in Congress held up in the election of 1976. Republicans could take encouragement from the fact that in the 1976 presidential election Gerald R. Ford, who replaced Agnew in 1973 and thus was on hand to serve out the final two and a half years of Nixon's presidency, came close to being elected over Carter.

After 1976 the Republicans did not stay down long. Changes in party procedure, economic thought, and the political climate helped produce a comeback in the 1980s. The Republican National Committee shifted fund-raising from large contributors to direct mailings and use of computer technology, acquiring substantially larger sums of money and a broader base. Several forces combined to produce an enlarged ultraconservatism, the New Right. First came the appeal in the nation, if not the world, of supply-side economics, the thesis that prosperity depended upon sharp reduction of taxes, especially in the highest brackets. Many people concluded that a divided and guilt-ridden America had become impotent in the aftermath of the Vietnam War, a charge seemingly made unchallengeable in the humiliating hostage crisis with Iran that began in 1979. Because Carter was president at the culmination of this post-Vietnam syndrome, blame was laid at his feet. Republicans continued to mobilize white voters in the South and Southwest, conspicuously through politicization of the religious right—white evangelicals disturbed with reform movements that favored affirmative action in the workplace and educational institutions, abortion, feminism, and homosexual rights. While strongest in the South, the religious right showed strength in other states.

The 1980s marked the high point of Republican domination during the post–World War II era. Ronald Reagan defeated Carter in 1980 by nearly 10 percent

of the popular vote and Republicans won control of the Senate for the first time since 1954. Despite gaining thirty-three seats in the House, they could come no closer to the Democrats than fifty-one. A man of strong feelings rather than intellect, Reagan was a superb communicator who emerged as spokesman of neoconservative ideas—hostility to social programs, freedom of economic enterprise (expressed mostly in lower taxes), traditional values, and patriotism expressed in U.S. military power. Inspired by a tax cut (with no corresponding reduction in government spending) and by the admonition that it was proper, even American, to seek personal gain, the economy began a long surge. Interest rates and inflation went down. Massive increases in military spending and the president's skirmishes with foreign adversaries such as the dictator of Libya were indications that America "was back." Seemingly every Republican (and some Democrats) signed on to the program of nationalism and conservatism; scarcely anywhere could one find anyone who wore the label of liberal Republican. The high point came in the election of 1984 when the ticket of Reagan and George Bush defeated Walter Mondale and Geraldine Ferraro with 59 percent of the popular vote; the Democrats won only Minnesota (Mondale's home state) and the District of Columbia.

The scope of the Republican victory in 1984 was illusory. Republicans retained control of the Senate but made a disappointing gain of only fourteen seats in the House, leaving Democrats with a margin of eighty-one seats. The erosion of Republican power began. Democrats recaptured the Senate in 1986 and established a ten-seat margin that would carry into the 1990s. The majority in the House grew and by 1991 had reached 100. Republicans did narrow Democratic domination of governors' races. By Reagan's second term, however, it was possible to charge that the benefits of Reaganomics, as the economic program was called, had gone largely to the wealthy. The boom of the 1980s rested on borrowed money, leading to soaring budget deficits and a trade deficit that for a single year passed $150 billion. Reagan's popularity continued to befuddle opponents, but his presidential style came under criticism, notably in the Iran-Contra affair, a drawn-out scandal that raised constitutional questions about the conduct of foreign policy within the White House.

If the Reagan revolution was not fully a Republican revolution it continued to promote party fortunes in retaining the presidency in 1988. Victory of the Republican ticket of Vice President Bush and Senator Dan Quayle (by 54 to 46 percent) rested on the same coalition that had elected Reagan: the South, Great Plains, Rocky Mountain area, California and key industrial states, white Protestants (notably evangelicals), and partial support of white Catholics. Out of conviction or expediency, the Bush administration pledged more conservatism, more Reaganism. Encouraged by unexpected developments in foreign affairs, the new president received a high approval rating, and at one juncture it passed even that of Reagan. In speed and apparent fullness of victory, the Gulf War of 1991 dazzled the American people. Republicans claimed that the collapse of communism and of the Soviet Union, which occurred during 1989–1991 also were victories of Presidents Reagan and Bush. Bush's fall from grace, if more gradual than the rise, was equally profound. Problems that appeared earlier in the 1980s caught hold—budget and trade deficits, plant closings, and increasing unemployment. Conservatives who had claimed that growth in the 1980s had come from diminished government activity could not now urge more government involvement. In Governor Bill Clinton and Senator Al Gore the Democrats in 1992 offered young opponents who promised something new for the nation. Entry into politics of Ross Perot, an eccentric and appealing billionaire, complicated the political picture. Perot's message that something was seriously wrong in Bush's America did not bode well for the incumbent Republican. On the surface the defeat of Bush and Quayle was devastating—less than 38 percent of the popular vote and more reduction of Republican strength in Congress. The magnitude of the loss was offset by the size of the Democrat victory—Clinton and Gore received only 43 percent of the popular vote.

Ending twelve years of Republican control of the presidency did not end the contest for party leadership and direction. The party reevaluated the wisdom of being identified as a rightist organization with narrowly defined social and economic positions. An immediate problem of the mid-1990s was how the party would treat the religious right, a group that pledged votes, vigor, and money but that angered some Republicans and showed signs of producing diminishing returns. If the Republicans had received their best marks in managing world affairs, they had to answer charges that they were a party of whites, a nativist group in a nation increasingly immigrant, a party whose policies favored an economic elite. Debates in Congress over post–cold war foreign policy, health care, and crime reinforced this view. By the 1994 midterm elections, the most conservative Republicans at the state and national level had won the battle

to redefine the party. Rallying around their "Contract with America," they marched to an astonishing partisan victory at the polls. Playing to the anxieties of Americans about big government and higher taxes, and perceptions of President Clinton's ambivalence and weakness as a leader, the Republican party gained its first Senate majority in eight years, its first majority of governors since 1970, and its first House majority in thirty years and only the second since 1930. Not a single Republican incumbent senator, governor, or House member was defeated. The formerly Democratic "Solid South" left Republicans with 16 of 28 southern and border senators, 7 of the 14 southern governorships, and 73 of 139 southern representatives. When the dust cleared, control of Congress and of the Republican party was in the hands of Majority Leader Robert J. Dole in the Senate and Speaker Newt Gingrich in the House. Many pundits predicted that the long-awaited national party alignment had taken place—from Democratic dominance to Republican—not unlike the shift that had taken place in 1930 and 1932. It remained to be seen how valid that assessment would be—if the remarkable Republican gains of 1994 would be far-reaching.

[Sidney M. Milkis, *The President and the Parties* (New York, 1992); A. James Reichley, *The Life of the Parties: A History of American Political Parties* (New York, 1992).]

ROSS GREGORY

See also **SUPP:** Democratic Party; Iran-Contra Affair; Reaganomics; Supply-Side Economics; Watergate, Aftermath of.

RESEARCH LABORATORIES exist in nearly every sector of the U.S. economy, straddling the boundaries separating government from private enterprise, the academic sector from the corporate, and the civilian from the military. During the cold war, U.S. laboratories became vital sources of economic, military, and intellectual power, producing new consumer goods and weapons. The cold war's sudden conclusion, as well as globalization of the economy and increased pressure from foreign and domestic competition, dramatically altered the political economy in which such laboratories flourished. In the early twentieth century, corporations and philanthropies separated research from teaching and created the first industrial and private research laboratories. After World War II the U.S. military created a new technical order by maintaining such wartime weapons laboratories as Los Alamos in New Mexico and the Johns Hopkins University Applied Physics Laboratory in

Maryland and by establishing new research laboratories, such as the Lincoln Laboratory at the Massachusetts Institute of Technology. By the 1990s corporations and the federal government were reassessing the role that laboratories might play in the new global economy. All agreed that the products of research laboratories were essential for economic competitiveness, but few agreed on who should support these powerful but fragile institutions.

In 1990 one-sixth of the nation's scientists and engineers were employed in more than 700 federally funded laboratories, including sixty-five Department of Defense and Department of Energy institutions, which had annual budgets ranging from $15 billion to $21 billion, depending on who and what is counted. The armed services research institutions expanded during the 1980s under President Ronald Reagan's vast and expensive arms buildup. Furthermore, Reagan's Strategic Defense and Computing initiatives pumped billions into corporate and university-based research organizations. With the end of the cold war, military research institutions were forced to justify their cost, and collaboration between weapons laboratories and the commercial sector became an essential part of economic planning, as was the once unthinkable—the elimination or combination of one or more of the Department of Defense's weapons laboratories to reduce costs. Academic laboratories and their university sponsors were especially hard hit by the decline in military support. Indirect overhead money from government contracts, at rates greater than 50 percent of a contract's value, were important sources of university funding. Increasingly, basic research, the strength of the American university, was viewed as a luxury rather than a necessity.

Corporate research laboratories also underwent a massive change during the 1970s and 1980s. The breakup of American Telephone and Telegraph (AT&T) in 1984 affected the research done at Bell Laboratories, famous for invention of the transistor and a tradition of allowing researchers to pursue their own ideas. By the mid-1990s Bell Lab managers were intent on harnessing the laboratories' research to the needs of AT&T's operating divisions. IBM's Thomas J. Watson Research Center began emphasizing research for securing that firm's market share in the volatile computer market. Competitive pressures also forced corporate research laboratories to demonstrate their market value. The 1980s also witnessed a new phenomenon—the growth of research consortia in which industrial, government, and university scientists and engineers worked together to develop new,

basic technologies. Perhaps the best known was Sematech, devoted to semiconductor manufacturing technology.

[Stuart W. Leslie, *The Cold War and American Science: The Military-Industrial-Academic Complex at MIT and Stanford* (New York, 1993); U.S. Congress, Office of Technology Assessment, *Federally Funded Research: Decisions for a Decade* (Washington, D.C., 1991).]

MICHAEL AARON DENNIS

See also **SUPP:** Think Tanks.

RESEGREGATION. *See* **Schools, Resegregation of.**

RESOLUTION TRUST CORPORATION. *See* **Savings and Loan Crisis.**

RETAILING INDUSTRY. Since the late 1970s sales revenues in the retail trade in the United States seemed to indicate robust growth, but several sectors of the industry were hit hard by poor sales, changing trends, and consolidation by retailers such as Wal-Mart. Mass-merchandise discounters, led by Wal-Mart, became the nation's dominant institutions, while specialty stores catering to individual consumer tastes grew in popularity. Several enterprises, including gasoline service stations, automotive dealers, food stores, and drugstores, underwent steady consolidation. The number of service stations, for example, fell by 28 percent, from 176,465 million in 1977 to 105,334 in 1992. Smaller retail stores went out of business or merged into larger national chains as it became difficult to compete in price and provide employees with competitive wages and benefits. Retail trade was relatively stagnant in 1977 when there were 1.8 million retail establishments. By 1992 the number had grown 17 percent, to 1.5 million. Total retail sales grew 171 percent, from $700 billion in 1977 to $1.9 trillion in 1992.

Virtually every facet of the U.S. economy grew more slowly from 1977 to the mid-1990s than in previous decades. With factories closing, unions declining, and the economy switching from industry to lower-paying services, consumers had to shop in stores—usually Wal-Marts and Kmarts—that offered the cheapest prices on basic goods. Workers able to take advantage of the service sector's highest salaries—lawyers, doctors, executives—had more money to spend on expensive goods, helping the growth of specialty stores.

The predominant trend, however, was the growth of

discounters. Between 1987 and 1992 discounters increased their number of stores 16 percent, from 58,000 to 67,000, with sales increasing 49 percent, from \$69.3 billion to \$103.4 billion. By comparison, conventional department stores such as Macy's suffered and their number of stores fell by 2 percent, from 24,000 to 23,000, while sales increased only 7 percent, from \$47.7 billion to \$51.3 billion. Epitomizing the trend was Arkansas-based Wal-Mart, which became the nation's top retailer, both in number of stores and sales. Founded in the early 1960s by Sam Walton, the company expanded from a chain located mostly in small towns in the South and Midwest to a national chain with a presence in large suburban markets and cities. The store relied on folksiness and the small-town common touch by using store greeters and such promotions as gerbil races in its pet departments. At the same time it became a leader in using technology to make the company more efficient, allowing it to keep prices as low as possible and still ring up profits that impressed Wall Street. It spent billions installing such devices as price scanners and computers that tracked inventories and took care of administrative details such as payrolls. It built its own satellite system, which allowed store managers scattered throughout the country to stay in contact with company headquarters in Bentonville, Ark. Such innovations allowed Wal-Mart to stay ahead of its main competitor, Kmart, founded in 1962, which had a bigger national presence during the 1960s and 1970s. Wal-Mart overtook it, however, as Kmart suffered from poor merchandise, bad management, and a poorly designed diversification scheme that led it into bookstores, sporting goods outlets, and a home materials supply company.

By the mid-1990s, however, Wal-Mart ran into its own problems, as it had difficulty maintaining the same rapid pace of revenue and profit growth. It also faced its toughest competition from Target, a division of Minneapolis-based Dayton Hudson Stores, Inc. Target attracted shoppers with more upscale stores but still featured low prices on basic goods. The company showed strong growth during the 1990s and was one success story that Dayton Hudson, which also owned ailing department stores, could boast of. The growth of Wal-Mart and Target caused many smaller, independent retailers, especially in the small towns where Wal-Mart expanded in the 1980s, to go out of business. Such retailers usually could not compete and found their customers leaving traditional downtown stores to shop in new Wal-Marts at the edges of towns.

Technology became more important for all U.S. retailers in the 1990s. Stores and chains adopted Wal-Mart technology to make themselves more efficient. Products such as computers and software, as well as televisions, videocassette recorders, and stereo systems, recorded strong sales and helped such companies as Best Buy, Circuit City, and Blockbuster Entertainment become staples of the suburban shopping center and strip mall. Technology, however, challenged traditional retailers by allowing consumers to buy goods without going into stores. At the lowest end of the technological spectrum, mail-order houses such as L. L. Bean and Lands' End flourished by sending catalogs to consumers. The late 1980s saw the emergence of cable television networks dedicated to selling goods twenty-four hours a day. The two most prominent were the Home Shopping Network and QVC. By 1995 merchandising had moved onto the global computer network known as the Internet, with companies accessing the computer network system to sell to consumers. Many observers predicted that the Internet would become a huge source of commerce, but problems with sending credit card numbers through the system plagued the medium.

[Robert Spector and Patrick D. McCarthy, *The Nordstrom Way* (New York, 1995); Sandra S. Vance and Roy V. Scott, *Wal-Mart: A History of Sam Walton's Retail Phenomenon* (New York, 1994).]

THOMAS G. GRESS

See also **SUPP:** Home Shopping Networks; Mail-Order Industry; Malls, Shopping.

RHODE ISLAND, which began as a colony in 1636 based on the separation of church and state and religious freedom, by 1905 was the first state to have a Roman Catholic majority (61.7 percent in 1990). Whites overwhelmingly dominated the state's 1990 population of 1,003,464 (91.4%), while African Americans made up only 3.9 percent of the population. From its earliest days, Rhode Islanders had to scratch and scramble to create a productive economy. Having a tiny coastal state without an exploitable hinterland, natural resources, large scale agriculture, or population, its people have had to live by their wits. In the colonial era they turned to ocean commerce, privateering, slave trading, and smuggling, after the American Revolution to the China trade, and then to manufacturing in the nineteenth century. The twentieth century brought extended economic difficulties. While most of the United States suffered through the Great Depression from 1929 to 1940, Rhode Island's depression began early in the 1920s and, except for the respite of World War II, lasted until the late 1950s. While Rhode Island shared in the general prosperity of New England from the 1960s to the mid-1980s, the state was particularly hard hit by the recession of the early 1990s. Unemployment exceeded both U.S. and New England levels as regional hard times tended to exaggerate conditions in the state. The largest civilian employer of Rhode Islanders, Electric Boat, a builder of submarines, reduced its workforce as defense contracts shrunk after the end of the cold war. The state's privately insured but corrupt credit union system collapsed in 1991, plunging the state into a deepened economic and political crisis.

Ranked as the nation's sixth-largest industrial center in 1900, Rhode Island steadily deindustrialized since then. Manufacturing, which employed 52 percent of the workforce in 1947, employed only 20 percent in 1993. In the 1980s manufacturing jobs fell by another 34,200; half of the remaining manufacturing jobs were in the jewelry industry. Of the twenty-one companies that employed 1,000 or more workers in 1941, only two remained in 1991. Several significant manufacturing concerns were based in Rhode Island, including Hasbro, one of the world's largest toy manufacturers, and GTECH, the world's largest supplier of on-line lottery systems. From being the first urban industrial state, Rhode Island began developing a postindustrial economy in the 1960s and 1970s. The population shifted out of the old industrial centers, and by 1990 nearly four times as many Rhode Islanders were employed in the service sector as in manufacturing. The leading economic enterprises became tourism, business and health services, and education. Rhode Island's recovery from the economic depression of 1990–1993 was slowed by the decline of defense employment, both in terms of defense manufacturing and by the withdrawal of the remaining naval vessels. The electronics industry that the state had hoped to build upon was hard hit in all of New England, and in 1993 the U.S. government ordered sharp restrictions on the fishing industry in order to permit depleted stocks to recover. When the U.S. Navy withdrew most of its operations from Newport after 1973, the city found its economic salvation in the tourist industry. Narragansett Bay remained a major asset and tourism continued to grow. Education constituted a significant "export" industry. While in the 1990s the state produced about 9,800 high school graduates each year, its colleges and universities awarded nearly 16,000 degrees, and most of the college students were from other states and nations.

After the Democratic party's capture of the state government in 1935, Rhode Island entered a period of one-party rule. Democratic domination was so pronounced that by the mid-1960s Rhode Island had the least interparty competition of any New England state, and the Republicans were so weak that they failed to offer even token candidates for more than half of the seats in the state's general assembly. In 1974, however, the first Republican to be elected mayor of Providence since 1938 won over a divided Democratic party. The first Republican U.S. senator since 1938 was elected in 1976, and the first Republican U.S. representative since 1940 won in 1980. By 1993 the minority party held half of Rhode Island's congressional delegation and three of five general state offices. Two significant factors promoted the waning of Democratic power—the rise of independent voting and the decline of ethnicity. Voters cast off party loyalty, allowing mavericks and Republicans to capture many important offices. Until the 1960s the four ethnic groups—Yankee, Irish, Italian, and French-Canadian—each representing about 20 percent of the population, dominated all the general state offices, the legislature, the mayoralties, and the congressional delegation. The Democratic party in particular had been built on a carefully balanced ethnic coalition, and it depended on ethnic loyalties to sweep the elections. Beginning in the 1960s, however, the old ethnic neighborhoods started to break up and the people scattered to the suburbs. Providence, which had 40 percent of the state's population in 1950, had only 15 percent by the 1990s. Consequently, individuals of small ethnic groups were elected by a public that cared little about ethnicity. For example, in 1992, in the most Catholic state in the Union, three of the five general state officers were Jewish, including the governor.

In the seventeenth century Rhode Island was tagged "Rogues' Island" by the neighboring Puritan colonies, which regarded the lack of a state church as wicked. In the last quarter of the twentieth century the state experienced such a stream of corruption in high and low places that "Rogues' Island" seemed a fitting name. Rhode Island suffered the embarrassment of seeing two consecutive chief justices of the state supreme court driven from the bench because of corruption. Revelations of corrupt and unethical practices embraced a former governor and three speakers of the state house and a number of legislators, mayors, and public officials. In the 1980s the mayors of Providence, North Providence, Pawtucket, and Cranston were charged with crimes and only one escaped conviction. Beginning in 1991 Rhode Island suffered a local version of the savings and loan scandal that hit several states in the 1980s. The failure of many banks and credit unions tied up one-third of the resources of the state's depositors and triggered a political uprising and major reforms in government.

[Patrick T. Conley, *An Album of Rhode Island History, 1636–1986* (Norfolk, Va., 1986); George H. Kellner and J. Stanley Lemons, *Rhode Island: The Independent State* (Woodland Hills, Calif., 1982); William G. McLoughlin, *Rhode Island: A History* (New York, 1978).]

J. STANLEY LEMONS

RICHMOND V. J. A. CROSON COMPANY, 488 U.S. 469 (1989), a Supreme Court case that considered whether the constitutionality of set-asides, affirmative action programs for minority businesses, permitted by a standard of strict scrutiny under the Fourteenth Amendment's equal protection clause should continue. Since 1942 Congress had approved legislation requiring businesses with federal contracts to draw up action plans for hiring minority workers. Until *Croson,* however, the Court had not questioned this practice. In 1983 the Richmond, Va., city council instituted a set-aside to remedy past discrimination by requiring prime contractors to whom the city awarded construction contracts to subcontract at least 30 percent of each contract's dollar amount to minority business enterprises. Prime contractor J. A. Croson Company did not comply with the program, whereupon the city awarded the contract to another company. Croson challenged the city's 30 percent quota as a violation of the Fourteenth Amendment's equal protection clause. The city responded that the quota merely copied federal policy guidelines. In a six-to-three vote, the Court decided in favor of Croson, signaling the Court's increased willingness to limit the states' use of quotas as a remedy for past discrimination.

TONY FREYER

See also **SUPP:** Affirmative Action; Set-Asides.

RIGHT-TO-DIE MOVEMENT. *See* **Euthanasia.**

RIOTS. The English Riot Act of 1715 made it a felony for twelve or more persons to gather together and disturb the peace. As part of the common law practiced in the American colonies and the United States, a riot could consist of as few as three persons, assembled for a common purpose, who behaved so as to cause observers to fear disturbance of the peace. Most events characterized as riots, however, involve more people, and sociologists and social psychologists now treat riots as instances of "collective behavior" or "crowd psychology." The common law definition of a riot allows public officials to break up even a peaceful assembly, if participants behave in such a way as to cause observers to fear disruption of civic peace. Whether actions of publicly assembled people cause a riot depends very much on point of view. The Boston Massacre of 1770 occurred when British troops fired into what they regarded as a rioting crowd, and the Boston Tea Party of 1773 was, to British authorities, another riot. From a later American perspective these were not unfortunate breaches of civic peace but events leading to the revolutionary war. When people protest against injustice they often view their action as a legitimate uprising, while those against whom the protest is directed are likely to define it as a riot.

The Constitution was a compromise between those who favored democratic self-government and those who feared that democracy would degenerate into mob rule. The First Amendment guarantees the "right of the people peaceably to assemble, and to petition the Government for a redress of grievances." Freedom of assembly establishes legitimacy of peaceful demonstrations, but it is widely held that crowds are more irresponsible than the individuals they comprise. From the perspective of those in authority, crowds must be kept under control. A riot is not just a failure to keep the people under control, but it is also an occasion for using force to gain control. The right of people to assemble is balanced by the right of authorities, established in common law, to declare an assembly a threat to civic peace.

One of the worst waves of riots was occasioned by the military draft during the Civil War. The Conscription Act of 1863 not only required men to fight for a cause in which many did not believe, but allowed any man drafted to avoid service by finding a substitute or paying $300. There were riots across the country, but the worst were in New York City in July 1863, where there were many poor Democrats who both sympathized with the South and resented the ability of the rich to buy out of military service. It took four days and a combination of police, militia, army, navy, and West Point cadets to quell the rioting.

The history of labor unions has been punctuated by civil disturbances. The weapon of unions has been the strike, and strikes have often resulted in violence. Workers struck against the Carnegie Steel Company in Homestead, Pa., in 1892, and the company hired Pinkerton detectives to protect the strikebreakers brought in by the company. The battle between strikers and detectives led the governor to call in the state militia, which broke the strike. Strikers often engage in picketing to publicize their grievances, discourage the public from patronizing the business being struck, and prevent strikebreakers from taking their jobs. Both strikes and picketing have resulted in court decisions and legislation to protect workers, owners, and the peace. The courts have usually frowned on protecting civil disorder or violence, most recently in the case of protesters outside of abortion clinics.

Veterans, impoverished by the Great Depression, marched on Washington, D.C., in 1932 and camped out in fields and government buildings. They were supporting passage of a bill to grant them immediate payment of their World War I bonus. After the bill was defeated in Congress approximately 2,000 of the 15,000 veterans refused to leave the capital, and some government officials feared that the veterans would disturb the peace. When attempts by local police to remove the veterans resulted in four deaths, Army Chief of Staff General Douglas McArthur, on orders from President Herbert Hoover, sent in U.S. troops, which set fire to the camps and drove the "bonus marchers" from the city.

The unpopular and undeclared Vietnam War, and the use of the draft to provide soldiers for it, was the occasion for many antiwar demonstrations. In the summer of 1968 civil rights and antiwar protesters joined in a march outside the Democratic National Convention in Chicago. One of the reasons for emphasis on nonviolence in the civil rights and antiwar movements in the 1960s was to make it more difficult for officials to declare a march or demonstration a riot. In Chicago, however, city and party officials viewed the march as a potential riot, and Mayor Richard J. Daley sent in busloads of police. Protesters and sympathizers described what happened as a police riot, claiming the protest peaceful and nonviolent until police attacked. Defenders of the police argued that television cameras recorded only violence of the police, not provocations of demonstrators.

A 1968 report of the National Advisory Commission on Civil Disorders identified white racism and resulting feelings of hopelessness and powerlessness on the part of African Americans as the cause of race riots during the 1960s. The same reasoning could be applied to actions taken by members of the American Indian Movement, who occupied Alcatraz in San Francisco Bay in 1969, and Wounded Knee on the Pine Ridge Reservation in South Dakota in 1973. Different factors, however, were identified as the causes behind the disturbances in Los Angeles during the summer of 1992, when Hispanics and Koreans as well as African Americans took to the streets. The actions followed the acquittal of white police officers who had beaten Rodney King, a black man. The beating was videotaped and shown so often on national television that many Americans, white as well as black, saw the acquittal as a miscarriage of justice. It was argued that the beating was only an occasion for the rioting, the latter being an expression of frustration on the part of poor racial groups in Los Angeles. According to this argument, the Los Angeles uprising of 1992 had more to do with class than with race. The difficulty Americans had in categorizing what happened in Los Angeles in 1992 demonstrates the continuing debate in the United States over what distinguishes a riot from legitimate protest over injustice.

[Robert Gooding-Williams, ed., *Reading Rodney King, Reading Urban Uprising* (New York, 1993); Barbara Salert, *The Dynamics of Riots* (Ann Arbor, Mich., 1980).]

RICHARD W. MOODEY

See also **DAH:** Draft Riots; Race Riots; **SUPP:** Alcatraz; American Indian Movement; Los Angeles Riots; Wounded Knee.

RLDS. *See* **Reorganized Church of Jesus Christ of Latter-day Saints.**

ROBBERIES. The United States experienced a boom in bank robberies in the 1990s, and in 1991 banks reported the greatest number in U.S. history. Los Angeles accounted for 20 percent of the robberies, with an average take of $3,000 and 85 percent of thieves caught. While robbers lacked the drama and flair of such bandits from earlier eras as Bonnie Parker and Clyde Barrow or Willie "The Actor" Sutton, the new generation brought about the reinstitution of past practices. A holdup that netted $434,000 drove a Wells Fargo bank to post a $10,000 reward, a practice unknown since the 1890s. Automatic teller machines (ATMs) brought theft increases. With more than 77,000 ATMs nationwide early in the 1990s, they became prime sites for small robberies. In some cases, hackers were able to crack computer codes and steal cash. In rare instances, thieves removed entire machines, opened them, and stole their contents.

While law enforcement officers were successful in tracking down most bank robbers, they were less successful with armored car robberies, solving only one-third of 340 armored car heists between 1988 and 1992. The nation's largest open-road armored car robbery, in which thieves netted $10.8 million, remains unsolved. The theft occurred June 26, 1990, outside a convenience store in Henrietta, N.Y. In January 1993, in nearby Rochester, N.Y., thieves held up a Brink's depot, escaping with $7.4 million. Authorities arrested four men, alleging that most of the money was funneled to the Irish Republican Army. In what may have been the largest cash theft in history, owners of Revere Armored Car, Inc., were charged in 1993 with stealing as much as $40 million from client businesses and banks over three years. Attempts to have charges dismissed because the government failed to preserve the company's records failed in 1994.

The Isabella Stewart Gardner Museum in Boston was the site of the biggest art heist in history on Mar. 18, 1990. Thieves stole thirteen pieces worth an estimated $200 million, including five works by Degas, a Vermeer, a Manet, and three Rembrandts. The thieves made their way through the museum, slicing paintings out of frames. On Sept. 15, 1993, a 1960s radical surrendered in one of the nation's most infamous robbery cases. Katherine Ann Power turned herself in to police twenty-three years after driving the getaway car in a small-time robbery that turned deadly. A student and Vietnam protester, Power was involved in a plot to rob a Boston bank on Sept. 23, 1970. While she waited in the car, an accomplice killed Boston police officer Walter Schroeder, father of nine children. Power fled, living as a fugitive in various cities before settling in Oregon in 1977 under the name Alice Metzinger. Unable to overcome her conscience, she surrendered to authorities and began serving an eight-to-twelve-year sentence in September 1993.

[Keith Middlemas, *The Double Market: Art Theft and Art Thieves* (Farnborough, Eng., 1975); Debra Weyermann, *The Gang They Couldn't Catch* (New York, 1993).]

KATHLEEN B. CULVER

See also **SUPP:** Crime; Crime, White-Collar.

ROBERTS ET AL. V. UNITED STATES JAYCEES,

468 U.S. 609 (1984), a case in which the Supreme Court ruled that the states may forbid sex discrimination not only in public accommodations but also in private associations whose membership is restricted. The Civil Rights Act of 1964 exempted private clubs from its coverage, but by the 1980s California and Minnesota had extended their bans on sex discrimi-

nation to cover these groups. Minnesota's law led to a confrontation between the local and national organizations of the Junior Chamber of Commerce (the Jaycees), which encouraged members to participate in community activities, including running for office. Membership is open to any eligible person who pays the dues, and the Jaycees have welcomed all races, religions, and nationalities since it was founded in 1920. Until 1984, however, only males between the ages of eighteen and thirty-five could be full members. Women began demanding Jaycee membership in the 1970s, arguing that exclusion denied them equal professional and civic opportunities. Some local chapters began admitting women, and when the national organization threatened to revoke the charters of the Minneapolis and Saint Paul chapters, the case ended up in the Supreme Court. The justices ruled unanimously that, in light of the Jaycees' traditionally inclusive membership, they "have demonstrated no serious burden on their male members' freedom of association." *Roberts* did not ban all sex discrimination in private associations; it held only that the Constitution did not bar the states from prohibiting sex discrimination in a group like the Jaycees. Nevertheless, one month after the decision, the national organization voted to admit women.

[Judith A. Baer, *Women in American Law* (New York, 1985–1991).]

JUDITH A. BAER

See also **SUPP:** *Rotary International* v. *Rotary Club of Duarte.*

ROBOTICS is the science of designing and building independent mechanical devices that perform actions in place of human beings. Karel Čapek coined the term in his 1921 play *R.U.R.* in which robots wage and win war against humans. The word is derived from the Czech word *robat*, meaning "compulsory service" or "compulsory labor." Popular culture generally depicts robots as simulating the movements, speech, and appearance of humans, an image that has raised public concern about the possibility of conflict between humans and robots. In a wildly popular series of science fiction novels and short stories relating to robots, the writer Isaac Asimov in 1950 proposed three immutable laws governing the behavior of robots: a robot may not injure a human being or, through inaction, allow a human being to come to harm; a robot must obey orders except where orders would conflict with the first law; and a robot must protect its own existence as long as such protection does not conflict with the first or second law. Other writers adopted his three rules of robotics.

The reality of robotics has been both more mundane and more far-reaching. Robotic devices have proved useful in a variety of applications, and robotics has drawn on—and stimulated—advances in artificial intelligence, because of the interrelatedness of the fields. The most common application for robotics is in industry. The Robotic Industries Association defines an industrial robot as a reprogrammable, multifunctioning manipulator designed to move materials, parts, tools, or specialized devices through variable programmed motions for the performance of a variety of tasks. In 1961 the first of three prototype machines was installed in the General Motors Turnstedt plant in Trenton, N.J.; the machines quenched hot parts produced by a die-making process. PUMA (Programmable Universal Machine for Assembly) is a computer-controlled robot arm developed in the 1970s that grew out of pioneering research by Massachusetts Institute of Technology researcher Victor Scheinman with financial support from General Motors. Since then, robots have been designed for a wide range of industrial tasks, including welding, inspecting parts, painting, gluing, and drilling. In most cases robots perform the same task over and over with little variation but with greater accuracy than humans would produce for such repetitive work. Robots also have been employed in assembling devices or objects from an array of pieces, but such robotic systems require more advanced technology than those performing repetitive tasks. The robot must be able to sort components, picking the proper ones, placing them precisely, and fastening them properly. Such an application demands the highest level of sophistication in several areas, such as robot vision and sensation of torques and touch.

Mobile robots offer new opportunities for exploring places that are either inaccessible or unsafe for humans to visit directly, such as other planets and deep undersea. Such robots are controlled through teleoperation, in which a distant human reviews data gathered by the robot and directs its activities in response. Dante, a semiautonomous, eight-legged robot built at Carnegie Mellon University, descended part way into Mount Erebus, a volcano in Antarctica, in 1993; the test demonstrated how teleoperated robots could explore Mars or other planets. Robots have also played a key role in exploration of the sea floor and objects on it, such as the wreck of the *Titanic;* images from the robot were beamed to schools around the United States via satellite. Advances in miniaturiza-

tion, originally developed for manufacturing semiconductors, promise to speed the creation of ultrasmall robots, using components called microelectromechanical systems, which are no bigger than one millimeter. These systems could be used to devise small robots for use in applications such as surgery.

[Tom Logsdon, *The Robot Revolution* (New York, 1984).]

VINCENT KIERNAN

See also **SUPP:** Artificial Intelligence; Cybernetics.

ROCKEFELLER COMMISSION REPORT (1991). The National Commission on Children, created by Congress in 1987, began its deliberations two years later and presented its report in 1991. Chaired by Senator John D. (Jay) Rockefeller IV of West Virginia, the committee was broadly based and included representatives of all levels of government, business and civic leaders, and child welfare administrators. Its purpose was to "assess the status of children and families in the United States and propose new directions for policy and program development." The resulting assessment was bleak: one in five children lived in poverty, two out of five were at risk for failure in school, one out of four was being raised by a single parent, and millions were involved in sexual promiscuity, drug and alcohol abuse, and crime. The commission recommended early intervention, support through government programs and workplace benefits, and a general shoring up of families. It gave more attention to moral development than had reports of previous years. Most controversial among the recommendations were a proposed $1,000 per child tax credit and a proposal that employers provide unpaid parental leave for births, adoptions, and other family emergencies. The commission proposed new federal spending of $52 to $56 billion annually, which gave rise to substantial public criticism and an uncertain future for the commission's recommendations.

[National Commission on Children, *Beyond Rhetoric: A New American Agenda for Children and Families* (Washington, D.C., 1991).]

ELLEN GRAY

ROCK MUSIC. *See* **Music, Rock and Roll.**

ROE **V. WADE,** 410 U.S. 113 (1973), which established a woman's constitutional right to choose to have an abortion, set one of the most controversial precedents in the history of the Supreme Court. By a vote of seven to two, the Court invalidated Texas and Georgia laws prohibiting abortion except when necessary to save the mother's life. "Jane Roe" was the pseudonym of Norma McCorvey, a pregnant woman who challenged the Texas statute. The law prevented her from terminating the pregnancy (she gave her daughter up for adoption), but her case won that right for other women. Justice Harry Blackmun's majority opinion relied on the right of privacy recognized eight years earlier in *Griswold* v. *Connecticut.* "This right," he declared, "is broad enough to encompass a woman's decision whether or not to terminate her pregnancy." The Court acknowledged that the right to choose an abortion based on a private decision between a woman and her doctor was not absolute. Like all rights it could be infringed if government had a compelling interest in doing so.

Texas had advanced two justifications for abortion laws: protecting the mother's health and preserving prenatal life. The Court ruled that each interest became compelling at a different stage of pregnancy. No restrictions were justified in the first trimester (three months). Concern for maternal health justified appropriate regulations, but not prohibition, in the second trimester, when abortion became more risky than going to term. The question of prenatal life was more complex. If, as many people believe, human life begins at conception, the state has not only the power but the duty to protect the constitutional rights of the fetus. *Roe* concluded that "the word 'person' as used in the Fourteenth Amendment does not include the unborn." The state's interest in "potential life" became compelling, however, when the fetus could survive outside the mother's body. Since viability occurred at approximately the end of the sixth month, a state could prohibit third-trimester abortions—except when necessary to save the mother's life.

Although *Roe* was not based on the equal protection clause, it was a victory for women's rights. The need for reproductive choice, regardless of the exact judicial rationale, is indicated by the fact that 1.5 million elective abortions are performed in the United States every year. The Court's opinion, however, received widespread criticism even from those who were positive or neutral about the result. The justices evinced little awareness of the considerable differences between birth control, the issue in *Griswold,* and abortion. If Justice Harry Blackmun emphasized the possible devastating effect of unwanted pregnancy, he did not explain why bearing an unwanted child was worse than many other things government forces upon individuals. *Roe* also did not

explain why, if no legal, medical, or philosophical consensus exists on when life begins, a state cannot decide that it begins at conception. The public reaction to *Roe* v. *Wade* made reproductive choice one of the country's most debated issues and even inspired presidential selection of justices expected to overturn *Roe.* Decisions upholding indirect restrictions have weakened the impact of *Roe.* In practice only adult women who have access to abortion and can afford it have the right to choice.

[Judith A. Baer, *Women in American Law* (New York, 1991); Joan Hoff, *Law, Gender and Injustice* (New York, 1991).]

JUDITH A. BAER

See also **DAH:** Woman's Rights Movement; **SUPP:** Abortion; *Griswold* v. *Connecticut; Planned Parenthood of Southeastern Pennsylvania* v. *Casey;* Pro-Choice Movement; Pro-Life Movement; *Rust* v. *Sullivan; Webster* v. *Reproductive Health Services;* Women's Movement; Women's Rights.

ROMAN CATHOLICISM. *See* **Catholic Church.**

ROTARY INTERNATIONAL V. ROTARY CLUB OF DUARTE, 107 Supreme Court 1940 (1987), upheld the second of two state laws prohibiting sex discrimination in private associations. This decision involved a California statute similar to the Minnesota law upheld in *Roberts* v. *United States Jaycees* (1984). Like *Roberts,* the case represented a conflict between a local chapter and its parent organization. Two Supreme Court justices had to recuse themselves from the case—Harry A. Blackmun because he was a member of the Rotary and Sandra Day O'Connor because her husband was a member. Rotary, it was clear, was not a private club. It describes itself as "inclusive, not exclusive" and, like the Jaycees, works to remove racial, religious, and cultural barriers—among males. The difference between *Rotary* and *Roberts* was that the Rotary has always been a less political and more selective group than the Jaycees. Rotary does not take positions on public issues, and local chapters determine their own admissions procedures (the international organization recommends selection committees). In rejecting Rotary International's claim that the state law violated the constitutional right to privacy recognized in *Griswold* v. *Connecticut,* the Court emphasized "factors such as size, purpose, selectivity, and whether others are excluded from critical aspects of the relationship." A year later, the Court, in *New York State Club Association* v. *New York,* upheld an ordinance banning sex discrimination in even the most elite "city clubs."

[Judith A. Baer, *Women in American Law* (New York, 1991).]

JUDITH A. BAER

See also **SUPP:** *Roberts* v. *United States Jaycees.*

RURAL LIVING. Many Americans have believed rural living to be remote, obsolete, and deprived. The rapid mechanization of farming in the twentieth century has meant combination of farms into ever-larger entities, sometimes known as agribusiness, with ever-fewer Americans working on farms. The boundaries between rural and urban actually no longer exist, however, because rural residents have imported more mass-society patterns of dress, food, and leisure. Agrarian society is increasingly subject to urban patterns of consumption. This melding of what hitherto were different ways in living is reflected in the U.S. Bureau of the Census definition of "rural" as non-metropolitan. "Rural," by census definition, does not refer to making a living on farms but to people who live outside cities and metropolitan areas. The rural population, so defined, increased slightly between 1970 and 1990, from 53,565,000 to 61,656,000, to 24.8 percent of the national population. Statistically, rural Americans are among the nation's poorest citizens. Rural states rank near the bottom in collections by the Internal Revenue Service, federal payments to individuals, state and government income, gross production, and per capita income. Rural states generally have more people below the poverty level and higher dropout rates among high school students. Some compensation can be found in that rural locations have increasingly attracted minor and low-paying, nonunionized industries and residue enterprises, such as prisons, landfills, and nuclear waste receptacles. Rural life is also undeniably safer than city living. Maine, Wyoming, Vermont, North Dakota, and South Dakota had only sixty-one murders combined in 1991. These states ranked near the bottom in virtually all crime statistics, including robberies and aggravated assaults, despite very low expenditures for police and penitentiaries.

Americans feel deep nostalgia for rural America. Garrison Keillor's radio show *Prairie Home Companion* spoke to urbanized America's longing for a romanticized version of rural simplicity. States such as Montana and Idaho have attracted wealthy real estate

investors seeking refuge from the stress of urban life. Ironically, services for such elite made rural life emulate the rest of the nation, with the introduction of satellite and cable television, automated banking, computer modems, fast food restaurants, sports centers, and rapid mail delivery. By the early 1990s such developments curtailed the isolation of national parks. Thus, rural areas now offer all comforts of urban living for those who can afford them.

[Gary Alampi, ed., *Gale State Rankings Reporter* (Detroit, 1994); Janet M. Fitchen, *Endangered Species, Enduring Places: Change, Identity, and Survival in Rural America* (Boulder, Colo., 1991).]

GRAHAM RUSSELL HODGES

See also **SUPP:** Urban Living.

RUSSIANS. *See* **Soviet Americans.**

RUSTBELT, an economic region of the United States concentrated in the formerly dominant industrial states of Illinois, Indiana, Michigan, Ohio, and Pennsylvania. By the 1980s the Rustbelt became what the Dust Bowl was to an earlier generation—the symbolic name for a devastating economic change. The 1984 Democratic presidential candidate, Walter Mondale, is generally credited with the origin of the term. During the campaign, the former vice president from Minnesota attacked the economic policies of incumbent President Ronald Reagan, stating that the Republican president was "turning our great industrial Midwest and the industrial base of this country into a rust bowl." The media, however, repeated and reported the notion as "Rustbelt" and the phrase stuck. It described the declining industrial heartland, especially the steel- and automobile-producing regions in the Northeast and Midwest. The phrase became synonymous with industrial decline in the once dominant U.S. heavy manufacturing and steel industries.

The Rustbelt has indefinite boundaries, although in 1979 Joel Garreau dubbed the same general region "the Foundry." Both terms—"Foundry" and "Rustbelt"—aptly characterized the region's economic history and its underpinnings. With readily available coal, labor, and inland waterways, the region was ideal for steel manufacturing. Moreover, the automotive industry—a major buyer of steel—developed nearby. The U.S. steel industry, however, underwent decline and lost its world dominance. The U.S. worldwide market share of manufactured steel went from

182

20 percent in 1970 to 12 percent by 1990. U.S. employment within the industry dropped from 400,000 to 140,000 over the same period. Starting in the late 1970s, steel factories began closing. Among the hardest hit communities was Youngstown, Ohio, where the closure of three steel mills starting in 1977 eliminated nearly 10,000 high-paying jobs. Also hard hit were foundries in Buffalo, N.Y., Johnstown, Pa., and Pittsburgh, where the last outmoded steel plant closed in the late 1980s. While steel is produced in thirty-five states, the large steel plants in the Rustbelt were particularly hard hit because their large open-hearth furnaces were unprofitable and outdated. Many were sulfur-burning, coal-fired steel plants, which had difficulty meeting stringent environmental regulations on smokestack emissions. Layoffs occurred even as worldwide demand for steel grew. New demand often was met with lower-cost and sometimes higher-quality steel produced abroad, particularly in Japan. The steel industry rebounded by developing low-cost, highly automated minimills, which use electric arc furnaces to turn scrap metal into wire rod and bar products, but the minimills employ fewer workers.

The region was the nation's industrial heartland with large, densely populated urban areas. Those cities, which began showing signs of decline, had initially served as the melting pot for early European migration and the destination point for a tremendous migration of African Americans north to join the industrial workforce following World War II. With the industrial decline, however, thousands of well-paid, benefit-laden, blue-collar jobs were permanently lost. Families left the Rustbelt and relocated to the Sunbelt and the West, seeking jobs and better living conditions. The black populations in the Chicago and Pittsburgh metropolitan areas declined, reversing the earlier northern migration patterns from the Deep South. The population shift meant fewer congressional representatives from the region following the 1990 reapportionment.

[Richard Florida, *The Breakthrough Illusion: Corporate America's Failure to Move from Innovation to Mass Production* (New York, 1990); Joel Garreau, *The Nine Nations of North America* (Boston, 1981).]

BRENT SCHONDELMEYER

See also **SUPP:** Illinois; Indiana; Michigan; Ohio; Pennsylvania; Pittsburgh.

RUST **V.** *SULLIVAN,* 111 Supreme Court 1759 (1991). Congress enacted a law in 1970 that supported family-planning services by making available federal funds under Title X but forbade the use of federal funds for abortions. Over a fifteen-year period the Department of Health and Human Services (HHS) so regulated use of the funds under the law, but in 1986 HHS tightened regulations, attempting to limit the ability of clinics to provide information about abortions. Two years later, with the strong support of President George Bush, HHS imposed a gag rule upon clinics and their physicians, prohibiting references to abortion in family-planning programs. The first issue in *Rust* was whether the 1970 law could be construed to allow the gag rule even though Congress had not granted federal authorities such power. The second was whether the regulations including the rule violated freedom of expression guaranteed by the First Amendment and the due process of law protected by the Fifth Amendment. On both issues the Court decided in favor of the government. Conceding that the intent of Congress was ambiguous, the Court nonetheless held that it should defer to the judgment of those charged with applying the law. Regarding the second issue, the Court found that discussion of abortions could occur outside the federal program and thus there was no violation of either the First or Fifth Amendment. *Rust* affected 4,500 facilities serving nearly 4 million women and raised the question of whether the government could impose free-speech restrictions on other institutions receiving Title X funds. It marked a further limit of a woman's right to an abortion since the Court's landmark decision of *Roe* v. *Wade* (1973). The impact of the decision declined, however, when the administration of President Bill Clinton lifted the gag rule in1993.

[David Garrow, *Liberty and Sexuality: The Right to Privacy and the Making of* Roe v. Wade (New York, 1994).]

TONY FREYER

See also **SUPP:** Abortion; Contraception; *Roe* v. *Wade; Webster* v. *Reproductive Health Services.*

S

SACRAMENTO, the major urban center of California's Central Valley, is located at the confluence of the American and Sacramento rivers. The region has been a crossroads of trade and commerce since its earliest habitation. John A. Sutter, a German-speaking Swiss adventurer, arrived in Sacramento in 1839 and built a fort as a frontier outpost for the Mexican government. The gold rush that began in 1848 led the following year to the platting of the city of Sacramento, which became the state capital in 1854. It was briefly the western terminus of the Pony Express in the early 1860s and of the first transcontinental railroad, which was completed in 1869. Located at the lower end of one of the world's highest-volume watersheds, Sacramento experienced its first flood in 1849. Completion of the Shasta Dam on the Sacramento River in 1949, Folsom Dam on the American in 1956, and Oroville Dam on the Feather in 1968 led to extensive development on the flood plains. A major flood in 1989, which eclipsed all previous runoffs, and local flooding in January 1995 caused local, state, and federal agencies to reassess land use patterns. The completion of Interstate Highways 5 and 80 in the 1960s reaffirmed Sacramento's role as a transportation hub. Several factors shielded the local economy from the problems that beset other regions of California after the cold war. In the 1990s housing and land prices were one-third lower than in the San Francisco Bay area, approximately eighty miles to the southwest. Local, state, and federal government employment provided a stable, albeit declining, share of the job market. With many institutions of higher learning, including community colleges, California State University, Sacramento, and the University of California, Davis, the region has a well-educated labor force. Since the 1970s data processing centers, high-tech manufacturing companies, biotechnology enterprises, and financial services companies were created in or relocated to Sacramento. The city's population increased from 275,741 in 1980 to 366,500 in 1990, when the Sacramento–Yolo County Consolidated Metropolitan Statistical Area had a population of nearly 1.5 million in 1990. From its inception in 1839, when Sutter arrived with a party that included ten Hawaiians, one Belgian, one German, and one Irishman, Sacramento has had a multicultural population. Like the state of California, but at a much slower pace, Sacramento has experienced increased ethnic diversity since the 1970s. In 1989 a national news magazine listed Sacramento as one of the ten best places to live in the United States. Among its amenities are its colleges and universities, a symphony, an opera company, a ballet, many theater companies, and the American River Parkway, which extends more than thirty miles upstream from the Sacramento River to Lake Folsom.

[Robert L. Kelley, *Battling the Inland Sea: American Political Culture, Public Policy, and the Sacramento Valley, 1850–1986* (Berkeley, Calif., 1989); Joseph A. McGowan, *Sacramento: Heart of the Golden State* (Woodland Hills, Calif., 1983).]

GREGG M. CAMPBELL

See also **DAH** and **SUPP:** California.

SAINT LOUIS, located in eastern Missouri, experienced a major population decline from its 1950 high of 856,796 residents to only 396,385 in 1990. Old legislation prevented the city from expanding beyond its 1876 limits, but the metropolitan area continued to advance, to 2.5 million in 1990. Beginning in the 1970s Saint Louis promoters touted an urban renaissance that included an extensively restored railroad station that is also a stylish shopping center. New sports facilities were built, including Busch Memorial Stadium, and the Saint Louis Zoo remains a major tourist attraction. The first parts of a new light rail system were opened to much acclaim. A comprehensive freeway binds much of the metropolitan area. Many old neighborhoods vanished, however, and urban decay, which began after World War II, was a depressing reality in the 1990s. School desegregation was far from complete, although 47 percent of the city's population was African American. For many years the largest city in Missouri, in 1990 Saint Louis fell behind its traditional rival, Kansas City.

[James Neal Primm, *Lion of the Valley: A History of St. Louis* (Boulder, Colo., 1981).]

LAWRENCE H. LARSEN

See also **SUPP:** Kansas City; Missouri.

SALARIES. *See* **Wages and Salaries.**

SALT. *See* **Strategic Arms Limitation Talks.**

SAMOA, AMERICAN, an unincorporated trust territory of the United States in the southern Pacific and consisting of seven islands of the Samoa group. American Samoa approved its first constitution in 1960, but the Samoans rejected the idea of electing their own governor until 1977, when Peter Tali Coleman won office. The Fono, American Samoa's legislature, is bicameral, with the senate made up of *matai* membership and elected representatives in the house. Since 1970 American Samoa has had an official representative in the U.S. Congress. In the 1960s American Samoa saw major changes, receiving congressional funding for roads, schools, and a hospital; economic development in tourism and fisheries; and an experimental television broadcast system in the schools. These efforts and subsequent programs brought about a more Westernized lifestyle than is evident in Western Samoa, along with dependence on U.S. aid. Tuna canning and tourism remained the major industries of American Samoa. Outmigration from the islands is a crucial factor in the economy; in the 1990s there were more Samoans living outside than within American Samoa, and large Samoan communities

existed in Hawaii and California. The 1990 population of American Samoa was 46,773, but it is estimated that more than 60,000 American Samoans lived in the United States. As U.S. nationals, American Samoans travel extensively between Samoan communities "abroad" and the home islands. This escape valve has alleviated the problem of jobs for graduates of the islands' high schools and the Community College of American Samoa. Samoans in the United States nonetheless faced the same problems as other immigrant groups, including the breakdown of traditional authority and kinship roles.

[Frederick Koehler Sutter, *Amerika Samoa* (Honolulu, 1984).]

KAREN M. PEACOCK

SAN ANTONIO, located in south-central Texas, was the tenth-largest city in the United States in 1995. Its culture is strongly influenced by a predominantly Hispanic population and a strong Mexican heritage. San Antonio's historical sites, such as the Alamo, as well as the lovely River Walk along the San Antonio River and family amusement parks, have helped make the city the state's leading tourist center. San Antonio also became a major livestock and agricultural center, but no single factor has shaped modern San Antonio as much as its close ties with the U.S. military. Almost from its beginning as a Spanish outpost in 1718, the city's economy benefited from the military, a relationship that continued well into the twentieth century. By the 1980s San Antonio contained Fort Sam Houston, a fixture in the city since 1879, and Lackland, Kelly, Brooks, and Randolph air force bases. More than 44,000 military personnel lived in San Antonio in the early 1990s and about 35,000 civilians worked for the military. The city experienced a surge of growth in the 1970s and 1980s not only because of the military but also because of an expanding service sector, including health care, thanks to the South Texas Medical Center and the University of Texas Health Center. San Antonio's population in 1990 reached 935,933, a 43 percent increase from its 1970 population of 654,153. The 1995 decision by the Defense Base Closing and Realignment commission to shut down Kelly Air Force Base posed real problems for the city's future prosperity because the closing eliminated 13,000 civilian jobs.

[John L. Davis, *San Antonio: A Historical Portrait* (Austin, Tex., 1978); David R. Johnson, John A. Booth, Richard J. Harris, eds., *The Politics of San Antonio: Community, Progress, and Power* (Lincoln, Nebr., 1983).]

ROBERT B. FAIRBANKS

See also **SUPP:** Texas.

SANCTUARIES. *See* **Wildlife Refuges and Sanctuaries.**

SAN DIEGO, a Pacific port and southern California city located near the border of Mexico's Baja (Lower) California. Occupied by Native Americans, called Kumeyaay, the area was first visited by Europeans when Juan Rodríguez Cabrillo entered the harbor in 1542. Sebastian Vizcaíno gave the city its name in 1602 to honor San Diego de Alcalá, a Spanish Franciscan brother. The region remained unsettled until 1769, when Gaspar de Portolá, governor of Baja California, and Father Junípero Serra founded a military post and mission. During Mexican rule (1821–1846) San Diego became a civilian pueblo occupying the site known today as Old Town. The Mexican War in 1846–1848 brought Americans into the area, and San Diego made a peaceful transition to U.S. control in 1850, the year the city was incorporated. William Heath Davis founded New Town three miles south and close to San Diego Bay in 1850, but the site did not become successful until promoted by Alonzo E. Horton in 1867. By 1872 major businesses and the courthouse had moved to New Town and the first water company was formed in 1873. Arrival of the Santa Fe Railroad in 1884 set off a boom, and although growth slowed during the 1890s, San Diego, with its ideal climate and sandy beaches, continued to prosper well into the twentieth century. San Diego Bay, a natural deepwater harbor, is headquarters for the U.S. Eleventh Naval District and a base of operations for a number of military installations. The San Diego Zoo, Old Globe Theatre, Sea World, Mission Bay Aquatic Park, the Cabrillo National Monument, and a new convention center made tourism a major part of the city's economy. Trends in the 1990s were toward transborder activities and an emphasis on information and high-tech industries, including aerospace, electronics, and biomedical research. The city's population increased from 334,387 in 1950 to 1,110,549 in 1990. It is the seat of San Diego County, which numbered 2,498,016 in 1990.

[Iris H. W. Engstrand, *San Diego: Gateway to the Pacific* (Houston, 1992).]

IRIS H. W. ENGSTRAND

See also **SUPP:** California.

SAN FRANCISCO in the mid-1990s was still one of the most cosmopolitan cities in the United States. Although surpassed in population in 1989 by its Bay Area neighbor San Jose, it remained a center for Pacific Rim finance and trade and a city noted for ethnic and cultural diversity. The fourteenth-largest city in the United States in 1990, and part of the fourth most populous metropolitan area, San Francisco boasted a population of 723,959 that year. From 1970 to the early 1990s its Asian and Pacific Island communities grew from about 13 percent to almost 30 percent of the population. The Hispanic community also expanded (primarily Mexican and Central American immigration), while white residents decreased to about half the population and African Americans to 11 percent.

Known as a liberal city, San Francisco has been an important site for a succession of political and countercultural movements, from the general strike of 1934 to the Beat Generation in the 1950s to the hippies of the 1960s who were drawn to the Haight-Ashbury section and large civil rights and antiwar demonstrations in the 1960s and early 1970s. In the 1990s there was a sizable gay and lesbian community, about 20 percent of the adult population, centered around the Castro district. Voters have elected Democratic mayors since 1963, with John Shelley, Joseph L. Alioto, George Moscone, Dianne Feinstein (the city's first female mayor, later elected to the U.S. Senate in 1992), and Art Agnos heading the city through the end of the 1980s. From his election in 1964 until 1983, the prominent liberal Phillip Burton served San Francisco in the U.S. House of Representatives. Building on a tradition of neighborhood politics and environmentalism, slow-growth movements opposed (with mixed success) local freeway projects and the continued construction of high-rise office buildings in the downtown district. An increasingly strained city budget in the 1980s, however, and the election in 1991 of conservative Democrat and former police chief Frank Jordan as mayor illustrated the many tensions facing the city's liberal politics.

San Francisco's manufacturing sector and seaport business began declining in 1970, but finance, insurance, high-technology, medical science, real estate, transportation, fashion, and low-paying service jobs gained increasing importance in the area's economy. The arts, entertainment, and tourism also played an important role. The city is known for its temperate climate, natural beauty, geographic compactness, abundance of restaurants, and eclectic mix of Victorian, Mediterranean, and postmodern architecture. Tourists and residents enjoy such local attractions and amenities as Golden Gate Park, the cable cars, Fisherman's Wharf, Chinatown, and the Bay Area Rapid Transit (BART), along with an array of museums and national sports teams. San Franciscans have encountered serious challenges since the 1980s. Despite the city's relatively high average income, by 1990 up to 7,000 residents were homeless. More than 7,000 people died in the 1980s of Acquired Immune Deficiency Syndrome (AIDS), the highest per capita rate in the United States. Other shocks included the 1978 murders of Mayor Moscone and gay city supervisor Harvey Milk, the 1989 Loma Prieta earthquake, and a statewide recession in the early 1990s. As San Francisco's population and economy declined relative to that of the surrounding South Bay and suburbs, its role as a hub city diminished, but it was likely to retain its standing as a global city.

[Richard Edward DeLeon, *Left Coast City: Progressive Politics in San Francisco, 1975–1991* (Lawrence, Kans., 1992); William Issel and Robert W. Cherny, *San Francisco, 1865–1932: Politics, Power, and Urban Development* (Berkeley, Calif., 1986).]

ERIC FURE-SLOCUM

See also **SUPP:** California; San Jose.

SAN FRANCISCO EARTHQUAKE (Oct. 17, 1989). At 5:04 P.M., shortly after a nationwide television audience tuned in to a World Series baseball game in San Francisco, the biggest earthquake since the great one of 1906 ripped northern California. Under the Santa Cruz Mountains, sixty miles southeast of the city, a section of the San Andreas fault had broken. As the earthquake vibrations raced outward they collapsed many buildings in small cities such as Santa Cruz and Watsonville near the epicenter and, to the surprise of many experts, also severely shook the low-lying and waterlogged soils near San Francisco Bay with devastating results. Falling buildings, bridges, highways, and other objects killed sixty-three people, most of them caught in cars under the collapsing Cypress Viaduct, a double-deck freeway on Interstate Highway 880 in Oakland, across the bay from San Francisco. In addition a section of roadway in the Bay Bridge connecting San Francisco and Oakland fell in, closing that vital span for a month. The quake injured at least 3,757 people, damaged 18,000 homes and 2,500 businesses, and left 12,000 people homeless. The cost of damage was $6 billion. Geologists refer to the event as the Loma Prieta Earthquake, after a mountain in the rugged region where it started. They place its magnitude at 6.9 to 7.1 and calculate that it ruptured twenty-five miles of fault, at depths from two to twelve miles. Some of the seismic waves may have bounced off deeper layers in the earth's crust and come up in the San Francisco area, possibly explaining why damage was so severe more than fifty miles from the source. Although the earthquake was large, it was far smaller than the 1906 San Francisco quake, which broke 250 miles of the fault and, with a magnitude of 8.0, released about thirty times more energy than the Loma Prieta quake.

[George Plafker and John P. Galloway, eds., *Lessons Learned from the Loma Prieta, California, Earthquake of October 17, 1989*, United States Geological Survey Circular 1045 (1989); State of California Office of Planning and Research, *Competing Against Time: Report to Governor George Deukmejian from the Governor's Board of Inquiry on the 1989 Loma Prieta Earthquake* (North Highlands, Calif., May 1990).]

CHARLES PETIT

See also **DAH:** San Francisco Earthquake; **SUPP:** Earthquakes; Oakland; San Francisco.

SAN JOSE, city in California, was organized in 1777 seven miles below the southern tip of San Francisco Bay in the fertile Santa Clara Valley, but not on navigable water. Despite serving as a depot for gold seekers and incorporation in 1850, it languished until acquisition of railroad connections in 1864. Improved transportation enhanced San Jose's role as an agricultural market, and by 1900 the city had 21,000 inhabitants. Over the next forty years it grew gradually, acquiring important agribusiness concerns. During World War II, under the innovative San Jose Plan, local businesses cooperated to obtain war contracts. The population reached 95,280 in 1950. During the second half of the twentieth century, tremendous growth occurred in San Jose and surrounding Santa Clara County, with the city reaching a population of 204,106 in 1960. The population more than doubled in the next decade, as the economy became more diversified. Electrical plants, military bases, and aerospace activities helped fuel the expansion, as did the rise of computer manufacturing in Silicon Valley. In 1990 San Jose was the eleventh-largest city in the United States with 782,248 people.

LAWRENCE H. LARSEN

See also **SUPP:** California; Silicon Valley.

SANTA CLARA PUEBLO V. MARTINEZ, 436 U.S. 49 (1978). In 1968 Congress enacted the Indian Civil Rights Act, applying certain provisions of the Bill of Rights to Native American tribal governments. Congress left principal responsibility for enforcing the law to tribal authorities. In criminal cases the act gave federal courts only a habeas corpus remedy. Over the years, however, federal judges developed an implied power to grant declaratory or injunctive relief or other civil remedies. As a result of this implied authority federal judges reviewed many policies of the tribal governments. A female member of the Santa Clara Pueblo tribe married a Navajo and had seven children. The Santa Clara Pueblo denied membership to the woman's children based on a tribal ordinance excluding children of female but not male members who married outside the tribe. Children excluded under the tribal ordinance could neither vote nor hold secular office and were not permitted to remain on the reservation in event of the mother's death or to inherit their mother's house or interest in communal lands. The mother asked the federal district court to enjoin enforcement of this gendered ordinance. The district court decided in favor of the mother on the merits, employing an implied jurisdiction to issue an injunction. The representative of the Santa Clara Pueblo appealed, arguing that the Indian Civil Rights Act did not authorize civil actions in federal court for relief against a tribe or its officials. Upon appeal, the Supreme Court through Justice Thurgood Marshall's opinion decided in favor of the tribe and held that the district court possessed no implied jurisdiction. The decision established strong tribal autonomy, except where Congress explicitly provided for federal judicial review.

[Catherine A. MacKinnon, *Feminism Unmodified: Discourses on Life and Law* (Cambridge, Mass., 1987); Susan Sanders Molander, "Case Notes: Indian Civil Rights Act and Sex Discrimination," *Arizona State Law Journal* 1 (1977).]

TONY FREYER

See also **SUPP:** Native Americans; Women's Rights.

SAVINGS AND LOAN CRISIS. One of the most dramatic financial stories of the 1980s was the collapse of hundreds of savings and loan institutions (S&Ls, also known as "thrifts") that had became insolvent in the wake of federal deregulation of the industry. As mandated by law, the government stepped in to protect the federally insured depositors of the failed thrifts, at a cost of billions of dollars. Traditionally, S&Ls had provided savings accounts and long-term residential mortgages and had been restricted by government regulation from offering most other types of financial services. With the failure of many S&Ls in the Great Depression, the Federal Savings and Loan Insurance Corporation (FSLIC) was created in 1934 to protect depositors' money. This system worked well in an environment of stable or falling interest rates, but the industry faced severe pressure from rising interest rates in the late 1960s and throughout the 1970s. S&Ls were forced to pay higher short-term rates to attract and keep deposits but could not increase revenue from the long-term, fixed-interest-rate home mortgages they had issued. In 1966 Congress placed a limit on the interest S&Ls could pay on deposits, setting it slightly higher than the rate allowed to banks. This limitation hurt S&Ls in the 1970s as investors began to shift money to higher-paying Treasury bills and newly created money market mutual funds. At the same time, most S&Ls continued to be prohibited from issuing adjustable-rate home mortgages.

Congress attempted to address these problems through a process of deregulation that started in 1980, when the Depository Institutions Deregulation and Monetary Control Act began to phase out interest-rate ceilings on deposits, allowed S&Ls to compete with banks in offering interest-paying checking accounts, and raised federal insurance on deposits to $100,000 per account. Problems continued and in 1981 for the first time the S&L industry as a whole was unprofitable. The Garn–St. Germain Depository Institutions Act of 1982 extended deregulation by authorizing S&Ls to issue adjustable-rate mortgages, permitting up to 40 percent of assets to be invested in nonresidential real estate loans and up to 10 in commercial loans and generally easing net worth and ownership requirements to give S&Ls more flexibility. Concurrently, several states liberalized their own regulation of state-chartered S&Ls, even as these non–federally chartered institutions still qualified for FSLIC deposit insurance.

The S&L industry grew dramatically. Assets soared from $686 billion in 1982 to $1.1 trillion in 1985. In the same period assets held in the traditional home mortgage market fell from 64.7 percent to 38.1 percent. Much of the increased asset base came from large (usually $100,000) deposits gathered nationally by "money brokers," such as Wall Street securities firms. Certain S&Ls, especially in Texas, Florida, Colorado, Arizona, and California, used their new powers to invest heavily in commercial real estate and even riskier investments, such as the high-paying, low-credit-rated "junk bonds" issued by Wall Street firms in the 1980s. The lavish personal expenditures and flamboyance of some S&L executives, many of whom were new to a traditionally low-key industry, garnered public attention. The fundamental problem that brought down many of these high-flying S&Ls was their inordinate exposure to high-risk and unsound investments that in the Southwest turned sour after oil prices plummeted in the mid-1980s. The high rates of interest paid to depositors and the fact that deposits were federally insured were a formula for disaster. Ultimately, government would be liable for the greed and excess of a certain part of the S&L industry.

As early as 1985 officials of the Federal Home Loan Bank Board (FHLBB), which regulated S&Ls, were aware of these problems and began to try to deal with them. They were hindered for several years by the failure of Congress to support them and by intervention of lawmakers on behalf of specific S&Ls. Still, quicker action by the FHLBB would not have eliminated the bad loans and investments already on the books of S&Ls. To close insolvent institutions required increased capitalization of the FSLIC insurance fund. Congress in 1987 approved a limited increase, inadequate to make much of a dent in the problem. Less money for the FSLIC meant fewer bad S&Ls could be closed, and House Majority Leader Jim Wright of Texas intervened on behalf of a group of Texas S&L owners. The FSLIC requested $15 billion in additional funds but received less than half that amount. The most celebrated case of successful lobbying to thwart federal regulators was that of the "Keating Five." Charles H. Keating, Jr., enlisted the aid of five senators—Alan Cranston of California, Dennis DeConcini and John McCain of Arizona, Donald W. Riegle, Jr., of Michigan, and John Glenn of Ohio—on behalf of his troubled Lincoln Savings and Loan. Keating contributed a total of $1.4 million to the campaign funds of these senators and was able to keep going until 1989, when Lincoln closed at an estimated cost to taxpayers of $2.5 billion. He later served a prison term for securities violations, and the five senators, particularly Cranston, were reprimanded by their colleagues.

Faced with limited congressional cooperation, the FHLBB in 1988 began to close insolvent S&Ls by arranging for their acquisition by outside investors; 205 S&Ls were disposed of in this fashion. The full dimensions of the problem, however, required the attention of President George Bush and Congress, which led in 1989 to the Financial Institutions Reform, Recovery, and Enforcement Act (FIRREA). This sweeping legislation authorized initial borrowing of an additional $50 billion to support the cleanup and established a new agency, the Resolution Trust Corporation (RTC), to carry out this task. The FHLBB was abolished and regulation of the remaining healthy S&Ls was lodged in the Office of Thrift Supervision in the Department of the Treasury. The FSLIC was merged into the Federal Deposit Insurance Corporation, which insured commercial bank deposits. Higher insurance premiums, much tighter net worth requirements, and restrictions on lending and investment practices were placed on S&Ls. This caused additional institutions that had not been greatly involved in the excesses of the 1980s to be closed or merged with banks. By 1995 the RTC had sold or merged 747 insolvent thrifts, leaving a smaller but presumably healthier industry. The cost to taxpayers under FIRREA was $180 billion, significantly higher than the initial expectations when the RTC was created but ultimately less than other estimates, which ranged as high as $500 billion. In any case, the savings and loan crisis was a sobering experience that raised many questions about business, government, and politics in the United States in the late twentieth century.

[Edward J. Kane, *The Gathering Crisis in Federal Deposit Insurance* (Cambridge, Mass., 1985); Lawrence J. White, *The S&L Debacle* (New York, 1991).]

JOHN B. WEAVER

See also **SUPP:** Banking and Finance; Corruption, Political; Deregulation; Junk Bonds; Real Estate Industry; Reaganomics.

SBA. *See* **Small Business Administration.**

SCANDALS. Political, financial, and sexual misconduct by government and business leaders, entertainers, and other well-known figures has occurred in every period of U.S. history. Since the 1970s, however, instances in which private misconduct becomes public scandal have increased dramatically with the burgeoning numbers and intensified scrutiny of news media as well as changing attitudes toward what constitutes "scandalous" behavior. As in the past, scandalous political behavior tends to involve blatant financial corruption such as taking bribes. In the early 1970s, however, the definition of political scandal took on new dimensions with the Watergate cover-up, in which revelations of the abuse of constitutional powers led for the first time to the resignation of a sitting president, Richard M. Nixon. Similarly, members of the Ronald Reagan administration involved in the Iran-Contra scandal of the 1980s were found to have subverted the democratic process for political ends. The 1980s also were marked by financial scandals in the private sector, chief among them the Wall Street insider-trading scandal, which resulted in prison terms for two of the market's most prominent figures, Ivan Boesky and Michael Milken; and the savings and loan debacle, in which some 2,000 deregulated thrift institutions failed because of the rampant greed of directors such as Charles H. Keating, Jr., who went to prison.

Scandals involving adultery and other forms of sexual misconduct have become far more frequent than in the past. Public figures, whether Hollywood stars or U.S. presidents, were once largely protected from exposure of their illicit affairs by journalists and public relations staffers. In the 1980s, however, even the most legitimate news organizations began to justify exposure of such activities as indicative of dishonesty or hypocrisy, as in the cases of the televangelists Jim Bakker and Jimmy Swaggart and of Senator Gary Hart, whose 1984 presidential campaign was derailed when he prevaricated about having an extramarital affair. Changing public mores fueled by the concerns of women also played a role by expanding the moral and legal definition of sexual misconduct to include date rape and sexual harassment and intensifying both censure of and criminal penalties for spousal abuse. Public discussions of these issues were carried on in large part through such widely publicized scandals as the rape trials of Senator Edward Kennedy's nephew, William Kennedy Smith, who was found innocent, and the heavyweight boxing champion Mike Tyson, who was convicted; the Hill-Thomas hearings in 1991 and sexual harassment charges against Senator Robert Packwood of Oregon in 1994–1995; and the 1995 trial of football star turned actor O. J. Simpson, who was acquitted of murdering his ex-wife after an earlier conviction for abuse during their marriage.

While the controversies surrounding these events have forced Americans to reevaluate their moral, religious, and political values, critics worried that the intense media coverage of these and literally hundreds of more minor scandals had created a "culture of scandal" that encouraged an unhealthy degree of public mistrust and cynicism. In an increasingly competitive media landscape, however, it seems a culture of scandal is here to stay.

[Sissela Bok, *Lying* (New York, 1978); Suzanne Garment, *Scandal: The Culture of Mistrust in American Politics* (New York, 1991); George C. Kohn, *Encyclopedia of American Scandal* (New York, 1989).]

JEFFREY M. MERRON

See also **SUPP:** Abscam Scandal; Celebrity Culture; Corruption, Political; Crime, White-Collar; Housing and Urban Development (HUD) Scandal; Iran-Contra Affair; Iraq-gate; Junk Bonds; Korea-gate; Savings and Loan Crisis; Sexual Harassment; Televangelism; Thomas Confirmation Hearings; Watergate, Aftermath of; Whitewater.

SCHOOLING, HOME, which refers to parents educating their children at home instead of sending them to a school, advanced from an eccentricity in the 1960s to a national movement by the 1990s. Home schooling was once a mainstay of education on the American frontier but never enjoyed great popularity in established urban areas. By the mid-1850s religious and political leaders, fearing negative consequences of radical individualism, placed great hope in a universal system of compulsory, public education that would provide the "engine of democracy" for the nation. Over the next century Americans learned, however, that their increasingly bureaucratized educational system could not prevent social ills. By the 1960s a small number of parents had turned to the family as the means of teaching children. While a census is impossible by virtue of the informal, noninstitutional nature of home schooling, the movement has experienced remarkable growth. According to the U.S. Department of Education, the number of children educated at home grew from 15,000 in the early 1970s to 300,000 by the early 1990s. Home-schooled children are most numerous in the West and South. The typical home-schooling family is economically prosperous and white, and at least one parent has some college education. In nine of ten such households the mother does most of the teaching. The average length of home education is one year.

Home-schooling families tend to subscribe to one of two rationales. The vast majority of parents—85 percent in one study—educate children at home for religious reasons. They want their children to learn doctrine that is denied in public schools and that in many cases also reflects a conservative political and social perspective. Other parents doubt that a child's intellectual growth and creativity can flourish in the rigidly structured, bureaucratic setting of most public schools. Home-schooled children perform better on standard tests than children in schools, but critics cite concerns about the social development of children isolated from peers. Researchers disagree as to whether home-schooled children have lower or higher self-esteem than children in school. The home-schooling movement has been marked by legal confusion as to whether children can be excused from school, what must be taught at home, and who is qualified to teach in the home. Home schooling is now legal in all fifty states, but there are no national standards for instruction. Within each state standards often vary from school district to district.

[Jane Van Galen and Mary Anne Pitman, eds., *Home Schooling: Political, Historical, and Pedagogical Perspectives* (Norwood, N.J., 1991); Alfie Kohn, "Home Schooling," *The Atlantic Monthly* 261 (April 1988); Anne Pedersen and Peggy O'Mara, eds., *Schooling at Home: Parents, Kids and Learning* (Santa Fe, N.Mex., 1990).]

PAUL S. VOAKES

See also **DAH** and **SUPP:** Education; **SUPP:** Education, Parental Choice in.

SCHOOLS, COMMUNITY, are committed to broad education and characterized by home, school, and community collaboration to achieve learning. Beginning in the mid-1960s, thousands of small alternative schools sprang up across the United States and Canada. They varied widely in programs and policies, but common factors were a disenchantment with conventional schooling, a desire to reform education, and the belief that schools should be controlled by the population served, including students, parents, teachers, and community members. The National Coalition of Alternative Community Schools was formed in 1976. Community schools include rural schools that serve as community centers, featuring educational and social programs; others are independent neighborhood schools meeting academic, social, and cultural needs of children of African Americans, Hispanic Americans, Latino Americans, Native Americans, and Asian Americans. The New York State Community School Program organized public inner-city schools as sites for the delivery of social services to needy children and their families. Community schools described as "integrative" have sought to bring disabled students into the regular school program. Corporate community schools created partnerships among business executives, educators, and community leaders to establish and operate business-sponsored elementary schools in inner cities. Their goal is to reform urban public education by setting standards and demonstrating instructional methods and school management that can be used across the country.

[Mary Leue, *Challenging the Giant* (Albany, 1992); Heleen Owen, "Community Schools and Service Integration in New York," *Equity and Choice* 6 (1990).]

MARY DEANE SORCINELLI

See also **SUPP:** Education.

SCHOOLS, FOR-PROFIT. The idea of schools for profit is rooted in the growing discontent with public schools that began in the 1960s, but an experiment in performance contracting, the hiring by public schools of private companies to provide instruction with remuneration dependent on student achievement, was deemed ineffective in a 1972 government report. Responding to widespread calls in the late 1980s for broad educational reforms, media entrepreneur Christopher Whittle and businessman John Golle offered for-profit school plans to redesign U.S. schools. In May 1991 Whittle announced the Edison Project, a plan for a multibillion-dollar chain of 150 to 200 private schools, which he declared would provide better instruction at lower per-pupil cost than public schools. A year later Whittle hired Benno C. Schmidt, Jr., president of Yale University, to head the project. After failing to raise sufficient capital, the project was scaled back, focusing instead on obtaining management contracts with existing schools or to winning public funds to establish new schools. In March 1994 Massachusetts became the first state to award charters for the project to operate schools. Meanwhile, Golle started Education Alternatives, Inc. (EAI), in 1986. His first schools, which opened in 1987, did not make money, so he turned to managing public schools. Following mixed results in Miami, Fla., and Duluth, Minn., EAI gained a $133 million contract to operate nine inner-city schools in Baltimore. At the end of its second year of operation, EAI showed significant positive changes in parent involvement, facilities maintenance, and student performance on standardized tests. Supporters of for-profit schools envision positive changes resulting from incentive management. Detractors declare dismay at the money-making and believe proliferation of private schools would further undermine the public schools and widen the existing chasm in educational quality between children from affluent and less-well-off families. Teachers' unions almost universally oppose for-profit schools.

[Kenneth Jost, "Private Management of Public Schools," *CQ Researcher* (Mar. 25, 1994); Myron Lieberman, *Privatization and Educational Choice* (New York, 1989).]

MYRNA W. MERRON

See also **DAH** and **SUPP:** Education.

SCHOOLS, MAGNET. A desire to help multicultural communities achieve academic excellence has led to the establishment of magnet schools in urban districts throughout the country. They differ from regular or zoned schools in three ways—by emphasizing a special core curriculum or special method of instruction, voluntary enrollment and open access beyond the geographic attendance zone, and by promoting student and parental involvement. In some big cities magnet schools have effected markedly reduced levels of racial, ethnic, and socioeconomic isolation in elementary and secondary schools.

[Mary Haywood Metz, *Different by Design: The Context and Character of Three Magnet Schools* (New York, 1986); Inger Morton, *Improving Urban Education with Magnet Schools* (New York, 1991).]

MARY DEANE SORCINELLI

See also **SUPP:** Education; Schools, Community.

SCHOOLS, PRIVATE. Enrollment in private elementary and secondary schools in the United States rose to nearly 6.4 million students in 1965, fell to 5 million during the 1970s, and since then has fluctuated between 5 and 5.7 million (approximately 10 to 13 percent of the total school population). Much of the decline was in Catholic schools, which in 1965 accounted for almost 90 percent of students in private schools but by 1990 enrolled only about 55 percent. The number of Catholic schools fell from a record 13,292 in 1965 to 8,587 in 1990 as Catholic migration to the suburbs and increased Catholic enrollment in public schools closed many inner-city schools. A growing number of non-Catholic religious schools, 11,476 by 1990 (46 percent of private schools), offset the Catholic school decline. Still, they only enrolled 31 percent of private school students, with approximately 4,483 nonsectarian institutions serving the rest. Nonsectarian schools frequently addressed particular educational concerns: preparatory schools provided rigorous training for college, military academies stressed discipline, and Waldorf and Montessori schools offered alternative educational philosophies. The increased number of non-Catholic religious schools came largely from growth of evangelical Christian academies. These academies responded to the concerns of parents about societal problems (drug abuse, violence, and sexual promiscuity) and the apparent unfriendliness of public schools toward Christianity, which critics attributed to an advancing secular humanist ideology. For similar reasons a rapidly increasing number of families—estimated in the 1990s at about 300,000—engaged in home schooling.

Private preschools also experienced a boom. Whether run by churches, employers, or entrepreneurs, these centers responded to the increased demand for child care created when growing numbers of women entered the labor force out of economic necessity or personal preference. The U.S. Department of Education study "A Profile of Child Care Settings" estimated that between 1976 and 1990 the number of child care centers increased from 18,307 serving 897,700 children to 55,960 serving 3.8 million.

Critics of the public schools proposed such reforms as tuition tax credits and school vouchers to enable private schools to compete for government funds, thereby increasing educational options for families and pressuring public schools to operate more efficiently. This "school choice" proposal gained national attention when President Ronald Reagan advocated it in 1981 and when President George Bush included it in the America 2000 Excellence in Education Act that he introduced in 1991. The religious nature of many private schools led to protests that school choice, besides undermining public education, would violate church and state separation. (Since the 1940s the U.S. Supreme Court has rarely allowed religiously affiliated private schools to have access to public funds.) President Bill Clinton consequently excluded school choice measures from his version of America 2000, the Goals 2000: Educate America Act of 1994. Nonetheless, several states—including California, Minnesota, New York, and Wisconsin—adopted or tested school choice programs.

[James C. Carper and Thomas C. Hunt, eds., *Religious Schooling in America* (Birmingham, Ala., 1984); Peter W. Cookson, *School Choice* (New Haven, Conn., 1994); Abbie Gordon Klein, *The Debate Over Child Care, 1969–1990* (Albany, N.Y., 1992).]

ALFRED LINDSAY SKERPAN

See also **SUPP:** Education; Education, Cooperative; Education, Experimental; Schooling, Home.

SCHOOLS, RESEGREGATION OF. In the landmark case *Brown* v. *Board of Education of Topeka* (1954), the Supreme Court decided school segregation was immoral and unconstitutional. Forty years later the desegregation of U.S. public schools remained unfinished. Even after court-ordered desegregation, a school district could remain segregated through what is termed "resegregation." School resegregation is the process that separates students by racial or ethnic groups within desegregated schools. Resegregation may result from allocating elementary students to separate classrooms or sorting them within classrooms according to ability. In junior and senior high schools, tracking or homogeneous grouping by ability reduces opportunities for cross-racial contact. Students of color may be disproportionately selected and removed from the classroom for special, compensatory, or bilingual education. Disciplinary policies may contribute to disproportionate suspension or expulsion of students of color. To reduce resegregation, schools have looked to alternatives. Recommendations have included assessing and assigning students to groups based on different and richer kinds of information standards; organizing instruction to encourage heterogeneous classrooms; and advocating cooperative learning as a model for mixed-ability grouping. Such techniques appear to have a positive effect on both race relations and achievement. Other measures include encouraging interracial contact in extracurricular activities and discipline that emphasizes keeping students in school rather than suspending them.

[Janet Eyler et al., *Resegregation* (Nashville, 1982).]

MARY DEANE SORCINELLI

See also **DAH**: *Brown* v. *Board of Education of Topeka;* Busing; Integration; **SUPP**: Civil Rights Movement; Education, Cooperative; Educational Testing.

SCHOOLS, SINGLE-SEX. Before the American Revolution most formal schooling was all-male. The common school movement of the mid-nineteenth century eliminated almost all single-sex primary schooling, while female seminaries and, later, colleges exposed women to some advanced subjects pursued by men in all-male colleges. High schools and some colleges and universities offered coeducational instruction by the late nineteenth century. Private schools and colleges have been virtually the only single-sex schools in the twentieth century, and large numbers of them became coeducational for financial reasons and as a result of the women's movement in the 1970s and 1980s. In 1986 only 6 percent of colleges and universities and 24 percent of private schools were single sex. In the 1980s proponents of the remaining women's colleges often argued that single-sex schooling best enables women to learn.

[David Tyack and Elisabeth Hansot, *Learning Together: A History of Coeducation in American Schools* (New Haven, Conn., 1990).]

CHRISTINE A. OGREN

See also **DAH**: Academies; **DAH** and **SUPP**: Colleges and Universities; **SUPP**: Coeducation; Colleges, Women's.

SCIENCE MUSEUMS. The first public science museum was the Ashmolean Museum, founded at Oxford University in England in 1683 and based on the natural history collections of the scholar, Elias Ashmole, and created to educate and entertain the English public. In the United States the Franklin Institute in Philadelphia (founded 1824) and the American Institute of New York (1828) were among the first organizations to hold exhibitions of scientific developments. For many years only natural history science museums existed, such as the Smithsonian Institution (1846), American Museum of Natural History (1869), and Chicago's Field Museum of Natural History (1893), which served as depositories for rich collections of specimens ranging from plants and animals to geological materials and human artifacts. By 1969 two different types of science museums existed—the traditional natural science museum with its collections for viewing and the science museum that incorporated science and technology with participatory activities. Oskar von Miller was the first person to create exhibits that were participatory in nature, with the establishment in 1903 of the Deutsches Museum in Munich, Germany. He called the exhibits "experimental exhibits." Almost all modern day science and technology museums emulated this style, including the National Air and Space Museum, which is part of the Smithsonian and opened in 1976. The majority of science and technology institutions are not involved in research, but are more involved in the hands-on interpretation of science. The traditional natural science museum is deeply involved in research and the care of collections, and are storehouses for the world's natural treasures.

Many science museums had their beginnings in world fairs. The first major international exhibition of a world fair of science was the 1851 Exhibition of the Industry of All Nations, better known as the Crystal Palace Exhibition and sponsored by the Royal Society of Arts in London; a similar exhibition with the same name was held in New York City in 1853. The well-known Museum of Science and Industry in Chicago occupies the sole surviving building from the 1893 World's Columbian Exhibition; it opened as a museum during the Century of Progress International Exhibition (1933–1934). The participatory science movement in the United States began in the 1970s, and by the 1990s there were 23 major science and technology centers and some 260 smaller institutions. The first major science and technology museum that did not house collections was the Exploratorium in San Francisco, which opened its doors in the early

1970s after a European tour of science museums by its founding director, Frank Oppenheimer. During his tour he had the opportunity to visit the Deutsches Museum and to bring back the museum's hands-on philosophy. The exhibits created at the Exploratorium proved to be so successful that Oppenheimer and his associates published a two-volume manual called *The Cookbook,* the first guidebook on building interactive exhibits. Many of the Exploratorium's exhibits have been copied and are in use by the majority of science centers that have been created since the early 1970s. These museums are constantly seeking ways to involve visitors. Science museums in the United States are a very diverse group. Many have gone through major additions, such as the Saint Louis Science Center (1959), which, in addition to pre-Columbian North American Indian artifacts, has modern interactive exhibits on the world we live in and the environment. Discovery Place in Charlotte, N.C. (1981), has a living rain forest and in 1991 added an omnimax theater and a large planetarium. Planetariums, such as Adler Planetarium (1930) in Chicago have also added interactive science exhibits. The California Museum of Science and Industry (1880) in Los Angeles houses exhibits on aerospace and computer-aided design and manufacturing. The Oregon Museum of Science and Industry (1944) in Portland has exhibits on earthquakes, computers, and electricity. Zoos, aquariums, and national parks have also added small science museums to their exhibit areas.

[Victor J. Danilov, *Science and Technology Centers* (Cambridge, Mass., 1982).]

FREDA H. NICHOLSON

See also **DAH:** Exhibition of the Industry of All Nations; Field Museum of Natural History; Science, Popularization of; Smithsonian Institution; World's Columbian Exposition; **SUPP:** Museums.

SCIENCE TELEVISION. Popular awareness of science in the United States is often linked to the launch of *Sputnik,* the first artificial satellite, by the Soviet Union in 1957. That event was covered on television by newscaster Walter Cronkite with the help of a blackboard and rudimentary animation and helped launch his career as America's first broadcast science journalist. Cronkite later became the narrator for the first network science shows, *21st Century* and *Universe.* In the early 1960s the British Broadcasting Corporation (BBC) launched a second channel with a mandate to develop popular science programming. The result was the forty-five-minute weekly series

Horizon, which began as a live studio-based show with filmed segments but soon developed into a documentary series with each episode shot entirely on film and devoted to a single science theme. American public television's first science programs were explicitly modeled on the BBC example. In 1974 Boston-based producer Michael Ambrosino recruited several *Horizon* producers and created the one-hour weekly Public Broadcasting System series *NOVA,* the longest-running science documentary series in the United States, reaching 25 million viewers a month. In 1980 astronomer Carl Sagan attracted an enormous audience with his lavishly produced thirteen-part series *Cosmos,* which set the stage for a decade of multipart science series backed by major corporations and featuring glossy production style and spectacular animation. In the 1990s cable-television stations, such as the Discovery Channel, broadened the range of outlets for science programming. Audience research has shown that certain subjects, notably archaeology, paleontology, and astronomy, consistently draw many viewers. Some subject areas, such as chemistry or theoretical physics, are notoriously difficult to present in the type of "story" format demanded by television viewers. Outstanding science programs for children are *Newton's Apple* and *3-2-1.*

EVAN HADINGHAM

SCIENTIFIC FRAUD. In the late 1970s and 1980s the media called attention to incidents in which scientists falsified research data or plagiarized the work of others. Although cases of fraud have been recorded throughout the history of science, disclosures of these new incidents suggested that many research universities had failed to investigate charges of fraud and that individuals who made charges (sometimes called "whistle-blowers") were frequently singled out for retaliation. In 1985 Congress required research institutions to develop an administrative process for handling reports of fraud in connection with biomedical and behavioral research supported by the Public Health Service. The new federal Office of Research Integrity was established in the Department of Health and Human Services to develop regulations and provide oversight for institutional reviews. In 1987 the National Science Foundation authorized its inspector general to develop similar regulations. The effort to devise regulations and procedures has been complicated by disagreement over definitions of fraud or misconduct in science, conflicts regarding division of labor between federal agencies and research institutions, and complexities of fact-finding and due process. The first case of scientific fraud to receive attention in a federal court involved a research scientist, Dr. Stephen E. Breuning, formerly at the Western Psychiatric Institute of the University of Pittsburgh Medical School. Dr. Breuning in 1988 pleaded guilty to two charges of providing false reports involving federally funded research, for which he was sentenced to a fine and community service. A central issue in discussions of scientific fraud is the extent to which the research environment contributes to misconduct. Although many scientists believe that fraud is rare, incentives such as the pressure to publish have been cited. Several research institutions therefore have developed guidelines that not only describe procedures for investigating charges of fraud but also address such issues as credit for contributions, exchange of materials or data, dissemination of preliminary research results, and peer review.

[Alexander Kohn, *False Prophets* (New York, 1986); National Academy of Sciences, Committee on Science, Engineering, and Public Policy, *Responsible Science: Ensuring the Integrity of the Research Process,* 2 vols. (Washington, D.C., 1992–1993).]

ROSEMARY CHALK

See also **SUPP:** National Science Foundation.

SCULPTURE. The late 1960s saw the rise of minimalism as the dominant art form in sculpture. Minimalism can be viewed as a logical extension and exploration of the ideas of late modernist sculpture produced by such artists as David Smith. Late modern sculpture was pushing toward a purified non-illusionistic form expressed through basic geometric structures. The pioneering minimalists, Donald Judd, Robert Morris, Dan Flavin, and Carl André, reduced their sculptures to essentials, removing the artist's touch. Judd's metallic boxes were factory fabricated according to his specifications. André's modular work used presized timbers and bricks. Minimalists dispensed with pedestals and bases, hoping to achieve engagement between viewer and art object without the artifice of illusion a formal "frame." If the ends of minimalism seemed simple enough, the means were multifaceted and intellectually charged. It explored notions of time and space, measurement, mathematics, proportional systems, and perceptual psychology. Minimalists included Beverly Pepper, Richard Serra, and southern California artists Robert Irwin and Larry Bell. Minimalism achieved acceptance in the 1970s, when it influenced the Inter-

national style of architecture favored by corporate America, but many artists felt constrained by the purity of minimalism. They could not ignore the social issues that were gripping the country—the Vietnam War, pollution, sexism, racism, and consumerism. Four movements followed minimalism, ushering in the postmodern era: process art, conceptual art, earth art, and performance art.

Eva Hesse, Jackie Winsor, and Hans Haacke were important process artists. Hesse created soft, organic hanging works that were rich with generative and sexual metaphor. She allowed materials and techniques to influence her sculpture and, in contrast to the minimalists, used such fragile and malleable materials as cheesecloth and latex. Winsor subjected her meticulously self-constructed cubes to fire and explosives. Haacke used the cube to create self-contained "weather boxes" that addressed the relation between nature and culture. In response to the increasing commercialism of the art world, conceptual artists focused on ideas behind their sculpture. Artists such as Sol LeWitt, Robert Morris, and Joseph Kosuth expressed their ideas through temporary installations. LeWitt's *All Variations of Incomplete Open Cubes* (1974) was an investigation of the mental possibilities of permutation. Morris's *Steam Cloud* (1969) represented an attempt at deobjectification. As early as 1965, with *One and Three Chairs,* Kosuth investigated the relation between language and visual art. His text-object sculpture continues to influence artists who often make reference to semiotics and linguistics.

Earth art is exemplified by *Spiral Jetty,* constructed in Utah's Great Salt Lake by Robert Smithson in 1970. Prompted by environmental concerns, large-scale earthworks were created throughout the 1970s with the aid of heavy machinery and complex engineering. Walter de Maria's *Lightning Field,* completed in 1977, and Michael Hiezer's *Double Negative* (1970) are striking examples of what was accomplished by earth artists. Prominent women sculptors of earth art include Alice Aycock, Nancy Holt, and Ana Mendieta. Influenced by sacred architecture, Holt was known for her precise celestial orientations. By the late 1970s many sculptors turned to performance art. Seeking to engage their audiences, Laurie Anderson, Chris Burden, and Bruce Nauman often used film or video. Performance art verges on theater but it also illustrates the interdisciplinary nature of contemporary art. Burden, known for his masochistic performances, created such politically charged installations as *The Reason for the Neutron Bomb* (1979).

Impressive public sculptures were commissioned throughout the 1970s and 1980s. Some commissions were publicly acclaimed, such as Isamu Noguchi's 1975 design for Hart Plaza in Detroit, while others, such as minimalist Serra's site-specific *Tilted Arc,* installed in Federal Plaza in New York City, met with negative criticism; *Tilted Arc* was removed in 1989. Maya Lin's abstract design for the Vietnam War Memorial in Washington, D.C., dedicated in 1982, so disappointed conservative critics that a figurative sculptural grouping of three soldiers by Frederick Hart was added.

The pluralistic sculpture of the 1980s was known as new image art. Minimalism had lost momentum and sculptors returned to figurative and metaphorical subjects borrowed from art history and science, appropriating it in surprising ways. The sculpture of Nancy Graves derived from study of taxidermy and fossils. Joel Shapiro constructed minimal stick figures from modules similar to those of André. Scott Burden's rock chairs seemed to be both natural rock formation and functional furniture. Jonathan Borofsky and Siah Armajani created multilayered sculptures that elude precise meaning. In the late 1980s Duane Hanson and John DeAndrea made hyperrealist sculpture. Countering it were the colorful and active neoexpressionist wall assemblages of Judy Pfaff and the brooding abstract bronzes of Julian Schnabel. The 1990s were characterized by variety, exemplified by exhibitions at New York City's Whitney Museum, in which the sculpture ranged from the sardonic pop-inspired objects of Jeff Koons to the elegant abstract pieces of Martin Puryear and the socially poignant installations of Jenny Holzer.

[Richard Armstrong and Richard Marshall, eds., *The New Sculpture, 1965–1975: Between Geometry and Gesture* (New York, 1990); Robert Atkins, *Art Speak: A Guide to Contemporary Ideas, Movements, and Buzzwords* (New York, 1990); Lucy Lippard, *Overlay: Contemporary Art and the Art of Prehistory* (New York, 1983); Daniel Wheeler, *Art Since Mid-Century: 1945 to the Present* (New York, 1991).]

PETER C. SUCHECKI

See also **SUPP:** Architecture; Painting.

SDI. *See* **Strategic Defense Initiative.**

SEALING AND WHALING. For centuries sealing and whaling were accepted means of extracting wealth from the sea. After Earth Day in 1970, however, U.S. citizens began to see these practices as cruel and unnecessary. Environmental groups that opposed sealing and whaling effectively used the media to gain support in the United States, where few people earned their livings from either pursuit. Sealing had long been an important livelihood on the northeast and northwest coasts of North America. On the Pribilof Islands in the Bering Sea, Aleuts working for private companies in 1867–1910 and then the federal government in 1910–1984 harvested adolescent male fur seals for the fashion industry. The government discontinued the harvest in 1984 when protests against sealing and the fur industry intensified. The harvesting of harp seal pups on the other side of the American subcontinent created a storm of protest. Young harp seals have beautiful, almost pure white coats that serve as excellent camouflage on ice floes against natural predators. Each spring, fishermen from Newfoundland seeking to supplement their meager incomes headed out to the ice floes to gather seal pelts, which involved clubbing the animal on the head and removing the skin. The killing spawned criticism from environmentalists who noted that furs were luxury items and that continued harvesting of the young threatened the species. Television crews filmed the appalling scenes of slaughter. Although harvesting of young seals was a minor problem in the long list of environmental crises facing the global community, the undeniable appeal of baby mammals made it a headline issue that fueled the growth of the environmental and animal rights movements.

Whereas protest against sealing revolved around the animals' appearance, protest against whaling depended largely on the rarity, intelligence, and awe-inspiring presence of whales. By the 1970s most whale species were approaching extinction. Environmental groups, such as Greenpeace and the American Cetacean Society, undertook an ambitious plan to educate U.S. citizens, harass whalers, and challenge the International Whaling Commission (IWC), which had worked ineffectually for decades to maintain whale stocks. In 1972 Congress passed the Marine Mammal Protection Act, which in conjunction with other legislation required the Commerce Department to restrict imports from any country that pursued any policy that harmed worldwide stocks of seals, whales, or dolphins. Throughout the 1970s and 1980s the United States was one of the leaders in pushing the IWC to action. U.S. resolve was crucial in halting most whaling.

[Briton Busch, *The War Against the Seals* (Kingston, Ont., 1985); Richard Ellis, *Men and Whales* (New York, 1991).]

KURK DORSEY

SEATTLE is located in the western part of Washington State, on Puget Sound 120 miles inland from the Pacific Ocean. With a 1994 population of 531,400 and 2.5 million more in the three-county Consolidated Metropolitan Statistical Area, Seattle is the largest city and leading commercial center of the Pacific Northwest. Its traditional economic base has rested on forestry, fishing, and transpacific trade, but during World War II the city became a center of the aircraft industry. Native Americans, including the chief for whom the city was named, had villages along the shore before the first Euro-Americans settled there in 1851. Fishing, timber cutting, and the milling of lumber destined for California were early industries as the village spread along Elliott Bay. Several early developments helped assure a permanent role for Seattle. The city acquired the territorial (later state) university in 1861, and a substantial business district was rebuilt after a fire in 1889 destroyed wooden buildings and piers. After becoming the terminus of the Great Northern Railway in 1893, Seattle emerged as a taking-off point and provision supplier for prospectors headed for the Klondike gold rush in 1897; the physical expansion of the city was made possible when hills were leveled early in the twentieth century to fill tideflats and ravines. A vital labor movement, highlighted by a citywide general strike in 1919, gave Seattle a radical reputation, but it also helped create a population of emerging middle-class homeowners and few extremes of rich and poor.

A growing identity and self-assurance followed World War II, but Seattle entered the 1970s suffering from a severe recession after the dominant Boeing Company experienced reverses common to the cyclical aircraft industry. Prosperity returned as Boeing and the area diversified. Container shipping facilities revitalized water-borne commerce, and an electronics and computer software industry emerged. The city struggled to offset the growth of burgeoning suburban areas and maintain a viable downtown while also seeking to strengthen neighborhoods. A covered stadium, an aquarium, a convention center, an art museum, and an underground bus tunnel were built downtown. Culturally, Seattle in the 1990s was marked by increasing ethnic diversification and influence, although the dominant white population remained three-fourths of the total; many newcomers arrived from small Asian nations. A popular youth culture of "grunge" dress and music became nationally influential. Seattle's reputation for surrounding natural beauty, increasing cultural and recreational amenities, and a casual lifestyle made the city attractive to visitors and potential residents even as officials wrestled with major transportation difficulties, educational inequities, and emerging crime problems.

[Murray Morgan, *Skid Road: An Informal Portrait of Seattle* (Seattle, 1982); Roger Sale, *Seattle Past and Present* (Seattle, 1976).]

CHARLES P. LEWARNE

See also **DAH:** Puget Sound; Seattle World's Fair; **DAH** and **SUPP:** Washington, State of.

SELF-HELP MOVEMENT is a vast collection of mostly small, local groups of people loosely linked through national newsletters or associations. These groups seek to reach, through mutual support, such goals as physical, mental, and spiritual enhancement; the ability to cope with loss or social stigma; upgrading occupational status; improving interpersonal relations; and achieving competence in specialized activities. Although physicians, social workers, therapists, clergy, and other professionals often initially form and convene self-help groups, their continued involvement is usually limited. Groups have not been the only vehicle through which self-help activities have been undertaken. With the development and growth in popularity of videocassettes and personal computers, along with books, magazines, and recordings, entrepreneurs have created a huge and thriving industry of self-help materials that consumers can use by themselves. This trend appears to have diminished the need for groups, making self-help less a grassroots social movement and more a vast sea of isolated individuals seeking personal change.

[Alfred H. Katz and Eugene I. Bender, *The Strength in Us: Self-Help Groups in the Modern World* (New York, 1976); Stephen Starker, *Oracle at the Supermarket: The American Preoccupation with Self-Help Books* (New Brunswick, N.J., 1989).]

NORMAN GEVITZ

SEMICONDUCTORS. The electrical conductivity of this class of solids is less than that of conductors but greater than that of insulators. Highly refined semiconducting elements such as silicon and germanium can be made more conductive by adding trace impurities, a process called doping. Electron-rich or electron-deficient elements produce negative (n-type) or positive (p-type) semiconductors that, when joined together, create one-way gates for electric current (diodes). More complex electrical junctions lead to devices that can amplify weak electrical signals (transistors), store electric charges (electronic memory), or convert electric energy to light (solid-state lasers and photodiodes).

Invention of the junction transistor in 1948 produced a revolution in the military and consumer electronics industries and allowed for the development of fast and efficient electronic computers. In little more than a decade transistors replaced bulky and inefficient vacuum tubes. Breakthroughs in technology enabled the coupling of diodes and transistors into integrated circuits and computer processing chips. Computer chips containing more than a million switches (bits) per square millimeter were commonplace by the 1990s, and three-dimensional stacks of these chips permitted densities exceeding one billion switches per cubic inch. Because electrical signals cannot travel faster than the speed of light, the increasing speeds at which computers processed information were linked to development of high-density microchips.

In addition to use in computers and consumer electronics, semiconductor devices find wide application in solar energy and in light-sensing, where large arrays of microscopic detectors (charge-coupled devices, or CCDs) produce highly sensitive, high-resolution video cameras and astronomical telescopes. Miniaturized chemical detectors also are possible by depositing thin reactive films onto semiconductors, with applications ranging from detecting polychlorinated biphenyl (PCB) vapors in office buildings and drug levels in the blood to monitoring hydrogen levels in the cabin of a space shuttle.

[Alan M. Litke and Andreas Schwarz, "The Silicon Microstrip Detector," *Scientific American* (May 1995); Gary Stix, "Toward 'Point One,'" *Scientific American* (February 1995); Ken Zweibel, "Thin Film Photovoltaic Cells," *American Scientist* (July-August 1993).]

DAVID K. LEWIS

See also **DAH** and **SUPP:** Computers; **SUPP:** Computer Industry.

SERIAL KILLINGS. According to the National Institute of Justice, serial killings, or serial murders, are series of two or more murders committed as separate events, usually but not always by one offender acting alone over a period of time ranging from hours to years. Often the motive is psychological, with the offender's behavior and the evidence reflecting sadistic, sexual overtones. Law enforcement officials estimate that in the 1990s there were between thirty and fifty serial killers active at any given time in the United States. Records of serial killings in the fif-

teenth and sixteenth centuries and the murders by Jack the Ripper in nineteenth-century England attest that the practice is not new, nor are serial killings strictly a U.S. phenomenon. The former Soviet Union bred a number of serial killers, although their existence did not become manifest until the collapse of communism in 1990. Andrei Chikatilo, a schoolteacher and factory procurer from the small coal-mining town of Shakti, holds the modern record—fifty-two known killings, mostly children under the age of twelve. The largest number of serial killers, however, have been North American. Although victims of serial murders are few in comparison with other murders, the twentieth century saw a marked increase in serial killings. Serial murders are committed by members of all races and both genders, acting in pairs or even in gangs, but the greatest number are committed by single white males. A small percentage of serial murderers act because of greed or the possibility of gain. Curiously, the number of female killers with such purposes is almost triple that for female serial killers who act for other reasons. Serial killings, once recognized, receive great attention from the media. Among the most notorious serial killers of the second half of the twentieth century are Ted Bundy, who raped and murdered women in several states in the 1970s and 1980s (executed in 1989); Albert DeSalvo, known as the Boston Strangler; New York's David Berkowitz, known as Son of Sam; Wayne Williams of Atlanta; Richard Ramirez of southern California; and Jeffrey L. Dahmer, who by his own admission tortured, killed, and dismembered men and boys in Milwaukee and was convicted in 1992 of killing fifteen. Sentenced to fifteen consecutive life terms, Dahmer was himself bludgeoned to death in prison in 1994.

[David Lester, *Serial Killers* (Philadelphia, 1995); Michael Newton, *Hunting Humans* (Port Townsend, Wash., 1990); Joel Norris, *Serial Killers* (New York, 1988).]

ROBERT M. GUTH

See also **DAH** and **SUPP:** Crime.

SET-ASIDES, a form of affirmative action used by governments in contracting government business, including programs that typically designate a percentage of government contracts or funds (either for services or construction of public works) for minority-owned businesses. In 1977 Congress passed a law that directed 10 percent of federal public works funds to minority-controlled businesses. The Public Works Employment Act defined these businesses as ones in which 50 percent of the business was held by African Americans, Hispanics, Asian Americans, Native Americans, Eskimos, or Aleuts. Set-asides are adopted in the belief that government support for minority-owned businesses will help overcome traditional economic disadvantages minorities have faced and promote economic development in minority communities. Like affirmative action programs generally, set-aside programs are controversial. Opponents claim that they constitute reverse discrimination and are not cost efficient, because contracts go to businesses that may not have been the lowest bidder or the most qualified.

Constitutional challenges to set-aside programs have met with mixed results. In *Fullilove* v. *Klutznick* (1980) the Supreme Court upheld the 1977 federal program, finding it did not violate the equal protection clause of the Fifth Amendment or Title VI of the Civil Rights Act of 1964 because it was a legitimate exercise of Congress's spending power. In *City of Richmond* v. *J. A. Croson Company* (1989), however, the Court struck down a municipal set-aside program, stating that the Fourteenth Amendment authorizes Congress, not state and local governments, to create remedies for racial discrimination. This decision called into question the constitutionality of similar programs in twenty-two states. In 1993 the Court permitted contractors in Jacksonville, Fla., to file suit against that city's program, which was modeled after the 1977 federal statute *(Northeastern Florida Chapter of the Associated General Contractors of America* v. *City of Jacksonville)*. Signaling a new level of skepticism about all such programs, in 1995 the Court held that the federal government must be subject to the same "strict scrutiny" as state and local governments when attempting to remedy discrimination. In *Adarand Constructors, Inc.* v. *PENA* the Supreme Court rejected a federal set-aside program established in the Small Business Act to aid "socially disadvantaged individuals."

[Kent Greenawalt, *Discrimination and Reverse Discrimination* (New York, 1983).]

KATY J. HARRIGER

See also **SUPP:** Affirmative Action; *Richmond* v. *J. A. Croson Company.*

SEXUAL HARASSMENT, the most common and often most subtle form of sexual abuse experienced by women in the United States, was frequently trivialized as unimportant until the Senate confirmation hearings of Clarence Thomas for the Supreme Court in October 1991. The testimony of Anita Hill, who worked for Thomas while he was director of the Equal Employment Opportunity Commission (EEOC), was met with sexist responses by senators who supported President George Bush's nomination of Thomas and gave sexual harassment prominence as a serious issue. By the mid-1990s the United States led the industrialized world with respect to sexual harassment legislation and guidelines, according to a 1992 report by the International Labor Organization. The Thomas confirmation hearings prompted such concern among women across the United States that in 1992 an unprecedented number ran for political office and won. Twenty-one obtained state executive office and 1,374 entered state legislatures. Eleven women ran for the U.S. Senate, several of them opposing men who had supported Thomas; five won, as did one female incumbent. Twenty-nine women (twenty-two of them new members) won in races for the House of Representatives, for a total of forty-eight. Also significant during the 1992 elections was the fact that a variety of sexual accusations became major issues in state and national races involving several male politicians. In 1993, for the first time in American history, a president had to take sexual harassment charges into consideration when making appointments to office. That same year the U.S. Navy issued guidelines to prevent sexual harassment within its ranks following the embarrassment, firings, and resignations caused by the Tailhook incident of 1991, when drunken naval aviators assaulted female officers at the aviators' annual convention.

In its broadest sense, sexual harassment is the unwanted imposition of sexual requirements in the context of a relationship of unequal power. As more technically defined by the 1980 guidelines of EEOC, sexual harassment can be any behavior that has the "purpose or effect of unreasonably interfering with an individual's work performance or creating an intimidating or hostile or offensive environment . . . [including] unwelcome sexual advances, requests for sexual favors, and other verbal or physical conduct of a sexual nature." Despite this inclusive federal definition, during the presidency of Ronald Reagan (1981–1989) the EEOC under Thomas did not make the enforcement of sexual harassment a top priority. It is estimated that anywhere from 30 to 70 percent of all working women will experience or have experienced some type of sexual harassment. (Figures for sexual harassment vary dramatically because there have been no national statistical studies that controlled for type of job—blue-collar, pink-collar, or white-collar female workers—let alone women in professional or executive positions.) In the mid-1970s surveys indicated that women in factories and the military experienced more sexual harassment than pink- or white-collar clerical personnel. A 1981 study of federal government workers indicated that 42 percent had been sexually harassed. In 1986 the Association of American Colleges documented that one-third of tenured female faculty members at Harvard University and half of untenured ones reported being sexually harassed. This same study estimated that as many as 40 percent of all undergraduate women and 29 percent of female graduate students had been harassed by faculty members. On most campuses, however, the 40 to 60 percent of female students who report being sexually harassed say that it is by other students. In 1986 the United Nations Ad Hoc Groups on Equal Rights for Women reported that half the women interviewed had been victims of sexual harassment on the job. A 1990 Defense Department study substantiated that two-thirds of female military personnel had endured such abuse.

Two types of sexual harassment are recognized under U.S. law. First, there is quid pro quo harassment—being fired or forced to quit for not complying with sexual demands. The second type is more subtle and occurs when the harassment becomes a pervasive condition of work, that is, constitutes a hostile work environment but for which dismissal or demotion is not necessary to prove employment discrimination. This type of sexual harassment was not recognized as sex discrimination under Title VII of the 1964 Civil Rights Act until the U.S. Supreme Court decision in *Meritor Savings Bank* v. *Mechelle Vinson* in 1986. Before *Meritor* the 1980 EEOC guidelines prohibited sexual harassment under various circumstances, including the creation of an "intimidating or hostile or offensive environment." The *Meritor* case marked the first time the Supreme Court attempted to interpret these guidelines, although they had been variously used between 1980 and 1986 by lower courts.

Because hostile work-environment harassment began to be recognized as actionable only in the late 1980s, so much confusion remained at the federal circuit court level in the early 1990s that the Supreme Court granted certiorari to resolve discrepancies between districts over how to determine the level of harm and employer liability. In the summer of 1993 the New Jersey Supreme Court took up this challenge to set standards that both employees and employers could understand and which the latter could enforce. In *Lehmann* v. *Toys 'R' Us, Inc.* (1993), the New Jersey court in a detailed decision outlined four standards. First, a plaintiff has a cause for action when "he or she alleges discriminatory conduct that a reasonable person of the same sex in the plaintiff's position would consider sufficiently severe or pervasive to alter conditions of employment and to create intimidating, hostile or offensive working environment," and that the plaintiff need not be the direct target of harassing conduct. Second, in cases of supervisory sexual harassment the cumulative effect of incidents and not just single incidents will determine whether the employer "will be held strictly liable for equitable damages and relief," regardless of whether such discrimination is intentional or unintentional. Third, in cases where supervisors act as the employers' surrogates or abuse their authority, employers will be vicariously liable under the principles of agency law for compensatory damages that exceed equitable relief. Fourth, employers will not be held liable for punitive damages unless they authorize, approve, or participate in creating an offensive working environment. *Lehmann* set forth the most logical set of tests and reasoned standards for state and federal courts to follow in deciding sexual harassment cases for the remainder of the 1990s.

[Joan Hoff, *Law, Gender, and Injustice,* rev. ed. (New York, 1994); Catharine MacKinnon, *Sexual Harassment and Working Women* (New Haven, Conn., 1979); Jane Mayer and Jill Abramson, *Strange Justice: The Selling of Clarence Thomas* (Boston, 1994).]

JOAN HOFF

See also **SUPP:** *Meritor Savings Bank* v. *Mechelle Vinson;* Tailhook Incident; Women's Movement; Women's Rights.

SEXUALITY. In the aftermath of the "sexual revolution" of the 1960s, Americans remained deeply ambivalent in their attitudes toward sex as the twentieth century neared its close. Despite their insatiable appetite for sexual images, manifested in the explosion of sexually oriented advertising, movies, videos, and talk shows, Americans had difficulty talking about sexual attitudes and practice and continued to cling to puritanical notions that relegated sexual matters to the privacy of the marital bedroom. In many respects, technology surged into the twenty-first century while attitudes remained frozen in the past.

This ambivalence toward sexuality inhibited much-needed scientific research into post–sexual revolution changes in sexual attitudes and practice. Without major support from either government or private foundations, research was conducted on a limited scale in sex clinics, specialized academic fields, and popular literature. Following the controversial *Kinsey Report* of the 1950s, researchers William H. Masters and Virginia C. Johnson pushed back the boundaries of sexual research in the 1970s by moving from the interviews Alfred C. Kinsey had employed to direct observation of sexual activity. From their Saint Louis institute, Masters and Johnson recorded sexual interplay of married couples in order to develop therapeutic methods for enhancing the desired responses. While they pioneered controversial methods for recording sexual response, their aim was conservative. Believing that human beings thrive in long-term, heterosexual, monogamous relationships, Masters and Johnson focused on achieving a working sexual relationship within marriage by curing dysfunction. Reflecting their emphasis on marriage, they explained a great deal about sexual response in middle and old age, offering information about the aging process designed to preserve sexual response in aging couples.

One of the most important areas of sex research to emerge from academe was in the field of cognitive development. In 1987 social scientists Lisa A. Serbin and Carol H. Sprafkin proposed a developmental model using schema theory to show the relationship between cognitive and sexual development. According to schema theory, our most basic cognitive development is linked to sexual identification. Beginning with pink and blue blankets in the nursery, infants are sexually marked. This early identification forms our most basic schema for sorting information. Serbin and Sprafkin identified differing developmental patterns in boys and girls. Because male sex organs are visible and more easily manipulated, boys reach the level of cognitive development needed to understand their sexual organs much earlier than girls. For boys, cognitive development is achieved at the same age as sexual maturity; whereas in girls, there is a five- or six-year gap between physical maturity and the cognitive development needed to understand their sexual organs. Serbin and Sprafkin suggested that this gap could account for the high rates of teenage pregnancy in the United States. In showing the relation between sexual and cognitive development, developmental theory can aid realistic sex education programs that take into account the stages of sexual development.

In other fields, scientific inquiry was polarized along the lines of the nature-versus-nurture debate. Research in the physical sciences, especially cell development, endocrinology, and brain function, stressed biological differences between male and female sexual development, whereas social scientists emphasized the importance of social and cultural conditioning in shaping human sexuality. This debate created a paradox wherein the physical sciences catalogued differences between men and women while social sciences noted similarities. In grappling with this paradox, researchers sought to understand the interaction between nature and nurture in the development of human sexuality. After twenty-five years of debate, the consensus suggested that biology (nature) physically determines male and female forms while culture (nurture) inscribes those forms with socially constructed, communally enforced gender roles to order sexual relations. Thus, while nature determines, nurture governs.

This principle was borne out in the 1990s by the most extensive survey of sexual practice in the United States since Kinsey. In 1987 the National Health and Social Life Survey (NHSLS) began as a response to the AIDS epidemic. Initially intended to survey the sexual practice of 20,000 Americans, the study was significantly scaled back when it lost government funding in 1991. Carrying on with private funds, the NHSLS surveyed more than 3,500 individuals. The results of the NHSLS survey contradicted results of popular surveys, suggesting that sexual practice was more conservative than what was described by the *Hite Report,* the *Janus Report,* and *Redbook* and *Playboy* magazines. While noting the dramatic change in sexual openness driven by popular culture, the NHSLS survey concluded that sexual attitudes are formed by social groups, sexual practice is prescribed by social norms, the choice of sexual partners is limited to individuals within social networks, and sexual events are scripted by social convention.

While Americans were less promiscuous and more convention-bound than reported by the popular surveys, the NHSLS report noted significant changes in sexual behavior after the 1970s. Americans were having more sexual partners over their lifetimes, but they tended to have one partner at a time and generally remain faithful to that partner while the relationship lasted. In refuting the myth of widespread promiscuity, the study asserted that only a few had many partners, while many had a few partners. Marriage remained the most popular institution for regulating sexual relations, although cohabitation was widely practiced as a precursor of marriage. Fewer women were virgins when they married, although the survey noted a slight increase in the number of male virgins. Americans were engaging in sexual activity both earlier and later in life and arrived at the peak of sexual activity in their twenties. In sum, the report concluded that Americans were having their first sexual experience at an earlier age, were marrying later, divorcing more, and having more sexual partners in the course of their lives.

[Paul R. Abramson and Steven D. Pinkerton, eds., *Sexual Nature, Sexual Culture* (Chicago, 1995); Robert T. Michael, John H. Gagnon, Edward O. Laumann, and Gina Kolata, *Sex in America: A Definitive Survey* (Boston, 1994); Paul A. Robinson, *The Modernization of Sex* (New York, 1976); Lisa A. Serbin and Carol H. Sprafkin, "A Developmental Approach: Sexuality from Infancy through Adolescence," in James H. Geer and William O'Donohue, eds., *Theories of Human Sexuality* (New York, 1987).]

MARIAN YEATES

See also **DAH:** Sexual Attitudes; **SUPP:** Marriage and Divorce; Sexual Orientation; Sexually Transmitted Diseases.

SEXUALLY TRANSMITTED DISEASES (STDs), formerly known as venereal diseases and now called sexually transmitted infections (STIs) or reproductive tract infections (RTIs), are a major health problem in the United States. Twelve million new cases of STDs occur each year, two-thirds of them among persons under age twenty-five. At that rate one American in four will acquire an STD at some time in his or her life. Until the early 1980s only five STDs—syphilis, gonorrhea, chancroid, lymphogranuloma venereum, and granuloma inguinale—were widely recognized. By the mid-1990s more than fifty organisms and syndromes were known to be transmitted sexually. With the possible exception of acquired immune deficiency syndrome (AIDS), none of the STDs on this expanded list is "new"; rather, advances in medical technology have permitted more accurate diagnosis of many of these infections. Still, there was a large increase in the incidence of STDs in the latter decades of the twentieth century. Changes in sexual mores increased the number of years in which individuals are sexually active. Many sexually active persons have several sexual partners (on average, adults have seven partners during their lifetimes), which raises their chances of encountering someone infected with an STD. Moreover, most people with multiple partners are not consistent users of condoms, which can substantially reduce the risk of infection. Some diseases, including chlamydia (the most common STD), gonorrhea, and syphilis, are caused by bacteria and can generally be cured easily with antibiotics if diagnosed early. STDs caused by viruses, however, such as genital herpes, human papilloma virus (HPV, or genital warts), hepatitis B, and human

immunodeficiency virus (HIV), the last of which causes AIDS, cannot be cured and can be passed on to sexual partners even when no symptoms are present. STDs have a disproportionate effect on women, because women become infected more easily than men, infections are harder to diagnose in women, and the complications of infection are more severe in women. Thousands of women each year become infertile or experience life-endangering fallopian-tube pregnancy (ectopic pregnancy) as a result of STD infection. Infected women can transmit an STD to their offspring during pregnancy or childbirth with devastating results. STDs exact a huge financial cost. The costs of just three diseases—chlamydia, gonorrhea, and herpes—are estimated at $5 billion annually.

[Allan M. Brandt, *No Magic Bullet: A Social History of Venereal Disease in the United States Since 1880* (New York, 1987); Patricia Donovan, *Testing Positive: Sexually Transmitted Disease and the Public Health Response* (New York, 1993).]

PATRICIA DONOVAN

See also **SUPP:** Acquired Immune Deficiency Syndrome.

SEXUAL ORIENTATION. A person's erotic, romantic, and affectional attraction to the other sex, the same sex, or both is referred to as sexual orientation. An individual who is attracted to the other sex is referred to as heterosexual or straight. A person attracted to the same sex is called homosexual, gay (a term more often applied to men), or lesbian if she is a woman. One who is attracted to both men and women is bisexual. The term "sexual preference" is sometimes used instead of "sexual orientation" but may be misleading because it implies conscious preference or choice. Sexual orientation is a part of sexual identity, a sense of self that also includes how one identifies in terms of gender. Identity as male or female is relatively independent of sexual orientation. Homosexuality is not synonymous with transsexuality; lesbian women do not believe themselves to be or wish to be men and gay men do not have a female gender identity. Sexual fantasies, sexual behavior, and the gender of the person with whom one falls in love are not always consistent and may change over a lifetime. A woman may live happily in a monogamous marriage for many years, never questioning her heterosexuality. Later she may fall in love with a woman and begin to develop a lesbian identity. Heterosexual men in prison may engage in sexual behavior with men because of the absence of female partners (referred to as situational or circumstantial homosexuality). When no longer imprisoned they may choose women partners exclusively. Such men identify as heterosexual although their lifetime behavior patterns might be considered bisexual.

Scientific concepts of sexual orientation have evolved since the late nineteenth century, when the terms "sexual inversion" and "homosexuality" were introduced by John Addington Symonds and Havelock Ellis. In the late 1940s Alfred C. Kinsey and his colleagues developed the concept of a bipolar continuum of sexual orientation ranging from exclusive heterosexuality to exclusive homosexuality, now known as the "Kinsey Scale." Prior to this many scholars regarded heterosexuals and homosexuals as distinct categories and bisexuals as homosexuals repressing their true identities and/or trying to "pass" as heterosexual. Since Kinsey, others have proposed more complex models to describe and quantify variability in sexual orientation. For example, homosexuality and heterosexuality may be seen as independent dimensions—a person high on both is bisexual, a person low on both is asexual; and persons high on one scale and low on the other are homosexual and heterosexual, respectively.

In 1956, at the annual meeting of the American Psychological Association, Evelyn Hooker presented a paper documenting normal psychological adjustment patterns in nonclinical samples of male homosexuals. Prior to this time, with the exception of Ellis and Kinsey's work, there was little scientific literature that was not founded in a pathological model for understanding homosexuality. Hooker's work was largely overlooked until 1967, when Stanley Yolles, director of the National Institute of Mental Health, appointed a task force on homosexuality. Its final report was issued in October 1969, six months after the Stonewall riots in New York City marked the beginning of the gay liberation movement. In addition to recommendations regarding further research, the report included recommendations related to social policy and others related to treatment and prevention. The former were welcomed positively by the organizing gay community, whereas the latter were less welcomed.

Despite growing evidence to the contrary, psychopathological explanations of homosexuality were still widely believed, particularly among psychoanalysts, but in 1973 the American Psychiatric Association removed homosexuality from its *Diagnostic and Statistical Manual of Mental Disorders*. Many psychiatrists, particularly those whose work was based in psychodynamic theory, remained opposed to "normalizing" homosexual behavior, citing writings of psychoanalysts reporting on homosexuality as a psychopathological condition that could be "cured" for at least some proportion of individuals through psychoanalytic techniques. As a compromise, in 1980 the term "ego-dystonic homosexuality" was included in the *Manual*. Further debate led to the removal of this term in 1986 and inclusion of a statement in a more neutral manner that some individuals may wish to change sexual orientation.

Attitudes toward homosexuality underwent many changes in the last decades of the twentieth century as a result of increased understanding of sexual orientation, further questioning of psychodynamic theory, and activism for gay and lesbian rights. Many psychoanalytically trained psychiatrists, however, still view homosexuality as psychopathological. Some religious and political groups also maintain that homosexuality is pathological or immoral. In the 1990s discrimination against homosexuals was common, and there were vocal groups on both sides of the issue regarding the acceptance of homosexuality as an alternate lifestyle or its condemnation as a perversion, sin against God, or transgression against society. Most professionals today question the ethics of using therapy to try to change a trait that is not a disorder and is such an important aspect of an individual's identity. In general, interventions to change sexual orientations of homosexuals have led to reduced sexual behavior and self-esteem rather than creating or enhancing attraction to the other sex.

Many theories about the etiology of sexual orientation have been put forward. Sigmund Freud did not view homosexuality as a mental illness but suggested that homosexual men tended to have weak or absent fathers and domineering mothers, seductive mothers, or unresolved oedipal feelings. Later psychoanalysts adopted a more pathological view. Others suggested homosexuality was caused by seductive other-sex parents, seduction by older persons of the same sex, rape (for lesbianism), or insufficient heterosexual opportunities during development. There is, however, little empirical support for these psychoanalytic and social environmental theories. Early gender nonconformity (sissy behavior in boys and tomboyism in girls), especially in the extreme, may be indicative of a predisposition toward homosexuality, but the cause of the gender nonconformity remains a question.

Later studies highlighted the potential role of biological factors in sexual orientation. These include findings suggesting genetic causes of homosexuality, reports of neuroanatomical and neuropsychological differences in the brains of homosexuals compared to heterosexuals, and evidence that the prenatal hormone environment may affect the relative masculinization/demasculinization or feminization/defeminization of the brain and thus influence behavioral development. By the 1990s, however, many experts thought nature (biological determinism) versus nurture (environment or social determinism) arguments overly simplistic. Sexual orientation appears to result from the interaction of nature and nurture, each influencing the other at critical periods. Likely to develop in stages, sexual orientation appears to be formed by complex interactions of biological, psychological, social, cultural, and circumstantial factors with multiple developmental pathways possible.

[Alan P. Bell, Martin S. Weinberg, and Sue Kiefer Hammersmith, *Sexual Preference: Its Development in Men and Women* (Bloomington, Ind., 1981); Richard Green, *The "Sissy Boy Syndrome" and the Development of Homosexuality* (New Haven, Conn., 1987); Dean H. Hamer and Peter Copeland, *The Science of Desire: The Search for the Gay Gene and the Biology of Behavior* (New York, 1994); Simon LeVay, *The Sexual Brain* (Cambridge, Mass., 1993); David P. McWhirter, Stephanie A. Sanders, and June M. Reinisch, eds., *Homosexuality/Heterosexuality: Concepts of Sexual Orientation* (New York, 1990).]

STEPHANIE A. SANDERS

See also **DAH:** Sexual Attitudes; **SUPP:** Gay and Lesbian Movement; Psychology; Sexuality.

SHIPPING INDUSTRY. *See* **Merchant Marine.**

SIDS. *See* **Sudden Infant Death Syndrome.**

SILICON VALLEY, located around Santa Clara and San Jose, California, is the home of many key U.S. corporations specializing in advanced electronic and information technologies. First called "Silicon Valley" in 1971 by a local newsletter writer, Donald C. Hoefler, the "Valley" became the center of technologies that many believed would revolutionize computers, telecommunications, manufacturing procedures, warfare, and even U.S. society itself. The name came to symbolize a type of high-risk business characterized by rapid success or failure, extensive job mobility, and informal behavior, traits thought by some to be the wave of the future. The location of such high-tech research, development, and manufacturing in an area once known as the "prune capital of America"

was not coincidental. Stanford University in nearby Palo Alto provided a research-oriented institution active in engineering and electronics. In 1951 Stanford established a research park where companies could build facilities and conduct research in cooperation with the university, the first such enterprise in the country.

If there was a founder of Silicon Valley it was William Shockley, an English-born physicist who worked on early concepts of the transistor at Bell Laboratories before World War II and became director of Bell's Transistor Physics Research Group. A restless person whose inquisitive mind and entrepreneurial aspirations did not find satisfaction in the larger corporation, he became a visiting professor at the California Institute of Technology in 1954 and the following year founded Shockley Semiconductor Laboratories just south of Palo Alto in the north end of Silicon Valley. Shockley's business acumen did not equal his skills in science and engineering. In 1957 eight of his engineers created Fairchild Semiconductor, supported by Fairchild Camera and Instrument. Their departure established a mobility that would characterize careers in Silicon Valley and elsewhere in electronics companies where employees shunned ties of corporate loyalty in favor of personal fulfillment and financial reward. Fairchild Semiconductor later lost employees as well. In 1968 Robert Noyce, Gordon Moore, and Andrew Grove left to establish Intel. Another Fairchild employee, W. J. Sanders III, founded Advanced Micro Devices soon thereafter. In the early 1970s one survey found forty-one companies in Silicon Valley headed by former Fairchild employees. This pattern continued into the 1980s with such companies as National Semiconductor, Atari, Apple Computer, LSI Logic, and Cypress Semiconductor having all or part of their origins in Silicon Valley.

To many observers the California location was central to the success and, later, the problems of Silicon Valley. The popular image of California, with its promise of individual and professional renewal, played a part, as did the cultural climate of the 1960s, which criticized large organizations for suppressing personal expression. The moderate climate of Silicon Valley combined with a pool of educated talent from California universities, and a largely nonunion work force attracted investors and corporations. Publicity about Silicon Valley in the 1970s generated discussion about options for U.S. industry, especially in electronics. The Valley to a degree represented a shift in political and economic power from the older industrialized Northeast and Midwest to the Pacific Coast. The rise of Silicon Valley occurred at a time when many electronics companies were affected by changes in financial markets and availability of capital. During the 1950s and early 1960s much of the Valley relied on military contracts, but this dependence declined as commercial and then personal markets for computers emerged. Investors hoping for a very high rate of return increasingly were willing to risk supporting these companies even if as many as 25 percent would fail after a few years. Demand for capital increased as the size of electronic components such as memory chips decreased. With smaller size came the need for more sophisticated and costly technologies in manufacturing. By the late 1980s companies estimated they needed as much as $1 billion to establish a manufacturing facility for the latest generation of semiconductors. Observers of investment practices and corporate strategies began to worry that this reliance on venture capital had created a pattern in U.S. business that stressed short-term profits rather than longer-term concerns about product development and competition from foreign corporations. Silicon Valley's success and the boost it gave to California's image and economy led such states as Oregon, Michigan, Texas, Colorado, New York, and Minnesota to invite or promote advanced electronic firms. In the 1990s, however, Silicon Valley remained the major indicator of the health of the industry.

Products such as memory and logic chips, microprocessors, and custom-made circuits are expensive to manufacture, subject to price-cutting in the market, and have a short product life (sometimes two years or less) before the next generation appears. Their sale depends on the health of important segments of U.S. industry, including computers, telecommunications systems, automobiles, and military contractors. Silicon Valley and its counterparts elsewhere in the United States thus are subject to cycles of boom and bust. The latter occurred in 1984–1986, when many of the Valley's companies found themselves with surplus products after a drop in the U.S. personal computer market. Companies had to lay off workers and some went out of business. Foreign competition, especially from Japan, was perhaps the greatest cause of problems for Silicon Valley. Business and political leaders debated whether or not trade policy needed to defend the interests of U.S. electronics firms more aggressively and whether U.S. companies should receive government funding to make them more competitive in the international market. Silicon Valley had begun to worry about

Japanese competition by the late 1970s. In 1981 U.S. companies controlled 51.4 percent of the world's semiconductor market; Japan's share was 35.5 percent. Within seven years the figures were virtually reversed, with Japan at 51 percent and the United States 36.5 percent. U.S. companies charged their Japanese counterparts with dumping semiconductors onto the U.S. market at low prices to undercut U.S. manufacturers while Japan kept much of its home market closed. The Semiconductor Industry Association, representing many companies in Silicon Valley urged bilateral agreements to open Japan's market. The first of these was signed in 1986 and a second followed in 1992. By the early 1990s it appeared that U.S. industry had started to recover some of the ground lost to Japan.

Meanwhile, the lure of Silicon Valley was lessened by several factors. New technologies, the ascent of successful electronic-component manufacturing elsewhere in the United States, and foreign competition moved attention away from Silicon Valley. People learned that the manufacturing of electronic components was not as environmentally clean or safe as some thought; the growth of the Valley led to traffic congestion and air pollution; and in the early 1990s California's economy experienced a serious recession. Silicon Valley remained a center of research, development, and manufacturing in the electronics industry but its symbolic role as a frontier of industrial and social organization was no longer certain.

[Tom Forester, *High-Tech Society* (Cambridge, Mass., 1987); Robert Teitelman, *Profits of Science* (New York, 1994).]

KENNETH B. MOSS

See also **SUPP:** California; Computer Industry; Computers.

SINGLE PARENTHOOD. *See* **Family.**

SKIING. During the 1980s skiing reached a peak of popularity as a recreational activity, and U.S. downhill skiers excelled on the international competitive circuit. Phil Mahre won World Cups from 1981 through 1983, Tamara McKinney won the women's World Cup in 1983, and the United States earned an unprecedented three gold medals in skiing at the 1984 Winter Olympics, including Bill Johnson's victory in the men's downhill. Weakened by injuries, the 1988 U.S. Olympic ski team gave a disappointing performance, but the sport's recreational popularity continued to rise as technological improvements in equipment made skiing safer. Lift-ticket sales increased from $51.4 million during the 1984–1985 season to more than $1 billion in 1986–1987, but sales declined to $900 million by 1989, partly because the price of an all-day lift ticket rose. Other alternatives to traditional skiing included snowboarding, mogul skiing, ski dancing, tree skiing, bordercross (a variation on snowboarding that is like a slalom but with five skiers on the course at once), aerial freestyle skiing, and heli-skiing. A turnaround in U.S. competitive alpine skiing fortunes occurred at the 1994 Winter Olympics in Lillehammer, Norway, capped by the efforts of Tommy Moe, who became the second American to capture the gold medal in the downhill. Diann Roffe-Steinrotter won a gold medal in the women's Super-G alpine skiing event.

[Ralph Hickok, *The Encyclopedia of North American Sports History* (New York, 1992); Richard Needham, *Ski: Fifty Years in North America* (New York, 1987).]

DAVID P. McDANIEL

See also **SUPP:** Olympic Games; Sports, New.

SKINHEADS. *See* **White Supremacists.**

SKYSCRAPERS. *See* **Architecture.**

SLANG, informal language of a highly picturesque and metaphorical nature, is often ingenious and amusing. It is usually created as a more convenient, more private, or more entertaining means of communication than anything available in the standard language. Its terms are only temporary but are widely dispersed during their popularity. Gradations between slang and standard English are often difficult to distinguish, because language is a living entity, constantly taking in new members and dismissing old ones. Terms such as "show off," "chisel," "bootlegger," "racketeer," "movie," and "OK" had risen from slang to standard English by the 1950s, and some of the slang of the 1960s, 1970s, and 1980s such as "dude," "online," and "boom box" achieved standard usage by the 1990s. Most slang, such as the language of citizens band radio users in the 1970s or "Valley girls" in the 1980s, faded before reaching acceptability. The improved communications systems of the twentieth century shortened the time it takes for slang terms to reach acceptance and caused the regional character of slang to decline. In the 1920s and 1930s slang of national currency was created and disseminated by radio, motion pictures, and nationally syndicated comic strips and gossip columns. The coming of television in the 1950s and cable TV in the 1980s added a still more powerful means of disseminating slang.

Little slang was used in the United States before the great westward movement of the nineteenth century. Freed from the conventionality of eastern settlements, pioneers expressed their exuberant optimism and individualism in dazzling extravagances. The humorous literature of the Old Southwest introduced such terms as "rambunctious," "skedaddle," "shebang," "galoot," "stewed," and "woozy." The books of Mark Twain are rich repositories of the slang of the mid-nineteenth-century Middle and Far West.

The objects, actions, and ideas described with slang are in some ways constant. Each generation's subcultures produce hundreds of new terms related to sex, alcohol (and more recently drugs), and bodily parts and functions. At any given time a society's slang also reflects the popular preoccupations of its culture. Slang of the early 1940s reflected a nation at war and was drawn mostly from the military. The beginning of the Space Age in the 1950s added such terms as "in orbit," "blast off," "countdown," and "A-OK." In the 1960s society's fascination with the hippie counterculture increased the slang of drug use, radical politics, and rock music ("far out," "freaked out," "strung out," "bummed out"). The 1980s saw the emergence of another counterculture, an urban, African-American youth culture that found its expression in rap music and the spread of its slang soon followed ("homey," "hood," "dissed"). Slang terms, like standard terms, undergo shifts in meaning. In the 1940s "dope" referred to a stupid person; by the 1960s dope was an illicit drug, usually marijuana, and by the 1990s dope had become an adjective meaning "excellent."

[Paul Dickson, *Slang! The Topic-by-Topic Dictionary of Contemporary American Lingoes* (New York, 1990); H. L. Mencken, *The American Language* (New York, 1963); Tony Thorne, *Dictionary of Contemporary Slang* (New York, 1990).]

PAUL S. VOAKES

See also **DAH:** Slang, American; Slang, Military.

SMALL BUSINESS ADMINISTRATION (SBA), founded in 1953 to assist small companies, particularly those serving military interests, traces its roots to 1932, when President Herbert Hoover established the Reconstruction Finance Corporation to provide loans for small businesses during the Great Depression. Ten years later President Franklin D. Roosevelt created the Smaller War Plants Corporation to bolster the ability of small companies to secure military contracts during World War II. The corporation was disbanded in 1946 but reinstated as the Small Defense Plants Administration during the Korean War. President Dwight D. Eisenhower and Congress then consolidated the Small Defense Plants Administration and the Reconstruction Finance Corporation into the SBA, which also took on responsibilities of the Office of Small Business in the Department of Commerce. SBA's initial role called for keeping an inventory of businesses that could serve a military purpose in peacetime, provide disaster relief, and offer loans and technical assistance. The agency oversaw a lending program for veterans who wanted to start or expand small businesses. The Equal Opportunity Act of 1964 expanded the SBA's role to include programs to assist minority-owned businesses. President Richard M. Nixon added a minority set-aside program known as the Philadelphia Plan, which allocated a share of federal procurement contracts for minority small businesses. Enterprises owned by women, the disabled, and Vietnam veterans benefited from set-asides. In the 1990s the SBA assisted businesses specializing in high technology, environmental resources, and exports. Its constituency comprises 21.5 million companies with fewer than 500 employees, or 99 percent of all businesses in the United States, but directly serves only 1 percent of such businesses. Small businesses accounted for all of the job growth in the nation from 1987 to 1992 and are considered the engine for the national economy. Employing 54 percent of the workforce, they account for half the gross national product.

ERIK BRUUN

See also **SUPP:** Enterprise Zones; Environmental Business; Minority Business; Set-Asides.

SMOKING. In 1900 per capita consumption of cigarettes among U.S. adults was forty-nine per year. By the mid-1960s per capita consumption stood at more than 4,300. The rise of cigarette smoking was characterized by consolidation of a major industry as well as by increased advertising and consumption. Since release of the surgeon general's *Report on Smoking and Health* in 1964 there has been a revolutionary change in attitudes and behavior regarding smoking in the United States. The report reviewed and evaluated epidemiological studies that began to appear in the 1940s and 1950s implicating cigarettes as a serious cause of lung cancer, heart disease, and other ill-

nesses. At the time of the report almost half of adult Americans were cigarette smokers. By 1994 the percentage of smokers in the general population had fallen to 26 percent, although it had begun to rise among high school students, particularly young women.

The surgeon general's report touched off a debate about controlling or restricting cigarettes. Congress the next year passed the Federal Cigarette Labeling and Advertising Act, requiring cigarette packages to be labeled "Caution: Cigarette Smoking May Be Hazardous to Your Health." By 1970, as the harmful effects of smoking were increasingly documented, Congress mandated a stronger label: "Warning: The Surgeon General Has Determined that Cigarette Smoking Is Hazardous to Your Health." Congress banned cigarette advertisements from television and radio. In 1984 Congress passed legislation requiring four rotating warning messages on cigarette packages. In 1986 the surgeon general released a report on the detrimental effects of passive (secondary) smoke. A 1993 report by the Environmental Protection Agency named environmental tobacco smoke (ETS) as a Class A carcinogen. In 1994 the FDA announced that nicotine was an addictive substance and congressional hearings accused the tobacco industry of secretly manipulating the nicotine level of cigarettes to keep smokers hooked.

Evidence of the harmful effects of cigarette smoke for nonsmokers has led since the late 1970s to increased restrictions on smoking in the workplace and public spaces. By the late 1980s more than forty states had restricted smoking in public places and thirty-three had legislated prohibitions on smoking on public transportation. The General Services Administration restricted smoking in its 6,800 buildings throughout the United States. In 1988 Congress directed domestic airlines to ban smoking on flights of two hours or less; in 1990 this ban was extended to all domestic flights. A few U.S. airlines have banned smoking on international flights.

Despite the dramatic decline in numbers of Americans who smoke and the increasing stigmatization of smokers in U.S. society, cigarettes continue to cause serious health effects. In the early 1990s cigarettes were associated with 30 percent of cancers, 21 percent of deaths from coronary artery disease, and 82 percent of deaths from chronic obstructive pulmonary disease. Since 1982 lung cancer has become the leading cause of cancer deaths among women, surpassing breast cancer—the epidemiologic result of the rise in smoking among women from the 1940s to the 1960s. The total economic cost of smoking-related disease is estimated at $60 billion a year. According to the

American Cancer Society, smoking causes 400,000 deaths each year in the United States. Conservative estimates from a 1995 study indicate that smoking by pregnant women annually causes at least 19,000 miscarriages, 32,000 low-birth-weight babies, 14,000 babies requiring intensive care at birth, 1,200 cases of sudden infant death, and 3,100 deaths of children by the age of one month from complications caused by tobacco smoke. As the U.S. market has declined since the mid-1970s the United States tobacco industry has worked diligently to open new markets abroad; critics also have charged the industry with targeting teenagers in its domestic advertising campaigns. In July 1995 President Bill Clinton proposed that the Food and Drug Administration regulate the sale and advertising of cigarettes to minors.

[Robert L. Rabin and Stephen D. Sugarman, eds., *Smoking Policy: Law, Politics, and Culture* (New York, 1993); Robert Sobel, *They Satisfy: The Cigarette in American Life* (New York, 1978); Susan Wagner, *Cigarette Country* (New York, 1971).]

ALLAN M. BRANDT

See also **DAH** and **SUPP:** Tobacco Industry.

SOCCER, the most popular sport in the world, earned little interest in the United States until the nation hosted the 1994 World Cup. Held every four years, that championship is the most-watched single-sport event. The fifty-two games of World Cup '94 broke all previous records, attended by 3.5 million and watched on U.S. television by 4.5 million households. Organizers hoped that U.S. interest in the World Cup would translate into success for the newly formed Major League Soccer (MLS), the country's first serious outdoor professional soccer. Slated to begin in April 1996, MLS has twelve teams competing in a six-month season in ten cities.

In a nation saturated with baseball, basketball, football, and hockey leagues, professional soccer has had a difficult time earning the recognition it has found abroad, despite a long history of the sport in the United States, dating from collegiate teams in the 1800s to formation of ethnic (for example, Scottish, Irish, Portuguese, and Brazilian) teams in major cities in the last two decades of the nineteenth century. Professional organizations have included the American Football Organization (1884), the first governing body for soccer in the United States; the United States Football Association (1913), which was recognized by the Zurich-based Fédération Internationale de Football Association; the Professional American Soccer League (1933); and the North American Soccer League (1968). Nonetheless, Americans have never caught the fever that leads to ecstatic victory celebrations in South America or mass crowd frenzy and violence in Great Britain. Although it is generally called "football" internationally, soccer does not resemble U.S. football, which is more closely associated with rugby. Because the clock virtually never stops and only the referee knows the official time, play stoppages are close to nonexistent in soccer. The game continues when penalties are committed and player substitutions are much less frequent than in football or basketball.

In 1975 the U.S. Cosmos signed Brazilian Edson Arantes do Nascimento, better known as Pele, who eventually scored 1,280 goals in 1,362 matched (400 goals is considered phenomenal for a player). His skill and star quality spurred children to flock to the sport in record numbers. According to a sports marketing group, soccer in 1993 was the fourth most popular sport for youths under eighteen and second only to basketball for those under twelve. Total soccer participation increased 8 percent from 1992 to 1993, when 16.4 million Americans played the game, 4.2 million of them adults. Increased interest led to the 1988 awarding of World Cup '94 to the United States, a move derided internationally because the country did not yet have a bona fide professional outdoor soccer league, and its national team had not even qualified for the Cup since 1950. The U.S. team did make the 1990 Cup but critics remained unconvinced about the prospects for 1994. In addition to the commercial success of World Cup '94, played by twenty-four teams in nine cities, the U.S. team fared better than it had since 1930. The team upset the favorite, Colombia, 2–1, aided in part by Colombian player Andres Escobar's mistaken deflection that sent the ball into his own goal. A pall was cast over the victory when Escobar was shot to death upon return to Colombia and officials announced that a fan irate about his mistake was responsible. Still, the victory wiped away previous U.S. failures in World Cup participation, and promoters reported a surge in demand for a professional outdoor league. The Major Indoor Soccer League, many of whose stars (Steve Zungal and Preki of Yugoslavia and Tatu of Brazil) came from outside the United States, enjoyed mixed success in the 1990s after being beset by disorganization and falling fortunes during the previous decade.

[Michael L. LaBlanc and Richard Henshaw, *The World Encyclopedia of Soccer* (Detroit, 1994); Christopher Merrill, *The Grass of Another Country* (New York, 1993); Gary Rosenthal, *Everybody's Soccer Book* (New York, 1981).]

KATHLEEN B. CULVER

SOCIAL SECURITY is the largest, costliest, and most successful domestic program in the history of the United States. Through its 1,300 local branches, ten regional headquarters, and central offices in Baltimore and Washington, the Social Security Administration issues 500 million checks a year. Officials deal with old-age and survivors benefits, assess the needs of disabled workers, and provide eligible senior citizens with hospital insurance and supplemental medical insurance under Medicare. The administration's error rate is under 3 percent—a remarkable achievement for any bureaucracy. Beginning in the 1980s fear arose because of the program's imminent bankruptcy, but a majority of Americans continued to express considerable confidence in the system. Social security, Democratic Senator Bill Bradley declared in 1983, is "the best expression of community that we have in this country today."

Social security was designed to enable ordinary people to cope with the "risks" associated with loss of wages. Although Americans now tend to view it as a program for the elderly, its New Deal architects perceived old-age dependency in the context of family networks that changed with the generations. As Franklin Delano Roosevelt told Congress in 1934, "If, as our Constitution tells us, our federal government was established among other things, 'to promote the general welfare,' it is our plain duty to provide for the security upon which welfare depends. . . . Hence I am looking for a sound means which I can recommend to provide at once security against several of the great disturbing factors of life, especially those which relate to unemployment and old age. . . . These three objectives—the security of home, the security of livelihood, and the security of social insurance—are, it seems to me, a minimum of the promise that we can offer to the American people."

The Social Security Act of Aug. 14, 1935, largely met Roosevelt's expectations by mounting a two-pronged attack on old-age dependency. A federal-state partnership was established under Title I, which gave men and women over sixty-five years of age assistance if deemed eligible. (Because no national guidelines were established, southern states managed to circumvent the spirit of the provision and maintain racial discrimination. Still, procedures were established to enable applicants to appeal; this made old-age assistance a right, not a gratuity.) To reduce old-age poverty, employers and employees were expected to contribute 0.5 percent each (for a total of 1 percent) of the first $3,000 of an employee's salary for a retirement pension. The 1935 act dealt with the needs of younger citizens as well. Titles III and IX established a mechanism for unemployment compensation. Title IV launched what would eventually become Aid for Families with Dependent Children; Title X assisted the blind. Under Title V states received money for crippled children, rural public health services, and vocational rehabilitation; the U.S. Public Health Service received training funds under Title VI. The Social Security Board was authorized (Title VII) to evaluate programs. Although Title XI gave Congress "the right to alter, amend, or repeal any provision of this Act," President Roosevelt knew his program was safe: "We put those payroll contributions there so as to give the contributors a legal, moral, and political right to collect their pensions and unemployment benefits. With those taxes in there, no damn politician can ever scrap my social security program."

In 1939 Title II benefits were extended to widows and other family members of contributing workers. Whereas private insurance would have required an increase in taxes on grounds of equity, no new Federal Insurance Contribution Act (FICA) taxes were levied, showing a social-welfare orientation. Disability provisions were added in the 1950s, medicare in 1965. The 1972 amendments combined assistance provisions into a supplemental security income program, which established the nation's first poverty floor. That same year automatic cost-of-living adjustments were added. As its creators envisioned in the depths of the Great Depression, by the mid-1970s nearly every worker paid taxes on his or her wages. In principle, nearly all U.S. citizens were eligible for entitlements at some point in their lives. President Gerald Ford (1974–1977) first confronted the fiscal problems associated with expanding social security. To strengthen the system, President Jimmy Carter (1977–1981) adjusted benefit schedules and imposed steep tax increases. Although the 1983 amendments shored up financing of the retirement program, public confidence in the system's future remained shaky. The disability insurance program remains volatile; neither experts nor policymakers seem able to define "disability" in a consistent manner.

[W. Andrew Achenbaum, *Social Security: Visions and Revision* (New York, 1986); Martha Derthick, *Agency Under Stress: The Social Security Administration in American Government* (Washington, D.C., 1990); Eric R. Kingson and Edward D. Berkowitz, *Social Security and Medicare: A Policy Primer* (Westport, Conn., 1993).]

W. ANDREW ACHENBAUM

See also **DAH:** Medicare; New Deal; Social Security; Taxation; **SUPP:** Medicare and Medicaid.

SOMALIA, RELATIONS WITH. Somalia, in northeastern Africa, is one of the few African states composed largely of people from the same ethnic group. Almost all Somalis are Muslim and most are pastoral herders. The people are divided into six clan-families of varying size. Historically these clans frequently fought each other. The British and the Italians conquered the Somalis in the nineteenth century and divided them into two colonies, which were combined in 1960, when Somalia gained independence. Many Somalis still live across the country's western border in Ethiopia. In 1969 the government was overthrown by the military led by Mohammed Siad Barre. During the 1970s Barre courted the Soviet Union, from which he acquired considerable military aid. In 1980 he switched sides and allied with the United States, which also poured in military aid. As the cold war ended Somalia lost its attraction as an ally. Partly because of reduced aid from the United States, Barre was overthrown in 1991. His ouster allowed clan rivalries, which his dictatorial rule had held in check, to erupt into civil war. The large number of weapons introduced during the cold war made the conflict especially devastating. The war and severe drought destroyed Somalia's economy, and thousands starved. In response to televised scenes of starving children the international community sent aid, which the war prevented from reaching its intended recipients. The United Nations in December 1992 introduced troops from several nations, under the command of the United States, to see that the food reached the starving people. This food mission initially succeeded, but when its commanders also tried to settle the civil war, troops were caught in a chaotic situation. Thirty U.S. soldiers lost their lives in the course of the conflict, the worst incident being an October 1993 army ranger raid in which eighteen U.S. soldiers were killed and their bodies paraded through the streets of Mogadishu, the capital city. The bloody exchanges caused the American public to demand a withdrawal of U.S. forces in early 1994. Other UN troops remained until U.S. marines helped evacuate them in March 1995. After more than two years and $2 billion the UN operation left Somalia with no government or administration and controlled by heavily armed rival clans.

R. L. WATSON

See also **SUPP:** Africa, Relations with.

SON-OF-SAM LAW. Adopted in New York State in 1977 as a response to the public outrage over profits made by convicted serial killer David Berkowitz (also known as "Son of Sam") for selling his story to a publishing house, the law required publishers to deposit money owed to persons either convicted of a crime or who confessed to having committed a crime in a fund used to compensate their victims. In *Simon and Schuster, Inc.* v. *Members of the New York State Victims Board* (1991) the Supreme Court struck down the New York law because it violated the First Amendment.

KATY J. HARRIGER

SORORITIES. *See* **Fraternities and Sororities.**

SOUTH AFRICA, RELATIONS WITH. U.S. interest in South Africa did not become sustained until the 1880s, after discovery of vast deposits of diamonds and gold in the briefly independent Boer Republics of Transvaal and the Orange Free State. U.S. mining engineers such as John Hays Hammond worked closely with British imperialist Cecil Rhodes in his pursuit of mineral wealth in South Africa. In the 1899–1902 war between Great Britain and the Boer Republics the U.S. government remained technically neutral but gave strong unofficial support to the victorious British. In subsequent years the United States gradually improved its relations with the white South Africans. After establishment as a Dominion of the British Commonwealth in 1910, the Union of South Africa bolstered its intense racial discrimination against the majority African population. Despite lingering dislike for Great Britain among many of the Dutch-descended Afrikaners (Boers), the Union of South Africa fought on the British and U.S. side in World Wars I and II. By the 1940s most Americans had come to see South Africa as a dependable ally and beacon of European civilization on a generally unenlightened continent, an amiable relationship personified by the South African military and political leader Jan Smuts.

After World War II relations gradually became difficult. The electoral defeat of Smuts in 1948 dismayed the U.S. government, especially because it came at the hands of the anglophobic Nationalist (later National) Party, the primary goal of which was to establish an even more rigid form of racial segregation and inequality known as apartheid. For a while the Nationalists' fervent anticommunism and total support for the U.S. position in the developing cold war proved more important than U.S. concerns about befriending the emerging antiracist Third World. The 1950 South African agreement to sell its extremely valuable uranium ore exclusively to the United States and Great Britain brought intimacy, despite diverging views of domestic race relations. U.S. trade and investment in South Africa expanded dramatically after World War II and continued to increase until the 1980s. Meanwhile, however, desegregation in the United States brought pressure to condemn Pretoria. U.S. administrations, especially that of President Jimmy Carter (1977–1981), distanced themselves at least rhetorically from South African practices. By the 1980s a vocal movement on college campuses and elsewhere demanded institutional divestiture of South African securities. In 1986, overriding the veto of President Ronald Reagan, Congress responded to public pressure by passing economic sanctions against South Africa. The release of African National Congress leader Nelson Mandela from prison in 1990 and his election as president of South Africa in 1994 in the nation's first all-races election led to the cancellation of those sanctions and much warmer relations between the United States and South Africa.

[Thomas Borstelmann, *Apartheid's Reluctant Uncle: The United States and Southern Africa in the Early Cold War* (New York, 1993); William Minter, *King Solomon's Mines Revisited* (New York, 1986); Thomas J. Noer, *Cold War and Black Liberation* (Columbia, Mo., 1985).]

THOMAS BORSTELMANN

See also **DAH:** African-American Relations; **SUPP:** Africa, Relations with.

SOUTH CAROLINA. The decline of agriculture in South Carolina has been one of the most important developments since the 1960s. As late as 1960 more than half the state's cotton was picked by hand. Over the next twenty years mechanization eliminated tens of thousands of jobs in rural counties. By 1990 only about 2 percent of South Carolinians lived on farms. Cotton is no longer king, and farmlands are being converted into timberlands. The decline of agriculture has had an effect on state government in which for nearly a century politicians from rural counties dominated the legislature. In 1973 the 100th General Assembly adjourned, the last in which representation was allocated by counties. The house of representatives and senate were reapportioned into single-member districts. Coupled with the federal Voting Rights Act of 1965, this change transformed South Carolina politics. The South Carolina Democratic party, which dominated the state for a century after Reconstruction, suffered serious losses in the 1994 elections. Republicans won all but one statewide constitutional office and control of the state house of representatives.

Nearly a half century after a school desegregation case in Clarendon County that would eventually become part of the landmark *Brown* v. *Board of Education* decision of 1954, South Carolina was a far different place from what it was even in the 1950s. African Americans were regularly elected to local and county offices and to the U.S. House of Representatives. Racial issues no longer played a major role in political campaigns, but politics had begun to take on racial characteristics, with African Americans supplying a core of voters for Democratic candidates and urban and suburban whites a core for Republicans. A panel of citizens was appointed in 1991 to study the structure of South Carolina government. Although initial reform efforts were unsuccessful, state agencies were reorganized and the executive branch given more authority. Many observers saw restructuring as the first step toward overhaul of every facet of state government. Education is a major issue and reform measures, the most important of which was the Education Improvement Act of 1984, have improved opportunities for all schoolchildren.

The closing of military installations made new jobs a pressing need and attracting industry a goal of the state's leadership. Since 1975 South Carolina has attracted a significant number of foreign corporations, including Michelin, which located its U.S. headquarters in the state. The stretch of Interstate 85 from the North Carolina line to Greenville is sometimes referred to as "UN Alley" because of the number of non-American companies located there. Nevertheless, there was increasing concern for the effect of new industries on land and water resources. This concern was especially pressing with regard to the tourist industry, which has been big business in the state since the 1950s. With a semitropical climate and relatively inexpensive land, South Carolina has been a developer's dream. Along the coast sleepy family beaches such as Myrtle Beach have grown into major tourist destinations. Barrier islands south of Charleston, such as Kiawah and Hilton Head, are playgrounds and retirement communities for wealthy outsiders. The state's attempts to manage coastal development in an orderly and environmentally sound manner have run afoul of federal court decisions. The U.S. Supreme Court in *Lucas* v. *South Carolina Coastal Council* ruled that the state, in forbidding construction on threatened beachfront property, had, in effect, seized the plaintiff's property without due process of law. The property owner was entitled to financial compensation from the state for the loss of the use of his property. As the billions of dollars in damage caused by Hurricane Hugo in 1989 graphically illustrated, there was a real need for the state to act.

In 1992 there were 3,603,227 South Carolinians, 69 percent of whom were white, 30 percent African American, and less than 1 percent Hispanic.

[Walter B. Edgar, *South Carolina in the Modern Age* (Columbia, S.C., 1992); Charles F. Kovacik and John J. Winberry, *South Carolina: The Making of a Landscape* (Columbia, S.C., 1989).]

WALTER B. EDGAR

See also **SUPP:** Charleston; Hurricanes.

SOUTH DAKOTA. The population of South Dakota grew by only 5 percent from 1970 to 1990, reaching a total just under 700,000, with residents about equally divided between rural and urban areas. The limited productivity of the land and a somewhat inhospitable climate restricted population growth to a rate supported by selective economic diversification. Occupations related to agriculture, tourism, mining, lumber, and wildlife industries plus federal assistance sustained the residents. The state's Native American population enrolled on its nine reservations was 75,400, nearly 4 percent of all Native Americans reported in the 1990 census. Since 1970 a renaissance in traditional American Indian culture, a revival in tribal governance, and the improvement of economic circumstances were the factors that led to the increase in the number of Native Americans living on or near the reservations.

When an experiment with state-sponsored socialism in 1917–1925 left South Dakota with several profitable tourist spots but also a $40 million debt, the state shifted away from its undiversified economy to federal support. Between 1952 and 1992 federal contributions to annual state expenditures rose from 20 percent to 39 percent. Federal support of farming and ranching—South Dakota's primary industry—reached a record $436 million in 1991–1992. Tourism flourished, especially at the Badlands National Park and the Mount Rushmore National Memorial, and brought in approximately $380 million per year. Low unemployment resulted from the presence of the U.S. Army Corps of Engineers along the Missouri River, the U.S. Forest Service overseeing the timberlands and grasslands, and Ellsworth Air Force Base. Thrifty fiscal management and administrative efficiency have been the hallmark of state officials since the 1970s. Legislators and administrators operated with constrained budgets to maintain a surplus while consolidating agencies and functions. By the mid-1970s

officials had merged 3,300 school districts into 200, consolidated 1,000 rural schools into fewer than 50, and collapsed 160 agencies into 16 departments. A cumbersome judicial system was replaced with a supreme court of five judges, thirty-six circuit judges for eight districts, and magistrate courts limited to criminal and minor civil matters. Officials modernized law enforcement under the attorney general and Department of Public Safety and replaced game wardens with conservation officers under a wildlife, parks, and forestry department.

By substantial majorities South Dakota voters have resisted economic improvements at the expense of ecological integrity. Instead of attracting manufacturing and chemical or nuclear-waste-disposal plants, South Dakotans have taken an interest in "clean" businesses. Because the state has no income tax and maintains a regressive tax system, banking giant Citicorp moved its credit card operations to Sioux Falls in 1981, and Gateway Computers, one of the largest mail-order suppliers of personal computers in the United States, established itself at North Sioux City and Sioux Falls. *Money* magazine in 1992 designated Sioux Falls as the most desirable urban center in the United States, not merely because of limited taxation but because of clean air, a network of roads and highways linked by bridges across the Missouri, and easy air transportation. The state's institutions of higher learning—sixteen colleges and universities serving 700,000 people—are fewer in number as compared to a generation earlier. During the 1980s Huron College became a vocational school, owned first by British and then Japanese investors. The state college campus at Springfield was converted into a prison, as was Yankton College.

Native Americans in South Dakota have flourished since the 1960s because of a new generation of political and cultural leaders. On each reservation an elected, constitutional government has been encouraged and empowered by Congress. The Indian Civil Rights Act of 1968 protected the national constitutional rights of individuals while it required tribal approval for state governmental intervention in jurisdiction rightly claimed by the tribes. The Indian Self-Determination and Education Act of 1975 consolidated previous efforts to affirm federal responsibility, encouraged tribal leaders to govern functions previously under the purview of the Bureau of Indian Affairs, and invited tribal participation in governing education, with the Tribally Controlled Community College Act of 1978 assuring federal grants. Since 1970 tribal leaders have reduced unemployment rates in some places by more than 80 percent with new occupational opportunities in the transportation and construction industries, livestock and agricultural production, wildlife management, and bingo operations and gambling casinos free from state taxation (under the National Indian Gaming Act of 1988).

[Herbert T. Hoover, *The Yankton Sioux* (New York, 1988); Herbert T. Hoover and Karen P. Zimmerman, *South Dakota History: An Annotated Bibliography* (Westport, Conn., 1993); Herbert T. Hoover and Larry J. Zimmerman, *South Dakota Leaders* (Lanham, Mo., 1975).]

HERBERT T. HOOVER

SOUTHEAST ASIAN AMERICANS is a term that encompasses several national and ethnic groups, the largest of which includes former citizens of the Philippines, Vietnam, Laos, Cambodia, and Thailand. Filipino Americans, numbering 1,406,770 in 1990, were the largest group. The 1990 census enumerated 614,547 Vietnamese Americans, 149,014 Laotian Americans, 147,411 Cambodian Americans, 91,275 Thai Americans, and 90,082 Hmong Americans (an ethnic group from Vietnam). Before 1975, when the first wave of Southeast Asian refugees arrived in the United States following the fall of the governments of South Vietnam, Laos, and Cambodia to communist forces, few immigrants from those countries settled permanently in the United States. During the 1950s fewer than fifty-five people emigrated per year, and during the 1960s the total gradually increased from about 100 at the beginning of the decade to 1,000 toward its end. Vietnamese constituted the greatest number, totaling 18,000 by 1974 as compared with fewer than 300 from Laos and Cambodia. Immigration from Vietnam, Laos, and Cambodia was, of course, linked to U.S. involvement in the Vietnam War and to Asian exclusion laws that prevailed until 1965. Many immigrants arrived between the 1960s and 1974 as spouses of U.S. servicemen in South Vietnam or as students, often under U.S. government sponsorship. They were distributed throughout the country, with 18 percent of Vietnamese living in California in 1974 and 7 percent in Texas. The immigration and settlement pattern changed dramatically in 1975 with the first wave of refugees, who greatly outnumbered the earlier arrivals, and the second wave, which reached a peak in 1980. Refugees, as opposed to immigrants, were individuals who arrived under the Indochina Migration and Assistance Act of 1975 and the Refugee Act of 1980.

The communist victory in Phnom Penh and Saigon in April 1975 triggered the flight of thousands of Cambodian government officials, military officers, and others together with their families and a massive and chaotic evacuation of Vietnamese government and military personnel. Many of the Cambodians sought refuge in Thailand, from whence some left to join the Vietnamese exiles as refugees in the United States. Laotian refugees were not allowed to enter under the provisions established for the first wave. Vietnamese, comprising 95 percent of the first group, and Cambodian refugees, more than 130,000 by August 1975, were taken to Guam, Thailand, the Philippines, Wake Island, and Hawaii, where they were processed by the Immigration and Naturalization Service before being transported to receiving centers in California, Arkansas, Florida, and Pennsylvania. The refugees were registered with voluntary agencies that found sponsors to help locate housing, clothing, food, and jobs and enroll children in school. The 1975 Refugee Assistance Act helped ease the burden of resettlement.

Because of the war's devastation, the Vietnamese government's persecution of minorities, particularly ethnic Chinese, the brutality of the Pol Pot regime in Cambodia, and the flight of Hmong and lowland Laotians, the flow of refugees continued. "Boat people," the majority of whom were ethnic Chinese, endured great privation at sea, were preyed upon by pirates, and were turned away on the beaches of Malaysia, Indochina, the Philippines, and Hong Kong. Totaling 500,000, perhaps as many as half perished. The numbers climbed throughout the late 1970s, with 20,400 arriving in the United States in 1978, 80,700 in 1979, and 166,700 in 1980. China took in 250,000 Sino-Vietnamese. Half of the refugees worldwide resettled in the United States, 761,000 by 1985, with Canada, Australia, and France admitting 100,000 each.

Policy initially was to disperse refugees throughout the United States ostensibly to minimize economic and cultural disruption in host communities and facilitate assimilation. Kin and ethnic isolation proved difficult and unpopular, and refugees moved to warm states like California. About 30,000 Hmong had settled in Fresno between 1980 and 1986, largely in response to appeals from leaders. The need for familial and cultural support in a strange and sometimes hostile environment compelled reexamination of policy and led to a strategy better accommodated to the desires of refugees, including recognition that ethnic clustering could yield beneficial results. The largest numbers of Vietnamese, Laotian, Cambodian, Thai, and Hmong Americans lived in California, according to the 1990 census, but many Vietnamese Americans lived in Texas, Laotian Americans in Washington and Minnesota, Cambodian Americans in Massachusetts and Washington, Thai Americans in New York and

Texas, and Hmong Americans in Minnesota and Wisconsin. Despite government assistance in alleviating problems of resettlement and refugee efforts directed at self-sufficiency, significant numbers continued to show economic and social need.

Refugees in the first wave were generally well-educated and skilled, proficient in English, and from wealthy social groups, whereas refugees of the second wave tended to be less educated and skilled, with limited English, and from poorer social groups. In 1980, among Vietnamese Americans, 76 percent of men and 63 percent of women age twenty-five to twenty-nine had completed high school as compared with 87 percent of white men and women students. For Southeast Asian Americans as a whole (excluding Filipino Americans), 3 percent were employed as managers in 1987, 22 percent were service workers, and 58 percent blue-collar laborers. Southeast Asian Americans established themselves through retention and adaptation recalling their long history in Indochina of resisting and receiving invaders and in keeping with their syncretic religious and world views. The family and extended kinship are foundations of the community, and families pool resources to bring other members from Southeast Asia. Changes are under way within the family structure because of the greater freedom of children in the United States and because more women are employed outside the household, which raises their standing. Catholic churches, Buddhist temples, and business districts provide points of convergence for the community and ways of linking Southeast Asian American communities within the wider American society. A goal of the Vietnamese Buddhist temple in Los Angeles, for example, is to promote cultural and religious dialogue between Vietnamese and other Americans.

In what some observers have described as a coming to terms with the Vietnam War, Congress in 1978 passed the Amerasian Homecoming Act, which provided for immigration of American-Vietnamese children born between January 1962 and January 1976 and certain of their family members. Often abandoned by their American fathers and ostracized by the Vietnamese, Amerasians were a sharp reminder of a war and a past that many had hoped to forget. They came to the United States poorly educated, were ambivalently received, and searched for identities. By 1989, 22,000 Amerasians had been admitted to the United States.

[James M. Freeman, *Hearts of Sorrow: Vietnamese-American Lives* (Stanford, Calif., 1989); David W. Haines, ed., *Refugees as Immigrants: Cambodians, Laotians, and Vietnamese in America* (Totowa, N.J., 1989); Paul James Rutledge, *The Vietnamese Experience in America* (Bloomington, Ind., 1992).]

GARY Y. OKIHIRO

See also **SUPP:** Filipino Americans; Japanese Americans.

SOVIET AMERICANS. The entry of more than 243,000 émigrés from areas within the former Soviet Union between 1981 and 1993 represents the second large wave of Russian/Soviet immigration to the United States. Between 1881 and 1920, 3.2 million people, the majority of them Jewish, came to the United States from areas of the former Soviet Union. Between these two eras immigration of both Soviet Jews and non-Jews was at very low levels. Public displays of anti-Semitism and lack of opportunities for social and economic advancement increased pressure on the Soviet government to allow the emigration of Soviet Jews during the late 1970s. The U.S. government responded by admitting more than 50,000 refugees from the Soviet Union, the majority of whom were Jews, between 1972 and 1980. Since 1980, 96 percent of immigrants to the United States from areas within the Soviet Union have entered as refugees. Since the late 1980s Soviet refugee streams have included increasing numbers of non-Jews as well as Jews. During the 1990s refugee arrivals from areas within the former Soviet Union ranged between 40,000 and 60,000 per year. For 1993 Congress authorized the admission of 49,775 Soviet refugees.

The communities of Russian and Soviet émigrés within the United States reflect each of these waves of large-scale migration. Between 1970 and 1990 the size of the U.S. population that had been born in the Soviet Union declined from 463,500 to 334,000, reflecting the aging of immigrants who entered at the turn of the century. Nearly two-fifths of the 1990 U.S. population of persons born in czarist Russia or the Soviet Union had entered in the previous ten years.

Since 1992 the U.S. Immigration and Naturalization Service has reported immigration from specific areas in the former Soviet Union. Of the 58,600 immigrants admitted from the former USSR in 1993, 31.3 percent were born in Ukraine, 20.6 percent in Russia, 10.7 percent in Armenia, and 8 percent in Belarus. More than half of recent Soviet immigrants are women and 30 percent are under the age of twenty, indicating the important role of the family in emigration.

As with other groups, Soviet émigrés are concentrated in specific geographic areas in the United States. In 1990, 48 percent of this population resided in the Northeast and 27 percent in western states; among Soviet immigrants arriving during the 1980s, 36 percent settled in California. The New York metropolitan region had the largest number of Soviet- and Russian-born people, and large communities of émigrés were formed in the Los Angeles–Long Beach area. Settlement of Soviet Jewish immigrants was aided in large part by private Jewish organizations in metropolitan areas throughout the United States. Results of survey research on resettled Jewish populations, moreover, indicate that Soviet Jewish émigrés to the United States expressed strong religious identities similar to Soviet émigrés to Israel.

Descendants of earlier waves of Russian immigration have been characterized by high levels of education and occupation. In the 1990 census half of the Russian-ancestry male population reported either professional specialties or executive, administrative, or managerial occupations; among Russian-ancestry women, 40 percent were in these occupations. These levels are significantly higher than those for other ancestry groups. Recent immigrants also have been distinctive in levels of education and occupation. Among Soviet immigrants admitted to the United States in 1993, one-third of those reporting occupations listed professional, executive, administrative, or managerial occupations. Occupations among recent Soviet Jewish immigrants are estimated to be proportionally even higher. Estimates for immigrants aided by the Hebrew Aid Society in 1989 suggest that two-thirds of Soviet Jewish immigrants were in professional, scientific, technical, and white-collar occupations prior to migrating.

[Stanley Lieberson and Mary C. Waters, *From Many Strands: Ethnic and Racial Groups in Contemporary America* (New York, 1988); Rita J. Simon, ed., *New Lives: The Adjustment of Soviet Jewish Immigrants in the United States and Israel* (Lexington, Mass., 1985).]

ELLEN PERCY KRALY

See also **SUPP:** Immigration; Jews, American; Refugees; Soviet Union, Relations with.

SOVIET UNION, RELATIONS WITH. Between the 1970s and 1990s relations between the United States and the Soviet Union experienced change unexpected in either scope or pace. At the end of the 1960s the two nations were opposing one another in a struggle for ideological domination of Indochina. Washington's prestige in the Third World was plummeting. Criticism of U.S. policies spread in Europe and relations within the U.S.-led North Atlantic Treaty Organization (NATO) were increasingly strained. At home the

Vietnam War provoked divisions within society. The economy suffered, inflation mounted, and social justice issues languished as the war diverted money and attention from the Great Society programs so optimistically unveiled just a few years before. In contrast, the Union of Soviet Socialist Republics (USSR) appeared to be in an improving position. Its economy, somewhat revived by the reforms of former Communist Party First Secretary Nikita Khrushchev, was producing increased amounts of industrial and agricultural goods. The administrative turmoil and political uncertainties stirred by Khrushchev had quieted since the accession of Leonid Brezhnev to the chief party post in 1964. The supremacy of the will of the Soviet Union over its satellites in Eastern Europe and its own alliance system, the Warsaw Pact, had been unchallenged—despite a certain degree of noncooperation on the part of Romania—since 1968, when the Soviets crushed Czech moves for democratic reform and independence from that alliance.

By the close of 1991, however, the former Soviet empire in Eastern Europe had come apart, the Warsaw Pact was dissolved, and the prestige of communism and Moscow as its leader in world affairs had fallen sharply. Economic and environmental crises were spreading throughout a fragmented country. Protests against mismanagement, misrule, and worsening living standards were turning into ethnic wars. The United States, if still troubled by persistent social and racial problems and a stagnant economy, seemed more self-confident. Moreover, its stature as a world leader had been reasserted by the Gulf War of 1991 that restored Kuwait's independence from Iraq. How this reversal of fortunes came about continues to be the subject of much inquiry by historians. Although some analysts have assigned substantial credit or blame to individual statesmen, consensus suggests the causes are multiple, rooted not only in individual decisions and national philosophies but also in factors ranging from technology to the environment, from economics to chance. Moreover, if economic and military pressures had much to do with the deterioration of the Soviet Union, subsequent developments have shown that those same forces also harmed the United States. The latter may have outlasted the Soviet Union, enabling it to claim victory in the cold war. Nevertheless, the toll levied on the U.S. economy, social programs, and capacity for future world leadership was considerable.

Domestic unrest and the untenable position of the United States in Vietnam at the beginning of the 1970s had much to do with diplomatic initiatives that altered Soviet-U.S. relations and affected the course of the cold war. Confident that the United States was weakening, the Brezhnev leadership expanded the Soviet role in Africa, South America, the Middle East, and Central Asia, ultimately invading Afghanistan in 1979. Activism in the Third World dictated an easing of tensions in Europe. An equilibrium had been achieved over the previous decades as both East and West became more comfortable with—or at least accustomed to—the de facto division of the continent. Unlike his predecessors, Brezhnev suspected that victory over capitalism did not rest solely on class struggle but also on technical knowledge as the determinant of new modes of production. It was in this area that the Soviets and their allies most seriously trailed the West. A relaxation of tensions might permit increased trade with the West, including the acquisition of machine tools and improved technologies. Such information also was necessary because China and its leader, Mao Zedong, increasingly challenged Soviet leadership of the communist world. Indeed, incidents along the Chinese border and the necessity of stationing more troops there emphasized the value of reducing confrontation in the West, lest the Soviets be confronted with simultaneous crises on borders more than 2,000 miles apart.

China also loomed large in the thinking of President Richard M. Nixon, who took office in January 1969. Because of his credentials as a strong anticommunist cold warrior, Nixon was one of the few U.S. politicians who could take the initiative in opening relations with the People's Republic of China without facing the criticism of being "soft" on communism. Nixon also saw the value of playing off China and the Soviet Union against one another. The Chinese, although mistrustful, also saw the utility of improving relations with the United States because they feared a Soviet preemptive air strike against their northern nuclear sites. Cautious approaches led to Nixon's visit to Beijing in February 1972 and U.S. rapprochement with the largest communist nation in the world. U.S.-China contacts did not pass unnoticed in Moscow, which consequently shifted to a more accommodating stance in disarmament talks that had proceeded desultorily since 1968. In May 1972 Nixon traveled to Moscow to sign the Strategic Arms Limitation Treaty (SALT I).

Thus was inaugurated a period of Soviet-U.S. relations known as détente, or relaxation of tensions, but the relaxation both desired did not conceal that the two nations interpreted détente differently. Soviet leaders believed history was evolving in the direction of communism and saw détente as a process that would allow that to happen with as few military encounters as possible. This arrangement, called "peaceful coexistence," did not imply any socialist retreat or even acceptance of a static situation. In particular the Soviets were willing to accept détente in Europe as long as they were able to continue expanding their role in the Third World. For U.S. leaders détente meant a way, other than traditional containment, to urge the USSR into behavior more like that of Western industrialized nations. The United States, too, thought time was on its side and that emerging countries, if left to themselves, would evolve toward democracy and industrial capitalism.

The SALT I arms agreement was modest, primarily limiting to two the number of antiballistic missile (ABM) systems each power could deploy. This proviso assured that neither power could launch a "safe" nuclear first strike, because neither could wipe out its opponent's retaliatory power or protect itself from a retaliatory strike, maintaining the possibility of mutually assured destruction (MAD) that had militated against outbreak of nuclear war between the superpowers. As for offensive weapons, the number of strategic missile launchers each possessed would be frozen for five years. In short, SALT I produced no reduction of armaments, just a reduction in their expansion to a rate acceptable to the strategic plans and economies of both powers. SALT I did, however, indicate that negotiation was possible. Other contacts were opened and in the summer of 1972 the Soviets arranged extensive grain purchase contracts with the United States. U.S. farmers cheered but consumers did not when it was discovered the Soviets had quickly and quietly purchased at prices subsidized by U.S. taxpayers more grain than warranted by national reserves, thus elevating bread prices in the United States. Disarmament talks continued. In November 1974 Brezhnev and President Gerald R. Ford agreed at a summit meeting in Vladivostok to limits on strategic missile launchers and a sublimit on multiple, independently targeted reentry vehicles (MIRVs). As construction of ABM systems was proving technologically difficult, both were willing to reduce such systems to one per country.

Arms reduction and other discussions stimulated by détente involved some alteration in the U.S. diplomatic posture toward the Soviet Union. Since 1947 the United States had followed a policy of containment, which by the 1960s had come to mean primarily the encirclement of the Soviet Union with military bases and nuclear weapons. Only limited effort had been expended on comprehensive negotiations. A diplomatic stalemate had resulted, with only isolated breakthroughs. Through détente and a concept known as linkage, Nixon and his national security adviser and later secretary of state, Henry Kissinger, attempted to move negotiations along a broader front than in the past by tying progress in one area to progress in another. The United States still wished to contain the Soviet empire but saw a need for new approaches at a time when Soviet prestige in the Third World was mounting and economic and political support for an active U.S. foreign policy and military role was waning. The United States also wanted help in leaving Vietnam and for the Soviets to restrain themselves in the Third World. In return, Nixon and Kissinger offered recognition of strategic parity, access to Western trade and technology, and some willingness to tolerate the record of the USSR and its satellites on human and democratic rights.

Détente and linkage had only minor influence on events outside Europe. The Soviets continued to press for advantage in the Third World, and the West endeavored to retain a strong influence there. In the Middle East, both the United States and the Soviet Union placed troop contingents on highest alert during the Yom Kippur War of 1973. The success of the Israelis in defending themselves against Egyptian-Syrian attack strengthened the U.S. position in the region, as did Egyptian expulsion of Soviet advisers. In Africa, by contrast, the success the Soviets and Cubans experienced in supporting Marxist-Leninists in Angola in the mid-1970s demonstrated the weakness of U.S. influence in that area. If détente faltered on the periphery it succeeded in Europe by temporarily facilitating the efforts of West German Chancellor Willy Brandt to improve relations between his country and Eastern Europe. Brandt already had achieved treaties with Poland and the Soviet Union. In 1972, with the Soviets and the West reaching agreements over access to Berlin, the East and West German governments signed what came to be called the Basic Treaty—each entered the United Nations the following year with approval of both superpowers. In 1973 Brezhnev and Nixon signed an agreement renouncing nuclear warfare between their countries and promising to try to prevent it among themselves.

Aside from armament limitation the 1975 Helsinki Accords were the major achievement of détente, but even these were very much a part of the cold war. A key Soviet goal had long been separation of the United States from its European allies and promotion of East-West understanding in Europe without U.S. involvement. Moscow also wanted formal acceptance of European borders arising from World War II. To

this end, in the spring of 1968 the Soviets proposed a conference solely of European states. Their heavy-handed actions in Czechoslovakia a few months later, however, strengthened the resolve of European NATO members not to be separated from their Canadian and U.S. friends. Eventually, foreign ministers of thirty-five nations, including all NATO partners, gathered in Helsinki in 1973 to initiate what has now become the larger Conference on Security and Cooperation in Europe (CSCE). In time the CSCE talks led to a tripartite statement of principles signed by the participants in 1975. Basket I dealt with security matters and essentially confirmed the status quo in Europe; Basket II called for cooperation on environmental, technological, and economic problems; and Basket III contained a statement of human rights that the signatories promised to protect. The Soviets initially considered the Helsinki Accords a triumph for their side because it confirmed the status quo in Eastern Europe. The West paid little attention or criticized the accords as an abandonment of Eastern Europe by the United States, its will and economy weakened by the Vietnam experience. In response the Ford administration tried to link U.S. acquiescence to Soviet and satellite promises to better human rights. These promises would be taken by East European reformers as a rallying point and leverage tool with which to demand transformation of their governments.

The election of Jimmy Carter to the U.S. presidency in November 1976 brought to the White House a novice in international affairs. For advice he turned to two able individuals of differing views, Secretary of State Cyrus Vance and national secretary adviser Zbigniew Brzezinski. Interested in arms control, Vance believed in strengthening détente and hoped for cooperation from younger Soviet officials who were not as dogmatically Marxist as the aging Brezhnev generation. He also worried that China might use the United States for its own ends, worsening Soviet-U.S. relations, and did not want Third World issues to dominate the Soviet-U.S. agenda. Brzezinski saw little use in trying to reach agreement with the Soviets or in waiting for them to assume a more cooperative stance. They needed to be countered everywhere, change in Kremlin attitudes was not to be expected, and the aid of the Chinese should be enlisted in challenging Moscow. According to Brzezinski the contest was a total one and compromise or concession a mistake.

Without serious challenge the Soviets and Cubans aided seizures of power by communist or pro-Soviet groupings in Angola, Ethiopia, Afghanistan, Cambodia, Grenada, and Nicaragua. Although they viewed the Carter regime as ineffectual, Soviets were angered by their exclusion from the Camp David talks wherein Carter achieved a breakthrough in fostering Israeli-Egyptian agreement. Meanwhile, Soviet successes and the nudgings of the Chinese, who indeed wanted to use the Americans against the Soviets, turned the U.S. electorate and Carter himself away from the views of Vance and toward Brzezinski's more traditional cold warrior tactics of confrontation.

Despite Soviet adventurism in the Third World and changing U.S. attitudes, détente still held possibilities for arms control. Although the European states of NATO were wealthier than those of the Warsaw Pact, they disliked the notion of sacrificing domestic programs for additional military expenditures. Efforts to achieve a mutual and balanced force reduction of conventional forces went nowhere, and in the late 1970s both sides determined to modernize their intermediate-range nuclear forces (INF) in the European theater. Discussions regarding long-range missiles made some headway. A SALT II treaty signed in June 1979 by Carter and Brezhnev upheld the agreements reached at Vladivostok and placed a sublimit on seaborne forces (but not seaborne launchers). It also postponed the possibility of the intercontinental ballistic missiles (ICBMs) of either side being vulnerable to attack, thus preventing either power from considering a preventive first strike. By this time, however, anti-SALT forces were strong in the U.S. Senate, where conservatives resented Carter's successful negotiations for the eventual relinquishment of control over the Panama Canal. Specious controversy arose over a brigade of Soviet troops that actually had been in Cuba for many years and represented no reinforcement of Soviet arms there. Doubts mounted over Brezhnev's assurance that the Soviet Backfire bomber, which had many performance characteristics of a strategic bomber, was not adaptable to intercontinental use. Any prompt ratification of SALT II became impossible.

Benefits anticipated by the Soviets from the granting of most-favored-nation trading status by the United States at the beginning of the détente period in return for settlement of old World War II lend-lease debts failed to materialize. Almost immediately Senator Henry M. Jackson of Washington, a noted cold war hawk, demanded revocation of an exit tax imposed by the Soviets on émigrés, intended to reimburse the cost of education provided by the state. His amendment to a trade bill forced the Soviets to cancel their tax. Jewish immigration from the USSR be-

came a substitute for ideological confrontation. The United States soon pressed the USSR to double the number of Jews it would allow to emigrate. Legislative restrictions were placed on Export-Import Bank loans, to be lifted only if the Soviets removed restrictions on emigration by all nationalities according to a schedule approved by the United States. Brezhnev and his advisers interpreted such legislative notions as meddling in Soviet civil affairs. Their annoyance with Carter mounted when he responded to the deployment of new Soviet missiles aimed at Europe by pressuring NATO allies to accept installation of Pershing and cruise missiles, both of which posed serious defensive problems for the Soviets.

While the value of détente was being questioned by both superpowers the dangers of ethnic factionalism and rising Islamic fundamentalism in Afghanistan led to Soviet military intervention in December 1979. The U.S. reaction was perhaps more severe than the Kremlin anticipated. Branding the USSR an aggressor nation, Carter imposed a grain embargo and declared that U.S. athletes would not participate in the summer Olympic Games to be held in Moscow. Détente was at an end and a renewed arms race appeared likely. This possibility seemed confirmed by the election as president of Ronald Reagan, an old-style cold warrior who characterized the Soviet Union as the "evil empire," but even he had to continue some form of arms negotiations. The U.S. proposal that both sides eliminate nuclear weapons in Europe was rejected by the Soviets. Their campaign to persuade European governments to resist deployment of new U.S. intermediate-range missiles failed; the Soviets then withdrew from both intermediate- and long-range missile talks. Further cooling of relations flowed from sympathy in the United States for the Solidarity movement in Poland. The United States imposed economic sanctions against that country when the Soviet Union pressured the Polish military into seizing power in Warsaw in 1981. By the end of 1983 U.S.-Soviet relations were at their lowest point in years.

During that year the Soviet Union was adjusting to new leadership. Brezhnev, too old and feeble to attempt any new policy orientation, had died in November 1982. His successor, Yuri Andropov, appeared aware that the USSR's expansionism in the Third World and its search for absolute security might be negatively affecting attitudes in Washington. Moreover, unrest in Poland and economic conditions in Russia were becoming increasing problems. At the end of August, Soviet fighters shot down a Korean jetliner that had strayed into Soviet airspace. Soviet spokesmen first denied responsibility then asserted that the airliner was serving as a spy plane. Reagan and the world harshly chastised the Soviets for wantonly taking civilian lives.

In the early years of containment the United States was content to "hold the line" while hoping for internal changes in the Soviet Union. Now it began to exert more pressure. U.S. troops were sent to Grenada in 1983 ostensibly to protect U.S. medical students; as a result, the island's government passed from the hands of Marxists to pro-Westerners. U.S. aid also was secretly funneled to the Contras opposing the Sandinista regime in Nicaragua as part of the Reagan Doctrine of supporting forces opposing pro-Soviet regimes throughout the world. The president traveled to China and reaffirmed what had been a weakening relationship there. Most notably, Reagan generally increased the U.S. defense budget and military forces. He also proposed in March 1983 the Strategic Defense Initiative (SDI). Although the Soviets protested that a new outer space defense against ballistic missiles violated the 1972 ABM treaty, the Americans forged ahead with research. The Soviets could ill afford to fall behind in the new arms race. If that race put severe strains on the United States, which markedly increased its national debt, it spelled near-disaster for the Soviets, who had fewer reserves and a less developed economy. Moreover, the death of Andropov in February 1984 and the succession of the geriatric Konstantin Chernenko meant a lack of strong leadership when it was most needed.

By the time the dynamic Mikhail Gorbachev became the first secretary of the party after Chernenko's death in March 1985 it was clear that a new course was necessary. As part of his new thinking, Gorbachev decided to reduce expenditures associated with Soviet commitments overseas, in Afghanistan where fruitless warfare continued, and even in Eastern Europe. Gorbachev's initiatives to achieve troop and arms reductions took Washington by surprise, but Reagan's genuine fear of nuclear war and his wish to make a historic contribution to the peace process meant Soviet offers would be favorably received. After months of negotiation and several summit meetings, an INF treaty was signed in December 1987. It entailed not just a limitation on deployments but an actual reduction in armaments. SDI remained a roadblock as well as an incentive for further talks regarding strategic missiles. Meanwhile, the Soviets announced a withdrawal of troops from Afghanistan, a process that was completed in February 1989.

Gorbachev's willingness in 1989 to allow East European countries to choose their own political paths, followed by his acquiescence to German reunification, had more to do with Soviet economic and political issues than with U.S. relations. It did, however, have the effect of wiping out many of the old quarrels that had contributed to the cold war and facilitating what Gorbachev understood his country badly needed to restructure its economy—more trade and investment from the West. During the Gulf War of 1991 he even reluctantly abandoned former Arab friends and aligned the USSR with the United States. Gorbachev's foreign policy and military cutbacks partially stimulated the failed August 1991 conservative coup that shifted governing power in the USSR to other leaders, such as the more radical Boris Yeltsin and heads of various republics who desired independence for their regions. They would declare the end of the Union of Soviet Socialist Republics as of Dec. 31, 1991. Ironically its demise occurred at probably the friendliest point in U.S.-Soviet relations since World War II. The cold war was over, but its legacy in placing stress on both the USSR and the United States would be felt for years to come.

Multiple issues remained to be resolved between the United States and the successor states to the Soviet Union. Sharp debates arose between Russia, the largest of the republics, and the United States despite mutual desire for good relations. How much financial aid would the United States provide for the reconstruction of the new Russia? To what extent would Russia welcome private U.S. investment? What role should the United States play in the dismantling of antiquated Soviet nuclear weapons and plants? Differing views were strongly held on the possible expansion of NATO to include former Soviet satellite states, on the treatment of crises in the Balkans, and on the extent of Russian and U.S. influence in the other successor republics. A half decade of such controversies firmly demonstrated that the road to true harmony in U.S.-Russian relations would require long traveling.

[Warren I. Cohen, ed., *The Cambridge History of American Foreign Relations,* vol. 4, *America in the Age of Soviet Power, 1945–1991* (New York, 1993); Walter LaFeber, *America, Russia and the Cold War, 1945–1991,* 7th ed. (New York, 1993); Don Oberdorfer, *The Turn: From Cold War to a New Era: The United States and the Soviet Union, 1983–1990* (New York, 1991).]

JONATHAN E. HELMREICH

See also **DAH:** Arms Race with the Soviet Union; Berlin Wall; Cuban Missile Crisis; Missiles, Military;

Russia, U.S. Relations with; **DAH** and **SUPP:** Cold War; North Atlantic Treaty Organization; Strategic Arms Limitation Talks; Summit Conferences; **SUPP:** Afghanistan, Invasion of; Arms Race and Disarmament; China, Relations with; Eastern Europe, Relations with; Gulf War of 1991; Strategic Defense Initiative; Summit Conferences, Presidential.

SPACE PROGRAM. The U.S. civil space program went into something of a holding pattern after completion of Project Apollo in December 1972. For the next decade the major program of the National Aeronautics and Space Administration (NASA) was the development of the Space Transportation System, a reusable space shuttle that was supposed to be able to travel back and forth between the Earth and space more routinely and economically than the spectacular but expensive series of missions that had followed the Apollo 11 moon landing on July 20, 1969. Between the autumn of 1969 and early 1972, NASA leaders worked to convince President Richard M. Nixon that the shuttle was an appropriate follow-on project to Apollo. They were successful on Jan. 5, 1972, when the president issued a statement announcing the decision to "proceed at once with the development of an entirely new type of space transportation system designed to help transform the space frontier of the 1970s into familiar territory, easily accessible for human endeavor in the 1980s and 1990s." The shuttle became the largest, most expensive, and most highly visible project undertaken by NASA after its first decade, and it has continued to be a central component of the space program.

The space shuttle that emerged in the early 1970s consisted of three primary elements: a delta-winged orbiter spacecraft with a large crew compartment, a fifteen-by-sixty-foot cargo bay, and three main engines; two solid rocket boosters (SRBs); and an external fuel tank housing the liquid hydrogen and oxidizer burned in the main engines. The orbiter and SRBs were reusable. The shuttle was designed to transport up to 45,000 pounds of cargo into near-Earth orbit for a planned space station, to be located 115 to 250 miles above the earth, and to accommodate a flight crew of ten (although seven would be more common) for a basic space mission of seven days. For its return to earth, the orbiter was designed to have a cross-range maneuvering capability of 1,265 miles to meet requirements for liftoff and landing at the same location after only one orbit. This capability satisfied Department of Defense requirements for a shuttle that could place in orbit and retrieve reconnaissance satellites.

NASA began developing the shuttle soon after the president's announcement with the goal of flying in space by 1978, but because of budgetary pressure and technological problems the first orbital flight was delayed until 1981. There was tremendous excitement when *Columbia,* the first operational orbiter, took off from Cape Canaveral, Fla., on Apr. 12, 1981, six years after the last U.S. astronaut had returned from space following the Apollo-Soyuz Test Project in 1975. After the two-day test flight, the nation watched with excitement as the shuttle landed like a conventional airplane at Edwards Air Force Base in California. The first flight was a success, and both NASA and the media proclaimed the beginning of a new age in space flight, an era of inexpensive and routine access to space for many people and payloads. Speculation abounded that within a few years shuttle flights would take off and land as predictably as airplanes and that commercial tickets would be sold for regularly scheduled "spaceline" flights.

As it turned out, the shuttle program provided neither inexpensive nor routine access to space. By January 1986 there had been only twenty-four shuttle flights; in the 1970s NASA had projected more flights than that for every year. Although the system was reusable, its complexity, coupled with the ever-present rigors of flying in an aerospace environment, meant that turnaround time between flights was several months instead of several days. Missions were delayed for all manner of problems, and it took thousands of work hours and expensive parts to keep the system performing. Observers began to criticize NASA for failing to meet expectations. Analysts agreed that the shuttle had proven neither cheap nor reliable, both primary selling points, and that NASA should not have used those arguments in building a political consensus for the program. By 1985 there was general agreement that the effort had been both a triumph and a tragedy. An engagingly ambitious program had developed an exceptionally sophisticated vehicle, one that no other nation on earth could have built at the time. At the same time, the shuttle's much-touted capabilities had not been realized. Criticism reached its height following the tragic loss of *Challenger* and its crew of seven in an explosion during a launch on Jan. 28, 1986. Pressure to get the shuttle schedule more in line with earlier projections had prompted NASA workers to accept operational procedures that fostered shortcuts and increased the opportunity for disaster, although that was not the entire reason for the explosion. Several investigations followed the accident, the most important being the blue-ribbon commission mandated by President Ronald Reagan and chaired by William P. Rogers. It found that the *Challenger* accident resulted from a poor engineering decision, an O-ring used to seal joints in the SRBs that was susceptible to failure at low temperatures.

Following the *Challenger* accident, the shuttle program went into a two-year hiatus while NASA redesigned the SRBs and revamped its management. James C. Fletcher, NASA administrator between 1971 and 1977, was brought back and given the task of overhauling the agency. NASA invested heavily in safety and reliability programs and restructured its management. Most important, engineers added a way for the astronauts to be ejected from a malfunctioning shuttle during launch. Another decision resulting from the accident was to increase the use of expendable launch vehicles. The space shuttle finally returned to flight on Sept. 29, 1988, with the launch of *Discovery*. Through April 1993 NASA launched an additional thirty shuttle missions without an accident. Each undertook scientific and technological experiments ranging from deployment of space probes, such as the *Magellan* Venus radar mapper in 1989 and the Hubble Space Telescope in 1990 to the continued *Spacelab* flights in 1991 for the European Space Agency (which NASA had undertaken in 1983) and a dramatic three-person extravehicular activity (EVA) in 1992 to retrieve a satellite and bring it back to earth for repair. Through all these activities, a good deal of realism about what the shuttle could and could not do began to emerge.

In addition to the shuttle, the space program initiated a series of spectacular science missions in the 1970s. Project Viking was the culmination of an effort begun in 1964 to explore Mars. Two identical spacecraft were built, each consisting of a lander and an orbiter. Launched on Aug. 20, 1975, *Viking 1* landed on July 20, 1976, on the Chryse Planitia (Golden Plains). *Viking 2* was launched on Sept. 9, 1975, and landed Sept. 3, 1976. One of the scientific activities of the project was an attempt to determine whether there was life on Mars, but the Viking landers provided no clear evidence for living microorganisms in soil near landing sites. One of the most important space probes undertaken by the United States was initiated because the Earth and all the giant planets of the solar system were due to gather on one side of the sun in the late 1970s. This geometric lineup made possible close observation of all planets in the outer solar system (with exception of Pluto) in a single flight, which was called the Grand Tour. The flyby of each planet would bend a spacecraft's flight path and increase velocity enough to deliver it to the next destination, which would occur through a complicated process known as gravity assist (something like a slingshot effect), thereby reducing the flight time to Neptune from thirty years to twelve. Project Voyager was a satellite reconnaissance in which two Voyager spacecraft were launched from Kennedy Space Center in 1977 to photograph Jupiter and Saturn. As the mission progressed, with achievement of all objectives at Jupiter and Saturn in December 1980, flybys of the two outermost giant planets, Uranus and Neptune, proved possible—and irresistible. *Voyager 1* and *Voyager 2* explored all the giant outer planets, including their rings and magnetic fields and forty-eight of their moons.

The $2 billion Hubble Space Telescope project received much media attention in the early 1990s. A key component of the telescope was a precision-ground 94-inch primary mirror shaped to within microinches of perfection from ultralow-expansion titanium silicate glass with an aluminum-magnesium fluoride coating. The telescope was launched from the space shuttle in April 1990, and the first photos provided much better images than pictures of the same target taken by ground-based telescopes. Controllers then began moving the telescope's mirrors for better focus, and although focus sharpened, the best image still had a pinpoint of light encircled by a hazy ring or "halo." Technicians concluded that the telescope had a spherical aberration, a mirror defect one twenty-fifth the width of a human hair that prevented Hubble from focusing all light to a single point. Many observers believed the spherical aberration would cripple the forty-three-foot-long telescope, and NASA received much criticism, but scientists found a way to work around the abnormality with computer enhancement. Because of difficulties with the mirror, NASA launched *Endeavour* in December 1993 on a mission to insert corrective lenses on the telescope and to service other instruments. During a weeklong mission *Endeavour*'s astronauts conducted a record five space walks and completed all programmed repairs. The images returned afterward were more than an order of magnitude better than those obtained before.

During the 1980s plans were put forth for a new generation of planetary exploration. The Reagan administration called for a permanently occupied space station in 1984. Congress made a down payment of $150 million for space station *Freedom* in the fiscal year 1985 NASA budget. From the outset both administration officials and NASA intended *Freedom* to be an international program. Partners abroad, many with their own rapidly developing space capabilities, could enhance the effort. NASA leaders pressed forward with international agreements among thirteen nations to take part, but almost from the outset *Freedom* was controversial. Debate centered on costs versus benefits. The projected cost of $8 billion had tripled within five years. NASA pared away at the budget, and in the end the project was satisfactory to almost no one. In the late 1980s and early 1990s a parade of space station managers and NASA administrators, each attempting to rescue the program, wrestled with *Freedom* and lost. In 1993 the international situation allowed NASA to include Russia in the building of an international space station, a smaller and cheaper successor to *Freedom.* On Nov. 7, 1993, a joint announcement was made by the United States and Russia that they would work with other international partners to build a station for benefit of all. Even so, the space station remained a difficult issue as policymakers confronted competing national programs. Even more troubling for the space program was the ambitious Space Exploration Initiative (SEI), which would return people to the moon by the year 2000, establish a lunar base, and, using the space station and the moon as bases, reach Mars by 2010. The price tag was estimated at $700 billion over two decades. Congress refused to fund SEI despite lobbying by Vice President Dan Quayle as head of the National Aeronautics and Space Council, an advisory group to President George Bush. Although the president castigated Congress for not "investing in America's future," members believed such a huge sum could be better spent elsewhere. "We're essentially not doing Moon-Mars," Senator Barbara Mikulski of Maryland declared bluntly.

By 1993 the highly successful *Magellan* mission to Venus had provided data about that planet. The *Galileo* mission to Jupiter had become a source of concern because not all systems were working, but it also returned useful data. The ill-fated *Mars Observer* reached its destination in 1993 but was lost as a result of an onboard explosion. Thus, as the U.S. space program approached the last years of the twentieth century its reputation had been tarnished by debates about the space station and SEI, the initial failure of the Hubble Space Telescope, and the deficiency of *Galileo,* to say nothing of the *Challenger* accident. The fate of the space station program was undecided in 1994, on the twenty-fifth anniversary of the first moon landing,

but both it and the stillborn Space Exploration Initiative pointed up the difficulty of building a constituency for large science and technology programs.

[Roger E. Bilstein, *Orders of Magnitude: A History of the NACA and NASA, 1915–1990* (Washington, D.C., 1989); Wernher von Braun, Frederick I. Ordway III, and Dave Dooling, *History of Rocketry and Space Travel,* 3rd ed. (New York, 1986); Roger D. Launius, *NASA: A History of the U.S. Civil Space Program* (Melbourne, Fla., 1994); Howard E. McCurdy, *Inside NASA: High Technology and Organizational Change in the U.S. Space Program* (Baltimore, 1993); Walter A. McDougall, *The Heavens and the Earth: A Political History of the Space Age* (New York, 1985).]

ROGER D. LAUNIUS

See also **DAH:** Astronautics; National Aeronautics and Space Administration; **SUPP:** Astronomy; *Challenger* Disaster; Hubble Telescope.

SPECIAL PROSECUTORS. When a prosecutor who would ordinarily be responsible for a given case has, or is perceived to have, a conflict of interest in its investigation and prosecution, a special prosecutor may be appointed. Special prosecutors are used in state and municipal government for investigations of public corruption but their prominence in U.S. history arises largely from their use in national politics. Calvin Coolidge appointed special counsel to investigate the Teapot Dome scandal of the 1920s, and special prosecutors appointed by President Richard M. Nixon figured prominently in the investigation of the Watergate scandal of the early 1970s. Watergate helped institutionalize use of special prosecutors at the national level. After Nixon dismissed Special Prosecutor Archibald Cox, public outcry forced him to appoint a successor, Leon Jaworski. Congress then began debating proposals that provided for independent special prosecutors. The Ethics in Government Act of 1978 arranged for judicially appointed independent counsel to investigate allegations of criminal misconduct against high-ranking executive officials. The act's provisions remained controversial throughout their existence. Opponents argued that appointment of independent prosecutors was an unconstitutional violation of the doctrine of separation of powers. In *Morrison* v. *Olson* (1989) the Supreme Court ruled that such arrangements were constitutional. Between 1978 and 1992, the year Congress failed to reauthorize the Ethics Act, its provisions were invoked in cases involving members of the Jimmy Carter and Ronald Reagan administrations. The most prominent and controversial of these involved the Iran-Contra scandal. In response to allegations of misconduct by President Bill Clinton in the Whitewater scandal, Republicans dropped their opposition to the provisions and they were reauthorized in 1994.

[Katy J. Harriger, *Independent Justice: The Federal Special Prosecutor in American Politics* (Lawrence, Kans., 1992).]

KATY J. HARRIGER

See also **DAH:** Teapot Dome Oil Scandal; Watergate; **SUPP:** Iran-Contra Affair; Scandals; Whitewater.

SPECIES, INTRODUCED. As humans settled in North America over the past 15,000 years, they brought with them a variety of species novel to the environment. Many introduced, or exotic, species, such as wheat, potatoes, cattle, pigs, and horses, were brought to the United States intentionally. Many organisms, however, have been unintentionally introduced, traveling in the holds of ships or planes, hitching rides on imported produce, or escaping from captivity. Both intentional and unintentional introductions can leave unforeseen and destructive economic and ecological effects. Although most introduced species are poorly adapted to a novel ecosystem and die out, some thrive. Arriving in an ecosystem that evolved without them, introduced species frequently have no predators. Native species may not have the defenses necessary to ward off a novel predator. Introduced species can outcompete native species and drive them to extinction or change an ecosystem by altering relationships within it.

The results of introductions of species, intentional and unintentional, are often dramatic. The ecosystems of Hawaii, which evolved in isolation, have been devastated by the introduction of exotic species. Since the arrival of Polynesians 1,000 years ago and Europeans 200 years ago, many of the islands' native plant, bird, and insect species have become extinct because of competition and predation by rats, cats, sheep, goats, and other introduced organisms. In the 1990s there were three times as many introduced species of plants on the islands as there were native plants. In an effort to produce domestic silk, the caterpillar of the gypsy moth was imported to the United States in the nineteenth century. Moths escaped in 1869 and spread throughout the country because they had few natural predators or parasites. Their effect reached a climax in the 1980s, but the insects continue to cause widespread damage to hardwood forests throughout North America. In 1890 European starlings were released in New York City by a birding enthusiast who wanted to establish in the United States all birds from William Shakespeare's writings. The population of these opportunistic and aggressive birds quickly increased as they displaced native cavity-nesting birds, and their range now includes most of North America.

In 1956 the African species of honeybee that had been imported into Brazil escaped from captivity and established colonies and hybridized with the European species of honeybee, itself an introduced species essential for the production of honey and pollination of fruit trees. Africanized honeybees began migrating north and crossed into Texas in October 1990. The Department of Agriculture predicted that the Africanized species will have substantial negative effects on U.S. agriculture. One of the most celebrated cases of an introduced species causing economic damage was the unintentional introduction of the Mediterranean fruit fly, or Medfly, in the 1970s in California. Imported on foreign produce, these small flies caused widespread fruit and vegetable damage. The spread of the Medfly spurred an eradication campaign in California that highlighted the pros and cons of pesticide use.

An introduced species that began causing widespread economic and ecological disruption in the 1990s was the zebra mussel, believed to have been released from the ballast of a European tanker in the Great Lakes in 1988. The mussel population exploded, displacing native mollusks, blocking water pipes and dam outlets, disrupting fisheries, and destroying native aquatic ecosystems. The projected cost to control the zebra mussel invasion is $5 billion by the year 2000. The urgency of the situation provoked Congress to pass the Nonindigenous Aquatic Nuisance Prevention and Control Act of 1990. Near the end of the twentieth century there were thousands of introduced species living in the United States. The Department of Agriculture estimated that introduced species were the primary factor in the population decline of approximately 225 of the nation's 660 endangered or threatened species.

[Marcia Barinaga, "Entomologists in the Medfly Maelstrom," and Mark H. Crawford, ed., "Africanized Bees Near Texas Border," *Science* 247 (1990); Allen Hammond, *World Resources Institute Environmental Almanac* (Boston, 1994); John Ross, "An Aquatic Invader Is Running Amok in U.S. Waterways," *Smithsonian* 24 (1994).]

DAVID W. CASH

See also **SUPP:** Ecology; Endangered Species; Pesticides.

SPEECH, FREEDOM OF. *See* **Freedom of Speech.**

SPERM BANKS. *See* **Reproductive Technology.**

SPIES AND SPYING. *See* **Espionage, Industrial; Intelligence, Military and Strategic.**

SPORTS, NEW. During the 1970s and 1980s a number of new sports appeared on the U.S. scene as a result of popular concerns about health and fitness and commercial promotion of nontraditional activities. These sports tend to be fast-paced, highly individualistic, and aggressive. Hang gliding began to flourish in California with development of a rigid and easily controllable wing design. The first soaring association, the Peninsula Hang Glider Club, organized in December 1971, became the U.S. Hang Gliding Association in 1973. It holds twelve regional meets each year leading to a national championship. Paragliding, a cross between hang gliding and skydiving that originated in Europe in the mid-1980s, was adopted in the United States in the mid-1990s. Other subspecies of skydiving included skysurfing (like skydiving except that the jumper has a board attached to his or her feet that facilitates stunts), and BASE jumping, which involves leaping from *b*uildings, *a*ntennae, *s*pans, and *e*arth.

Frisbee games such as freestyle and Ultimate came into their own during the 1970s. Freestyle is an individual sport in which players are judged on their style and tricks while throwing and catching. Ultimate is a seven-player team sport played on a sixty-by-forty-yard field with thirty-yard end zones. The disk must be passed from player to player and a catch made in the end zone is worth one point. Bicycle sports such as cyclo-cross and trail-bike riding also became competitive events. Riders traverse difficult terrain and at least once must carry their bikes across a body of water. Cyclo-cross peaked in the early 1970s and has since declined, while the noncompetitive mountain biking remained popular. Like many sports, competitive freestyle skiing grew out of a recreational activity, in this case the stunts and tricks performed by downhill skiers known as "hot-dogging." The first meet was held in 1971 and two years later devotees formed the National Freestyle Skiers Association. Inclusion of freestyle skiing as a demonstration sport at the 1988 Winter Olympics represented the coming of age of this entertaining activity.

Perhaps the most grueling of new sports, the triathlon, began in Hawaii in 1978, when on a whim several men decided to compete in the Waikiki Roughwater Swim, the Around Oahu Bike Race, and the Honolulu Marathon all in the same day. Their efforts inspired the Hawaii Ironman Triathlon (in which both sexes participate). After portions of the event were televised in 1982, the popularity of the sport increased dramatically. By the 1990s an estimated 750,000 triathletes took part in 2,000 races worldwide. In 1994 triathlete Karen Smyers won her fifth consecutive national women's championship. Sailboarding became a competitive sport in the early 1980s. A sailboard is essentially a surfboard with a pivoting mast and a triangular sail of sixty square feet. Competitions among riders of these wind-driven boards involve course racing, slalom, and freestyle. The United States Boardsailing Association, organized in 1980, governs this sport. Other new sports since 1970 include arena football, indoor soccer, roller blading, jet-ski boating, parasailing, Wally ball, and ski orienteering. They represent the U.S. public's insatiable desire for varied competitive and recreational activities.

[Ralph Hickok, *The Encyclopedia of North American Sports History* (New York, 1992); Thomas C. Jones, *The Great American Sports Book* (Geneva, Ill., 1990).]

DAVID P. MCDANIEL

See also **SUPP:** Aerobics; Fitness; Marathons; Olympic Games; Skiing; Tennis; individual sports.

SSC. *See* **Supercolliding Super Conductor.**

STAGFLATION, a term referring to transitional periods when the economy is simultaneously experiencing the twin evils of inflation and high unemployment in the early stages of stagnation, a condition many economists as late as the 1950s considered atypical of the U.S. economy. Stagflation occurs when the economy is moving from an inflationary period to a recessionary one. If the economy goes through an overheated period in which prices rise because of increases in wages, machinery, credit, and/or natural resources, the reaction of business firms is to produce less and charge higher prices. The term first came into use in the mid-1970s, when inflation soared to 12 percent and the unemployment rate nearly doubled to 9 percent. This inflation was caused by the quadrupling of oil prices by the Organization of Petroleum Exporting Countries (OPEC), increases in the price of raw materials, and the lifting of government-imposed wage and price controls. At the same time, the economy went into recession. In 1980–1981 the country entered a period of stagflation so severe that a new term, "slumpflation," was used. After years of double-digit inflation the Federal Reserve Board (FRB), under Paul Volcker, raised interest rates to record levels of 20 percent to induce a recession and break the inflation cycle. Subsequently the FRB pursued a monetary policy designed to head off significant increases in inflation, but in 1994–1995 seven FRB increases in short-term interest rates failed to moderate economic growth. This led to speculation that in a global economy, domestic monetary policy may not be as effective in controlling either stagflation or slumpflation as previously thought.

ERIK BRUUN

See also **DAH:** Inflation; **SUPP:** Banking and Finance; Federal Reserve System; Oil Crises.

STARK **INCIDENT.** On May 17, 1987, an Iraqi fighter plane attacked the U.S. frigate *Stark* in the Persian Gulf and killed thirty-seven of the crew. The vessel was on patrol to demonstrate freedom of navigation in international waters during the Iran-Iraq War. Claiming the attack was a mistake, Iraq paid the United States $27 million in compensation, but the attack and a U.S. decision two days later to protect eleven Kuwaiti oil tankers triggered congressional debate over both U.S. foreign policy and the dangers facing U.S. forces in the Persian Gulf before the 1991 war against Iraq.

[George P. Shultz, *Turmoil and Triumph: My Years as Secretary of State* (New York, 1993).]

KENNETH B. MOSS

See also **SUPP:** Gulf War of 1991; Iran-Iraq War; Middle East, Relations with.

STAR WARS. *See* **Strategic Defense Initiative.**

STATE, DEPARTMENT OF. The Constitution empowers the president to appoint diplomats and consuls to represent the United States abroad. Since 1789 their work has been directed by the Department of State. For much of the nineteenth century, appointments to the diplomatic and consular services were used to reward political contributors and the party faithful. The 1890s witnessed the first lasting steps to end this arrangement and to base appointments on demonstrated merit. By the time the United States

entered World War I not only had the consular service and that portion of the diplomatic corps below the rank of ambassador or minister been taken out of politics, but the foundations and structural outline for a career foreign service had been put into place.

Appointments now were made to the services only after examination and incumbents were not turned out of office when the other political party captured the White House. The State Department's operations and its links with the field foreign service were systematized, primarily through development of the geographic bureaus, which have been the basis for much of the department's organization ever since. In 1924 the Rogers Act, drafted in the State Department, merged the diplomatic and consular services into the Foreign Service of the United States. Many of the reforms of prior years, such as appointment only after competitive examination, were given statutory authority.

In the 1990s, there were approximately 4,700 Foreign Service officers (FSOs) working at some 250 diplomatic and consular offices abroad as well as at the State Department in Washington, D.C., in four major areas: political reporting and analysis; economic reporting and analysis; consular affairs (primarily handling visa applications and assistance to U.S. citizens); and administration. Even before the Rogers Act, the proportion of chiefs of mission coming from the career service had reached 50 percent. In the decades that followed, and particularly with the great increase in the number of nations after World War II, roughly a 70:30 ratio came to prevail. From the 1960s to the mid-1990s about 70 percent of such appointments went to career FSOs and 30 percent to political appointees. That ratio was slightly more favorable for FSOs under President Jimmy Carter (75:25) and slightly less favorable under Ronald Reagan (67:33). Some commentators have observed that the United States is the only major country that chooses large numbers of its envoys from outside its career service and that both Republican and Democratic presidents have dealt in "bought commissions" for ambassadorial appointments. Others note that in some instances a president may need to appoint to a foreign capital a person in whom he has confidence or with whose views he is in agreement. This sentiment is by no means new, as illustrated by Woodrow Wilson's letter, four months into his presidency, to a State Department official: "Every day, I feel more and more keenly the necessity of being represented at foreign courts by men who easily catch and instinctively themselves occupy our point of view with regard to public matters."

Since the Rogers Act, changes in the organization of the Foreign Service have demonstrated an almost continuous effort to adapt the foreign affairs machinery to changing circumstances. The Foreign Service Act of 1980, for example, created a Senior Foreign Service for older officers, fostering the advancement of younger FSOs. A principal problem for the State Department has been that it has not been alone in representing the nation abroad, much less in helping the president formulate and conduct foreign policy. The State and Commerce departments have clashed over certain issues involving foreign trade promotion since the Commerce Department was created in 1903, and since World War II foreign affairs agencies have proliferated. One observer counted sixty-one in 1971 and a study in 1993 found eighty-seven. At the typical U.S. embassy abroad fewer than 20 percent of the personnel are State Department people. At home, the department has had to contend in policy planning matters not only with a much enlarged Defense Department but with agencies traditionally domestic in their orientation, such as the Departments of the Treasury and Agriculture, as foreign and domestic questions have become more intertwined.

The State Department's chief competitor in Washington, D.C., has been the National Security Council (NSC), created in 1947 by the National Security Act. Particularly since the John F. Kennedy administration (1961–1963), the NSC has built a large staff to contend with State for the ear of the president and his staff. Several presidents have relied more on the national security adviser than the secretary of state, and they have appointed strong and articulate academics to the former post, such as Kennedy's McGeorge Bundy, Richard Nixon's Henry Kissinger, and Jimmy Carter's Zbigniew Brzezinski. An example of a president bypassing the secretary of state occurred in the summer of 1980, when Secretary of State Edmund Muskie and other State Department officials learned only from newspaper accounts that President Carter had two weeks earlier issued a directive revising the U.S. nuclear war strategy; by contrast, the Defense Department and the NSC had taken part in the decision.

During the Ronald Reagan (1981–1989) and George Bush (1989–1993) administrations, the secretary of state's role vis-à-vis the national security adviser was strengthened, primarily because of the forcefulness of Secretaries of State Alexander Haig, George P. Shultz, and James Baker. Yet even Secretary Shultz felt obliged in 1986 to cable all U.S. ambassadors with a warning not to bypass him by communicating directly with the national security adviser. It is clear that the traditional concept of a State Department serving the president as the only agency for foreign policy development, as well as having nearly total responsibility for official contacts and relations with other nations, has not been a viable one since at least the late 1940s. Critics frequently have called upon the State Department to coordinate the activities of the various foreign affairs agencies, a task more easily said than done.

Another problem for the State Department has been its lack of a domestic constituency. During the first years of the twentieth century, department officials were able to mobilize support from the business community for their work on behalf of promoting foreign trade and reforming the consular and diplomatic services. Most of this support was soon diverted to the Commerce Department's commercial attachés. Other agencies, such as the Departments of Defense and Agriculture, have developed powerful domestic pressure groups lacking in the Department of State.

Social changes in the United States and the world also have left their marks on the State Department and Foreign Service. Among these are changes in the roles of women. Increasingly, wives of FSOs have demonstrated a strong desire for careers of their own, yet traditionally they have acted as unpaid hostesses and until 1972 were even included as an element in their husbands' annual performance evaluations. In 1978 the department established the Family Liaison Office, which received legislative sanction in the Foreign Service Act of 1980, to help with careers for spouses. The 1980 act also provided for retirement and survivor benefits for divorced spouses. Women Foreign Service officers likewise gained ground. As late as 1971 a woman FSO was expected to resign if she married and women were routinely assigned to consular rather than to diplomatic work. Also in 1971 the first sex discrimination suit was filed against the department. *Palmer* v. *Shultz* (1985) held that the department did not discriminate but was reversed the next year, resulting in cancellation of the 1989 foreign service examination while the department worked to take corrective action as prescribed by the court.

Concern that the Foreign Service contained too small a proportion of minorities and women led to concerted efforts to recruit and retain persons from both groups. Hence, the department has pursued affirmative action, as it did in the early twentieth century for white male Democrats from the South in order to create the fact and the image of greater political diversity in the foreign service. By the late 1980s and early 1990s the department's efforts were achieving results. From 1987 to 1993 women and minorities eligible for promotion were advanced at rates slightly higher than other eligible FSOs. The push for affirmative action did not slacken with the advent of the Bill Clinton administration and its advocacy of a government that "looks like America." Meanwhile, with much less attention, the composition of the service also has been changing in terms of the college background of officers, with a pronounced decline in the proportion possessing Ivy League degrees and a significant rise in the fraction of alumni from state universities.

Another development greatly affecting the Foreign Service has been the growing incidence of terrorism directed at U.S. embassies abroad, of which the Iranian hostage situation of 1979–1981 was only the most prominent and dramatic. By 1981 the State Department was offering a two-day seminar on how to avoid and survive terrorist attacks, and by early 1983 some 15 percent of the department's expenditures were used to protect U.S. personnel and facilities. In 1986 the Bureau of Diplomatic Security was established at State, and in that same year Congress voted to provide U.S. government employees taken hostage by terrorists cash payments of not less than half the worldwide average per diem. The reference by Secretary of State John Foster Dulles (1953–1959) to Foreign Service officers as "soldiers in the front line trenches of our foreign policy" was taking on additional meaning in the last quarter of the twentieth century.

[Barry M. Rubin, *Secrets of State: The State Department and the Struggle Over U.S. Foreign Policy* (New York, 1985); Andrew L. Steigman, *The Foreign Service of the United States: First Line of Defense* (Boulder, Colo., 1985); Richard Hume Werking, "Department of State," in Donald R. Whitnah, ed., *Government Agencies* (Westport, Conn., 1983).]

RICHARD HUME WERKING

See also **SUPP:** Commerce, Department of; Defense, Department of; Hostages, Middle East; Terrorism.

STOCK MARKET. *See* **Financial Exchanges; Options Exchanges; Wall Street.**

STOCK MARKET CRASH OF 1987. *See* **Black Monday Stock Market Crash.**

STRATEGIC ARMS LIMITATION TALKS (SALT). From November 1969 until June 1979, the United States and the Soviet Union negotiated limitations on their strategic nuclear arms. Two sets of agreements

were reached—the SALT I accords signed at the first summit meeting of President Richard M. Nixon with Soviet leader Leonid I. Brezhnev in Moscow in May 1972, and the SALT II Treaty signed at the only summit meeting between President Jimmy Carter and Brezhnev, in Vienna in June 1979. These were the first substantial arms control agreements between the two countries. Originally proposed by the United States in December 1966, the Soviet Union equivocated until May 1968, when the Soviets had numerical strategic parity in sight. A planned opening of SALT at a summit meeting in September 1968 was derailed by the Soviet-led Warsaw Pact occupation of Czechoslovakia in August. With the defeat of the Democrats in the 1968 presidential election, SALT had to await a new administration and its review of defense and foreign policies. The delay of the opening of SALT from fall 1968 to late fall 1969 had one significant adverse effect; during that year the United States successfully tested and developed deployable MIRV (multiple, independently targeted reentry vehicle) warheads for its strategic missiles—five years ahead of the Soviet Union. As a result, the negotiations placed no restrictions on MIRV technology, seriously undercutting the value of the SALT I and SALT II agreements limiting strategic offensive arms.

Two SALT I accords were reached in January 1972—the Antiballistic Missile (ABM) Treaty, which severely limited ABM defenses, and the Interim Agreement on the Limitation of Strategic Offensive Arms, which froze the total number of strategic missile launchers pending further negotiation of a more comprehensive treaty limiting strategic missiles and bombers. (A separate agreement on measures to avert accidental use of nuclear weapons had been concluded in September 1971.) The ABM Treaty, of indefinite duration, restricted each party to two ABM sites, with 100 ABM launchers at each. (In the only later amendment to the treaty, a 1974 protocol, the two parties agreed to forgo one of those sites, so that each was thereafter limited to a single deployment location.) Further constraints included a ban on the testing and deployment of land-mobile, sea-based, air-based, and space-based systems. Only fixed, land-based ABM systems could be deployed at the one allowed site. The Soviet Union kept its existing ABM deployment around Moscow. The United States completed its deployment at a site for defense of intercontinental ballistic missile (ICBM) launchers near Grand Forks, S.Dak., but in 1975 mothballed the complex as too expensive. The ABM Treaty was a solid achievement in arms limitation, although agreement was facilitated by doubts on both sides as to the cost-effectiveness of available ABM systems. While the treaty headed off a costly and useless ABM deployment race, it did not have the desired effect of also damping down deployment of strategic offensive missiles, especially because MIRVs were not constrained.

The Interim Agreement froze the level of land- and sea-based strategic missiles (permitting completion of launchers already under construction). The Soviet Union had a quantitative advantage with 2,348 missile launchers to 1,710 for the United States. This was, however, offset in two important ways. First, neither strategic bombers nor forward-based nuclear delivery systems were included, and the United States had a significant advantage in both categories. Second, although the Soviet Union had more missile launchers and deployed missiles, the United States had a larger number of strategic missile warheads and by 1972 had already begun deploying MIRV warheads. Overall, the Interim Agreement placed only modest limits on strategic missiles. In contrast to the ABM Treaty, it was not significant as an arms control measure.

SALT II was the name given to the follow-on negotiation of a treaty to replace the SALT I Interim Agreement. These talks lasted from November 1972 to June 1979. The SALT II Treaty provided equal levels of strategic arms (2,400, to be reduced over time to 2,200, strategic delivery vehicles) and included strategic bombers as well as strategic missiles. Intended to be in effect for ten years, during which a third SALT negotiation for further reductions was envisaged, the SALT II Treaty fell afoul of the collapse of the Soviet-American détente of the 1970s after the Soviet occupation of Afghanistan in 1979 and was never ratified. Its major constraints, however, were formally observed by both sides until 1986, and for all practical purposes even after the dissolution of the Soviet Union.

In 1982, under the administration of President Ronald Reagan, a new series of negotiations, the Strategic Arms Reduction Talks (START), succeeded SALT. In July 1991 the START I Treaty was signed in Moscow by President George Bush and Soviet President Mikhail Gorbachev. In January 1993 the START II Treaty was also signed in Moscow, by Bush and Russian President Boris Yeltsin. The treaties involved increasingly substantial reductions, but even so, START I brought the level of strategic warheads down only to about the SALT II level, and START II down to the SALT I level.

The SALT process was a success in demonstrating that adversaries could reach arms limitation agreements, but owing to the very cautious and conservative approaches of both sides, the limitations on strategic offensive arms were unable to keep up with the military technological advances given precedence by the two countries. The ABM Treaty, buffeted mainly by revived U.S. interest in President Reagan's Strategic Defense Initiative (SDI) of 1983, survived the decade before the SDI was abandoned. It remained an effective arms control agreement. Pursuant to the SALT I agreements a Standing Consultative Commission (SCC) was established to resolve questions regarding the meaning of and compliance with the SALT agreements. It was also stipulated that there would be no interference with the use of national technical means of verification, such as observation satellites. SALT thus helped at least to stabilize, if not greatly reduce, the military balance. The SALT process and the agreements reached, while causing some friction and disagreements, contributed to the overall political détente of the 1970s. While not sufficient to sustain that détente, the SALT process helped ensure that even under renewed tension the risk of nuclear war remained low.

[John Newhouse, *Cold Dawn: The Story of SALT* (New York, 1973); Gerard C. Smith, *Doubletalk: The Story of SALT I* (New York, 1980); Strobe Talbott, *Endgame: The Inside Story of SALT II* (New York, 1979); Thomas W. Wolfe, *The SALT Experience* (Cambridge, Mass., 1979).]

RAYMOND L. GARTHOFF

See also **SUPP:** Arms Race and Disarmament; Cold War; Soviet Union, Relations with; Strategic Defense Initiative.

STRATEGIC ARMS REDUCTION TALKS (START). *See* **Arms Race and Disarmament.**

STRATEGIC DEFENSE INITIATIVE (SDI), known to its critics as "Star Wars," was introduced in 1983 by President Ronald Reagan as a new and highly effective program to protect the United States from nuclear attack. SDI would have employed infrared detectors and exotic weapons, such as high-powered lasers to identify, track, and destroy incoming ballistic missiles. Traveling at the speed of light, a satellite-based laser beam could engage an enemy missile soon after launch. According to President Reagan, SDI would safeguard the nation, making nuclear weapons "impotent and obsolete." Despite its attraction, the proposal evoked immediate opposition. Critics questioned the legality of SDI because space-based antimissile weapons were prohibited by the 1972 ABM (antiballistic missile) Treaty. Moreover, they claimed that the system would require many major technological breakthroughs and would be prohibitively expensive (estimates ran as high as $1 trillion). They also claimed that SDI would be vulnerable to many countermeasures, and the immensely complex computer code required for battle management could never be tested and was unlikely to work. The administration argued that all the technical problems could be overcome with an aggressive research program, which was legal under its interpretation of the ABM Treaty. During the Reagan administration and that of George Bush (from 1981 to 1993), Congress funded the program at levels substantially below administration requests. As technical difficulties arose, the program was modified to emphasize more conventional weapons such as small heat-seeking rockets ("brilliant pebbles"). President Bill Clinton's first secretary of defense, Les Aspin, promoted theater missile defenses by substituting ground-based missile defense systems for space-based ones. In effect this proposal put an end to SDI, a course made easier by the collapse of the Soviet Union and the end of the cold war.

[Steven Anzovin, ed., *The Star Wars Debate* (New York, 1986); Robert M. Lawrence, *SDI: A Bibliographic and Research Guide* (Boulder, Colo., 1987).]

LEO SARTORI

See also **SUPP:** Arms Race and Disarmament.

STRIKES. Since the late eighteenth century, workers have used strikes, or organized work stoppages, to secure union recognition and better working conditions, wages, and benefits from employers. In the 1980s, however, fundamental changes both in the structure of the U.S. economy and in labor practices severely undercut the efficacy of the strike as a pressure tactic, resulting in fewer and shorter strikes involving substantially fewer workers. In 1974 the Department of Labor reported 424 strikes at businesses with 1,000 or more employees, involving nearly 1.8 million workers. After 1981 strikes numbered fewer than 100 annually, dropping as low as 35 in 1993.

The strength and militancy of the union movement declined as global competition, deregulation, and other factors forced massive layoffs and plant closures in such bastions of organized labor as the steel and automobile industries. Workers were increasingly displaced in heavy industry by automated manufacturing. The automobile industry relocated plants to southern states, where unionization was traditionally opposed, or to such countries as Mexico. These developments resulted in dramatic changes in the U.S. workforce as higher-paying, unionized industrial jobs gave way to lower-paying, generally nonunionized service-sector work. As late as 1960, for example, 30 percent of all U.S. employees were union members. By 1994 membership had dropped to 15.5 percent. The movement showed no appreciable growth as baby boomers and women joined the workforce and boosted employment to record levels. Employers increasingly turned to part-time employees or independent contractors who generally received none of the benefits provided by union contracts. Job growth occurred in small entrepreneurial companies, usually technology firms where unions had never existed.

The most dramatic setback suffered by labor was the 1981 strike by the more than 11,000-member Professional Air Traffic Controllers Organization (PATCO). The controllers, who were federal employees, struck for higher wages, shorter hours, better retirement benefits, and better equipment, saying that such changes would improve air safety. President Ronald Reagan responded by dismissing all the striking controllers and replacing them with supervisors, nonunion controllers, and military controllers. Reagan, who led a Screen Actors Guild strike in 1960, said he respected the right of workers in the private sector to strike but that the government had to "provide without interruption the protective services which are government's reasons for being." He pointed to the no-strike oath each controller had signed as a condition of federal employment. Reagan's position was reminiscent of the stance taken by his political hero Calvin Coolidge, who as governor of Massachusetts in 1919 opposed a strike by Boston police, stating that "there is no right to strike against the public safety by anybody, anywhere, anytime." The PATCO strike did massive damage to the labor movement. The strike was not honored by other airline unions, and the air traffic control system was rebuilt with little apparent effect upon public safety.

Perhaps the most serious consequence of the strike for labor was that the firing of the controllers encouraged private employers nationwide to thwart other strikes by hiring "replacement workers" even when the strike involved skilled employees. One prominent labor action involving replacement workers was the 1994–1995 Major League Baseball strike. Minor league and replacement players were brought into spring training in 1995, although the strike ended just prior to opening day. No agreement had been reached between owners and the Players' Association as the 1996 season approached. The city of Decatur, Ill., known as a union town, endured two strikes and a lockout in the 1990s. On July 12, 1994, 3,000 members of the United Rubber Workers went on strike at six locations of Bridgestone-Firestone. The Japanese owners of the company hired 2,300 replacement workers in February 1995, and the union accepted the company's contract offer and ended its strike in August, in a decision union members said was aimed at forestalling a union decertification election. Other strikes in the 1990s included that of nine of ten unions that went on strike against the *New York Daily News* in 1990; the union and British publisher Robert Maxwell, who bought the failing paper from the Tribune Company of Chicago, reached a contract agreement in the summer of 1991. On June 20, 1994, the United Auto Workers (UAW) struck eleven plants of Caterpillar, the world's leading maker of earth-moving and construction equipment. It was the tenth strike in three years by 10,000 UAW members, who had an average of twenty-four years on the job.

Deregulation weakened unions in industries where they had previously been the strongest, such as airlines, trucking, and railroads. Management engaged unions in negotiations over "give backs," including wage concessions and work rules. From the union-side, the negotiations shifted to job security, health insurance, and seniority. The agreements often changed unions' relation to management. Sometimes the agreements gave unions seats on boards. In other cases, particularly in the airline industry, unions became owners. Organized labor's strength shifted to the public sector, where 7.1 million workers (federal, state, and local) were union members in 1994, 38.7 percent of total public sector employment. Federal and often state laws restricted strikes by public sector employees. Out of forty-five major strikes in 1994 only eight involved public-sector employee unions. Of those disputes, five involved education. Labor's political clout waned. Traditionally, organized labor supported Democratic congressional and presidential candidates, but election of Republican majorities in both houses of Congress in 1994 undercut what little ability labor had to protect hard-won bargaining rights under federal law. President Bill Clinton did manage to sidestep Congress in 1995 by issuing an executive order barring federal agencies from granting contracts in excess of $100,000 to companies that permanently replaced striking workers.

Indicative of labor's troubles and attempts to revivify the movement was the forced resignation in 1995 of longtime AFL-CIO president Lane Kirkland. After the first contested election for the presidency in the union's history, he was succeeded by reform candidate John J. Sweeney, who campaigned on a record of aggressive organizing in the service sector as president of the Service Employees International Union. A new generation of union leaders called for a return to civil disobedience and confrontational tactics to stem the decline of unionism in the United States, but the increasingly international nature of the U.S. economy made the success of such efforts uncertain.

[David Brody, *Workers in Industrial America,* 2nd ed. (New York 1993); Charles B. Craver, *Can Unions Survive?* (New York, 1993); William Winpisinger, *Reclaiming Our Future: An Agenda for American Labor* (Boulder, Colo., 1989); Robert H. Zieger, *American Workers, American Unions,* 2nd ed. (Baltimore, 1994).]

BRENT SCHONDELMEYER

See also **SUPP:** Air Traffic Controllers Strike; Automobile Industry; Aviation Industry; Baseball Strike of 1994–1995; Labor Unions.

STYLE. *See* **Fashion and Style.**

SUBMARINES. Because neither light nor radar can penetrate water to any appreciable extent, a submerged submarine is very hard to locate. The ships are very quiet in order to avoid detection by sonar. All these factors make submarines the least vulnerable of any ship to attack. Modern missile-carrying submarines are nuclear-powered and can stay submerged for months. Submarines are used as launch platforms for submarine-launched ballistic missiles (SLBMs); the long range of these missiles gives the submarine a large operating area. SLBMs are the most numerous component of the U.S. strategic triad, which also includes land-based intercontinental ballistic missiles (ICBMs) and strategic bombers. Beginning with the Poseidon missile (1970), all U.S. SLBMs have carried multiple warheads, dubbed multiple independently targeted reentry vehicles (MIRVs). The most modern U.S. submarine, *Trident*, carries twenty-four Trident C-4 or D-5 missiles, each loaded with eight warheads. The Soviet Union had more submarines but fewer total warheads. In 1988 the United States had 6,600 warheads on thirty-two submarines and the Soviet Union 3,400 warheads on sixty-three submarines. Both forces have been reduced under the terms of the first Strategic Arms Reduction Talks Treaty (START I). Once the January 1993 START II agreement was implemented the United States planned to download its missiles in order to maintain a force of about 1,700 warheads on eighteen submarines. Early SLBMs were fairly inaccurate in large part because of uncertainty in the location of the submarine. The accuracy was greatly improved with the introduction of the global positioning system (GPS). Signals emitted from satellites in orbit enable the missile's computers to calculate its position with very high precision. With GPS guidance, the Trident missile is estimated to be accurate to within 100 meters, as good as that of the most accurate ICBMs.

[Thomas B. Cochran et al., *Nuclear Weapons Databook*, vols. 1 (Cambridge, Mass., 1984) and 4 (New York, 1989).]

LEO SARTORI

See also **SUPP:** Arms Race and Disarmament.

SUBSTANCE ABUSE, the improper consumption of harmful chemicals, includes excessive or habitual drinking of alcohol; use of such illegal drugs as cocaine, heroin, and marijuana; improper use of medications such as tranquilizers, stimulants, and steroids; and less common practices such as inhaling fumes of cleaning fluids. Cigarette smoking is also referred to as substance abuse in some contexts, especially since a 1994 FDA advisory committee voted unanimously that "the amount of nicotine delivered by currently marketed cigarettes [is] likely to lead to addiction in the typical smoker." In addition to direct physical and emotional harm, substance abuse is frequently cited as an important factor in crime, family strife, and other social problems. Substance abuse has been a concern throughout the nation's history but became prominent after 1960. Developing a national consensus or effective strategy to deal with it has proved difficult, because of contradictory beliefs about drugs and alcohol. As a result, government policies have shifted a number of times.

People use alcohol and drugs for a variety of reasons. Alcohol produces pleasurable sensations and a sense of escape from reality; certain drugs can heighten awareness and stimulate energy, while others can dull the user's consciousness and offer a sense of relaxation. The difference between use and abuse depends on many factors, including legitimate benefits, detrimental physical and psychological effects, and circumstances of the user. Distinctions may reflect religious and other values, social beliefs, and

interpretation of scientific research. There are varying degrees of abuse. Addicted people have extreme physical and psychological needs and can suffer withdrawal. Others are not addicted but habitually misuse substances and find it difficult to stop. Many people abuse substances only on rare occasions, such as drinking too much at a party.

In the nineteenth century cocaine and opium were widely sold and used in medications, nonmedicinal "health tonics," and other products. Concern about their addictive qualities and other effects increased, and local and state governments passed laws limiting use. The federal government established drug policies with the Harrison Act of 1914. This initiative ended common use of opiates and other narcotics except for medical purposes. Although alcohol was not considered to be in the same category as narcotics, liquor became a focus of controversy and many localities restricted or banned it. The Eighteenth Amendment made liquor illegal nationally in 1920. The amendment was repealed in 1933 but concern remained, and liquor continued to be regulated and remained illegal in some localities. Ironically, drinking gained social acceptance during and after Prohibition and was further encouraged by advertising, movies, and customs such as the cocktail party. Drug abuse became an increasing problem throughout the twentieth century, especially among the poor. A criminal economy developed to supply illegal narcotics. Addicts stole money or engaged in other illicit activities to obtain money for drugs. New tranquilizers, stimulants, and prescription medications led to problems among middle- and upper-income groups.

After 1960 the nation entered a period of social and political upheaval, and drugs became an important part of a larger national polarization of values and lifestyles. Early in that decade a small group of nonconformists known as hippies emerged, most visibly in the San Francisco area. The use of drugs was central to their spiritual exploration and free-spirited hedonism. Most hippies disapproved of liquor and depressant narcotics because they dulled the senses. They favored drugs that they believed heightened perception and expanded spiritual consciousness. Among these were marijuana, which is usually inhaled from pipes or smoked in cigarettes, and more powerful drugs known as psychedelics, such as LSD (lysergic acid diethylamide), which caused hallucinations and other vivid and bizarre mental experiences. The hippies' unusual, flamboyant lifestyle attracted increasing national attention and spread to other communities. Many young people, and some older ones, adopted the music, clothing, and attitudes of this new movement, often called the counterculture.

Problems associated with the proliferation of drug use soon became evident. While many users had no apparent ill effects from drugs like LSD and marijuana, others suffered frightening emotional experiences and long-lasting traumas. Some users even killed themselves. Warnings were raised by scientists about genetic damage and other long-term harm. Many users were continually under the influence of drugs and some turned to new, particularly dangerous substances such as "speed" (methamphetamine), a stimulant that caused erratic behavior and serious physical damage. The drug-related deaths of such popular cultural figures as rock musicians Janis Joplin and Jimi Hendrix focused attention on the dangers of substance abuse. At all levels of government, officials tried to update existing drug laws and policies to reflect the changing situation. Federal drug-control authority expanded and became more flexible. The Bureau of Narcotics was established in the Treasury Department in 1930. In 1968 the bureau was moved to the Justice Department and was combined with other agencies into the new Bureau of Narcotics and Dangerous Drugs, which in 1975 became the Drug Enforcement Administration. The efforts of federal agencies active in drug-law enforcement led to the Controlled Substances Act of 1970, which established classifications and penalties for types of drugs. The government also became active in prevention programs. The Community Mental Health Centers Act of 1963 provided drug-abuse treatment. State and local authorities revised their laws.

Drugs proliferated and the illegal markets that supplied them became more pervasive. Controversies continually arose over strategies to control drugs. Some observers believed that all drugs were dangerous and that the best way to control them was through stringent laws and vigorous enforcement. Others contended that many illegal drugs were harmless and should be legalized. There were shades of opinion between these extremes. One debate was whether to concentrate on drug education and treatment or on enforcement. People who disapproved of marijuana nevertheless believed it was improper to punish otherwise law-abiding citizens who used it. Others countered that so-called "soft drugs" such as marijuana led users to more dangerous hard drugs such as heroin. It was also contended that trying to stop trade in controlled substances was a losing battle and that it would be more effective to legalize but tightly regulate drugs, as had been done with alcohol after

Prohibition. Opponents of legalization argued that making drugs more available would only increase drug abuse. Despite widespread public support for fighting drug-related crime, efforts to strengthen enforcement also raised objections that such actions would erode civil liberties and hinder drug-related scientific research.

Drugs affected foreign policy because much of the supply of heroin, cocaine, and other hard drugs originated in other nations, especially in Latin America and Asia. Treaties encouraged international cooperation in the fight against drug trafficking. Coordination proved difficult to achieve. In 1969 a federal anti–drug smuggling initiative called Operation Intercept offended the government of Mexico in part because extensive searches of vehicles at the U.S.-Mexico border caused traffic delays.

As the 1970s progressed stronger psychedelic drugs such as LSD went out of fashion and the generation that had embraced the hippie ethic became more conservative. Marijuana lost much of its divisive symbolism. Although it remained illegal and was disapproved by a majority of citizens, many people used it as a recreational drug and nonusers became more tolerant. Oregon and other states "decriminalized" marijuana, reducing the penalties for possession of small amounts. Use began to level off and declined after 1979. New types of recreational drug abuse emerged, including medical depressants known as downers. Cocaine resurfaced after many years of obscurity. Although it was considered a recreational drug with a glamorous image when it reappeared, this view of cocaine quickly changed because of the drug's side effects.

After the 1960s the drug problem in low-income inner-city communities began to increase. This trend escalated in 1985 when a concentrated form of cocaine known as crack appeared. Because crack is immediately addictive it became associated with increasing violence. The lucrative market for cocaine and heroin also stimulated the growth of domestic gangs and international crime organizations. Drugs began to spread the fatal disease AIDS through the use of unsanitary hypodermic needles. As drugs became more closely linked with violence, the scope of activities and amount of money allocated to enforcement and treatment programs increased dramatically. The U.S. military began to try to control international drug trafficking, and public and private groups launched education and treatment programs. First Lady Nancy Reagan became the spokesperson for a nationwide educational campaign to discourage drug abuse among young people based on the motto "Just say no." By 1988 the federal budget reached $10 billion for the "war on drugs." That year Congress passed the Anti-Drug Abuse Act, which included the Office of National Drug Control Policy to oversee prevention, enforcement, and treatment, with a director referred to as the nation's "drug czar."

As the war on hard drugs raged the prevailing view of alcohol changed markedly. People became critical of alcoholism, drinking among young people, and other social problems created by alcohol abuse such as family violence and drunk driving. A 1973 report by the National Commission on Marijuana and Drug Abuse (a joint congressional and presidential committee) emphasized the similarities between alcohol and other drugs. The view of alcoholism as a biological disease among people susceptible to becoming dependent on liquor gained increasing acceptance. The parallel between drugs and alcohol was reinforced by psychological theories that all addictions stem from common emotional and mental patterns regardless of the substance. The same parallel between tobacco and other drugs began to be drawn, a view that was bolstered in 1994 when the FDA asserted that nicotine is an addictive substance.

Despite setbacks the push to bring the problem of substance abuse under control achieved some success. Many alcoholics and drug abusers joined self-help groups such as Alcoholics Anonymous or checked into rehabilitation clinics and other treatment programs, a trend that became known as the twelve-step recovery movement. By the late 1980s statistics indicated that fewer people were using illegal drugs or drinking excessively. Stringent laws and awareness campaigns against drunk driving changed the social habits of many citizens. Smoking and other forms of tobacco consumption were on the decline overall and smoking was banned or restricted in many locations. Popular culture and attitudes shifted from messages that condoned or encouraged substance abuse to emphasis on moderation or abstinence. By the early 1990s sobriety had become as fashionable as indulgence once had been. Nevertheless, substance abuse remained a widespread problem. In the early 1990s there were signs of a new cycle of abuse, with a resurgence in the use of tobacco, marijuana, and LSD among young people. The issues surrounding use and abuse of chemical substances were becoming more complex. Advances in medical research were expanding the level of knowledge about the human brain and psyche. Popularly accepted theories about alcoholism and other addictions were challenged and new forms

of treatment developed. A new generation of psychiatric drugs was emerging, such as the antidepressant Prozac, which offered the ability to control emotions and behavior in increasingly subtle and powerful ways. These drugs added to the basic social questions and debate about the role that chemical substances should have in shaping human behavior.

[John C. Burnham, *Bad Habits* (New York, 1993); H. Wayne Morgan, *Drugs in America* (Syracuse, N.Y., 1981); Stanton Peele and Archie Brodsky, *The Truth About Addiction and Recovery* (New York, 1991); Elaine Shannon, *Desperadoes, Latin Drug Lords, U.S. Lawmen, and the War America Can't Win* (New York, 1989).]

JOHN TOWNES

See also **DAH:** Drug Addiction; Prohibition; **SUPP:** Food and Drug Administration; Smoking; Tobacco Industry.

SUBURBAN LIVING. American suburban life is unique in several respects: affluent and middle-income citizens live in areas far from their workplaces, in houses they own, and with yards that by urban standards are enormous. The first suburbanites left urban problems far behind, but this was no longer true in the 1990s. Between 1950 and 1980, suburban living markedly increased. By 1980 two-thirds of the nation's housing units were for single-family living in a single dwelling surrounded by an ornamental yard. Dependence on the automobile surrounded bucolic suburbs with massive ropes of highways. One-time minor roads became the main streets of suburbs. Near or along the roaring corridors are strips of fast-food chains, inexpensive motels, quick-stop gas stations, and malls. Long considered centerless, suburbs after 1980 were reshaped by construction of corporate headquarters, in flight from high taxes and congestion in city cores. Suburbs offered parking and open space.

The original uniformity of suburbs gave way to extraordinary diversity. The most dynamic growth areas in the nation, suburbs since the mid-1970s turned into a broad patchwork of inner suburbs, office parks, retail centers known as edge cities, and large suburban cities. Nor are they exclusively white and middle-income. The racial character of suburbs changed dramatically between 1980 and 1990. The black suburban population increased by one-third, from 5.9 million to 8 million. The Hispanic population rose from 5.1 million to 8.7 million (a 69.3 percent increase) and the Asian population from 1.5 million to 3.5 million (125.9 percent). Rapid changes within suburbia were not without problems. Construction produced housing gluts, which combined with the economic recession of the late 1980s to induce record mortgage defaults. Central city problems of drug and alcohol abuse, petty property crime, and family violence reappeared in the suburbs. In 1990 one-third of poor Americans lived in the suburbs. Politically, suburban residents regard themselves as less and less connected to the welfare of urbanites and the fiscal condition of city governments. Through reapportionment, suburban communities gained larger political power in state legislatures and Congress. Increased power allows suburbanites to ignore urban problems in allocation of federal resources, sustaining a fallacious belief in separate destinies, urban and suburban.

[Kenneth T. Jackson, *Crabgrass Frontier* (New York, 1985); Anthony Towns, *New Visions for Metropolitan America* (Washington, D.C., 1994).]

GRAHAM RUSSELL HODGES

See also **SUPP:** Urban Living.

SUDDEN INFANT DEATH SYNDROME (SIDS),

sometimes referred to as crib death, is a medical term for the decease of an apparently well infant and describes a death that remains unexplained after all known and possible causes have been ruled out through autopsy, investigation of the scene, and review of the child's medical history. SIDS was first identified as a separate medical entity and named in 1969. SIDS causes the death of 7,000 infants each year in the United States. It occurs most frequently in the third and fourth months and is the most common cause of death in children between their first week and first birthday. SIDS more frequently affects males than females, non-Caucasians than Caucasians, and infants in poverty than those in higher-income situations. Most at risk are infants born prematurely, infants whose mothers smoked during pregnancy or after delivery, children with a history of severe apnea (periods of rapid breathing followed by periods of not breathing), and those whose siblings have died of SIDS. Deaths usually occur during sleep and are more likely during cold months. The cause of SIDS is unknown. Theories include an unidentified birth defect, stress in a normal baby caused by infection or other factors, and failure to develop. Scientists have explored the nervous system, brain, heart, breathing and sleep patterns, body chemical balances, autopsy findings, and environment. It is likely that SIDS, like many medical disorders, will prove to have more than one explanation. There are many popular misconceptions about the cause of SIDS, including belief that the child has suffocated in its bedclothes or inhaled its own vomit. Because no definitive cause can be found and because parents are totally unprepared for such a loss, the death often causes intense feelings of guilt.

JACK HANDLER

SUICIDE. *See* **Euthanasia.**

SUMMIT CONFERENCES, PRESIDENTIAL, denote personal diplomacy at the highest levels of government. They are based on the assumption that U.S. presidents, possessing the ultimate power over questions of peace and war, can in direct conversations with other heads of state resolve disagreements too long protracted, perhaps dangerously, by lesser officials. For that reason well-publicized exchanges between national leaders, even when they achieve nothing, offer reassurance to a troubled world that current conflicts, however bitter, exist far below the threshold of war. Presidential summitry implies that the country's interests, power, and prestige are directly engaged in the issues of the day. There were occasions before the dramatic events of the late 1930s when presidents participated in international gatherings or conferred privately with leaders of other countries, but those occasions scarcely passed as summit conferences, which supposedly address troublesome international issues head-on. Formal or ceremonial state visits had slight diplomatic significance, or perhaps none at all.

It is not strange, therefore, that the experience of the United States in summitry began with Franklin D. Roosevelt's efforts to influence the course and consequences of World War II. At the Atlantic Conference aboard the *Augusta* off Newfoundland in August 1941, Roosevelt and British Prime Minister Winston Churchill framed the Atlantic Charter to define their wartime goals. At Casablanca in January 1943 Roosevelt and Churchill agreed on basic war plans, and Roosevelt proclaimed the Allied goal of unconditional surrender. In late November 1943 Roosevelt conferred with China's Chiang Kai-shek in Cairo and then continued on to Tehran for his first tripartite summit with Churchill and the Soviet leader Joseph Stalin. Early in December he returned to Cairo for a minor summit with Churchill and President Ismet Inönü of Turkey. At Yalta in February 1945 Roosevelt held his second and final summit with Churchill and Stalin. President Harry S. Truman terminated the wartime tripartite summits at Potsdam in July and

August of 1945. With the emergence of the cold war, summit conferences with the Soviet Union were rendered elusive by Washington's demands that the Kremlin first abandon its objective of advancing world revolution, discard its aggressiveness, and appear ready to fulfill any international agreements by demonstrating its good faith.

Churchill used the term "summit" in calling for a conference at the highest level in the spring of 1953. Denying that the USSR was prepared to fulfill one or more of the country's established requirements, President Dwight D. Eisenhower refused for two years to attend a summit with the Soviet leaders. Retreating under domestic and world pressure, Eisenhower attended the Geneva Big Four Conference of July 1955. Despite its outward display of cordiality, the Geneva summit achieved very little. In November 1957 Kremlin leaders launched a crusade for another summit. The Eisenhower administration demanded that any future summits have adequate preparation, an agreed-upon agenda, and reasonable assurance of success. It was also decided to seek the approval of regional allies, usually registered in a presummit foreign ministers conference. Soviet leaders argued that presummit conferences eliminated the possibility of diplomacy among equals. Again with considerable reluctance, Eisenhower attended the Paris summit of 1960 only to face an angry Nikita Khrushchev, who quickly terminated the conference because of the president's refusal to apologize for sending spy planes across Soviet territory.

For President Richard M. Nixon summitry became symbolic of his effort to advance the spirit of détente between the United States and the communist powers. His summitry began with his trip to China in February 1972—a spectacular media event. His Moscow summit with Soviet leader Leonid Brezhnev in late May 1972 marked the high point of official Soviet-American cordiality during the cold war. In addition to the SALT I Treaty on nuclear weapons, the two leaders signed a variety of lesser agreements to extend the interests binding the two countries together. The two succeeding Nixon-Brezhnev summits, in Washington and Moscow, were anticlimactic. Both countries had reached the outer limits of successful coexistence. Nixon's East-West summits never overcame the doubts and antagonisms that characterized the cold war. President Ronald Reagan's four summits with Mikhail Gorbachev, beginning with the Geneva summit of November 1985 and ending with the Moscow summit of May 1988, marked the beginning of the end of the cold war itself. President George Bush's summit with Gorbachev at Malta in December 1989 continued that trend into the post–cold war era.

Noted critics of summitry, such as British diplomat Harold Nicolson and former U.S. ambassador George F. Kennan, warned that diplomacy among heads of states would lack the time and knowledge that professionals could bring to the task. In practice the summits scarcely engaged those present in diplomacy. Such gatherings permitted an exchange of views, extensive socializing, and photo opportunities in abundance, interspersed occasionally with the signing of agreements prepared laboriously by professional diplomats over long periods of time. Thus, summitry was designed less to settle disputes then to publicize agreements already reached. In personalizing such agreements, summits enabled those attending to exaggerate their achievements and thereby enhance their stature as world leaders. Presidents, responding to global expectations, possessed the authority to make concessions not permitted to those obligated to defend established policies. In practice, however, successive presidents refrained from exercising their special prerogatives as heads of the nation's foreign policy establishment. Still, their presence at the summits was a reminder that presidents, not others, carried the responsibility for the country's external policies. Summits invariably reflected the political, military, and diplomatic realities of the time with little capacity to change them. If presidents on occasion chose to be their own secretaries of state, they seldom revealed that proclivity at the summits.

[Elmer Plischke, *Summit Diplomacy: Personal Diplomacy of the President of the United States* (Westport, Conn., 1974), and *Diplomat in Chief: The President at the Summit* (New York, 1986).]

NORMAN A. GRAEBNER

See also **DAH:** Atlantic Charter; Cairo Conferences; Casablanca Conference; Geneva Conferences; Paris Conferences; Potsdam Conference; Summit Conferences; Tehran Conference; Yalta Conference; **DAH and SUPP:** China, Relations with; Cold War; Soviet Union, Relations with; Strategic Arms Limitation Talks; **SUPP:** Arms Race and Disarmament.

SUNBELT, comprising the states of the South and Southwest, is a term coined to describe both the warm climate of these regions and the rapid economic and population growth that have been characteristic since the 1960s. The Sunbelt stretches approximately from Virginia south to Florida and west to California but also includes western mountain states, such as Colorado and Utah, that have experienced similar economic growth. Historically, most of the nation's population and economic power has been based in the Northeast and upper Midwest. The Southeast had a smaller population, a less robust economy, and hot, humid summers that many northerners considered uncomfortable. Much of the Southwest was settled later and remained sparsely populated well into the twentieth century because of its remote location and an inhospitable desert climate that regularly reached triple-digit temperatures in summer. With the advent of air conditioning, however, year-round comfort became possible in both regions.

A shift from northeastern dominance was evident by the early 1970s. The term "New South" came into use to describe economic progress and social changes in the Southeast. California and oil-rich Texas were established as thriving economies, and newer regions of prosperity were emerging throughout the West. This pattern intensified in following decades as many states in the North lost population and industries. Domestic and international businesses were attracted to the Sunbelt for many reasons, including lower non-union wages and energy costs, state policies favorable to business, and, in the West, proximity to the increasingly important Pacific Rim nations. A national emphasis on developing domestic fuel sources in the early 1970s stimulated growth in Texas, Colorado, and other states. Many newcomers were attracted by the lifestyles and natural beauty of Sunbelt states. Southern and western states gained increasing political and economic power. All six winners of U.S. presidential elections between 1964 and 1992 were from the Sunbelt. Southern culture and values became influential, such as the nationwide popularity of country and western music. Hispanic cultures of the Southwest and Florida gained prominence.

The Sunbelt also faced difficult issues, including social problems that many people hoped to escape by moving there. Despite areas of prosperity the Southeast continued to have many sections of poverty. Texas and other energy-oriented states experienced a steep, if temporary, economic decline in the mid-1980s because of a fall in oil prices. California suffered serious economic recession and social stresses in the late 1980s and early 1990s, which caused a significant migration of businesses and residents to other nearby states. The impacts of growth and development became matters of urgent concern, as many Sunbelt communities experienced suburban sprawl, congestion, and pollution, along with an erosion of

their regional characteristics and identities. These trends provoked many controversies, which continued into the 1990s. Some people opposed the changes, but others saw them more positively as signs of progress and prosperity. Nationally, experts predicted that the economic growth and increasing influence of the Sunbelt marked a permanent change in the demographic, economic, and political structure of the nation.

[Donald J. Bogue, *The Population of the United States: Historical Trends and Future Projections* (New York, 1985); Charles Reagan Wilson and William Ferris, eds., *Encyclopedia of Southern Culture* (Chapel Hill, N.C., 1989).]

JOHN TOWNES

See also **SUPP:** Entries on individual states and cities.

SUPERCONDUCTING SUPER COLLIDER (SSC), a federally financed project abandoned in 1993 that would have been capable of accelerating subatomic particles to energy levels forty times that previously achieved by researchers. For reasons of national prestige and international economic competitiveness the Ronald Reagan administration in 1982 encouraged U.S. high-energy scientists to devise a challenging national accelerator project. Physicists responded with plans for the most ambitious particle accelerator ever attempted, a superconducting super collider. It was to be a proton collider far more energetic than existing ones, employing the superconducting magnetic technology recently developed at the Fermi National Laboratory in Illinois. The primary justification for the machine was a search for particles known as Higgs bosons. The machine was to produce 40 TeV protons (where 1 TeV, or tera-electron volt, is 1 trillion electron volts). This determined the size (a fifty-four-mile-long ring) and the projected cost ($4.4 billion). Federal funding for the machine required justification. Support from the Texas congressional delegation and the promise of $1 billion toward the project from the state of Texas led to the decision to build the accelerator in Waxahachie, Tex., rather than near Fermilab. In the autumn of 1993 the House of Representatives, faced with a more than doubled price tag, voted overwhelmingly to kill the project. By then $2 billion had been spent, the superconducting magnets had been tested, one-third of the ring had been excavated, and two teams of a thousand physicists and engineers from around the world were working out detailed designs of the two enormous particle detectors to observe and analyze proton collisions in the TeV energy range.

SUPERCONDUCTIVITY

[Daniel J. Kevles, *The Physicists: The History of a Scientific Community in Modern America,* 2nd ed. (Cambridge, Mass., 1995); James Trefil, "Beyond the Quark: The Case for the Super Collider," *New York Times Magazine* (Apr. 30, 1989); Steven Weinberg, *Dreams of a Final Theory* (New York, 1992).]

See also **SUPP:** Fermi National Accelerator Laboratory; Superconductivity.

SUPERCONDUCTIVITY. An electrical conductor becomes superconductive when, at low temperatures, its resistance to electric current decreases to zero. A solid in its superconducting state repels magnetic materials. The most important use of superconductive materials is in construction of electromagnets capable of producing high magnetic fields. The phenomenon was discovered in 1911 by Heike Kamerlingh Onnes, who noted that electrical resistance of frozen mercury suddenly drops to zero at temperatures below –269° C, or 4.2 kelvins (4.2 degrees above absolute zero). Repulsion of magnetic materials by superconductors was described by Walther Meissner and R. Ochsenfeld in 1933. In 1957 the physicists John Bardeen, Leon N. Cooper, and John R. Schrieffer presented a theoretical description of the behavior of electrons in superconductors, for which they received the Nobel Prize in 1972.

Thirty-six elements and hundreds of alloys are superconductive, most at very low temperatures. J. Georg Bednorz and K. Alex Muller in 1986 reported a lanthanum-barium-copper oxide that becomes superconductive at about –240° C (33 K). They received the 1987 Nobel Prize in Physics. This set off an immense international effort to produce composites in which the transition to superconductivity occurs at even higher temperatures. The effort was successful and by the mid-1990s materials that are superconductive at temperatures above –145° C (128 K)—the boiling temperature of commonly available liquified nitrogen—were available. The search continued for superconductive materials that do not require cooling.

Superconductors have found wide application despite the need for cooling to low temperatures. High-field electromagnets make possible such medical diagnostic techniques as magnetic resonance imaging, the related nuclear magnetic resonance spectroscopy widely used by chemists to identify molecules, and accelerators used by nuclear physicists. Applications envisioned for the future include smaller and more efficient electrical motors and generators, magnetically levitated trains, and controlled nuclear fusion.

[Paul C. W. Chu, "High-Temperature Superconductors," *Scientific American* 273 (September 1995).]

DAVID K. LEWIS

See also **SUPP:** Fermi National Accelerator Laboratory; Magnetic Resonance Imaging; Physics; Superconducting Super Collider.

SUPERFUND, officially the Comprehensive Environmental Response, Compensation, and Liability Act of 1980, began as a $1.6 billion, five-year program created by Congress to expedite cleanup of the nation's worst hazardous waste sites. National concern over the release of hazardous wastes buried beneath the residential community at Love Canal in western New York State prompted its passage. The term also refers to the Superfund Amendment and Reauthorization Act (SARA) of 1986, which comprehensively revised the original act and added $9 billion to the fund. In response to a 1984 tragedy in Bhopal, India, in which 3,000 people died and hundreds of thousands were reported to be affected by exposure to deadly methyl isocyanate gas that leaked from a Union Carbide plant, Congress included provisions in SARA requiring corporations to inform host communities of the presence of dangerous materials and to develop emergency plans for dealing with accidental releases of such materials. From the beginning Superfund met with harsh, and often justified, criticism. President Ronald Reagan's commitment to reduce government regulation of industry undermined the effectiveness of the legislation. At the end of five years the money was gone, and only 6 of the 1,800 hazardous waste sites identified at that time had been cleaned up. Another 18,000 suspected sites remained to be investigated. Caution over a Superfund provision holding a single polluter financially liable for the cleanup of wastes created by many polluters caused additional delays. The Environmental Protection Agency's focus on the legal process rather than on the actual cleanup routinely prevents polluters who are willing to restore a site from doing so because the legal issues are not resolved to EPA's satisfaction. Such delays can postpone cleanups for five to ten years. Many believe that Superfund's fundamental problems cannot be overcome without a legislative overhaul.

[Michael D. LaGrega, Phillip L. Buckingham, and Jeffrey C. Evans, *Hazardous Waste Management* (New York, 1994); Robert A. Taylor, "$1 Billion Later, Toxic Cleanup Barely Begun," *U.S. News & World Report* (Apr. 22, 1985); WMX Technologies, "Superfund Reform," *Views on Responsible Environmental Management* 2 (Winter 1994).]

JOHN MORELLI

See also **SUPP:** Bhopal Explosion; Environmental Protection Agency; Hazardous Waste; Love Canal.

SUPPLY-SIDE ECONOMICS, based on the premise that high tax rates hurt the national economy by discouraging work, production, and innovation, represented a major shift in U.S. economic thinking and policy in the 1980s. Supply-side theory was far from new, its basic ideas dating back to the early-nineteenth-century works of Jean-Baptiste Say and David Ricardo. It had been ignored in the United States since the New Deal, however, because of the demand-side theories of the British economist John Maynard Keynes, who believed in raising income and reducing unemployment by expanding demand even if the government does so through deficit spending. Supply siders, as they were dubbed, argued that high tax rates hurt the national economy because high taxes discourage work and encourage nonproductive investments in tax shelters or outright tax avoidance. Their recommendation was to cut taxes, particularly those of high income groups. In the 1980s supply siders found an audience looking for an alternative to deficit-oriented, demand-side policies. The idea was popularized by Arthur B. Laffer, who said that cutting taxes would increase government revenues. With lower tax rates there would be more incentives for business and for individuals to work and less reason to avoid taxes. There would be more jobs, a more productive economy, and more government revenues.

This theory fitted nicely into the conservative political agenda because it meant smaller government and less interference with the economy. Supply-side economics dominated the administration of President Ronald Reagan, who instituted major tax cuts in 1981 and 1986, reducing the top U.S. rate from 70 percent to roughly 33 percent. Deficits soared to record levels, which many supply siders attributed to the failure at the same time to adopt a balanced budget amendment that would control federal spending. Thus, in the view of some advocates, supply-side theories remained untried. The legacy of supply-side economics has been more political than economic. In the mid-1990s Republican House Speaker Newt Gingrich observed that supply-side economics has "relatively little to do with economics and a great deal to do with human nature and incentives." It contributed to the larger debate about the respective roles of government, individuals, and incentives in U.S. society as the nation faced a global economy.

[Victor A. Canton, Douglas H. Joines, and Arthur B. Laffer, *Foundations of Supply-Side Economics* (New York,

1983); Federal Reserve Bank of Atlanta, *Supply-Side Economics in the 1980s* (Westport, Conn., 1982).]
BRENT SCHONDELMEYER

See also **SUPP:** Budget, Federal; Conservatism; Gramm-Rudman-Hollings Act; Laffer Curve Theory; Reaganomics.

SUPREME COURT. In 1969 Chief Justice Earl Warren retired from the Supreme Court, bringing to an end the "Warren revolution," a period of unprecedented judicial activism in protection of personal rights ranging from the landmark *Brown* v. *Board of Education of Topeka,* 347 U.S. 483 (1954), which fueled the civil rights movement of the 1950s and 1960s, to *Miranda* v. *Arizona,* 384 U.S. 436 (1966), which protected citizens from arbitrary police interrogation. While many observers expected the Court of Warren Earl Burger (1969–1986), with four justices including the chief justice appointed by President Richard M. Nixon, to undo the Warren revolution, matters did not turn out that way. No important Warren Court decision was overruled; some were narrowed but others were not only applied but expanded.

During the Warren Court years, a new activism in protection of personal rights became the judicial hallmark. Strict scrutiny became the primary legal tool to broaden individual rights by reinterpreting the First Amendment, the procedural guarantees of the Bill of Rights (incorporated into the Fourteenth Amendment), the equal protection clause of the Fourteenth Amendment. For the most part the Burger Court continued this liberal jurisprudential trend, but it did more than merely confirm Warren Court jurisprudence. It reintroduced substantive due process to protect personal rights—a doctrine not employed widely since the first quarter of the twentieth century, under which due process was employed to review the reasonableness of laws. The outstanding example was the decision in *Roe* v. *Wade,* 410 U.S. 113 (1973), which ruled that there was a constitutional right to an abortion during the first three months of pregnancy. The right was based on the constitutional right of privacy that had been recognized by the Warren Court. *Roe* was as activist as any Warren Court decision—based on "policy" judgments that led to recognition of a new right not enumerated in the Bill of Rights.

The Burger Court also substantially expanded other women's rights. While it never declared sex a suspect classification under the Fourteenth Amendment, it did establish a "middle" or "heightened" level scrutiny test for sex discrimination cases as the result of three decisions between 1971 and 1976. In the first of these rulings, *Reed* v. *Reed,* 404 U.S. 71 (1971), the Supreme Court invalidated for the first time in its history a statute on the grounds of sex discrimination. In the second, *Frontiero* v. *Richardson,* 411 U.S. 677 (1973), the Court came within one vote of declaring sex a suspect classification. In the third, *Craig* v. *Boren,* 429 U.S. 190 (1976), the Court ruled that "classification by gender must serve important governmental objectives and must be substantially related" to the achievements of these objectives. This new standard has been applied to cases involving women since 1976.

The Burger Court also aided the cause of desegregation of public schools with its decision in *Swann* v. *Charlotte-Mecklenburg Board of Education*, 402 U.S. 1 (1971), which vested broad remedial power in the courts to ensure desegregation, including extensive busing. The *Brown* principle was also expanded to uphold affirmative action programs. As Justice Sandra Day O'Connor, the first woman justice to sit on the Court, later concluded, "We have reached a common destination in sustaining affirmative action against constitutional attack." The same was true in other areas, including the First Amendment, reapportionment, and equal protection. In all these areas the Warren principles remained. The Burger Court dealt with other crucial constitutional issues. *United States* v. *Nixon*, 418 U.S. 683 (1974), brought the Court into the Watergate scandal by ruling that the president could not retain subpoenaed tapes by claiming executive privilege. Its decision led directly to the first resignation of a U.S. president.

Under Chief Justice William H. Rehnquist (1986–), the Court reflected the rightward tilt in U.S. politics affirmed in the 1994 midterm congressional elections, in which Republicans gained control of Congress for the first time since the 1950s. Under the leadership of this conservative activist the Court began to shape a new constitutional case law undoing some of the work of its predecessors. A definite change in direction was manifested in the Rehnquist Court's decisions on civil rights and criminal law. In *Richmond* v. *J. A. Croson Company,* 488 U.S. 469 (1989), the Court struck down a Richmond, Virginia, affirmative action plan, known as set-asides, under which prime contractors awarded city contracts were required to subcontract at least 30 percent of each contract to minority business enterprises. Set-asides represented a form of affirmative action introduced by the Nixon administration, but the Rehnquist Court ruled that the Fourteenth Amendment required strict scrutiny of all race-based action by state and local governments. Without proof of intentional discrimination by the city, the Richmond plan could not be upheld. The argument that the city was attempting to remedy discrimination, as shown in the disparity between contracts awarded in the past to minority businesses and the city's minority population, was rejected. The Burger Court, in *Fullilove* v. *Klutznick*, 448 U.S. 448 (1980), had sustained federal works programs that set aside 10 percent of the value of contracts for businesses owned by blacks and other minorities. In *Adarand Constructors* v. *Peña* 115 S.Ct. 2097 (1995), however, five justices of the Rehnquist Court cast grave doubt on the continued validity of *Fullilove*. Although neither the federal construction program involved in the case or federal affirmative action in general was declared unconstitutional, strict scrutiny was for the first time applied to federal as well as state affirmative action programs, casting doubt on the validity of many such programs.

Other Rehnquist Court decisions shifted the burden of proof in civil rights cases, holding that plaintiffs, not employers, had the burden of proving that a job requirement shown statistically to screen out minorities was not a "business necessity." Employers were permitted to show by only a preponderance of the evidence rather than by clear and convincing evidence (a higher burden of proof) that refusals to hire were based on legitimate and not discriminatory reasons. The Rehnquist Court also refused to invalidate a death sentence imposed upon a black defendant despite a detailed statistical study that showed black defendants who killed white victims were far more likely to receive the death penalty than white defendants. The Court stressed that there was no proof that the decision-makers in this particular case acted with discriminatory purpose.

From 1973 to 1989 the Supreme Court struck down most attempts by states to place restrictions on women's constitutional right to abortions. In *Webster* v. *Health Reproductive Services,* 492 U.S. 490 (1989), the Rehnquist Court upheld restrictions on abortions but refused to overrule the fundamental right to abortion declared in *Roe*. In *Planned Parenthood of Southeastern Pennsylvania* v. *Casey,* 112 S. Ct. 2791 (1992), the Rehnquist Court again declined to overrule *Roe,* although it did uphold a variety of other restrictions on abortion.

Rehnquist Court decisions also marked the beginning of a trend in favor of property rights. For the first time in years, the Court began to stress the constitutional prohibition against taking property without compensation. Noteworthy in such cases was the Court's use of heightened scrutiny to review the merits of land-use regulations in deciding whether a challenged regulation required judicial invalidation in the absence of compensation. Indeed, the Court implied that claims of unconstitutional takings (whether by acquisition or regulation) fall into a particularly sensitive constitutional category comparable to that of freedom of speech. As the chief justice stated in a 1994 case, "We see no reason why the Takings Clause . . . should be relegated to the status of poor relation." The Court's decisions on takings without compensation signaled a tilt in favor of property rights and away from the strong preference given to personal rights by the Warren and Burger courts. Nonetheless, significant Warren Court criminal-procedure decisions remained a part of Rehnquist Court jurisprudence. The key Warren criminal trilogy—*Gideon* v. *Wainwright,* 372 U.S. 335 (1963); *Mapp* v. *Ohio,* 367 U.S. 436; and *Miranda* v. *Arizona,* 384 U.S. 436 (1966)—continued to be followed, although some of their doctrines were narrowed. When the Rehnquist Court struck down New York City's legislative apportionment in *Board of Estimate* v. *Morris,* 489 U.S. 688 (1989), it relied on the Warren Court's one-person, one-vote principle.

By the end of the Court's session in 1995 a conservative majority began to assert itself in a series of five-to-four decisions. Thus, it ruled that race cannot be the primary factor in redrawing congressional districts, held against Kansas City's ambitious court-ordered program for desegregating schools, permitted Boston's St. Patrick's Day parade organizers to exclude homosexuals from participating, upheld drug-testing of student athletes, limited lawsuits by prisoners protesting prison conditions, decided that the University of Virginia violated the free speech rights of students when it denied funding for a Christian student newspaper, and similarly found that Ohio could not prevent the Ku Klux Klan from erecting a cross in a public park.

[David P. Currie, *The Constitution in the Supreme Court: The Second Century, 1888–1986* (Chicago, 1990); Robert McCloskey, *The American Constitution,* 2nd ed. (New York, 1994); David M. O'Brien, *Storm Center: The Supreme Court in American Politics,* 2nd ed. (New York, 1990); William H. Rehnquist, *The Supreme Court: How It Was, How It Is* (New York, 1987); David G. Savage, *Turning Right: The Making of the Rehnquist Court* (New York, 1992); Bernard Schwartz, *The Ascent of Pragmatism: The Burger Court in Action* (Reading, Pa., 1990), *A History of the Supreme Court* (New York, 1993), and *Decision: How the Supreme Court Decides Cases* (New York, 1996);

James F. Simon, *The Center Holds: The Power Struggle Inside the Rehnquist Court* (New York, 1995); William M. Wiecek, *Liberty Under Law: The Supreme Court in American Life* (Baltimore, 1988).]

BERNARD SCHWARTZ

See also **DAH:** *Brown* v. *Board of Education of Topeka;* Gideon Case; *Miranda* v. *Arizona;* **SUPP:** *Craig* v. *Boren; Frontiero* v. *Richardson; Planned Parenthood of Southeastern Pennsylvania* v. *Casey; Reed* v. *Reed; Richmond* v. *J. A. Croson Company; Roe* v. *Wade;* Watergate, Aftermath of; *Webster* v. *Reproductive Health Services.*

SURGERY since the 1960s has undergone a revolution. Treatments have been devised for conditions previously thought beyond the surgeon's reach, such as replacing failed organs or unblocking clogged arteries. Technological advances have allowed surgeons to shrink the size of incisions and hasten recovery time. In some cases surgery has been replaced by other treatments. Transplantation of human organs was the most exciting advance. Early attempts were stymied because the recipient's immune system mounted an attack against the foreign organ. In 1954 Joseph E. Murray performed the first successful human kidney transplant in Boston. He avoided the problem of rejection by taking the donor kidney from the patient's identical twin brother. In 1990 he won the Nobel Prize for his work on kidney transplantation. Thomas E. Starzl performed the first human liver transplant in 1963. Until immunosuppressant drugs began to be developed in the 1960s, surgeons tried to stave off rejection by disabling patients' immune systems, which left recipients vulnerable to infection. The advent of drugs that diminish but do not shut down immune response made possible more than 10,000 kidney transplants and 3,000 liver transplants in the United States each year.

The first experimental heart transplant in the United States was performed at Stanford University soon after Christiaan Barnard's groundbreaking operation in South Africa in 1967. The procedure, however, was not widely accepted until introduction of the immunosuppressant drug cyclosporine in 1984. Ten years later 2,300 heart transplants were being performed in the United States annually, and by the mid-1990s 77 percent of heart-transplant recipients were still alive two years later. Transplants of bone marrow, corneas, bone, and heart valves also were performed. In 1987 research groups in the United States, Mexico, and Germany transplanted fetal brain tissue into brains of people with Parkinson's disease, but the procedure remained controversial. Many sick people cannot be helped because there are not enough suitable organs. Artificial body parts are more readily available. In the 1990s artificial implants included pacemakers (electrical devices that help the heart beat at a steady rate), eye lenses, heart valves, joint replacements, hearing aids, and penile prostheses. The first artificial heart was implanted in a human patient in 1982, but repeated experiments show that these devices can sustain life only for a limited time. They are used only to keep people alive while they wait for a suitable donor organ.

The era of open-heart surgery began in 1953 when John H. Gibbon of Philadelphia used a heart-lung machine to do the work of heart and lungs while those organs were temporarily stilled by anesthesia. In the 1990s the most common cardiac operation was coronary artery bypass, first performed in 1967. To improve blood flow to the heart surgeons remove a length of a blood vessel from elsewhere in the body (usually the leg or chest) and use it to carry blood past a narrowed or blocked coronary artery. In 1971, 24,000 of these operations were performed in the United States; by 1992 the number had soared to 468,000 each year. No sooner did coronary artery bypass surgery catch on than a clever surgeon learned how to unclog coronary arteries without cutting open the patient's chest. The Swiss surgeon Andreas Gruntzig introduced balloon angioplasty to the United States in 1979. In this procedure the surgeon threads a catheter through the blood vessel to the blockage. There, a balloon on the catheter tip is inflated to stretch the constricted area and break up the obstruction. More than 300,000 of these procedures were performed in the United States each year in the mid-1990s, but one study found that more than half the patients who had balloon angioplasty needed either coronary-artery bypass surgery or repeat angioplasty within a three-year period. Researchers began developing other less invasive ways to reopen clogged vessels, such as using lasers to burn away fatty deposits. Drugs also helped people relieve the symptoms of coronary artery disease without undergoing surgery.

Doctors used to call upon surgeons when they needed to know what was amiss inside the body. Computer imaging techniques have made exploratory surgery almost obsolete but have increased medical costs. Computerized axial tomography (CAT) was introduced to the United States in the mid-1970s. It involves using a computer to generate cross-sectional views of the body that are clearer and more detailed than those made by conventional X-ray techniques. Magnetic resonance imaging (MRI) came in the mid-1980s. MRI uses electromagnetic waves to produce detailed images of the body in any plane. A few state-of-the-art operating rooms include an MRI device that can repeatedly scan the patient during an operation. Sensors attached to surgical instruments allow surgeons to see exactly where they are in the body.

There were also major advances in the use of endoscopes, tubes to view the inside of the body. Nineteenth-century surgeons attempted to see inside the body using rigid telescope-like tubes. By the 1930s the invention of semiflexible gastroscopes allowed doctors to examine the stomach visually. In the 1960s flexible endoscopes with fiber-optic viewing made it possible to inspect the inner reaches of the body. Surgeons began using endoscopes to perform laparoscopic or "band-aid" surgery. Traditionally, major procedures required an incision large enough for the surgeon's hands and tools. In laparoscopic surgery endoscopes with tiny cameras transmit an image of the body cavity to a video screen and allow surgeons to operate with tiny instruments inserted through incisions of five to ten millimeters. U.S. surgeons first used laparoscopy in 1988 for gall bladder removal. Five years later more than 85 percent of gall bladder operations in the United States were performed laparoscopically. Surgery for gallstones, appendicitis, perforated ulcers, and hernias can be done this way. Laparoscopic surgery causes less tissue damage, is less painful, requires a shorter hospital stay, and speeds recovery. It is not perfect, however, because surgeons cannot rely on sense of touch, and the tiny incisions restrict the range of movement of operating instruments. In 2 percent of cases complications occur and the surgeon has to open up the patient.

Surgery has been changed by the realization that lasers, originally developed for military use, could help surgeons perform bloodless operation on parts of the body too delicate for conventional instruments. A laser produces a narrow beam of intense energy that can cut through tissue. In 1964 a laser beam was used to stop abnormal bleeding in the retina. Thirty years later lasers were used in many eye operations, particularly to repair retinal tears, and were also used to seal bleeding arteries in peptic ulcers, destroy early malignant tumors, reopen blocked fallopian tubes, and remove tattoos and skin blemishes. Microsurgery was another advance made possible by technological innovations. Surgeons use a specially designed pedal-operated microscope, tiny instruments, and delicate stitches to work on minute nerves, blood vessels, or other structures. Ophthalmologic surgeons pioneered microsurgical techniques but today the most celebrated use of microsurgery is reconstructive. Surgeons have been able to reattach severed fingers, toes, penises, and limbs.

Cataract removal is the most commonly performed operation in the United States. Nearly 2 million of these operations are carried out each year, and in 90 percent of cases the patients go home immediately following the procedure. This was not always the case. Until the 1950s cataract operations were agonizing. Patients had to spend two weeks lying in a dark room in the hospital with their heads held in place by sandbags because movement could tear out the stitches. Improvements in stitches, bandages, and painkillers made it possible for patients to recover at home. Large incisions and stitches are no longer required because ophthalmologists can use ultrasound to break up the cataract and remove it in fragments through minuscule cuts that heal themselves and artificial lenses that fold for insertion.

Advances in treatment of cancer show the changing role of surgery. In the case of breast cancer, surgery is used less extensively and usually paired with such adjunct treatments as radiation and chemotherapy. Until the 1960s radical mastectomy (complete removal of the affected breast, chest and underarm lymph nodes, chest muscle, and additional fat and skin) was the standard treatment for breast cancer. In the 1950s surgeons began reporting that simple mastectomy (removal of internal tissue from the affected breast) and radiation could be just as effective. Today surgeons often recommend lumpectomy (removal of cancerous tissue) or quadrantectomy (removal of affected tissue plus a wedge of surrounding tissue) and radiation.

Methods for evaluating surgical outcomes also changed. Researchers now use clinical trials to determine what surgical interventions are most effective and whether procedures that are technically successful improve the patient's quality of life. These measures assess not only traditional procedures but innovations that sound like science fiction. Scientists are experimenting with technology that may allow surgeons to operate on patients that are miles away. Although the potential for new procedures seems limitless, the money to pay for them is not. Surgeons soon may be faced with not only deciding whether an operation is medically feasible but whether it is economically sound.

[W. F. Bynum and Roy Porter, *Companion Encyclopedia of the History of Medicine* (New York, 1993); Charles B. Clayman, ed., *The American Medical Association Encyclopedia of Medicine* (New York, 1989); John Duffy, *From Humors to Medical Science: A History of American Medicine* (Urbana, Ill., 1993); Knut Haeger, *The Illustrated History of Surgery* (New York, 1988); Ira M. Rutkow, *Surgery: An Illustrated History* (St. Louis, Mo., 1993).]

PETA GILLYATT

See also **SUPP:** Cancer; Cardiovascular Disease; Chemotherapy; Clinical Research; Computerized Axial Tomography; Heart Implants; Hospitals; Laser Technology; Magnetic Resonance Imaging; Medicine; Transplants and Organ Donation.

SURROGATE PARENTHOOD. A surrogate parent is one who bears a child for someone else to raise. While the term "surrogate father" may describe a sperm donor, "surrogate parent" usually refers to a woman who is artificially inseminated by a man whose wife is infertile. In rarer cases the woman may be implanted with a fertilized egg and carry the child to term for another couple. The infertile couple generally pays a fee, typically $10,000, to the surrogate mother in addition to medical costs. While informal surrogacy arrangements are referenced as far back as the Bible, in the United States the controversial practice of surrogacy contracts and the emergence of surrogate parenting clinics began in the mid-1970s. As of 1988 it was estimated that 2,000 children had been born to surrogate mothers. Until the 1988 "Baby M" court case in New Jersey, the practice received little public attention or scrutiny. Since then reneged surrogacy agreements and complex developments in infertility treatment have routinely commanded the media spotlight. In the Baby M case, the birth mother, Mary Beth Whitehead, kept the baby against the terms of a surrogacy contract with the Sterns. After a protracted court trial, custody was given to the Sterns, although Whitehead was granted visitation rights. While the majority of surrogate parenting arrangements proceed without legal complication, in rare cases the contracts go awry, with devastating consequences to the surrogate, the would-be parents, and the child. In 1993 the California Supreme Court became the first court to uphold a surrogacy contract, and by 1994 a few other states had passed legislation to uphold such contracts. On the other hand, at least ten states had passed legislation declaring surrogacy contract unenforceable. While new technologies and the fluctuations of human intent continued to raise controversy, as of 1995 there was no legal consensus regarding the validity of surrogacy contracts.

[Martha A. Field, *Surrogate Motherhood: The Legal and Human Issues* (Cambridge, Mass., 1988); Amy Z. Overvold, *Surrogate Parenting* (New York, 1988).]

ANNE C. WEISS

See also **SUPP:** Fertility; Reproductive Techniques.

SUSTAINABILITY, a central premise of the environmental movement, expresses the idea that societies that overexploit natural resources and destroy ecosystem integrity cannot be maintained indefinitely and therefore must make their economic and social goals compatible with the limits to growth established by the natural environment itself. By the late 1980s sustainable development had transformed debates about socioeconomic growth worldwide and become the stated goal of virtually all international development agencies. The term also is associated with preserving ecosystem viability and biological diversity.

[Donella H. Meadows, *Beyond the Limits* (Post Mills, Vt., 1992); World Commission on Environment and Development, *Our Common Future* (New York, 1987).]

BRON R. TAYLOR

See also **SUPP:** Bioregionalism; Conservation Biology; Environmental Business; Environmental Movement.

T

TAILHOOK INCIDENT (1991). The Tailhook Association, named for the arresting gear on carrier-based aircraft, is a private group of navy and marine aviators that has worked closely with the U.S. Navy hierarchy. During the association's 1991 annual convention in Las Vegas, eighty-three women, many of them naval officers, alleged that they had been sexually assaulted passing through a hotel hallway filled with male officers. Secretary of the Navy H. Lawrence Garrett III and Chief of Naval Operations Admiral Frank B. Kelso II attended the convention, but both said they witnessed no improper behavior. A subsequent navy investigation was indecisive, and on June 18, 1992, Secretary Garrett asked the Defense Department's inspector general to take control of the inquiry. The next week several female victims, led by navy Lieutenant Paula A. Coughlin, a helicopter pilot and aide to Rear Admiral John W. Snyder, Jr., brought charges. They described their mistreatment in interviews with newspaper and television reporters. On June 26 Secretary Garrett resigned. Members of Congress criticized the pace of the investigation, the commitment of investigators, and the stonewalling of Tailhook members whose memories of the incident could not be refreshed. In July the Senate Armed Services Committee approved 1,126 promotions for navy and marine officers only after the committee had been assured that those officers had not attended the convention. The 1993 defense appropriation barred the Tailhook Association from receiving federal funds. In April 1993 the Defense Department's Inspector General accused 140 officers of indecent exposure, assault, and of lying under oath. About fifty were fined or disciplined. Accusations in more prominent cases did not lead to court-martial convictions or even demotions. On Feb. 8, 1994, a navy judge ruled that Admiral Kelso had misrepresented his activities at the convention and had tried to manipulate the subsequent investigation. Denying these charges, Kelso decided to retire two months early with a full pension, in return for a tribute from Defense Secretary John J. Dalton that stated Kelso was a man of the "highest integrity and honor." During that same week Coughlin announced her resignation, saying her career in the navy had been ruined because she had chosen to bring charges. Commenting on these two distinctly different career endings, Democratic Representative Pat Schroeder of Colorado concluded that the investigation of Tailhook had been "mishandled from its tawdry beginning to its embarrassing finale." Coughlin sued the Tailhook Association and received a monetary award in a September 1994 out-of-court settlement (the amount was not disclosed). Her negligence suit against the Hilton Hotels Corporation and the Las Vegas Hilton Corporation, which claimed that inadequate security was provided during the convention, went to trial in October, and she received $6.7 million in damages, a decision that set the stage for other lawsuits against Hilton.

[Congressional Quarterly, "Tailhook," *Congressional Quarterly Almanac* 48 (1992).]

IRWIN N. GERTZOG

See also **SUPP:** Sexual Harassment; Women in Military Services.

TALK SHOWS. Television talk shows have been a staple of viewers since Sylvester L. (Pat) Weaver, Jr., produced *Today* starring Dave Garroway, Jan. 14,

1952, on NBC. Because they are the least expensive type of show to produce, they are the bread and butter of daytime television. More than 4,000 interview programs are broadcast daily throughout the United States, ensuring that most of the 192 million television sets in the United States are tuned in to at least one such show. More than 1.7 million guest bookings occur each year. Talk shows are either syndicated, such as Donahue (with host Phil Donahue), aired on any station that buys the program, or network programs such as *The Tonight Show,* aired on one network. Types of telecasts are talk shows (*Face the Nation* and *Meet the Press*); talk-variety (*Tonight* and *The Late Show with David Letterman*) in which celebrities make up the majority of guests; talk-service programs (*Charlie Rose, The Oprah Winfrey Show,* and *Donahue*) in which bookings relate to controversial issues; and talk-religious shows (*Oral Roberts*), which are geared to an audience of a specific religious persuasion. Interview techniques vary from the straight one-on-one interviews of William F. Buckley's *Firing Line* to Larry King's discussions with call-in viewers to telephone interviews with guests in remote locations. The longevity of this type of program depends on the personality of the celebrity in charge. The longest-running talk show in prime time is *The Tonight Show,* which premiered Sept. 27, 1954, on NBC with Steve Allen as host. He was succeeded by Ernie Kovacs and then by Jack Paar and guest hosts. Johnny Carson and Ed McMahon made their debut as host and co-host on Oct. 2, 1962, and gathered the largest talk-show viewing audience on Dec. 17, 1969, with the televised wedding of Tiny Tim, a bizarre celebrity of the day, and his bride, Miss Vicki. Carson relinquished the host chair to Jay Leno in May 1992. Talk shows can be educational, enlightening, entertaining, and even serve the political process. Both John F. Kennedy and Robert F. Kennedy appeared with Jack Paar on *The Tonight Show*; both before and after their election in 1992, President Bill Clinton and Vice President Al Gore made extensive use of popular talk shows.

[Richard Mincer and Deanne Mincer, *The Talk Show Book* (New York, 1982).]

JOHN J. BYRNE

See also **SUPP:** Radio; Television.

TAYLOR V. LOUISIANA, 419 U.S. 522 (1975), a Supreme Court decision that represents an early judicial response to the reemergence of feminism in the late twentieth century. Ironically, the defendant, Billy Taylor, who won this early male sex discrimination case, was accused of rape. The Supreme Court sustained Taylor's claim that a state law infringed on his right to a jury trial by exempting women from jury duty. In Louisiana women could be called for jury service only if they filed a written declaration of their willingness to serve. As a result most Louisiana juries, including the one that convicted Taylor of kidnapping, were all-male. Louisiana's practice was similar to one that the Court had unanimously upheld in *Hoyt* v. *Florida* (1961), a decision that sustained the Florida law as a reasonable concession to women's family responsibilities. As a result of the *Hoyt* decision a woman accused of murdering her husband could be tried by a jury almost certain to consist entirely of men. The Court had implied acceptance of states' exclusion of women from grand juries as recently as 1972, but *Taylor* ended special treatment for women, invalidating all remaining state laws restricting jury duty on the basis of gender. The Court quoted from an earlier case: "Who would claim that a jury was truly representative of the community if all men were intentionally and systematically excluded from the panel?" but defendants had no right to a "representative" jury or even one that included both women and men despite the Sixth Amendment, which "affords the defendant in a criminal trial the opportunity to have the jury drawn from venires [a jury pool] representative of the community." Since *Taylor* jury duty has been a responsibility shared equally by men and women.

[Judith A. Baer, *Women in American Law* (New York, 1991).]

JUDITH A. BAER

TEACHER CORPS. The Higher Education Act of 1965 created the Teacher Corps after Senators Gaylord A. Nelson of Wisconsin and Edward M. Kennedy of Massachusetts proposed the legislation and President Lyndon B. Johnson gave the idea a name. During its seventeen-year life the corps conducted more than 650 projects in cities, small towns, and rural areas, focusing on educational innovation. The first broad concern of the Teacher Corps was to improve education for the disadvantaged. In the mid-1960s policymakers likened it to the Peace Corps—idealistic young people would bring energy and commitment to schools in blighted urban areas and poor rural communities. The corps encouraged graduates of liberal arts colleges and members of minority groups to join. The perspectives of these nontraditional teachers led to curricular innovation in individual instruction and multicultural education. A second innovation was in teacher training. After eight weeks of training, interns spent two years engaged simultaneously in university study, work-study in the schools, and work in communities, which included after-school recreation activities, home visits, and health programs. During its last years the Teacher Corps was more concerned with in-service training for teachers already in schools, focusing on professional development and innovations among veteran teachers. Cooperation among educators was important to the Teacher Corps. The Department of Health, Education and Welfare provided funds. At the state level college and university teachers instructed interns and consulted with local schools. School districts and community groups used the interns. Controversy surrounded the Teacher Corps from the beginning. The corps threatened the traditional rights of the states in educational matters, and issues of trust and authority simmered beneath the surface of relations between teachers and interns, school districts and universities, the national office and local educators. Community groups were concerned about being shuffled aside. By the late 1970s the mission of the corps became difficult to define, its varied constituents hard to satisfy. In an effort to cut back federal involvement in education, President Ronald Reagan officially eliminated the corps as part of the 1981 Education Consolidation and Improvement Act and it ceased operations in 1983.

[Ronald G. Corwin, *Reform and Organizational Survival: The Teacher Corps as an Instrument of Educational Change* (New York, 1973).]

CHRISTINE A. OGREN

See also **SUPP:** Education; Education, Department of; Education, Experimental.

TEACHER TRAINING in the United States began in 1794, when the Society of Associated Teachers was formed in New York City to establish qualifications for teachers in that city. The Free School Society, established in 1805, also in New York City, began training teachers using public funds and organized a teacher-training course. In 1885 Brown University began to offer students courses in pedagogy, establishing one of the first university-level departments of education. When the study of teaching methods was recognized as a valid program in the twentieth cen-

tury, the certification standards for teachers were raised throughout the United States. By the end of the twentieth century, almost all U.S. teachers received preservice training in institutions of higher education with programs that complied with state guidelines for certification. These institutions usually have separate schools or departments of education and prospective teachers are education majors. Nearly every teacher holds a bachelor's degree, and the vast majority have additional credits, with more than half holding one or more advanced degrees. Many states require graduate education for permanent certification. Education students must take courses in pedagogical techniques, and prospective secondary teachers need a specified number of credit hours in the specific subject they plan to teach. Training includes a student teaching requirement, a period of classroom teaching under the supervision of a certified teacher. States vary in their course content and credit requirements. Critics of teacher training programs cite an overemphasis on methods and psychological studies, the neglect of academic subjects, the need for accountability to ensure that training and certification are based less on academic credits and more on ability to function in the classroom, and the lack of uniform requirements among states. *A Nation at Risk,* the 1983 report of the National Committee on Excellence in Education, appointed by President Ronald Reagan, alerted the American public to the need to attract high-quality teaching candidates and to improve their training. By the mid-1990s most states offered alternative routes to certification to mid-career people and liberal arts graduates via programs that provide on-the-job supervision.

MYRNA W. MERRON

TELECOMMUNICATIONS. Beginning in the 1870s the Bell Telephone Company dominated the nation's phone network, known as the Bell System, including long-distance service under its subsidiary, American Telephone & Telegraph (AT&T). In the late 1960s, however, AT&T faced pressure from the U.S. government to break its protected monopoly. In 1969 government regulators allowed MCI Communications to sell long-distance service and connect with the AT&T network. In 1984 a federal court decision allowed AT&T to retain its long-distance service and manufacturing and research operations but forced the company to divest itself of the seven regional Bell operating companies, the so-called Baby Bells, and agree to purchase equipment from other companies besides its subsidiaries. The implications of the divestiture of AT&T in 1984 were far-reaching. At first there was confusion as customers began paying phone bills to both a local phone company and a long-distance company. Soon consumers adjusted to a variety of long-distance companies, such as AT&T, MCI, and Sprint, and many companies began to sell phone equipment to consumers.

By the mid-1990s new technologies had rapidly changed the telecommunications market. The expanded use by the 1980s of fiber-optic cable in network systems enabled companies to transmit telephone calls by digital technology, which conveys information about the transmitted signal through a numerical code rather than representing it, as is done with analog technology. This change resulted in improved clarity on phone lines, but in the mid-1990s as many as half the phones in the United States still relied on analog technology to send a signal between the network system and the home or office. For computers and fax systems to use analog technology, it was necessary to provide them with a modem, which converts the digital message into audio signals. Increasingly, some argued that telephones did not need to rely on traditional network systems and that a radio signal or even a satellite transmission could be used, which was the basis of the expanding mobile and cellular phone business. Between 1990 and 1992 the number of cellular phones in the United States increased from 4 million to 9 million. In fact, because of the accelerating integration of technologies related to computers, telephones, and cable television, and other entertainment media seemed uncertain by the mid-1990s. Companies that provided the network system for telephones wanted changes in U.S. laws that would enable them to carry entertainment shows into homes in order to challenge cable television. During the early and mid-1990s a number of agreements and mergers between telecommunications and entertainment companies occurred that reflected new technological capabilities. Likewise, the regional Bell companies wanted Congress to revise existing laws so that they could compete directly against AT&T and other companies in the manufacture of telecommunications equipment.

[Irwin Lebow, *Information Highways and Byways: From the Telegraph to the 21st Century* (New York, 1995); Steven Lubar, *InfoCulture: The Smithsonian Book of Information Age Inventions* (Boston, 1993).]

KENNETH B. MOSS

See also **DAH:** Telephone; **SUPP:** Communications Industry; Computers; Fiber Optics; Internet; Office Technology.

TELEVANGELISM. The propagation of the Christian gospel over the airwaves, dubbed "televangelism," is a natural extension of evangelicalism's exploitation of communications technology. Throughout U.S. history evangelicals (those who interpret the Bible literally and who believe in the centrality of the conversion, or "born-again," experience) have been pioneers in mass communications, from George Whitefield's open-air preaching in the eighteenth century to Charles G. Finney's use of newspapers in the nineteenth century to the radio programs of Aimee Semple McPherson and Charles Fuller early in the twentieth century. When Billy Graham emerged as a cultural phenomenon after World War II, he turned first to radio and then to television.

Because of changes in television, evangelists gained even larger audiences in the 1970s. The Federal Communications Commission (FCC) mandated that all local stations allocate time to religious broadcasting. Network policy forbade local affiliates to accept money for such programming. With increased independence of local stations, however, and with the blessing of the FCC, stations began accepting money for religious broadcasts. Evangelists seized upon the opportunity, recognizing that they could draw in donations that would pay for the inexpensive airtime available on Sunday mornings. The nature of religious programming changed dramatically. Whereas religious broadcasts once had been dominated by the staid liturgies of Roman Catholicism and mainline Protestantism, evangelicals, drawing on the long evangelical tradition of mixing religion and entertainment, translated the gospel into what some critics said was show business. The "electronic church" took many forms: the pentecostal and healing emphasis of Kathryn Kuhlman, Oral Roberts, and Ernest Angley; the positive-thinking messages of Rex Humbard, Robert Schuller, and Robert Tilton; the inimitable theatrics of Jimmy Swaggart; the conservative politics of James Robison and Jerry Falwell; and the talk-show format of Pat Robertson and, later, Jim and Tammy Faye Bakker, whose programs were modeled after Johnny Carson's *Tonight Show*. Televangelism thus became profitable. Many televangelists received millions every year, far exceeding the budgets of some denominations. Robertson's ability to garner audiences turned his network, the Christian Broadcasting Network (CBN), into a formidable organization that provided the foundation for his campaign for the Republican presidential nomination in 1988.

By the middle of the 1980s scandal caught up with many of the televangelists. Bakker's flamboyant lifestyle led to financial improprieties that eventually sent him to prison but did not bar him from returning to television upon his release at the end of 1994; Swaggart was caught in dalliances with a prostitute in Louisiana; and Roberts declared that God would "take [him] home" unless God's people ponied up $4.5 million to save his flagging empire. Early in the 1990s Tilton was reeling from an ABC news exposé that cast serious doubts on his integrity. The effect of the scandals was a sag in ratings and revenues. Many of the larger televangelist organizations cut back on operations but the proliferation of cable television beginning in the early 1990s opened the doors for new televangelists and new networks.

[Quentin J. Schultze, *Televangelism and American Culture: The Business of Popular Religion* (Grand Rapids, Mich., 1991).]

RANDALL BALMER

See also **DAH:** Evangelism, Evangelicalism, and Revivalism; Finney Revivals; **SUPP:** Fundamentalism; Pentecostal Churches; Protestant Churches; Religion.

TELEVISION. At the end of the twentieth century television was the primary leisure activity of most Americans and their most likely source for news. The medium had changed markedly since the mid-1970s, when three national networks, ABC, CBS, and NBC, dominated television; 87 percent of all TV stations were affiliated with a network. In the evening, when most Americans watched television, 90 percent of all sets were tuned to a network program. The networks fought for first place in audience ratings. Because advertisers sponsoring programs paid more for large audiences, high ratings meant millions of dollars. The networks spared no expense to lure viewers.

Network rivalries were fierce in the mid-1970s. ABC, long the weakest of the three networks in terms of popular programming and affiliates, gradually achieved parity with CBS and NBC, winning younger viewers with situation comedies like *Happy Days* and *Three's Company.* The latter's sexually teasing qualities, apparent in another ABC hit, *Charlie's Angels,* about three female private detectives, encouraged imitation by CBS and NBC. ABC also poured resources into its long-dormant news division, which by the 1980s enjoyed an equal rating with its competitors. ABC also benefited from television sets equipped to receive ultra high frequency (UHF) channels 14 through 83, relying on UHF stations for affiliates. In 1967 just under half of all viewers had sets equipped to receive UHF; eight years later the number was 90 percent. UHF ultimately undermined all three networks; UHF stations began operations without network affiliation. "Independent stations" increased from 13 percent in 1975 to 39 percent in 1987. They began counterprogramming, especially in the early evening, with game shows and other entertainment to compete with the network news shows. Availability of stations unaffiliated with ABC, CBS, or NBC encouraged formation of a fourth network, Fox, in 1986.

The three original networks underwent changes in ownership in 1986. General Electric purchased NBC, Capital Cities purchased ABC, and the investor Lawrence Tisch bought CBS. To their dismay the new proprietors found themselves in a cost squeeze. In the 1970s inflation had allowed networks to pass along to advertisers higher production expenses. Sponsors, affected by the inflation psychology, did not protest. A decade later, with inflation falling, demand for national time softened; the networks no longer enjoyed a seller's market. Although programming costs continued to rise, advertisers refused to make up the increases. Even network news divisions, sources of industry pride, had to lower expenses. Staffs were cut and domestic and overseas bureaus pared or shut. Each network looked for cheaper programming, including more news shows. Despite lavish salaries awarded a few newscasters, news programs such as CBS's *48 Hours* cost less than entertainment series. The networks produced the news shows and did not have to share their profits with independent producers in Hollywood. Despite reductions in operating expenses the three networks' woes worsened; profits fell 50 percent between 1984 and 1988. By the mid-1990s Fox emerged as a serious rival of the big three. Like ABC in the 1970s, Fox succeeded with comedies like *The Simpsons* and *Married . . . With Children,* as well as a sexy dramatic series, *Beverly Hills 90210,* which appealed to the younger viewers coveted by advertisers. In 1994 Fox outbid CBS for the rights to telecast National Football League games, which the latter network had aired since the 1950s. A year later Fox led CBS in many large TV markets.

Cable television proved the greatest blow to the networks' oligopoly. Cable required a monthly fee to enhance reception but offered many more choices in programming. In a typical viewing area in the 1980s a noncable household had seven channels; a cable household thirty-three. In the 1990s experts predicted as many as 500 cable channels might eventually be available. Cable systems had entered some areas to improve reception, not choice, as early as 1949, but the Federal Communications Commission (FCC) and local governments, which regulated underground wiring connecting households to cable, discouraged the new system until the mid-1970s. Over the next years government oversight relaxed. Households with cable increased from 15 percent in 1975 to 60 percent in 1994. It was not until the late 1980s that the networks recognized cable's threat. Earlier they had started cable channels but their involvement was half-hearted; their emphasis remained over-the-air broadcasting.

Meanwhile, the Public Broadcasting System (PBS), established in 1967 and partly supported by federal and state sources, lost viewers and programming to cable outlets emphasizing culture. The Cable News Network (CNN) established a small but devoted following and was boosted by the Gulf War of 1991 and the sensational murder trial of O. J. Simpson four years later. In 1992 CNN programs combined with radio talk shows to assist the independent presidential candidacy of the Texas billionaire Ross Perot, initially ignored by the networks. Democratic nominee Bill Clinton similarly used "alternative media," including the all-music MTV channel.

Communication satellites benefited cable TV. In the mid-1970s several companies, including independent stations in Atlanta, New York, and Chicago, began relaying signals off satellites and making them available to cable companies across the country. Pay-cable outlets led by Home Box Office offered recently released and uncut feature films together with original programming. In late 1993 more than one-fourth of all households with television sets received one or more pay cable outlets. The videocassette recorder (VCR) delivered another blow to the networks. Sales of VCRs began in the early 1980s and by the mid-1990s four out of every five households with televisions had VCRs. Although some owners used VCRs to tape network shows to watch later, many more rented feature films, especially on weekends, which greatly reduced TV viewing. The effects of cable and VCRs were clear by the early 1990s. The network share of evening prime time fell to 60 percent. In 1980 three-fourths of viewers tuned to network evening newscasts; by 1992 that share had fallen almost to half.

One response to cable, seen at NBC in the early 1980s, was to make programs more "realistic," more like uncut movies on pay channels, with explicit treatment of sex and violence. Relaxed standards in feature films and popular music inspired this new realism. Being frank about sex and violence on television, however, infuriated parents, members of Congress, and conservative pressure groups, who accused the networks of contributing to a decline of national morality. In 1992 Vice President Dan Quayle condemned the TV series *Murphy Brown* for having the title character give birth out of wedlock. Relatedly, the news divisions were anxious to boost their programs' appeal and compete with many more channels. Network newscasts began to mimic local stations, which had never taken their responsibilities as seriously as had the networks. Especially at CBS, less attention was devoted to international and national news and more to human interest stories and segments on helping viewers cope with medical and financial matters. News programs competing against entertainment shows in the evening began to imitate the "tabloid" or sensational programs aired by Fox and independent producers.

[Ken Auletta, *Three Blind Mice* (New York, 1992); James L. Baughman, *The Republic of Mass Culture* (Baltimore, 1992).]

JAMES L. BAUGHMAN

See also **SUPP:** Advertising; Cable News Network; Music Television; Radio; Science Television; Talk Shows; Televangelism.

TELEVISION, SCIENCE. *See* **Science Television.**

TENNESSEE. Experiencing steady growth throughout its 200 years, Tennessee in 1970 had a population of 3,925,164; by 1990 that figure had grown to 4,877,187, an increase of more than 24 percent. The population became concentrated in urban areas, and many rural counties suffered substantial declines. Crockett, Obion, and Gibson, in the northwestern part of the state, lost substantially, as did the middle counties of Lawrence, Lewis, and Lincoln. Most eastern counties remained stable or reflected gains. Cheatham, Montgomery, Wilson, Sumner, Rutherford, and Williamson—all in close proximity to Nashville—each grew 20 percent or more in the 1980s. Among the cities, Memphis, with a population of 610,337, remained the state's largest, while Nashville's growth of 7.2 percent pushed the capital city's population to a half million. Knoxville, just ahead of Chattanooga, lost 5.7 percent, with a 1990 population of 165,121.

Industry expanded as well. Nissan Motor Manufacturing Company opened a $300 million truck-assembly plant near Murfreesboro in the 1980s; by 1994 it was worth $1.2 billion and manufactured trucks, buses, and Sentra passenger cars. By 1994 Japanese companies had invested $4.7 billion in Tennessee, and more than half of the 114 Japanese-owned operations were related to the automobile. Agriculture remained an important industry; principal crops were corn, tobacco, cotton, wheat, and soy beans. Beef cattle and dairying were also important. The number of farms continued to decline as construction of automobile and other plants led increasing numbers of Tennesseans to give up farming in order to take more lucrative jobs in factories. Many moved to the towns and cities. Others continued to raise crops and livestock on the farms while commuting to nearby plants for their principal incomes.

The expansion of industry and increasing population brought changes in politics. Traditionally part of the Democratic solid South, Tennessee in the 1990s was substantially a two-party state. During the 1970s and 1980s, Republicans, concentrated primarily in the eastern counties and the major cities, battled Democrats on an about-even basis. Republicans held the office of governor for twelve years between 1970 and 1990, both U.S. Senate seats for six years, and won the state's electoral votes in four of the six presidential elections through 1992. Democrat Ned Ray McWherter served two terms as governor but Republicans returned to power in the landslide of 1994. That year, even as native son Al Gore, a Democrat, served as U.S. vice president, they elected the governor, both U.S. senators, and five of the nine congressmen. Democrats retained control of the state legislature immediately after that election but within a few months lost the senate because of defections to the Republicans.

Tennessee is known as the country music capital of the world, and the "Nashville sound" means to millions not only country music but Western and religious music as well. In the literary field, Alex Haley, a Henning native and retired sailor, in 1976 published the most successful book ever written by a Tennessean. His *Roots,* translated into twelve languages and adapted for a television film seen in twenty-eight countries, gained new respect for the heritage of African Americans. By the mid-1990s, however, the state had not come to grips with the needs of state-supported education. In urging the legislature to build more schools, Governor John Brown in 1873 referred to his state as "third in ignorance"; Tennessee's rank was not much improved 100 years later. Although Governor Lamar Alexander's "better schools program" and Governor McWherter's increase in the sales tax kept the program respectable, educators and tax reformers alike argued that only a state income tax would place the state's educational program on a par with that of other states. In higher education the state in the 1970s authorized a medical school at Johnson City and several two-year colleges, but Tennesseans serving on a nationwide panel in 1993 to study offerings at 3,400 colleges and universities joined with other members in a highly critical statement of their own state's programs. They called on administrators to concentrate on improved academic offerings and the strengthening of values. Some of the trauma of racial integration during the 1960s continued into the next two decades, but schools were no longer segregated, although African Americans continued to experience job discrimination.

As in the country as a whole, crime and health care were major issues by the early 1990s. Problems of overcrowding, violence, idleness, and filth in the prisons resulted in the federal government's taking temporary control in 1982. After six new prisons accommodating 1,000 prisoners each were opened, the system was returned to state control in 1993. In the following year, more than a third of a billion dollars went into operating the prisons. In health care, TennCare was substituted for Medicaid. With federal approval the plan enabled the state to use federal money to purchase health care from providers for uninsured workers and Medicaid recipients. The controversial plan, begun early in 1994, was designed to expand health care and save money at the same time.

[Robert E. Corlew, *Tennessee: A Short History* (Knoxville, Tenn., 1989); William F. Fox and Patricia A. Price, *An Economic Report to the Governor of the State of Tennessee on the State's Economic Outlook* (Nashville, 1993).]

ROBERT E. CORLEW

See also **SUPP:** Memphis; Nashville.

TENNIS. In the late 1960s tennis began to undergo great changes, in part because of improvements in technology. For nearly one hundred years after the introduction of tennis in the United States during the 1870s, the best tennis rackets were made from wood but that changed with invention of the steel racket, which first appeared in the United States in 1967. Other innovations involving new materials followed. Aluminum rackets appeared in 1968 and graphite and fiberglass rackets during the 1970s. In 1976 Prince Manufacturing introduced an oversized racket with a head more than 50 percent larger in surface area than conventional models. During the 1970s and 1980s wood and metal rackets gave way altogether to new synthetic materials and conventional head sizes disappeared in favor of oversized and new intermediate, midsized heads. Rackets in use in the 1990s were simultaneously larger, lighter, and stronger than older wood or metal rackets. Another significant innovation appeared in the United States in 1987. Called the "widebody" because of the thickness of the racket head, this racket generates greater power than older designs. By the mid-1990s it had not yet gained wide acceptance among professional men players but was almost universally used by professional women players.

Competitive techniques and styles of play were greatly affected by the new racket technology. The two-handed backhand, popularized during the 1970s by Bjorn Borg, Jimmy Connors, and Chris Evert, proved to be ideally suited to the new, larger racket heads and became a staple of the competitive game; in 1970 none of the world's top ten men or women used the stroke, but five of the top men and six of the top women did in 1992. The greater power and flexibility of the two-handed shot made the backhand an offensive weapon for more players. In general, the newer rackets made it possible to hit harder with less effort and, consequently, increased the rewards for offensive tactics. The new racket technology was clearly responsible for a greater reliance on power in both women's and men's competitive tennis in the 1990s.

Tennis also underwent major economic changes. Until the late 1960s the sport's most prestigious competitions were open exclusively to amateurs. The arrival of Open tennis in 1968 led to the establishment of money prizes for all world-class tournaments. Since then the amount of prize money has increased dramatically. In 1969 the world's top male player, Rod Laver, earned a total of $124,000; in 1993 Pete Sampras won $4.1 million and Steffi Graf $2.8 million. Financially, tennis became one of the elite professional sports; *Forbes* magazine placed nine tennis players on its list of the world's forty highest-paid athletes in 1991. In 1993 Ivan Lendl led all men players in career prize money, with total earnings of $21 million, while Martina Navratilova led all women with $19.4 million. The professionalization of competitive tennis changed the careers of players. In the amateur era, players were typically young, and few players could afford to play full-time for more than a few years after college because of the difficulty of earning a living as a tennis player under the rules governing amateur status. After the advent of Open tennis, the mean age of competitive players rose sharply, as many found they could earn more playing tennis than in other careers. At the same time increasing prize money brought about the intensive training of young players. Junior competitions and training programs proliferated, and tennis academies were established where promising young players could live and train year-round. This more intensive training made many teenage players more advanced technically than young players of the past. Consequently, another feature of the Open era was the entry of small numbers of gifted players into adult competition at very young ages.

Tennis has long been one of the most international of sports, but the growing prize money and publicity of the Open era increased its geographic extent. During the 1990s the rankings of the world's top players for both men and women have consistently included citizens of more than twenty different countries, but the United States remains the single most important source of world-class players. At the end of 1991 there were seventeen Americans ranked among the world's top 100 men, and twenty-five Americans among the top 100 women; no other country had even half as many players in either group. The sport's champions have also been Americans in disproportionate numbers. Between 1970 and 1993 six American men—Stan Smith, Jimmy Connors, Arthur Ashe, John McEnroe, Jim Courier, and Pete Sampras—held the world's top ranking in ten of twenty-four years, and Ivan Lendl, a naturalized American, added another three. In the same period Americans Billie Jean King, Chris Evert, and Tracy Austin held the top women's ranking in a total of eight years, while Martina Navratilova, a naturalized American, added another seven. Tennis enjoyed a remarkable growth in popularity in the United States during the 1970s. An estimated 10 million Americans played the sport in 1970 but that number more than tripled to 32–34 million in 1974–1978. After a period of declining popularity during the 1980s, interest in the sport revived and an estimated 23 million Americans played during 1993.

[Bud Collins and Zander Hollander, eds., *Bud Collins' Modern Encyclopedia of Tennis* (Detroit, 1994).]

DAVID W. GALENSON

TERRORISM uses low levels of violence or intimidation for political ends. U.S. terrorist groups have been racist (Ku Klux Klan, Black Panthers), nationalist (Puerto Rican Liberation Army), opposed to a strong central government (Posse Comitatus), antiwar (Weathermen, Symbionese Liberation Army), and xenophobic and anti-Semitic (neo-Nazi skinheads). From 1985 to 1993 there were five to ten terrorist incidents in the United States annually, mostly bombings and arson, with about the same number of suspected and prevented incidents. The first incident of international terrorism against the United States occurred just before the Algeciras Conference in 1904, when the Moroccan chief Ahmed ibn-Muhammed Raisuli kidnapped Ion Perdicaris, a naturalized American citizen, from his villa near Tangier. Secretary of State John Hay telegraphed the U.S. consul-general in Tangier demanding "Perdicaris alive or Raisuli dead." The public acclaimed the tough handling of the incident, but an unpublished part of the telegram had warned the consul to avoid force without specific instructions.

The Department of State has kept statistics on international terrorism since 1968. The data show that U.S. citizens and property have been the most frequent targets of terrorism—about 20 percent of all international incidents in 1985 and more than 40 percent in 1990. In 1975 American citizens suffered 36 percent of the casualties from international terrorism; in 1985, 21 percent; and in 1990, only 5 percent. U.S. casualties peaked at 386 (271 fatalities, 115 wounded) in 1983, when on October 23, 241 marines died when a member of the Islamic Jihad drove a truck loaded with dynamite into the barracks at the Beirut International Airport. The level of terrorism has been directly related to U.S. foreign policy. There were, for example, some 160 terrorist attacks worldwide within six weeks of the start of the Gulf War in January 1991. The most significant international terrorist act against the United States was the seizure of the U.S. embassy in Tehran, Iran, on Nov. 4, 1979. Fifty-two Americans were held for 444 days with the collusion of the Iranian government. They were released on Jan. 20, 1981, in return for the $6 billion in Iranian assets frozen in U.S. banks. The event helped defeat Jimmy Carter in the 1980 presidential election. The worst incident of international terrorism within the United States was the Feb. 26, 1993, bombing in New York City of the World Trade Center, the tallest building in the nation's most populous city. Six people were killed and more than 1,000 injured by explosives equal to 1,500 pounds of TNT.

The U.S. government has demanded the extradition of terrorists, trained foreign antiterrorist forces, launched air strikes, and enforced trade sanctions against states that support terrorism. It also has traded weapons to Iran for hostages kidnapped in Lebanon and reportedly paid $3 million to Sheik Mohammed Hussein Fadlallah, who organized the 1983 bombing of the marine barracks, not to attack U.S. interests in Beirut again. International terrorism accounted for fewer than 2,000 deaths during 1970–1979 and just over 4,000 fatalities during 1980–1989. Terrorism has been more frightening and dangerous than these statistics indicate, however, because terrorists have targeted civilians and attempted to destabilize governments.

[Walter Laqueur, *The Age of Terrorism* (Boston, 1987); John L. Scherer, ed., *Terrorism* (Minneapolis, 1986– , quarterly); U.S. Department of State, *Patterns of Global Terrorism* (Washington, D.C., annually); Alexander Yonah, ed., *Terrorism: An International Journal* (New York, 1977–1991, quarterly).]

JOHN L. SCHERER

See also **SUPP:** Beirut Bombing; Fundamentalism; Hostage Crises; Oklahoma City Bombing; White Supremacists; World Trade Center Bombing.

TEXAS. The Lone Star State achieved a new level of prosperity and recognition in the 1970s. During that decade Texas not only grew at a tremendous pace but caught the imagination of Americans as never before. This success grew out of a series of developments that began in World War II, when massive government spending for defense injected needed capital into the state's economy and boosted industrial development, particularly in aircraft manufacturing, petrochemicals, and shipbuilding as well as oil and natural gas. Oil production increased after the war with the growing popularity of the automobile. High oil prices precipitated by the Arab oil embargo of 1973 sent profits skyrocketing and brought even greater prosperity to the state. The rapid migration to Texas of people eager to take part in its expanding economy set off a building boom that provided more job opportunities and lured even more workers from the stagnating North. Between 1950 and 1980 the population of Texas doubled from 7 million to 14 million. Some 58 percent of that growth during the 1970s came from migration from other states. Many factors other than the oil economy were responsible for that growth; the state particularly benefited from the expansion of manufacturing, tourism, transportation, international trade, and the continued military buildup begun during World War II and necessitated by the cold war. Growth of the computer and electronics industries after 1960 made an even greater impact on the state's economic health. A number of companies established regional offices and some national corporations such as American Airlines relocated their headquarters to Texas.

The postwar transportation revolution played a significant role in the state's expansion. Improvement of commercial aviation and construction of new airports in Texas, including the massive Dallas–Fort Worth International Airport in 1974, helped make the state more accessible. The interstate highway system initiated in the 1950s and cheap fuel costs lessened the state's isolation and helped attract manufacturers. Low taxes and a probusiness, antiunion climate also did not hurt. The importance of the automobile to the state's development is illustrated by the fact that Texas has more than 220,000 miles of municipal and rural highways. The growing use of air conditioning in the 1950s and 1960s for home and car also lured newcomers to the state by making the hot summer days more tolerable.

The country's ongoing defense buildup continued to have a major impact on Texas. The Manned Spacecraft Center in Houston (which opened in 1963), the aircraft and high-tech industries of north Texas, and the presence of military posts throughout the state played a critical role in stimulating the economy. Texas thus evolved from one of the nation's most rural states to one of its most urban. By 1990 it had three of the ten largest cities in the United States—Houston, Dallas, and San Antonio. Texas contained 298 municipalities with a population of at least 5,000, and more than 80 percent of its residents lived in urban areas. Its total 1990 population was 16,986,510. Demographic changes occurred in the 1980s. Population increased by 19 percent during the decade, with Hispanic Americans accounting for more than 45 percent of that growth. The African-American population also rose at a more rapid rate than Anglos, and there was a significant influx of Asian Americans. Indeed, Texas attracted unprecedented numbers of legal and illegal immigrants and became a much more ethnically diverse state than ever before. The economy also underwent changes in the 1980s. The oil boom that gave Texas one of the nation's healthiest economies during the 1970s soured in the 1980s as the price of oil plummeted from $40 a barrel in 1981 to $18 a barrel in 1992. The state suffered from banking failures in the 1980s, losing 163 banks between 1987 and 1988, and the building boom of the 1970s came to an abrupt halt. An economy that once depended on oil, natural gas, and cotton increasingly relied on high-tech industries and the service sector, including tourism, health, and education.

The state has experienced both political and social transformation. At the beginning of the twentieth century, white males in the Democratic party controlled the state and minorities had few rights or op-

portunities. For example, the Texas legislature approved a poll tax in 1902 and later barred blacks from the Democratic primary. The state also passed Jim Crow segregation laws and showed little tolerance of African Americans or the growing number of Mexican Americans streaming into the state. Change occurred, however, when the Supreme Court's *Smith* v. *Allwright* decision (1944) voided the state's white Democratic primary and gave the state's large minority populations the opportunity to participate more fully in politics. The civil rights movement of the 1950s and 1960s that led to the Voting Rights Act of 1965 further strengthened the political hand of the state's minorities. By 1978 the Texas House of Representatives included fourteen African Americans and seventeen Mexican Americans. In 1980 almost 1,000 Mexican Americans held public office in local government although the number of African Americans remained below 200. Despite sending prominent liberals to the U.S. Senate after World War II, such as Lyndon B. Johnson and Ralph Yarborough, Texas voters retained their conservative tendencies even during the presidencies of John F. Kennedy and native son Johnson. The election of Republican William P. Clements in 1978 as governor signaled the rise of a two-party system in Texas. The Democrats, however, reclaimed the governor's mansion in 1982 with the election of Mark White. Eight years later Texas voters selected another Democrat, Ann Richards. Under her administration women and minorities gained unprecedented opportunities to participate in the state's government and development. Texans supported Jimmy Carter, a Sunbelt Democrat, for president in 1976 but voted Republican in the next three presidential contests. Indeed, in 1992 Bill Clinton became the first Democrat in the history of the United States to lose Texas and win the presidency. Two years later Republican George W. Bush, son of the former president, beat Ann Richards for state governor. Meanwhile, Republican Kay Bailey Hutchison in 1993 became the first woman to represent Texas in the U.S. Senate. Her election marked the first time Texas had two Republican senators since 1875. This victory, along with the defeat of Clinton in Texas a year earlier, clearly suggested the growing strength of the Republican party in a state that historically had been Democratic.

[David G. McComb, *Texas: A Modern History* (Austin, 1989); Robert S. Maxwell, *Texas Economic Growth, 1890 to World War II* (Boston, 1981); Char Miller and Heywood T. Sanders, eds., *Urban Texas: Politics and Development* (College Station, Tex., 1990); David Montejaño, *Anglos and Mexicans in the Making of Texas, 1836–1986* (Austin, 1987).]

ROBERT B. FAIRBANKS

See also **SUPP:** Austin; Dallas; El Paso; Fort Worth; Galveston; Houston; San Antonio; Sunbelt.

TEXTBOOKS constitute the de facto curriculum in many disciplines. American history, especially at the secondary level, where 85 percent of the nation's students take courses before graduation, is a controversial area because of disputes over content and interpretation. U.S. history texts include the study of continental geography, political history, economic development, social history, and diverse cultures. Private corporations provide textbooks to state and local governments for a profit, an arrangement that differs from most industrialized countries, where the national government creates the curriculum and publishes textbooks. The total domestic market for instructional materials was an estimated $5 billion in 1992, of which more than $2 billion represented elementary and high school materials.

Changes in textbooks since 1970 have been particularly considerable in U.S. history and social studies, as social history, revisionism, and multiculturalism influenced curriculum composition. Publishers expended considerable effort to make texts redress earlier omissions. Still, as state-level controversies of the late 1980s and early 1990s in California and New York indicated, textbook publishers remained beset by special-interest groups, including ethnic activists, feminists, the disabled, environmentalists, homosexuals, and religious groups, all desiring favorable and prominent treatment. Such pressures make it difficult for publishers to balance academic integrity against market requirements. Several federal court cases in the 1980s reflect the perennial disputes over textbook censorship, content, and interpretation. Challenges have arisen over biology, health, literature, and history texts. Three significant federal cases originated in local complaints that textbooks promote secular humanism (*Smith* v. *Board of School Commissioners of Mobile County,* 1986), atheism (*Mozert* v. *Hawkins County Public Schools,* 1987), and the theory of evolution (*Aguillard* v. *Edwards,* 1987).

Textbooks remain useful and efficient devices for learning in all formal subjects. Offering organized, convenient sequences of ideas and information, they structure teaching and learning. In the 1990s schools at all levels began to experiment with CD-ROMs and other video technologies as curriculum supplements.

The classroom use of CD-ROM reference works, electronic atlases, and on-line databases was growing, but it was not certain that such media would supplant textbooks in the future.

[Philip G. Altbach et al., *Textbooks in American Society* (Albany, N.Y., 1991); Joan Del Fattore, *What Johnny Doesn't Know: Textbook Censorship in America* (New Haven, Conn., 1992).]

GILBERT T. SEWALL

See also **SUPP:** American Studies; Cultural Literacy; Curriculum; Education; Multiculturalism.

THEATER. Profound changes began to occur in theater during the 1960s, establishing patterns that prevailed into the 1990s. The major development was decentralization of the professional theater, which provided careers for artists outside New York City and made professional theater accessible to audiences throughout the United States. Theaters were most often established as not-for-profit operations, heavily dependent on local and federal support. The regional shift occurred because rising production costs in New York discouraged risk taking and admission prices gradually increased (in 1994 Broadway theater tickets reached a high of $75). By the early 1990s, 300 not-for-profit professional theaters were playing to more than 16 million people annually. Despite the demise of forty theaters between 1980 and 1993, largely the result of economic pressure, in the early 1990s not-for-profit theaters were a $366 million industry.

One interesting result of the spread of American theater was transference of successful productions by regional theaters to New York (and national or international recognition), beginning with the Washington, D.C., Arena Stage production of Howard Sackler's *The Great White Hope* in 1976. Since then major American plays have frequently originated outside New York: David Mamet's *Glengarry Glen Ross* (Chicago's Goodman Theatre, 1984), Marsha Norman's *'night, Mother* (American Repertory Theatre in Cambridge, Mass., 1983), Herb Gardner's *I'm Not Rappaport* and *Conversations with My Father* (both presented first at the Seattle Repertory Theatre), and all of the plays by African-American playwright August Wilson, beginning with *Ma Rainey's Black Bottom* (Yale Repertory Theatre, 1984). Sixteen of the seventeen Pulitzer Prizes in drama (1976–1993) went to plays developed by not-for-profit companies. The winner of the 1992 prize, Robert Schenkkan's *The Kentucky Cycle* was seen first in Seattle in 1991. The

1993 winner, Tony Kushner's *Angels in America,* received the prize several weeks before its Broadway opening, after development in London, San Francisco, and Los Angeles.

A residual effect of the socially committed, aesthetically radical theater artists of the late 1950s and early 1960s, and in opposition to theater epitomized by Broadway, was an avant-garde theater centered in the Off-Broadway and Off-Off-Broadway districts and in major cities throughout the country. This avant-garde theater paralleled the winding down of the Vietnam War. Stimulated by the English-born director Peter Brook and the Polish national Jerzy Grotowski, it sought to strip away old conventions and reach what Brook and Grotowski called a "holy" core or essence. Experiment led to changes in style and structure and encouraged new topics and such cross-disciplinary hybrids as dance-theater, performance art, docudrama, environmental theater, guerrilla theater, and New Vaudeville. Eschewing conventional plots and characters, director-playwrights Richard Foreman, Lee Breuer, and Robert Wilson emerged in the 1970s, and such ensembles as Mabou Mines and the Wooster Group turned from polemic to self-reflective visionary and aural images. In the 1980s a more conservative atmosphere encouraged radical artists—for example, Eric Bogosian, Laurie Anderson, Karen Finley, Spalding Gray, and Anna Deavere Smith—to explore social and political issues in more personal ways. The controversial authorial voice of stage directors, which began in the 1970s, intensified in the work of JoAnne Akalaitis, Meredith Monk, Elizabeth LeCompte, Anne Bogart, and Peter Sellars.

All the while there was an expansion of demographics on stage and in the audience. The voices of African Americans, Latinos, Asians, gays, and women, in the past on the fringe, reached the centers of theater. Previously marginalized artists moved into positions of considerable visibility. Pulitzer Prizes were won by Beth Henley (*Crimes of the Heart,* 1981), Marsha Norman (*'night, Mother,* 1983), and Wendy Wasserstein (*The Heidi Chronicles,* 1989), raising by half the number of Pulitzers in drama awarded to women since their inception in 1918. The African-American director George C. Wolfe became producer of the New York Shakespeare Festival, a major not-for-profit theater established by Joseph Papp (1921–1991). In 1993 the National Endowment for the Arts appointed as its head actress Jane Alexander, the first artist to hold this post.

Commercial theater since the early 1970s, despite unwillingness to experiment and despite soaring production costs, has enjoyed considerable prosperity, with long runs of spectacular musicals, many imported from abroad, such as *Cats, Les Misérables, Phantom of the Opera, Miss Saigon, Sunset Boulevard,* and others with small-cast plays. Major figures included playwright Neil Simon, whose *Lost in Yonkers* (1991) won the Pulitzer Prize, and composer-lyricist Stephen Sondheim, who continued to be the most original American creator of musical theater. Playwrights who first gained attention in the 1970s, such as John Guare, Terrence McNally, and August Wilson, became major voices in the theater by the late 1980s. By the mid-1990s, however, despite productions dealing with controversial subjects (*Kiss of the Spider Woman, Angels in America*), Broadway continued to be dominated by musical revivals (*Guys and Dolls, Crazy for You, She Loves Me, Joseph and the Amazing Technicolor Dreamcoat, My Fair Lady, Damn Yankees, Show Boat*).

[C. W. E. Bigsby, *Modern American Drama, 1945–1990* (New York, 1992); Mary C. Henderson, *Theater in America: 200 Years of Plays, Players, and Productions* (New York, 1986); Don B. Wilmeth and Tice L. Miller, *Cambridge Guide to American Theatre* (New York, 1993).]

DON B. WILMETH

THEME PARKS. The origins of the theme park trace back to late-nineteenth-century beach clubs, such as those along Coney Island in Brooklyn, N.Y., where people drank, socialized, and watched musical productions in pavilions. Mechanical rides were added to these resorts and to picnic parks that were developed by trolley companies to build weekend and holiday use of local transit systems. By the 1930s these areas had developed into amusement parks. In 1955 Walt Disney built the first amusement theme park, Disneyland, in Anaheim, Calif., where he combined fantasy with rides, food, and shows in a safe, clean, family environment. In the 1990s there were ten major types of theme park: multi-theme, such as Disneyland and Six Flags Great Adventure (N.J.); water theme, such as Water Country USA (Va.); holiday and Santa Claus theme, such as Holiday World (Ind.); imaginary character theme, such as Dogpatch USA (Ark.) and Sesame Place (Pa.); movie theme, such as Disney-MGM Studios (Fla.) and Universal Studios (Fla.); musical theme, such as Dollywood (Tenn.) and Opryland USA (Tenn.); marine life theme, such as Marineland (Fla.) and Sea World (Fla.); historic theme, such as The Old Country (Va.); western theme, such as Frontier City (Okla.); and animal and nature theme, such as Busch Gardens' The

Dark Continent (Fla.) and Waimea Falls Park (Hawaii). The largest theme park in the world is Walt Disney World in Lake Buena Vista, Fla. With almost 28,000 acres, it is twice the size of Manhattan and admits more than 20 million visitors each year.

[American Automobile Association, *The AAA Guide to North America's Theme Parks* (New York, 1992).]

JOHN J. BYRNE

THINK TANKS are policy-oriented research organizations that have proliferated in twentieth-century America, but no precise count or unambiguous definition exists for such organizations. They perform studies that result in policy recommendations; they usually publish their findings; they may undertake research for a client on a grant or contract basis or initiate their own studies; and most, not all, have non-profit status. Their work frequently is of an interdisciplinary character in contrast to the more traditional disciplinary studies of university scholars. Think tank examples include the Rand Corporation, Brookings Institution, American Enterprise Institute, Hudson Institute, and such newer entities as the Heritage Foundation and the Cato Institute. The creation of think tanks came in three waves. The earliest ones were established in the Progressive Era as part of the movement to bring efficiency to government. A second wave came after World War II when many think tanks such as the Rand Corporation were set up to advise the federal government, especially in defense. In the 1970s a third wave emerged that reflected a political policy or ideological orientation. Think tanks engage in dialogue with one another and are often cited or referred to by government officials or by political protagonists, although their effect on policy remains a matter of debate. In their number, variety, and intellectual vitality, think tanks are a U.S. phenomenon, and they contribute to the dynamism, openness, and pluralism of the nation's policymaking process.

[Joseph C. Kiger, ed., *Research Institutions and Learned Societies* (Westport, Conn., 1982); Bruce L. R. Smith, *The Advisors* (Washington, D.C., 1992), and *The Rand Corporation* (Cambridge, Mass., 1966); James Allen Smith, *The Idea Brokers* (New York, 1991).]

BRUCE L. R. SMITH

THIRD PARTIES AND INDEPENDENTS. The decline since 1960 in identification among the electorate with either the Republican or Democratic parties contributed to a proliferation of minor parties and two of the most successful independent presidential tickets in U.S. history. Third parties in the United States have always been quite diverse in goals and organization. With the exception of Alabama Governor George Wallace's American Independent party in the presidential election of 1968, the only aspect such parties have had in common is their failure to influence the electoral process. Wallace's party exemplified the third party as protest vote, and his strength at the polls (13.5 percent of the total) inspired the administration of Richard M. Nixon to adopt rhetoric and policies specifically designed to capture Wallace's traditionally Democratic followers for the Republican party. Wallace competed in the Democratic primaries in 1972 but was shot in an assassination attempt, and the party he founded faded into obscurity.

Most third parties are ideologically based, and purity of doctrine is more important than pragmatic efforts to build a campaign organization and establish a coalition of voters. The Marxist parties—Socialist Workers, Communist, Socialist Labor, Workers World, Socialist—are cases in point. All remained active through the 1980s, but none received more than one-tenth of 1 percent of the votes cast, in part because state laws make it difficult for third-party candidates to qualify to be on ballots. The Libertarian party has achieved greater success on the far right of the political spectrum. Emphasizing individual freedom, an unregulated market economy, and voluntarism (even to the extent of opposing the power of taxation), the Libertarians have contested most national and many state offices. Their presidential candidate in 1980, Ed Clark, received just over 1 percent of the vote, and the 1992 candidate, Andre Marrou, .28 percent. A few minor parties focus essentially on a single issue, much like interest groups. The Prohibition party continued to field presidential candidates, although it drew only a few thousand votes per election and only 985 votes in 1992. The Citizens party, founded by Barry Commoner in 1969 and similar to the Green parties in Europe, qualified for federal matching funds in 1984 but attracted only 72,000 presidential votes. The Right-to-Life party, which opposes abortion, has received even fewer votes.

Far more impressive than third parties has been a series of independent candidates. Former Democratic Senator Eugene McCarthy drew almost 1 percent of the vote nationally in the 1976 presidential election. Republican John Anderson qualified for federal matching funds in 1980, initially while contesting his own party's primaries and then as an independent in the general election. He spent almost $15 million on the campaign and captured 6.6 percent of the popular vote. In 1990 maverick Republican Lowell Weicker won the governorship of Connecticut as an independent, while Bernard Sanders of Vermont ran as an independent for the U.S. House of Representatives and became the first Socialist elected to Congress since World War I. In the 1992 presidential campaign Texas billionaire Ross Perot ran as an independent and captured almost 19 percent of the popular vote (the best third-party showing since Theodore Roosevelt ran as a Progressive in 1912), even though he dropped out of the race for ten weeks in midsummer. Perot created a tightly controlled campaign organization, designed primarily to obtain signatures to qualify him for the ballot in every state. He spent tens of millions of his own dollars on lengthy network television "infomercials," $3 million on election eve alone. He was also the first third-party candidate to be included in televised presidential debates. Perot's success illustrated both widespread disaffection with the major parties and the crucial importance of money in politics.

[Earl R. Kruschke, *Encyclopedia of Third Parties in the United States* (Santa Barbara, Calif., 1991); Frank Smallwood, *The Other Candidates: Third Parties in Presidential Elections* (Hanover, N.H., 1983).]

KEITH IAN POLAKOFF

THOMAS CONFIRMATION HEARINGS (1991). President George Bush's nomination of Clarence Thomas in July 1991 to succeed Associate Justice Thurgood Marshall on the Supreme Court proved controversial from the beginning. Opponents argued that Thomas was minimally qualified and had done a poor job of enforcing civil rights laws as director of the Equal Employment Opportunity Commission (EEOC). Despite the fact that the Senate Judiciary Committee sent the Thomas nomination to the floor with no recommendation on Sept. 27, 1991 (the committee split seven to seven), it appeared that Thomas would be confirmed in a close vote by the full Senate. Then, shortly before the Senate was to act, news was leaked that Anita Hill, a former employee of Thomas, had accused him of sexual harassment during his directorship of the EEOC, forcing the Senate Judiciary Committee to reopen its hearings.

On the weekend of Oct. 11–13, 1991, millions of Americans watched the televised hearings, during which Hill accused Thomas of repeated unwanted sexual advances and the use of graphic sexual language in the office. Eighty-four percent of the public reported watching at least one hour of the hearings. More than half (52.4 percent) thought the reopened hearings were "an orchestrated campaign to discredit

the nominee's character" (*Los Angeles Times* poll). Ultimately, Thomas and his supporters were able to save his nomination by using hearsay and innuendo against Hill, thus taking advantage of the fact that Senate hearings do not adhere to standard courtroom procedures, such as burden of proof or rules of evidence. Republican Senators Alan Simpson, Orrin Hatch, and Arlen Specter were especially aggressive in questioning Hill. Thomas indignantly defended himself from what he called a "high-tech lynching of an uppity black." His reference to "lynching" galvanized much support among African Americans. With his white wife visible behind him throughout the hearings, Thomas evoked an earlier era of black persecution. Democrats on the committee demonstrated no strategic plan for questioning witnesses or, like Senator Edward Kennedy, were reduced to ineffectual roles because of their own sexual history. For many Democratic senators, the Thomas vote became an issue of racial loyalty rather than qualifications, ideology, or even sexual conduct. One study showed that a moderate Democratic senator from a state that was one-third black was two-thirds more likely to support Thomas's nomination than a similar senator from a state that had no blacks, but hundreds of African-American women took out a full-page ad in the *New York Times* protesting the "racist and sexist treatment" of Hill and expressing their "vehement opposition to the policies represented by the placement of Clarence Thomas on the Supreme Court." Ultimately, the confirmation of Thomas squeaked through the Senate by a vote of fifty-two to forty-eight, the closest margin for a Supreme Court appointment in more than 100 years.

Although public support for Thomas was about the same before and after the hearings, it would be wrong to overlook the political and social impact of this event. First, it heightened awareness of sexual harassment of women in the workplace because of Hill's testimony. Second, the perception that Hill was unfairly treated by the all-male Judiciary Committee contributed to the political "year of the women" in 1992, when an unprecedented number of women were elected at all levels of government. Third, the Senate came under attack for its status as an all-white, mostly male institution that was "out of touch" and "just didn't get it." By 1994 the Senate was less white, less male, and more sensitive to gender-related issues, in part because of the Thomas confirmation hearings.

[John C. Danforth, *Resurrection: The Confirmation of Clarence Thomas* (New York, 1994); Jane Mayer and Jill

Abramson, *Strange Justice: The Selling of Clarence Thomas* (Boston, 1994); Timothy M. Phelps and Helen Winternitz, *Capitol Games: The Inside Story of Clarence Thomas, Anita Hill, and a Supreme Court Nomination* (New York, 1993).]

DAVID T. CANON

See also **SUPP:** Sexual Harassment; Women in Public Life, Business, and the Professions.

THREE MILE ISLAND, site of the worst nuclear power program mishap in the history of the United States, is located in the Susquehanna River near Harrisburg, Pennsylvania. The event, which could easily have become a major disaster, shook public confidence in nuclear technology. The seven-day emergency began on Mar. 28, 1979, at Unit 2, one of two nuclear power plants built on the island in the early 1970s. The plant's operators initially mishandled the accident, and the resulting emergency was poorly managed by technical experts as well as state and federal officials responsible for public safety. The seriousness of the accident became clear, however, when both Governor Richard L. Thornburg of Pennsylvania and President Jimmy Carter visited the stricken plant while its operators were still struggling to resolve the menacing situation. A combination of faulty design and human error caused the problem. An overheated reactor core whose protective coolant was largely gone resulted in reactor temperatures as high as 4,300 degrees and the accidental release of radiation into the atmosphere. The event could have led to core temperatures so high (5,200 degrees) that the core would have melted through its base, resulting in unprecedented damage to the containment structure. Although a nuclear meltdown had never occurred, there was little doubt that such an event could have caused a release of deadly radiation into the atmosphere many times greater than the fallout created by the atomic bomb exploded at Hiroshima in the final days of World War II. The population around Three Mile Island and possibly—depending on prevailing winds—hundreds of miles away would have been in deadly peril. Government analysts calculate that, at the height of the crisis, the Three Mile Island reactor was within approximately one hour of a meltdown. The lessons learned at Three Mile Island led to stricter supervision and design modifications that, together with the prospects of high cleanup costs, such as those incurred at the stricken Pennsylvania plant, made earlier profit expectations unrealistic. Thus, the accident had a strong negative effect on the nuclear power industry's plans for building new plants.

[Philip L. Cantelon and Robert C. Williams, *Crisis Contained: The Department of Energy at Three Mile Island* (Carbondale and Edwardsville, Ill., 1982); Fred Clement, *The Nuclear Regulatory Commission* (New York, 1989); Daniel F. Ford, *Three Mile Island: Thirty Minutes to Meltdown* (New York, 1982); Mike Gray and Ira Rosen, *The Warning: Accident at Three Mile Island* (New York, 1983); President's Commission on the Accident at Three Mile Island, *The Need for Change: The Legacy of Three Mile Island* (Washington, D.C., 1979).]

ROBERT M. GUTH

See also **SUPP:** Nuclear Power; Nuclear Regulatory Commission; Pennsylvania.

TIANANMEN SQUARE PROTEST (Apr. 15–June 4, 1989) began in Beijing, China, as peaceful prodemocracy demonstrations by students calling for political liberalization and an end to official corruption. The protests in the square and at gathering places in other Chinese cities soon escalated into massive demonstrations involving people from all walks of life. In June the government used heavily armed troops to crush the movement. Soldiers killed more than 1,000 protesters and bystanders, many of them workers, and a much larger number were injured. These acts of repression horrified many Americans, who watched the movement unfold on television and sympathized with the protesters. President George Bush responded by imposing minor diplomatic sanctions against the Chinese regime.

[Jeffrey N. Wasserstrom and Elizabeth J. Perry, eds., *Popular Protest and Political Culture in Modern China: Learning from 1989* (Boulder, Colo., 1992).]

JEFFREY N. WASSERSTROM

See also **SUPP:** China, Relations with.

TIMBERLANDS. The use of fire by Native Americans had altered American forests by the time of European arrival, and European settlers accelerated forest change. The expansion of agriculture cleared vast areas of forest, and Europeans employed wood for a multitude of purposes—for houses, of course, not to mention roads (for a while), ships, tools, and many other items. In the mid-1990s forests in the United States covered 70 percent of the area that was forested in the early seventeenth century. Seventy percent of America's timberland is east of the Mississippi, where hardwood forests predominate. Nearly three-fourths of U.S. timberland is privately owned.

Nonindustrial private owners hold half of all timberlands; what one might describe as industrial forests account for 14 percent of U.S. forests. National forests, subject to careful rules, comprise most of the federal land. The bulk of timber harvested in the nation comes from privately owned land. Forest conservation programs have reversed forest loss. In the 1920s timber growth nationally was about half the rate of harvest. Annual forest growth in the 1990s was more than three and one-half times the 1920 rate, and the ratio of timber growth to harvest was 1:1.33. The rehabilitation of America's forests is one of the world's greatest conservation success stories. Changing public attitudes toward the purposes of forests have generated pressure for changes in the use of public forests, away from timber to recreation, wildlife, and ecosystem management. Timber production increasingly is concentrated on privately owned forest lands.

[Douglas S. Powell et al., *Forest Resources of the United States: 1992* (Fort Collins, Colo., 1994); Michael Williams, *Americans and Their Forests* (New York, 1989).]

HAROLD W. WISDOM

TIMES BEACH, a town in Missouri, came to national attention in December 1982, when Environmental Protection Agency (EPA) officials received laboratory reports indicating that soil samples taken from the town's dirt roads contained dioxin, a toxic chemical by-product, in concentrations hundreds of times higher than levels considered safe for human exposure by the Centers for Disease Control. The EPA had investigated sites where a contractor hired by Times Beach had sprayed waste automotive oil onto dirt roads to control dust. The contractor, a waste hauler named Russell Bliss, had disposed of industrial sludge from a defunct chemical company by mixing it with the waste oil. The EPA purchased all property in Times Beach and permanently evacuated its 2,000 residents. The buyout was the first under the Superfund program.

[Linda Garmon, "Times Beach: The Long Road to Recovery," *Science News* (Apr. 23, 1983); Michael Posner, "Anatomy of a Missouri Nightmare," *Maclean's* (Apr. 4, 1983).]

JOHN MORELLI

See also **SUPP:** Environmental Protection Agency; Hazardous Waste; Missouri; Superfund.

TOBACCO INDUSTRY. Despite decades of turmoil caused by medical evidence that tobacco use creates a health hazard, in the mid-1990s the tobacco industry still maintained its important position in the U.S. economy. The industry enjoyed political and social approval during the first half of the twentieth century, although its pricing policies and advertising practices sometimes drew public ire. After the Supreme Court broke up the American Tobacco Trust in 1911, six corporations—American Tobacco, R. J. Reynolds, Philip Morris, Brown and Williamson, Liggett and Myers, and P. Lorillard—dominated cigarette manufacturing. Cigar, pipe, and chewing tobacco manufacturers likewise tended toward concentration, led by U.S. Tobacco. In 1946 the Supreme Court upheld lower court findings that cigarette manufacturers had tacitly fixed prices, albeit through collusion rather than formal agreement. Beginning in the 1950s the Federal Trade Commission (FTC) regularly issued cease-and-desist orders against tobacco manufacturers for misleading advertising, which made health claims in such slogans as "A Treat Instead of a Treatment" and "Not a Cough in a Carload." Despite such interventions cigarette smoking was encouraged by the government and even the Red Cross during both world wars and was adopted by many Americans as chic, convenient, and socially acceptable. Movies, advertising, and Prohibition promoted increased use of tobacco products. In 1920 the industry sold 298,590 metric tons of tobacco (or 11.3 grams per adult per day); by 1950 that number had risen to 511,880 (12.7 grams per adult per day). Increased use of cigarettes accounted for most of the growth. More than half of men and about a third of women smoked regularly in 1950.

Medical studies regarding the safety of cigarette smoking threatened tobacco's economic and political status. During the early 1950s British and U.S. physicians, together with organizations like the American Cancer Society, began to publicize epidemiological studies showing a long-suspected association between cigarette smoking and cancer as well as heart disease and other ailments. Newspapers and magazines such as the *Reader's Digest* published articles condemning smoking, producing the first national health scare. As a result, in 1953 and 1954 both tobacco stock prices and cigarette consumption declined. Manufacturers responded in several ways: exporting to other markets, producing filter-tip cigarettes, and launching new advertising and public relations campaigns. Exports climbed after 1955, from 15 million cigarettes to 25 million ten years later; they increased more rapidly after 1970. The popularity of filter tips grew because smokers thought they were safer than regular cigarettes. Before 1953 just one brand of filtered cigarettes was sold in the United States, but each of the major companies put at least one brand on the market in 1953 or 1954; market share grew from 1 percent in 1950 to 19 percent in 1955. The industry spent $38 million on television, magazine, and newspaper advertising in 1954. It promoted filtered cigarettes, although not all filters were effective and some, such as one made of asbestos, were harmful.

Forbidden by a 1911 antitrust order to form a trade association, cigarette manufacturers engaged a New York public relations agency, Hill and Knowlton, which advised company presidents to recruit public relations firms, growers, and warehouses to create the Tobacco Industry Research Committee (TIRC). TIRC's mission was to provide research money for study of issues related to smoking and cancer and to conduct a public relations program. TIRC representatives insisted that because a clinical link between smoking and lung cancer had not been proven (which was true) more research should be conducted. In 1958 the Hill and Knowlton agency created the Council for Tobacco Research, responsible for scientific research only, and the Tobacco Institute, the industry's lobbying and public relations arm.

The 1964 U.S. surgeon general's *Report on Smoking and Health* created a second national health scare. Based on more than 4,000 published studies on tobacco use, the report indicated that without question smoking was hazardous and that the problem warranted remedial action. Two-thirds of the adults in a government survey that year said they believed smoking caused lung cancer, up from two-fifths the previous year. This widespread and growing belief brought a threat of federal regulation but neither the FTC or the Food and Drug Administration took decisive action, and the U.S. Department of Agriculture continued to provide subsidies to tobacco farmers. Congress divided on the issue of tobacco and health, usually to the industry's benefit. The first hearings on smoking and health took place in 1957, when a House committee found that the FTC had not adequately reacted to deceptive advertising about filters. After the surgeon general's report Congress in 1965 passed the Cigarette Labeling and Advertising Act, which required that all cigarette packages and advertisements contain the warning label "Caution: Cigarette Smoking May Be Hazardous to Your Health." Critics found the warning weak because it said "may be" rather than "is" and because it did not include warnings about lung cancer or other diseases.

The industry opposed any label but accepted the 1965 version; ironically, the label later provided legal protection for the industry, which could prove that after 1965 smokers had been aware of potential risks associated with tobacco use but chose to smoke anyway.

Congressional investigation of cigarette advertising and an aggressive campaign that used the Federal Communications Commission's Fairness Doctrine to gain free air time for antismoking messages led manufacturers in 1970 to remove all cigarette ads from television and radio, while Congress continued to fund research on how to grow more and better tobacco. Revenue from tobacco taxes made it difficult for Congress to be decisive about regulating cigarette smoking. In 1964 annual federal taxes on cigarettes totaled $2 billion; state taxes brought in well over $1 billion.

Despite growing criticism of the industry, tobacco manufacturers never acknowledged that their products were harmful or addictive, although they offered filter tips and took steps to lower the amounts of tar and nicotine in cigarettes. Tobacco remained a legal product and tobacco interests gained exemptions from such measures as the Consumer Product Safety Act, the Fair Packaging and Labeling Act, the Hazardous Substances Act, and the Toxic Substances Control Act. During the 1980s tobacco corporations diversified by purchasing less controversial companies, such as Nabisco and General Foods, which helped protect stock prices. Exports, especially to Asia, continued to rise. Fifty years after the first major health scare the tobacco industry was valued at $50 billion and had 50 million consumers worldwide.

A wave of civil lawsuits against the tobacco industry also reflected smokers' concerns; between the mid-1970s and 1995 more than 400 unsuccessful lawsuits were filed. The companies responded with a no-compromise legal strategy. They defended every claim regardless of cost through trials and appeals. Tobacco attorneys outspent and outlasted plaintiffs who ran out of money or died while litigation lingered. In 1994, however, the first class-action suits were brought against tobacco companies, including a suit by sixty law firms in five states. The suit represented up to 40 million smokers and 50 million former smokers claiming to be addicted or damaged or both by tobacco products. The solidarity of the tobacco companies against lawsuits and regulation was shattered in March 1996, when the Liggett Group (the fifth-largest company but with only a 2 percent market share) agreed to settle its part of the suit. Liggett agreed to payments for an antismoking campaign, not to oppose new government regulations, and to make the first damage payments ever by a tobacco company. Shortly thereafter, two former Philip Morris employees confirmed charges against the tobacco companies of manipulation of nicotine levels to keep smokers hooked. Other class-action suits were pending as well, including one against Philip Morris involving 60,000 flight attendants who said they were forced to inhale secondary smoke in airline cabins before smoking on airplanes was banned. In February 1994 the state of Florida decided to sue the tobacco companies for the Medicare costs it incurred in treating smokers; West Virginia, Minnesota, and Mississippi filed similar suits.

[John C. Burnham, *Bad Habits* (New York, 1993); A. Lee Fritschler, *Smoking and Politics,* 4th ed. (Englewood Cliffs, N.J., 1989); Robert L. Rabin and Stephen D. Sugarman, eds., *Smoking Policy: Law, Politics, and Culture* (New York, 1993); Robert Sobel, *They Satisfy: The Cigarette in American Life* (Garden City, N.Y., 1978); Susan Wagner, *Cigarette Country* (New York, 1971); Thomas Whiteside, *Selling Death* (New York, 1971).]

KAREN S. MILLER

See also **SUPP:** Advertising; Environmental Protection Agency; Food and Drug Administration; Smoking; Substance Abuse.

TOKYO ROUND. *See* **General Agreement on Tariffs and Trade.**

TOLEDO, the fourth-largest city in Ohio in the 1990s, began as a French trading post (1680) and fortification (1700). Ceded to the British in 1763, it was incorporated into the U.S. Northwest Territory in 1787, but permanent settlement did not begin until after the War of 1812. Canals and railroads helped establish Toledo as a major inland port and center of industry on the Maumee River estuary at the western end of Lake Erie. In 1835 the city was claimed by both Ohio and Michigan, in the so-called Toledo War, and the dispute was settled by Congress, which awarded the city to Ohio (and the Upper Peninsula to Michigan). During the Progressive Era in the early twentieth century Toledo won national recognition for urban reform through the works of Mays Samuel "Golden Rule" Jones and Brand Whitlock. Historically, Toledo has been a major producer of glass and automotive products, but these industries declined, and from 1970 to 1990 employment in the Toledo metropolitan area decreased markedly. During this same period population declined from 383,062 to 332,943. Toledo

has experienced other problems. A 1967 race riot caused extensive property damage, injuries, and arrests. Public schools were closed for several weeks in 1976 and 1978 because of teacher strikes. In July 1979 a bitter dispute between the city government and police and firemen led to a two-day general strike and costly arson fires. The mood of those years was caught by John Denver's satiric 1973 song "Saturday Night in Toledo, Ohio." In the 1980s and 1990s Toledo sought to emphasize its strong medical, cultural and higher educational institutions. New downtown buildings and the Portside festival marketplace along the Maumee was indicative of business leaders' commitment to the city.

[Morgan Barclay, *Toledo: Gateway to the Great Lakes* (Tulsa, Okla., 1982); Melvin D. Berger, *Toledo: Focused for the Future* (Chatsworth, Calif., 1991).]

JOHN B. WEAVER

See also **DAH:** Toledo War; **DAH** and **SUPP:** Cincinnati; Cleveland; Columbus (Ohio); Ohio.

TORNADOES are products of thunderstorms of unusual power. Major thunderstorms extend from the ground up through the jet stream to the stratosphere. They often produce a double vortex, the upper vortex turning in a direction opposite to the circular motion of the lower. The latter normally stretches from the bottom of the storm cloud to the ground and commonly has a funnel-like shape. The typical tornado is in contact with the ground for only about six miles, and its path may be no more than 500 feet wide. Tornadoes typically travel at about thirty miles per hour but can move as rapidly as sixty miles per hour, with wind speeds exceeding 250 miles per hour. Although tornadoes can occur anywhere in conjunction with thunderstorms, they are most common in the central United States as a result of the topography. The west-to-east flow of air across the United States is interrupted by the Rocky Mountains, which pushes the air currents up; they fall suddenly when they reach the Great Plains. If moisture-laden air is pulled in from the Gulf of Mexico and meets the high dry air over the plains, that confluence creates the conditions for a tornado. The average number of tornadoes in the United States ranges between 700 and 800 a year, but in some years, notably 1973, 1982, 1990, and 1992, the total has exceeded 1,000. In 1992 a total of 1,300 were recorded, the greatest number since 1950, when records were first kept. Texas generally has the most tornadoes, followed by Oklahoma and Kansas. Fatalities have tended to be higher in the Deep South and generally total fewer than 100 per year. The year 1974 was an exception; 350 people died on April 3–4 in Alabama, Georgia, Tennessee, Kentucky, and Oklahoma. Tornadoes cause one-fifth of natural disaster losses each year in the United States. The National Severe Storms Forecast Center, in Kansas City, Mo., is responsible for issuing warnings of approaching tornadoes. It bases its predictions on meteorological conditions in combination with unusual patterns on the weather radar. Although the approach of a tornado can be forecast only 50 percent of the time, warnings have been important in reducing the death toll.

[Joe R. Eagleman, *Severe and Unusual Weather* (Lenexa, Kans., 1988).]

NANCY M. GORDON

See also **SUPP:** Disasters, Natural and Environmental.

TOURISM, one of the leading industries in the United States in the 1990s, generated more than $300 billion per year in transportation, lodging, eating and drinking, and amusement and recreation services, and more than 10 million people were employed in these services. Half of the tourist trade consisted of domestic travelers touring the United States and half of foreign visitors coming to this country. When U.S. citizens go on vacation 31 percent choose to visit cities, with Washington, D.C., and New York City the favorite choices, while 26 percent favor the oceans and beaches. Twenty-two percent visit small towns, 10 percent favor the mountains, while the remainder go to lakes, streams, and other places. Each year 1.3 billion trips are taken, 500 million of which are to visit friends and relatives, 500 million to pursue other pleasure, and the rest traveling for business and to attend conventions. Collectively, U.S. families enjoy 900 million vacation trips and 770 million weekend trips. Since the 1980s several factors have favored domestic travel, including expansion of international terrorism, the decline in the U.S. dollar that makes travel abroad more expensive, and the low price of gasoline.

While Florida's Disney World is the most popular vacation spot, attracting 22 million visitors per year, California is the number-one state for domestic travel. After California and Florida, U.S. travelers spend most of their vacation money in New York, Texas, and Illinois, while the fewest dollars are spent in South Dakota, North Dakota, Delaware, Vermont, and Wyoming. During the winter Florida is by far the most popular destination of U.S. tourists, followed by Hawaii, Colorado, California, and Nevada. In Wash-

ington, D.C., the top sites visited are the Holocaust Museum, the National Air and Space Museum, the National Gallery of Art, and the National Museum of Natural History. The White House on a busy day attracts 7,000 people—compared to 4,000 per day who tour Graceland, Elvis Presley's house in Memphis, Tenn. The travel industry is the top employer in thirty-nine states. California and Florida have the highest budgets for tourism and receive the greatest benefits, while Kansas, North Dakota, and Nebraska spend the least, $1 million per year. More than $168 million a year is spent for network travel advertising.

In the early 1990s tourism became the country's leading source of foreign currency. In 1990 foreign visitors spent $43 billion on vacations in the United States, $450 million more than Americans spent abroad. In 1992 foreign visitors spent $53.8 billion. Each year sets a new record. By the mid-1990s more than 50 million foreign tourists were expected to arrive and spend more than $61 billion. In 1993 for the first time overseas visitors exceeded the total visitors from Canada, which, along with Mexico, is the greatest single source of the U.S. tourist trade. Most visitors to the United States coming for pleasure are from the United Kingdom, Germany, France, Japan, China, Korea, Brazil, Venezuela, and Argentina. Japan's 4 million yearly tourists do not comprise the greatest number of visitors but they spend the largest amount of money in the United States—$13.8 billion. Overseas travelers spend six times more per person per day on a one-trip basis in this country than domestic travelers.

The average stay of foreign visitors of almost three weeks is five times longer than the average domestic vacation of four nights. One in every seven hotel rooms in the United States each night is rented to a visitor from overseas. Tour operators have increased overseas promotions so that foreign visitors have exceeded the previous year's total each year since the late 1980s. Hotels and restaurants provide bilingual clerks and waiters, and airports have signs in several languages advising passengers of delays. The bombing of the World Trade Center in New York City and the murders of foreign tourists in Florida have not stopped the massive influx. The most frequently visited place for first-time visitors from abroad is New York City, where foreigners make up 22 percent of the city's 25 million yearly visitors and where they spend $1.6 billion a year for shopping. The Disney parks are next in attendance, and the number-one destination of all visitors to the United States is Disney World. One attraction for foreign visitors is shopping at malls. The average visitor to this country spends $539 per capita on gifts and souvenirs and malls have developed their own promotional material for tourists. Sawgrass Mills, an outlet mall just west of Fort Lauderdale, Fla., attracts the most foreigners. Nearly half of its 18 million annual visitors come from abroad, making it the second-largest tourist attraction in Florida.

[Peter E. Tarlow and Mitchell J. Muehsam, "Wide Horizons: Travel and Tourism in the Coming Decades," *The Futurist* (Sept.-Oct. 1992).]

JOHN J. BYRNE

See also **SUPP:** California; Florida; New York City; Parks, National; Recreation; Theme Parks; Washington, D.C.

TOWER COMMISSION. Appointed by President Ronald Reagan in November 1986, the Tower Commission investigated and reported on allegations involving arms sales to Iran in exchange for U.S. hostages in Lebanon and the diversion of money from arms sales to the Nicaraguan contras in violation of congressional legislation. Headed by former Senator John Tower, the commission was charged with explaining events surrounding these allegations and proposing changes in the National Security Council (NSC) to prevent any such action in the future. Its report, released in February 1987, concluded that members of the NSC staff were responsible for the secret diversion of funds and that President Reagan was out of touch with the actions of his own White House. It exonerated Vice President George Bush who later as president unsuccessfully tried to appoint Tower as secretary of defense. A House-Senate investigation confirmed much of the Tower Report, but after an eight-year investigation Special Prosecutor Lawrence E. Walsh concluded that although neither Reagan nor Bush knew of the diversion of money to the contras or violated any criminal statutes, Bush was aware, contrary to his earlier claims, of the arms-for-hostages deal.

[Harold Hongju Koh, *The National Security Constitution: Sharing Power After the Iran-Contra Affair* (New Haven, Conn., 1990); President's Special Review Board, *The Tower Commission Report* (New York, 1987).]

KATY J. HARRIGER

See also **SUPP:** Iran-Contra Affair; Nicaragua, Relations with.

TOXIC SHOCK SYNDROME (TSS), a rare, sometimes fatal disease that caused widespread panic among women during the early 1980s when the Centers for Disease Control (CDC) and other public health organizations linked the growing number of cases of TSS with the increasing popularity of high-absorbency tampons. First identified in 1978, the earliest reported cases of TSS occurred among seven children. All were linked with the presence of *Staphylococcus aureus*. Symptoms of the disease include vomiting, diarrhea, high fever, and sunburnlike rash. A dramatic upsurge in cases reported to the CDC occurred in 1980, when 890 cases were reported, 812 of which were among women whose illness coincided with the start of their menstrual periods. Fatalities among early TSS patients were around 8 percent. This striking association of TSS with menstruating women stimulated careful epidemiological analysis. When information collected by the Utah Department of Health suggested that a particular tampon brand, Rely, had been used by many women with TSS, a detailed study was devised by the CDC in September 1980 to examine tampon brand use. This study found that 71 percent of a test group of women with TSS had used Rely tampons. On Sept. 22, 1980, Procter and Gamble recalled all Rely tampons on the market and all tampon manufacturers subsequently lowered the absorbency of their tampons. The Food and Drug Administration began requiring that all tampon packages carry information on TSS advising women to use tampons with the minimum absorbency needed to control menstrual flow and to change tampons frequently. Although cases of menstrually related TSS fell off dramatically after 1984, the overall number of cases is suspected to have risen as the staphylococcal bacteria that produces the deadly toxin spread to more people. By the 1990s only about half of the cases of staphylococcal toxic shock syndrome were connected with menstruating women in part because of the increased use of sanitary napkins in the wake of the TSS scare. TSS has been reported in men, children, and older women and in conjunction with surgery, influenza, sinusitis, childbirth, and intravenous drug use; a wound, abscess, boil, cut, or even an insect bite; and use of a contraceptive sponge, cervical cap, or diaphragm.

[Maria E. Donawa et al., "Toxic Shock Syndrome: Chronology of State and Federal Epidemiologic Studies and Regulatory Decision-Making," *Public Health Reports* 99 (1984); Elizabeth W. Etheridge, *Sentinel for Health: A History of the Centers for Disease Control* (Berkeley, Calif., 1982).]

SUZANNE WHITE-JUNOD

See also **SUPP:** Centers for Disease Control and Prevention; Epidemiology.

TRADE, BALANCE OF. *See* **Balance of Trade.**

TRADE, DOMESTIC. Between 1970 and 1995 the U.S. domestic economy went from being manufacturing based to information and service based. Partly as a result of this change, and primarily as a result of competition from abroad, U.S. industry spread throughout the globe. Many everyday consumer products, such as cars, personal computers, and home electronics, were manufactured both overseas and in the United States, making the definition of "domestically produced" a highly subjective one. The difficulties underlying understanding of the new domestic economy became evident when in the 1980s many Americans reacted to a large foreign trade deficit by encouraging citizens to "buy American." During this period many articles appeared in the popular press explaining that most Honda (a Japanese firm) automobiles purchased in the United States were actually made in Ohio, while many personal computers made by U.S. companies such as Compaq, Apple, and IBM were manufactured wholly or in part by overseas firms. In 1994 the Federal Trade Commission (FTC) accused the Boston-based shoemaker New Balance of deceiving customers by labeling its shoes "Made in the USA" even though the soles were imported from Asia. A competitor, Hyde, which produced Saucony shoes, agreed to use the phrase "Made in the USA of domestic and imported components."

Large U.S. manufacturing firms, primarily automakers and other producers of durable goods, suffered from imports during the last quarter of the twentieth century. In the 1970s and 1980s foreign firms had the advantage of much cheaper labor, but their labor costs began rising and U.S. costs were declining because of the increasing weakness of U.S. labor unions. The competitiveness of foreign manufacturers, however, increased in terms of shipping goods, as the slow, expensive ships of former times gave way to huge and efficient container vessels. The once-considerable costs of communication began to lessen with computer and satellite technologies. The decline of large manufacturing firms in the United States led to a resurgence in small businesses (firms with fewer than 500 employees). In the early 1990s small businesses provided 56 percent of private sector employment and represented fully half of the gross national product. Few small companies engaged in manufacturing but those that did prospered, producing 37.4 percent of the nation's total manufacturing output in 1986. Meanwhile, larger manufacturers were downsizing plants, with pre-1970 plants averaging about 650 employees and post-1970 plants averaging only about 250 workers.

The primary cause for the growing importance of small businesses in domestic trade was their ability to adapt to rapidly changing conditions. As new technologies, such as personal computers, fax machines, and computer networks, became cheaper, smaller firms were better able to compete with larger companies. CAD, CAM, and CAE (computer-aided design, manufacturing, and engineering) became standard for both small and large companies. Enhanced communications and networking enabled small companies to cooperate and allowed larger corporations to subcontract work more easily. These changes were most evident in the automobile and computer industries. The big three automakers—General Motors, Ford, and Chrysler—lost their domestic dominance in the 1970s and 1980s as high-quality, inexpensive, and fuel-efficient imports from Japan attracted consumers. Because of the energy crises of 1973 and 1979 the federal government stipulated fuel-efficient cars. At the same time Detroit failed to anticipate the importance of imports and when it became evident failed to react swiftly. It was not until the late 1980s and early 1990s that U.S. automakers, due in part to cooperative design agreements with Japanese automakers, U.S.-Japanese trade agreements, and real declines in gasoline prices, were able to recover some of their market share.

Domestic industries responded to the fast-changing global economy in an inconsistent fashion. Demand for electronic components was strong in the early 1990s but that industry gained, especially by cutting its workforce. Manufacturing in the United States in the mid-1990s was dependent on growth in five industries: automobiles, housing, computers, health care, and environmental equipment. Computers were the fastest-growing industry between 1973 and 1988, health care equipment between 1987 and 1994. Still, in 1991 the gross domestic product of the United States was $6 trillion, the largest in the world. Despite ups and downs throughout the late 1970s, 1980s, and early 1990s domestic trade grew in a fairly consistent pattern. Manufacturing nearly tripled in income during this period, from $317.5 billion in 1975 to $873.8 billion in 1992. Agricultural income more than doubled, from $46.5 billion in 1975 to $95.6 billion in 1992. Transportation tripled from $48 billion in 1975 to $144.8 billion in 1992. The most dramatic change occurred in communications, where income quadrupled, from $26.8 billion in 1975 to $98.6 billion in 1992. Other developments indicated continued strength for domestic trade. The North American Free

Trade Agreement, linking the Canadian, Mexican, and U.S. economies, went into effect on Jan. 1, 1994, providing for elimination of many tariffs by the year 2005. A trend toward business deregulation that began with the administration of President Ronald Reagan (1981–1989) continued to remove barriers for interstate commerce.

[Mansel G. Blackford, *A History of Small Business in America* (New York, 1991); Barry Bluestone and Bennett Harrison, *The Deindustrialization of America* (New York, 1982).]

JEFFREY M. MERRON

See also **SUPP:** Agriculture; Automobile Industry; Balance of Trade; Commerce, Department of; Communications Industry; Economic Indicators; Foreign Investment in the United States; Manufacturing; North American Free Trade Agreement; Real Estate Industry; Retailing Industry; Small Business Administration; Trade, International; Trade Agreements; Transportation Industry.

TRADE, INTERNATIONAL. Between the 1970s and the mid-1990s the U.S. post–World War II dominance of world trade came to an end. Major changes in transportation, finance, corporate structures, and manufacturing restructured the global economy, erasing the significance of international economic boundaries. This process was painful for some and profitable for others. The uncertain and uneven impact of trade liberalization contributed to anxiety, controversy, and political divisiveness. Whole industries in the United States were largely eliminated, unable to compete effectively against cheaper and often better imports. In labor-intensive industries, such as textiles, shoes, and assembly work, the competition came from low-wage developing countries; in the automobile, steel, and electronics industries it came from technological innovators abroad who developed new products and efficient manufacturing.

The United States continued to be the world's largest internal economic market, but this did not isolate the United States from international trade, as it willingly imported goods and services and eagerly exported goods and know-how. The United States sought a role in the global economy, as evidenced by the North American Free Trade Agreement (NAFTA) and major revisions in the General Agreement on Tariffs and Trade (GATT). NAFTA, which became effective in January 1994, created a major regional trading block including Canada, the United States, and Mexico. This far-reaching agreement reduced tariffs

over a fifteen-year period, eased cross-border transportation, and opened Mexico to U.S. and Canadian investments, even in banking and state-owned energy monopolies. Labor unions opposed NAFTA, asserting that corporations would transfer jobs and plants to Mexico because of lower wages and lax environmental regulations. GATT negotiations were protracted. Revisions were negotiated by three presidents—Ronald Reagan, George Bush, and Bill Clinton—who supported cutting tariffs among 123 nations. The GATT agreement known as the Uruguay Round reduced tariffs by 40 percent, cut agricultural subsidies, extended patent protection, and set out rules on global investment. Disputes were to be resolved by the World Trade Organization (WTO), a powerful arbitration board that would decide whether a nation's domestic laws violated the agreement. Proponents estimated that the latest revisions to GATT, when they become fully effectively in 2004, would create jobs and pump up to $100 billion annually into the U.S. economy. (This figure represents less than 2 percent of the nation's total economic output.) Opponents said decisions by the WTO would violate U.S. sovereignty and environmental protection laws.

The arguments for trade liberalization through NAFTA and GATT were the classic economic arguments of comparative advantage originally articulated by the early nineteenth-century British economist David Ricardo. The idea was simple—nations should specialize in products they can produce cheaper or better. Deciding what products that would mean for the United States was problematic. The last U.S. trade surplus (U.S. exports exceeding imports) occurred in 1975, when the nation enjoyed a $12.4 billion surplus. By 1984, however, the United States was posting $100 billion-plus trade deficits each year, reaching a record $166 billion in 1994. The trade deficit is a summary statistic for a more complicated set of relationships that includes country-to-country deficits and surpluses and differences between economic sectors. In 1993, for example, the United States ran a trade surplus of $12.8 billion for foods, feed, and beverages but had large deficits in automotive vehicles ($50 billion) and consumer goods ($79.4 billion).

U.S. productivity lost its advantage when other industrializing nations used new technologies and lower wages to gain access to the vast U.S. market, outcompeting domestic manufacturers. A television-addicted nation sat glued in front of foreign-produced sets. The last U.S. television factory—operated by Zenith Electronics Corporation in Springfield, Mo.—

closed in 1992, leaving more than 1,300 workers jobless when production shifted to Mexico. Japan cut into several consumer markets—electronics, cameras, computers, automobiles. Japanese brand names became household words: Sony, Mitsubishi, Toyota, Nissan, Honda, Hitachi, Mazda, Sharp, Canon, Panasonic. The United States turned to quotas to stem Japanese imports. Japan responded by opening plants in the United States that employed U.S. workers but still diverted dollars abroad.

Labor unions urged the public to "buy American," but identifying the products was far from easy. A car "made in America" contained components built in more than a dozen countries on three continents and ultimately assembled in a U.S.-based factory. Was the car American made? A General Motors executive in 1952 testified before Congress: "What is good for the country is good for General Motors." The reasoning no longer held as GM moved jobs and facilities to East Asia or to Mexican plants along the U.S. border. Displaced from well-paying jobs, U.S. workers and managers found reentering the workforce difficult. Even in a growing economy, new jobs paid less. The Census Bureau found that workers who left or were laid off between 1990 and 1992 saw their weekly wages fall 23 percent when they regained employment, often without health insurance and other benefits.

The international economy developed an infrastructure of transportation, financing, and communications that made the movement of money, information, and goods easier and cheaper. Corporations moved money around the world to finance trade, protect against currency fluctuations, or to seek higher returns on investments. Meanwhile U.S. individual and institutional investors looked overseas for investments, often financing enterprises that competed against U.S.-based companies. Huge amounts of capital that otherwise might have been invested in domestic companies found its way abroad into emerging markets in Eastern Europe, Latin America, and the Pacific Rim. Money could be moved instantaneously around the world. Capital's loyalties were not to governments or domestic economies but to the best rate of return. Development of global finance introduced volatility into world financial markets. This new world economic order in effect placed increased burdens on the United States to stabilize or prop up other economies. The Mexican economy collapsed in December 1994 under a severe currency devaluation, leaving the U.S. government and the International Monetary Fund to come up with loan guarantees to stabilize the economy. This bailout followed a 1982 collapse in Mexico and South America wherein the U.S. government intervened to bail out U.S. banks with substantial loans in the region. U.S. financial intervention was selective, however, as little assistance was provided the former republics of the Soviet Union when they experienced a currency collapse in 1994.

Making the United States competitive internationally was easier to advocate than accomplish. It put pressures on corporations to reduce employment and improve production. Competition stimulated corporations to undertake organizational change based on ideas in an influential book by Michael Hammer and James Champy, *Re-Engineering the Corporation* (1993). The authors offered a harsh critique of the modern business companies: "Inflexibility, unresponsiveness, the absence of customer focus, an obsession with activity rather than result, bureaucratic paralysis, lack of innovation, high overhead—these are the legacies of one hundred years of American industrial leadership." In their business manifesto the authors urged corporations to reinvent themselves through a "fundamental rethinking and radical redesign of business processes." Typically, "reinvented" companies had fewer employees and fewer managerial levels and used technology to achieve improved performance. Some observers believed the United States needed a "national industrial policy," whereby the government would undertake measures to stop the deindustrialization resulting from corporations moving jobs and capital abroad. Individuals favoring a national industry policy pointed to Japan, where the powerful Ministry of International Trade and Industry worked closely with business. Economists, however, questioned government's ability to pick industrial winners and whether the industrial policies of Japan, France, and Germany were as successful as portrayed, noting that the two European countries were also losing manufacturing jobs.

Problems created in the United States by trade liberalization remained largely unaddressed by the mid-1990s. For the public, trade liberalization was complicated and confusing, with contradictions that were difficult to explain or accept. If trade agreements were good for the nation, why were jobs lost and industries hurt? In 1994 the United States displaced Japan as the world's most competitive economy, based on an annual index by the World Economic Forum. The international economy subjected the U.S. labor force to new economic pressures—job insecurity, stagnant wages for nonskilled labor, and fewer company-sponsored benefits, particularly health insurance. U.S. wage rates were substantially lower than those in Germany and Japan, but within the United States something else occurred—a long-term trend of widening income inequality between the nation's rich and the poor and middle classes. Between 1989 and 1994 the share of income earned by the top 5 percent of Americans increased from 18.9 percent to 21.2 percent, while that earned by the middle 50 percent of Americans fell from 49.3 percent to 46.8 percent. The middle class, accustomed to higher wages and rising living standards in the post–World War II economic boom, found the going tough. Major corporations, even while making record profits, reorganized, eliminating jobs of well-paid middle managers. Meanwhile, the domestic economy was transforming itself, moving from an industrial age to the information age, one for which many workers were ill prepared. The questions were how many high-tech, well-paying jobs could the economy realistically create and how could those stuck in low-wage jobs in the growing service section support themselves and their families.

[John J. Accordino, *The United States in the Global Economy* (Chicago, 1992); Donald B. Bartlett and James B. Steele, *America: What Went Wrong?* (Kansas City, 1992); Michael Hammer and James Champy, *Re-Engineering the Corporation* (New York, 1993); Paul R. Krugman, *The Age of Diminished Expectations* (Cambridge, Mass, 1990).]

BRENT SCHONDELMEYER

See also **SUPP:** Balance of Trade; Foreign Investment in the United States; General Agreement on Tariffs and Trade; International Monetary Fund; North American Free Trade Agreement; Trade, Domestic; Trade Agreements; Wages and Salaries.

TRADE AGREEMENTS. When two or more nations wish to establish or modify economic relations and set tariffs on international commerce they enter into a trade agreement. Any authorized government official may negotiate such an agreement but all participating governments must formally ratify the proposed treaty before it becomes effective. As a result, domestic political forces and interest groups exert considerable influence over the provisions of any trade agreement. The United States negotiated few trade agreements in the eighteenth and nineteenth centuries. Domestic political pressures determined how high or low import taxes (tariffs) would be. From the earliest debates in the First Congress, some political leaders favored low tariffs designed to raise revenue while others favored much higher rates to protect domestic producers from foreign competition.

Lower rates generally prevailed through the 1850s but protectionist tariffs were sponsored by the dominant Republican party during and after the Civil War. To encourage particular types of trade within the forbiddingly high post–Civil War tariff structure some leaders favored bilateral trade agreements in which each nation agreed to reduce rates in return for reciprocal reductions.

In the 1870s the United States signed a reciprocal trade agreement with the then-independent Hawaiian government that gave Hawaiian sugar exporters tariff-free access to the U.S. market. In the early 1890s Secretary of State James G. Blaine negotiated reciprocal trade agreements that softened the effect of the highly protectionist McKinley Tariff Act of 1890, but the 1894 Wilson-Gorman Tariff Act made such agreements impossible. With the exception of the Underwood Act, which passed in 1913 but never went into effect because of World War I, protectionist rates remained until the Great Depression, when it appeared that the nation's high import duties were not only detrimental to world trade but also might be harmful to the domestic economy. The Reciprocal Trade Agreements Act of 1934 permitted reduction of trade barriers by as much as half in return for reductions by another nation. In the late 1930s and 1940s U.S. negotiators arranged a great number of bilateral trade agreements.

Concessions to one nation through bilateral negotiations were often extended to all others through the most-favored-nation principle. Many international agreements included a clause stating that the parties would treat each other in the same way they did the nation their trade policies favored the most. If in bilateral negotiations the United States agreed to reduce its import duties on a particular commodity, that same reduction was automatically granted to imports from any nation with which the United States had a most-favored-nation arrangement. The high tariff walls surrounding the United States were gradually chipped away through bilateral agreements that established much lower rates for all its major trading partners.

The next step was to move negotiation to a multinational setting. When a proposed international trade organization proved unpopular with Congress after World War II, officials tied their hopes to the General Agreement on Tariffs and Trade (GATT), the world's first major multinational trade agreement. GATT resulted from negotiations involving twenty-three nations in 1947. In subsequent decades it served as the primary trade agreement for the noncommunist world and underwent numerous revisions and extensions.

Through eight formal rounds of negotiations, tariff rates on industrial goods dropped to an average of only 4 percent. Multinational negotiations proceed in much the same way as the bilateral negotiations that preceded GATT. A supplier enters into discussions with its primary customer and each side offers incentives it hopes are mutually beneficial. Once such an agreement has been reached it extends to all signatories of the multinational agreement through most-favored-nation provisions. Since 1934 U.S. trade negotiations have been an executive responsibility, but Congress has maintained a strong interest in both procedures and outcomes. In the 1960s and 1970s it called upon the U.S. Tariff Commission to identify "peril points," where reduction of specific duties might cause serious damage to U.S. producers or suppliers. Other federal legislation provided for relief measures if increased imports cause injury to a domestic industrial sector.

The world's acceptance of more liberal trade agreements has had different effects on U.S. producers. Most likely to benefit are those engaged in the nation's traditionally export-oriented agricultural sector. Production costs are relatively low in the U.S. heartland, so a freer market tends to benefit domestic agricultural exporters. At the same time, labor-intensive industries, such as textiles, electronics, and automobiles, have suffered from the gradual reduction of import restrictions. U.S. wage rates range far higher than comparable rates in certain countries that have built very efficient textile mills and fabrication plants for electronic devices and appliances. The recovery of the U.S. auto industry in the 1990s, however, demonstrated that increasing the use of industrial robotics and automated assembly lines can help undermine the cost advantage of foreign manufacturers. As more liberal trade agreements promote competition among producers, each nation is likely to develop stronger and weaker economic sectors that complement those of its global trading partners. The ultimate trade agreement is one in which all national barriers disappear. The European Union (formerly the European Economic Community) represents an approximation of that goal, as does the 1993 North American Free Trade Agreement (NAFTA) among the United States, Canada, and Mexico. NAFTA cancels all major barriers to exchange of goods and services among the participants, leaving the GATT structure in control of imports and exports outside the free trade area.

[Ricardo Grinspin and Maxwell A. Cameron, eds., *The Political Economy of North American Free Trade* (New York, 1993); Joseph A. McKinney and M. Rebecca Sharpless, eds., *Implications of a North American Free Trade Region* (Ottawa, Ont., 1992).]

JOHN M. DOBSON

See also **DAH:** Reciprocal Trade Agreements; Tariffs; **SUPP:** European Community; Foreign Investment in the United States; General Agreement on Tariffs and Trade; North American Free Trade Agreement; Trade, Domestic; Trade, International.

TRANSPLANTS AND ORGAN DONATION. The first successful human organ transplant, in 1954, was a kidney donated by a young man to his identical twin. Since then transplantation has rapidly become a major part of medical care. By the 1990s there were transplant programs for kidneys, hearts, lungs, livers, and pancreases. Dramatic improvements in understanding the human immune system and ability to control immune responses vastly improved the success rate of transplants. Recipients receive organs that are antigen-matched to their own immune systems. Antirejection drugs have fewer side effects. Supply and distribution of donor organs is coordinated nationally.

Between 1980 and 1990, 102,879 organ transplants were performed in the United States. The vast majority (81,283) were kidney transplants. While such established forms of transplant experienced substantial growth, others went from being experimental to relatively common. There were twenty-six liver transplants in 1981 and 2,656 by the end of the decade. Although transplants increased dramatically, demand increased even more. Between 1987 and 1991 waiting lists for every type of organ increased—for kidneys, there was a 67 percent increase. The majority of patients receive transplants from cadavers. Depending on the quality of the organs, a single cadaver can provide many organs; consequently, identifying and obtaining consent from every possible donor is essential. Twenty-one percent of the kidneys transplanted in 1991 were from living donors. With other organs living donation is rare, although there are programs to transplant segments of liver and, more recently, lung.

There has been a chronic shortage of transplant organs in the United States despite a number of programs aimed at increasing the available supply. In 1968 a congressional committee drafted a Uniform Anatomical Gift Act, which allows adults to donate their bodies after death for transplantation and was adopted in some form by every state by 1973. All fifty states and the District of Columbia have some form of donor card associated with driver's licenses. In the early 1980s it was hypothesized that in some cases health care professionals were failing to offer families the opportunity to donate organs because of fear of legal liability. In response, required request laws, which protect health care professionals from liability and require that they ask families of eligible donors to donate organs, were enacted. By 1989 required request laws had been adopted by most states and were linked to Medicare reimbursement and hospital accreditation. Such legislation increased awareness of transplantation but did not result in more donated organs.

As transplant programs developed and expanded so did formal and informal mechanisms for obtaining, sharing, and allocating organs. In 1977 the United Network for Organ Sharing (UNOS) was established to coordinate the distribution of kidneys nationally and to maintain a registry of persons awaiting transplant. UNOS was granted the federal contract to establish the Organ Procurement Transplant Network, mandated by Congress as part of the Omnibus Budget Reconciliation Act of 1986. All transplant centers were required to join the newly established network and abide by its rules. Only one organ procurement organization is allowed to function in each of the eleven national regions. Nevertheless, the shortage of organs persists.

The first kidney transplant raised questions about whether the chances of success were great enough to justify the risks; similar concerns were later expressed about living donations of liver and lung tissue. The difficulty of deciding who will receive a particular organ is exacerbated by the shortage of supply, which has raised questions about the policy prohibiting a donor from designating a recipient. Presumed consent laws and programs allowing payment for donation are being examined for their potential effect on the number of donated organs and on the values underlying donation. The question is constantly being raised of whether there are undiscovered potential donors who might increase supply. Specific groups being considered include anencephalic infants, non-heart-beating cadaver donors, and unrelated living donors. Such possibilities, however, necessarily raise concerns about risks to society, families, and donors.

[Rick Hanson, *Spare Parts: Organ Replacement in American Society* (New York, 1994).]

BETH A. VIRNIG

See also **SUPP:** Cardiovascular Disease; Medicine; Surgery.

TRANSPORTATION, DEPARTMENT OF. In a message to Congress in March 1966, President Lyndon B. Johnson outlined a proposal for a unified transportation authority, and in October Congress established the Department of Transportation (DOT). In April 1967 President Johnson activated the new department, which was headed by a cabinet-level secretary of transportation. The new department, which brought together about 90,000 employees from more than thirty formerly separate agencies, was given responsibility for federal investments in transportation and for creating an economical, efficient, and safe national transportation system, taking into account environmental standards and national defense. It did not take over the regulatory activities of the Civil Aeronautics Board (dissolved in 1984), the Interstate Commerce Commission, or Federal Maritime Commission. In 1981, however, the Maritime Commission, renamed the Maritime Administration, was transferred by Congress to DOT. Officials responsible for the nation's overall system of transportation report to the secretary of transportation, as do the administrators of nine special operating divisions, most of which are devoted to specific modes of transportation. Responsible for the general transportation system are a deputy secretary, a general counsel, and assistant secretaries for budget and programs, policy and international affairs, governmental affairs, public affairs, and administration. The nine operating divisions are the United States Coast Guard, Federal Aviation Administration, Federal Highway Administration, Federal Railroad Administration, National Highway Traffic Safety Administration, Urban Mass Transportation Administration, Saint Lawrence Seaway Development Corporation, Research and Special Programs Administration, and Maritime Administration. Although the administrators of these divisions report to the secretary of transportation, they are appointed by the president and must be confirmed by the Senate.

Railway transportation was in crisis in the late 1960s, and DOT participated in the creation of the National Railroad Passenger Corporation (Amtrak), established in 1971, and Consolidated Railroads (Conrail), established in 1976 primarily as a freight carrier. Both were chartered by the federal government as quasi-public, profit-making corporations. They have not been profitable, however, and have required federal subsides. In 1987 the federal government sold its shares of Conrail stock as part of President Ronald Reagan's privatization program. Amtrak, however, through a combination of rate hikes, cost cutting, and effective marketing, managed to reduce its reliance on federal subsidies. The secretary of transportation is one of the nine members of the Amtrak board.

A related but autonomous agency is the National Transportation Safety Board (NTSB), established by the same act that created DOT. NTSB is a five-member board, appointed by the president, that reports directly to Congress. It is responsible for investigating accidents involving all forms of transportation, taking over investigations formerly carried out by the Civil Aeronautics Board and the Interstate Commerce Commission. In practice, much of the initial accident investigation is carried out by the operating division within DOT that has jurisdiction over the mode of transportation involved in the accident.

[Robert C. Lieb, *Transportation: The Domestic System,* 2nd ed. (Reston, Va., 1981); Roy J. Sampson, Martin T. Farris, and David L. Shrock, *Domestic Transportation: Practice, Theory, and Policy,* 5th ed. (Boston, 1985).]

RICHARD W. MOODEY

See also **SUPP:** Transportation Industry.

TRANSPORTATION INDUSTRY. The United States always has been a mobile society, and this trend accelerated in the 1970s even though the future did not look bright for most U.S. transportation industries in that decade. The automobile industry rapidly lost market share to Japan, and energy crises in 1973 and 1979 made drivers wait in long lines to buy gas that had more than doubled in price by the end of the decade. Congested roads around major urban areas frustrated commuters. The greatest achievement of the 1970s and 1980s was the completion of the Interstate Highway System, a network of 45,493 miles of superhighways that was begun when President Dwight D. Eisenhower signed the Federal-Aid Highway Act (also known as the Interstate Highway Act) of 1956. By the late 1980s the system supported 20 percent of the nation's traffic and 49 percent of truck-trailer traffic.

Commuters continued to favor the car into the 1990s but commuting patterns shifted dramatically. In the early 1970s most commuters drove from suburban houses to jobs in the city. Twenty years later many commuters traveled from suburb to suburb or to newly created "edge" cities, where many companies

had relocated because of lower taxes and greater convenience for workers. Inexpensive computers and fax machines enabled companies to disperse from city centers and also enabled some workers to "telecommute." This trend was reflected in the number of workers working at home, which rose from 2,179,863 in 1980 to 3,406,025 in 1990, an increase of more than 56 percent. Another trend was the twenty-four-hour, time-shifted workday. Increasingly workers went to and returned from work at irregular hours, creating around some cities all-day rush hours. These changes resulted in greater congestion around urban areas as commuters resisted carpooling because it was not convenient and gas prices were reduced. While the percentage of all commuters traveling by car, truck, or van rose only 2 percent between 1980 and 1990, the percentage of commuters traveling alone increased by 9 percent; in 1990, almost three out of every four (73 percent) commuters rode to and from work by themselves. The percentage of commuters carpooling dropped from 19 percent in 1980 to 13 percent in 1990 and all forms of public transportation declined in popularity. The one bright spot for urban commuters, however, was the resurgence in light-rail trolley systems. San Diego, Portland, Sacramento, Buffalo, and Denver all had systems operating by the mid-1990s and many other cities were planning them.

Passenger railroad service did not rebound from a lengthy decline despite the establishment in 1971 of Amtrak, a national railroad that covered 24,000 miles in forty-five states by the 1980s. Although aided by government subsidies, the railroad could not compete with automobiles and airlines. Long-distance rail fares often were more expensive than airline fares, and the safety of the system was called into question with several derailments resulting in deaths in the 1990s. The country's aging track system limited trains to relatively slow speeds. In late 1994 Amtrak announced severe cutbacks in long-distance routes, and the company's future looked poor.

The airline industry, however, continued to grow. The airplane manufacturing industry, dominated by Boeing and McDonnell-Douglas, was one of the few businesses in which the United States remained technically and economically superior worldwide, with the companies ranking first and seventh in exports in 1992. Deregulation of the airline industry in the late 1970s led to the formation of scores of new airlines, many offering inexpensive fares and shuttle service along the Northeast corridor (Boston–New York–Washington) and between San Francisco, Los Angeles, and San Diego. One of the first and most success-ful of these airlines, People's Express, succeeded for a short time but then went out of business. Deregula-tion resulted in a greater concentration among air-lines, with three major carriers—United, American, and Delta—dominating domestic service in the mid-1990s, although these were being challenged by new "no frills" carriers like Kiwi and Southwest. Mean-while such giants as Pan Am and Eastern Airlines went out of business. The U.S. airline industry re-mained the dominant world player, boasting a fleet of 4,000 large jets carrying more than 450 million pas-sengers a year. The future of the U.S. aviation indus-try was uncertain. There was wide agreement by the 1990s that the air traffic control system was outdated and that major airports had reached their carrying ca-pacity limits. The reliability of the air traffic control system was first questioned in 1981 after President Ronald Reagan fired 11,500 striking controllers. The Federal Aviation Administration and the airlines de-veloped new technologies, including computer sys-tems, radar signaling devices on planes, and auto-mated control systems. It was hoped these would result in a great reduction in the number of air-traffic controllers needed. Despite technological advances and statistics showing that air travel was one of the safest means of transport, safety concerns rose to the forefront in the 1980s and 1990s. While the number of fatalities declined steadily from 2.2 per 100,000 passenger hours in 1975 to 1.3 per 100,000 passenger hours in 1991, deregulation and the aging air traffic control system resulted in reduced maintenance re-quirements and more congestion on the ground in centers designated as "hubs" by the remaining major airlines.

[Brad Edmondson, "Alone in the Car," *American Demo-graphics* (June 1994); Stephen B. Goddard, *Getting There: The Epic Struggle Between Road and Rail in the American Century* (New York, 1994); Mark H. Rose, *Interstate: Ex-press Highway Politics, 1939–1989,* rev. ed. (Knoxville, 1990); Anthony Sampson, *Empires of the Sky: The Poli-tics, Contests and Cartels of World Airlines* (New York, 1984).]

JEFFREY M. MERRON

See also **SUPP:** Aircraft Development and Transport; Air Traffic Controllers Strike; Automobile Industry; Rapid Transit; Transportation, Department of.

TREASURY, DEPARTMENT OF THE, established in 1789, consisted in 1995 of sixteen departmental offices and eleven operating bureaus: the Customs Service (established in 1789); U.S. Mint (1792); In-ternal Revenue Service (1862); Bureau of Engraving and Printing (1862); Office of the Comptroller of the Currency (1863); Secret Service (1865); Bureau of the Public Debt (1919); Financial Management Ser-vice (1920); Federal Law Enforcement Training Cen-ter (1970); Bureau of Alcohol, Tobacco, and Firearms (1972); and the Office of Thrift Supervision (1989). The Treasury Building in Washington, D.C., was de-clared a national historic landmark on Oct. 18, 1972. Secretary of the Treasury Salmon P. Chase's Civil War office, the office used by President Andrew Johnson for six weeks in 1865, and the Cash Room were restored with private funds.

The secretary of the Treasury is the chief adviser to the president on fiscal and financial affairs and plays a key role in the formulation and execution of domes-tic and international economic policy. Since 1970 the Treasury Department has played a central role in im-portant international events. The Treasury, with sup-port from other U.S. agencies, developed comprehen-sive proposals for reform of the international monetary system after the collapse in the early 1970s of the Bretton Woods system (the world payments system of fixed exchange rates for major currencies centered on the dollar and its convertibility into gold). It took the lead in the Smithsonian Agreement of 1971 (a last attempt to realign fixed rates and bol-ster the Bretton Woods system); revision of the ar-ticles of the International Monetary Fund in the mid-1970s, the basis for a new system of management of floating exchange rates; and the Plaza Accord of 1985 (the first substantive effort by the United States, United Kingdom, France, Germany, and Japan to co-ordinate their economic policies, including exchange rate policies). Through the Office of the Assistant Secretary for International Affairs, the Treasury De-partment was also the architect of the U.S. govern-ment's yen-dollar talks and two other bilateral finan-cial consultations with Japan in the 1980s aimed at liberalizing Japan's capital markets.

Treasury played a key role in the major tax reforms of the 1970s and the 1980s. Significant peacetime U.S. tax reforms took place during the administration of President Ronald Reagan (1981–1989), when the economic and legal staffs of the Office of the Assis-tant Secretary for Tax Policy helped draft the Eco-nomic Recovery Tax Act of 1981 and the Tax Reform Act of 1986. The staffs also played a key role in the formulation of the deficit reduction bills passed in 1990 and 1993. The Treasury Department also ad-ministered the revenue sharing program, an initiative of President Richard M. Nixon's administration that distributed $82.6 billion among 39,000 states, cities, and other general-purpose local governments between the program's enactment in 1972 and its repeal in 1986.

The Office of the Assistant Secretary for Economic Policy participated actively in the formulation of the four phases of wage and price controls (Aug. 15, 1971–Apr. 30, 1974); studied the impact of changes in the financing and benefit structure of the Social Security Trust Fund and provided input for the major reforms enacted in 1983; analyzed the hospital cost containment proposal of President Jimmy Carter's administration in 1980 and President Bill Clinton's health care reform proposal of 1993–1994; and analyzed the deficit reduction packages of the George Bush and Clinton administrations.

The U.S. government securities market is the largest and most liquid securities market in the world. Sales of Treasury securities to the public raise funds to cover the shortfall between the government's receipts and expenditures and to refinance debt. The public debt amounted to $371 billion on June 30, 1970. On Sept. 30, 1994, it was $4.7 trillion. More than half that amount, $2.7 trillion, was in marketable securities held by private investors. Nonmarketable Treasury securities, including U.S. savings bonds, and marketable debt held by government accounts and the Federal Reserve System, make up the rest of the public debt.

The Office of the Under Secretary for Domestic Finance, which develops the legislative and regulatory financial institutions policy for each presidential administration, developed the Financial Institutions Reform, Recovery, and Enforcement Act of 1989, which addressed the savings and loan crisis. The Fiscal Assistant Secretary's Office manages the government's cash balances. The Office of the Under Secretary for Enforcement oversees the government's second largest law enforcement complement. The Internal Revenue Service (IRS), the largest bureau of the Treasury Department, collects more than $1 trillion each year in tax revenue. Although income taxes account for the bulk of this amount, the IRS also collects corporate, excise, and estate and gift taxes. Electronic filing of tax returns was initiated in 1986, and passage of the Taxpayer's Bill of Rights in 1988 strengthened protections for individual taxpayers. The Bureau of Engraving and Printing produced U.S. paper money only in its Washington, D.C., plant until 1991, when it opened a second currency facility in Fort Worth, Texas. The savings and loan crisis of the 1980s led to

the creation of the Office of Thrift Supervision in 1989, replacing the Federal Home Loan Bank Board.

[Mark Walston, *The Department of the Treasury* (New York, 1989).]

ABBY L. GILBERT

See also **SUPP:** Banking and Finance; Budget, Federal; Savings and Loan Crisis.

TRIALS. Between 1975 and 1995 Americans were fascinated, indeed obsessed, with famous trials and trials of the famous. This interest must be seen as part of a long tradition of public fascination with trials, facilitated in the modern era by radio and then television, making law a spectator sport. The most prominent political trials of the era were in connection with the Iran-Contra affair, in which officials of President Ronald Reagan's administration, including national security advisers John M. Poindexter and Robert C. McFarlane and National Security Council aide Lt. Col. Oliver North, conspired illegally to sell arms to the government of Iran and use the money to aid the contras, right-wing guerrillas in Nicaragua. A federal jury in April 1990 found Poindexter guilty on five counts of perjury, including lying to Congress and conspiracy. North was convicted of destroying documents, misappropriating money for personal use, and obstructing a congressional investigation. Lesser defendants were convicted on a variety of counts. The Poindexter and North cases were subsequently dismissed by federal judges because key evidence came from congressional hearings. All defendants claimed they were acting with the support of President Reagan but he denied any knowledge of the illegal activities. Before leaving office President George Bush pardoned six former officials who remained convicted of or were faced with charges, including McFarlane and former Secretary of Defense Caspar Weinberger.

The longest and costliest criminal case in U.S. history was the McMartin-Buckey child abuse trial. Police in 1983 began to investigate allegations of sexual abuse of children at a Los Angeles County day-care center, which led to the arrest of seven people, although only two, Peggy McMartin Buckey and Raymond Buckey, faced trial, which took place in an atmosphere of hysteria supported by questionable police activities, grandstanding by publicity-seeking prosecutors, and media coverage of dubious objectivity. The children in the case accused the defendants of wholly impossible or utterly fantastic acts, including taking them for airplane rides in the middle of their preschool classes and practicing satanic rituals not witnessed by any of the other children in the school. During the trial one prosecutor quit, complaining about the coaching of child witnesses and expressing doubt about the credibility of the initial adult witness, who subsequently died from alcoholism. On Jan. 18, 1990, a jury acquitted the defendants on fifty-two counts and remained deadlocked on twelve other charges against Raymond Buckey. In his retrial on those counts in July 1990 the jury deadlocked again. In January 1991 the presiding judge declared a mistrial and dismissed all remaining counts. The judge noted the case had "poisoned everyone who had contact with it."

Beginning in the 1970s notable cases involved serial killers. In January 1989 the state of Florida executed Theodore R. "Ted" Bundy for the 1978 murder of twelve-year-old Kimberly Leach. By the time of his death Bundy had been linked with as many as forty murders, mostly of young women, in Washington, Colorado, and other western states as well as in Florida. Jeffrey L. Dahmer was arrested in July 1991 by Milwaukee police. He confessed to seventeen murders beginning in 1978, mainly of gay and/or nonwhite men and teenage boys. Evidence of necrophilia and cannibalism added to the already gruesome details of the trial. Dahmer pleaded not guilty by reason of insanity to fifteen counts of murder, but a Wisconsin jury determined he was legally sane and sentenced him to fifteen terms of life imprisonment. On Nov. 28, 1994, an inmate at Columbia Correctional Institution in Portage, Wis., murdered Dahmer.

The nation's war on drugs led to a few high-profile trials. In 1983 federal agents arrested the automobile executive John Z. DeLorean on drug trafficking charges, accusing him of selling drugs to obtain money to start his own company. After a twenty-two-week trial and twenty-nine hours of deliberation a Los Angeles jury acquitted him in the belief that the government had entrapped him and that federal agents were seeking to gain political support for the war on drugs. The federal government was only marginally more successful in its prosecution of the mayor of Washington, D.C., Marion S. Barry, arrested on Jan. 18, 1990, on various drug-related charges. Barry was filmed buying and smoking $60 worth of crack cocaine. After a six-week trial Barry was convicted on only a single misdemeanor count of possession; he was acquitted on one count and the jury deadlocked on twelve others. Complicating the case were allegations, which the jury apparently believed, that the George Bush administration had tar-

geted Barry because he was black. Some jurors believed the government may have entrapped him by using a friend who had become an informant to lure him into a hotel room where she offered him crack cocaine. After serving less than two years Barry was released. In 1994 he was reelected mayor of Washington, D.C.

A more successful case was the federal prosecution of General Manuel Antonio Noriega, the former head of the government of the Republic of Panama. After the invasion of Panama in 1989 federal officials removed Noriega to Florida and charged him with international drug trafficking. Noriega's trial began in September 1991 and ended when a jury convicted him on eight of ten counts of cocaine trafficking, racketeering, and conspiracy. Noriega wanted to present evidence that the Central Intelligence Agency (CIA) had been involved in drug trafficking to raise funds to aid anticommunist guerrillas in Central America. The court accepted the government's contention that national security required the defense not to discuss the CIA's involvement with Noriega or his longtime role as a CIA informant.

The 1980s and 1990s saw a number of other high-profile trials. In connection with the Wall Street insider-trading scandal of the mid-1980s the arbitrageur Ivan F. Boesky agreed in 1986 to pay $100 million in fines, settled civil suits for $50 million, and served two years of a three-year prison term for violation of securities laws, while the wealthy stockbroker Michael Milken began a prison sentence in 1991 for illegal stock and bond manipulations. Child and spousal abuse became a national issue with the case of Joel B. Steinberg and Hedda Nussbaum in New York City. Charged with murdering the couple's six-year-old adopted daughter, Lisa, Steinberg was convicted in January 1989 after Nussbaum, whom he had battered for years, testified against him. In 1993 the actress Mia Farrow and the director Woody Allen traded accusations in highly publicized hearings over custody of their children. A Florida jury in 1991 acquitted William Kennedy Smith of rape in a highly publicized trial. Smith was the nephew of Senator Edward M. Kennedy, the late Senator Robert Kennedy, and the late President John F. Kennedy. The case against Smith was never strong and some commentators believed the prosecutor may have proceeded with it to avoid charges of favoritism. At the same time as the Smith case, an Indiana jury convicted Michael Tyson, the heavyweight boxing champion of the world, of raping a beauty queen contestant, Desiree Washington. After serving nearly three years in jail

Tyson was given a hero's welcome in Harlem, New York, in June 1995.

Televised court proceedings meanwhile reached new heights of sensationalism with the 1993–1994 trial of Lyle and Erik Menendez, who admitted killing their parents with shotguns. The brothers claimed their father had emotionally and sexually abused them and thus justified the murders. The presiding judge ultimately declared mistrials when the jurors could not decide between verdicts of first-degree murder and a lesser charge. In a class by itself was the 1994–1995 trial in Los Angeles of one of the nation's greatest football players, O. J. Simpson, for the murder of his ex-wife, Nicole Brown Simpson, and her friend Ronald L. Goldman. The live televised proceedings were followed by millions of viewers and engendered a frenzy of media coverage. The trial raised issues about race (Simpson was black, his ex-wife and her friend were white), domestic abuse (Simpson had frequently abused his wife during their marriage), and the role of money in the U.S. system of justice (the bill for Simpson's defense ran into the millions of dollars). Sloppy police work called into question the legitimate use of DNA evidence, and police racism became a key issue when one of the prosecution's chief witnesses, Los Angeles police detective Mark Fuhrman, was revealed on audiotape to be a vicious racist who boasted of planting evidence in cases involving African-American suspects, thus bolstering defense allegations that crucial evidence had been planted to frame Simpson. In a verdict that shocked many observers who had thought the evidence against Simpson was overwhelming despite the failings of the L.A. Police Department, the jury took only three hours to find Simpson not guilty.

Trials always have been part of U.S. life but took on a new role in the late twentieth century. In a popular television show, *The People's Court,* a retired California judge heard disputes that ordinarily would be settled in small claims court. One cable television network, *Court TV,* devoted all of its programming to televised trials. The line between entertainment and life in the world of law increasingly blurred. In the glare of publicity caused by cameras in the courtroom and the emerging celebrity status of defendants and attorneys, it was not at all clear that justice was being achieved.

PAUL FINKELMAN

See also **SUPP:** Corruption, Political; Crime, White-Collar; Domestic Violence; Iran-Contra Affair; Los Angeles Riots; Scandals; Serial Killings; Wall Street.

TRUST TERRITORY OF THE PACIFIC ISLANDS. Captured by U.S. forces during the Pacific campaigns of World War II, some 2,000 Micronesian islands became the Trust Territory of the Pacific Islands (TTPI) in 1947, a United Nations strategic trusteeship administered by the United States. The TTPI included the Marshalls, Ponape (later Pohnpei), Truk (Chuuk), the Northern Marianas, Yap, and Palau. Initially administered by the U.S. Navy, the islands came under civilian control of the Department of the Interior in 1951, with the exception of Saipan (Northern Marianas), which reverted to the navy soon thereafter. A high commissioner appointed by the president held the chief executive office in the TTPI, which comprised six districts: Marshalls, Pohnpei, Marianas, Yap, and Palau. In 1966 the Congress of Micronesia was created and three years later its Joint Committee on Future Status began the long process of negotiating with the United States over the question of self rule. Micronesia was far from unified in its quest for self-government, and in 1972 the Marianas initiated separate talks that in 1975 led to creation of the Commonwealth of the Northern Marianas (CNMI), made up of Saipan, Rota, Tinian and the tiny Northern Islands. This arrangement is comparable to the status of Puerto Rico. Further fragmentation occurred when the Marshalls and Palau, both concerned that they might be forced to share their economic potential with less wealthy neighbors, held their own negotiations. In 1978 Pohnpei, Kosrae, Chuuk, and Yap approved the constitution that created the Federated States of Micronesia (FSM). The Republic of the Marshall Islands (RMI) and the FSM in 1986 moved into free association with the United States. The fifteen-year agreements arranged by Micronesian and U.S.negotiators gave the new entities control over internal and external affairs, guaranteed U.S. financing for the island governments, and put defense matters under U.S. control. Because of the conflict between U.S. military interests and the nuclear-free provisions of their constitution, citizens of the Republic of Palau (Belau) voted in repeated referenda without reaching the 75 percent approval required by Palauan law to accept the free-association compact. In 1993, having amended the 75 percent requirement of the constitution to a simple majority, Palau approved the compact. On Oct. 1, 1994, the agreement took effect, and the world's last trusteeship ceased to exist.

[P. F. Kluge, *The Edge of Paradise: America in Micronesia* (Honolulu, 1993); Arnold H. Leibowitz, *Defining Status: A Comprehensive Analysis of United States Territorial Relations* (Boston, 1989).]

KAREN M. PEACOCK

TUBERCULOSIS

See also **DAH:** Guam; Trust Territory of the Pacific; **DAH** and **SUPP:** Samoa, American.

TUBERCULOSIS, cited by the National Institute of Allergy and Infectious Diseases (NIAID) as the leading cause of death by disease in the United States in the nineteenth century, appeared to be vanishing by the mid-1970s. The decline brought a decrease in tuberculosis programs and research. NIAID, the major tuberculosis research center of the National Institutes of Health, gradually reduced its research through the 1970s. New York and New Jersey, for example, closed tuberculosis sanatoriums and hospital wards, transferred tuberculosis care to local clinics and community care on an outpatient basis, and decreased money for programs. Physicians attributed the disappearance of tuberculosis to the combination therapy of streptomycin, isoniazid, and PAS (para-aminosalicylic acid) and possibly with one or more other newer drugs. They believed that a short period of such therapy eliminated the contagious nature of persons infected with the disease, but some experts worried that the monitoring of drug therapy among outpatients in a community-based setting was far more lax than that for hospitalized patients.

Early warnings of the disease's resurgence came from the American Lung Association, the leading lobbying and support organization for tuberculosis research. Predicting an epidemic, the association's president in 1979 urged Congress not to abolish programs. By 1985 the long decline in tuberculosis cases was over. In 1989 the number of cases in New York City alone increased 68 percent from those recorded in 1980 with a high incidence in females aged twenty-five to forty-four. Researchers connected the rise to multidrug resistance, emergence of the human immunodeficiency virus (HIV) and its development into the acquired immunodeficiency syndrome (AIDS), and the discovery that short-term drug treatment did not eradicate the contagion. Some blamed the resurgence on the difficulties of organizing health services to diagnose, treat, and prevent the disease. Others pointed to lack of new drugs to combat multidrug-resistant tuberculosis and absence of a successful vaccine.

AIDS increasingly played a part in tuberculosis expansion. The correlation of tuberculosis with AIDS increased from 2.5 percent of all AIDS sufferers in 1984 to 17.42 percent in 1992 according to twenty-eight major metropolitan health departments in the United States. Tuberculosis hospitalizations associated with AIDS doubled between 1988 and 1992. By 1995 the World Health Organization announced that tuberculosis was the leading cause of death worldwide among HIV-infected people. To curb the rise, the American Thoracic Society and the Centers for Disease Control and Prevention (CDC) jointly published guidance on diagnosis, treatment, prevention, and control. In the early 1990s a voluntary group of thirty-four scientists and public health officials issued *The Tuberculosis Revival,* urging that close observation of outpatient drug therapy be required. Acknowledging tuberculosis as a public health concern, the CDC in 1992 counted 26,673 active cases in all the states, a 20 percent increase over cases reported in 1985. The disease was affecting all societal groups but hurting the poor and minorities the most. Nevertheless, experts considered tuberculosis preventable and curable, especially if caught early and monitored. In response to the rise in tuberculosis, NIAID increased research support from seven projects and $514,000 in 1979 to more than 100 projects and $28 million in 1994. Thus, the effort continued to wipe out this disease in the United States and the rest of the world.

[National Institute of Allergy and Infectious Diseases, *Tuberculosis: Resurgence of an Old Problem* (Bethesda, Md., 1993); Frank Ryan, *The Forgotten Plague: How the Battle Against Tuberculosis Was Won and Lost* (Boston, 1993).]

RUTH ROY HARRIS

TUCSON, the second-largest city in Arizona, takes its name from a Papago Indian village across the Santa Cruz River at the base of the Stjukshon mountain, or present-day Sentinel Peak. Situated in the lower Sonora Desert basin, Tucson is surrounded by the Santa Catalina and Santa Rita mountains, which serve as natural fortifications against unchecked urban sprawl. In 1700 Jesuit missionary Eusebio Francisco Kino founded San Xavier del Bac Indian Mission, and the Spanish established the Presidio de San Augustin de Tuguison in 1775. Tucson became part of U.S. territory with the Gadsden Purchase in 1853 and served as the capital of Arizona Territory from 1867 to 1877. The Southern Pacific Railroad reached Tucson in 1880 and the city was incorporated in 1883.

Following World War II the city experienced rapid growth, and since the 1960s the former Spanish settlement turned southwestern metropolis nearly doubled in size and quadrupled in diversity. The 1970 population figure of 262,933 grew to 405,390 residents by 1990, with the metropolitan area claiming 660,880 inhabitants. Through booster campaigns and individual initiative, Tucson's economy in the 1990s embraced every pursuit from agriculture to state-of-the-art electronics. The accelerated growth and development threatened a dwindling water supply; in 1980 Tucson was depleting water tables by four to five feet per year. The Central Arizona Project began supplying Colorado River water to Tucson in 1991. Although conservation strategies were put into place, the availability and cost of water remained a widespread concern. Both as a result of its traditional political liberalism and mass awareness of the water issue, Tucson is one of the most environmentally conscious cities in Arizona. The first city to offer municipally supported recycling, Tucson is home to both the Biosphere experiment and many national environmental groups.

With its eclectic appearance and scenic setting, Tucson offers activities for every taste and pocketbook. Wilderness enthusiasts enjoy the reaches of Mount Lemmon, the mysteries of Sabino Canyon, and vast stretches of desert graced with towering saguaros. Wealthy tourists and celebrities favor the amenities of the many expensive resorts, while more modest spenders patronize the Desert Sonora Museum and the "Old Town" restaurants and movie set that has served as the site for more than 200 feature-length films. The University of Arizona is at the center of cultural life in Tucson. In recent years, Arizona's second-largest university has sponsored ground-breaking medical and agricultural research. Since the late 1970s the university faculty has included such critically acclaimed writers as Native American authors Leslie Marmon Silko and N. Scott Momaday. Although Tucson suffered in the recession of the late 1980s, prosperity and optimism returned in the 1990s. While elected officials plotted new economic strategies, residents reaffirmed their long-standing desire to avoid the traffic congestion and rampant modernity of their historic rival, the capital city of Phoenix.

[Nat de Gennero, ed., *Arizona Statistical Abstract: A 1990 Handbook* (Tucson, 1990); C. L. Sonnichsen, *Tucson: The Life and Times of an American City* (Norman, Okla., 1982); Henry P. Walker, *Historical Atlas of Arizona* (Norman, Okla., 1979).]

EVELYN S. COOPER

See also **DAH** and **SUPP:** Arizona; **SUPP:** Phoenix; Sunbelt.

TULSA, city in northeastern Oklahoma, was part of Indian Territory and was settled by the Talasi band of Creek Indians who journeyed from their native Alabama to the banks of the Arkansas River in 1832. Other settlers arrived after the railroad in 1882, and the city became a transportation center. Discovery of oil in the area led to Tulsa's rapid growth early in the twentieth century, which continued during World War II, when several large industries were established there. Once known as the "oil capital of the world," Tulsa in the 1990s was headquarters for more than 1,000 energy-related corporations that accounted for 10 percent of total employment. The boom-and-bust of international oil prices had a sobering effect upon the city. After a few years of rapid rise and fall, the city's population steadied at 367,302 in 1990. Among the more notable qualities of Tulsa's population is that 5 percent are at least one-quarter Indian and 8 percent define themselves as Native American. The city's white population (80 percent) and African-American population (14 percent) grew with the rise of the oil industry in the 1920s, aircraft production in the 1940s and 1950s, and manufacturing and electronics firms. Tulsans regard themselves as different from other Oklahomans, and that view is often seconded by others, particularly those in Oklahoma City. Oklahoma has grown more conservative while traditionally Republican Tulsa has become more independent and moderate in its own politics. Another difference is that Tulsa prides itself on its cultural life, which includes opera, ballet, and theater companies and a symphony orchestra together with the Thomas Gilcrease Institute of American History and Art and the Philbrook Museum of Art.

[Angie Debo, *Tulsa: From Creek Town to Oil Capital* (Norman, Okla., 1943).]

DANNEY GOBLE

See also **DAH** and **SUPP:** Oklahoma City; Oklahoma.

U

UFOs. *See* **Unidentified Flying Objects.**

UNEMPLOYMENT. Few economic indicators are as important politically as unemployment. A rise in unemployment can bring down a presidency, while a decline in unemployment is welcome news, a sign that prosperity may be just around the corner. To be unemployed, a person must not have a job, must be able to take a job if one were offered, and must have actively looked for work in the preceding four weeks. To be considered employed, one must work for pay or profit or work at least fifteen hours without pay in a family-run business. The labor force is defined as the sum of the employed and unemployed, and the unemployment rate is the number of unemployed divided by the labor force. The unemployment rate is controversial because the definition of unemployment excludes "discouraged workers," persons who do not have jobs and are not actively seeking them because they believe that a job search would be fruitless; this exception makes the unemployment rate seem lower than it actually is.

Economists distinguish between frictional, seasonal, structural, and cyclical unemployment. Frictional unemployment refers to normal turnover of workers in any dynamic capitalist economy. Seasonal unemployment occurs because production varies over the year. Thus, for example, unemployment between 1976 and 1986 was 20 percent higher on average in January and February than in October. Structural unemployment refers to a mismatch between workers and jobs. The mismatch can be spatial—for example, entry-level jobs may go begging in suburbs because unemployed youths in central cities cannot get to them—or it may be skill-based. Together, frictional and structural unemployment define a natural rate of unemployment, one to which the economy tends in the long run. The natural rate usually ranges between 4 and 5 percent, but it has risen since the 1970s. This rise is partly due to the changing composition of the U.S. labor force. Minorities make up an increasing part of the labor force but have higher unemployment rates than average. In 1993 the unemployment rate for black males ages sixteen to nineteen was 40.1 percent, approximately six times the national average of 6.8 percent. Structural unemployment has also worsened since 1970. Cyclical unemployment arises during a recession and can be combated by fiscal or monetary policy. During the recession of the early 1980s the unemployment rate peaked at 9.7 in 1982. Most unemployed workers are covered by unemployment insurance, which provides benefits that vary with previous earnings and are normally paid for up to twenty-six weeks, although they can be extended if unemployment in a state is unusually severe or if Congress votes an extension. Unemployed workers may also be eligible for a variety of government programs that provide training for new employment opportunities, for example, the programs established by the 1982 Job Training Partnership Act.

There is no accepted theory of unemployment. Some economists believe that all unemployment is voluntary, because there are always job openings, even in a recession. Instead of taking such jobs, the unemployed rationally choose to wait for better offers. Other economists, influenced by John Maynard Keynes, hold that unemployment arises because wages are too high in terms of demand and supply. Wage "stickiness" has been attributed to the tendency of companies to pay efficiency (higher than market-clearing) wages in the belief that highly paid workers are more loyal and more productive. The insider-outsider theory posits that the employed (insiders) resist wage cuts, which lower their incomes but make more jobs available to the unemployed (outsiders). Insider-outsider theory is popular in Europe, where many countries experienced double-digit unemployment rates through the 1980s.

[Bruce E. Kaufman, *The Economics of Labor Markets and Labor Relations* (New York, 1989).]

ROBERT A. MARGO

UNIDENTIFIED FLYING OBJECTS (UFOs). The

U.S. Air Force examined thousands of reports of UFOs since the first sighting in 1947 until 1969, since when no U.S. agency has claimed to be involved in investigating UFOs. During that period the air force investigated 12,618 reports, of which 701 were unexplained. Investigations found nonextraordinary causes (for example, birds, weather balloons, and marsh gases) for 95 percent of reported sightings, some of which were hoaxes. Thus far, no one has convincingly proved the existence of UFOs. The great majority of scientists discount the possibility that UFOs are extraordinary phenomena. Those who believe otherwise have various theories, ranging from alien visitors from outer space to symbols of deep religious belief to near-death experiences. UFOs became part of popular culture because of many black-and-white amateur films and low-budget science fiction motion pictures that contributed to the cult status of UFOs and because of the success of two major Hollywood films, *Close Encounters of the Third Kind* (1977) and *E.T.: The Extra-Terrestrial* (1982), both of which remain on the list of all-time favorite movies. A special telephone line offers callers tips regarding UFO sightings, alien abductions, and extraterrestrial anatomy. The Center for the Study of Extraterrestrial Intelligence attempts to contact UFOs by broadcasting sounds allegedly made by UFOs, by flashing lights, and by trying to establish telepathic contact. Each year at the University of Wisconsin, a conference is held for people who believe they have been abducted by extraterrestrials or have been through episodes involving UFOs. In 1993 folk-rock star Richie Havens and ALOID and the Interplanetary Invasion, a band billing itself as "the world's first UFO rock group," performed at a UFO convention in New York City.

They believed that entertainment was the best way to inform the public about UFOs.

[Robert T. Rood and James Trefil, *Are We Alone?* (New York, 1981); Dennis Stacy, "The Omni Open Book Field Investigator's Guide: Part Two," *Omni* (April 1995); Pamela Weintraub, "Let the Project Begin," *Omni* (November 1994).]

JOHN J. BYRNE

UNIONS. *See* **Labor Unions.**

UNITED KINGDOM, RELATIONS WITH. Strong ties have long existed between the United States and the United Kingdom: a common language, culture, and legal system as well as a political alliance forged in the crucible of two twentieth-century world wars. The so-called special relationship, however, is not one between equals. Since the end of World War II the United States has dominated the relationship politically, economically, and militarily.

In the 1980s the countries were led by like-minded leaders, Prime Minister Margaret Thatcher and President Ronald Reagan. Their mutual relationship was singular, a striking convergence of ideologically driven conservatives who shared similar domestic agendas and a common foreign policy. Both led domestic political revolutions—supply-side economics, increased defense spending, privatization, deregulation, and an overall conservative agenda. Reagan was the Great Communicator, Thatcher the Iron Lady. The two were great friends. In 1982 the United States tried to mediate a dispute between Great Britain and Argentina over territorial control of the Falkland Islands, located in the south Atlantic Ocean. When mediation failed, the United States supported Great Britain by quietly providing logistical support and military intelligence during the three-month conflict. Reagan and Thatcher's mutual trust had great effect, particularly with regard to the Soviet Union. In 1984 Thatcher became the first Western political leader to meet with Mikhail Gorbachev before his ascension to the Soviet presidency. As Thatcher told the world, "We can do business together." That assessment shifted Western political rhetoric from East-West confrontation to conciliation and support for internal democratic reform in the Soviet Union. Reagan adopted Thatcher's view, largely abandoning his own harsh depiction of the Soviet Union as the "focus of evil in the modern world." The collapse of the Soviet Union, however, lessened U.S. military need for a trusty friend in Europe. Thus, U.S. relations with

Great Britain began to focus more on trade and economic issues.

Within the United Kingdom the focus shifted toward development of an "ever closer union" with the other nations of the European Community. The long-ruling Conservative party split over the issue of Europe. Thatcher, who wanted to keep Great Britain an island apart, was forced to resign in November 1990. She was replaced by Conservative John Major, who wanted the nation to be "at the heart of Europe." In 1991 the United Kingdom approved the Maastricht Treaty on political union and a common currency among democratic European states, although it opted out of some provisions. Tensions continued over the extent to which the United Kingdom would be part of a United States of Europe. Meanwhile, the larger political interests of the United States focused on Japan and Germany—two huge economies that affected international trade and currency-exchange rates.

Politically the United States retained a keen interest in Northern Ireland. Americans claiming Irish heritage numbered 44 million in 1995, compared to 5 million residents of Ireland and Northern Ireland. The United States pressured Irish nationalists to call a cease-fire in August 1994 and maintained consistent pressure on both the Irish Republic and the United Kingdom to reach a political settlement in the long-standing war. The Republic of Ireland pressured the Irish Republican Army (IRA) to halt its military terrorist campaign so that Sinn Féin, the IRA's political wing, could join all-party talks to create a new governmental structure for Northern Ireland. In 1995 Bill Clinton became the first U.S. president to visit Northern Ireland and urged the embattled Protestant and Catholic communities to "take risks for peace."

In the 1980s and 1990s Americans were eager consumers of such cultural exports as British rock music and BBC television productions and remained entranced with the continuing melodrama of the British royal family, especially the marital travails of Charles and Diana, prince and princess of Wales.

[Geoffrey Smith, *Reagan and Thatcher* (New York, 1991); Margaret Thatcher, *The Downing Street Years* (New York, 1993).]

BRENT SCHONDELMEYER

See also **SUPP:** European Community; Falklands War.

UNITED NATIONS (UN). The United States played a key role in the founding of the United Nations and maintained a strong if sometimes troubled relationship with the organization throughout the United Nations' first fifty years. The United Nations had its beginnings in a meeting between British Prime Minister Winston Churchill and President Franklin D. Roosevelt on Aug. 14, 1941, four months before U.S. entry into World War II. This meeting produced the Atlantic Charter, pledging "the final destruction of the Nazi tyranny" and proposed a postwar "establishment of a wider and permanent system of general security." In February 1945 Roosevelt met with Churchill and the Soviet leader Joseph Stalin at Yalta in the Soviet Crimea. There, even before the war's end, it was agreed to proceed with a United Nations Conference and draw up a UN Charter. Roosevelt believed that through the United Nations he could build a peaceful world and predicted that "the Crimean Conference . . . spells the end of the system of unilateral and exclusive alliances and spheres of influence and balances of power." He soon had misgivings about Stalin, however. On the day Roosevelt died, April 12, 1945, he asserted "that the spirit of Yalta was being betrayed by the Soviets." Thirteen days after Roosevelt's death the United Nations Conference convened in San Francisco. Two months later, on June 25, the delegates unanimously approved the UN Charter, and on July 28 the U.S. Senate ratified it by a vote of eighty-nine to two. The United Nations came into being on Oct. 24, 1945, with the approval of the required majority of the fifty-one participating nations.

An early concern was finding a permanent home for the new organization. The initial site of meetings was London, where the first General Assembly convened in January 1946. Several other European cities sought to have the UN headquarters, including Paris, Geneva, and The Hague. On Mar. 21, 1946, the Security Council moved into temporary quarters in the United States, the gymnasium on the Bronx Campus of Hunter College in New York City, while the search for a permanent home continued. When classroom space was needed by Hunter, the Security Council moved to the Sperry Gyroscope plant at Lake Success on Long Island and the General Assembly convened on the site of the 1939 New York City's World's Fair in Flushing Meadow, Queens. Then Robert Moses, New York's dynamic builder of bridges, tunnels, parks, and roads, suggested a permanent home in the Turtle Bay area of midtown Manhattan, six blocks of slaughterhouses and slums along the East River. The real estate entrepreneur William Zeckendorf put the parcels together, and on Dec. 11, 1946, John D. Rockefeller, Jr., offered to give $8.5 million to buy the site. The General Assembly accepted the offer by a vote of forty-six to seven. The UN complex, comprising a thirty-nine-story Secretariat building, a General Assembly hall, and a conference building for the Security Council on eighteen acres of land, was designed mainly by Wallace K. Harrison, one of the architects for Rockefeller Center. With the work completed in less than six years, the United Nations settled into its own complex in 1952, but a number of the specialized agencies occupied the old League of Nations sites in Geneva, with others in Vienna.

From the beginning, the UN atmosphere was quarrelsome because of the burgeoning cold war between the United States and the Soviet Union, both permanent members of the UN Security Council, which deliberates questions of peace and war. In 1946, only days after the election of the first UN Secretary-General, Trygve Lie of Norway, Stalin announced a new Five Year Plan for Soviet economic development that emphasized armaments rather than consumer goods. Stalin declared that the Soviet Union had to defend itself against "all kinds of eventualities" because "no peaceful international order is possible." Supreme Court Justice William O. Douglas described the speech as "the declaration of World War III." On Mar. 5, 1946, Winston Churchill, in company with President Harry S. Truman, delivered the address in which he described the Soviet takeover of Eastern Europe as an "iron curtain" that had descended across the Continent. Stalin declared the address "a call to war with the Soviet Union."

In those early years the pattern was set for the next four decades. The General Assembly, to which all member nations belonged, had no authority other than to recommend. The authority of the Security Council, which held the powers of peace or war or other punitive measures, was consistently blocked by the Soviet Union, which had veto power by virtue of its being a permanent member of the Security Council. After the United States joined with eleven other nations to form the North Atlantic Treaty Organization (NATO) to deter communist aggression, in April 1949, NATO nations had to resort to Article 51 of the UN Charter, which sets forth "the inherent right of individual or collective self-defense," when they decided to intervene militarily.

The first real test of the United Nations came with the Korean conflict in 1950. In an emergency meeting, the Security Council granted President Truman the authority to conduct a "police action" to counter North Korea's attack on South Korea. This approval was possible only because of the absence of the Soviet Union, which at the time was boycotting the Se-

curity Council in an attempt to force it to seat the communist People's Republic of China. On July 7, 1950, the Security Council set up a unified UN command with soldiers from fifteen nations under General Douglas MacArthur. Through the persuasion of the U.S. ambassador to India, Chester Bowles, India introduced in the UN General Assembly a cease-fire resolution on Dec. 3, 1952, that was adopted by fifty-four nations. President-elect Dwight D. Eisenhower, en route to the United States from Korea, a few days later sent an open message heard around the world asking General MacArthur to meet him in New York City at the president's residence at Columbia University to plan a strategy to end the war. This psychological warfare strategy worked. Talks began between the UN Command and the North Koreans at Panmunjom at the thirty-eighth parallel on Apr. 27, 1953. So began the process that finally brought the armistice on July 27, 1953. Ironically, Secretary-General Lie was a victim of the armistice process when the Soviets charged that during the negotiations he had sided with the United States. The effectively ostracized Lie resigned in April 1953 and was succeeded by Dag Hammarskjöld, a member of the Swedish cabinet. Lie warned his successor that "the task of Secretary-General is the most impossible job on earth."

The Middle East was a concern of the United Nations from its inception. On Nov. 20, 1947, the UN General Assembly adopted a resolution that ended the British mandate in Palestine and, against Arab wishes, partitioned the country into an Arab state and a Jewish state. Jerusalem, in which the holy places of the three great religions were located, was to be under international administration. Immediately the Arab delegation marched out of the assembly and announced they would not be bound by this decision. Not dissuaded, the Provisional State Council in Tel Aviv proclaimed the birth of Israel at midnight, May 14, 1948. Within eleven minutes President Truman had announced recognition of Israel. The president's action cut off a UN move for a temporary trusteeship. Full-scale war, which immediately erupted between Israel and its Arab neighbors, was ended in January 1949 by a cease-fire negotiated by Dr. Ralph Bunche, a member of the UN Secretariat. Bunche returned to New York an international hero and became the first African American to be awarded the Nobel Peace Prize. In May 1949 Israel was admitted to the United Nations.

The United Nations emerged as a strong moral force during the Suez crisis of 1956, with the establishment of the use of UN peacekeepers. On July 26, 1956, Egypt seized the Suez Canal, which had been built by the French and was of great commercial importance to both France and Great Britain. Over the objections of the UN Security Council, those two countries, joined by Israel, launched an armed attack against Egypt. With the support of both the United States and the Soviet Union, the United Nations intervened by sending in a UN Emergency Force numbering 6,000 men, known as Blue Helmets, to supervise a cease-fire and the withdrawal of troops. In retrospect, this must be viewed as one of the most significant UN military interventions in its first half century.

The growth of Third World countries and their entry into the United Nations in large numbers after 1960 made it increasingly difficult for the United States to control votes in the General Assembly. (From 51 nations in 1945, UN membership grew to 185 by 1995.) These primarily poor nations paid an extremely small part of total UN operating costs, which bothered some Americans, even though the United States was often in arrears in its own dues payments. As the former British, French, Portuguese, German, Belgian, Dutch, and Italian colonies in Africa and elsewhere emerged as nations, many were taken over by regimes backed by the Soviets, thus increasing resistance in the UN General Assembly toward the U.S.-led Western alliance.

In 1961, Secretary-General Hammarskjöld personally led UN Swedish troops into the seceding Katanga portion of the Congo, with the full support of President John F. Kennedy, in an effort to stop the fighting. Hammarskjöld was killed in a plane crash during the operation and was posthumously awarded the Nobel Peace Prize for 1961. Despite the presence of 20,000 Blue Helmets, it took until 1964 to achieve a cease-fire. The United Nations did not intervene with a major military force again until the 1992 operation in Somalia.

During the 1960s the United Nations, led by Hammarskjöld's successor, U Thant of Burma, was ineffectual in dealing with the escalating conflict in Vietnam. U Thant did, however, succeed in sending the Blue Helmets to Cyprus to keep Greeks and Turks from conflict on that newly independent island. Another notable accomplishment was the General Assembly's 1968 approval of the Treaty on Nonproliferation of Nuclear Weapons.

The United Nations continued to play a role in events in the Middle East. Blue Helmets had occupied outposts between Egypt and Israel since the 1956 Suez emergency. In 1967, however, Egypt demanded their withdrawal. To the consternation of Great Britain and the United States, U Thant complied. A few weeks later the Six-Day War broke out between Israel and Arab forces (Egypt, Jordan, and Syria), and continued sporadic fighting led eventually to the Yom Kippur (or October) War of 1973. Cease-fire agreements in 1974 established a UN peacekeeping force and buffer zone between the two armies.

In December 1971, Kurt Waldheim of Austria succeeded U Thant as the fourth secretary-general of the United Nations; in 1982 Waldheim was forced to resign in the face of allegations that he had been a member of the Nazi party during the Third Reich. He was succeeded by Javier Pérez de Cuéllar of Peru, who presided over the General Assembly's 1987 adoption of a resolution with terms for ending the Iran-Iraq War, which had raged since 1980. In 1988 the Nobel Peace Prize was awarded to UN peacekeeping forces. By the end of 1991, the last day for Pérez de Cuéllar as secretary-general, peace was also coming to civil war–ravaged El Salvador, in part due to both U.S. and UN efforts.

When Iraq invaded Kuwait on Aug. 2, 1990, President George Bush, a former U.S. ambassador to the United Nations, immediately asked for UN action. For the first time Arab nations did not vote as a block and, with Russian and American support, the United Nations authorized "all necessary means," which meant force to repel the invasion of Kuwait. UN forces led by the United States swiftly defeated the Iraqi army, and the now greatly enhanced Security Council appeared to have become what Roosevelt had envisioned—the heart of the United Nations. The Gulf War of 1991 was the third time the United Nations was an important instrument of the president of the United States during an international security crisis, just as it had been for Truman in 1950 and Eisenhower in 1956.

Boutros Boutros-Ghali, a former Egyptian diplomat and law professor, became the sixth secretary-general in 1991. Peacekeeping clearly had become the chief business of the United Nations in the post–cold war era. In its first four decades the Security Council had authorized only thirteen peacekeeping missions. In its fifth decade, 1985–1995, twenty were authorized. In 1995 alone the United Nations operated seventeen peacekeeping missions with 73,000 troops and police. During this era there were successful missions in Cambodia, Mozambique, and Haiti. A mission in December 1992 to end famine in Somalia was flawed, however, because it failed to impose political order despite the presence of 38,000 Blue Helmets, 25,000 of them from the United States. From March 1992 to October 1995, 20,000 UN peacekeepers also failed to stop the slaughter, known as ethnic cleansing, in the former Yugoslavia, the "safe areas" never being made safe. While the United States provided minimal air cover, it did not contribute ground soldiers to this effort.

The UN failure in Bosnia, combined with the desire of NATO to play a post–cold war role, set the stage for U.S. Secretary of State for European Affairs Richard Holbrooke to broker an agreement in Dayton, Ohio, among the Serbs, Croats, and the Bosnian government in October 1995. Signed in Paris in December 1995, the accord withdrew the UN from Bosnia and replaced them with a NATO-directed force of 60,000, including 20,000 Americans. (Russian personnel outside of NATO were also included.) In 1993 the United Nations established in The Hague an eleven-member war crimes tribunal; under the Dayton agreement the parties were to send indicted war criminals to The Hague for trial. The replacement of UN forces did not spell the end of peacekeeping as a basic mission of the United Nations but rather a failure in this instance without the dominant force of the United States.

From the beginning, UN policies were affected by the atrocities committed during World War II. It almost immediately appointed a human rights commission, which, under the leadership of Eleanor Roosevelt, issued the 1948 United Nations Universal Declaration of Human Rights. Since then the United Nations has endorsed other human rights treaties or covenants that the U.S. Senate has yet to ratify: the Convention on the Elimination of All Forms of Discrimination Against Women; the American Convention on Human Rights; the International Covenant on Economic, Social, and Cultural Rights; and the International Convention on the Elimination of All Forms of Racial Discrimination. The United Nations also sponsored four international conferences on women between the 1970s and 1995.

Although the primary mission of the United Nations was to eliminate "the scourge of war," the preamble of its charter also states its purpose "to promote social progress and better standards of life in larger freedom" and "to employ international machinery for the promotion of the economic and social advancement of all people." On these grounds the UN specialized agencies were created. The International Labor Organization (ILO) of 1919 was revived. Added were the Food and Agriculture Organization

(FAO), World Health Organization (WHO), and United Nations Educational, Scientific, and Cultural Organization (UNESCO). In all, by the 1990s there were nineteen specialized agencies with combined budgets far exceeding the operation of the United Nations itself (save for peacekeeping missions) and with more employees than the UN Secretariat. Clearly it had become a bureaucracy requiring reform. In the case of UNESCO, the United States withdrew from the organization in 1984 after a scathing critique of it by U.S. Ambassador Jeane Kirkpatrick. Still, there were some remarkable accomplishments among the specialized agencies. In 1980, for example, WHO announced global eradication of smallpox, and global eradication of polio was expected by the year 2000.

As leaders from 140 countries gathered in New York City in October 1995 to celebrate the fiftieth anniversary of the United Nations, there was a clear need for change and reform. The possible addition of states as permanent members of the Security Council remained a subject of dispute, as was the bloated UN bureaucracy. Yet for all its troubles, the world organization domiciled in New York proved its worth in its first fifty years; surely the world would have been a much more ugly, less satisfying place without it.

[Sidney D. Bailey, *The United Nations: A Concise Political Guide*, 3rd. ed. (Lanham, Md., 1995); William Jacobs, *Search for Peace: The Story of the United Nations* (New York, 1994); David Evan Trant Luard, *The United Nations: How It Works and What It Does* (New York, 1994); Stanley Meisler, *United Nations: The First 50 Years* (New York, 1995).]

R. GORDON HOXIE

See also **DAH:** North Atlantic Treaty Organization; United Nations Conference; United Nations Declaration; **SUPP:** Bosnia-Herzegovina; Gulf War of 1991; Middle East, Relations with; North Atlantic Treaty Organization; Somalia; Soviet Union, Relations with; State, Department of.

UNIVERSITIES. *See* **Colleges, African-American; Colleges, Women's; Colleges and Universities; Free Universities.**

URBAN LIVING. Between 1970 and 1990 the urban population of the United States grew from 150 million to 187 million, or from 73.6 percent to 75.2 percent of the total. Major cities (more than 2.5 million people) slipped from 6.92 percent to 5.46 percent. Major metropolitan areas lost or gained slightly in population during the same years. Greater New York dropped 0.4 percent annually, while Chicago posted only a 0.4 percent annual gain; by contrast Los Angeles grew by 2.1 percent per year. The biggest increases occurred in such Sunbelt cities as Tampa–Saint Petersburg, Orlando, Miami, and Houston. Many urban dwellers left for the suburbs. Among the forty-four metropolitan areas in 1990 with more than 1 million residents, the suburbs of forty-two gained population; the central cities of eighteen lost, weakening the power of cities in state legislatures and Congress.

Urban problems spiraled in the 1980s. Population losses translated into job flight to the suburbs, which captured more than 95 percent of new metropolitan manufacturing jobs from 1976 to 1980. One study of urban decline demonstrated that between 1960 and 1989, eighteen of the seventy-seven largest American cities lost employed residents. Pittsburgh, Newark, Saint Louis, Louisville, Buffalo, Cleveland, and Detroit lost more than one-fourth of employed residents. Lower-income people became increasingly concentrated in central cities. Because poverty begets social problems, the 1980s saw sharp increases in urban crime, drug use, unemployment, and births out of wedlock. Social plagues included severe illnesses such as AIDS. All these problems translated into higher costs for police and fire protection, judicial systems, jails, and public hospitals. Expenses translated into higher property and other taxes.

Cities remained centers for intellectual activities, cultural endeavors, and specialized retail facilities, including high-fashion stores, symphonies, medical centers, and institutions of higher learning. Cities still are the nodes for technology, transportation, and housing for low-income workers and newly arriving immigrants. Cities have experienced revivals as highly educated, upwardly mobile young people flooded into their core areas. Attracted by inexpensive housing and services, many such returned urbanites gentrified decaying neighborhoods with refurbished housing, restaurants, and stores. The economic uniformity of these "yuppies," as they were sometimes disparagingly called, also undercut the pluralism of cities. At worst, they forced long-term residents, especially the aged, from their homes and indirectly caused an increase in homelessness. Homosexuals have also concentrated in formerly decaying downtown areas; in addition to well-known gay neighborhoods like Greenwich Village in New York City and the Castro District in San Francisco, communities have arisen in Los Angeles, Houston, Seattle, Denver, Cincinnati, and Saint Louis.

[Anthony Downs, *New Visions for Metropolitan America* (Cambridge, Mass., 1994).]

GRAHAM RUSSELL HODGES

See also **DAH:** Cities, Growth of; Urban Structure; **SUPP:** Crime; Demographic Changes; Housing; Poverty; Suburban Living; Unemployment; Urban Renewal and Development.

URBAN RENEWAL AND DEVELOPMENT. In the 1950s and 1960s the federal government poured billions of dollars into massive "urban renewal" projects in an attempt to revitalize disintegrating U.S. cities. These projects, while sometimes creating successful public institutions, such as performing arts complexes and civic centers, typically involved razing vast sections of the affordable-housing stock and displacing poor and elderly residents, whose housing alternatives were then often limited to bleak-looking public-housing high rises. By the early 1970s the term "urban renewal" had taken on distinctly negative connotations, and policymakers began to search for new approaches to the problem of urban revitalization in an era of increasing scarcity, austerity, and privatization.

With the passage of the Housing and Community Development Act of 1974, which established the Community Development Block Grant program (CDBG), privatization emerged as the central thrust of federal urban-improvement policy. This act brought "revenue sharing" to the nation. It empowered the federal government to issue block grants to local governments for a wide range of improvement projects. Since then the federal government has affected central-city revitalization through a tangle of programs, especially those administered by the Department of Housing and Urban Development (HUD). These include Section 8 and Section 810 of the 1974 Housing and Community Development Act, which set up a national demonstration program with the help of HUD. Block grants were intended primarily for private and public housing rehabilitation and located in low- and moderate-income areas. Urban renewal, model cities, water and sewer line subsidization, open-space procurement, and housing rehabilitation were subsumed by these block grants.

President Jimmy Carter advanced three different urban policies during his tenure, specifically, a $16 billion "economic stimulus" package in 1977, the enactment of the Urban Development Action Grants

(UDAG) program, and a new emphasis on "targeting" aid to distressed cities. This package represented a 25 percent increase in intergovernmental aid to big cities. During the Carter years, $3.5 billion was awarded in direct financial assistance to central-city government as a kind of bonus revenue sharing. UDAG, which fostered central-city revitalization, provided a new and more flexible form of urban renewal in which federal assistance could sweeten development deals negotiated between local government and private builders. UDAG targeted communities with declining populations and large per-capita income disparities, poverty populations, and blocks of substandard houses. It also provided capital for developments that promised increases in jobs and local tax bases. (In 1979, $487 million in federal grants were matched by $2.86 billion in private investment.) By 1980 nearly 700 grants across 400 cities had been authorized, totaling $1.3 billion. Cities with these funds established some 160,000 temporary construction jobs, retained 92,000 old jobs, and created 200,000 permanent openings.

The Carter program also stressed a "new partnership" among various levels of government, the private sector, neighborhoods, and voluntary associations, but Congress proved unwilling to extend the antirecessionary measures of 1977. Carter's new partnership was mostly symbolic. Its $12 billion in proposals contained nothing for the Community Service Administration (successor organization to the Office of Economic Opportunity), only $40 million to ACTION to initiate an "urban volunteer corps," and a mere $15 million for a HUD program of small grants to neighborhood groups.

During Carter's presidency, antirecessionary fiscal assistance, the Comprehensive Employment and Training Act (CETA), and local public works were all phased down or cut out. Taken together, Carter's last two budgets (1979 and 1980) failed to achieve either general welfare reform or enactment of the more limited but equally critical youth employment idea. Nor did the programs ensure that needy central-city residents got the jobs created or retained by subsidies to private capital. Neighborhood revitalization was promoted by the Neighborhood Housing Services (NHS) program, a joint effort between HUD and the Federal Home Loan Board, and by urban homesteading, in which city-owned houses were distributed for little or no money to individuals who agreed to renovate and reside within them. Neither program, however, went very far toward combating urban decay.

By 1979, 86 percent of all cities with more than 50,000 people had created revitalized neighborhoods, but this typically was manifested in gentrification, a more benign form of urban renewal marked by trendy restaurants, boutiques, and overpriced specialty stores. Cynically attacked by critics as "private urban renewal," "reinvasion," or "reverse blockbusting," successful gentrification usually was followed by a substantial bidding-up of property values. For example, UDAG grants were awarded in 1980 to build department-store and office space in downtown Detroit and luxury harborside housing and a downtown office and shopping complex in Baltimore. This process of "devitalization," some economic critics claimed, produces no real active street life. Gentrification rehabilitates the cream of a city's older housing stock but in such a way that only upper-income residents benefit, meanwhile displacing longtime residents.

In the 1980s the administration of President Ronald Reagan emphasized placing urban redevelopment in the hands of the private market and relying on state rather than federal intervention to solve urban ills. Reagan's National Urban Policy Report of 1982, put out by HUD, outlined the Republican urban philosophy of New Federalism, which called for more revenue sharing and the creation of "enterprise zones"—areas excluded from many locally imposed taxes, zoning restrictions, and other regulations—to attract new businesses to impoverished areas. In 1984 Reagan's second Urban Policy Report recognized the problems of particularly distressed cities of the Rustbelt/Frostbelt. The limited amount of federal funding earmarked for urban growth and other local development was increasingly divided between tax incentives for large corporate projects and small-scale ancillary projects, such as street lighting and neighborhood spruce-up projects. While UDAG money under Republican supervision continued to finance new development that attempted to fill the gaps created by abandoned housing, it was parceled out stingily (from 1981 to 1985 UDAG funding fell from $440 million to $235 million), presaging its total demise by decade's end. Federal housing assistance and job training funds also fell precipitously. The Reagan administration halted virtually all government-subsidized rental-housing construction and instead began issuing vouchers for families, another policy in keeping with the trend toward "privatizing" housing subsidies. Responding to these Republican-initiated strategies, the U.S. Conference of Mayors in 1985 called for the protection of urban-directed programs, such as general revenue sharing, urban development action grants, subsidized housing, mass transit assistance, student loans, and jobs programs.

During the presidency of George Bush, Secretary

of Housing and Urban Development Jack Kemp continued to emphasize enterprise zones as the keystone of federal urban policy. Under Bush, states and localities that offered the most favorable incentive programs were given preferential treatment in determining enterprise zone eligibility. While commendable, Kemp's priorities for HUD—employment, home ownership, revitalized inner cities, and care for the homeless—were never fully pursued, however. President Bill Clinton, like his Republican predecessors, also relied on privatization as the solution for urban renewal. His presidency saw the implementation of many economic-growth initiatives set forth by the country's mayors, including stronger community-assistance programs, targeted fiscal assistance to cities in direst need, summer-jobs initiatives and training programs for inner-city youth, a crackdown on discriminatory "redlining" by lending and insurance institutions and other forms of housing discrimination, and the enforcement of a revitalized Community Reinvestment Act.

[John A. Jakle and David Wilson, *Derelict Landscapes: The Wasting of America's Built Environment* (Savage, Md., 1992); Michael H. Lang, *Gentrification and Urban Decline: Strategies for America's Older Cities* (Cambridge, Mass., 1982); John H. Mollenkopf, *The Contested City* (Princeton, N.J., 1983); Donald B. Rosenthal, ed., *Urban Revitalization* (Beverly Hills, Calif., 1980); Jon C. Teaford, *The Rough Road to Renaissance: Urban Revitalization in America, 1940–1985* (Baltimore, 1990); Morris Zeitlin, *American Cities: A Working Class View* (New York, 1990).]

TIMOTHY C. COOGAN

See also **SUPP:** Housing; Housing and Urban Development, Department of; Urban Living.

URUGUAY ROUND. *See* **General Agreement on Tariffs and Trade.**

USDA. *See* **Agriculture, Department of.**

UTAH, a state of 84,916 square miles of diverse geographic features—desert basins, broad plateaus, deep canyons, prehistoric dry lake beds, river valleys, salt flats, and the Wasatch and Uinta mountains, with the state's highest point, Kings Peak, at 13,528 feet—had a population of 1,722,850, in 1990, a 17.9 percent increase since 1980. Eighty percent of Utah's land is under the stewardship of the federal government. Utah's native people include the nomadic Shoshone, Paiute, and Ute, from which the state received its name, which means "home on the mountaintop." All three groups adapted to the region's extremely harsh conditions by living in caves or in portable brush lodges and by gathering seasonal harvests of wild plants as well as hunting, fishing, and trapping.

Economically, Utah mirrored the nation during the hardship years of the Great Depression and the subsequent economic upsurge generated by the demands of World War II. Between 1980 and 1990 the state's economy, like those of many other states, shifted away from the production of goods and toward the production of services. The energy boom of the 1970s became an energy bust of the 1980s. With a decline in mining and construction, and only modest gains in manufacturing, the employment growth in the service-producing industries accounted for 97 percent of all new jobs in the 1980s. In 1990 approximately 80 percent of all nonagricultural workers were employed in the service-producing industries. In the 1980s fewer than 13,000 families farmed, compared with a maximum of 132,000 in 1910. Despite this decline, land values and rural ways continued to reflect strong sentiments and preferences, evidenced in the vitality of state and county fairs at which livestock, rural, and home exhibits were avidly patronized. Tourism became a major part of Utah's economy during the last quarter of the twentieth century, thanks to the state's ski areas, five national parks, six national monuments, and two national recreation areas. By 1991 visits to Utah's 45 state parks had exceeded 5 million. A 1986 government study showed that approximately 11 million people visited the state each year, which increased to 14 million in the early 1990s, and that 50,000 Utahans were employed in the tourism industry. In the 1990s tourism accounted for $2.9 billion in revenue annually.

Utah's innovations in scientific research include the first artificial heart implant in Barney Clark in 1982 and the pioneering of artificial eyes, ears, and arms. The state saw the first renal transplant in 1965. Continued progress in thoracic surgery led to teams of surgeons doing heart transplants in four Utah hospitals, and the 90 percent survival rate in the 412 transplants performed from 1985 to 1992 was one of the best in the country. Among the products developed and produced in Utah in the last quarter of the twentieth century were computers, electronic devices, aircraft, rockets, and computer software. LDS Hospital had become a world model for the most sophisticated system of using computers in total patient care.

The Church of Jesus Christ of Latter-day Saints (LDS), whose membership numbered more than 8 million on a worldwide basis in 1991 and made up some 70 percent of Utah's population at the same time, continued to play a prominent role in the economic, political, and social life of the state. Economically, its building programs, educational institutions, and other activities were major sources of employment, and the businesses it operated, such as the Deseret Book Company, the *Deseret News,* and the broadcasting facilities of Bonneville International Corporation, provided employment and an important tax base. The racial climate in Utah improved after the LDS church announced in 1978 that the priesthood was open to "all worthy male members of the Church . . . without regard to race or color." This had an immediate effect upon the status of blacks in the church and doubtless that of all African Americans residing in Utah. Professional basketball franchises also improved Utah's racial climate. After the American Basketball Association's Los Angeles Stars moved to Salt Lake City in 1970 and changed their name to the Utah Stars, many of their black players were popular not only because of their athletic ability but also for their individual contributions to the community. In 1979 the National Basketball Association's New Orleans Jazz relocated to Salt Lake City and became the Utah Jazz. The popularity of the NBA elevated some Jazz players to celebrity status, and they were looked upon as role models on and off the court.

After World War II there was an expansion of the state's cultural institutions, such as the Utah Symphony Orchestra, the Mormon Tabernacle Choir, and Ballet West. The Sundance Institute, established by actor-director Robert Redford in 1981, gained international recognition for developing and exhibiting films.

[Dean L. May, *Utah* (Salt Lake City, 1987); Richard D. Poll, ed., *Utah's History* (Provo, Utah, 1978); Allan Kent Powell, ed., *Utah History Encyclopedia* (Salt Lake City, 1994).]

KAREN MARY SHREEFTER

UTOPIANISM. The lure of utopia (the Greek word *outopos* (literally "no place") has been strong throughout American history, especially in a land that so long boasted a western frontier. Many were experiments in social engineering; most of the utopian communities that flourished in the eighteenth and nineteenth centuries had religion at their core, such as the Protestant monasticism of the Ephrata Colony; the belief in Christ's second appearing for the Shakers; the postmillennialism of Oneida; and the transcendentalism of Brook Farm and Fruitlands. Others, notably New Harmony in Indiana, the Fourier Phalanxes, and the Icarian communities were socialist. All shared an aspiration to show the wider world how to organize society. After an attenuation of utopian fervor in the latter half of the nineteenth century, the utopian impulse revived somewhat in the twentieth. Some communities, like Estero, founded in Florida in 1900, were based on pseudoscientific notions, while others, like the Hutterites in the Dakotas and Canada and the Society of True Inspiration in eastern Iowa, sought to perpetuate a particular lifestyle derived from religious principles. The late 1960s saw another flowering of utopian communities; nearly all of them, from Total Loss Farm in Vermont to the various communes on the West Coast, were strongly identified with the counterculture of that era.

[Robert Fogarty, *Dictionary of American Communal and Utopian History* (Westport, Conn., 1980).]

RANDALL BALMER

See also **SUPP:** Communes and Communitarian Groups.

VEGETARIANISM, the practice of subsisting on a diet composed primarily or wholly of vegetables, grains, fruits, nuts, and seeds, with or without eggs and dairy products, was endorsed in the United States in 1838 by the American Health Convention. It enjoyed a rebirth with the counterculture of the 1960s. Still, in 1971 only 1 percent of U.S. citizens described themselves as vegetarians. By 1992 the number had jumped dramatically to 7 percent. Half of all vegetarians abstain from meat for health reasons and 15 percent are most concerned about animal welfare. In 1991 the National Restaurant Association endorsed vegetarianism, encouraging restaurants to carry vegetarian dishes because one-third of restaurant patrons had indicated they would order them if offered.

[Waverley Lewis Root and Richard de Rochemont, *Eating in America: A History* (New York, 1976).]

JEFFREY M. MERRON

See also **SUPP:** Animal Rights Movement; Health Food Industry; Nutrition.

VENEREAL DISEASES (VD). *See* **Sexually Transmitted Diseases.**

VERMONT. After World War II, but particularly starting in the 1980s, Vermont's political and economic landscape was transformed. Locally owned marble, granite, and machine tool companies that early in the twentieth century had surpassed agriculture as the prime source of income, were absorbed by international conglomerates, only to decline in favor of other industries, notably electronics. In 1880 the Vermont Marble Company was the state's largest employer; in 1980 it was IBM. Tourism also flourished: at peak season more people were employed on Vermont's ski slopes than in farming. In 1990 there were 2,381 dairy farms, down 8,000 from 1948, and while the size of individual herds increased, there was a significant decrease in acreage. The 263,000 cows in 1948 produced 1.2 billion pounds of milk as compared to the 167,000 cows that produced 2.1 billion pounds in 1990. A federal program to curb overproduction, the "whole herd buyout," ran from 1983 to 1984 and from 1986 to 1987 and attracted many Vermont farmers who, after accepting buyouts, sold their land to developers. As an incentive to retain land in agriculture, the state imposed a use tax in 1980, as distinguished from market value property tax.

The emergence of a two-party system in the state, with the rise of the Democratic party in the early 1960s, brought marked changes. Since Philip H. Hoff in 1962 became the first Democratic governor in 109 years, the governor's office has rotated between the parties. After 1970 both houses of the state assembly had occasional Democratic majorities. In 1974 the first Democratic senator since the founding of the Republican party was elected. In 1995 the Vermont congressional delegation consisted of Republican Senator James M. Jeffords, Democratic Senator Patrick J. Leahy, and independent socialist Representative Bernard Sanders—respectively Protestant, Catholic, and Jewish. The old power structure had disappeared. The gender barrier was breached in 1984, when Vermont elected its first woman governor, Madeleine M. Kunin, who served three terms.

Recent anthropological and historical studies that substantiate an Abnaki Indian presence in northwestern Vermont since 9000 B.C. kindled assertions of aboriginal rights and land titles. Unsuccessful in securing federal tribal recognition, the Abnaki Tribal Council has looked to the state for support. A lame-duck governor's executive order in 1976 accorded the Abnaki tribal status, but it was revoked by his successor the following year. Another temporary victory was won in 1989, when a Vermont court recognized the Abnaki claim to "unextinguished fishing rights" by dismissing charges of fishing without a license against the chief and other tribe members. In 1992 a higher court reversed the decision by concluding that a series of historical events, "the increasing weight of history," had extinguished aboriginal rights.

Showing a 14 percent population gain over the preceding decade, the 1970 census was the first since 1830 to record a more than 10 percent increase in residents, and the 1980 census showed 15 percent growth. A sluggish economy and state regulations restricting development contributed to slower growth during the 1980s, but gains remained substantial at 10 percent; in 1990 the state's population stood at 563,000. The cause of population growth was the interstate highway system, especially the interstate into Canada built in the 1960s. Having long promoted a pastoral retreat from urban life, Vermont became accessible to 40 million urban dwellers within a three-hour drive. Farms, hillsides, and roadsides were converted to vacation uses, including ski resorts and associated developments. Beginning in 1970 the state began to redirect its policies from reversing rural depopulation to preserving rural identity and landscape. Popularly known as Act 250, the legislation mandated permits for developments of more than 10 acres, with burden of proof for ecological soundness of a proposal resting upon the developer. In 1984 the statewide planning provision of the act was repealed, but four years later the legislature passed Act 200 to facilitate "growth management" by encouraging towns to develop plans. Opponents of Acts 250 and 200 alleged that the permit process had become so cumbersome and expensive that it inhibited sound development. A second source of opposition came from property owners organized for repeal of land management legislation as a denial of property rights and local control. During the early 1990s the administrators of land management legislation made accommodations to these sentiments. Vermonters in favor of more strict compliance with the two acts, however, could take heart: in June 1993 the entire state was designated an "endangered place" by the National Trust for Historic Preservation, becoming the first state so designated. The 1990 census figures show that despite Vermont's population growth in the 1980s, Vermont remained a white state of small towns. Asian-Pacific Islanders, American Indian, and African-American populations grew, but their numbers remained very small.

[Madeleine Kunin, *Living a Political Life* (New York, 1994); Harold A. Meeks, *Time and Change in Vermont: A Human Geography* (Chester, Conn., 1986); Joe Sherman, *Fast Lane on a Dirt Road: Vermont Transformed, 1945–1990* (Woodstock, Vt., 1991).]

SAMUEL B. HAND

VETERANS AFFAIRS, DEPARTMENT OF. In 1987 President Ronald Reagan threw his support behind a movement to raise the Veterans Administration, an independent government agency since its creation in 1930, to a cabinet-level department, and in 1988 he signed a bill creating the Department of Veterans Affairs (VA). In 1989 the secretary of veterans affairs became the fourteenth member of the president's cabinet. The VA is the second-largest cabinet-level department of the government; only the Department of Defense is larger. The VA is responsible for administering a wide variety of benefits for military veterans and their dependents. Within it are the Veterans Health Services and Research Administration, the Veterans Benefits Administration, and the National Cemetery System. Their heads and the general counsel for the VA are appointed by the president and confirmed by the Senate. Health benefits administered by the VA include hospitals, nursing homes, and outpatient medical and dental care. More than half the practicing physicians in the United States received part of their training within the health care system administered by the VA. There is a Prosthetics Assessment and Information Center, and programs include vocational as well as physical rehabilitation. The VA oversees military pensions, compensation for disabilities and death, and insurance and loans for veterans. The GI Bill of 1944 provided housing and educational benefits for World War II veterans, and benefits have been continued for veterans of the Korean and Vietnam Wars, all administered by the VA.

[Donald R. Whitnah, ed., *Government Agencies* (Westport, Conn., 1983).]

RICHARD W. MOODEY

VICE PRESIDENCY. The office of the vice president of the United States continued carrying a mixed legacy as the United States approached the end of the twentieth century. While the conception of its duties and its process of selection were flawed, the vice presidency has more or less performed the function the framers of the U.S. Constitution intended and has not—as some critics feared—led the nation into deep trouble. Choosing the vice-presidential candidate, and thus a vice president, remains above all an instrument for assisting in election of the president. The presidential candidate made the selection in every race between 1976 and 1992, as a rule picking someone with an appeal different from his. While traditional geographic and ideological "ticket balancing" remained alive—as in Jimmy Carter's selection of Walter Mondale in 1976—other considerations took on importance. Because Americans after the mid-1970s preferred presidential candidates (other than incumbents) from outside the ranks of national elective officeholders, running mates were insiders from Capitol Hill. Of the ten major party vice-presidential candidates between 1976 and 1992, all had served in Congress, seven of them in the Senate.

Recent years have seen innovations in the selection process. Mondale's choice in 1984 of the first woman, Geraldine Ferraro, acknowledged a changing political climate and created a new form of ticket balancing. George Bush's naming of Dan Quayle, a little-known senator with seemingly not much to offer the ticket or the nation, provoked much puzzlement, concern, and ridicule. Bill Clinton seemed to defy conventional logic in 1992, when he picked Senator Albert Gore, producing a ticket of two white males of similar age and ideology, both Baptist and both from southern states. Gore, however, enhanced an image that Clinton wished to project, and as a popular insider was strong in areas where Clinton was weak. None of these choices challenged the proposition that a vice-presidential candidate's responsibility was to help elect a president, nor did Ronald Reagan's selection in 1980 of Bush, a "moderate" balance to Reagan's conservatism and a candidate who could help the ticket in Texas, a critical state.

The people who have held the office—and who have run for it—since the 1970s generally have been capable, experienced individuals of sober judgment. The most apprehension arose from the candidacy of Quayle, who seemed ill-equipped and ill-prepared for the job despite several years in Congress. Recent presidents have made a point of having their vice presidents at important meetings and giving them special assignments. The issue of temporary succession came up twice during the presidency of Ronald Reagan, first when Reagan was shot on Mar. 30, 1981, and rushed into surgery, leaving it unclear as to who was in charge. When Reagan had surgery again in July 1985, he signed a transfer of power to the vice president for the period of his operation. For all the effort to promote the visibility of recent vice presidents, there is little to suggest they have had a major impact on policy. Indeed, Bush proudly asserted that he was not "in the loop" of decisions about the unpopular Iran-Contra episode. The most encouraging sign of change came with the Clinton administration in the mid-1990s. Clinton treated Gore as an equal partner during the election of 1992, and the two often campaigned together. Upon taking office Gore represented the new administration on environmental issues, operated behind the scenes in key congressional votes, and in 1993 presented the administration's case in a heralded debate with Ross Perot on the North American Free Trade Agreement. Projecting a refreshing self-confidence on most aspects of policy, Gore had a promising start.

Despite the persistence of jokes about its impotence and suggestions that it be changed, even abolished, the vice presidency remains firmly established in the U.S. government. Critics continue to insist that the vice president become more active and that the office serve as a training ground for the presidency. The process of selection, flawed—even risky—as it is, remains entrenched in party politics and is unlikely to change. The best the nation can hope for is that in choosing a running mate, the presidential nominee will give more heed to expertness in governance and less to politics, with the people making anyone pay who does not. Experience since the 1970s, and more broadly since 1945, has affirmed that in picking a running mate a presidential nominee probably is choosing a future presidential candidate. This proved true even of the most ridiculed of recent vice presidents, Quayle, whose national book tour in 1994 catapulted him into a potential presidential candidacy (before illness ruled it out).

[The Twentieth Century Fund, *A Heartbeat Away: Report of the Twentieth Century Task Force on the Vice Presidency* (New York, 1988); Jules Witcover, *Crapshoot: Rolling the Dice on the Vice Presidency* (New York, 1992).]

ROSS GREGORY

See also **SUPP:** Presidency.

VIDEO GAMES are electronic games played on "closed platform" game consoles—hand-held por-

291

tables, cartridge players that connect to a television set or arcade systems—that can only run software from publishers who have paid fees to the system manufacturer. In contrast, personal computers are an "open platform" system: PC software publishers do not pay system manufacturers. Video games emerged in the early 1970s with the development of the microprocessor. The first game released in the United States was Atari's Pong, which approximated Ping-Pong. The game systems of the early 1980s—Atari, Intellivision, ColecoVision—seem primitive compared with the first Nintendo Entertainment System (NES), released in 1985, which used an eight-bit processor. The NES was soon surpassed by the sixteen-bit Super Nintendo Entertainment System (SNES), Sega Genesis, and Sega CD, a CD-ROM player that connects to the Genesis system. Since the mid-1970s the video game industry has been dominated by two manufacturers, Nintendo and Sega. In 1994 more than one-third of American homes had a video game system, the video arcade had become a teen gathering place in malls nationwide, and the industry projected annual sales of $7 billion. The popularity of video games was paralleled by controversy over their purported health risks and benefits. One measure of a game's success is its "addictiveness," and parents are encouraged to monitor the content and duration of children's play. In late 1993 a U.S. Senate subcommittee addressed concerns about violence in video games, resulting in industry-generated ratings. Video games are growing increasingly realistic. Both Sega and Sony released CD-based systems with thirty-two-bit processors in 1995, and Nintendo was expected to release a sixty-four-bit-system in 1996. Further developments are likely to include interactive "movies" for multiple players delivered via fiber-optic cable networks, and virtual reality games.

[Steven A. Schwartz, *Parent's Guide to Video Games* (Rocklin, Calif., 1994); David Sheff, *Video Games: A Guide for Savvy Parents* (New York, 1994).]

CAROL GASKIN

See also **SUPP:** CD-ROM Technology; Fiber Optics.

VIETNAM. *See* **Prisoners of War and Missing in Action.**

VIETNAM WAR MEMORIAL. The Vietnam Veterans Memorial was dedicated on the Washington Mall in November 1982. Maya Ying Lin, a Yale University architecture student who won the national design competition, erected two elongated, tapered walls of black granite that joined at the higher ends at a 125-degree angle to form an open "V." The back sides of the walls were landscaped to be even to the ground. Open front sides sloped downward into the earth to a depth of ten feet where the wings meet. The names of the 57,939 American men and women dead or missing in action in the war were etched, chronologically, in white on the polished granite. At the dedication, veterans and family members read the names of the dead in alphabetical order, which required more than three days. The organizers of the Vietnam Memorial intended their project as a symbol of reconciliation. Their nonpolitical memorial would not comment on the rightness or wrongness of the Vietnam War. By focusing simply on those who served and died, the organizers hoped to conciliate the war's supporters and opponents. Their choice of a site across from the Lincoln Memorial meant, as one veteran put it, that "no one could ignore it." The wall's stark design offended some conservatives and veterans groups, who agitated for a more heroic memorial. As a compromise, sculptor Frederick Hart prepared a statue of three U.S. soldiers—one black, one white, and one Eurasian—as a counterpoint to the abstract simplicity of the wall. Since its unveiling, the Vietnam Memorial has been the third most-visited site in Washington.

[Wilbur J. Scott, *The Politics of Readjustment: Vietnam Veterans Since the War* (New York, 1993).]

J. GARRY CLIFFORD

See also **SUPP:** Prisoners of War and Missing in Action; War Memorials.

VIGILANTES. On the U.S. frontier of the nineteenth century, vigilantes were self-appointed groups of property owners organized to keep order and put down illegal activity. Vigilante committees were organized when citizens found law enforcement absent or inadequate. By the turn of the century, as law enforcement increased, most committees disbanded. The term "vigilante" has since been used to describe actions by groups or individuals who take the law into their own hands or punish real or perceived wrongdoings outside the legal system. Dissatisfaction with law enforcement or the legal process remains the principle motive. Typically that dissatisfaction is shared by other individuals who see vigilante actions as heroic. Among the many cases receiving media coverage in the late twentieth century was that of Bernard Goetz. His 1984 shooting of four black youths, who he believed were attempting to rob him in a New York City subway car, gained Goetz national celebrity status. Admirers provided bail when he was arrested and letters of support from victims of similar crimes appeared in the press. In the early 1990s attention focused on a vigilante incident dating back to 1923, when a large group of white attackers torched the black-populated town of Rosewood, Fla. The invasion was caused by a questionable accusation that a black man had assaulted a white woman in nearby Sumner and that the assailant was a Rosewood resident. When he could not be found, a group of Sumner men took it upon themselves to resolve the matter. In May 1994 the state of Florida paid $2 million to nine of the survivors, the first time in U.S. history that a state awarded damages to citizens for failing to properly defend them. Additional compensation was set aside for scholarships for the descendants of residents. Both the Goetz and Rosewood cases illustrate vigilantism in its modern meaning—unlawful retribution by private citizens.

ROBERT M. GUTH

VIOLENCE, DOMESTIC. *See* Domestic Violence.

VIOLENCE AGAINST WOMEN BILL was introduced in Congress in January 1991 by Senator Joseph Biden of Delaware. Biden, chairperson of the Senate Judiciary Committee, and the cosponsors were motivated by the high incidence of assaults, aggravated assaults, murders, and rapes committed against women. In 1991 an estimated 4 million women were victims of domestic violence, with 20 percent of all assaults that were reported to the police occurring in the home. The bill was made part of the Violent Crime Control and Law Enforcement Act and was signed into law on Sept. 13, 1994, by President Bill Clinton. The act authorized $1.6 billion to be spent over six years on the creation of rape crisis centers and battered women's shelters and authorized additional local police, prosecutors, victim advocates, and a domestic violence hotline; funds were also made available to train judges who hear domestic violence cases. Provisions of the act expanded rape shield laws, created offenses for interstate spousal abuse, and allow women who are victims of gender-based crimes to sue those responsible in federal court. Under the latter section of the act victims have to prove the crime was not random and was motivated by animus toward their gender, a finding similar to that required to prove racially motivated crimes. Por-

tions of the act not originally part of the Violence Against Women Bill include restrictions on gun purchases for persons guilty of domestic abuse; safeguards to protect the confidentiality of information kept by state motor vehicle bureaus, with the aim of preventing stalkers and other criminals from finding their victims; and increased penalties for hate crimes in which the victim is targeted on the basis of race, gender, religion, or sexual orientation. An eleventh hour Republican effort to remove domestic violence provisions from the act, on the grounds that funding them constituted government waste, was defeated narrowly in the House of Representatives and by a cloture vote ending a filibuster in the Senate.

[Congressional Caucus for Women's Issues, *Update* (September-October, 1994); U.S. Senate, Majority Staff of the Committee on the Judiciary, *Violence Against Women: A Week in the Life of America* (Washington, D.C., 1992).]

IRWIN N. GERTZOG

See also **SUPP:** Domestic Violence; Women's Rights.

VIRGINIA. Beginning in the 1960s the state of Virginia increasingly reflected national patterns in society and politics. Its black population ended a long relative decline and held at just under 19 percent in the censuses of 1970, 1980, and 1990. Meanwhile, residents of Asian ancestry increased from a negligible number at the time of the 1965 Immigration Act to a figure approaching 4 percent of all Virginia residents by the 1990s. The state's total population grew from 4,648,494 in 1970 to 5,346,818 in 1980 (a 15 percent increase) and to 6,187,358 in 1990 (a 16 percent increase). Net in-migration accounted for fully half the growth in each decade, and by 1990 only 54 percent of all residents were Virginia natives. Such developments illustrated significant changes in Virginia's recent history, as the state had been a large exporter of people throughout the nineteenth century and well into the twentieth. Virginians lived increasingly in urban or suburban areas. The city of Virginia Beach offers one measure; by 1990 it had grown to a population of 393,069, the nation's thirty-seventh largest. The core cities of Norfolk, the state's port city and adjacent to Virginia Beach, and Richmond, the state capital, each lost between 15 and 20 percent of their population between 1970 and 1990. Nonetheless the urbanization of northern and eastern Virginia proceeded rapidly. The counties bordering Richmond—Henrico and Chesterfield—displayed massive growth. Some largely rural counties, such as Prince William and Loudoun, found themselves absorbed into metropolitan Washington, D.C. Others, mostly in the southern and western parts of the state, lost population as rural residents moved to urban areas.

Political changes dating from the 1960s continued over the ensuing decades. In 1964 the Twenty-fourth Amendment ended the poll tax as a condition of voting in federal elections, and in a 1966 case that arose in Virginia the U.S. Supreme Court struck down the tax in state elections as well. The Supreme Court rendered decisions that forced reapportionment in elections to Congress and to the Virginia state legislature. These changes led to the defeat of long-term incumbents, such as U.S. Senator A. Willis Robertson and U.S. Representative Howard W. Smith. The newly reapportioned legislature enacted a sales tax in 1966, and in 1969 a Republican, A. Linwood Holton, won the governorship, breaking the stranglehold of rural white Democrats on Virginia politics. Republicans won again in 1973 with former Democrat Mills E. Godwin, Jr., and in 1977 with John N. Dalton, but Charles S. Robb retrieved the state executive office for the Democrats in 1981. Gerald L. Baliles and L. Douglas Wilder held it for the Democrats in 1985 and 1989, but the Republican candidate, George F. Allen, won in 1993. In legislative races Republicans and Democrats faced each other as equals in the 1990s. As late as 1975 the hundred-member Virginia House of Delegates included only seventeen Republicans, but by 1994 the number was forty-seven. Meanwhile, Virginia became a Republican state in presidential elections. As early as 1948, although President Harry S. Truman took the state that year, Virginia Democrats had begun to abandon their party in presidential elections. Black Virginians abandoned the Republican party and embraced the Democrats, but were swamped by the stream of white voters heading in the other direction, who together with many new residents voted Republican. From 1952 through 1992 the Democratic presidential candidates won Virginia's electoral votes only in 1964.

In terms of race and gender, Virginia politics in the 1990s differed greatly from the 1960s. In the late 1960s, for the first time since the 1880s, black candidates won election to the state legislature, and the number of women, most of them white, increased slowly as well. By the 1994 session thirteen of the legislature's 140 members were black and sixteen were women. Meanwhile, after the 1985 elections, Mary Sue Terry began the first of two terms (eight years) as state attorney general. L. Douglas Wilder, after sixteen years in the state senate, was elected lieutenant governor in 1985 and in 1989 became the

first African American elected governor of any state. The declining significance of race in Virginia politics can be seen in the fact that while a majority of white voters pulled the Republican lever, Wilder's victory depended on the support of far more whites than blacks. As for the judiciary, in 1983 John Charles Thomas became the first black justice of the Virginia Supreme Court, and in 1988 Elizabeth B. Lacy became the first female justice. In 1986 James Randolph Spencer became Virginia's first black federal judge, and in 1989 Rebecca Beach Smith became the first woman appointed to such a position. After the 1992 elections Virginia's congressional delegation, like the state legislature, was no longer all white and all male. Robert C. Scott became only the second African American to win a seat from the Old Dominion, 104 years after John Mercer Langston's election in 1888, and Leslie L. Byrne became the first woman ever elected to Congress from Virginia, although Byrne lost her bid for reelection in 1994.

Major changes occurred in higher education in Virginia in the last decades of the twentieth century. Such changes were related to public finance, numbers of students, the racial desegregation that came to Virginia in the 1950s and 1960s, and expansion of opportunities for women. The 1966 legislature inaugurated a statewide system of community colleges. By the 1990s three universities—Virginia Polytechnic Institute and State University, Virginia Commonwealth University, and George Mason University—each enrolled more than 20,000 students, as did Northern Virginia Community College. The University of Virginia was not far behind. Before the 1950s only one public institution of higher education in Virginia (now known as Virginia State University) admitted black students; by the 1990s blacks attended every school, although the numbers were still well below the African-American percentage of Virginia residents. Women were first admitted to the University of Virginia as undergraduates only in 1970; by the 1990s men and women attended in almost equal numbers. Although women had begun attending law school there in 1920, they comprised 10 percent of the total number of law students only after congressional enactment of Title IX in 1972. By the 1990s women comprised one-third of each graduating class. In the 1990s the state reversed a quarter-century-long trend and trimmed its spending on higher education; those budget cuts drove up tuition costs.

Virginia's economy made major shifts between the 1970s and the 1990s. The reduction of the U.S. military in the 1990s meant the loss of thousands of military-related jobs, from the Radford Arsenal to the Newport News Shipbuilding and Drydock Company. Agriculture, although still a large part of the economy, continued to decline in relative importance, while tobacco became less important among agricultural commodities. Tourism remained a major industry; Virginia's beaches and mountains as well as its shrines to the colonial era, the American Revolution, and the Civil War—Colonial Williamsburg, the Blue Ridge Parkway, George Washington's Mount Vernon—were among the leading attractions. Manufacturing—electronics and transportation equipment, textiles and apparel, paper and printing—increased only 16 percent and dropped from first to fourth in total employment between 1970 and 1990. Services rocketed from fourth to first; jobs in trade climbed from third to second; employment in government slipped from second place to third. In the same twenty-year period, the per capita income of Virginians rose from 94 percent to 105 percent of the national average.

In the 1990s Virginia had a growing population that was increasingly urban, a diverse economy, and a two-party political system. Virginians as different as tennis player Arthur Ashe and evangelist Jerry Falwell had an effect on people far from Old Dominion. Students from foreign countries came to Virginia for college and university educations, foreign investment in Virginia mounted, and Virginia governors went overseas in quest of export markets for the state's products.

[Frank B. Atkinson, *The Dynamic Dominion: Realignment and the Rise of Virginia's Republican Party Since 1945* (Fairfax, Va., 1992); Thomas C. Parramore, Peter C. Stewart, and Tommy L. Bogger, *Norfolk: The First Four Centuries* (Charlottesville, 1994); Marie Tyler-McGraw, *At the Falls: Virginia and Its People* (Chapel Hill, N.C., 1994); Peter Wallenstein, "'These New and Strange Beings': Women in the Legal Profession in Virginia, 1890–1990," *Virginia Magazine of History and Biography* 101 (April 1993).]

PETER WALLENSTEIN

See also **SUPP:** Virginia Beach.

VIRGINIA BEACH, a resort city of hotels, casinos, and beaches in Princess Anne County, Va., and located on Chesapeake Bay. First developed in 1880, Virginia Beach was incorporated as a town in 1906 and became an independent city in 1952. During and after World War II the Hampton Roads region, with its naval and shipbuilding facilities, ballooned in employment and population, but the number of residents of Virginia Beach had reached only 8,091 in 1960. In 1959 the city of Norfolk annexed a large portion of Princess Anne County, and to thwart further annexation political leaders and residents of Virginia Beach and what remained of the county initiated a merger, ratified by referendum in 1962 and approved by the Virginia legislature the same year. The new city of Virginia Beach became a reality on Jan. 1, 1963. With an area of 256 square miles—more than four times that of Norfolk or Richmond, the cities with the largest populations in the state—Virginia Beach had ample room to grow. By 1970 it ranked third among Virginia cities with 172,106 residents. Its population grew by 52 percent in the 1970s and another 50 percent in the 1980s. By 1990, with 393,069 residents, it had become Virginia's most populous city and the thirty-seventh largest in the nation. By 1990 the city's population was 80 percent white, 14 percent black, and 4 percent Asian. Virginia Beach borders Norfolk International Airport and it contains First Landing State Park. Military installations in the city include the Oceana Naval Air Station, and facilities for higher education include the Virginia Beach campus of Tidewater Community College.

[Stephen S. Manfield, *Princess Anne County and Virginia Beach: A Pictorial History* (Norfolk, 1989); Thomas C. Parramore, Peter C. Stewart, and Tommy L. Bogger, *Norfolk: The First Four Centuries* (Charlottesville, 1994).]

PETER WALLENSTEIN

See also **SUPP:** Virginia.

VIRGIN ISLANDS. By the 1970s economic and social change was under way in the U.S. Virgin Islands—Saint Thomas, Saint Croix, and Saint John. The once-dominant sugar industry ceased production in 1966, and within a few years virtually all other agriculture had disappeared, except for a few small-scale fruit and vegetable farms on Saint Croix. Agriculture and commercial fishing gave way to tourism, especially on Saint Thomas and Saint John, and to petrochemical and aluminum production on Saint Croix. Displaced native farmers and fishers resented the influx of migrants from the U.S. mainland, Puerto Rico, and other Caribbean islands who came to take the new industrial and tourist-related jobs. These arrivals helped swell the population from 63,000 in 1970 to 102,000 in 1990. High-living tourists, mostly white, incurred the wrath of natives influenced by the contemporary U.S. and Caribbean black power movement. A wave of violent crimes against tourists broke out during the administration (1971–1975) of the first elected governor of the U.S. Virgin Islands, Republican Melvin H. Evans, a native black physician. Eight persons, seven of them white, were murdered at Fountain Valley Golf Club on Saint Croix in September 1972, a crime for which five members of the Nation of Islam were convicted. More than a dozen other whites died during the next two years in apparently racially motivated crimes on Saint Croix. The situation was less tense on Saint Thomas and Saint John, but all the islands suffered drastic reductions in tourist revenues due to publicity about the crimes.

Governor Evans lost his reelection bid in 1974 and was succeeded by Cyril E. King of the populist Independent Citizens Movement (ICM). The new legislature, however, was composed of nine Democrats, five ICM members, and one Republican, which set the pattern for the next dozen years, with the ICM controlling the governorship, the Democrats dominating the legislature, and the Republicans marginalized. Attempts to restructure the territorial government failed as island voters rejected four proposed constitutions during the 1970s and 1980s, leaving the 1954 Organic Act in force. The propensity of territorial legislators to vote themselves hefty salary increases made voters leery of constitutional changes that would create a local bureaucracy to replace federal civil servants in the administration of the islands. Democrat Alexander A. Farrelly was elected governor in 1986 and soon launched a study of the territory's public administration needs, hiring Marion S. Barry, Jr., mayor of Washington, D.C., as a consultant. In 1989 it was revealed that $260,000 was squandered on lavish living by Washington city employees sent to advise Farrelly on personnel policy. Despite the scandal, the governor was reelected for another four-year term in 1990.

As the crime wave subsided, the tourist industry revived, although racial tensions remained beneath the surface and gave rise to sporadic outbreaks of violence throughout the 1980s, especially on Saint Croix. In 1989 Hurricane Hugo devastated that island. Saint Thomas and Saint John largely escaped the effects of the hurricane, and their sheltered waters continued to provide a prime playground for visiting yachts. In the early 1990s large cruise ships annually disembarked more than 1 million visitors at Saint Thomas, and increasing numbers of ecotourists were attracted to the surrounding coral reefs and the national park that covers two-thirds of the adjacent island of Saint John. In 1995 Hurricane Marilyn swept through the islands, causing damage amounting to more than $800 million and leaving more than half the structures on Saint Thomas destroyed or seriously damaged.

[Isaac Dookhan, *A History of the Virgin Islands of the United States* (Kingston, Jamaica, 1994); Earle B. Ottley, *Trials and Triumphs: The Long Road to Middle Class Society in the U.S. Virgin Islands* (Saint Thomas, 1982); Ralph M. Paiewonsky and Isaac Dookhan, *Memoirs of a Governor: A Man of the People* (New York, 1990).]

NEILL MACAULAY

VIROLOGY. *See* **Bacteriology and Virology.**

VIRTUAL REALITY refers to computer-generated, three-dimensional simulations that allow a participant to experience and interact with a setting or situation. In the most advanced forms of virtual reality, a participant wears a large headset that incorporates high-resolution video displays and audio speakers. The headphones provide the participant with the visual and auditory sensations of being immersed in the simulation. The participant also wears a special glove or body suit studded with sensors that monitor all movements by the participant. Data from the sensors are fed back into the computer, which modifies the simulation accordingly. For example, a simulation might include the image of an object in front of the participant. If the participant moves toward the object, the virtual reality system will change the participant's apparent angle of viewing the object. If the participant moves a hand to lift the object, the display is revised accordingly. In a more theoretical sense, virtual reality systems allow a participant to experience, navigate through, and manipulate cyberspace, a hypothetical area filled with imaginary structures and objects. The term "cyberspace" is often regarded as a synonym for virtual reality; the writer William Gibson first used it in his 1984 novel *Neuromancer*. By the mid-1990s virtual reality technology was limited to simulating the senses of sight and hearing. Virtual reality systems provided, for example, little or no sensation of weight when the participant is supposed to be carrying an object.

Computers have often been used to produce simulations, such as those used to train airline pilots. The advent of inexpensive but powerful computers, combined with the development of sophisticated computer graphics techniques, has enabled virtual reality systems to operate more quickly and to generate more detailed simulations, adding to the reality of the experience. A major use for virtual reality technology is likely to be entertainment; it can provide consumers with a choice of exotic, surreal, or breathtaking experiences without the need to take any physical risk. Virtual reality technology also can be employed for more serious ends. Astronauts at the National

Aeronautics and Space Administration used virtual reality devices as part of their training for the 1993 space shuttle flight, during which they repaired the flawed Hubble Space Telescope. Experts at the Department of Energy use a virtual reality version of a nuclear weapon in a shipping container to train emergency workers to handle trucking accidents involving such weapons. Another application of virtual reality technology is telepresence, or giving the participant a sensation of being in a distant location. Telepresence systems allow a physician in a hospital to perform emergency surgery on a soldier by remote control while the soldier is still on the battlefield, rather than having to wait for the soldier to be transported to the hospital. Telepresence can also be used to operate robotic rovers on the moon or on Mars for scientific purposes or for profit-making entertainment ventures.

[Michael Heim, *The Metaphysics of Virtual Reality* (New York, 1993); Howard Rheingold, *Virtual Reality* (New York, 1991).]

VINCENT KIERNAN

VOICE OF AMERICA (VOA) is a multilingual radio broadcasting service begun in 1942 and administered since 1953 by the United States Information Agency (USIA), known from 1978 to 1982 as the International Communications Agency. The agency is an organization responsible for the dissemination of U.S. policy and information to foreign countries. In administering the VOA, the director of the USIA reports to the secretary of state and the president of the United States. Under its congressionally mandated charter, the VOA seeks to broadcast reliable news stories, present a balanced view of U.S. culture, and report on U.S. policy. Programming is intended for non-U.S. audiences, and under provisions of the Smith-Mundt Act (1948) and a clarifying amendment in 1972 programs may not be broadcast within the United States without congressional approval. VOA broadcasts have been blocked by communications services in some countries, which have criticized its programming as anticommunist propaganda, but the agency has continued to receive support from Congress and U.S. presidents into the early post–cold war years. Voice of America continued its work in the 1990s with programs ranging from the promotion of democracy to the war on drugs. Its programs reach an estimated 130 million people. In 1983 VOA established the International Broadcast Training Center in Washington to train broadcasters from developing countries and to demonstrate the value of a free press. In

1985 VOA founded Radio Marti for broadcasting to Cuba, and in 1990 it expanded efforts to deliver uncensored news to that nation with the establishment of TV Marti. In 1987 VOA began programming aimed at drug addiction and narcotics trafficking.

[Holly Cowan Shulman, *The Voice of America: Propaganda and Democracy, 1941–1945* (Madison, Wis., 1990); Thomas C. Sorensen, *The Word War: The Story of American Propaganda* (New York, 1968).]

KERRY A. BATCHELDER

VOLCANOES are mountains with a central tube from which molten material from deep within the earth can spew under the appropriate conditions. Volcanoes have existed for geologic eons but many are no longer active. The number of volcanoes worldwide in the mid-1990s viewed by earth scientists as active, that is, that could possibly erupt, was about 500. Volcanoes are usually located at the junction of the earth's lithospheric plates. In the United States, most active volcanoes are located in the state of Hawaii, which consists of a group of islands formed by earlier volcanic eruptions, or in Alaska; a relatively inactive zone occurs on the West Coast of the continental United States. The two principal volcanoes in the United States are Mauna Loa and Kilauea on Hawaii Island in the Hawaiian island chain. Mauna Loa is the world's largest volcano. Its most recent eruptions occurred in 1975 and 1984. Kilauea is in almost continuous eruption, notable events occurring in 1977, 1984, 1986, and 1990. Alaskan eruptions occurred in 1986, involving an unnamed volcano on Augustine Island in Cook Inlet, 180 miles southwest of Anchorage; in 1989, when Mount Redoubt, along Cook Inlet 115 miles southwest of Anchorage, erupted; and in 1992, when Mount Spurr erupted. Although not in the United States, Mount Pinatubo in the Philippines, which erupted in 1991, had a significant cooling effect on U.S. climate for several years as a result of the ash projected into the stratosphere. Eruptions in the lower forty-eight states are rare but certainly not unknown. The eruption of Mount Saint Helens in Washington State in 1980 was widely publicized. Despite dire predictions, and the fact that a minor eruption occurred in 1990, the area surrounding Mount Saint Helens has largely recovered from the effects of the 1980 eruption. Two volcanic observatories exist in the United States. One was established on Kilauea in 1912, the second oldest in the world. (The oldest is in Italy on Vesuvius.) Following the eruption of Mount Saint Helens in 1980, an observatory was established there.

[Robert W. Decker, *Mountains of Fire: The Nature of Volcanoes* (New York, 1991); Alwyn Scarth, *Volcanoes* (College Station, Tex., 1994).]

NANCY M. GORDON

See also **SUPP:** Alaska; Hawaii; Mount Saint Helens.

VOLUNTEER ARMY. Throughout most of its history, the United States has relied on volunteers to fill the ranks of its military forces, resorting to conscription only for brief periods in times of great peril. The cold war marked a departure from that tradition. Beginning in 1948 the drafting of young males—a system known as Selective Service—became the preferred means of sustaining the military establishment. By the late 1960s, however, perceived inequities in the draft and opposition to the Vietnam War had undermined the legitimacy of the Selective Service system. To undercut the antiwar movement, President Richard M. Nixon in 1972 announced that he would abolish the draft. Although Selective Service legislation remained on the books and eighteen-year-old U.S. males continued to register for the draft, monthly draft calls were reduced to zero. The military establishment created by this shift in policy was known as the All-Volunteer Force or the Volunteer Army. Throughout the 1970s efforts to attract recruits in the quantity and quality required achieved only mixed success, and these difficulties prompted critics to question the feasibility of relying exclusively on volunteers. In the 1980s, however, recruiting methods and the quality of recruits improved. Several factors contributed to that turnaround: improved pay and benefits; skillful marketing of the armed forces; expanded career opportunities for women; and the fading memory of Vietnam. By the late 1980s and early 1990s, a string of U.S. military successes—most notably in the Gulf War of 1991—seemed to vindicate Nixon's decision to revert to the volunteer tradition.

[William Bowman et al., *The All-Volunteer Force After a Decade* (New York, 1986); John Whiteclay Chambers, *To Raise an Army* (New York, 1987); Richard Halloran, *Serving America: Prospects for the Volunteer Force* (New York, 1988).]

ANDREW J. BACEVICH

See also **SUPP:** Draft.

VOLUNTEERISM, broadly defined as socially beneficiary activities by individuals and groups that are noncompulsory and not profit oriented, has become more significant since the 1970s, with increasing numbers of people contributing time and expertise to community organizations, mutual aid societies, and social welfare programs. As a national phenomenon volunteerism dates back to World War I, when Herbert Hoover and others encouraged individuals and especially businesses to cooperate in such wartime activities as food rationing and price controls. When volunteerism failed during the Great Depression its reputation diminished, only to be temporarily rescued during World War II. In addition to being associated with national cooperation efforts, volunteerism since the nineteenth century has denoted the unpaid philanthropic, social service, and political work of American women. The recession of the early 1970s and the subsequent ebbs and flows of the national economy led to an increasing reliance on technology, which resulted in a greater need for more highly trained workers. Unemployment plagued the economy, straining public assistance and social service programs. When the great numbers of children born in the decade following World War II entered the workforce in the 1970s, jobs were often unavailable for them. The jobs that were available often required training that traditional educational institutions could not provide.

Volunteerism became one solution to these many social challenges. A few government programs supporting volunteer activity had been created in the 1960s, most notably the Peace Corps, Volunteers in Service to America (VISTA), the Foster Grandparents Program, and the Retired Senior Volunteer Program (RSVP). These programs set the stage for President Richard M. Nixon to inaugurate a major national volunteer force. In 1971 a new governmental agency, ACTION, was created to coordinate the existing programs and encourage participation on a national level. At the same time a nongovernment agency, the National Center for Voluntary Action, was created by Congress to centralize and promote volunteerism throughout the country. Older workers, who were increasingly encouraged to make way for younger employees by taking early retirement, were targeted as an important volunteer pool for community-based and public-sector social programs. Volunteerism by the young was emphasized as a solution to the need for both service to the community and specialized training not provided by the educational system. Since the 1970s "service learning" components have been incorporated into elementary, high school, and college curricula.

Aimed at decentralizing government welfare functions, the federalist policies of Presidents Ronald Reagan and George Bush in the 1980s continued the trend of the previous decade. Both administrations heralded community volunteerism as the ideal solution to social problems, and Reagan and Bush believed that cuts in government social services would stimulate voluntary community service. The leaders of many volunteer organizations, however, stated that voluntary efforts could not compensate for federal cuts. Volunteerism was also a significant concern of President Bill Clinton, who emphasized community service, the integration of education with labor needs, and grass-roots organizing against crime and other social problems. In 1993 Congress passed President Clinton's plan allowing students to repay federal college loans through community service. In the 1990s volunteer labor became an entrenched sector of the economy wherein volunteers engaged in "co-production" along with traditional public- and private-sector providers.

[Susan J. Ellis and Katherine H. Noyes, *By the People: A History of American Volunteers* (San Francisco, 1990); Jon Van Til, *Mapping the Third Sector: Voluntarism in a Changing Social Economy* (New York, 1988).]

JULIET NIEHAUS

See also **DAH:** ACTION; **SUPP:** Peace Corps.

W–Z

WACO SIEGE (1993). The deaths of four federal agents and seventy-eight members of the Branch Davidian religious group during a fifty-one-day siege of their commune headquarters outside Waco, Texas, provoked widespread controversy over the use of force in dealing with dissident sects. A botched and bloody attempt on Feb. 28, 1993, to arrest the group's leader, David Koresh, on a weapons charge led to stalemate until U.S. Attorney General Janet Reno ordered the use of force on Apr. 19 to end the standoff. Fire engulfed "Ranch Apocalypse," killing seventy-two, including Koresh and seventeen children. Although some surviving members of the sect were tried for manslaughter and found not guilty, they were convicted of lesser charges and received extremely harsh sentences.

[Martin King and Marc Breault, *Preacher of Death: The Shocking Inside Story of David Koresh and the Waco Siege* (New York, 1993); Dick J. Reavis, *The Ashes of Waco: An Investigation* (New York, 1996); James D. Tabor and Eugene V. Gallagher, *Why Waco?: Cults and the Battle for Religious Freedom in America* (Berkeley, Calif., 1996).]

BRUCE J. EVENSON

WAGES AND SALARIES. From the end of World War II to 1973, average wage and salary earnings in the United States, adjusted for inflation, more than doubled for men working in full-time, year-round employment, from $15,257 to $30,578 (in 1987 constant dollars). This favorable situation reflected U.S. dominance in global markets and a large base of high-wage manufacturing jobs. The pattern in wages and salaries since 1973 has been much slower growth and significant declines for certain groups within the population. Young males (ages 25–34) with a high school education or less have seen the greatest drop in earnings, as many manufacturing jobs disappeared because of foreign competition and greater productivity. In 1973, 64 percent of such persons earned annual incomes of $20,000 or more (1987 dollars); by 1986 the percentage was down to 40 percent. Before the 1980s the difference in earnings between college-educated and non–college-educated persons had been narrowing, as the first wave of the baby-boom generation born after World War II flooded into higher education and then the job market. Since 1980, however, the gap has steadily widened. Men with at least a four-year degree represented the only group in manufacturing to see an increase in real earnings between 1973 and 1986. Productivity gains were much slower to translate into job reductions in the service sector of the economy.

For women the change in wage and salary patterns was different. The increasing proportion of married women working full-time caused average female earnings to rise at a faster rate than male earnings since 1973. The shift from manufacturing to service-sector employment was of relatively greater advantage to women. Although they continued to earn less than men, the difference was shrinking, from a ratio of women's to men's earnings of 57 percent in 1973 to 85 percent in 1993. While educational level became a more powerful determinant of income level, even women with five years of college education earned only 69 percent of what was earned by men with the same amount of schooling. Another group whose salaries became the object of much public attention in the 1980s was that of corporate business executives. Their average incomes rose dramatically. In 1980 the ratio of a chief executive officer's (CEO) salary to that of a factory worker was 42:1. By 1991 this ratio had risen to 104:1, far higher than in other industrial countries. The average CEO earned more than $1 million in salary plus other forms of compensation.

For some commentators the image of a "vanishing middle class" emerged out of this economic data. The most rapidly growing segments of the population were families making less than $20,000 or more than $50,000 a year. While per capita income continued to increase after 1973, this was largely because of more women entering the labor force and a lower birth rate, trends expected to level off and thus have less impact on income levels. Stagnation of wages and salaries was identified as a key factor behind public resistance to higher taxes, the large federal budget deficit, and low rates of personal savings. Proposed solutions ranged from immigration restriction to improved education and job training.

[Frank Levy and Richard Michel, *The Economic Future of American Families: Income and Wealth Trends* (Washington, D.C., 1991); Lawrence Mishel and Jared Bernstein, *The State of Working America, 1994–1995* (Armonk, N.Y., 1994).]

JOHN B. WEAVER

See also **SUPP:** Poverty; Unemployment.

WALL STREET. No other street or location in the United States evokes the idea of money, financial power, and capitalism as does Wall Street, the financial district of capitalism, and that was never more true than during the 1980s and early 1990s, when a series of "bull" markets sent stock and bond prices on an upward spiral, doubling or tripling prices and encouraging Americans to invest. Interestingly, however, by this time New York City's Wall Street no longer was the epicenter of the nation's finance; there were also financial markets in London, Frankfurt, Tokyo, and Sidney. Smaller exchanges appeared in Western and Eastern Europe and in Latin America, all attracting money away from Wall Street. Computers, fax machines, and electronic wire transfers made location largely irrelevant. In minutes, trades and deals could be executed and money moved anywhere. Because of world differences in time, it also became possible to trade around the clock. A sign that every street in the world was becoming a competitor to Wall Street was the loss of occupants in prestigious buildings on "the street"; office vacancies were said

to amount to eight empty buildings as large as the Empire State Building.

All the while there were new kinds of investors, new products, and new rules. Perhaps the greatest factor in change was the tremendous influx and influence of institutional money in all its configurations—public and private pension funds, corporate treasuries, and mutual funds. The mutual funds took on strength during bull markets, profoundly changing investing while enriching millions of middle-class Americans who previously had shied away from taking market risks. Everything seemed to be changing. Consider what happened with mutual funds in the 1980s and early 1990s. First offered in Boston in 1924, such investments initially had attracted little investor interest because growth was hampered by a legality—the "prudent man" rule obligated investment managers to preserve capital and avoid risks. It was a play-it-safe approach in which investing was done with an eye to not losing money rather than to achieving growth. Quantitative economic research developed ideas about managing portfolios of risk. Investments could be grouped and managed so that losses in one investment likely would be offset by gains in others. This key development—assisted by the growing ability to number-crunch data—liberated money managers. Mutual funds offered a convenient way for middle-income investors to obtain part of the riches being generated in financial markets at home and abroad in emerging markets. For investments of as little as $50 or $100, investors could buy into diversified portfolios. As stocks soared, mutual funds swelled, with millions of Americans moving money out of passbook savings and certificates of deposits. More money meant more funds. In 1980 there were roughly 500 mutual funds, with a total asset value of $135 billion. By 1995 there were about 5,300 mutual funds with $2.2 trillion in assets. One-third of U.S. households owned part of at least one fund.

The funds of the Boston-based Fidelity Investments firm illustrates the vast growth of mutual funds. Founded in 1946, the firm grew into a financial powerhouse. By 1994 it managed assets of nearly $300 billion, making it comparable to some of the largest banks. Its Magellan Fund, managed by Peter Lynch, generated double-digit returns and grew into the nation's largest mutual fund. Lynch himself became a star, writing best-selling books on investing, making television appearances, and finding his opinions regularly quoted by financial writers. It was, of course, difficult for fund managers to outperform the market. Lynch's successes, as well as the even greater investing success of Warren Buffett, an Omaha investor who ran Berkshire Hathaway, called into question the prevailing academic theory about Wall Street, called the efficient market theory (EMT), which claimed that Lynch and Buffett's methods of examining company performance and prospects in hopes of finding an undervalued stock were worthless. EMT maintained that a stock could neither be overpriced nor underpriced; each day the market correctly set a stock's price because the price reflected all the information about a company known that day. A popular book by Burton Malkiel, *A Random Walk Down Wall Street*, introduced EMT to the general public in the early 1970s.

EMT became the accepted gospel as classic market economics regained exalted status in political, academic, social, and economic circles, but holes in EMT began to pop open. The *Wall Street Journal* ran a six-month contest comparing the performance of four stocks selected by investment professionals to four stocks—expected to represent EMT—selected by throwing darts at a stock table pinned to a dart board. The experts, however, beat the dart board, albeit by a narrow margin. Meanwhile, Lynch, Buffett, and other investment managers, such as John Neff and John Templeton, punched more holes in the EMT by repeatedly outperforming the market by large margins. Nonprofessionals also gave EMT fits. A group of sixteen Illinois women—ages forty-one to eighty-seven and known as the Beardstown Ladies—created an investment strategy that generated an annual return of 23 percent between 1983 and 1994, outperforming the Standard & Poor's 500 index for the same period.

The flow of money into mutual funds helped sustain a strong bull market that started in October 1990 and by spring 1995 had become the third longest such market in Wall Street history. It was exceeded only by the six-year bull market from 1924 to 1929 and the five-year market from August 1982 to August 1987. The market of the early 1990s pushed the Dow Jones Industrial Average (DJIA) ever upward. Quoted in points instead of dollars, the index reflects the closing stock prices of thirty widely held companies. The companies represented one-fifth of the New York Stock Exchange's total value. In November 1972 the Dow Jones broke the 1,000-point barrier, although it collapsed during the recession associated with the oil embargo imposed by the Organization of Petroleum Exporting Countries. It was not until 1987 that the DJIA broke 2,000. The 3,000 barrier was broken in 1991 and the 4,000 and 5,000 barriers in 1995.

Wall Street became populated by aggressive, take-no-prisoners business school graduates attracted by the prospect of getting rich. Much money was made in corporate takeovers in which bankers, accountants, attorneys, and management made big fees and substantial bonuses. Buffett regularly criticized chief executives who "possess an abundance of animal spirits and ego" that send them hunting for deals. "When such a CEO is encouraged by his advisers to make deals," Buffett said, "he responds much as would a teenage boy who is encouraged by his father to have a normal sex life." He added: "It's not a push he needs." Often the deals left companies awash with debt, forcing them to divest holdings, fire employees, or plunge into bankruptcy to protect themselves from creditors. James Grant, writer of an influential New York investment newsletter, noted at the time (like Buffett employing a sexual metaphor) that "the 1980s are to debt what the 1960s were to sex."

Unfortunately, the market craze had a darker side. The get-rich mentality of the 1980s led some Wall Streeters to engage in criminal practices such as insider trading. The scandals of the decade landed some of the nation's best-known financiers in jail, including Michael Milken, who had pioneered the use of junk bonds in corporate takeovers, and Ivan Boesky, who specialized in securities arbitrage. Prosecutors snared a *Wall Street Journal* reporter who was trading stocks based on information gathered from a broker who was a source for stories. The scandals provided grist for a movie, *Wall Street* (1987), directed by Oliver Stone, in which a character similar to Milken and Boesky proclaimed that "greed is good."

The stock market's upward climb was not without fast and dangerous falls. One of those was the Oct. 19, 1987, market crash, known as Black Monday. That day the exchanges almost broke under the trading volumes. The DJIA plunged a record 508 points—a 22.6 percent decline. It was the largest single-day decline in percentage terms in stock market history. The crash, which unregulated computer-directed sell orders helped accelerate, left investors wary, but they surprised observers of the market, who expected smaller investors to cash out. Instead, money was shifted into less aggressive stock investments, where the cash stayed while investors waited for the market to improve. Eventually the markets shrugged off the losses. Volume grew from 26.2 billion shares in 1982 to 103.4 billion shares in 1992. Much trading shifted from the New York Stock Exchange (NYSE) to the National Association of Securities Dealers Automated Quotations (NASDAQ). In 1983 the NYSE had 55 percent of the 39.5 billion shares traded on the U.S. exchanges, with NASDAQ responsible for 40 percent and the American Stock Exchange for 5 percent. By 1992 NASDAQ's share percentage had increased to nearly half. The tradition-bound NYSE found itself challenged by NASDAQ, which advertised itself as "the market for the next hundred years." Advertisements featured NASDAQ's stellar stocks, many of them high-technology companies that went public during the 1970s and 1980s, including Microsoft, the software corporation; Apple Computer, maker of the Macintosh computer; and Intel, whose microprocessors powered personal computers.

Throughout these years of change there was a dropping away of government and exchange rules, known as deregulation. The abolition of rules was international. In 1973 a nearly forty-year period of fixed rates for currency exchanges under the Bretton Woods Agreement of 1944 ended when major Western governments allowed currencies to be traded against each other. Supply and demand would determine the value of each currency. Freely traded currencies opened up a whole new arena for markets in which to speculate or protect against changes in currency values. Trading currencies—the U.S. dollar, Japanese yen, German mark, French franc, English pound—linked what previously were largely separate and isolated financial markets across the world. A second and this time internal U.S. deregulation occurred in 1975, when Congress forced the New York Stock Exchange to end its 183-year-old practice of fixed brokerage commissions, a reform that the Securities and Exchange Commission and others both inside and outside the exchange had pushed for years. Announced on May 1, the decision was dubbed Mayday—the international distress-call signal. For some brokerages it was just that, but others like the new brokerage house of Charles Schwab thrived. Schwab established a brokerage that offered no financial advice, merely trades at rock-bottom prices. Interestingly, the first office opened in San Francisco, not on Wall Street.

A landmark in U.S. financial deregulation was the elimination in the early 1980s of Regulation Q, established by the Federal Reserve in 1933, which had limited the interest rates banks could pay on deposits. In 1966 the regulation had been extended to savings and loans. With its termination in 1982, banks and thrifts found they had to pay higher interest to attract depositors. Savers woke up to rates, looking harder at where they deposited money. Banks and thrifts had to compete for business—paying more for deposits and earning less.

The 1980s and early 1990s saw a constant expansion of new investments, and in the early 1990s a novelty known as derivatives began to raise questions. It was not easy to understand, even for professionals. In 1994 and 1995 professionals who invested heavily in derivatives, investment instruments tied to interest rates, incurred large losses when rates rose. Wealthy Orange County in southern California filed for protection from bankruptcy in 1994 because of $1.3 billion in losses in its investment in derivatives. A twenty-eight-year-old British trader in Singapore lost $1.5 billion in 1994, pushing the 233-year-old House of Baring Bank in London into bankruptcy. Also in 1994 a government bond trader at Kidder Peabody was accused of fabricating $350 million in phony profits to boost his year-end bonus; Kidder claimed it was unaware of what was going on, but was so damaged by the deals that it was sold to another brokerage. Losses resulted in calls for new regulations, although the general experience was that regulations never could keep abreast with innovations. Moreover, Wall Street regulations only encouraged trading in other markets, often those abroad.

[Marshall E. Blume, Jeremy J. Siegel, and Dan Rottenberg, *Revolution on Wall Street: The Rise and Decline of the New York Stock Exchange* (New York, 1993); Paul Gibson, *Bear Trap: Why Wall Street Doesn't Work* (New York, 1993); Michael Lewis, *Liar's Poker: Rising Through the Wreckage on Wall Street* (New York, 1989); Joseph Nocera, *A Piece of the Action: How the Middle Class Joined the Money Class* (New York, 1994).]

THOMAS G. GRESS
BRENT SCHONDELMEYER

See also **SUPP:** Banking and Finance; Black Monday Stock Market Crash; Crime, White-Collar; Deregulation; Financial Exchanges; Financial Services Industry; Junk Bonds.

WARD'S COVE PACKING COMPANY V. ATONIO, 490 U.S. 642 (1989), briefly redefined the nature of the disparate-impact theory of employment discrimination. Since 1971 courts had been following the standards of the *Griggs* v. *Duke Power Company* case for disparate-impact situations. If a plaintiff could show that an employer action harmed a protected group then the employer had the burden of proving that its actions were a business necessity. The *Ward's Cove* case was widely regarded as shifting the burden of proof to employees, making it harder to prove discrimination. The *Ward's Cove* plaintiffs (nonwhite employees) sued the Alaskan salmon canning company on the basis of a disparate impact theory, providing statistical evidence on the disparity in the racial composition of jobholders in skilled and in unskilled cannery work, thereby establishing a prima facie case. The Supreme Court held that the plaintiffs had to do more than show disparate impact; they had to prove the specific relationship between employer practices and a discriminatory outcome. In addition, employers no longer had to prove that their actions were based on business necessity; a less stringent "business justification" standard would suffice as a defense. Critics argued that the reasoning and conclusion in this case, and other recent Supreme Court decisions of the 1980s, eroded civil rights. The outcry stimulated civil rights groups to seek substantive legislative amendments, an effort that ultimately succeeded with the passage of the Civil Rights Act of 1991. That legislation overturned the decision, restoring the *Griggs* standards for disparate-impact suits.

[Vincent J. Apruzzese, "Selected Recent Developments in EEO Law: The Civil Rights Act of 1991, Sexual Harassment, and the Emerging Role of ADR," *Labor Law Journal* 43 (June 1992).]

GILBERT J. GALL

See also **SUPP:** Civil Rights Act of 1991; *Griggs* v. *Duke Power Company.*

WAR MEMORIALS. The Minuteman Statue, Liberty Bell, Tomb of the Unknowns, U.S.S. *Arizona* Memorial, Rough Riders Monument, Holocaust Memorial, and Vietnam War Memorial are all artifacts that reflect the importance of conflicts in American memory. The National Park Service maintains in pristine condition the memorials and sites of the American Revolution and Civil War. The American Battle Monuments Commission preserves the cemeteries, landscapes, and memorial chapels of Americans who died in the two world wars. Smaller conflicts, such as the Korean War and the War of 1812, have fewer shrines. Belated recognition of African Americans and women killed in war suggests that earlier memorials were a reflection of American prejudice as well as sacrifice.

[James M. Mayo, *War Memorials as Political Landscape* (New York, 1988).]

J. GARRY CLIFFORD

See also **SUPP:** Vietnam War Memorial.

WAR POWERS ACT (1973), officially the War Powers Resolution. According to the Constitution, the president as chief executive is also commander-in-chief of U.S. armed forces, but the Constitution explicitly assigns to Congress the authority to declare war. Rather than distinguishing clearly between the authority to initiate war and the authority to wage it, this effort to distribute war-making authority has fostered ambiguity and political controversy. In practice, chief executives have employed the U.S. military without congressional mandate virtually as a matter of routine throughout much of U.S. history, especially during the cold war. The purposes for which presidents have deployed U.S. forces range from a show of force to minor hostilities to large-scale warfare. Although such actions have not been uniformly popular, the existence of a consensus regarding U.S. foreign policy generally muted any complaint about presidents exceeding their constitutional prerogatives.

That consensus collapsed with the Vietnam War. Presidents Lyndon B. Johnson and Richard M. Nixon cited the Tonkin Gulf Resolution of August 1964 as congressional authorization for involvement in Vietnam and escalation of the U.S. role in the war. The conflict proceeded without benefit of any formal declaration of war, becoming increasingly unpopular as it dragged on. Within the federal government, opposition to the war was lodged in the Congress. Critics attributed the costly U.S. involvement in the Vietnam War to a failure to prevent successive presidents from usurping authority that rightly belonged to the legislative branch. This perception provoked calls for a reassertion of congressional prerogatives to check future presidential adventurism. Such thinking culminated in passage of the War Powers Resolution of November 1973, which was passed despite President Nixon's veto. The resolution directed the president to consult with Congress prior to introducing U.S. forces into hostilities; it required the president to report to Congress all nonroutine deployments of military forces within forty-eight hours of their occurrence; and it mandated that forces committed to actual or imminent hostilities by presidential order would be withdrawn within sixty days unless Congress declared war, passed legislation authorizing the use of U.S. forces, or extended the deadline. The sixty-day time limit could be extended to ninety days if the president certified that additional time was needed to complete the withdrawal of U.S. forces.

Heralded as a congressional triumph, the War Powers Resolution proved to be of limited use. Presidents continued to insist that the resolution was an unconstitutional infringement on executive authority. Time and again they circumvented or disregarded its provisions: Gerald Ford in 1975 at the time of the *Mayaguez* operation; Jimmy Carter in 1980 with the Desert One hostage rescue attempt; Ronald Reagan in 1983 with the intervention in Grenada and in 1986 with the air attack on Libya; and George Bush with the 1989 invasion of Panama. Even the U.S. military response to the Iraqi invasion of Kuwait in August 1990 was launched without benefit of congressional mandate. President Bush relied on executive authority in ordering the U.S. buildup of 500,000 troops in the Persian Gulf. When it came to legitimizing his action, the president showed more interest in securing the endorsement of the United Nations Security Council than of the U.S. Congress. It was only when U.S. forces were in place and the decision to use force had effectively been made that Bush consulted Congress, even then acting less for constitutional than for political reasons. On Jan. 12, 1991, Congress narrowly passed a resolution authorizing Bush to do what he clearly intended to do anyway—forcibly eject Iraqi troops from Kuwait. When four days later Operation Desert Storm began, the usefulness of the War Powers Resolution seemed more problematic than ever and the goal of restoring a division of warmaking powers appeared ever more elusive.

ANDREW J. BACEVICH

See also **DAH:** War, Declaration of; War and the Constitution; War Powers of the President; **SUPP:** Grenada Invasion; Gulf War of 1991; Panama Invasion.

WASHINGTON, D.C., or the District of Columbia, came of age in a political sense during the mid-1970s, a time of high expectations. In 1973 Congress approved the Home Rule Act, giving the 700,000 residents the right to elect local officials, including a mayor and city council. Since 1874 congressional committees, often run by avowed southern segregationists, had controlled the nation's capital, to the detriment of the large African-American population. While the Home Rule Act continued Congress's control over the city's budget and laws, the new era ushered in opportunities for local politics and perhaps eventually statehood. By 1976 social changes begun in the late 1950s had created a polarized city. Many middle-class families, white and black, moved to the suburbs of Maryland or Virginia. The remaining white residents—who made up 30 percent of the population—generally were wealthy liberals who lived west of Rock Creek Park in the city's northwest quadrant. Middle-class blacks lived between the park

and the Anacostia River. East of the Anacostia the residents were predominantly poor and black. The races and classes rarely mixed, either in social or business settings. The district's story had become a tale of five cities: the federal city of government and monuments that attracted millions of tourists; the international city of embassies and diplomats; white neighborhoods of lawyers, journalists, and government officials; stable black communities of physicians, clerks, and government officials; and poor black neighborhoods.

Could a new political system, dominated by African Americans, bring the classes and races together and lift the poor? Marion Barry, Jr., promised to do just that in 1978 when he won a slim victory in the crucial, three-way Democratic primary and then scored a landslide in the general election to become the city's second mayor under home rule. He cut a dashing figure as a former civil rights activist, appealing to white liberals and the city's underclass. The city's African-American elite rejected him, but they were a minority. In his first term, he opened the doors of the District Building to the entire city and brought services to people who had been neglected for years. After 1982, when Barry was elected to his second four-year term, the nation's capital experienced a commercial real estate boom that created local millionaires and transformed the central business area. Pennsylvania Avenue—between the Capitol and the White House—was rejuvenated. Investors from Toronto to Tokyo bought high-priced ground in America's capital city. The downtown blossomed with new restaurants, hotels, and nightclubs. The revenues from the building boom, however, were never applied to the city's pressing problems of poverty, a dismal school system, and high infant mortality. Barry instead used the money to create a bloated bureaucracy and wasted millions of dollars. His administration never "took the boards off" public housing, as he had promised. Public housing complexes festered and became breeding grounds for drugs and violence, just as Barry cut funds for the police department.

By the late 1980s the U.S. capital city had earned the infamous label "murder capital." More people were killed in proportion to the population in the District of Columbia than in Detroit, Miami, or New York. Drug gangs fought over the right to control sections of the city that were awash in crack cocaine. In 1991, 489 were slain. It was a murder rate essentially in black, not white: few whites were killed, and fewer than five murders occurred in white neighborhoods.

As the city succumbed to crack, so did Mayor Barry, by then in his third term. His drug habit was no secret. Metropolitan police had covered up for him for years, but in 1989 a team of local police and federal agents conducted an investigation and set up a "sting" operation to catch Barry in the act. On Jan. 18, 1990, they made a videotape, later shown around the world, of Barry drawing on a crack pipe. Convicted of one misdemeanor count of possession, he was sentenced to a six-month jail term.

The District of Columbia suffered but there was hope once again in the election of 1990, which brought Sharon Pratt Dixon to office as mayor. A sparkling and articulate African-American utility executive, she was accepted on Capitol Hill as a "breath of fresh air" but had a difficult time governing. She ran up deficits, alienated supporters, and couldn't keep professional football's Washington Redskins from moving to the suburbs. Meanwhile, in the early 1990s the district's more prosperous blacks began streaming out of the city because of high crime and poor schools, leaving it with fewer taxpayers and role models. Hispanic immigrants from Central America began taking up residence in the Adams Morgan and Mount Pleasant neighborhoods, and Korean merchants took over inner-city stores. The city began to take on an ethnic tone, but the population had plummeted to 570,000. The failure of local government to control spending and deliver services seemed to be holding back the city's progress. Toward the end of 1994 and throughout 1995 Congress began taking back power that it had given to the district in the Home Rule Act twenty years before. It installed a federal control board to take control of the city's purse strings. Meanwhile, Barry staged a miraculous comeback by returning from jail and running successfully for mayor in 1994, which only served to deepen the city's crisis and inflame Congress. Statehood for the District of Columbia was all but dead.

[Constance McLaughlin Green, *Washington: A History of the Capital, 1800–1950* (Princeton, N.J., 1976); Harry S. Jaffe and Tom Sherwood, *Dream City: Race, Power, and the Decline of Washington, D.C.* (New York, 1994).]

HARRY S. JAFFE

WASHINGTON, STATE OF. Two events in 1974 served as harbingers of what would prove the predominant factor in the life of Washington in the modern era. Host to two previous world's fairs in Seattle in 1909 and 1962, Washington opened its third fair in Spokane in 1974. The theme for Expo '74 was the effect of human beings on the environment. Earlier that year Judge George Boldt of the federal district court in Tacoma made what proved to be a landmark ruling in *United States* v. *Washington,* declaring that the state's Native American peoples were entitled to fish at all of their "usual and accustomed places," borrowing a phrase from treaties enacted in the 1850s. Indeed, the treaties used language stipulating that incoming American settlers could fish "in common with" Indians, from which Judge Boldt determined that the Native Americans' modern-day descendants were entitled to one-half of all of the harvestable catch. No event in Indian-white relations for the previous one hundred years superseded this decision in importance. A century or more of grievances originating in broken promises had led to a sequence of Indian demonstrations and counter-demonstrations along the banks of the Nisqually and Puyallup rivers in western Washington. This agitation, including occasional violent encounters between Indian and white fishermen and fisheries officials of the state of Washington, was brought to a crisis when the federal Department of Justice joined the Indians and sued the state. Not only were the tribes' treaty rights reaffirmed by Judge Boldt's decision (upheld by the Supreme Court in 1979), the one-half set-aside for native fishermen enhanced the competition among white commercial interests and sports fishermen for a resource increasingly recognized as being in rapid decline.

Developments in Washington during the previous forty years were the telling influence in this story. Dams built on the Columbia and Snake rivers and their many tributaries, plus increased urbanization, and particularly suburbanization in the Puget Sound lowlands, severely affected the environment. So critical had the situation become that by 1993 the Snake River salmon were on the verge of being listed as an endangered species.

The Spokane World's Fair and the Boldt decision served as more general indicators of the state of Washington's evolving environmental consciousness. The state's timber stands—the principal source of industrial employment from the time of American settlement in the 1840s until the late 1930s—became as much an environmental battleground as had the state's rivers and streams, and several concerns also brought an era of limits to the timber industry. One was the loss of scenic quality because of the clear-cutting of timber on privately held land—and more particularly the state's several national forests. Another was the damage to watersheds that such practices engendered. A third, emerging in the early

1990s, involved the northern spotted owl's survivability. Similarly, the environmental consequences of the Hanford Project near Richland in eastern Washington, site of the Manhattan Project's World War II plutonium facility, became a major public issue in the early 1980s. The Washington Public Power Supply System, an ambitious nuclear power plant consortium, defaulted on $2.25 billion in bond payments in 1983 because of large cost overruns associated with the construction of five nuclear power plants. This development, the largest municipal bond default in American history, soon was compounded by the end of the cold war and, accordingly, the diminished need for plutonium. Thousands of layoffs led to an economic crisis in the Richland area, the capital of Washington's nuclear industry. The state's evolving environmental consciousness, however, proved to be that locale's economic savior as federal, state, and community support for cleaning up the waste left from forty years' worth of nuclear production resulted in what is now the most expensive public works project in the state's history. In fiscal year 1994 alone, the federal government invested $1.6 billion in the clean-up effort, which was estimated to require decades to complete.

Concurrently, Washington from 1970 to 1990 developed a sizable tourism and hospitality industry, which surpassed the old staples of fishing and logging as a source of employment. An "attraction economy" of ski resorts, wineries, national parks, and modern museums supplanted the world of "wigwam" incinerators of sawmill waste and purse seine fishing nets. Washington proved to be an attractive destination for permanent residents as well as tourists. Population growth in the largest cities continued unabated, as did a few of the more rural areas, such as the San Juan Islands, an appealing destination for retirees from other regions, especially California. Seattle was regularly listed in the popular press as one of the nation's "most livable" cities.

Washington's population in 1970 stood at 3.4 million. By 1993 it was estimated to be 5.2 million. A leading factor in this growth was the great expansion of the Boeing Company's production of airplanes from 1985 to 1990 plus the emergence of a robust high-technology sector lead by the Microsoft Corporation. Despite repeated attempts to diversify the economy after the aerospace busts of the early 1970s and the 1980s, the most important factor in the economic health of the state remained the economic fortunes of Boeing.

The state of Washington's coming of age since the 1970s was reflected in the maturing of its arts and cultural scene. A particularly noteworthy and trend-setting arts phenomenon with its roots in Washington was the Art in Public Places program, resulting from legislation passed in 1974. Although this program engendered its share of controversy, many pieces of modern art were placed in Washington's schools and urban settings. Two of the nation's most respected architects earned commissions for the design and construction of the state's flagship cultural enterprises. A new downtown version of the Seattle Art Museum, credited to postmodernist Robert Venturi, opened in 1992. Charles Moore, also a postmodernist, won an international design competition for the new Washington State History Museum in Tacoma, for which ground was broken in December 1993.

The best-known development in Washington since 1970 was the volcanic eruption of Mount Saint Helens on May 18, 1980, which killed sixty people and reinforced in the minds of residents and observers how the natural environment of Washington continues to serve as a principal factor in shaping events in the state.

[Robert E. Ficken and Charles P. LeWarne, *Washington: A Centennial History* (Seattle, 1988); Carlos Schwantes et al., *Washington: Images of a State's Heritage* (Spokane, 1988).]

DAVID L. NICANDRI

See also **SUPP:** Environmental Movement; Mount Saint Helens; Nuclear Power; Seattle.

WASTE DISPOSAL. Societies have always had to deal with waste disposal, but what has been defined as waste, as well as its ultimate destination, has varied greatly over time. Large-scale waste disposal is primarily an urban issue because of the waste disposal needs of population concentrations and the material processing and production-type activities that go on in cities. Waste is often defined as "matter out of place" and can be understood, as the noted sanitary engineer Abel Wolman wrote, as part of a city's metabolic processes. Cities require materials to sustain their life processes and need to remove wastes resulting from consumption and processing to prevent "nuisance and hazard." Well into the nineteenth century, many U.S. cities lacked garbage and rubbish collection services. Cities often depended on animals such as pigs, goats, and cows, or even buzzards in southern cities, to consume slops and garbage tossed into the streets by residents. In the middle of the century, health concerns stimulated such larger cities as New York to experiment with collection, often by contracting out. Contractors and municipalities often discarded wastes into nearby waterways or placed them on vacant lots or the city fringe.

Rapid urbanization in the late-nineteenth century increased the volume of wastes and aroused concern over nuisances and hazards. Garbage had been viewed as a nuisance, but the public health movement, accompanied by widespread acceptance of anticontagionist theory, emphasized the rapid disposal of organic wastes to prevent epidemics. Municipalities were driven to consider collection, usually setting up their own services, granting contracts, or allowing householders to make private arrangements. By the late nineteenth century, cities were relying on contractors, although there were shifts between approaches. Cities apparently preferred contracting to municipal operation because of cost as well as the absence of a rationale for government involvement in a domain with many private operators.

During the first half of the twentieth century, municipal control over collection gradually increased to between 60 and 70 percent, largely for health and efficiency reasons. Just as they had moved from private to public provision of water because of concerns over inability of the private sector to protect against fire and illness, cities began to question leaving waste removal to contractors. Contractor collection was often disorganized, with frequent vendor changes, short-term contracts, and contractor reluctance to invest in equipment. Municipal reformers concluded that sanitation was too important to be left to profit-motivated contractors. Initially, responsibility went to departments of public health, but as the germ theory of disease replaced anticontagionism, control over the function shifted to public works departments. Garbage collection was increasingly viewed as an engineering rather than a public health problem, and municipal concern shifted from health to fire hazards and the prevention of nuisances such as odors and flies.

Changes in both composition of wastes (or solid wastes, as they were now called) and collection and disposal methods occurred after World War II. A major fraction of municipal solid wastes before the war had been ashes, but as coal was displaced by heating oil and natural gas, ashes became less important. The solid wastes generated by individuals did not decrease, however, because there were sharp rises in the amount of nonfood materials, such as packaging and glass. Another change occurred in regard to disposal sites. Before the war cities had disposed of wastes in dumps, on pig farms (a form of recycling), by ocean dumping, or by incineration; a few cities used garbage reduction or composting. For nuisance and health reasons, cities found these methods unacceptable, and in the decades after 1945, they adopted the so-called sanitary landfill method of waste disposal, which involved the systematic placing of wastes in the ground using a technology such as a bulldozer or a bull clam shovel. The sanitary landfill, or tipping, had been widely used in Great Britain before the war. It was developed in the late 1930s by Jean Vincenz, director of public works in Fresno, California. Vincenz used the sanitary landfill to deal with solid wastes at army camps during the war. Public works and public health professionals and municipal engineers viewed the technique as a final solution to the waste disposal problem. Between 1945 and 1960 the number of fills increased from 100 to 1,400.

A further development, starting in the late 1950s, involved a rise in private contracting. Firms that provided economies of scale, sophisticated management, and efficient collection absorbed smaller companies and replaced municipal operations. Sharp rises in the costs of disposal as well as a desire to shift labor and operating costs to the private sector also played a role. In the 1980s private contracting grew rapidly because it was the most cost-effective method available.

In the 1960s the environmental movement raised questions about solid waste disposal and the safety of sanitary landfills, both in terms of the environment and health. Environmental regulations were strengthened by states in the 1950s, while the federal government followed with the Solid Waste Act in 1965 and the Resource Conservation and Recovery Act in 1976. Higher standards for landfills raised costs. Increasingly, society sought disposal methods such as recycling that were protective of health and environmentally benign. By the last decade of the twentieth century, as new techniques for utilizing recycled materials and controlling waste generation developed, society seemed on its way to a more sustainable balance; the tendency of Americans to consume ever-increasing amounts of goods, however, dampened the rate of improvement.

[Martin V. Melosi, *Garbage in the Cities: Refuse, Reform, and the Environment, 1880–1980* (College Station, Tex., 1981); William Rathje and Cullen Murphy, *Rubbish! The Archaeology of Garbage* (New York, 1992).]

JOEL A. TARR

See also **SUPP:** Hazardous Waste; Recycling.

WATERGATE, AFTERMATH OF. The term "Watergate" has resonated in America's collective consciousness since the scandals and crimes committed during the 1972 presidential election campaign by members of President Richard M. Nixon's administration became public. The exposé published by the *Washington Post,* which revealed that the burglary of National Democratic Party headquarters on June 17, 1972, at the Watergate apartment-office complex in Washington, D.C., was committed by employees of the Committee to Reelect the President, arguably encouraged investigative journalism and accentuated the adversarial relationship between government and media. Congress acted quickly after the Senate Watergate hearings in 1973 by enacting laws limiting executive control over foreign policy, notably the War Powers Act of 1973, passed in November over President Richard M. Nixon's veto shortly after what came to be called the "Saturday Night Massacre," when Nixon fired Special Watergate Prosecutor Archibald Cox. Congress enacted campaign finance reforms, conflict-of-interest legislation, stronger freedom of information statutes, and protection of privacy laws. The Ethics in Government Act of 1978 provided for judicially appointed special independent prosecutors to investigate executive wrongdoings.

The Iran-Contra affair of 1985–1986 during President Ronald Reagan's administration—with a similar cast of characters, embattled presidential aides, televised congressional hearings and special prosecutor—evoked a sense of Watergate déjà vu, although this time Congress stopped short of impeaching a popular president. The suffix "-gate" became a descriptive label to denote political scandals: "Koreagate" involved bribes of members of Congress by South Korean agents in 1976–1978; "Billygate" referred to President Jimmy Carter's brother Billy and his connection to the Libyan government; and "Iraqgate" concerned secret and illegal loans to Iraq by the administrations of Reagan and George Bush before the Persian Gulf War of 1991. Other terms that emerged during the Watergate investigations and hearings—"smoking gun," "dirty tricks," "enemies list," and "stonewall"—have remained in political parlance.

Political analysts noted a "post-Watergate morality," a new set of expectations about the ethical behavior of public officials. Remembrance of past transgressions led to watchful surveillance. Law schools offered more courses on legal ethics. Public-interest organizations such as Common Cause tripled in membership. In 1977 the House and Senate passed new codes of conduct for its members on financial disclosure, imposed limits on outside income, and added new restrictions on campaign fund-raising. States passed similar laws. Private as well as public morality of government officials came under scrutiny, such as when a special prosecutor was appointed to investigate a presidential aide accused of cocaine use. As the media investigated the sexual behavior of presidential candidates and Supreme Court nominees, some people reportedly shunned public office lest they endure the media circus and public exposure mandated by post-Watergate reforms. Whether a healthy concern for public ethics had become an obsession, Watergate irrevocably changed political mores in the United States.

Debate continues over whether Watergate was a constitutional crisis or a personal aberration. Investigations in the aftermath of Watergate exposed assassination plots by the Central Intelligence Agency and other abuses of power by presidents before Nixon. Defenders of Nixon made it seem that his greatest crime was in getting caught. It became less clear which Watergate offenses Nixon alone had perpetrated (obstruction of justice) and which had become routine during an arrogant, imperial presidency. A conservative interpretation thus depicted Watergate as more scandal than crisis, a morality play in which Nixon's liberal enemies in the press and Congress harried the president from office over minor offenses. A British historian called Watergate "the first media Putsch in history, as ruthless and anti-democratic as any military coup by bemedaled generals with their sashes and sabers." The liberal interpretation downplayed the media story and depicted Watergate as raising "weighty questions of governance, especially concerning the role of the presidency and its relation to other institutions in the governmental apparatus." Liberals advocated a number of campaign financing reforms and limitations on presidential power, including a special prosecutor mechanism to prevent future Watergates, none of which has operated very effectively. Conservatives contended that the system worked without the need for additional safeguards. By contrast, radical historians characterized Nixon's 1974 resignation and subsequent pardon by President Gerald Ford as "an inexpensive expiation" that prevented a fundamental reevaluation of the American national security state and reinforced a two-tier system of justice that does not hold top U.S. politicians accountable for illegal or unconstitutional actions.

A 1987 Gallup Poll asked Americans what major events had most affected their thinking. Only 5.9 percent listed Watergate, placing it behind the Vietnam War, Ronald Reagan's presidency, and the Great Depression. Apparently, most Americans remember Watergate more as a frothy scandal than as a serious constitutional crisis. Nixon's later efforts at political rehabilitation reflected the continuing ambiguity of Watergate. In televised interviews in 1977, he claimed he "did not commit a crime, an impeachable offense," although "I did let down our system of government." His memoirs, published the following year, asked for public acceptance and public sympathy. Watergate, he predicted, would get only a footnote when future historians assessed his foreign policy triumphs. With more books on foreign affairs, international trips, op-ed pieces, the opening of the Nixon Library in 1990, his advice solicited by Presidents Reagan, Bush, and Bill Clinton, Nixon seemed to achieve the status of elder statesman before he died in 1994, but his Gallup Poll approval rating in 1990 had risen to only 38 percent (from 24 percent in 1974), indicating that Watergate remained "the spot that will not out." The eulogies at Nixon's funeral notwithstanding, the subsequent publication of diaries by key individuals involved in Watergate and documentaries commemorating the twentieth anniversary of Watergate reminded everyone that Nixon was the first president to resign because of a constitutional crisis.

[Stephen E. Ambrose, *Nixon: Ruin and Recovery* (New York, 1991); Katy Harriger, *Independent Justice* (Lawrence, Kans., 1991); Godfrey Hodgson, *All Things to All Men: The False Promise of the Modern American Presidency* (New York, 1980); Joan Hoff, *Nixon Reconsidered* (New York, 1994); Stanley Kutler, *The Wars of Watergate: The Last Crisis of Richard Nixon* (New York, 1980); Tom Wicker, *One of Us: Richard Nixon and the American Dream* (New York, 1991).]

J. GARRY CLIFFORD

See also **DAH:** Nixon, Resignation of; Watergate; **SUPP:** Iran-Contra Affair; Iraq-gate; Korea-gate.

WATER POLLUTION. Widespread water pollution in the United States, including contamination of major rivers and large portions of lakes and estuaries, was primarily a product of three nineteenth-century trends—natural resource exploitation, industrialization, and urbanization. Although development of natural resources, especially lumbering and mining, caused the despoliation of many lakes and rivers, urbanization and industrialization were the primary causes of water pollution. Effluents generated by cities and factories produced widespread contamination of waterways and municipal water. Water pollution increasingly posed a threat to human health in the last decades of the nineteenth century as cities constructed sewer systems discharging millions of gallons of untreated sewage per day into rivers and lakes. By 1904 about 28 million people lived in cities with sewers, but only 1.1 million had their sewage treated. Deaths from such waterborne diseases as typhoid fever rose sharply in cities whose water supplies came from nearby rivers and lakes.

In the early 1890s biologist William T. Sedgwick directed an interdisciplinary group in Massachusetts for clarifying the relation of typhoid fever to sewage. By 1905 thirty-six states had enacted legislation protecting drinking water, with enforcement by state boards of health; most laws, however, were weak. In 1912 concern over pollution and health led Congress to assign the Public Health Service (PHS) to investigate "the diseases of man and conditions influencing the propagation and spread thereof, including sanitation and sewage and the pollution, either directly or indirectly, of the navigable streams and lakes of the United States." The PHS investigations focused on the effects of sewage and industrial waste on stream quality, the assimilative characteristics of streams, and the measurement of pollution. In 1914 the PHS set the first water quality standards for interstate commerce, based on bacterial methods of water analysis. Reduction of waterborne disease, however, was accomplished primarily through water and sewage treatment. Experiments in the 1890s showed how slow sand and mechanical filters could treat sewage-polluted waters used for drinking. Many inland cities then installed filters, resulting in an impressive decline of typhoid fever as well as other waterborne diseases. Advances were also made in sewage treatment methods, but implementation proceeded at a much slower rate because sewage treatment benefited primarily downstream cities.

In the 1920s the PHS undertook investigations regarding industrial wastes, especially where they contributed to drinking water problems, but all action to control water pollution in that decade was at the state level. The Pennsylvania Sanitary Water Board, created in 1923, established a widely emulated classification scheme to balance environmental quality and industrial progress, protecting streams used for drinking water but designating others for waste disposal. Conservation groups such as the Izaak Walton League protested this approach, because waste disposal affected recreational use of waterways. As regulation lagged, pollution of waterways accelerated. During the 1930s, President Franklin D. Roosevelt created the Water Planning Committee of the National Resources Board and the Special Advisory Committee on Water Pollution Control. Under New Deal programs, the federal government aided in the construction of 1,165 new municipal sewage treatment plants, while the population served by sewage treatment increased from 21.5 million in 1932 to more than 39 million in 1939. While some federal officials and conservation organizations pushed for federal water control, Congress balked and so left power in state hands. By World War II water quality had improved in river basins with treatment plants. The war exacerbated the problem because of emphasis on production. Not only were such traditional industries as metals, food, and petroleum expanded without attention to pollution control, but many new substances capable of producing long-lasting environmental damage were produced. Among them were rayon, artificial rubber, the chlorinated hydrocarbons (DDT, chlordane, endrin, and others), and synthetic detergents.

Congress approved the Water Pollution Control Act in 1948. It kept standards enforcement at the state level but provided federal technical assistance, research, and comprehensive planning, and matching funds to localities for construction of sewage treatment plants. Although it provided for $27 million annually for five years, only $8.5 million was actually allocated under the program. In 1956 Congress approved the Federal Water Pollution Control Act Amendments, which maintained the "primary responsibilities and rights of the states" to control water pollution while providing them with assistance. In 1960 President Dwight D. Eisenhower vetoed legislation that would have increased federal grants for sewage treatment facilities by $90 million annually. In 1961, however, President John F. Kennedy persuaded Congress to approve the Federal Water Pollution Control Act Amendments, which extended federal enforcement to coastal and interstate waters and provided $570 million over six years for construction.

The Water Quality Act of 1965 marked a new direction for water pollution control. It redefined the federal effort as being one "to establish a national policy for the retention, control, and abatement of water pollution." It established water quality standards, to be set by the states, for interstate waters. If the states failed to establish them, they were to be developed by the Department of Health, Education, and Welfare (HEW). The act created the Federal Water Pollution Control Administration within HEW. It provided that pollutant discharges resulting in "sub-

standard" interstate water quality would be subject to federal proceedings. The Clear Waters Restoration Act of 1966 provided new funds for construction and research. The 1965 and 1966 legislation, however, relied on state standards, which were prey to delays by poorly funded state programs. A more effective approach was required.

The Federal Water Pollution Control Act Amendments of 1972 (commonly known as the Clean Water Act) marked a major shift in policy by moving control to the federal government. Passed over President Richard M. Nixon's veto, the act sought complete elimination of pollutant discharges (zero discharge) by the mid-1980s. It called for industry's implementation of the "best practicable" water control technology by mid-1977 and the "best available" technology by mid-1983. Municipalities had to offer secondary treatment or better by mid-1977 and "best practicable" treatment by mid-1983. The act was amended in 1977, 1981, and 1987 to extend deadlines, permit "innovative and alternative" technologies in meeting effluent standards, and allow for state management of nonpoint pollution, such as urban runoff. Issues of groundwater pollution remained. The constant generation of new chemicals and suspicions about older ones such as chlorine, plus the ability to detect ever smaller amounts of pollutants, suggest that concerns over water pollution will be an issue long into the future.

[Earl Finbar Murphy, *Water Purity: A Study in Legal Control of Natural Resources* (Madison, Wis., 1961); Philip V. Scarpino, *Great River: An Environmental History of the Upper Mississippi, 1890–1950* (Columbia, Mo., 1985); Joel A. Tarr, *The Search for the Ultimate Sink: Urban Pollution in Historical Perspective* (Akron, Ohio, 1996).]

JOEL A. TARR

See also **DAH:** Sanitation, Environmental; **SUPP:** Hazardous Waste; Public Health Service; Recycling; Waste Disposal.

WEAL. *See* **Women's Equity Action League.**

WEATHER SATELLITES, robotic spacecraft that observe changes in terrestrial weather patterns, play a key role in weather forecasting. The satellites are credited with sharply reducing deaths from hurricanes and other violent weather. The first weather satellite, TIROS I, was launched in 1960 and functioned only eighty-nine days. TIROS (an acronym for Television and Infrared Observation Satellite) recorded television images of cloud patterns below, enabling meteorologists to track the movement of weather patterns and fronts with new accuracy. Since then, weather satellites have grown much more durable and can register more data, including wind speeds, atmospheric and surface temperatures, water temperatures, wave heights, and height of the polar ice caps. Weather satellites have been fielded by the United States, the Soviet Union and Russia, the European Space Agency, Japan, India, and China. The U.S. government operates separate weather satellite programs for civilians and the military.

Weather satellites fall into two types. A geostationary satellite remains parked over a given point of the Earth's equator, allowing it to keep continuous watch over a large portion of the Earth from an altitude of 22,000 miles. A polar-orbiting satellite flies at a much lower altitude—about 500 miles—in an orbit that carries it nearly over the Earth's north and south poles. Such a satellite views a much smaller portion of the Earth than a geostationary satellite but can make more detailed observations. Also, the polar-orbiter's orbit is designed so that the sun is at the same angle on every orbit, eliminating the confusion of shifting shadows on the Earth's surface below. For civilian weather forecasting the U.S. government typically has maintained two geostationary satellites and two polar-orbiting satellites in orbit at all times, but satellite weather forecasting ran into a snag in 1989, when the GOES-6 failed in orbit. A replacement, GOES-8, was to have been launched on a space shuttle mission, but the *Challenger* shuttle explosion interrupted all shuttle launches. The replacement was further delayed until 1994 by technical problems with the instruments on the satellite, the first of an improved model of geostationary spacecraft. To fill the gap a European weather satellite was repositioned over the Atlantic Ocean to provide coverage of the eastern United States. The new line of geostationary satellites does not have to spin to remain stable; its two principal instruments can operate simultaneously rather than taking turns, and its instruments gather more data than previous models.

[William James Burroughs, *Watching the World's Weather* (New York, 1991); P. Krishna Rao et al., eds., *Weather Satellites: Systems, Data, and Environmental Applications* (Boston, 1990).]

VINCENT KIERNAN

See also **SUPP:** Weather Service, National.

WEATHER SERVICE, NATIONAL. In the late twentieth century the National Weather Service (NWS) increased its computerization of ground and upper-air data and thereby enhanced its forecasting and climatological services. The excellent Doppler radar for tornadoes and other severe weather was a leading example, but technological advance was plagued by slow and allegedly faulty manufacturing of equipment and huge cost overruns by private companies. Also seemingly retarding progress was mismanagement within the National Aeronautics and Space Administration, which sponsored development of weather satellites for the NWS that included the Geostationary Operational Environmental Satellites (GOES) and Landsat series. Public users of forecasts and other data continued to criticize errors in this inexact science. In federal court Delta Airlines pilots, rather than air traffic controllers, who used NWS forecasts on the thunderstorms, received blame for negligence (misuse of NWS data) in landing during a thunderstorm crash at Dallas–Fort Worth in 1985. Meanwhile, the NWS impressed Congress as being a sound operation. Budget cutbacks in the 1980s and threats of privatization were apparently ended in 1994. The service even sought increased funding, particularly for personnel but also to develop better technology for tracking hurricanes as well as predicting wind shear and microbursts at airports.

[Donald R. Whitnah, *A History of the United States Weather Bureau* (Urbana, Ill., 1961), and "National Weather Service," in *Government Agencies* (Westport, Conn., 1983).]

DONALD R. WHITNAH

See also **SUPP:** Weather Satellites.

WEBSTER V. REPRODUCTIVE HEALTH SERVICES, 492 U.S. 490 (1989), marked a significant change in the Supreme Court's approach to abortion rights and demonstrated the influence of President Ronald Reagan's appointments to the Court. Appointing conservative judges, particularly those opposing *Roe* v. *Wade* (1973), was a top priority of the Reagan administration, which went to unprecedented lengths to ensure the ideological acceptability of judicial candidates, subjecting them to a stringent legal "litmus test" before their nominations went to the Senate. During Reagan's first term only one Supreme Court vacancy occurred, which he filled with Sandra Day O'Connor. Her consistent votes to uphold abortion restrictions, and the government's frequent appearance as an amicus curiae (third party) in these cases, were reflected in the Court's changed attitude toward parental consent laws. Nonetheless, the Court did not overrule *Planned Parenthood* v. *Danforth* (1976), which had invalidated a consent law. *Planned Parenthood* v. *Ashcroft* (1983) even sustained a regulation including a "judicial bypass" (a provision allowing a minor to obtain permission from a judge if her parents refused consent). The Court continued to invalidate restrictions on adult access to abortion. As late as 1986, *Thornburgh* v. *American College of Obstetricians and Gynecologists* reaffirmed the principle of abortion rights and struck down most of a Pennsylvania law that imposed various obstacles to abortion.

When Chief Justice Warren Burger, a member of the *Roe* majority, retired in 1986, Reagan promoted William Rehnquist to the chief justiceship, and replaced him with Antonin Scalia, an appeals court judge of impeccable conservative credentials. Lewis Powell's retirement in 1987 and the appointment of Anthony Kennedy further eroded the support for *Roe*. When Reagan left office in 1989, only four justices committed to abortion rights remained on the Court: Harry Blackmun, William Brennan, Thurgood Marshall, and John Paul Stevens. The reversal of *Roe* v. *Wade,* a long-awaited conservative victory, seemed within reach. Anti-choice activists (those opposed to a woman's right to choose an abortion, also known as pro-lifers) put increased pressure on state legislatures to forbid abortion outright.

Webster came to the Court from Missouri, a stronghold of the anti-choice movement. The Missouri legislature had tried to limit abortions ever since *Roe*; both *Planned Parenthood* v. *Danforth* and *Planned Parenthood* v. *Ashcroft* were Missouri cases. A third Missouri law, passed in 1986, began, "The general assembly of this state finds that the life of each human being begins at conception." Among this statute's provisions were a ban on abortions in public facilities or by public employees, a requirement that all abortions after sixteen weeks of pregnancy take place in a hospital, and mandated "viability" testing after twenty weeks. Reproductive Health Services, a clinic, joined a class-action suit asking a federal court to declare the law unconstitutional. The plaintiffs won in the lower courts. William Webster, the state's attorney general, obtained Supreme Court review. The Justice Department filed an amicus curiae brief urging the Court to overturn *Roe* v. *Wade*. The decision was a clear warning that women were in danger of losing the right to choose abortion. *Thornburgh*'s five-to-four vote to invalidate restrictions became a five-to-four vote to sustain them. *Webster* did not allow states to forbid abortion, although journalists who covered the Court reported that in internal court discussions, Rehnquist almost succeeded in getting *Roe* overturned. His plurality opinion, joined by White and Kennedy, minimized the need to follow precedent in constitutional cases and dismissed the possibility that "legislative bodies, in a nation where more than half the population is women," would "enact abortion regulations reminiscent of the dark ages." The plurality described the law's preamble a "value judgment" without coercive effect and ruled that *Roe*'s viability testing provision "permissibly furthers the state's interest in protecting potential human life." Since testing was required well before the end of the sixth month, the plurality of justices eviscerated the "trimester" framework of *Roe*. Justice O'Connor concurred in the opinion but disavowed much of the wording, while Justice Scalia's sarcastic opinion accused the plurality of attempting to "prolong this Court's self-awarded sovereignty over a field where it has little proper business." Justice Blackmun's dissent was equally passionate: "I fear for the future. I fear for the liberty and equality of millions of women."

Webster was a victory for opponents of abortion. The Court extended the state's power to regulate, hinted that new laws limiting abortion would receive sympathetic consideration, and accepted three new cases for the next term, but the predicted rush by state legislatures to pass new antiabortion laws did not materialize. Only nine states and one territory had done so by the end of 1991, the first full legislative year after *Webster*; only three of these laws forbade most early abortions. Two events in 1992—the Court's weak but explicit reaffirmation of abortion rights in *Planned Parenthood* v. *Casey* and the election of Bill Clinton, a Democrat, to the presidency—indicated that the anti-choice movement may have gone as far as it could.

[Barbara Hinkson Craig and David M. O'Brien, *Abortion in American Politics* (Chatham, N.J., 1993).]

JUDITH A. BAER

See also **SUPP:** Abortion; *Planned Parenthood of Southeastern Pennsylvania* v. *Casey;* Pro-Choice Movement; Pro-Life Movement; *Roe* v. *Wade;* Supreme Court.

WEEA. *See* **Women's Educational Equity Act.**

WEIGHT CONTROL seeks to promote good health and prevention of obesity, which carries such attendant risks as cardiovascular disease and diabetes. In the mid-1990s more than 30 million adult Americans were overweight and the number was increasing. To reduce further incidence, the risks of obesity were being emphasized to promote better health care in the home and in the workplace. Attempts were made to improve the quality of school meals, to reduce the fat content of "fast foods" eaten daily by millions of Americans, and to discourage advertisement of other foods contributing to obesity. By encouraging physical activity and improved diet, obesity can be prevented in many cases.

[Reva T. Frankle and Mei-Uih Yang, *Obesity and Weight Control* (Rockville, Md., 1988); Albert J. Stunkard and Thomas A. Wadden, eds., *Obesity: Theory and Therapy,* 2nd ed. (New York, 1993).]

PETER H. WRIGHT

See also **SUPP:** Eating Disorders; Fitness, Physical; Food, Fast; Health Food Industry.

WELFARE in the United States generally refers to the complex of social insurance programs such as social security, disability insurance, Medicare, and public assistance programs of two varieties: in-kind programs, such as food stamps, the Special Supplemental Food Program for Women, Infants, and Children (WIC), and Medicaid; and income maintenance programs, such as Aid to Families with Dependent Children (AFDC), generally known as welfare, and General Assistance (GA), relief provided by the states. In the years since these programs came into being, social welfare policy has been constantly debated and adjusted. Public assistance of the 1990s had its roots in the Social Security Act of 1935. The Great Depression shattered many of the myths about the ability of the United States to provide full employment to all citizens, and the ability of people to "pull themselves up by their own bootstraps." Although private assistance was available from voluntary organizations and from churches, these services could not meet the great need in the 1930s. In the 1960s the Great Society programs of President Lyndon B. Johnson's administration were established. Welfare reform in these years consisted of extending AFDC to families with unemployed fathers, authorizing work training, and adding social services to move people off the welfare rolls. The trend of poverty and welfare programs also was to increase benefits to the elderly. There were new in-kind programs, such as housing subsidies, public housing units, and nutritional programs. In 1970 Congress made food stamps available at no cost to families below the poverty line, mostly welfare recipients, and at a small price to those just above the poverty line, the so-called working poor.

Most of the increase in welfare spending during the last quarter of the twentieth century was in the AFDC program. In addition to loosened eligibility, participation rates among the eligible rose sharply. One reason for the increase was worsening economic conditions for black Americans due to the mechanization of southern agriculture, which pushed blacks northward into cities where automation and deindustrialization were greatly reducing the number of factory jobs. Another reason for higher participation rates was the "feminization of poverty," due to the increasing divorce rate, increased out-of-wedlock births, continuing gender discrimination in employment, and increased activity by welfare rights organizations. The overall poverty rates declined in 1960–1986. By some accounts white poverty decreased by 38 percent, black poverty by 26 percent. Child poverty, although dropping precipitously between 1960 and 1974 (from 27 percent to 15 percent), subsequently increased to 21 percent in 1986. The rise in female-headed households was largely responsible for this trend.

Although always controversial, welfare became a political target in the mid-1970s, when large-city and federal deficits increased tremendously. The "welfare state" was characterized as out of control. In many states General Assistance was the first program cut through "welfare reform," because it was the program whose recipients were most "employable." Young single people who were not parents, regardless of their skills or prospects for finding or holding a job providing a living wage, were cut from the GA rolls. Despite talk of job training or retraining, very few of these individuals went into the workforce. They were more likely to end up in homeless shelters, whose numbers were growing. Other public assistance benefits slipped between the mid-1970s and the mid-1980s. The maximum AFDC benefit dropped by one-third and the combined AFDC and food stamp benefits dropped by one-fifth.

In the 1980s major welfare cuts were enacted during the administration of President Ronald Reagan. Supplemental Security Income (SSI), granted to people of any age unable to work for at least one year because of disabilities since the 1960 and 1965 amendments to the Social Security Act, was withdrawn from 200,000 recipients. People with mental disabilities were particularly vulnerable to being ruled ineligible. AFDC sustained a large cut. By 1983, 408,000 people lost eligibility, and 299,000 lost their benefits. The average dollar loss to an AFDC family was $1,555 per year, and the savings to federal and state governments were $1.1 billion. Between 1982 and 1985 total funds spent on unemployment insurance went down 6.9 percent, food stamps went down 12.6 percent, child nutrition programs were cut 27.7 percent, housing assistance 4.4 percent, and low-income energy assistance 8.3 percent. Only WIC was increased.

Welfare policy was criticized by both political parties, by conservatives and liberals, and by other groups. One conservative argument is that welfare is antilibertarian. This criticism is based on the assumption that welfare redistributes income. Conservatives also state that welfare has failed to end poverty, crime, and lack of education. A third argument is that welfare costs too much, given the lack of significant results. Another is that the federal role in welfare programs is too great and constitutes "social engineering." Another argument is that welfare erodes family values. Liberal arguments against welfare claim that it has failed to reduce economic inequality, that welfare programs cannot counteract the distributive injustice resulting from a capitalist system, and that welfare does not promote collective responsibility, but provides scapegoats for workers who have been able to find employment.

A feminist criticism of welfare is that while gender has been a fundamental organizing principle of the welfare system, it has been largely invisible. When gender is brought into view, it becomes apparent that there is a double standard for men and women: welfare policy accepts the premise that women, particularly mothers, should be at home and supported by men. The alternatives offered to women are dependence on the state through AFDC or independence through work. Because programs to train and employ AFDC recipients have never been wholeheartedly supported by sufficient funding and private sector cooperation, and because backing in the larger society in the form of equal job opportunities for women, equal pay, and high-quality affordable day care have been slow in coming, it can be surmised that as a society, Americans prefer to keep women dependent. The stigmatizing of recipients makes welfare an unattractive alternative to being supported by men. Therefore, it can be argued, the welfare system in the United States functions to keep women dependent on men and men dependent on work.

In the public discourse on welfare, a distinction is made between the "deserving" and "undeserving" poor. Throughout welfare history there has always been a preoccupation with such groupings. The deserving poor are those who "through no fault of their own" have fallen from a higher economic level to a temporary and reluctant dependency on the state. The undeserving are characterized as dependent by nature, having different values and aspirations than productive Americans, and lacking morality, restraint, and decorum. There is also a racial element in these characterizations, with the undeserving poor most often assumed to be African American. There are still other presumed shortcomings of the welfare system. One is that public assistance grants are too small to permit a decent standard of living and do nothing to get recipients out of poverty. By design these programs do not allow recipients to build equity of any kind, and therefore it is extremely difficult for them to improve their situation. Public assistance recipients (less so for recipients of social insurance) are stigmatized in U.S. society. Prior to the passage of the Family Support Act of 1988, only twenty-eight states had AFDC-UP (Aid to Families with Dependent Children–Unemployed Parent [father]) programs. Elsewhere, families with two parents were ineligible for assistance, which encouraged fathers to desert wives and children so they could obtain assistance. Even three years after the passage of that act only 7.1 percent of AFDC recipients received benefits based on unemployment in a two-parent family. Another criticism is that AFDC and other public assistance programs are bureaucratized, overregulated, and hence inefficient. Further, there are loopholes in eligibility. It is possible to be very poor with no real prospect of work and still be ineligible for assistance. Potential recipients can be denied benefits in some states until the sixth month of pregnancy with their first child; if they are under eighteen and not in school; if their income has dropped within two months from a level at which they would be ineligible; or if there is a stepfather living in the home, regardless of his willingness to support the applicant child.

Although welfare is usually discussed in terms of the altruistic and moral purposes that this set of programs serves, or fails to serve, historical analysis shows the expansions and contractions of welfare benefits in functional terms. Some researchers assert that the two principal functions of welfare are maintaining civil order and enforcing work. The assistance programs begin or expand during times of widespread unemployment and civil unrest and decrease when order is restored to provide an incentive for work.

[Linda Gordon, ed., *Women, the State, and Welfare* (Madison, Wis., 1990); Michael B. Katz, *In the Shadow of the Poorhouse: A Social History of Welfare in America*

(New York, 1986), and *The Undeserving Poor: From the War on Poverty to the War on Welfare* (New York, 1989); Frances Fox Piven and Richard A. Cloward, *Regulating the Poor: The Functions of Public Welfare* (New York, 1971); William J. Wilson, *The Truly Disadvantaged: The Inner City, the Underclass, and Public Policy* (Chicago, 1987).]

ELLEN GRAY

See also **SUPP:** Budget, Federal; Cost of Living Adjustment; Health Care Reform; Medicare and Medicaid; Poverty; Unemployment.

WEST BERLIN DISCO BOMBING. On Apr. 5, 1986, a bomb killed two U.S. soldiers and a Turkish woman and injured more than 200 others in a West Berlin discotheque popular with U.S. military personnel. U.S. and German intelligence sources linked the bombing to the Libyan government of Mu'ammar al-Gadhafi. Already worried about a wave of anti-American terrorist actions by groups from Syria, Iran, and Libya, President Ronald Reagan ordered air strikes against Libyan targets, including Gadhafi and his family, on Apr. 14, 1986, to signal a tough U.S. policy toward terrorism. Nevertheless, Libya continued to support terrorist organizations, although its role in terrorist incidents in Europe decreased.

[Brian L. Davis, *Qaddafi, Terrorism, and the Origins of the U.S. Attack on Libya* (New York, 1990); George P. Shultz, *Turmoil and Triumph: My Years as Secretary of State* (New York, 1993).]

KENNETH B. MOSS

See also **SUPP:** Terrorism.

WEST VIRGINIA remained near the top or bottom of every social and economic ranking from the 1970s to the mid-1990s. With few exceptions the state was dominated by the Democratic party. In the presidential contest of 1980 Jimmy Carter carried West Virginia over Ronald Reagan by 33,000 votes; in the same year Democrat John D. Rockefeller IV won a second term as governor by defeating Republican Arch A. Moore, a popular two-term governor (1969–1977). Although the state legislature went Democratic by a huge margin in 1980, Republicans Michael "Mick" Staton, a South Charleston banker, and Cleve Benedict, a Greenbrier County farmer, capitalized on national trends to win congressional seats, creating a split state delegation of two Republicans and two Democrats; two years later, however, the delegation became solidly Democratic and remained so through the 1994 elections. In 1984 President Ronald Reagan carried the state, while Moore

regained the governorship for an unprecedented third term over Democrat Clyde See. That year, Rockefeller reportedly spent $11 million of his own money to win the U.S. Senate seat vacated by Jennings Randolph; in 1990 he won reelection. Rockefeller joined a stalwart among West Virginia politicians, Robert C. Byrd, in the Senate. Since entering Congress in 1953 as a U.S. representative, Byrd had been the state's most durable vote-getter. As Democratic majority leader and chairman of the Senate Appropriations Committee, he steered hundreds of millions of federal dollars into the state as well as several thousand federal jobs. In the early 1990s he was instrumental in securing the establishment of a large Federal Bureau of Investigation fingerprinting facility at Clarksburg.

In the 1988 presidential election Democrat Michael Dukakis carried the state handily over George Bush; four years later Bill Clinton won over President Bush, although third-party candidate Ross Perot received 109,000 votes. In state politics Democrat Gaston Caperton, a Charleston insurance executive, won the governorship in 1988 over Arch Moore; in the same election former Republican Congressman Cleve Benedict was elected agriculture commissioner to break the Democratic monopoly on state elective offices. Caperton was reelected in 1992. The state's political scene was rocked in 1990 when former Governor Moore received a seventy-month prison term after pleading guilty to extortion, mail fraud, tax evasion, and obstruction of justice. The Democratic president of the state senate was sentenced to federal prison on unrelated corruption charges. In 1994 the director of the state lottery went to prison.

After the state's population fell from 1,949,000 in 1980 to 1,793,000 in 1990, West Virginia lost one of its congressional seats. The population drop stemmed from decreased economic activity. Per capita income of $15,065 in 1992 placed the state forty-ninth in national rankings. The poverty rate among whites was the highest in the nation. Coal production, one of the state's mainstay industries, rose from 121.6 million tons annually in 1980 to 171.2 million in 1990, but the number of mining employees fell from 55,500 to 28,900. Attempts by conservatives to enact right-to-work legislation failed in the legislature, but union membership plummeted nonetheless. The state had one of the nation's lowest high school and college graduation rates. Aside from the usual mining and industrial fatalities, floods in 1985 devastated river valleys. The floods resulted from a tropical storm that swept through the southeastern United States from the

Louisiana coast. The West Fork River at Clarksburg crested at 18.5 feet—11 feet above flood stage. An estimated forty-four people in eight counties lost their lives and many citizens incurred staggering property losses. In an outpouring of public support, all fourteen of the state's television stations participated in a telethon featuring prominent West Virginians, including Governor Moore, Senator Rockefeller and wife, the supersonic pilot Charles "Chuck" Yeager, and the astronaut Jon McBride. The popular singer John Denver helped in the effort to raise funds for flood relief. Despite its troubles, West Virginia in the mid-1990s continued to enjoy one of the nation's lowest crime rates.

[Otis K. Rice and Stephen W. Brown, *West Virginia: A History,* 2nd ed. (Lexington, Ky., 1993).]

PAUL D. CASDORPH

WETLANDS. The term "wetland" refers to any of an array of habitats, including marshes, bogs, swamps, estuaries, and prairie potholes, in which land is saturated or flooded for some part of the growing season. According to the U.S. Fish and Wildlife Service, wetlands contain water-loving plants (hydrophytes) and hydric soils. Since 1780 human activity has destroyed more than half the wetlands of the United States—more than 60 acres per hour. Wetlands serve many ecological and practical purposes. They provide habitat and breeding sites for fish, shellfish, birds, and other wildlife and help maintain biological diversity (biodiversity). They reduce the effect of floods by diverting and storing floodwaters; provide protection from storm waves and erosion; recharge ground waters; and improve water quality by filtering out sediments, excess nutrients, and many chemical contaminants. Wetlands provide recreational, research, and aesthetic opportunities, such as fishing, boating, hunting, and observing and studying wildlife. Wetlands comprise only 5 percent of the land surface of the contiguous forty-eight states, or 104 million acres, but they are extremely productive, exceeding even the best agricultural lands and rivaling rain forests in quantity and diversity of plant and animal life. More than half of the saltwater fish and shellfish harvested in the United States and most of the freshwater sport fish require wetlands for food, reproduction, or both. At least half of the waterfowl that nest in the contiguous states use the midwestern prairie potholes as breeding grounds. Wetland-dependent animals include bald eagles, ospreys, beaver, otter, moose, and the Florida panther.

The value of wetlands was not recognized until the mid-1970s. Before then, most people considered wetlands to be wastelands. They were destroyed by draining, ditching, diking, or filling so they might be used for other purposes, primarily agriculture and development. Early legislation, such as the Swamp Lands acts of 1849, 1850, and 1860, allowed fifteen states on the Mississippi River to "reclaim" wetlands for cultivation. By the middle of the twentieth century, accumulating evidence, including U.S. Fish and Wildlife wetlands inventories in 1954 and 1973, made clear that destruction of wetlands was causing declines in fish and waterfowl. Federal, state, and local laws—notably the federal Clean Water Act of 1972 and amendments in 1977—attempted to regulate destruction. Development, agriculture, and increasing pollution still threaten U.S. wetlands. One-third of wetland losses occurred in midwestern farmbelt states. All but three states (Alaska, Hawaii, and New Hampshire) have lost more than 20 percent of their wetlands. Biologists and economists agree that preserving wetlands is less expensive than attempting to restore damaged wetlands. There is still controversy regarding whether it is possible to restore wetlands and how scientists might measure restoration. The economic and biological feasibility of restoration is hotly debated when a developer seeks permission to build on a wetland, thus destroying it, and offers (or is required) to attempt to rehabilitate a second, already degraded site in return. Many biologists feel that because a degraded site cannot be fully restored, it may not be acceptable to allow this trade-off in any but the most desperate circumstances.

[Council of Environmental Quality, *Environmental Trends* (Washington, D.C., 1989); National Research Council, *Restoration of Aquatic Ecosystems: Science, Technology, and Public Policy* (Washington, D.C., 1992).]

SUSAN J. COOPER

See also **SUPP:** Environmental Movement; Environmental Protection Agency; Fish and Marine Life; Wildlife Refuges and Sanctuaries.

WHALING. *See* **Sealing and Whaling.**

WHITE-COLLAR CRIME. *See* **Crime, White-Collar.**

WHITE SUPREMACISTS. Since World War II the number of whites who profess belief in racial equality has steadily increased, but there continue to be many Americans who proudly proclaim their belief in white supremacy. White supremacist organizations in the United States tend to be short-lived, but new organizations always take the place of those that die. The best known of these groups is the Ku Klux Klan (KKK), a name that a number of organizations have used. A group of ex-Confederate soldiers, who were mainly interested in amusing themselves with pranks and practical jokes, started the first Klan in Pulaski, Tenn., in 1866. It grew rapidly in the former Confederate states, but was breaking up into separate groups by the time it was suppressed by the federal government under legislation passed in 1871. Since then there have been several periods when a number of new Klans sprung up, a large group after World War I and smaller ones in the 1960s during the civil rights movement and still again in the late 1970s and 1980s. In the 1990s there were numerous Klans active under a variety of names. A partial list of other white supremacist groups in the 1990s includes the American Nazi Party, Nazi Skinheads, Posse Comitatus, Aryan Nations, The Order, the National Alliance, Populist Party, Liberty Lobby, White Patriot Party, the John Birch Society, and the Church of Jesus Christ Christian. These groups varied in the degree to which they advocated armed violence as a means to realize their goals. Many white supremacists are Identity Christians, who believe that white "Aryans" are the only true descendants of the Israelites, God's chosen people.

[Mark S. Hamm, *American Skinheads* (Westport, Conn., 1993); James Ridgeway, *Blood in the Face: The Ku Klux Klan, Aryan Nations, Nazi Skinheads, and the Rise of a New White Culture* (New York, 1990).]

RICHARD W. MOODEY

See also **DAH:** Ku Klux Klan; **SUPP:** Militias.

WHITEWATER, a scandal involving charges against President Bill Clinton and his wife, Hillary Rodham Clinton. Scandals have bedeviled modern U.S. presidents as much as failed foreign policies and budget deficits. Watergate forced Richard M. Nixon from the White House, and the Iran-Contra scandal stained Ronald Reagan's final term. Both scandals originated in the White House and involved constitutional questions about abuse of executive power. Although Whitewater raised questions about the actions of President Clinton and his aides during his White House tenure, the scandal had its origins in a 1978 Arkansas land development deal. The issue was whether he, while Arkansas governor, and his wife, a Little Rock lawyer, used political influence with state banking officials for the benefit of a partner in the land development deal in return for campaign contributions and other financial favors from the partner. The Clintons' partners in the Whitewater Development Corporation were a longtime friend, James McDougal, and his wife, Susan. After investing in Whitewater, McDougal bought a Little Rock savings and loan known as Madison Guaranty. Under McDougal's stewardship Madison apparently dispensed loans to board members and prominent Arkansas politicians, with the loans sometimes only partially repaid or not repaid at all. McDougal also threw a fund-raiser in 1985 at Madison to help Clinton repay campaign debts undertaken in his successful run for governor the previous year.

Madison was poorly run, and federal regulators eventually declared it insolvent, but one of the main Whitewater charges was that Governor Clinton in 1985 appointed a new state banking commissioner specifically to protect McDougal. The banking commissioner's actions allegedly kept Madison from being shut down in 1985, increasing the savings and loan's loss when federal regulators finally closed it in 1989. After Clinton became president, congressional Republicans arranged hearings about the matter, with Republican Senator Alfonse D'Amato spearheading the probe. The scandal took on darker dimensions when Clinton's deputy White House counsel, Vincent Foster, apparently in charge of the Clintons' taxes and Whitewater files, committed suicide in July 1993. In 1994 Clinton legal confidant Webster Hubbell, a partner of Hillary Clinton's in a Little Rock law firm, pleaded guilty to fraud charges resulting from false billings he made while with the firm. The billings were discovered as part of the Whitewater investigation. Meanwhile, in 1994 independent prosecutors Robert B. Fiske and then Kenneth W. Starr began looking into contacts between White House and Treasury Department officials over Whitewater; no criminal charges were brought, but a top Treasury official, Roger Altman, resigned the same year. In 1995 the independent prosecutor scrutinized the actions of White House aides and of Susan Thomases, a New York lawyer who was a close friend and adviser to Hillary Clinton. Republicans, gaining strength from their congressional election victories in 1994, initiated Senate hearings that continued into 1996.

[Robert L. Bartley, ed., *Whitewater: From the Editorial Pages of the* Wall Street Journal (New York, 1994).]

THOMAS G. GRESS

WILDFIRES have shaped the landscape of America since long before the arrival of humans. Those fires were all caused by lightning, and lightning is still a major cause of wildfires, particularly in the West. In the twentieth century, governments at all levels tried to suppress wildfires. In the second half of the century, the environmental movement introduced the notion that wildfires were ecologically beneficial, and in 1972 the National Park Service adopted, experimentally, a policy of letting some wildfires burn; in 1976 the policy was adopted generally and became known as the "let-burn" policy. In 1978 the U.S. Forest Service adopted the same policy. Most such fires, designated "prescribed fires," burned less than 100 acres. In years of drought, however, there were major problems. In 1977, 175,000 acres of California wilderness burned in the Marble Cone fire. In 1979 wildfires in California, Oregon, Idaho, Montana, and Wyoming burned more than 600,000 acres. In 1981 a swamp fire in Florida consumed 300,000 acres. Three years later 250,000 acres of Montana forest and range burned, and in 1987, 200,000–300,000 acres in Oregon burned. The worst wildfire season since World War II came in 1988; more than 6 million acres burned, 2.2 million of them in Alaska. Fires around Yellowstone National Park were shown on television and had a major public effect. As drought in the West persisted, wildfires continued to pose major risks. Yosemite National Park closed temporarily in 1990 because of a nearby wildfire. In 1991 a wildfire raced through a residential section of Oakland, Calif., killing at least twenty-four people. In 1993 a spectacular wildfire in the brushland north and south of Los Angeles burned the houses of many celebrities and caused nearly $1 billion in damage. In 1994 more than fourteen firefighters were killed fighting wildfires in Colorado and elsewhere in the West; acreage burned again exceeded one million acres.

[Stephen J. Pyne, *Fire in America: A Cultural History of Wildland and Rural Fire* (Princeton, N.J., 1982).]

NANCY M. GORDON

WILDLIFE REFUGES AND SANCTUARIES. The first wildlife refuge in the United States was a 3.5-acre area on Pelican Island, Fla., designated by President Theodore Roosevelt in 1903 as a breeding refuge for such shore birds as pelicans, herons, and egrets. By 1993 the U.S. Fish and Wildlife Service administered 500 refuges encompassing 90 million acres in the National Wildlife Refuge System, with an additional 2.1 million acres of wetlands designated for 174 waterfowl production areas. Elements of society supporting the federal wildlife refuge system have been quite diverse. Conservation organizations such

as the National Audubon Society, sport hunting clubs such as the Boone and Crockett Club and Ducks Unlimited, and scientific associations have supported the refuge system. Extinction of the passenger pigeon in 1914 persuaded sport hunters and conservationists like Roosevelt to take steps to deal with declining waterfowl populations. Most people blamed decreasing numbers on the meat and apparel markets, which traded waterfowl and other game animals as commodities. In 1934 the federal government began purchasing private property with money collected from duck stamps, which were fees imposed on waterfowl hunters. Previously such refuges as the National Elk Refuge in Jackson Hole, Wyo., were acquired by philanthropists and donated to the federal government. Other refuges were established by nongovernmental organizations, such as the National Audubon Society and Nature Conservancy. States and municipalities also created refuges to facilitate public recreation on state lands as well as to benefit wildlife populations.

Scientific interest in nongame animals and ecosystem management increased throughout the twentieth century. Refuges became field laboratories in addition to game reservoirs. Prior to the 1960s refuge managers worked to protect game populations important to hunters and wildlife observers. Perhaps one of the more famous examples of protecting game animals at the expense of others is that of Aldo Leopold, known for his books *Game Management* (1933) and *A Sand County Almanac* (1949) and who pushed the wolf population on the Kaibab Plateau (in Arizona and Utah) to extermination in an effort to increase the deer population. This policy resulted in a deer overpopulation that led to a massive natural die-off from starvation. After the 1960s, drawing on such examples, managers focused on ecosystem health rather than the well-being of particular species.

[Laura and William Riley, *Guide to the National Wildlife Refuges* (Garden City, N.Y., 1979).]

DENNIS WILLIAMS

See also **DAH:** Bird Sanctuaries; Conservation; **SUPP:** Conservation Biology; Ecology; Endangered Species.

WINE AND SPIRITS INDUSTRY has grown in size since the 1970s, despite a growing public awareness during the late 1980s and 1990s of the dangers of excessive alcohol consumption, and its products have improved in quality. The number of wineries burgeoned, especially in California but also in Oregon and Washington, and these wineries, particularly those that employed European vinifera, were producing ever-better wines. Wineries also sprung up elsewhere in the United States, but they rarely used local grapes; instead they imported grapes and their juices, sometimes frozen, for their winemaking activities and thus did little for production of truly local wines. Although American wines continued to improve in taste and longevity, they were not extensively marketed in the Far East, and their prices remained relatively high, often exceeding those for well-known European wines. Bourbon continued to be the most significant contribution of the United States to the spirits industry. Small and exclusive distilleries produced superior whiskeys that commanded respect and ever-higher prices throughout the world.

[Barbara Ensrud, *American Vineyards* (New York, 1990); Harold Grossman and Harriet Lembeck, *Grossman's Guide to Wines, Beers, and Spirits*, 8th rev. ed. (New York, 1995).]

COOPER P. SPEAKS

WISCONSIN. The "Rustbelt" phenomenon—the decline of the traditional heavy goods manufacturing economy—took its toll in Wisconsin beginning around 1970, as it did in the neighboring western Great Lakes and upper Mississippi River states. Major industrial firms such as Allis-Chalmers ceased to exist; others moved away or expanded only out-of-state or cut back their Wisconsin workforce and output; and a few survived by adjusting their product lines. The resulting decline in well-paid employment, both managerial and production, proved devastating to organized labor and by the mid-1990s was probably not complete. There was, however, some recovery of employment in manufacturing (printing, publishing, and papermaking were strong), and employment increases in service fields left the state with a below-average unemployment level for the region and nation—although the new jobs generally paid lower rates than the lost jobs.

From the 1970s to the 1990s less dramatic but important changes occurred in dairying, for a century the backbone of the state's agriculture. Income from dairying fell, although the state remained a leading milk producer and especially a producer of milk products such as cheese. Milk prices remained flat while government regulations and mechanization raised production costs. The result was declining numbers of farms and farmers, an increase in average farm size, and a concern over the impact of such technology as bovine growth hormone. The state's other major farm products, such as processed vegetables

and fruits, remained stable. Private and government tree farming was important to the northern half of the state, but lumbering remained modest. Despite periodic efforts, especially in copper, the state's mining production was small. The strength of financial institutions—banks, insurance companies, and securities firms—contributed to the economy's survival in the 1970s and 1980s.

The effect of a major convulsion in industry and a continuing decline in farming was felt in politics. From the pre–Civil War decade to the mid-twentieth century, Wisconsin was dependably Republican. Early in the twentieth century, the La Follette Progressives reinforced that bias, while adding a commitment to the use of state government for the general welfare, especially in regulation, taxation, and social programs. Despite the creation by the La Follette Progressives of their own party in the 1930s, Republicans resumed ascendancy before World War II and remained dominant for a decade thereafter. With new leadership and the help of organized labor and distressed farmers, the Democrats became fully competitive with the Republicans beginning in 1957–1958, dominating the state assembly and sharing the governor's office, the nine-member delegation to the U.S. House of Representatives, the two U.S. Senate seats, and presidential electoral votes. By the mid-1990s, Wisconsin's politics were centrist. Radical positions on social and cultural issues—abortion, race, ethnicity, lifestyle, education, crime, and gambling—were neither partisan nor sustainable. Overall the state's politics were moderate, and two post–World War II governors regarded as moderates—Republicans Walter J. Kohler, Jr. (1951–1957), and Warren Knowles (1965–1971)—were acknowledged to have been highly successful. Conversely, three governors who failed of reelection—Republican Vernon W. Thomson (1957–1959) and Democrats John Reynolds (1963–1965) and Anthony Earl (1983–1987)—were apparently perceived as out of the mainstream on social and economic issues. Republican Tommy Thompson (1987–), who stressed economic development, sought consensus with Democratic legislators on many statewide issues.

Economic development had bipartisan support. Democrats tilted toward organized labor, marginal farmers, and minorities but supported initiatives to control spending, limit taxes, and adjust the three major sources of state and local revenue—the income tax, sales and excise taxes, and the property tax, which until the 1990s produced roughly equal amounts of revenue. Democrats launched the selective sales tax in 1962, cut a property tax on business, and acquiesced in the Republican initiative to reduce income taxes and phase out the inheritance tax, all departures from La Follette Progressive traditions. In 1995 the governor and legislature adopted measures to provide two-thirds of local public school funding by 1997, in order to reduce the pressure on local property taxes. Growing public dissatisfaction with school performance, especially in inner cities, brought approval of extensive school choice and other reforms.

Since about 1970 Wisconsin has sought business expansion, especially by changes in administrative and regulatory rules, tax relief, and loans and grants. It was difficult to focus business recruitment because of the state's location, climate, and limited natural resources. One exception was renewed emphasis on tourism, especially to offset declines in heavy industry and agriculture and depression in small towns and the northern cutover. Wisconsin has had an above-average tourist appeal since the late nineteenth century, owing to its varied scenery, abundant lakes and rivers, broad temperature ranges, and a corresponding recreational and vacation appeal to residents of Chicago, metropolitan Milwaukee, and Minneapolis–Saint Paul. These factors were still in play in the mid-1990s but with a changed emphasis. The lakes of southeastern Wisconsin had been converted from resorts and cottages to all-year residences. Central and northern Wisconsin lost some of their "mom and pop" resort culture but acquired additional summer residents from all three metropolitan areas. The north retained its fishing and hunting allure and added a skiing and snowmobiling clientele. To such traditional tourist attractions as the Wisconsin River Dells and the Door County peninsula were added the unique House on the Rock near Madison, the Victorian mansion of beer baron Frederick Pabst in Milwaukee, and the annual July fly-in of more than 2,300 planes held by the Experimental Aircraft Association at Oshkosh. Big league sports teams are another attraction. The major ones in Wisconsin are the Green Bay Packers, an original National Football League team; the Milwaukee Brewers, an American League baseball team since 1970; and the Milwaukee Bucks of the National Basketball Association, who play in the Bradley Center, a $73 million gift in 1990 from heirs to the Allen-Bradley fortune. Tourism was promoted along four themes: the ethnic settlements along the Lake Michigan shore on the east; the Fox-Wisconsin River route diagonally across the state; the Lac du Flambeau in the Chippewa Indian reservation area; and architect Frank Lloyd Wright's heritage,

especially his studio-school, Taliesin, near Spring Green.

In 1987 the state legislature and the electorate approved a dramatic break with the past by authorizing a state lottery and limited gambling. Two considerations led to this step—expectation of property tax relief and competition for tourist dollars. Lottery receipts disappointed taxpayer hopes, and the four greyhound racetracks had varying profitability. Because gambling did not develop exactly as legislators and voters had expected, there was little disposition to expand it in the mid-1990s. As a consequence of federal legislation, however, the state's Native American population—39,387 in 1990—qualified for seventeen casino gambling operations that since 1991 dramatically improved the economic status of the tribal organizations.

Despite economic problems, the state continued to show a stable growth pattern. The incidence of unemployment was, however, highly uneven. Black migrants from the South since World War II disproportionately settled in the heavy goods industrial centers—Milwaukee, other Lake Michigan cities, and Madison and the Rock River Valley—which were most heavily hit by the Rustbelt phenomenon. Unemployment and underemployment among young black males, especially in Milwaukee, increased welfare dependency and impeded family formation and stability. In metropolitan Milwaukee stubborn residential segregation complicated the economic and social consequences of black unemployment, especially in public schools, and led to some outmigration. Hispanic migrants to the state, smaller in numbers, later in time, and handicapped by language but not as much as blacks by color, experienced problems similar to those of blacks in the same industrial centers. The state's population (4,891,769 in 1990) showed declining growth: 11.8 percent in 1960–1970; 6.5 percent in 1970–1980; and 4.0 percent in 1980–1990. In 1990, 92.2 percent of residents were white, compared with 98.8 percent in 1950. Outmigration, chiefly for jobs and a milder climate, was offset by black and Hispanic inmigration and post–World War II increases in Native Americans to the highest level in history, three times their 1940 numbers. In 1990 blacks constituted 5 percent of the population, Hispanics 1.9 percent, and Native Americans 0.8 percent. The Native American increase was due to state and federal assistance programs and migration to urban areas, some of it seasonal. Improvements in tribal self-government, following reversal in 1973 of the experiment in the 1950s in defederalization with the Menominee, brought two developments in the 1980s—the Indian casino gambling boom, a significant contributor to employment and to tribal coffers, and a more aggressive tribal effort to enforce broad hunting and fishing rights, guaranteed by land cession treaties of the mid-nineteenth century and enforced by federal courts.

Post-secondary education in the state was dominated by two systems reorganized in the 1960s and 1970s. Vocational, technical, and adult education, a Progressive Era program, became regional rather than local, with more state funding and a junior college role; eventually, the program had almost half a million enrollees annually. The University of Wisconsin system resulted from merger of the university's four four-year campuses, its two-year centers, and its extension unit with the nine campuses of the Wisconsin State University cluster. One of the largest systems in the nation, it enrolled more than 150,000 students in the 1993–1994 academic year. The Madison campus retained its preeminence in the biological and physical sciences, chemical engineering, computer science, sociology, and economics. Since the Vietnam era protests, which culminated in the Mathematics Research Center bombing of 1970 that involved one fatality, the Madison campus has lost some of its reputation for student radicalism.

[Robert C. Nesbit and William F. Thompson, *Wisconsin: A History,* 2nd rev. ed. (Madison, Wis., 1990); Wisconsin Legislative Reference Bureau, *State of Wisconsin Blue Book* (Madison, Wis., 1853–).]

FREDERICK I. OLSON

See also **SUPP:** Milwaukee; Rustbelt.

WOMEN IN CHURCHES. Since colonial times women have made up more than half the membership of American churches. In the Society of Friends, for example, women had leadership roles in congregations and as traveling missionaries as early as the seventeenth century. In the nineteenth century Catholic nuns pioneered in the founding of schools, hospitals, and orphanages. Protestant women led revivals and founded home and foreign missionary societies. New religious movements, such as the Shakers and Christian Science, were founded by women. Social reform movements, such as abolitionism, prison reform, temperance, and the suffrage movement were led by Christian women. Women also began to demand the right to be ordained. At the first women's rights convention, held in 1848 at Seneca Falls, N.Y., the delegates called for women's ordination. In 1853 the Congregationalists ordained the first woman to the

ministry, Antoinette Louise Brown Blackwell. Methodists, Lutherans, and Episcopalians created orders of deaconesses in the late nineteenth century to channel women's desire for ministry. It was not until 1953 that the Methodist and Presbyterian churches voted to ordain women. The growing numbers of women ministers and theological professors brought women's issues into theology and seminary education. Many churches revised their liturgies to use gender-inclusive language for human beings, but female imagery for God became a source of controversy in most churches.

[Rosemary R. Ruether and Rosemary S. Keller, *Women and Religion in America,* 3 vols. (San Francisco, 1981).]

ROSEMARY RADFORD RUETHER

WOMEN IN MILITARY SERVICE. Major changes in the status of women in the military occurred during the last three decades of the twentieth century. In 1975 Congress ended the prohibition on female matriculation at the military academies. The creation of an all-volunteer force in 1973 prompted the services to recruit more women. Whereas prior to 1967 no more than 2 percent of each service could be women, more than 10 percent of each service was female by the early 1990s. In the early 1970s most occupational specialties were opened to women. By 1994, 91 percent of all army career fields and 67 percent of all positions were accessible to women, and they constituted 12.9 percent of the active army. These changes called attention to imbalances in the rights and responsibilities of service personnel, and several landmark court cases leveled the playing field. In *Frontiero* v. *Richardson* (1973) the Supreme Court held that male spouses of female service personnel were entitled to the same benefits as those received by female spouses of servicemen, even when the servicewomen were not the chief sources of financial support for their spouses. The decision in *Crawford* v. *Cushman* (1976) forbade dismissal of a woman because she became pregnant. The *Owens* v. *Brown* (1978) decision allowed servicewomen to be assigned to ships other than hospital or transport ships. In 1981, however, the Supreme Court said that Congress had not violated women's rights by excluding them from the draft (*Roskter* v. *Goldberg,* 1981). The Court held that women's ineligibility for combat justified exclusion from the draft.

Several events in the 1980s and early 1990s prompted reconsideration of women's combat roles. The invasion of Panama in December 1989 marked the first time in modern U.S. military history that women soldiers engaged in combat. In the Gulf War of 1991 women made up more than 7 percent of the 540,000 troops deployed to the region. They received the same $110 a month imminent danger pay as servicemen. Thirteen women were killed. In May 1991 Democratic Representatives Patricia Schroeder of Colorado and Beverly Byron of Maryland succeeded in amending the 1992 defense authorization bill to remove combat restrictions on women air force and navy pilots. A second amendment to the bill established a fifteen-member presidential commission (Commission on the Assignment of Women in the Armed Forces) to study women's roles in the military and report its recommendations to the president by Nov. 15, 1992. The commission of nine men and six women was chaired by retired Air Force General Robert T. Herres and called for few changes. It voted eight to seven to retain the prohibition on flying combat missions, ten to zero to exclude women from land combat units, and eleven to three to continue ineligibility for the draft. The panel voted eight to six to allow women to serve on all combat ships except submarines and amphibious vessels. Secretary of Defense Richard Cheney said he would allow the incoming administration of President Bill Clinton to respond to the report. On Apr. 28, 1993, Secretary of Defense Les Aspin ordered the armed services to drop most of their restrictions on women in air and naval combat. He also ordered the navy to draw up legislation for Congress to permit assignment of women to ships on combat missions.

[Martin Binkin and Shirley J. Bach, *Women in the Military* (Washington, D.C., 1977); Judith Hicks Stiehm, *Arms and the Enlisted Woman* (Philadelphia, 1989); Carol Wekesser and Matt Polesetski, eds., *Women in the Military: Current Controversies* (San Diego, 1991).]

IRWIN N. GERTZOG

See also **SUPP:** *Frontiero* v. *Richardson;* Tailhook Incident.

WOMEN IN PUBLIC LIFE, BUSINESS, AND THE PROFESSIONS. The 1970s witnessed the most energetic feminist activism since suffrage, a new women's movement committed to a redefinition of social roles for both men and women. The new feminist credo urged that women play a larger public role and men take on more private responsibility for family care. In 1950, 34 percent of women worked for pay; by 1970 that figure had grown to 43 percent. In the two decades that followed the growth rate was even steeper. By 1990, 57.5 percent of all women worked outside the home. Employment of married women with children younger than six rose sharply from 14 percent in 1951 to 30.3 percent in 1970 to 59 percent in 1990. Two-thirds of them were working full time. Until 1991 African-American women consistently worked at rates higher than white women. In that year the median earnings for all women who worked full time and year round increased to 70 percent of those for men, up from 60 percent in 1971. Black women's median earnings rose in that period from 52 percent to 62 percent of those for men.

Economic participation resulted primarily from pressure on family incomes, and working women in 1990 continued to concentrate in clerical, service, and sales work, as well as the historically female professions of teaching, nursing, library service, and social work, but feminist activism for enforcement of laws protecting job rights and enactment of legislation prohibiting sex discrimination in education permitted women to pursue more occupations. Between 1975 and 1990 women doubled their ranks in executive and managerial jobs (from 5.2 to 11.1 percent) and more entered the historically male professions and occupations. Between 1970 and 1991 the proportion rose from 4.7 to 19 percent of lawyers; 12.1 to 18.1 percent of physicians; and 2.7 to 14 percent of police officers. Although engineering remained virtually unbreached (women made up 8.2 percent of engineers in 1991), women advanced in most of the sciences, from less than 10 percent in 1973 to more than 25 percent by 1991. In 1988, 47 percent of Fortune 1000 companies reported women on boards of directors, up from 13 percent in 1976. In 1982 women owned 25 percent of U.S. firms (mostly sole proprietorships), and in 1987 receipts from women-owned firms accounted for 14 percent of the U.S. total.

As women claimed a full public role they sought political positions at every level with the support of new national and local feminist political organizations. In 1971 women occupied 4.5 percent of the seats in state legislatures; by 1993 the proportion had grown to 20.4 percent. Seven women held mayoralties in 1971; twenty years later there were 151. From fifteen women in the 92nd Congress (1971–1973) numbers climbed slowly to thirty-two (three senators and twenty-nine representatives) on the eve of the 1992 election. With that election Congress expanded to fifty-four women members, forty-eight in the House and six in the Senate. The latter included the first African-American woman senator, Carol Moseley Braun of Illinois; in the House there were nine African-American women, one Asian/Pacific-

American woman (Patsy Mink of Hawaii), and three Latinas. Women obtained a fairer share of places in the judiciary. By 1970 only six women had ever been named to the federal district and circuit courts; by 1992 they composed 13.4 percent of federal judicial officers and a year later two of the nine Supreme Court justices, Sandra Day O'Connor and Ruth Bader Ginsburg. By the 1990s the legitimacy of women in politics and the workforce was beyond question. The assumption by men of a larger responsibility for family life was slow to emerge, however, and women continued to face the burden of meeting the frequently conflicting demands of their private and public roles.

[Cynthia Costello and Anne J. Stone, eds., *The American Woman, 1994–1995: Where We Stand* (New York, 1995).]

CYNTHIA HARRISON

See also **SUPP:** Affirmative Action; Equal Employment Opportunity Commission; Equal Pay Act; Family Leave Act; Pregnancy Discrimination Act; Sexual Harassment; Women in Churches; Women in Military Services; Women's Equity Action League; Women's Movement.

WOMEN'S COLLEGES. *See* **Colleges, Women's.**

WOMEN'S EDUCATIONAL EQUITY ACT (1974) was passed as part of the Special Projects Act contained in the Education Amendments of 1974. The purpose of the act is to promote educational equality for women in the United States, an equality that Congress had mandated two years before in Title IX of the 1972 Education Act Amendments. The act also authorized federal grants to develop and evaluate curricula and textbooks; to promote educational equity for disabled women and girls; to help unemployed women and female drop outs; and to encourage women to develop math and science skills. The congressional appropriation in 1991 to achieve these goals was about $2 million.

[U.S. Department of Education, *Women's Educational Equity Act Program: Report of Activities, 1988–1992* (Washington, D.C., 1992).]

IRWIN N. GERTZOG

WOMEN'S EQUITY ACTION LEAGUE (WEAL), founded in Ohio in 1968 and headquartered in Washington, D.C., draws its members largely from the ranks of professional women and has taken a conservative stand on the issue of abortion to distinguish itself from the larger, more liberal National Organization for Women (NOW). WEAL developed from a small, volunteer organization into a national society of thousands of members. In 1970 it initiated the first sex-discrimination case on behalf of women in educational institutions, which led to the hiring of more female faculty. WEAL set up a tax-exempt fund to support lawsuits and to monitor implementation and enforcement of Title IX legislation of the 1972 Education Act Amendments dealing with academic discrimination and economic equity. It also sought to remove gender as a factor in insurance ratings and joined the fight to pass the Pregnancy Discrimination Act of 1978. Initially dependent on federal funds, the organization was able to secure grants from the Ford Foundation after 1980. WEAL published *WEAL Washington Report, Better Late Than Never: Financial Aid for Older Women*, and newsletters on issues of concern to women including executive and legislative actions and court decisions.

[Joyce Gelb and Marian Lief Palley, *Women and Public Policies,* rev. ed. (Princeton, N.J., 1987).]

GRAHAM RUSSELL HODGES

See also **SUPP:** Women in Public Life, Business, and Professions; Women's Educational Equity Act; Women's Movement.

WOMEN'S HEALTH. During the 1960s and 1970s the women's movement publicized and politicized the experiences of women as medical providers, investigators, and patients, as well as the objects of research. Feminist health activists argued that notions of female inferiority undergirded medical theory, research, and practice. Threatened with a sex discrimination class-action suit in 1970, medical schools dramatically increased enrollment of women medical students. Nonetheless, the gendered concentration of women physicians in such fields as pediatrics and primary care continued. Self-help groups and alternative clinics, such as the Feminist Women's Health Collective of Los Angeles sought to demystify medical knowledge and expose medical sexism. *Our Bodies, Ourselves* (1975), written by the Boston Women's Health Book Collective, became the "bible" of the feminist health movement. By the 1990s the National Women's Health Network, a coordinating lobby group founded in 1975, represented 500 women's health organizations. Activists worked with such groups as the National Abortion Rights Action League to demand legal reform in the name of equal rights. Instead, the Supreme Court in *Roe* v. *Wade* (1973) ruled that abortion was governed by the right to privacy and that the state could not intervene until the fetus was "viable"—a term that has shifted in meaning with improving medical technologies. Access to abortion, especially by poor women, was severely limited by the Hyde Amendment (1976) and such legal decisions as *Maher* v. *Roe* (1977), *Webster* v. *Reproductive Health Services* (1989), *Rust* v. *Sullivan* (1991), and *Planned Parenthood of Southeastern Pennsylvania* v. *Casey* (1992). In addition, the training of doctors qualified to perform abortions declined dramatically in the 1980s as did the number of counties with clinics or hospitals providing abortion services.

In the 1960s the feminist health movement was made up mainly of white middle-income women who shared a liberal integrationist view; with the establishment of black, Latina, and Native American health groups a broader movement embraced class, racial, and ethnic diversity and the resulting heterogeneous perspectives on women's health issues. Debates over women's choice and state control have been exacerbated by new reproductive technologies, especially in vitro fertilization, embryo transfer, sophisticated prenatal tests, and the contraceptives Norplant and Depo-Provera. The feminist health critique encouraged greater use of birthing centers and patient consent forms and more open public discussions about sexuality, breast cancer, mental illness, surrogate motherhood, and eating disorders.

Risks of sterility, disease, and death were recognized in the high-estrogen pill, the synthetic hormone DES, the Dalkon Shield and other intrauterine devices, and high-absorbency tampons. Fear of legal action led some companies to exclude women from jobs exposing them to chemicals harmful to their reproductive capacities, raising complex issues of civil rights and gender discrimination. In 1991, however, the Supreme Court in *Automobile Workers* v. *Johnson Controls* ruled in favor of women's, not fetal, rights, saying that employers could not discriminate against fertile women by excluding them from jobs that might harm a fetus. In the 1980s activists increased public awareness of the absence of women subjects in long-range studies of diseases, such as heart disease, that affect both men and women, as well as the lack of resources devoted to research of diseases, such as breast cancer, that primarily affect women. In response to calls for new categories and methods of research, Congress in 1993 passed legislation requiring scientists of the National Institutes of Health to include women in research designs and analyses.

[Rima D. Apple, ed., *Women, Health, and Medicine: A Historical Handbook* (New York, 1990); Flora Davis, *Moving the Mountain: The Women's Movement in America Since the 1960s* (New York, 1991).]

NAOMI ROGERS

See also **SUPP:** Abortion; *Automobile Workers* v. *Johnson Controls;* Cancer; Childbirth; Contraception; Eating Disorders; *Planned Parenthood of Southeastern Pennsylvania* v. *Casey;* Reproductive Technology; *Rust* v. *Sullivan;* Toxic Shock Syndrome; *Webster* v. *Reproductive Health Services;* Women's Movement; Women's Rights.

WOMEN'S MOVEMENT. The reemergence of the women's movement in the United States in the late 1960s is commonly referred to as the second wave of feminism, which serves to distinguish it from the period more than a century earlier when women first organized around demands for full citizenship. While this modern wave of feminism changed during its first three decades, the demand for greater equity and self-determination for women in the United States remained its core. Through its many struggles and achievements, the women's movement remained a salient force for social justice and equity in the 1990s. The roots of the second wave lay in large-scale structural changes that occurred in the United States after 1960. Demographic change, including a rapidly falling birth rate, increased longevity, a rising divorce rate, and an increase in the age at which people married, radicalized the expectations of girls and women. They flooded into the full-time labor force, stayed in school longer, secured college and postgraduate degrees in increasing numbers, and linked their newfound sexual freedom with the desire to control their own reproduction.

What women found as they emerged from the relative shelter of wife and mother roles, however, was a society reluctant to accept them as full and equal participants. This contradiction variously produced disappointment, outrage, anger, and finally a social movement determined to acquire for women full rights of citizenship. The earliest organized forms of second-wave feminism were modeled on the civil rights movement's successful challenge to racial injustice in the United States. Many early activists in the women's movement had participated in the civil rights and antiwar movements or in the New Left politics and counterculture of the 1960s. The organizing lessons learned and the contacts developed served as the basis for their own attempts at change.

The ideology of the movement was diverse from

the beginning, but there were underlying themes common to all those who sought to improve women's status. One was that of sexism—the notion that there are political and social institutions as well as deep-seated cultural attitudes that discriminate against women, denying them the opportunity to reach their fullest potential. A second theme was the goal of individual self-determination—the claim that women should be free to choose their own paths in life, perhaps helped by but not constrained by men or other women. Finally, perhaps the most widely publicized theme was that the "personal is political," the conviction that the only way to change women's individual problems in the form of battering, rape, low-paying jobs, unfair divorce laws, discriminatory education, or degrading notions of femininity is through political organizing and political struggle.

Organizations and small groups appeared in the late 1960s and the 1970s as feminists grappled with the difficult question of how to act on these themes and insights. The largest and most structured of the new feminist organizations, the National Organization for Women (NOW), founded in 1966, fought legal and legislative battles in an unsuccessful attempt to secure passage of the Equal Rights Amendment, intended to eliminate discrimination against women in education and the labor force and safeguard women's reproductive freedom. In contrast, the small, loosely organized consciousness-raising groups typical of the early women's liberation movement held intimate discussions in which women explored their struggles to become more assertive and to resist a socialization process that had taught them to be passive and self-denigrating.

Some feminists believed that street protests were the most effective way to communicate feminism's message to large numbers of people. Direct-action tactics included protests at the Miss America pageant in 1968; the hexing of the New York Stock Exchange by women dressed as witches; the Women's Strike for Equality on Aug. 26, 1970, involving more than 100,000 women throughout the country; and, later, huge demonstrations to assert women's right to abortion. Other activists worked for a feminist vision of change by organizing alternative institutions. Rape hot lines and battered women's shelters were established; women's health clinics, food stores, publishers, a symphony orchestra, art galleries, bookstores, banks, and bars provided outlets for creative energies and entrepreneurial skills. Although there was much disagreement within the movement about which of these disparate tactics was most effective, their combined effect was staggering. They touched the lives of millions of Americans and began to transform the ways people thought about and acted toward women.

In the 1990s the women's movement faced new challenges and problems. Despite substantial gains in many areas over thirty years, sexist attitudes and behavior endured. The gap between women's and men's incomes narrowed but persisted, with women earning approximately 25 percent less than men regardless of education. Abortion rights, while guaranteed, came under renewed attack and in some states were eroded. Sexual harassment was a recognized crime but continued to compromise women's full equality. More women were running for and winning elective office than ever before but in 1994 women constituted only 10 percent of the Congress. Many women earning their own incomes had to work a "second shift" because they remained responsible for most or all of their families' care, even in two-earner households. These and other concerns shaped the ideological debates within feminism at the end of the twentieth century. The women's movement continued to contain within itself a plethora of differing analyses and opinions concerning women and social change.

One such debate focused on the issue of sexual violence. Feminists were divided about the role of pornography in engendering and encouraging the sexual violence rampant in the United States. Many who believed that pornography was a major cause of woman-centered violence called for strict regulation or outlawing of pornography as a violation of women's civil rights. Other feminists were concerned about the difficulty of defining pornography, claiming that the real causes of violence against women are complex and rooted deep within our culture and social institutions. They argued that pornography is a form of free speech—however abhorrent—that must be tolerated in a democratic society. Disagreements were apparent as well on the question of how to define and punish such problems as sexual harassment, date rape, and marital rape. Some questioned the legitimacy of a "battered woman defense," giving women victims of systematic violence the right to strike back against their abusers. While all feminists agreed that gender-based crimes against women, including violent acts against lesbian women, were a virulent form of sexism that must be eradicated, they differed in their analyses of and remedies for these problems.

Another debate divided "difference" feminists from "equality" feminists. Difference feminists stressed that women resemble one another and differ from men in fundamental ways. They focused on the value of presumed feminine characteristics, claiming women's greater empathy, cooperation, intuition, and care and posited these as superior to those thought to characterize men. Although they frequently pointed to socialization rather than biology as the source of sex differences, these feminists believed women's characteristics are shared by all women and difficult if not impossible to alter. Equality feminism, in contrast, rejected the view that there are basic social and psychological differences between women and men. It focused on eliminating barriers to fulfilling individual potential. Equality feminism defined social justice in a gender-neutral fashion, anticipating a future that would provide women and men with opportunities to exercise individual choice on a wide range of issues, including reproduction, education, employment, legal rights, sexual orientation, and personal relationships. It rejected the traditional idea that women's differences from men are inherent or can ever be legitimately used to justify either sex's exclusion from any aspect of society or social life. The political ramifications of difference and equality feminism were many. They divided feminists who advocated special provisions for women in the labor force and the law from those who wanted equal treatment for women and men. One practical aspect of this debate concerned the appropriate remedy for the persistent disadvantages of women in the labor force. When compared to men, women earned less, were promoted less frequently, and continued to be segregated in "female" occupations. Most harmful of all was the pattern of interrupted work histories that characterized large numbers of women as they continued to drop out of the labor force in order to almost single-handedly rear children and care for their homes.

Insisting on preserving women's special relationship to home and children, difference feminists addressed women's disadvantaged position in the workforce with such solutions as the "mommy track." This special arrangement of part-time work enables female lawyers, for example, to spend more time at home without forgoing their law practices. Women retain their relationships with firms even though the ability to qualify as partners is delayed and salaries are considerably lower than are those of full-time lawyers. Equality feminists, however, rejected such special protections. Their search for remedies focused rather on finding ways to equalize men's and women's responsibilities for home and child care. Many equality feminists believed that parental leaves of absence from work when children are young or ill, expanded availability of low-cost and high-quality day care, and greater participation of men in fairly

dividing responsibilities for housework and child rearing were the only real solutions to women's dual-workload problem. By the middle of the 1990s, however, neither difference nor equality feminists had been able to exercise the political power necessary to resolve women's continuing disadvantages in the labor force.

The ideologies of difference and equality separated feminists with respect to strategies for building the movement itself. Difference feminists tended to be wary of coalitions, especially those with men. They were generally pessimistic about the possibility of changing what they saw as men's essentially intractable sexist attitudes and behavior and frequently claimed that only women can understand and fight women's oppression. As a result, feminists influenced by a difference model tended to be separatist, inward looking, and focused on what they saw as women's inevitable victimization. Their activism often took the form of trying to shield women from sexism, especially by separating them from its sources. Thus, one of their primary goals was the creation of all-women environments that were considered safe spaces, such as those at women's music festivals or retreats.

The ideology of equality feminism, in contrast, concentrated on eradicating sexism by removing its causes. For many equality feminists this included working in coalition with men to change their attitudes and behavior toward women. They focused on issues that could unite women and men of different social classes and races, such as the disproportionate poverty of U.S. women and their children, federal funding for abortions, and the need for day care. Their goal was to change those aspects of the society that engender sexism. They fought for fair laws and nonsexist legislation and staged large demonstrations and protests to create a broad-based, diverse, and effective movement for ending sexism.

The difference and equality debate raged within academic institutions. The establishment of women's studies courses and programs in almost every institution of higher education in the country was unquestionably one of the women's movement's most significant achievements. These programs and the women's centers with which they were often associated on college campuses altered the way scholars and students thought about issues of gender. Reversing a situation in which women and their contributions to history, science, and society were almost entirely ignored, women's studies courses educated millions of young people about the importance of both women and men to our cultural heritage and contemporary world. Despite their success, women's studies programs faced an identity crisis in the 1990s. On one side, equality feminists argued that the subjects of women and gender should be integrated into the curriculum and not require separate courses or programs. To them the primary goal of women's studies programs was to facilitate that integration. In contrast, difference feminists claimed that only an independent women's studies curriculum could fulfill the continuing need for courses dedicated to women's unique place in and approach to the world. Thus, feminists celebrated the many accomplishments of women's studies programs even as they disagreed about the strategy that should be adopted by such programs.

The women's movement remained a forum for debate, with issues, strategies, and tactics subject to controversy. While such diversity may have confused a public looking for simple definitions or perplexed those who wanted to know, finally, "What do women want?" its multifaceted nature was the movement's strength. The women's movement had room for everyone who agreed that sexism has no place in a society dedicated to social justice. The most important contribution of the women's movement of the late twentieth century was to improve women's lives by reducing obstacles to the full expression of their desires and choices. Feminists contributed to the wider society as well, because their activism was an important element in the continuing struggle for a more equitable and just society for all.

[Alice Echols, *Daring To Be Bad: Radical Feminism in America, 1967–1975* (Minneapolis, 1989); Sara M. Evans, *Born for Liberty: A History of Women in America* (New York, 1989); Jo Freeman, *The Politics of Women's Liberation* (New York, 1975); Victor R. Fuchs, *Women's Quest for Economic Equality* (Cambridge, Mass., 1988); Arlie Hochschild, *The Second Shift* (New York, 1989); bell hooks, *Ain't I A Woman? Black Women and Feminism* (Boston, 1981); Wendy Kaminer, *A Fearful Freedom: Women's Flight from Equality* (New York, 1990); Kristin Luker, *Abortion and the Politics of Motherhood* (Berkeley, Calif., 1984); Susan Schechter, *Women and Male Violence* (Boston, 1982); Carol Tavris, *The Mismeasure of Woman* (New York, 1992).]

JOAN D. MANDLE

See also **SUPP:** Abortion; Affirmative Action; Comparable Worth; Contraception; Domestic Violence; Ecofeminism; Equal Employment Opportunity Commission; Equal Pay Act; Equal Rights Amendment; Family; Family Leave Act; Gay and Lesbian Movement; Marriage and Divorce; Pornography; Pregnancy Discrimination Act; Pro-Choice Movement; Pro-Life Movement; Rape; Rape Crisis Centers; Sexual Harassment; Violence Against Women Bill; Women in Churches; Women in Public Life, Business, and the Professions; Women's Educational Equity Act; Women's Equity Action League; Women's Health; Women's Rights; Women's Studies.

WOMEN'S RIGHTS. The demands of U.S. women for equal rights reached a high point during the 1960s and 1970s as they sought to alter their political, social, and economic status. The modern women's rights movement was known as the feminist movement or the women's liberation movement. It was also known as the second wave of feminism in acknowledgment of the nineteenth-century activism for women's rights that led in 1920 to passage of the Nineteenth Amendment, which gave women the right to vote. Feminists in the 1960s were responsible for placing the issue of women's inequality on the public policy-making agenda. Women formed such groups as the National Organization for Women (1966), the Women's Equity Action League (1968), and the National Women's Political Caucus (1971) to give greater force to their demands for equality. Women's rights advocates generally agreed on a common set of goals. For the most part, they believed in equal employment opportunity, equal pay for equal work, an end to sexual harassment in the workforce and educational institutions, more equitable divorce and child-custody laws, and greater concern with violence against women. Most also supported pay equity or comparable worth, reproductive rights (including abortion), and greater domestic autonomy. They believed that many of these reforms would occur when the numbers of women at all levels of government increased.

Early successes of the women's rights movement included the 1963 Equal Pay Act, the 1964 Civil Rights Act, laws prohibiting discrimination in educational and credit opportunities, and Supreme Court decisions expanding the civil liberties of women. In 1972 Congress sent the Equal Rights Amendment to the states for ratification; despite approval from more than half the states it failed to obtain the necessary two-thirds needed by 1982. Subsequent gains included the Civil Rights Restoration Act of 1987, the Civil Rights Act of 1991, the Family and Medical Leave Act of 1993, and the Violence Against Women Act of 1994. Victories in state legislatures included laws establishing greater protection for battered women and victims of violent crime, reform of rape statutes, and laws providing for more equitable distribution of marital property following divorce, made necessary by the negative impact of no-fault divorce laws on women. At the same time, many states placed restrictions on women's constitutional right to obtain abortions and often interpreted no-fault divorce laws in ways that harmed women's economic status.

For all their successes, women's rights advocates in the 1990s regarded the battle as far from over. While advocates won many victories in the 1960s and 1970s, a backlash against women's rights occurred in the 1980s and violence against women spread. In the 1990s women continued to be paid less than men and were underrepresented in government, corporations, and educational institutions; access to abortion clinics diminished; and families headed by single women were among the poorest in the nation.

[Nancy E. McGlen and Karen O'Connor, *Women, Politics, and American Society* (Englewood Cliffs, N.J., 1995); Susan Gluck Mezey, *In Pursuit of Equality: Women, Public Policy, and the Federal Courts* (New York, 1992); Sheila Ruth, ed., *Issues in Feminism,* 3rd ed. (Mountain View, Calif., 1995);Virginia Sapiro, *Women in American Society,* 3rd ed. (Mountain View, Calif., 1994).]

SUSAN GLUCK MEZEY

See also **SUPP:** Abortion; Affirmative Action; Civil Rights Act of 1991; Civil Rights Restoration Act of 1987; Comparable Worth; Domestic Violence; Equal Pay Act; Equal Rights Amendment; Family Leave Act; Marriage and Divorce; Pregnancy Discrimination Act; Rape; Sexual Harassment; Violence Against Women Bill; Women in Public Life, Business, and the Professions; Women's Equity Action League; Women's Health; Women's Movement; Women's Studies.

WOMEN'S STUDIES. Between the late 1960s and early 1990s hundreds of U.S. colleges and universities developed interdisciplinary women's studies courses, majors, undergraduate and graduate programs, departments, and research institutes. Not confined to the United States, women's studies extended a presence internationally, especially in Canada, New Zealand, Australia, and the Netherlands and subsequently in Kenya, Great Britain, Vietnam, Russia, India, Italy, and Poland. The regional and institutional diversity of their settings imparted great variety to women's studies enterprises. Much of the impetus behind the work of women's studies founders was compensatory. In virtually every field, research and teaching was male-dominated or reflected unduly the experiences and perspectives of men. New knowledge about women was needed to redress the bias, but when research and publication of vast new bodies of knowledge about women's history, literature, art, music, sociology, politics, economics, religion, and science failed to alter in any substantial way the ordinary workings of disciplines, it became clear that feminist scholarship was an insufficient catalyst for change. Some feminist scholars initiated a fundamental questioning of masculine investments in the existing disciplinary forms and the inherent limitations of those forms, encouraging an interdisciplinary approach for women's studies teaching and research.

Achievements of women's studies programs in their first twenty-five years included the founding of such influential journals as *Signs* and *Feminist Studies;* the sorting out of challenging teaching methods; the involvement of a wide range of faculty and students; self-criticism about issues of race, class, sexual orientation, and other differences among women; the scrutiny of the gender biases of knowledge-making itself; and practical participation in public policy governing gender relations. Administrators of women's studies typically preferred loosely structured interdisciplinary programs over departmental organization. At the 1994 National Women's Studies Association conference, program directors argued that institutional weakness characterized programs without tenured faculty and where the principal focus of activity is undergraduate teaching. Few Ph.D. programs in women's studies existed in the United States by the mid-1990s; the highest degree achieved by most women's studies majors was the master's degree.

Debates within women's studies in the 1990s addressed the departmentalization, professionalization, and fund-raising necessary to secure viable programs into the twenty-first century. They distinguished between monodisciplinary feminist research and interdisciplinary women's studies scholarship. Some observers questioned the continued viability of the term "women's studies" for a field that also analyzed gender, masculinity, and cultural aspects of sexuality. Others questioned whether women's studies should describe itself as an interdisciplinary field or as an interdisciplinary method. It remained to be seen whether women's studies would transform traditional approaches to knowledge or whether it would succumb to the same theoretical and political differences that fragmented the women's movement in the 1990s.

[Judith A. Allen, "Feminist Critiques of Western Knowledges," in K. K. Ruthven, ed., *Beyond the Disciplines: The New Humanities* (Canberra, 1992); Catharine R. Stimpson, *Women's Studies in the United States* (New York, 1986).]

JUDITH A. ALLEN

See also **SUPP:** Colleges and Universities; Colleges, Women's; Curriculum; Multiculturalism; Women's Movement.

WOODSTOCK (1969 and 1994). Near the end of the 1960s, with the anti–Vietnam War and counterculture movements peaking in strength, a series of rock music festivals crisscrossed the United States, especially in 1969. The Woodstock Music and Art Fair was the high point of the festivals and, many would argue, of the decade as well. From 400,000 to 500,000 people crammed onto a farm in Bethel, N.Y., near Woodstock, to camp, listen to music, and commune with nature. The festival attracted many of the top musicians and bands of the 1960s, including Janis Joplin, Jimi Hendrix, Joan Baez, Santana, The Who, Joe Cocker, and Crosby, Stills, Nash, and Young. The festival also attracted many of the era's favorite recreational drugs, including marijuana and LSD, although the latter sometimes came laced with toxic substances. Added to the mix of music and drugs, heavy rains turned the farmland into acres of mud and led thousands to shed their clothes. A benevolent chaos and anarchy ruled the festival, with many attendees cutting down the gates surrounding the farm to avoid the eighteen-dollar ticket charge. For many in the counterculture and antiwar movement, Woodstock represented the best of the 1960s. Reality, however, tarnishes the myth. For all of its antiestablishment underpinnings, a corporate and government presence constantly hovered over the festival. Organizers later said that their main goal was to make money from the festival; Warner Brothers had cameras present and produced an Academy Award–winning movie, while Atlantic Records recorded the festival for a multi-record set. When food and water ran out, helicopters ferried in those supplies along with medicine—the same type of helicopters that ferried soldiers and munitions during the Vietnam War, the target of much of the counterculture's wrath.

Woodstock organizers staged a reunion concert in Saugerties, N.Y., in August 1994. This festival was openly corporate, with Pepsi, Häagen Dazs ice cream, and MCI among the sponsors. It was also expensive: advance tickets cost $135 each; those attending found a Häagen Dazs ice cream bar selling for $3 dollars and a cup of Pepsi for $2 while an official program cost $15. This second concert's music lineup was geared toward the tastes of baby boomers' children, with "alternative" rock and punk bands such as Green Day, Nine Inch Nails, and Porno for Pyros as the headliners. On the other hand Bob Dylan performed this time, while several Woodstock I performers showed up, including Cocker, Santana, and Crosby, Stills, and Nash. Moreover, two stalwarts of the original festival—drugs and mud—reappeared. Many concertgoers used marijuana and LSD, despite the efforts of a large security force to confiscate the contraband, but there was less drug use than in 1969. Heavy rains left the more than 300,000 people in attendance covered with muck.

[Joel Makower, *Woodstock: The Oral History* (New York, 1989); Robert Stephen Spitz, *Barefoot in Babylon: The Creation of the Woodstock Music Festival, 1969* (New York, 1979).]

THOMAS G. GRESS

See also **SUPP:** Music, Rock and Roll; Music Festivals.

WORLD'S FAIRS are one-time international expositions that feature exhibits showcasing developments in science, technology, industry, and the arts. Held in cities, they typically run for six months, from spring to fall. Exhibitors include governments, corporations, and large private organizations. The Crystal Palace Exhibition held in London in 1851 began the modern era of international expositions. Staged to demonstrate the superiority of British industry, it housed exhibits of machinery, art, and crafts and attracted more than 6 million visitors. Since the Crystal Palace world's fairs have become more than demonstrations of industrial progress and have acquired symbolic purposes. The Philadelphia Centennial Exposition of 1876 commemorated the anniversary of the Declaration of Independence. The 1893 World's Columbian Exposition at Chicago celebrated the anniversary of the discovery of America. In 1915 the San Francisco Panama-Pacific International Exposition honored the opening of the Panama Canal and the city's recovery from the earthquake of 1906.

Fairs held in the United States during the 1930s helped visitors cope with the Great Depression. In 1933–1934 Chicago's Century of Progress International Exhibition took shape around the theme of scientific and industrial progress since the city's founding. It marked the first time that such firms as General Motors constructed pavilions to display their products. The 1939–1940 New York World's Fair, billed as "The World of Tomorrow," drew more than 44 million visitors. It introduced television and promoted suburban living and pollution-free, automated factories. World War II and its aftermath precluded international expositions until the late 1950s. The United States did not host a postwar world's fair until the

1962 Century 21 Exposition in Seattle. The inspiration for this fair came in part from the cold war; after the Soviet Union launched *Sputnik* in 1957, U.S. leaders and scientists wanted to demonstrate the nation's scientific prowess. The Seattle fair featured the 605-foot Space Needle, a monorail, an amusement park, and many exhibits. In 1964–1965 the New York World's Fair drew more than 51 million visitors, offered striking pavilion architecture, and pioneered audiovisual display techniques. It included 200 buildings and the Unisphere, a 140-foot-high stainless steel globe signifying "Peace Through Understanding." In response to the ecological crisis of the 1970s the United States hosted three fairs dealing with energy conservation and the environment: Spokane (1974), Knoxville (1982), and New Orleans (1984). The Bureau of International Expositions, which since 1928 has overseen world's fairs, authorizing dates and enforcing exhibition standards, authorized three events through the year 2000: Expo 96 in Budapest, Hungary; Expo 98 in Lisbon, Portugal; and Expo 2000 in Hanover, Germany.

[John E. Findling and Kimberly D. Pelle, eds., *Historical Dictionary of World's Fairs and Expositions, 1851–1988* (Westport, Conn., 1987); Robert W. Rydell, *World of Fairs: The Century-of-Progress Expositions* (Chicago, 1993).]

ANDREW FELDMAN

See also **DAH:** Centennial Exposition; Century of Progress International Exhibition; New York World's Fairs; Panama-Pacific International Exposition; Seattle World's Fair; World's Columbian Exposition.

WORLD TRADE CENTER BOMBING. On Feb. 26, 1993, Islamic terrorists exploded a car bomb in the underground garage to the World Trade Center in New York City, killing six people and injuring more than 1,000. Federal authorities soon arrested Sheik Omar Abdel Rahman, a blind fundamentalist Islamic cleric implicated in the assassination of Egypt's Anwar el-Sadat a decade earlier, and nine co-conspirators. Following a nine-month trial, during which a Federal Bureau of Investigation informant who had infiltrated the group provided secretly videotaped evidence, Rahman and his followers were convicted of plotting to blow up the United Nations, FBI offices, highway tunnels, and the George Washington Bridge, in addition to the World Trade Center. Sheik Rahman and El Sayyid Nosair received life sentences and the other conspirators prison terms ranging from twenty-five to fifty-seven years. Notwithstanding

Rahman's claim that the trial was part of the "American war against Islam," U.S. Attorney Mary Jo White denied any "prosecution of Islam or any other religion" and hailed the sentences as "strong and appropriate."

[Laurie Mylroie, "The World Trade Center Bomb," *National Interest* 42 (Winter 1995–1996).]

J. GARRY CLIFFORD

See also **SUPP:** Middle East, Relations with; Terrorism.

WORLD WIDE WEB, also called WWW, the Web, or W3, is an information environment that links computers around the globe to form a literal web of machines distributing hypermedia—text, images, audio, video, and computational services—on the Internet. The WWW uses a standard set of protocols and conventions, which makes it easy for anyone on the Web to roam, browse, and participate in electronic exchanges. According to late 1995 estimates, 18 million people use the WWW at tens of millions of sites, or computers connected and serving hypermedia on the Web. The WWW uses the Hypertext Transfer Protocol (HTTP) as its core communications protocol on the Internet. Documents are written in Hypertext Markup Language (HTML), which controls the formatting and presentation of the hypertext on each Web site. Hypertext allows users to make selections and navigate further into the text through keywords and interrelated links that can point to hypertext documents contained on one isolated Web site or another site around the globe. The World Wide Web project was begun in 1989 by Tim Berners-Lee at CERN, the European Particle Physics Laboratory, who formed the World Wide Web Consortium—an industry consortium run by the Laboratory for Computer Science at the Massachusetts Institute of Technology—to develop common standards for the evolution of the Web.

[Graphics, Visualization, and Usability Center, *Fourth WWW User Survey* (Atlanta, 1995); Ed Krol, *The Whole Internet User's Guide and Catalog* (Sebastopol, Calif., 1992).]

MICHAEL REGOLI

See also **SUPP:** Internet.

WOUNDED KNEE. The confrontation between Native Americans and U.S. authorities at Wounded Knee in 1973 emerged out of a long history. The incident was also influenced by the civil rights activism of the 1960s and the growth of confrontational politics, especially on behalf of racial minorities. The radical American Indian Movement (AIM), formed in 1968, provided leadership in the seizure of Alcatraz Island in November 1969 and the occupation of the Bureau of Indian Affairs (BIA) building in Washington, D.C., in November 1972. The small Indian settlement of Wounded Knee on the Pine Ridge Sioux Reservation in South Dakota was significant as the site of a mass grave resulting from the last "battle" of the Indian wars of the nineteenth century, a brutal episode revisited in Dee Brown's best-selling *Bury My Heart at Wounded Knee* (1971). Pine Ridge also signaled a division in Native American ranks between largely urban militants and the more conservative tribal leadership of the Oglala Sioux. On Feb. 27, 1973, some 200 armed men, most belonging to AIM, seized the village at Wounded Knee by taking eleven elderly hostages and destroying seven Indian homes, two churches, and a museum. The action was designed to publicize Indian grievances and challenge the elected local tribal head, Richard Wilson. Only the government's decision to place U.S. marshals on the road to Wounded Knee prevented these two groups of Native Americans from attacking one another. Even so, the government's action produced a military standoff and a crisis. While a full-blown shootout did not transpire in the seventy-day siege, exchange of gunfire did lead to the deaths of two Indians and serious injury to a federal marshal. The end came on May 8, 1973, with agreement that the insurgents would lay down their arms and the government would discuss grievances. Charges against AIM leaders were either dropped or rejected in court; a judge dismissed charges against AIM leaders Russell Means and Dennis Banks in 1974. The disagreement among the Oglala Sioux did not end, nor did friction between AIM and the government. A shootout at Pine Ridge in June 1975, which killed one Indian and two FBI agents, led in 1977 to a controversial trial and a life sentence for murder for AIM leader Leonard Peltier. The episode and its aftermath gave Wounded Knee new meaning to Native Americans and produced a broadened awareness of Indian problems. Before and after the Wounded Knee standoff, the administration of President Richard M. Nixon increased the BIA budget and supported reform legislation that led to passage of the Indian Self-Determination and Educational Assistance Act of 1975.

[Peter Matthiessen, *In the Spirit of Crazy Horse* (New York, 1983); Wilcomb E. Washburn, ed., *History of Indian-White Relations* (Washington, D.C., 1988).]

ROSS GREGORY

See also **SUPP:** American Indian Movement; Native Americans.

WYOMING, the least populated of the fifty states, with a 1990 population of 453,588 and a land area that is ninth largest, with 97,104 square miles. Sixty-five percent of the state's population lived in areas defined as urban. The Great Plains extend into the eastern part of the state, the land rising to mountains and high plateaus in the west. Winter temperatures can fall as low as minus sixty degrees, although humidity is extremely low. Brisk winds add to the generally harsh climate. Vast distances separate the towns and cities. Because of the small and homogenous population, the state has been characterized as a "small town with a long main street."

Natural resource exploitation, livestock raising, irrigation farming, and tourism have been the main industries. Manufacturing is almost nonexistent, even in the larger towns. Oil and coal, along with trona (a source of sodium compounds discovered in 1938) and uranium (discovered in 1918 but not produced until the 1950s), have made Wyoming susceptible to economic booms and busts. Wyoming's economy was locked into two decades of stagnation until 1973, when the Arab oil embargo caused energy prices to rise dramatically. By the mid-1970s oil exploration had brought hundreds of new workers to Wyoming, but the coal industry experienced the greatest growth. The industry practically died in the 1950s when the railroads switched from coal-burning locomotives to diesels. Public utilities began building coal-fired plants across the country, including plants in Wyoming at Rock Springs, Kemmerer, Glenrock, and Wheatland during the 1970s, which brought thousands more workers to the state. During the decade the population soared from 320,000 to 469,000. By the 1990s, 98 percent of the state's electricity was provided by steam-powered plants.

The coal beds in Wyoming, estimated to underlie 40 percent of the land area, are often close to the surface, making strip mining practical in most areas. More than 96 percent of the coal is subbituminous with a relatively low heat content. Nonetheless, it contains sulfur, making it a more acceptable fuel for meeting clean air standards. The area of greatest expansion in coal production was the Powder River Basin in northeastern Wyoming. For example, the state's total production in 1974 was just 20 million tons. In 1992 the Black Thunder Mine near Gillette was producing 28.6 million tons annually. Coal production in

333

Wyoming was greater than in any other state from 1989 (171 million tons) to 1995 (263 million tons).

The mineral boom of the 1970s brought with it increasing demands for government services and local amenities. The small ranching communities could not provide enough facilities to accommodate all of the new arrivals. In 1969 the state had adopted a severance tax on minerals, and with increasing prices and production of minerals, the tax raised hundreds of millions of dollars by the late 1970s. Some of the funds were directed back to local communities in order to build new water and sewer systems, streets, schools, and jails.

In the 1980s energy prices declined and pushed Wyoming into its worst economic depression. The population fell 3.4 percent from 1980 to 1990. By the early 1990s the state's economy was stagnant and, except for some resort towns, most places continued to lose population. Tourism flourished, however, especially at Yellowstone National Park, Grand Teton National Park, and Devil's Tower National Monument (generating approximately $1.5 billion in revenue annually in the 1990s), but it did not offset the loss of highly paid jobs in the minerals sector. Jackson Hole, nationally renowned for the beauty of the nearby Tetons and for outdoor sports, grew rapidly, causing housing prices to inflate to West Coast levels. The federal government controlled 46.5 percent of the state's land in 1993. Although many residents resented the federal presence, a substantial number relied on federal assistance, particularly in the livestock, tourism, and mineral industries.

Republicans have dominated politics for much of Wyoming's history, but party affiliation has been less important than strong personalities and constituent service. Although Republicans have dominated the state legislature, the governors from 1974 to 1993 were Democrats. During the early 1970s Wyoming voters kept Democrat Gale McGee and Republican Clifford Hansen in the U.S. Senate. McGee sought reelection in 1976 but lost to rancher and businessman Malcolm Wallop. In 1978 Hansen, a former governor, retired from the Senate to his Jackson Hole ranch. His successor was Alan K. Simpson, the son of former governor and senator Milward Simpson. Democrat Teno Roncalio retired in 1978 after five terms in Congress. Republican Richard Cheney, former chief of staff to President Gerald R. Ford, succeeded Roncalio in Wyoming's only seat in the U.S. House of Representatives; he was reelected every two years until 1989, when he resigned to accept the post of secretary of defense. Cheney's successor, Republican

Craig Thomas, went on to the Senate in 1995 after Wallop retired. Democrat Ed Herschler was first elected governor in 1974 and was the first governor to be elected to three terms. He retired in 1986 and was replaced by another Democrat, Michael J. Sullivan, who served two terms. The Democrats lost the governorship to Republican Jim Geringer in 1994, when Sullivan ran unsuccessfully against Thomas for Wallop's Senate seat. That same year the one seat in the House was won by Republican Barbara Cubin, the first woman elected to Congress from Wyoming.

[Loren Jost, ed., *Wyoming Historical Blue Book,* 3rd ed. (Cheyenne, Wyo., 1990); T. A. Larson, *History of Wyoming* (Lincoln, Nebr., 1979); Clynn Phillips et al., *Wyoming Data Handbook* (Cheyenne, Wyo., 1991); Phil Roberts et al., *Wyoming Almanac,* 3rd rev. ed. (Laramie, Wyo., 1994).]

PHIL ROBERTS

YUGOSLAVIA. *See* **Bosnia-Herzegovina.**

ZOOLOGY is the study of the structure, function, and ecology of animals. Throughout the eighteenth and nineteenth centuries, zoological study in the United States focused on identifying and classifying the abundant and diverse animals found on the North American continent. Researchers such as John James Audubon undertook massive cataloging efforts, identifying and describing animal natural history. During this time a parallel effort was also made in the field of botany. At the end of the nineteenth century, zoology evolved into a more integrative science, encompassing the fields of natural history, morphology (the study of the structure of animals), and physiology (the study of the functions in animals). As advances were made in genetics in the early twentieth century, zoology began to focus on that area. The fields of ecology, comparative anatomy, embryology (fetal development), cytology (cell development), parasitology (parasite biology), systematics (classification of organisms), and protozoology (microorganism biology) all were part of the overarching field of zoology.

The discovery of DNA, the molecule that transfers genetic information in all organisms, in the 1950s brought molecular biology to a central position in the field of biology, which it continued to dominate for the rest of the century. Throughout the 1960s, 1970s, and 1980s, as interest in molecular biology increased, interest in whole organisms and morphology decreased. In the 1970s the effort to integrate the branches of zoology gained ground, partly in response to the growing interest in ecology. By studying the ecology of animals, zoologists joined their understanding of the molecular biology of animals with their understanding of how animals fit into the larger picture of ecosystems and environments. Articles in zoology journals focused on the roles animals play in their ecosystems and on how they interact with their environment, as zoologists studied the interrelationships among animals, plants, microorganisms, and physical factors.

The trend toward a more ecological approach was grounded in increased concern over environmental degradation during the 1980s and 1990s. As zoologists noted the precipitous decline in animal populations in the wild, they sought to explain the reasons for the decline and to develop methods to reverse it. In the years since the passage of the Endangered Species Act in 1973, zoologists have played a central role in the research necessary for the implementation of the act. Zoologists have also studied species extinction. The threat to global biodiversity has caused alarm among biologists, and efforts have been undertaken to document which animals are threatened, which animals have become extinct, and the causes of the decline in biodiversity. Ironically, this concern has created a need to catalog animals that parallels the early zoological efforts in the eighteenth and nineteenth centuries in the United States. E. O. Wilson, a Harvard University biologist and an expert on biodiversity, called for a major effort to identify, classify, and catalog the millions of species that remain unknown, arguing that the effort to protect the world's habitats and thus animal diversity must begin with a comprehensive knowledge of which animals live where.

Although cataloging has become one area of increased zoological interest, the major thrust has been on the interaction between animals and their environments. A specific area of this research that is gaining in prominence is the investigation of the influence of human activity on animals. Changes in the environment caused by pollution, habitat destruction, climate change, and hunting all affect animal survival. Examination of these influences is increasingly falling into the domain of zoologists. In addition to identifying how human activity affects animals, zoologists study ways of remediating human impacts. Zoos have begun making captive breeding programs a priority among their activities. These programs will permit the restoration of endangered animals into the wild. Zoologists play a key role, not only in understanding the reproductive biology and ecology of animals, but in determining the most effective methods of reintroduction. Issues like species extinction are extraordinarily complex. The integration of the expertise of many fields is essential for solving the problems that affect the world's animals. Zoologists therefore collaborate with botanists, soils experts, land and water resource specialists, atmospheric scientists, and policymakers in their joint effort to understand and maintain the earth's biological resources.

[Keith R. Benson and Brother C. Edward Quinn, "The American Society of Zoologists, 1889–1989: A Century of Integrating the Biological Sciences," *American Zoologist* 30 (1990); C. Leon Harris, *Concepts in Zoology* (New York, 1992); E. O. Wilson, *The Diversity of Life* (Cambridge, Mass., 1992).]

DAVID W. CASH

See also **DAH** and **SUPP:** Ecology; **SUPP:** Endangered Species; Species, Introduced.

ALPHABETICAL LIST OF ENTRIES

ALPHABETICAL LIST OF ENTRIES

INDEX

Numbers in boldface refer to the main entry on the subject. Museums are listed under "Museums"; orchestras under "Orchestras"; legal cases, other than Supreme Court cases, under "Legal cases"; and Supreme Court cases under "Supreme Court cases." Titles of radio programs appear under "Radio programs" and titles of television programs and shows under "Television programs."

A

A. H. Robins, **1:**157a
Aaron, Hank, **1:**70b
AARP. *See* American Association of
    Retired Persons (AARP)
Abbas, Mahmoud, **1:**336b
Abbott Laboratories, **1:**316b
ABMs. *See* Antiballistic missiles (ABMs)
Abnaki Tribal Council, **2:**290a
Abortion, **1:3a–6a,** 200b
    Catholic Church opposition to, **1:**101a
    children's rights and, **1:**116a
    Christian conservatives and, **1:**154b
    clinics harassed by pro-life movement,
        2:146a
    and Food and Drug Administration,
        1:255b
    and genetic engineering, **1:**281a
    Harris v. *McRae* (1980), **1:**292b
    as issue in Minnesota politics, **2:**37a
    as issue in presidential campaign of
        1984, **1:**94b
    laws, **2:**181a
    legislation in Pennsylvania, **2:**111a
    not discussed in presidential campaign of
        1976, **1:**93b
    and pregnancy discrimination Act,
        2:137b
    and privacy, **1:**287b
    rights, **2:**327b, 329b–330a
    and Supreme Court, **2:**240b, 313b–314b
    and Women's Equity Action League,
        2:325b
Abourezk, James, **1:**40b, 362a

Abruzzo, Ben, **1:**66a
Abscam scandal, **1:6a–b,** 151b, 159a, 165b
Abu-Lughod, Ibrahim, **2:**104a
Academic freedom, **1:6b–7a**
Academic research, **1:**7a
Accidents, **1:7a–b**
    alcohol as cause of, **1:**60b
Accounting
    firms in New York City, **2:**72a
    jobs in, **2:**8a
Achille Lauro, **1:7b–8a**
Acid rain, **1:8a–b,** 31b, 201b, 215a, 224a
Acquired Immune Deficiency Syndrome
        (AIDS), **1:8b–11b,** 64a,b, 104a, 296b;
        2:16b, 17a, 59a
    activists' pressure on health care system,
        1:298a
    in Africa, **1:**19a–b
    benefit concerts for, **1:**74a
    in California, **1:**92b
    as cause of death, **1:**181b, 367b
    and dance, **1:**174b
    and drug use, **2:**233b
    and Food and Drug Administration,
        1:255b, 256a
    and gay liberation, **1:**274b
    identification of virus, **2:**29b
    international conferences, **1:**10a
    as metaphor for gay writers, **1:**372a
    in New York City, **2:**72b
    and prostitution, **2:**146b
    pure food and drug movement, **2:**156a
    in San Francisco, **2:**188a
    and sexuality, **2:**202b, 203a,b
    and tuberculosis, **2:**276a–b

Acreage Reduction Program, **1:**243a
Act for Better Child Care (1990), **1:**114b
ACTION, **2:**298b
ACT UP (AIDS Coalition to Unleash
        Power), **1:**10b, 256a, 274b
Acupuncture, **2:**19b–20a, 66b
ADA. *See* Americans with Disabilities Act
        (ADA)
Ada County, Idaho, **1:**315a
Adams, Abigail, **1:**247a,b, 376b
Adams, John, **1:**278a; **2:**49b
    on language, **1:**205a
Adams, Oscar, **1:**33b
Adams County, Colo., **1:**183b
Addiction, **2:**232a–b
Adena culture, **1:**41a–b
Adler, Mortimer J., **1:**207a; **2:**58b
Administrative convenience, **2:**167a
Adoption, **1:11b–13b,** 236b, 262b
    laws for assistance, **1:**116a
    See also Foster care
Adoption Assistance and Child Welfare Act
        (1980), **1:**12b, 262b
Advanced Micro Devices, **2:**205b
Advertising, **1:13b–15a**
    and direct mail, **1:**187a
    firms in New York City, **2:**72a
    infomercials, **2:**5a
    in magazines, **2:**3b
    of mail-order business, **2:**4b
    in newspapers, **2:**71a
    as outlet for photographers, **2:**123b
    psychology applied to, **2:**150a
    tobacco industry, **2:**260b, 261b
Aerobics, **1:15a–b**

INDEX

INDEX

INDEX

354

INDEX

G

INDEX

INDEX

INDEX

397

INDEX

INDEX

400

INDEX

INDEX

X

Xenografts, **1:**281a
Xerography, **2:**90a
Xerox Corporation, **1:**152b; **2:**90a

Y

Yachting, **2:**3a
Yale College, **1:**281a
Yale University, **1:**152b
  deconstructionist literary criticism,
    2:135b
  Lyme disease, **1:**382b
Yalow, Rosalyn S., **2:**76a
Yalta Conference, **1:**198b; **2:**235b, 281b
Yamaguchi, Kristi, **2:**95b, 96a
Yankton College (S.Dak.), **2:**213b
Yap. *See* Trust territory of the Pacific
    Islands
Yarborough, Ralph, **2:**254b
Yastrzemski, Carl, **2:**131a
Yasui, Minoru, **1:**342b
Yeager, Charles "Chuck," **2:**318a
*Yearbook of American and Canadian
    Churches,* **2:**148a
Years of Potential Life Lost Before Age
    Sixty-Five (YPLL), **1:**367b
Yellowstone National Park, **1:**154a; **2:**42a,
    164b, 334a
  disaster in, **1:**195a
  fires in, **1:**328a
  and wildfires, **2:**320a

wolves in, **1:**328a
Yellow Thunder Camp (1981-1984), **1:**37a
"Yellow Wallpaper, The" (Gilman), **1:**377a
Yeltsin, Boris, **2:**220b
  arms control, **1:**48b; **2:**229a
  and Bosnia, **1:**83a
Yerkes, Robert, **1:**208b
Yeshiva University, **1:**345a
YMCA (Young Men's Christian
    Association), **2:**164a
Yoakum, Joseph, **1:**252a
Yoga, **1:**169a; **2:**20a
Yolles, Stanley, **2:**204a
Yolo County, **2:**185b
Yom Kippur War (1973), **1:**131a; **2:**31a,
    218a, 283b
  as cause of first oil crisis, **2:**92a
York County, Maine, **2:**5b
Yosemite National Park, **2:**320a
Yosemite Valley, **2:**164b
Young, Al, **1:**91a
Young, Andrew, **1:**18b, 58a, 283a
Young, Coleman, **1:**186b; **2:**27b
Young, Frank E., **1:**255b
Young, Kevin, **2:**96b
Young, La Monte, **2:**51b
Young, Milton R., **2:**82b
Young, Purvis, **1:**252b
Youngstown, Ohio, **1:**138b; **2:**90b
  steel industry in, **2:**183a
Yucatán Peninsula, meteor craters in,
    1:282b

Yugoslavia, **1:**199a, 228b, 230a.
  breakup of, **1:**197b, 199b
  creation of, **1:**198a
  See also Bosnia-Herzegovina
Yurchenko, Vitaly, **1:**326b
YWCA (Young Women's Christian
    Association), **2:**164a–b

Z

Zahn, Johannes, **2:**42b, 42b
Zahnister, Howard, **1:**221a
Zaidan, Mohammad Abul Abbas, **1:**8a
Zaire, U.S. relations with, **1:**18b
Zane, Arnie, **1:**174b
Zappa, Frank, **1:**97b
Zebra mussel, **2:**224b
Zeckendorf, William, **2:**281b
Zeldis, Malcah, **1:**252a
Zenith Electronics Corporation, **1:**316b;
    2:266b
Zero discharge, **2:**312b
Zhou Enlai, **1:**117a
Zigler, Edward, **1:**295b
Zimbabwe, U.S. relations with, **1:**18a
ZIP (Zone Improvement Program) code,
    2:135a
Zoology, **2:334b–335b**
Zooplankton, **1:**248a
Zukor, Adolph, **2:**43a,b
Zungal, Steve, **2:**209b
Zwilich, Ellen Taaffe, **2:**51b